Structured COBOL Programming

Robert T. Grauer, Ph. D.
University of Miami, Florida

PRENTICE-HALL, INC., Englewood Cliffs, New Jersey 07632

Library of Congress Cataloging in Publication Data

Grauer, Robert T. 1985
Structured COBOL programming,

Includes index.
1. COBOL (Computer program language) 2. Structured programming. I. Title.
QA76.73.C25G7373 1985 001.64'24 84-26358
ISBN 0-13-854217-1

Editorial/production supervision: Lynn S. Frankel
Interior and cover design: Anne T. Bonanno
Manufacturing buyer: Gordon Osbourne

Printed in the United States of America

10 9 8 7 6 5

ISBN 0-13-854217-1 01

Prentice-Hall International, Inc., London
Prentice-Hall of Australia Pty. Limited, Sydney
Editora Prentice-Hall do Brasil, Ltda., Rio de Janeiro
Prentice-Hall Canada Inc., Toronto
Prentice-Hall Hispanoamericana, S. A., Mexico
Prentice-Hall of India Private Limited, New Delhi
Prentice-Hall of Japan, Inc., Tokyo
Prentice-Hall of Southeast Asia Pte. Ltd., Singapore
Whitehall Books Limited, Wellington, New Zealand

To Marion, Benjy, and Jessica

The following information is reprinted from COBOL Edition 1965, published by the Conference on Data Systems Languages (CODASYL), and printed by the U.S. Government Printing Office:

Any organization interested in reproducing the COBOL report and specifications in whole or part, using ideas taken from this report as the basis for an instructional manual or for any other purpose is free to do so. However, all such organizations are requested to reproduce this section as part of the introduction to the document. Those using a short passage, as in a book review, are requested to mention "COBOL" in acknowledgment of the source, but need not quote this entire section.

COBOL is an industry language and is not the property of any company or group of companies, or of any organization or group of organizations.

No warranty, expressed or implied, is made by any contributor or by the COBOL Committee as to the accuracy and functioning of the programming system and language. Moreover, no responsibility is assumed by any contributor, or by the committee, in connection therewith.

Procedures have been established for the maintenance of COBOL. Inquiries concerning the procedures for proposing changes should be directed to the Executive Committee of the Conference on Data Systems Languages.

The authors and copyright holders of the copyrighted material used herein:

FLOWMATIC (Trade mark of the Sperry Rand Corporation), Programming for the Univac (R) I and II, Data Automation Systems copyrighted 1958, 1959, by Sperry Rand Corporation; IBM Commercial Translator Form No. F28–8013, copyrighted 1959 by IBM; FACT, DSI 27A5260–2760, copyrighted 1960 by Minneapolis-Honeywell

have specifically authorized the use of this material in whole or in part, in the COBOL specifications. Such authorization extends to the reproduction and use of COBOL specifications in programming manuals of similar publications.

Contents

3 The Identification, Environment, and Data Divisions 42

4 The Procedure Division 61

5 Writing a Report Program 88

6 Debugging 121

7 Structured Programming and Design 145

11 Table Processing 270

12 Sorting 311

Preface

Structured COBOL Programming is a truly comprehensive work, providing in a single source all subjects normally covered in the one-year COBOL sequence. The scope is extensive, ranging from an introduction to COBOL to maintaining sequential and nonsequential files. The single-volume presentation affords a unified approach and eliminates the need for separate texts in the two semesters. This is especially valuable when students transfer schools (e.g., from a community college) for the second semester, as it eliminates the problem of what may or may not have been previously covered.

Structured COBOL Programming represents several years of effort, encompassing many revisions to earlier books by the same author. It embodies suggestions from hundreds of individuals, both students and instructors, who have used one Grauer book or another. Many new features have been added, while others have been retained, with the following of special interest:

- *Immediate entry into COBOL programming,* beginning in Chapter 1. Programming is learned by doing, and the book has the student writing a complete program from the very beginning. Chapter 2 continues the discussion, by having the reader "punch and run" the program of Chapter 1 in a thorough introduction to the programming process.
- *Twenty-Two Complete COBOL Programs,* which reinforce the discussion in the text and serve as both pedagogical aids and subsequent reference material. Each illustrative program is presented in a uniform and detailed format including program narrative, record layouts, report layouts, test data, and processing specifications.
- *Increased Number of Programming Assignments,* which appear at the end of each chapter. The assignments are presented in the same format as the illustrative programs.
- *Abundant and Challenging Exercises,* at the end of each chapter. The number of exercises has been increased from earlier books, and the problems are constructed to reinforce and stimulate the reader's ability in COBOL.
- *New Debugging Workshops,* featuring an additional eight COBOL programs to give students practice in an area where it is needed most.
- *Ten Programming Tips,* which go beyond the syntactical rules of COBOL and suggest stylistic considerations to make programs easier to read. Many of the tips take the form of coding standards and are typical of what the student will encounter in "the real world."
- *Extensive Use of Graphic Aids,* including a two-color presentation and abundant use of tints. This enables important elements, such as COBOL syntax and 8X changes and enhancements, to be consistently highlighted from chapter to chapter.

- *New System Concept Presentations,* at the beginning of each of the advanced COBOL chapters. Instruction in COBOL has come to require additional material, beyond the language itself. These discussions include control breaks, data validation, logical versus physical records, techniques for table lookups and initialization, sorting, Report Writer, the balance line algorithm for file maintenance, and organization of indexed files.
- *Thorough presentation of structured methodology,* with emphasis on hierarchy charts and pseudocode, and deemphasis of the traditional flowchart. Material is also included on stepwise refinement, top-down testing, and Nassi–Shneiderman diagrams.
- *Substantial coverage of the 8X compiler,* which is both thorough yet nonconfusing to those familiar with COBOL 74.

APPROACH TO THE NEW COMPILER

The text is designed for users of both the 74 compiler and the new 8X version. All listings were run under COBOL 74 and are upwardly compatible. In addition each chapter contains a concluding section that presents the relevant 8X changes and enhancements. Appendices A, B, and C contain still more COBOL 8X material, including a sample program. Appendix D contains the 8X Language Summary.

The moderate approach to the new compiler was carefully chosen. It would have been possible, for example, to inundate the reader with new features of COBOL 8X to the point of making the illustrative programs totally incompatible with COBOL 74. To have done so would have greatly weakened the book's overall impact. It took many years for industry to convert from COBOL 68 to COBOL 74, and history has a tendency to repeat itself.

ACKNOWLEDGMENTS

The author wishes to thank the many people who have made this book possible. He acknowledges the contributions his students have made over the years through their many suggestions and active class participation. He is indebted to the in-depth analysis provided by his reviewers, including: Professor Earl Adams (Illinois Central College), Professor Carol C. Grimm (Palm Beach Community College), Professor Margot Hummer (University of Miami), Professor Lewis Myers, Professor James Payne (Kellog Community College), Professor Joel Stutz (University of Miami), Professor Terry Walker (University of Southwestern Louisiana), and Mr. Richard Weiland.

Cathy Benway, Jackie Clark, and Lita Fox, all of the University of Miami, helped to proofread the book. Each made a significant contribution. Ms. Sheila Grossman typed, then retyped the manuscript, always maintaining her sense of humor.

Jim Fegen and Marcia Horton are the acquisition editors responsible for this project. Lynn Frankel, the production editor, put all pieces together in her expert way. Anne Bonanno designed the book and its cover. Herb Daehnke did his usual expert job on the computer listings. Karen Fortgang put on the finishing touches. Last, and certainly not least, thanks to Joe Heider, marketing manager, for making the book a success.

A final word of thanks to the hundreds of unnamed students in MAS223 at the University of Miami who made it all worthwhile.

ROBERT T. GRAUER

Introduction

1

Overview

This book is about computer programming. In particular it is about COBOL, a widely used commercial programming language. Programming involves the translation of a precise means of problem solution into a form the computer can understand. Programming is necessary because, despite reports to the contrary, computers cannot think for themselves. Instead they do exactly *what they have been instructed to do, and these instructions take the form of a computer program. The advantage of the computer stems from its speed and accuracy. It does not do anything that a human being could not do, given sufficient time.*

All computer applications consist of three phases: input, processing, *and* output. *Information enters the computer, it is processed (i.e., calculations are performed), and the results are communicated to the user. Input can come from punched cards, a diskette, magnetic tape, a hard disk, computer terminals, or any of a variety of other devices. Processing encompasses the logic to solve a problem, but in actuality all a computer does is add, subtract, multiply, divide, or compare. All logic stems from these basic operations, and the power of the computer comes from its ability to alter a sequence of operations on the basis of the results of a comparison. Output can take several forms. It may consist of the ubiquitous 11 × 14⅞ computer listing or printout, or it may be payroll checks, computer letters, mailing labels, magnetic tape, etc.*

We begin our study of computer programming by describing a single problem and then developing the logic and COBOL program to solve it. This rapid entrance into COBOL is somewhat different from the approach followed by most textbooks, but we believe in learning by doing. *There is nothing very mysterious about COBOL programming, so let's get started.* □

THE FIRST PROBLEM

Our first problem involves a set of student records, one record per student. Each record contains the student's name, number of completed credits, and the student's major.

We are to produce *a list of engineering students who have completed at least 110 credits*. Our problem is to develop a COBOL program that can process the set of student records to generate the desired report.

Implicit in the preceding problem statement are the definitions of three fundamental terms in data processing: *field, record,* and *file*. A *record* is a set of facts (or *fields*) about a logical entity. In our example, each student record contains three fields: name, major, and credits. A *file* is a set of records. For example, if there were 1,000 students enrolled in the university, there would be 1,000 student records, which make up a single student file.

A student record must be precisely designed with respect to the location of the individual fields. Figure 1.1 shows that the student's name is contained in positions 1–25, the number of credits in positions 26–28, and the student's major in positions 29–43. Every record in a given file will have the identical record layout, as shown in Figure 1.1.

FIGURE 1.1 Student Record Layout

In similar fashion, the report produced as output is also precisely designed. Figure 1.2 shows a print layout chart, in which the names of selected students appear in columns 9–33 of each printed line. Note that the location of the name field is different in the input and output records (positions 1–25 and 9–33, respectively). Observe also that each input record contains three fields but that each line of output contains only one field.

Program Specifications

The requirements of a program, i.e., the programming specifications, must be provided in a clear, uniform, and unambiguous fashion. Accordingly, the author has adopted the format shown in Figure 1.3, which will be used throughout the text for both illustrative programs and student assignments.

As can be seen, Figure 1.3 begins with the program name and a brief narrative overview. This is followed by a description of the input, output, and processing requirements. The specification document, such as Figure 1.3, should be entirely self-contained. If the person preparing the specifications has done a complete job, there should be no need for the programmer to seek additional information.

Required Logic

Let us imagine momentarily that the student records are physically in the form of manila folders, stored in a filing cabinet, and further that a clerk is available to do our bidding. Our problem therefore reduces to instructing the clerk

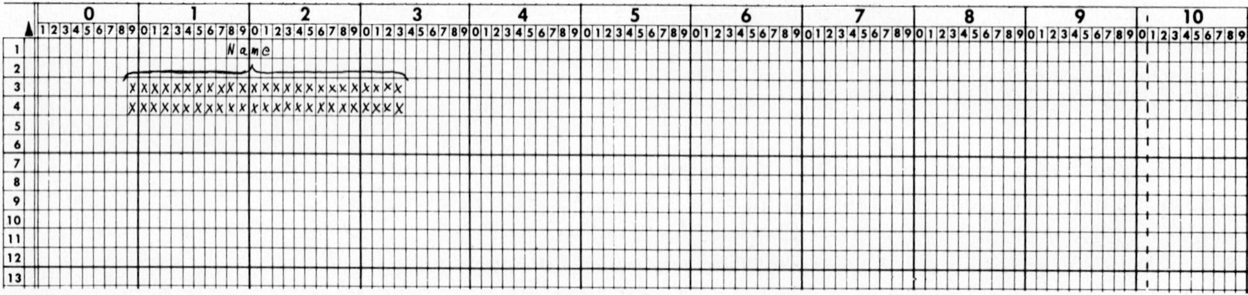

FIGURE 1.2 Print Layout

Programming Specifications

Program Name:
Engineering Senior Program

Narrative:
This program processes a file of student records and prints the name of every student who is an engineering major with at least 110 credits.

Input File(s):
STUDENT-FILE

Input Record Layout:
See Figure 1.1.

Report Format:
See Figure 1.2.

Processing Requirements:
1. Read a file of student records.
2. For every record read, determine whether that student has a major of engineering *and* has completed 110 credits or more.
3. Print the name of every student who satisfies the requirements in item 2 above. Single-space the output.

FIGURE 1.3 Program Specifications

on how to go through the folders. We would say something to the following effect:

Repeat steps 1, 2, 3, and 4 for every folder; stop when finished:

1. Pull the next folder.
2. Examine the folder to see if this student is an engineering major with at least 110 credits.
3. If the student meets both qualifications, write the student's name on a running list.
4. Return the folder to the file cabinet.

In essence, we have prepared a series of instructions for the clerk to follow. If our instructions are correct and if they are followed exactly, then the clerk will produce the desired results.

A *computer program* is a set of instructions, written according to a precise set of rules, which the computer interprets and subsequently executes. Unlike the clerk, however, the computer always follows our instructions exactly. In other words, *the computer does what we tell it to do, which is not necessarily what we want it to do.* A human clerk, on the other hand, has a mind of his or her own and can question or alter erroneous instructions. Since the computer does precisely what it is told, it is imperative that one strives to write correct programs. Accordingly, one must expend significant effort in the *design phase* of a project, *prior to actual coding,* in order to develop a program's logic correctly. Two common techniques for expressing that logic are *flowcharts* and *pseudocode*.

Flowcharts

A flowchart is a pictorial representation of the logic inherent in a program. It is the translation of a problem statement into a logical blueprint that is subsequently incorporated into the COBOL program. A flowchart to list the engineering students with at least 110 credits is shown in Figure 1.4.

A flowchart uses blocks with specific shapes to indicate the nature of an operation. Using Figure 1.4 as a guide, we see that a diamond-shaped block indicates a decision, a parallelogram depicts input or output, an ellipse shows the beginning or end, and a rectangle implies straightforward processing.

To understand the flowchart in Figure 1.4, consider the nature of a READ statement. The function of a READ instruction is to obtain a record, but there will always be a point when a READ is attempted and no record is found, i.e., when all the records in the file have already been read. Since one does not know in advance how many records a file contains, the READ instruction must also test for the *end-of-file* condition. Thus if a file contains two records, it is actually read three times (once for each record, and once to sense the end-of-file condition).

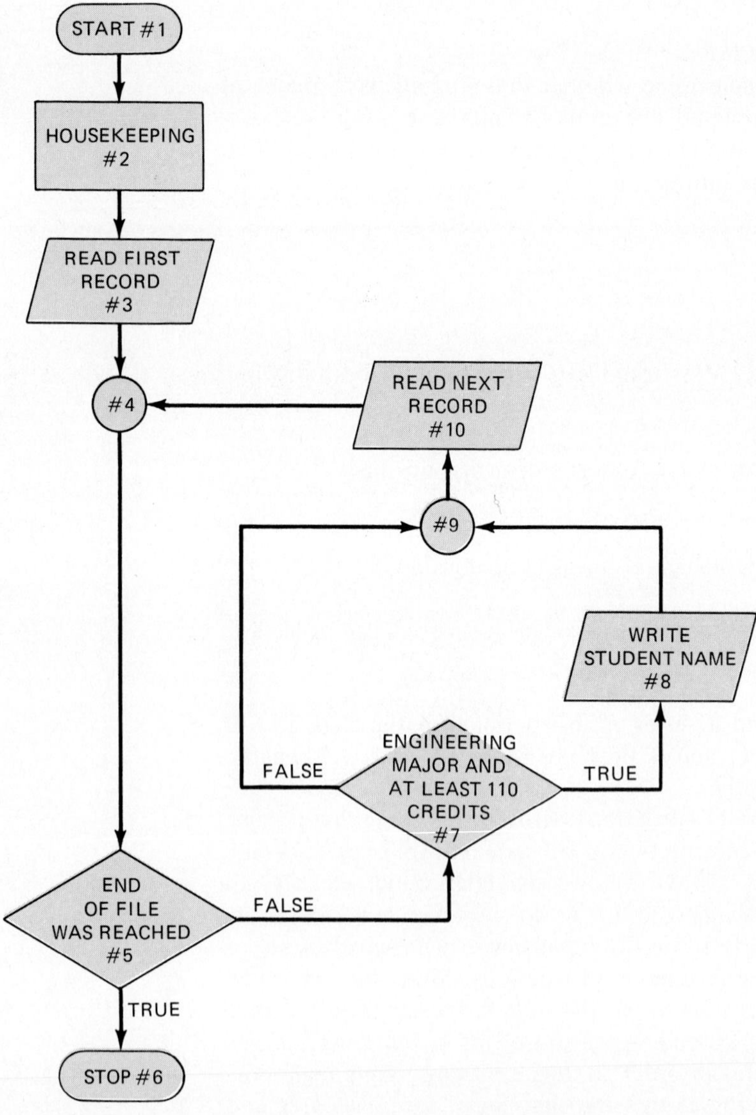

FIGURE 1.4 FLowchart to Select Engineering Majors with 110 Credits or More

The flowchart in Figure 1.4 begins with a start block (block 1), and continues with a housekeeping block (block 2). Housekeeping consists of statements that are done once at the start of processing, e.g., writing a heading at the start of a report. Block 3 is a READ statement, to obtain the first student record. Control then passes to a connector block (block 4) and through to a decision statement (block 5).

If the end of file has not been reached, control goes to the decision block (block 7) to determine if the record just read meets both qualifications. If so, that student's name is written to the output report in block 8; if not, control goes directly to the connector in block 9. *Observe that both the true and false branches from the condition block meet at a single connector in block 9.* The next record is read in block 10, after which control flows through the connector in block 4 to the end-of-file test in block 5. Eventually, when the end of file has been reached, control will pass to the stop statement in block 6.

To aid in further understanding how the flowchart works, we concoct some test data for the problem statement and run it through the flowchart. Assume that data have been prepared for four students as follows:

STUDENT NAME	CREDITS	MAJOR
John Adams	90	political science
Adam Smith	120	economics
Orville Wright	115	engineering
Francis Key	80	music

The flowchart begins execution with the start and housekeeping blocks. The third block reads the first record, John Adams. The end of file has not been reached, so block 5 directs flow to block 7, the test for engineering majors with at least 110 credits. John Adams "fails" the test; hence control passes through the connector in block 9 to the READ in block 10. The data for Adam Smith are now stored in the computer's memory. Control flows through the connector of block 4 to the end-of-file test in block 5. Adam Smith fails the test of block 7, causing flow to pass directly to the connector in block 9. So far, the data for two students, Adams and Smith, have been completely processed, but neither has passed the qualification test.

Control flows from the connector of block 9 to the READ in block 10, whereupon Orville Wright is read into memory. Since Wright is an engineering major with 110 credits, his name is written in block 8.

Francis Key is next read into memory in block 10. Control flows through the connector in block 4 to the end-of-file test in block 5. (Although Key is the last record, the end-of-file condition has *not* yet been detected.) Key fails the qualification test, whereupon control flows to the READ in block 10. This time the end of file is detected so that, when control again reaches the end-of-file test in block 5, processing will be directed to the STOP statement in block 6.

It is useful to summarize this discussion by tabulating the number of times each block in Figure 1.4 is executed:

BLOCK NUMBER		TIMES EXECUTED	EXPLANATION
1	Start	1	At beginning of program
2	Housekeeping	1	At beginning of program
3	Initial read	1	At beginning of program to read first record, i.e., Adams
4	Connector	5	Entered five times (marks the beginning of the repetition or loop structure)

5	End-of-file test	5	Once for each of four records; once to sense end-of-file condition
6	Stop	1	Executed once, at program's end
7	Qualification test	4	Once for each student
8	Write	1	Executed for Wright only, since no one else passed test of block 7
9	Connector	4	Entered four times (marks the end of the selection structure)
10	Read	4	Reads every record *but* the first and senses end of file

Pseudocode

Students, in general, do not like flowcharts. Nor do practicing programmers, who draw flowcharts only after a program has been written, and then only to satisfy a manager. However, both groups typically write notes to themselves before coding, and such notes are a form of *pseudocode*.

Pseudocode is a relatively new technique that expresses a program's logic more concisely than a flowchart. One definition of pseudocode is "neat notes to oneself," and since programmers do this naturally, pseudocode has come to replace the traditional flowchart. Consider Figure 1.5, which contains the identical logic as the flowchart in Figure 1.4, albeit in a more concise fashion.

As shown in Figure 1.5, the logic of most programs can be divided into three major portions: initialization, repetitive processing (i.e., a loop), and termination. Initialization is done once at the start of processing, e.g., reading the *first* record in a file. This is followed by a series of instructions that are executed repeatedly, once for each incoming record; hence, each record is evaluated for an engineering major with the requisite number of credits. If both conditions are met, the name will be written on the registrar's list; if the conditions are not met, nothing further is done with the particular record. When *all* the records in the file have been read, the loop is finished, and a termination routine is entered to print a total or simply stop processing.

Figure 1.5 also contains vertical lines connecting the words IF and ENDIF, and DO and ENDDO. This notation serves to indicate two basic building blocks *(selection* and *iteration)* of a discipline known as *structured programming*. The latter is explained fully in Chapter 7.

Pseudocode uses instructions similar to those of a computer language to describe program logic. However, it is *not* bound by precise syntactical rules as are formal programming languages. For example, the vertical lines referred to previously are the author's convention and do not necessarily appear in the

```
Initialization—read first record
┌DO while data remains
│  ┌IF engineering major with at least 110 credits
│  │     Write student's name on registrar's list
│  │ELSE
│  │     Do nothing more with this student
│  └ENDIF
│   Read next record
└ENDDO
Termination—stop
```

***FIGURE 1.5** Pseudocode for the Engineering Senior Problem*

pseudocode of others. Nor is pseudocode bound by any rules for indentation, which is done strictly at the discretion of the person using it. The purpose of pseudocode is simply to convey program logic in a straightforward and easily followed manner.

A FIRST LOOK AT COBOL

We now proceed to the COBOL program in Figure 1.6, which corresponds to the flowchart in Figure 1.4 and the pseudocode in Figure 1.5. The syntactical rules for COBOL are extremely precise, and you are certainly *not* expected to

```
       IDENTIFICATION DIVISION.
       PROGRAM-ID.    FIRSTTRY.
       AUTHOR.        JACKIE CLARK.

       ENVIRONMENT DIVISION.
       CONFIGURATION SECTION.
       SOURCE-COMPUTER.  IBM-4341.
       OBJECT-COMPUTER.  IBM-4341.
       INPUT-OUTPUT SECTION.
       FILE-CONTROL.
           SELECT STUDENT-FILE ASSIGN TO UT-S-SYSIN.
           SELECT PRINT-FILE   ASSIGN TO UT-S-SYSOUT.

       DATA DIVISION.
       FILE SECTION.
       FD  STUDENT-FILE
           LABEL RECORDS ARE OMITTED
           RECORD CONTAINS 80 CHARACTERS
           DATA RECORD IS STUDENT-IN.
       01  STUDENT-IN.
           05  STU-NAME                PIC X(25).
           05  STU-CREDITS             PIC 9(3).
           05  STU-MAJOR               PIC X(15).
           05  FILLER                  PIC X(37).

       FD  PRINT-FILE
           LABEL RECORDS ARE OMITTED
           RECORD CONTAINS 133 CHARACTERS
           DATA RECORD IS PRINT-LINE.
       01  PRINT-LINE.
           05  FILLER                  PIC X(8).
           05  PRINT-NAME              PIC X(25).
           05  FILLER                  PIC X(100).

       WORKING-STORAGE SECTION.
       01  DATA-REMAINS-SWITCH         PIC X(2)      VALUE SPACES.

       PROCEDURE DIVISION.
       MAINLINE.
           OPEN INPUT  STUDENT-FILE
                OUTPUT PRINT-FILE.
           READ STUDENT-FILE
               AT END MOVE 'NO' TO DATA-REMAINS-SWITCH.
           PERFORM PROCESS-RECORDS
               UNTIL DATA-REMAINS-SWITCH = 'NO'.
           CLOSE STUDENT-FILE
                 PRINT-FILE.
           STOP RUN.

       PROCESS-RECORDS.
           IF STU-CREDITS NOT < 110 AND STU-MAJOR = 'ENGINEERING'
               MOVE SPACES TO PRINT-LINE
               MOVE STU-NAME TO PRINT-NAME
               WRITE PRINT-LINE.

           READ STUDENT-FILE
               AT END MOVE 'NO' TO DATA-REMAINS-SWITCH.
```

Identification Division

Environment Division

Data Division

Procedure Division

FIGURE 1.6 The First COBOL Program

remember them after a brief exposure to Figure 1.6. The author believes, however, *that immediate exposure to a real program is extremely beneficial in stripping the mystical aura that too often surrounds programming*. Further, Figure 1.6 will become easier to understand after some brief explanation.

Every COBOL program consists of four divisions, which must be in a specified order:

Identification Division	This division contains the program name and author's name. It can also contain other identifying information such as date written or installation name.
Environment Division	This division mentions the computer on which the program is to be compiled and executed (usually one and the same). It also specifies the I/O devices to be used by the program.
Data Division	This division describes the data; for example, it specifies the incoming and outgoing positions in a record where various fields are located.
Procedure Division	This division contains the program logic, i.e., the instructions the computer is to execute in solving the problem.

Since COBOL is intended to resemble English, you may be able to get an overall sense of what is happening, merely by reading the program. We provide an intuitive explanation and reiterate that you should in no way be concerned with the precise syntax of the language. *Our present intent is to teach COBOL by example, with the short-term objective of achieving a conceptual understanding of a COBOL program.* We proceed with an overview of each of the four divisions.

Identification Division (Lines 1–3)

The Identification Division appears at the beginning of every program. It serves to identify the program (FIRSTTRY) and the author (Jackie Clark). There is nothing complicated about this division, and it has no effect on the results of the program.

Environment Division (Lines 5–12)

Although COBOL is intended to be machine independent, certain parts of every program are dependent on the hardware on which the program is actually run. The Environment Division is the link between the theoretically machine-independent program and its physical environment.

The Environment Division consists of two sections: the Configuration Section (lines 6–8) and the Input-Output Section (lines 9–12). The former contains the Source-Computer and Object-Computer paragraphs, which serve only for documentation.

The Input-Output Section describes the files used by the program. The Engineering Senior Program required two files, an input file containing the student records and an output file for the report. The names chosen by the programmer for these files (i.e., STUDENT-FILE and PRINT-FILE) are assigned to physical devices by the SELECT statement and associated ASSIGN clause. Line 11, for example, ties the incoming STUDENT-FILE to the physical device, UT-S-SYSIN; this tells the operating system to read the file containing the incoming student records from the device UT-S-SYSIN. (The name of the device, such as UT-S-SYSIN, is installation dependent and varies from computer to computer.)

Data Division (Lines 14–36)

The Data Division describes all data elements used by the program. It is divided into two sections, the File Section (lines 15–33) and the Working-Storage Section (lines 35–36). The File Section contains file description (FD) entries for files previously defined in SELECT statements. The FD for STUDENT-FILE extends from line 16 to line 19 and contains clauses to describe the physical characteristics of the file, e.g., a record length of 80 characters. The FD is followed by a record description which defines the various fields within a record.

The data elements themselves are preceded by *level numbers,* e.g., 01 and 05. The level number 01 is special and indicates that this line begins a *record description* entry. The fields within a record are defined through a series of PICTURE clauses (PIC is an acceptable abbreviation), which indicate the *type* and *length* of the field. A picture of 9's indicates a numeric field, whereas a picture of X's implies an alphanumeric field. The number in parentheses indicates the *length* of the field; for example, PIC 9(3) indicates a three-position numeric field, and X(25) is a 25-position alphanumeric field. The PICTURE clauses in lines 21–24 of Figure 1.6 are consistent with the record description in the original problem statement.

The Working-Storage Section is used to define any data names that do not appear in an input or output file. Its use will be made clearer after an examination of the Procedure Division.

Procedure Division (Lines 38–57)

The Procedure Division is the part of the program that "actually does something"; it contains the logic required to solve the problem. The Procedure Division is divided into paragraphs, each paragraph consisting of one or more sentences.

The first paragraph, MAINLINE, extends from line 39 to line 48. It begins by opening the two files defined previously and reading the first student record. It then *transfers control* to the paragraph PROCESS-RECORDS, which processes incoming student records until the data file is exhausted.

The IF statement in line 51 determines whether an incoming record meets both qualifications, i.e., whether the student is an engineering major with at least 110 credits. If *both* conditions are met, that student's name is written to the output report. The IF statement is terminated by the period in line 54; that is, if the condition in line 51 is met, every statement between the condition and the period in line 54 will be executed. Note that three COBOL statements are required to produce a detail line; the print line is cleared in line 52, the incoming name is moved to the output name in line 53, and the line is finally written in line 54.

The action of the PERFORM statement is explained with the aid of Figure 1.7. The PERFORM statement in line 44 transfers control to the paragraph PROCESS-RECORDS UNTIL DATA-REMAINS-SWITCH = 'NO', i.e., until the data file is empty. Accordingly the last statement of the performed routine is a READ statement to read the next record. When the end of file is reached, the AT END clause of the READ statement will move NO to DATA-REMAINS-SWITCH to terminate the perform. Control then returns to the statement under the PERFORM statement, that is, to line 46, which closes the files and terminates the run.

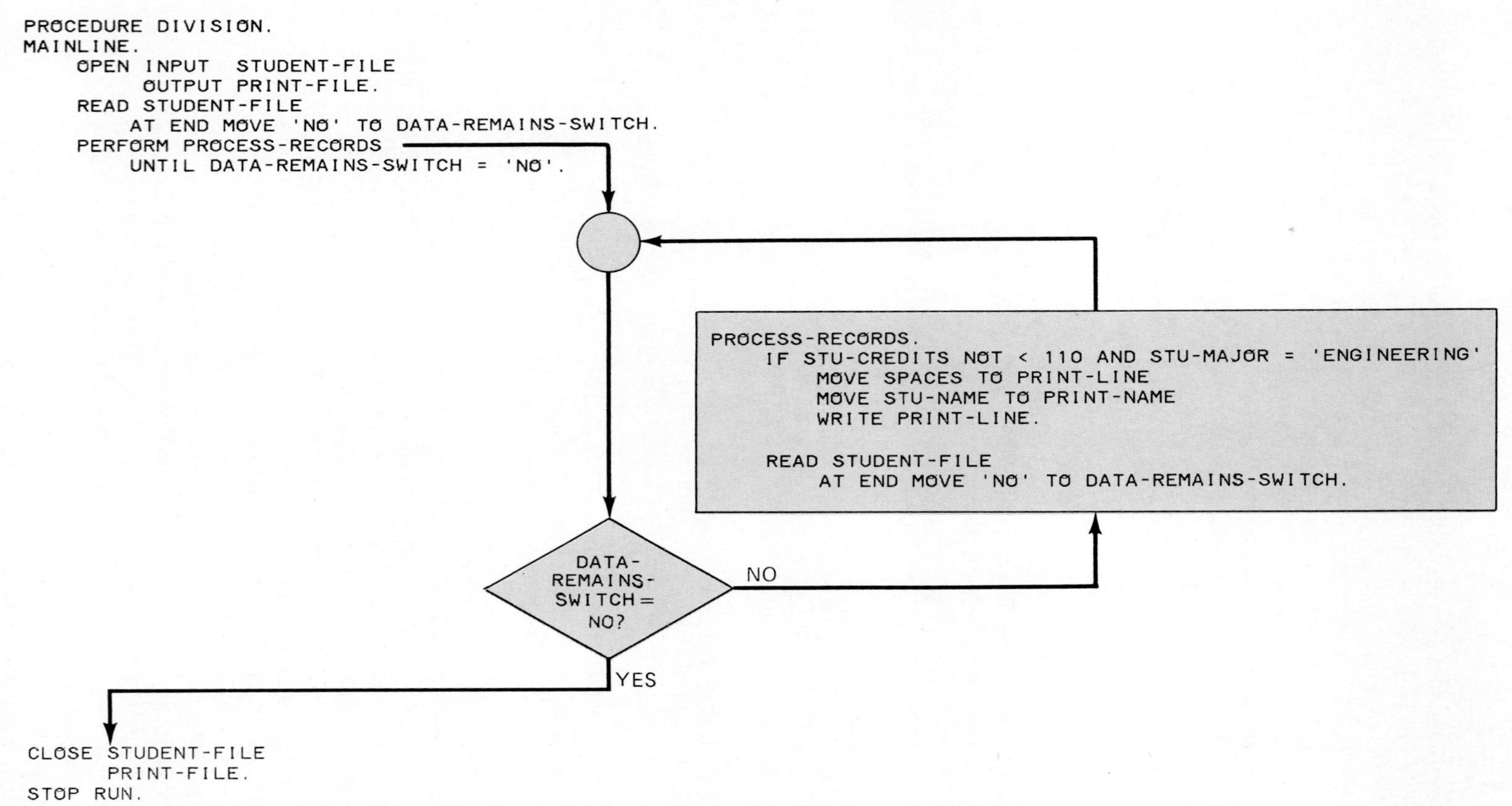
PROCEDURE DIVISION.
MAINLINE.
OPEN INPUT STUDENT-FILE
OUTPUT PRINT-FILE.
READ STUDENT-FILE
AT END MOVE 'NO' TO DATA-REMAINS-SWITCH.
PERFORM PROCESS-RECORDS
UNTIL DATA-REMAINS-SWITCH = 'NO'.
PROCESS-RECORDS.
IF STU-CREDITS NOT < 110 AND STU-MAJOR = 'ENGINEERING'
MOVE SPACES TO PRINT-LINE
MOVE STU-NAME TO PRINT-NAME
WRITE PRINT-LINE.
READ STUDENT-FILE
AT END MOVE 'NO' TO DATA-REMAINS-SWITCH.
DATA-REMAINS-SWITCH = NO?
NO
YES
CLOSE STUDENT-FILE
PRINT-FILE.
STOP RUN.

FIGURE 1.7 *Procedure Division for Engineering Senior Program*

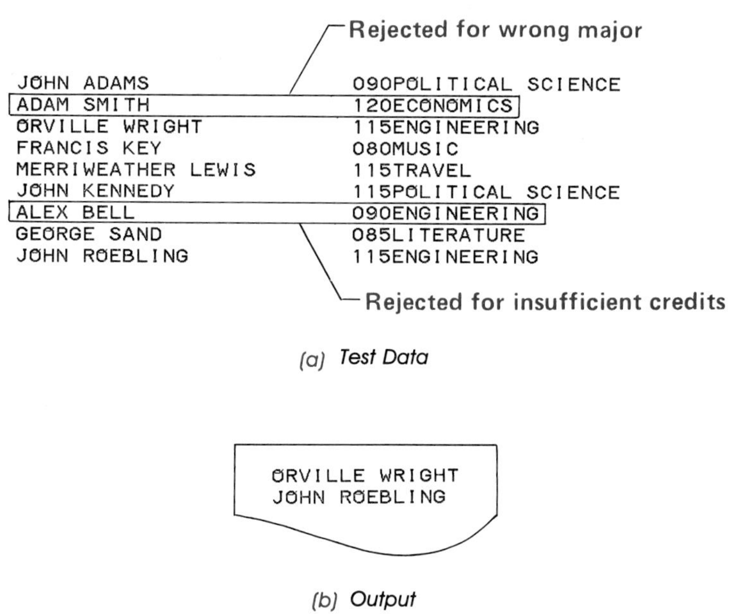

Rejected for wrong major
JOHN ADAMS 090POLITICAL SCIENCE
ADAM SMITH 120ECONOMICS
ORVILLE WRIGHT 115ENGINEERING
FRANCIS KEY 080MUSIC
MERRIWEATHER LEWIS 115TRAVEL
JOHN KENNEDY 115POLITICAL SCIENCE
ALEX BELL 090ENGINEERING
GEORGE SAND 085LITERATURE
JOHN ROEBLING 115ENGINEERING
Rejected for insufficient credits
ORVILLE WRIGHT
JOHN ROEBLING

(a) Test Data

(b) Output

FIGURE 1.8 Test Data and Output for Engineering Senior Problem

Test Data

Figure 1.8 contains test data and the associated output produced by the program in Figure 1.6. (The first four records in Figure 1.8*a* were discussed previously in conjunction with the flowchart.) You should be able to state the reasons why individual records were not selected; e.g., Adam Smith and Alex Bell were rejected for the wrong major and an insufficient number of credits, respectively. (Can you identify all nine of our famous students?)

ELEMENTS OF COBOL

Although you are *not* yet expected to write a COBOL program, you should be able to follow simple programs like the one in Figure 1.6 intuitively. This section begins a formal discussion of COBOL so that you will eventually be able to write an entire program.

COBOL consists of six language elements: reserved words, programmer-supplied names, literals, symbols, level numbers, and pictures. *Reserved words* have special significance to COBOL and are used in a rigidly prescribed manner. They must be spelled correctly, or the compiler will not be able to recognize them. The list of reserved words varies from compiler to compiler, and a comprehensive list is given in Appendix C. The beginner is urged to refer frequently to this appendix for two reasons: (1) to ensure the proper spelling of reserved words used in his or her program, and (2) to avoid the inadvertent use of reserved words as *programmer-supplied* names.

The programmer supplies names for paragraph, data, and file names. A *paragraph name* is a tag to which the program refers, e.g., PROCESS-RECORDS or MAINLINE in Figure 1.6. *File names* are specified in several places throughout a COBOL program, but their initial appearance is in the Environment Division, e.g., STUDENT-FILE and PRINT-FILE in Figure 1.6. Data names are the elements on which instructions operate, e.g., STU-NAME, STU-CREDITS, and STU-MAJOR in Figure 1.6. A programmer supplies paragraph, file or data names within the following rules:

- ☐ A programmer-supplied name may contain the letters A to Z, the digits 0 to 9, and the hyphen (-). No other characters are permitted, not even blanks.
- ☐ Data names must contain at least one letter. Paragraph and section names may be all numeric.
- ☐ A programmer-supplied name may not begin or end with a hyphen.
- ☐ Reserved words may not be used as programmer-supplied names.
- ☐ Programmer-supplied names must be 30 characters or less in length.

The following examples illustrate the rules associated with programmer-supplied names:

PROGRAMMER-SUPPLIED NAME	*EXPLANATION*
SUM	Invalid—reserved word
SUM-OF-X	Valid
SUM OF X	Invalid—contains blanks
SUM-OF-X-	Invalid—ends with a hyphen
SUM-OF-ALL-THE-XS	Valid
SUM-OF-ALL-THE-XS-IN-ENTIRE-PROGRAM	Invalid—more than 30 characters
GROSS-PAY-IN-$	Invalid—contains a $
12345	Valid as a paragraph name but invalid as a data name

A *literal* is an exact value or constant. It may be *numeric* (i.e., a number) or *nonnumeric* (i.e., enclosed in quotes). Literals appear throughout a program and are frequently used to compare the value of a data name to a specified constant. Consider line 51 of Figure 1.6:

```
IF STU-CREDITS NOT < 110 AND STU-MAJOR = 'ENGINEERING'
```

In the first portion STU-CREDITS is compared to 110, a numeric literal. The second part contains a nonnumeric literal, ENGINEERING. Nonnumeric literals are contained in quotes and may be up to 120 characters in length. Anything, including blanks, numbers, and reserved words, may appear in the quotes and be part of the literal. Numeric literals can be up to 18 digits long and may begin with a leading (leftmost) plus or minus sign. A numeric literal may contain a decimal point but may not end with a decimal point. Examples are shown:

LITERAL	*EXPLANATION*
123.4	Valid numeric literal
'123.4'	Valid nonnumeric literal
+123	Valid numeric literal
'IDENTIFICATION DIVISION'	Valid nonnumeric literal
123.	Invalid numeric literal—may not end with a decimal point
123−	Invalid numeric literal—the minus sign must be in the leftmost position

TABLE 1.1 COBOL Symbols

CATEGORY	SYMBOL	MEANING
Punctuation	.	Denotes end of COBOL entry
	,	Delineates clauses
	;	Delineates clauses
	" " or ' '	Sets off nonnumeric literals
	( )	Encloses subscripts or expressions
Arithmetic	+	Addition
	−	Subtraction
	*	Multiplication
	/	Division
	**	Exponentiation
Relational	=	Equal to
	>	Greater than
	<	Less than

Symbols are of three types, punctuation, arithmetic, and relational, and are listed in Table 1.1.

The use of relational and arithmetic symbols is described in detail later in the text, beginning in Chapter 3. Commas and semicolons are used to improve the readability of a program, and their omission (or inclusion) does not constitute an error. Periods, on the other hand, should be used after a completed entry, and their omission could cause difficulty. Thus, there are two rules with respect to punctuation symbols. The first is an absolute requirement; violation will cause compiler errors. The second is strongly recommended; violation will *not* cause compiler errors but could cause execution errors.

1. A space must follow and may not precede a comma, semicolon, or period. (Thus a space is a valid and necessary symbol.)
2. All entries should be terminated by a period.

Consider these examples:

1. OPEN INPUT STUDENT-FILE, OUTPUT PRINT-FILE.
2. OPEN INPUT STUDENT-FILE OUTPUT PRINT-FILE.
3. OPEN INPUT STUDENT-FILE, OUTPUT PRINT-FILE
4. OPEN INPUT STUDENT-FILE , OUTPUT PRINT-FILE.
5. OPEN INPUT STUDENT-FILE,OUTPUT PRINT-FILE.

Examples 1 and 2 are perfect. Example 3 is missing a period; although that is not an error, it does violate our second guideline. In example 4, the comma is preceded by a space. Example 5 is missing a space after the comma.

Level numbers and pictures are discussed more fully in Chapter 3 under the Data Division. Level numbers describe the relationship of items in a record. For example, under STUDENT-FILE in Figure 1.6, there was a single 01-level entry and several 05-level entries. In general, the higher (numerically) the level number, the less significant the entry; thus 05 is less important than 01. Entries with higher numeric values are said to belong to the levels above them. Thus, in Figure 1.6 the several 05-level entries belong to their respective 01-level entries.

Pictures describe the nature of incoming or outgoing data. A picture of 9's means the entry is numeric; a picture of X's means the entry is alphanumeric, i.e., it can contain letters, numbers, and special characters. (Alphabetic pictures,

```
00001           IDENTIFICATION DIVISION.
00002           PROGRAM-ID.    FIRSTTRY.
00003           AUTHOR.        JACKIE CLARK.
00004
00005           ENVIRONMENT DIVISION.
00006           CONFIGURATION SECTION.
00007           SOURCE-COMPUTER.  IBM-4341.
00008           OBJECT-COMPUTER.  IBM-4341.
00009           INPUT-OUTPUT SECTION.
00010           FILE-CONTROL.
00011               SELECT STUDENT-FILE ASSIGN TO UT-S-SYSIN.
00012               SELECT PRINT-FILE   ASSIGN TO UT-S-SYSOUT.
00013
00014           DATA DIVISION.
00015           FILE SECTION.
00016           FD  STUDENT-FILE
00017               LABEL RECORDS ARE OMITTED
00018               RECORD CONTAINS 80 CHARACTERS
00019               DATA RECORD IS STUDENT-IN.
00020           01  STUDENT-IN.
00021               05  STU-NAME                PIC X(25).
00022               05  STU-CREDITS             PIC 9(3).
00023               05  STU-MAJOR               PIC X(15).
00024               05  FILLER                  PIC X(37).
00025
00026           FD  PRINT-FILE
00027               LABEL RECORDS ARE OMITTED
00028               RECORD CONTAINS 133 CHARACTERS
00029               DATA RECORD IS PRINT-LINE.
00030           01  PRINT-LINE.
00031               05  FILLER                  PIC X(8).
00032               05  PRINT-NAME              PIC X(25).
00033               05  FILLER                  PIC X(100).
00034
00035           WORKING-STORAGE SECTION.
00036           01  DATA-REMAINS-SWITCH         PIC X(2)      VALUE SPACES.
00037
00038           PROCEDURE DIVISION.
00039           MAINLINE.
00040               OPEN INPUT  STUDENT-FILE
00041                    OUTPUT PRINT-FILE.
00042               READ STUDENT-FILE
00043                   AT END MOVE 'NO' TO DATA-REMAINS-SWITCH.
00044               PERFORM PROCESS-RECORDS
00045                   UNTIL DATA-REMAINS-SWITCH = 'NO'.
00046               CLOSE STUDENT-FILE
00047                     PRINT-FILE.
00048               STOP RUN.
00049
00050           PROCESS-RECORDS.
00051               IF STU-CREDITS NOT < 110 AND STU-MAJOR = 'ENGINEERING'
00052                   MOVE SPACES TO PRINT-LINE
00053                   MOVE STU-NAME TO PRINT-NAME
00054                   WRITE PRINT-LINE.
00055
00056               READ STUDENT-FILE
00057                   AT END MOVE 'NO' TO DATA-REMAINS-SWITCH.
```

Programmer-supplied file name appears in several places (see lines 40, 42, and 46).
PICTURE clauses describe the incoming record and are consistent with Figure 1.1.
Reserved words (see Appendix C).
Programmer-supplied paragraph name.
Nonnumeric literal
Numeric literal

FIGURE 1.9 The First COBOL Program

with a picture of A, are seldom used; even names can contain apostrophes or hyphens, which are alphanumeric rather than alphabetic in nature.)

Consider now Figure 1.9, a relabeled version of our first COBOL program (Figure 1.6). This time our intention is to emphasize the various COBOL elements as they appear in a complete program. Observe, for example, the definition of a *file name,* STUDENT-FILE, in the SELECT statement of line 11, and its subsequent appearance in the FD of line 16, and the OPEN, READ, and CLOSE statements of lines 40, 42, and 46. Notice the definition of the various *data names* in lines 21–23 (accomplished through level numbers and PICTURE clauses) and the subsequent appearances in the Procedure Division. Note the consistency of the paragraph name in the PERFORM statement of line 44 and the paragraph header in line 50. Observe that literals appear in the IF statement of line 51 and in the AT END clause of the READ statement (line 57). Finally, note the abundant use of COBOL reserved words (PROCEDURE, DIVISION, WORKING-STORAGE, SECTION, etc.) throughout.

DIFFERENT VERSIONS OF COBOL

COBOL was first introduced in 1959, largely through the efforts of Captain Grace Murray Hopper of the United States Navy. At its inception, COBOL was designed to be "open ended and capable of accepting change and amendment." It was also intended to be a highly *portable* language; i.e., a COBOL program written for an IBM computer should also run on a UNIVAC, a TRS-80, or any other machine that supports the language. Over the years the needs of an evolving language and the desire for compatibility among vendors have given rise to several COBOL standards, notably COBOL 68, COBOL 74, and most recently COBOL 8X.

All listings in this text (with the exception of those in Appendix B) were run under the 74 compiler (specifically the IBM OS/VS compiler). The 74 listings in this book are *upwardly compatible,* i.e., they will run under an 8X compiler with no modification whatever. The converse is not true; one *cannot* take an 8X listing from Appendix B and expect it to run unchanged under the earlier compiler. This is because the 8X examples are written to take advantage of enhancements in the newer compiler.

This book is intended for use in installations with either COBOL 74 or COBOL 8X. Accordingly, many chapters will describe relevant differences between the two COBOL standards in a concluding section entitled "COBOL 8X: Changes and Enhancements." In order to avoid confusion, all 8X material is color tinted. If you are running under COBOL 74, there is no need for you to read any of the tinted material. However, if you have access to the new compiler, the tinted sections will be very interesting.

Summary

This chapter is intended as an introduction to COBOL programming and the text that follows. A substantial amount of material has been presented, the true significance of which will be better appreciated as you progress through the text. In the meantime, a recap should prove helpful:

- ☐ *Every computer application consists of input, processing, and output.*
- ☐ *Input and output must be precisely specified as to content and location.*
- ☐ *The computer cannot think for itself but must be told precisely what to do. This is done through a series of instructions known as a program.*
- ☐ *The computer does not do anything that a human being could not do if given sufficient time. The advantages of a computer stem from its speed and accuracy.*
- ☐ *A flowchart and/or pseudocode are representations of the logic embodied in a computer program.*
- ☐ *COBOL contains six language elements: reserved words, programmer-supplied names, literals, symbols, level numbers, and pictures.*
- ☐ *COBOL is intended to be an evolving language, with portability between different vendors. The differences between the 74 and 8X versions will be highlighted throughout the text.*

True/False Exercises

1. Nonnumeric literals may not contain numbers.
2. Numeric literals may not contain letters.
3. A data name may not contain any characters other than letters or numbers.
4. The rules for forming paragraph names and data names are exactly the same.
5. A data name may not consist of more than 30 characters.
6. A nonnumeric literal may not contain more than 30 characters.
7. A numeric literal may contain up to 18 digits.
8. There are four divisions in a COBOL program.
9. The divisions of a COBOL program may appear in any order.
10. Data description appears in the Identification Division.
11. A record contains one or more fields.
12. A file is a set of records.
13. Computers can think for themselves.
14. No statement in a computer program may be executed more than once.
15. A rectangle is the standard flowchart symbol for a decision block.
16. Reserved words may appear in a nonnumeric literal.
17. Reserved words may be used as data names.
18. Pseudocode serves the same function as a flowchart.
19. Pseudocode must be written according to precise syntactical rules.
20. There are subtle differences between the COBOL 74 and COBOL 8X compilers.

Problems

1. Indicate whether the entries below are valid as data names. If any entry is invalid, state the reason.

   (a) NUMBER-OF-TIMES
   (b) CODE
   (c) 12345
   (d) ONE TWO THREE
   (e) IDENTIFICATION-DIVISION
   (f) IDENTIFICATION
   (g) HOURS-
   (h) GROSS-PAY
   (i) GROSS-PAY-IN-$

2. Classify the entries below as being valid or invalid literals. For each valid entry, indicate whether it is numeric or nonnumeric; for each invalid entry, state why it is invalid.

   (a) 567
   (b) 567.
   (c) −567
   (d) +567
   (e) +567.
   (f) '567.'
   (g) 'FIVE SIX SEVEN'
   (h) '−567'
   (i) 567−
   (j) 567+
   (k) '567+'

3. Indicate whether the following entries are acceptable according to the COBOL rules for punctuation. Correct any invalid entries.

(a) CLOSE STUDENT-FILE,PRINT-FILE.
(b) CLOSE STUDENT-FILE PRINT-FILE.
(c) CLOSE STUDENT-FILE, PRINT-FILE
(d) CLOSE STUDENT-FILE , PRINT-FILE.
(e) CLOSE STUDENT-FILE, PRINT-FILE.

4. (a) Which division(s) do not contain paragraph names?
(b) Which division(s) contain the SELECT statement(s)?
(c) Which division(s) contain level numbers?
(d) Which division(s) contain data names?
(e) Which division(s) contain reserved words?
(f) Which division(s) contain PICTURE clauses?
(g) Which division(s) do not contain file names?

5. Given the COBOL program in Figure 1.6, indicate what changes would have to be made if

(a) We wanted music students rather than engineering students.
(b) We wanted students with 60 or fewer credits.
(c) The student major was contained in columns 60–74 of the incoming record.
(d) We wanted engineering students *or* students with 110 credits or more.

Note: Treat parts (a), (b), (c), and (d) independently.

6. Which division in a COBOL program contains

(a) The Configuration Section?
(b) The File Section?
(c) Statements to open and close files?
(d) The description of incoming data?
(e) The description of outgoing data?
(f) The author's name?
(g) The program's name?
(h) Statements to read information?
(i) Statements to write information?

Note: Use Figure 1.6 as a guide, and indicate specific line numbers where the information is found.

7. Your programming supervisor has drawn a flowchart for you to code. He left the flowchart on his dining room table at home, and unfortunately his three-year-old son, Benjy, cut it up into pieces with a pair of scissors. Your supervisor has collected the pieces (shown in Figure 1.10) and has asked you to rearrange them properly into a correct flowchart; do so. The flowchart is to read a file with each record containing three *unequal* numbers, A, B, and C. Write out the *greater* of the two sums (A + B) and (B + C) for each record *only* if A is less than 50. *Develop the equivalent pseudocode.*

8. World Wide Sales, Inc., wishes to promote one of its employees to head the South American Division. The selected employee must speak Spanish, be 40 or younger, and hold a college degree. The programming manager has prepared the necessary flowchart (see Figure 1.11), but unfortunately Benjy and his scissors got to it first (see Problem 7). Your job is to put the flowchart together. Note that there may be more than one employee who qualifies for the position. Accordingly, the flowchart includes the necessary logic to count and print the number of qualified employees and to print the name of every such employee. *Develop the equivalent pseudocode.*

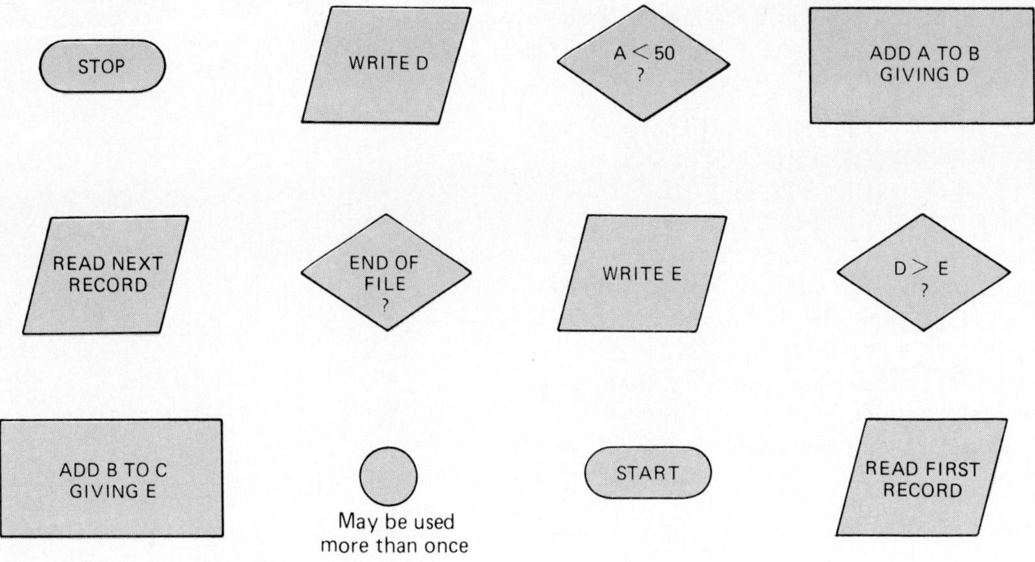

FIGURE 1.10 Flowchart Blocks for Problem 7

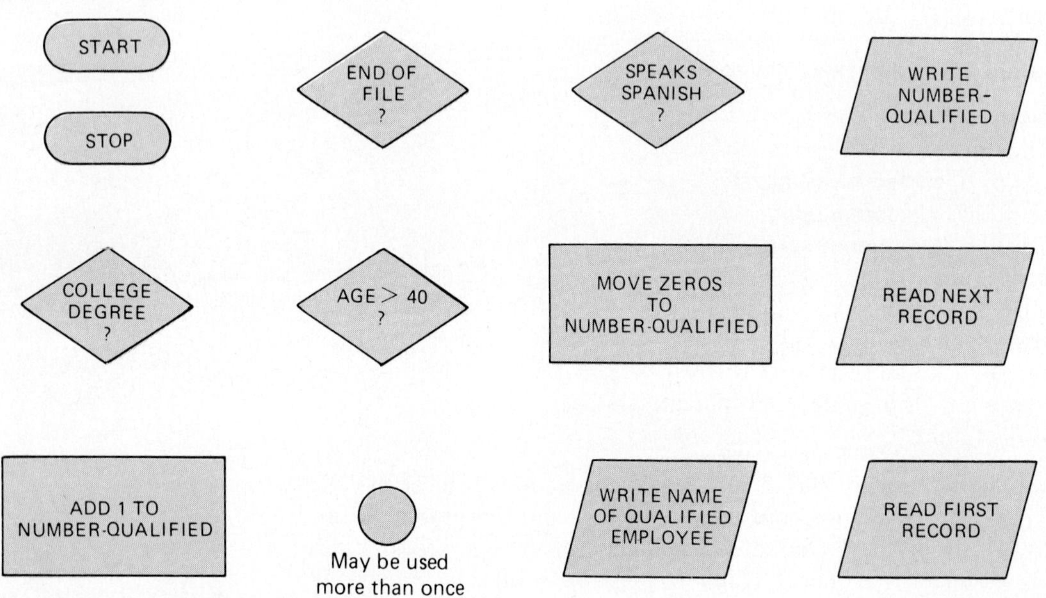

FIGURE 1.11 Flowchart Blocks for Problem 8

9. Figure 1.12 contains a COBOL program to process a file of employee records and print the names of programmers under 30. Using Figure 1.6 as a guide, restore the missing information so that the program will run as intended.

```
       IDENTIFICATION DIVISION.
       PROGRAM-ID.    FIRSTTRY.
       [            ]  JACKIE CLARK.                          (1)

       ENVIRONMENT DIVISION.
       CONFIGURATION SECTION.
       SOURCE-COMPUTER.  IBM-4341.
       OBJECT-COMPUTER.  IBM-4341.
       INPUT-OUTPUT SECTION.                                  (2)
       FILE-CONTROL.
           SELECT EMPLOYEE-FILE   ASSIGN TO UT-S-SYSIN.
           [      ] PRINT-FILE    ASSIGN TO UT-S-SYSOUT.

       [              ]                                       (3)
       FILE SECTION.
       FD  EMPLOYEE-FILE
           LABEL RECORDS ARE OMITTED
           RECORD CONTAINS 80 CHARACTERS
           DATA RECORD IS EMPLOYEE-CARD.
       01  EMPLOYEE-CARD.
           05  EMP-NAME              PIC X(25).
           05  EMP-TITLE             PIC X(10).
           05  EMP-AGE               PIC 99.
           05  FILLER                PIC XX.
           05  EMP-SALARY            PIC 9(5).
           05  FILLER                PIC X(36).               (4)

       FD  PRINT-FILE
           [             ] ARE OMITTED
           RECORD CONTAINS 133 CHARACTERS
           DATA RECORD IS PRINT-LINE.                         (5)
       01  PRINT-LINE.
           05  FILLER                PIC X(1).
           05  PRINT-NAME            [         ]
           05  FILLER                PIC X(2).
           05  PRINT-AGE             PIC 99.
           05  FILLER                PIC X(3).
           05  PRINT-SALARY          PIC 9(5).                (6)
           05  FILLER                PIC X(95).

       [                      ]
       01  END-OF-DATA-FLAG          PIC X(3)  [           ]  (7)

       PROCEDURE DIVISION.                                    (8)
       MAINLINE-ROUTINE.
           [    ] INPUT  EMPLOYEE-FILE
                  OUTPUT PRINT-FILE.
           MOVE SPACES TO PRINT-LINE.
           MOVE ' SALARY REPORT FOR PROGRAMMERS UNDER 30' TO PRINT-LINE.
           WRITE PRINT-LINE AFTER ADVANCING 2 LINES.
           READ EMPLOYEE-FILE
               AT END MOVE 'YES' TO END-OF-DATA-FLAG.         (9)

           [       ] PROCESS-EMPLOYEE-RECORDS
               UNTIL END-OF-DATA-FLAG = 'YES'.
           CLOSE EMPLOYEE-FILE
                 PRINT-FILE.
           STOP RUN.
                                                              (10)
       PROCESS-EMPLOYEE-RECORDS.
           IF EMP-TITLE = 'PROGRAMMER' AND EMP-AGE < 30
               MOVE [         ]  TO PRINT-LINE
               MOVE EMP-NAME     TO PRINT-NAME                (11)
               MOVE [         ]  TO PRINT-AGE
               MOVE EMP-SALARY TO PRINT-SALARY
               WRITE PRINT-LINE AFTER ADVANCING 2 LINES.
                                                              (12)
           READ EMPLOYEE-FILE
               AT END MOVE [     ] TO END-OF-DATA-FLAG.
```

FIGURE 1.12 COBOL Listing for Problem 9

The Programming Process

2

Overview

One objective of this book is to teach you COBOL programming. A broader objective is to teach you how to solve problems using the computer. To this end, we shall present a generally accepted problem-solving procedure consisting of seven steps:

1. *Problem statement and analysis*
2. *Flowcharting and/or pseudocode*
3. *Coding and data entry*
4. *Preparation of test data*
5. *Preparation of job control statements*
6. *Program testing: phase 1 (compilation)*
7. *Program testing: phase 2 (execution)*

This chapter continues to focus on the engineering senior problem of Chapter 1 and covers specifics to enable you to run your own program. We discuss the COBOL coding form, use of a text editor, and submission to the computer. We cover the "compile, link, and go" sequence and discuss the differences between problem- and machine-oriented languages. We prepare you for the errors you will almost inevitably make and discuss fundamentals of debugging.

At the conclusion of this chapter we shall ask you to submit the program of Chapter 1 to your computer center. *"Seeing is believing" is especially pertinent to data processing. After you have seen computer output from your own program, many of your questions will answer themselves. Although it would not be surprising if you felt a bit confused after reading Chapter 1, the sooner you get down to running a program, the sooner things will resolve themselves. You will need to supplement this book by extensive interaction with the computer.* □

A PROBLEM-SOLVING PROCEDURE

Figure 2.1 contains a flowchart that depicts the various steps in solving a problem through use of a computer. The first step is to obtain a clear statement of the problem containing a complete description of the input and desired output.

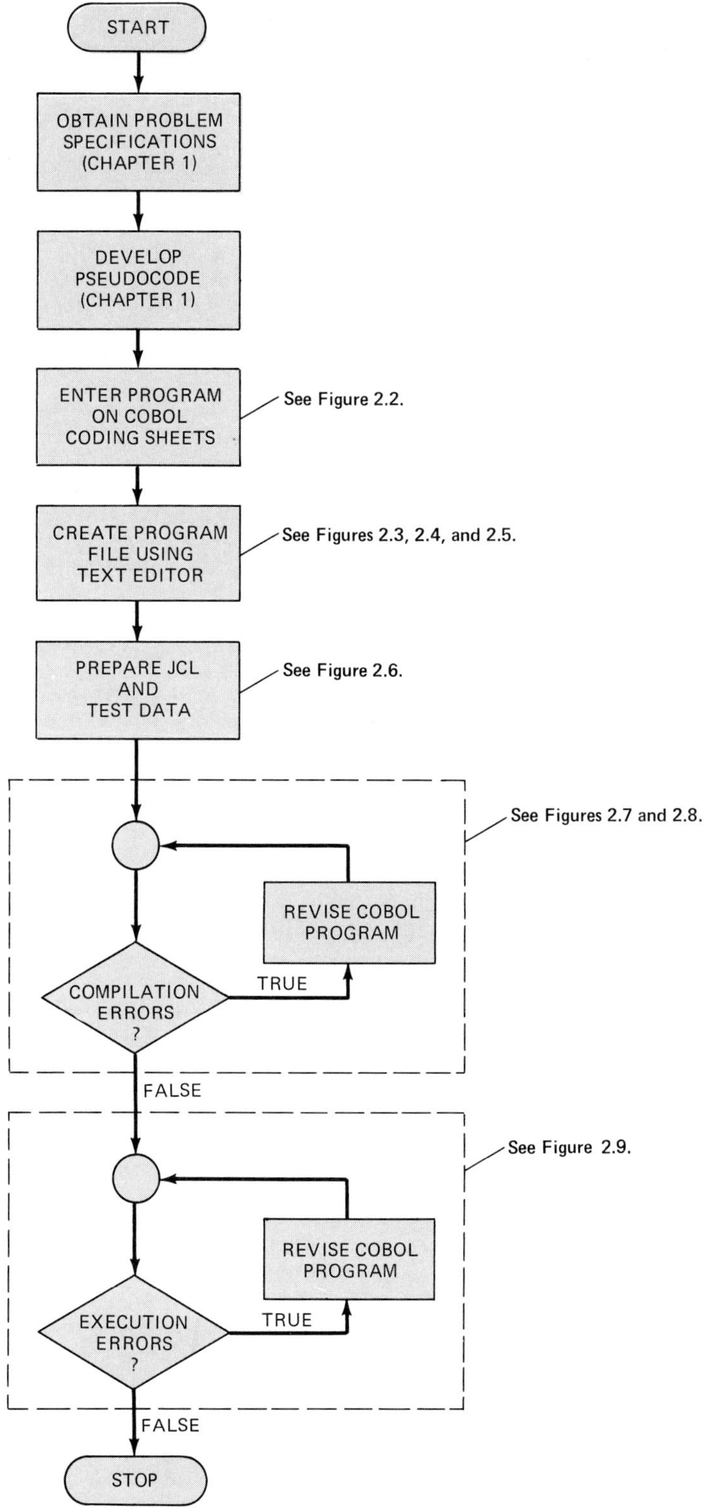

FIGURE 2.1 The Programming Process

The problem statement should also contain processing specifications. It is not enough merely to say "calculate a student's quality point average (QPA)." The method for calculating QPA must be given as well.

Once the input, output, and processing specifications have been enumerated, a flowchart is drawn or pseudocode is developed. Either technique summarizes the logic to be used in solving the problem. Careful attention to this step simplifies subsequent coding.

Coding is the translation of a flowchart or pseudocode into COBOL. Coding must be done within well-defined COBOL rules and coding conventions and must adhere to "rules of the coding sheet."

After the program is written on coding sheets, it is put into machine-readable form through a *text editor*. Unlike COBOL, which is constant from machine to machine, text editors vary greatly from computer to computer. Nevertheless, we cover very basic principles, and there should be little difficulty in adapting this information to a particular installation.

The COBOL program is submitted in conjunction with a set of *job control statements*. The latter provide information to a computer's operating system as to the location of the COBOL program and/or its associated data. *Job control language* (JCL) also varies greatly from installation to installation.

After a program is submitted, *compilation* begins. (A *compiler* is a computer program that translates a higher level language, such as COBOL, into a machine language.) Initial attempts at compilation are apt to identify several errors, which may be due to misspellings, missing periods, misplaced parentheses, etc. Corrections are made, and the program is recompiled. Only after the compilation has been successfully completed can we proceed to execution.

During *execution* one is apt to encounter logical errors. In this step the computer does *exactly* what it is instructed to do, but it may have been instructed incorrectly. For example, assume the word OR replaced the word AND in line 51 of Figure 1.6, the engineering senior problem. The program would then select *either* engineering majors *or* seniors. Either way, it would function differently from the original, logically correct version. The program would still compile perfectly in that the COBOL syntax was correct. However, it would not execute as intended. Corrections are made, the program is recompiled, and testing continues.

The presence of two decision blocks in Figure 2.1 indicates the iterative nature of the entire process. Few, if any, programs compile correctly on the first try—hence the need to recode specific statements. Similarly, few programs execute properly on the first test and thus the need to reflowchart, recode, recompile, etc.

We return now to the engineering senior problem of Chapter 1. Our purpose in the opening chapter was to provide a rapid introduction to COBOL to give you an immediate feeling of what programming is all about. *The present objective is to enable you to execute the program.* Hence we shall discuss the COBOL coding form, use of a text editor, submission to the computer, and debugging.

THE COBOL CODING FORM

The COBOL compiler is very particular about the information it receives; certain positions (columns) of each statement are reserved for specific elements of COBOL. For example, division and section headers are required to begin between columns 8 and 11, whereas most other statements may begin in or past column 12. Further, there are additional rules for continuation (what happens if a sentence does not fit on one line), comments, optional sequencing of source statements in columns 1–6, and program identification in columns 73–80. Rules of the coding sheet are summarized in Table 2.1 and illustrated in Figure 2.2. The latter shows completed forms for the engineering senior problem of Chapter 1.

Several features in Figure 2.2 bear mention. Note in particular the wavy

TABLE 2.1 Rules for the COBOL Coding Form

COLUMNS	EXPLANATION AND USE
1–6	Optional sequence numbers: If this field is coded, the compiler performs a sequence check on incoming COBOL statements by flagging any statements out of order. Although some commercial installations encourage this option, we advise against it, especially if you are entering your own programs.
7	Used to indicate comments and for continuation of nonnumeric literals: A comment may appear anywhere in a COBOL program and is indicated by an asterisk (*) in column 7. Comments appear on the source listing but are otherwise ignored by the compiler.
8–11	Known as the "A margin": Division headers, section headers, paragraph names, FD's, and 01's all begin in the A margin.
12–72	Known as the "B margin": All remaining entries begin in or past column 12. COBOL permits considerable flexibility here, but individual installations have their own requirements. We, for example, begin PICTURE clauses in the same column, e.g., column 37, for better readability. (We shall discuss this further in Chapter 5.)
73–80	Program identification: a second optional field, which is ignored by the compiler. Different installations have different standards regarding use of this field.

line under various PIC entries to indicate that identical information is to be entered on subsequent lines. Of greatest import, however, is the conformity between the entries in Figure 2.2 and the COBOL requirements of Table 2.1.

Though use of coding sheets is not mandatory, their use is highly recommended. The information in Figure 2.2 is not *machine readable,* i.e., the COBOL statements must still be entered into the computer via a *text editor,* which is discussed in the next section. However, *your life will be greatly simplified if you organize your task as fully as possible before entering your computer center.* A good start is to have your program *neatly* coded in the appropriate columns.

USE OF A TEXT EDITOR

Once a program has been entered on coding sheets, it must be put into machine-readable form and submitted to the computer. Previous COBOL texts, written for use during the 1960s and early 1970s, discussed the punched card as the primary storage medium for student programs, the keypunch as the associated means of data entry, and batch processing (often with turnaround times of several hours or more) as the way in which programs were submitted.

The student of the 1980s is far more fortunate in the technology available. You will use terminals to a large mainframe, and/or a stand-alone microcomputer. Either way, the days of carrying (and dropping or losing) card decks are over. Of greater import is the use of *interactive* computing, which enables students to obtain several executions at a single session instead of having to wait hours (or days) to retrieve a single run, wait hours more for the next run, etc. This is accomplished through use of a *text editor,* a program that enters and manipulates COBOL statements.

There are many different editors available, and needless to say, we will not attempt to consider all of them. Instead, we will briefly cover the underlying principles and leave you to brush up on the system available at your installation.

Figure 2.3 is yet another version of the Engineering Senior Program. The *line* numbers that appear at the left of this listing are associated with a *text editor.* These line numbers begin with 10 and continue to 570 in increments of

Columns 1 - 6 for optional sequence numbers (not used in this program)

COBOL CODING FORM

PROGRAM FIRST TRY	REQUESTED BY	PAGE 1 OF 3
PROGRAMMER J. CLARK	DATE 9/1Ø/85	IDENT. 73 80

PAGE NO. 1 3 | LINE NO. 4 6 | 7 | A 8 | 11 | B 12 | 16 | 20 | 24 | 28 | 32 | 36 | 40 | 44 | 48 | 52 | 56 | 60 | 64 | 68 | 72 Z

```
IDENTIFICATION DIVISION.
PROGRAM-ID.     FIRSTTRY.
AUTHOR.         J. CLARK.

ENVIRONMENT DIVISION.
CONFIGURATION SECTION.
SOURCE-COMPUTER.   IBM-4341.
OBJECT-COMPUTER.   IBM-4341.
INPUT-OUTPUT SECTION.
FILE-CONTROL.
    SELECT STUDENT-FILE ASSIGN TO UT-S-SYSIN.
    SELECT PRINT-FILE   ASSIGN TO UT-S-SYSOUT.

DATA DIVISION.
FILE SECTION.
FD  STUDENT-FILE
    LABEL RECORD ARE OMITTED
    RECORD CONTAINS 8Ø CHARACTERS
    DATA RECORD IS STUDENT-IN.
Ø1  STUDENT-IN.
    Ø5  STU-NAME             PIC X(25).
        STU-CREDITS              9(3).
        STU-MAJOR                X(15).
        FILLER                   X(37).
```

Division, section, and paragraph headers; FD and 01 entries begin in column 8.

Picture clauses begin anywhere after data names end; column 37 was chosen.

FIGURE 2.2 *The COBOL Coding Form*

COBOL CODING FORM

PROGRAM FIRSTTRY | REQUESTED BY | PAGE 2 OF 3

PROGRAMMER J. CLARK | DATE 9/10/85 | IDENT.

```
       FD  PRINT-FILE
           LABEL RECORDS ARE OMITTED
           RECORD CONTAINS 133 CHARACTERS
           DATA RECORD IS PRINT-LINE.
       01  PRINT-LINE.
           05  FILLER                    PIC X(8).
           ~~  PRINT-NAME                ~~  X(25).
           ~~  FILLER                    ~~  X(100).

       WORKING-STORAGE SECTION.
       01  DATA-REMAINS-SWITCH           PIC X(2)      VALUE SPACES.

       PROCEDURE DIVISION.
       MAINLINE.
           OPEN INPUT  STUDENT-FILE
                OUTPUT PRINT-FILE.
           READ STUDENT-FILE
               AT END MOVE 'NO' TO DATA-REMAINS-SWITCH.
           PERFORM PROCESS-RECORDS
               UNTIL DATA-REMAINS-SWITCH = 'NO'.
           CLOSE STUDENT-FILE
                 PRINT-FILE.
           STOP RUN.
```

Wavy lines indicate identical information is to be coded on subsequent statements.

Blank lines added for readability.

FIGURE 2.2 (continued)

COBOL CODING FORM

PROGRAM FIRSTTRY — PROGRAMMER J. CLARK — REQUESTED BY — DATE 9/10/85 — PAGE 3 OF 3 — IDENT.

```
PROCESS-RECORDS.
    IF STU-CREDITS NOT < 110 AND STU-MAJOR = 'ENGINEERING'
       MOVE SPACES TO PRINT-LINE
       MOVE STU-NAME TO PRINT-NAME
       WRITE PRINT-LINE.

    READ STUDENT-FILE
       AT END MOVE 'NO' TO DATA-REMAINS-SWITCH.
```

Optional indentation to indicate these statements "belong" to the IF.

Procedure Division statements begin in or past column 12.

FIGURE 2.2 *(continued)*

Line numbers belonging to a text editor.

```
 10.          IDENTIFICATION DIVISION.
 20.          PROGRAM-ID.    FIRSTTRY.
 30.          AUTHOR.        JACKIE CLARK.
 40.
 50.          ENVIRONMENT DIVISION.
 60.          CONFIGURATION SECTION.
 70.          SOURCE-COMPUTER.  IBM-4341.
 80.          OBJECT-COMPUTER.  IBM-4341.
 90.          INPUT-OUTPUT SECTION.
100.          FILE-CONTROL.
110.              SELECT STUDENT-FILE ASSIGN TO UT-S-SYSIN.
120.              SELECT PRINT-FILE   ASSIGN TO UT-S-SYSOUT.
130.
140.          DATA DIVISION.
150.          FILE SECTION.
160.          FD  STUDENT-FILE
170.              LABEL RECORDS ARE OMITTED
180.              RECORD CONTAINS 80 CHARACTERS
190.              DATA RECORD IS STUDENT-IN.
200.          01  STUDENT-IN.
210.              05  STU-NAME             PIC X(25).
220.              05  STU-CREDITS          PIC 9(3).
230.              05  STU-MAJOR            PIC X(15).
240.              05  FILLER               PIC X(37).
250.
260.          FD  PRINT-FILE
270.              LABEL RECORDS ARE OMITTED
280.              RECORD CONTAINS 133 CHARACTERS
290.              DATA RECORD IS PRINT-LINE.
300.          01  PRINT-LINE.
310.              05  FILLER               PIC X(8).
320.              05  PRINT-NAME           PIC X(25).
330.              05  FILLER               PIC X(100).
340.
350.          WORKING-STORAGE SECTION.
360.          01  DATA-REMAINS-SWITCH      PIC X(2)      VALUE SPACES.
370.
380.          PROCEDURE DIVISION.
390.          MAINLINE.
400.              OPEN INPUT  STUDENT-FILE
410.                   OUTPUT PRINT-FILE.
420.              READ STUDENT-FILE
430.                  AT END MOVE 'NO' TO DATA-REMAINS-SWITCH.
440.              PERFORM PROCESS-RECORDS
450.                  UNTIL DATA-REMAINS-SWITCH = 'NO'.
460.              CLOSE STUDENT-FILE
470.                    PRINT-FILE.
480.              STOP RUN.
490.
500.          PROCESS-RECORDS.
510.              IF STU-CREDITS NOT < 110 AND STU-MAJOR = 'ENGINEERING'
520.                  MOVE SPACES TO PRINT-LINE
530.                  MOVE STU-NAME TO PRINT-NAME
540.                  WRITE PRINT-LINE.
550.
560.              READ STUDENT-FILE
570.                  AT END MOVE 'NO' TO DATA-REMAINS-SWITCH.
```

Line 510 will be changed.

FIGURE 2.3 Line Numbers Associated with Text Editor

10. (This is very different from the *compiler statement* numbers in Figure 1.6, which went from 1 through 57.) *Compiler statement* numbers are always consecutive, whereas line numbers for a text editor generally leave gaps for subsequent insertion of additional lines.

The availability of a text editor facilitates making changes in a program. Assume, for example, that one is interested in *all* students with at least 110 credits, irrespective of their major. Accordingly, it is necessary to replace line 510 of the program. Given that one is interested in all majors, we would further modify the program to include the student's major in the report. This in turn requires insertion of additional fields in a print line; we would insert additional COBOL statements after line 320 (to define the fields) and after line 530 (to move

```
?REPLACE 510
?           IF STU-CREDITS NOT < 110
?INSERT 321
?           05 FILLER             PIC X(15).
?INSERT 322
?           05 PRINT-MAJOR        PIC X(15).
?CHANGE '100' TO '70' IN 330
?           05 FILLER             PIC X(70).
?INSERT 531
?           MOVE STU-MAJOR TO PRINT-MAJOR
```

FIGURE 2.4 Hypothetical Text Editor Dialogue

```
 10.          IDENTIFICATION DIVISION.
 20.          PROGRAM-ID.    FIRSTTRY.
 30.          AUTHOR.        JACKIE CLARK.
 40.
 50.          ENVIRONMENT DIVISION.
 60.          CONFIGURATION SECTION.
 70.          SOURCE-COMPUTER.  IBM-4341.
 80.          OBJECT-COMPUTER.  IBM-4341.
 90.          INPUT-OUTPUT SECTION.
100.          FILE-CONTROL.
110.              SELECT STUDENT-FILE ASSIGN TO UT-S-SYSIN.
120.              SELECT PRINT-FILE   ASSIGN TO UT-S-SYSOUT.
130.
140.          DATA DIVISION.
150.          FILE SECTION.
160.          FD  STUDENT-FILE
170.              LABEL RECORDS ARE OMITTED
180.              RECORD CONTAINS 80 CHARACTERS
190.              DATA RECORD IS STUDENT-IN.
200.          01  STUDENT-IN.
210.              05  STU-NAME                PIC X(25).
220.              05  STU-CREDITS             PIC 9(3).
230.              05  STU-MAJOR               PIC X(15).
240.              05  FILLER                  PIC X(37).
250.
260.          FD  PRINT-FILE
270.              LABEL RECORDS ARE OMITTED
280.              RECORD CONTAINS 133 CHARACTERS
290.              DATA RECORD IS PRINT-LINE.
300.          01  PRINT-LINE.
310.              05  FILLER                  PIC X(8).
320.              05  PRINT-NAME              PIC X(25).
321.              05  FILLER                  PIC X(15).
322.              05  PRINT-MAJOR             PIC X(15).
330.              05  FILLER                  PIC X(70).
340.
350.          WORKING-STORAGE SECTION.
360.          01  DATA-REMAINS-SWITCH         PIC X(2)      VALUE SPACES.
370.
380.          PROCEDURE DIVISION.
390.          MAINLINE.
400.              OPEN INPUT  STUDENT-FILE
410.                   OUTPUT PRINT-FILE.
420.              READ STUDENT-FILE
430.                  AT END MOVE 'NO' TO DATA-REMAINS-SWITCH.
440.              PERFORM PROCESS-RECORDS
450.                  UNTIL DATA-REMAINS-SWITCH = 'NO'.
460.              CLOSE STUDENT-FILE
470.                    PRINT-FILE.
480.              STOP RUN.
490.
500.          PROCESS-RECORDS.
510.              IF STU-CREDITS NOT < 110
520.                  MOVE SPACES TO PRINT-LINE
530.                  MOVE STU-NAME TO PRINT-NAME
531.                  MOVE STU-MAJOR TO PRINT-MAJOR
540.                  WRITE PRINT-LINE.
550.
560.              READ STUDENT-FILE
570.                  AT END MOVE 'NO' TO DATA-REMAINS-SWITCH.
```

Lines 321 and 322 have been inserted.
PICTURE clause has been changed.
Line 510 has been modified.
Line 531 has been inserted.

FIGURE 2.5 Modified Engineering Senior Program

the major prior to printing). Finally, one would have to change the FILLER entry in line 330 to accommodate additional fields in the print line.

Figure 2.4 shows hypothetical statements to accomplish these changes, and Figure 2.5 the modified listing. The preceding discussion is the barest of introductions to the subject of text editors. However, it did present the concept of commands to replace, insert, and change program statements. The reader will require a few hours of practice to become proficient with the system he or she will use.

SUBMITTING A PROGRAM TO THE COMPUTER

Modern computers are highly sophisticated devices capable of executing many different kinds of programs. Accordingly, a computer must be told precisely what program to execute, where the program is coming from, and where to obtain the data. These tasks are accomplished through the operating system and JCL (job control language). An *operating system* consists of a series of programs, that enables the computer to function. The operating system is supplied by the computer manufacturer because it is far too complex to be developed by individual installations. *Job control language* is the method of communication with the operating system.

The Compile, Link, and Go Sequence

The job control language needed to execute a COBOL program *varies greatly from installation to installation,* but the underlying concepts remain the same. Simply stated, the JCL instructs the operating system about which programs to execute, and this is not as apparent as it seems initially. Figure 2.6 depicts what is necessary for the simple Engineering Senior Program of Chapter 1.

As can be seen from Figure 2.6, there are three distinct steps in the overall process, with *three separate programs.* In other words, in order to produce a list of engineering students, three different programs have to execute. The process begins with the COBOL compiler, which accepts a COBOL program (or *source program*) as input and produces a machine language program (or *object program)* as output.

The output of the compilation, the object program, is input into a second program (called the *linkage editor* on IBM systems) which combines the object program with subroutines and other object modules to produce a *load module.* (Even a simple program, such as the Engineering Senior Program, requires external subroutines for input/output operations.)

Execution of our program finally takes place in the third step, in which the load module produced by the linkage editor accepts our input data and produces an output report.

Your instructor may wish to supplement this material with a handout from your computer center, with the specific job control language necessary to execute your program at your installation.

Output

You will receive a variety of outputs associated with your job, depending on the particular compiler, its associated options, and the success or failure of the program itself. At the very least, you should expect a listing of your program. In addition, one may see a *cross-reference listing,* of the type shown in Figure 2.7.

A cross-reference listing is an alphabetized list of all data names used in a

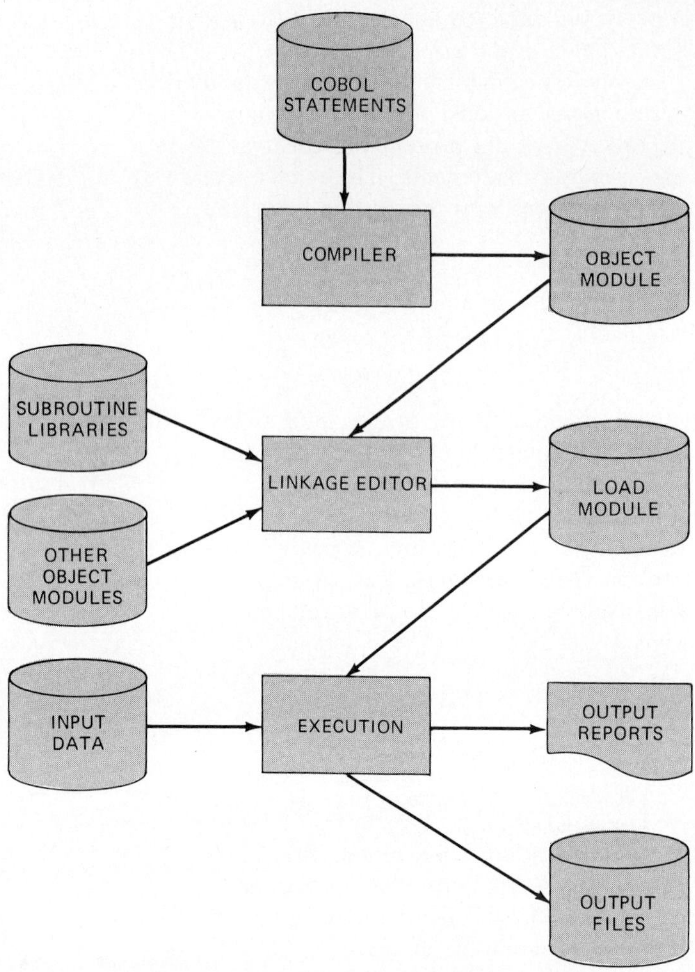

FIGURE 2.6 *Compile, Link, and Execute Sequence*

program. It shows the line number in the Data Division where the data name was first defined and all subsequent Procedure Division references.

The cross-reference listing in Figure 2.7 is associated with the Engineering Senior Program in Figure 1.6. The data name PRINT-LINE, for example, is defined in line 30 of the Data Division and used in lines 52 and 54 of the Procedure Division.

Observe also that Figure 2.7 is in two parts. Figure 2.7*a* contains only *data names,* whereas Figure 2.7*b* refers to *paragraph* names. (Other compilers will combine Figures 2.7*a* and *b* into a single listing.)

PUTTING IT TOGETHER

"One learns by doing." This time-worn axiom is especially true for programming. We have covered a lot of material since you first began reading Chapter 1. Now it is time to put everything together and actually run your first program. *Follow the steps in Figure 2.1 as they relate to the engineering senior problem.* Enter the program on the coding sheets in Figure 2.2, using the text editor at your installation. Prepare the appropriate job control statements. Create your own test data, or use Figure 1.8*a*. Submit the job and retrieve your output.

We believe—in fact, we are very sure—that after you receive your first computer printout, many things will fall into place. Nevertheless, certain pitfalls may confront you along the way.

PRINT-LINE is defined in line 30.

```
DATA NAMES                     DEFN      REFERENCE

DATA-REMAINS-SWITCH            000036    000043  000044  000057
PRINT-FILE                     000012    000040  000046  000054
PRINT-LINE                     000030    000052  000054
PRINT-NAME                     000032    000053
STU-CREDITS                    000022    000051
STU-MAJOR                      000023    000051
STU-NAME                       000021    000053
STUDENT-FILE                   000011    000040  000042  000046  000056
STUDENT-IN                     000020
```

PRINT-LINE is referenced is referenced in lines 52 and 54.

Datanames are listed in alphabetical order.

(a) Data Name Cross Reference

Lists all paragraphs in the Procedure Division.

```
PROCEDURE NAMES                DEFN      REFERENCE

MAINLINE                       000039
PROCESS-RECORDS                000050    000044
```

(b) Procedure Name Cross Reference

FIGURE 2.7 Cross-Reference Listings

Murphy's Law

The first program you submit is in many ways the most difficult you will ever attempt. The difficulty is not in the program's complexity (the engineering senior problem is logically trivial). Nor is it in the COBOL syntax, in that Figure 1.6 uses only a fraction of the COBOL features you will eventually employ. The problems arise in interacting with the computer, using the text editor, preparing JCL, finding your output, etc.

Murphy's Law is perhaps the most eloquent statement of what the truly uninitiated beginner may expect. Once you have found the computer center, be prepared for any or all of the following:

- *Errors associated with using the text editor:* These are potentially the most damaging, especially if one spends an hour entering the program and then forgets to save it, saves it incorrectly, or deletes it unintentionally. A suggested course of action is to enter only the first two lines, save these, *log off the system,* then log on and retrieve the file. Other frequent errors are to enter information in the wrong columns, to misuse a tab key, etc.
- *Incorrect or incomplete job control language:* The syntax of any job control language, especially that of IBM's JCL, is particularly stringent. The jobstream submitted with the COBOL program *must* be syntactically correct, or everything else will fail. Invalid jobstreams often result in the system being unable to execute the job, leaving the student with a totally frustrating message of the form "Job not run due to JCL error."
- *Compilation errors:* These occur because the student has violated a rule of the COBOL grammar, for example, by misspelling a word or omitting or misplacing a period. The compiler is unable to translate a portion of the COBOL program. Consequently, subsequent execution, if attempted, will not be correct. (Figure 2.8)
- *Execution errors:* These occur after a program has compiled correctly and are usually due to errors in logic. (Figure 2.9)

The discussion for Figures 2.8 and 2.9 follows on page 34.

```
00001          IDENTIFICATION DIVISION.
00002          PROGRAM-ID.    FIRSTTRY.
00003          AUTHOR.        JACKIE CLARK.
00004
00005          ENVIRONMENT DIVISION.
00006          CONFIGURATION SECTION.
00007          SOURCE-COMPUTER.  IBM-4341.
00008          OBJECT-COMPUTER.  IBM-4341.
00009          INPUT-OUTPUT SECTION.
00010          FILE-CONTROL.
00011              SELECT STUDENT-FILE ASSIGN TO UT-S-SYSIN.
00012              SELECT PRINT-FILE   ASSIGN TO UT-S-SYSOUT.
00013
00014          DATA DIVISION.
00015          FILE SECTION.
00016          FD  STUDENT-FILE
00017              LABEL RECORDS ARE OMITTED
00018              RECORD CONTAINS 80 CHARACTERS
00019              DATA RECORD IS STUDENT-IN.
00020          01  STUDENT-IN.
00021              05  STU-NAME             PIC X(25).
00022              05  STU-CREDIT           PIC 9(3).
00023              05  STU-MAJOR            PIC X(15).
00024              05  FILLER               PIC X(37).
00025
00026          FD  PRINT-FILE
00027              LABEL RECORDS ARE OMITTED
00028              RECORD CONTAINS 133 CHARACTERS
00029              DATA RECORD IS PRINT-LINE.
00030          01  PRINT-LINE.
00031              05  FILLER               PIC X(8).
00032              05  PRINT-NAME           PIC X(25).
00033              05  FILLER               PIC X(100).
00034
00035          WORKING-STORAGE SECTION.
00036          01  DATA-REMAINS-SWITCH      PIC X(2)      VALUE SPACES.
00037
00038          PROCEDURE DIVISION.
00039          MAINLINE.
00040              OPEN INPUT  STUDENT-FILE
00041                   OUTPUT PRINT-FILE.
00042              READ STUDENT-FILE
00043                  AT END MOVE 'NO' TO DATA-REMAINS-SWITCH.
00044              PERFORM PROCESS-RECORDS
00045                  UNTIL DATA-REMAINS-SWITCH = 'NO'.
00046              CLOSE STUDENT-FILE
00047                    PRINT-FILE.
00048              STOP RUN.
00049
00050          PROCESS-RECORDS.
00051              IF STU-CREDITS NOT < 110 AND STU-MAJOR = 'ENGINEERING'
00052                  MOVE SPACES TO PRINT-LINE
00053                  MOVE STU-NAME TO PRINT-NAME
00054                  WRITE PRINT-LINE.
00055
00056              READ STUDENT-FILE
00057                  AT END MOVE 'NO' TO DATA-REMAINS-SWITCH.
```

Data Division definition is inconsistent with Procedure Division reference.

(a) COBOL Listing

COBOL statement number where error occurred.

```
CARD    ERROR MESSAGE

51      IKF3001I-E      STU-CREDITS NOT DEFINED. TEST DISCARDED.
```

(b) Compiler Diagnostics

FIGURE 2.8 Engineering Senior Problem with Compilation Errors

```
IDENTIFICATION DIVISION.
PROGRAM-ID.    FIRSTTRY.
AUTHOR.        JACKIE CLARK.

ENVIRONMENT DIVISION.
CONFIGURATION SECTION.
SOURCE-COMPUTER.  IBM-4341.
OBJECT-COMPUTER.  IBM-4341.
INPUT-OUTPUT SECTION.
FILE-CONTROL.
    SELECT STUDENT-FILE ASSIGN TO UT-S-SYSIN.
    SELECT PRINT-FILE   ASSIGN TO UT-S-SYSOUT.

DATA DIVISION.
FILE SECTION.
FD  STUDENT-FILE
    LABEL RECORDS ARE OMITTED
    RECORD CONTAINS 80 CHARACTERS
    DATA RECORD IS STUDENT-IN.
01  STUDENT-IN.
    05  STU-NAME             PIC X(25).
    05  STU-CREDITS          PIC 9(3).
    05  STU-MAJOR            PIC X(15).
    05  FILLER               PIC X(37).

FD  PRINT-FILE
    LABEL RECORDS ARE OMITTED
    RECORD CONTAINS 133 CHARACTERS
    DATA RECORD IS PRINT-LINE.
01  PRINT-LINE.
    05  FILLER               PIC X(8).
    05  PRINT-NAME           PIC X(25).
    05  FILLER               PIC X(100).

WORKING-STORAGE SECTION.
01  DATA-REMAINS-SWITCH      PIC X(2)       VALUE SPACES.

PROCEDURE DIVISION.
MAINLINE.
    OPEN INPUT  STUDENT-FILE
         OUTPUT PRINT-FILE.
    READ STUDENT-FILE
        AT END MOVE 'NO' TO DATA-REMAINS-SWITCH.
    PERFORM PROCESS-RECORDS
        UNTIL DATA-REMAINS-SWITCH = 'NO'.
    CLOSE STUDENT-FILE
          PRINT-FILE.
    STOP RUN.

PROCESS-RECORDS.
    IF STU-MAJOR = 'ENGINEERING'
        MOVE SPACES TO PRINT-LINE
        MOVE STU-NAME TO PRINT-NAME
        WRITE PRINT-LINE.

    READ STUDENT-FILE
        AT END MOVE 'NO' TO DATA-REMAINS-SWITCH.
```

Credits test is missing.

(a) COBOL Listing

Erroneous record.

```
ORVILLE WRIGHT
ALEX BELL
JOHN ROEBLING
```

(b) Erroneous Output

FIGURE 2.9 Engineering Senior Problem with Execution Errors

Discussion

Consider Figure 2.8*a*, a slightly modified version of the Engineering Senior Program in Figure 1.6 (Line 22 has been changed to produce a compilation error.)

Figure 2.8*b* contains a compiler diagnostic, stating that the data name STU-CREDITS, referenced in COBOL statement 51, has *not* been previously defined. Your initial reaction is that STU-CREDITS was indeed defined, in line 22. But look *carefully* at the two data names; notice that STU-CREDIT is defined in line 22 but that STU-CREDITS is referenced in line 51. We know they refer to the same quantity, but the compiler does not; hence the error. Compiler diagnostics are discussed fully in Chapter 6.

Figure 2.9*a* is a second modified version of Figure 1.6. Figure 2.9 compiled cleanly but produced the erroneous output in Figure 2.9*b*. (Review the test data and expected output of Figure 1.8, which indicates that Alex Bell should not be selected because of an insufficient number of credits.) Recall that *a computer does exactly what we tell it to do, which is not necessarily what we want it to do*. The credits test was omitted in line 51 of Figure 2.9*a*; hence its logic was incorrect and the associated output erroneous. The error associated with Figure 2.9 occurs during the *execution* phase, after its compilation has been successfully completed.

A computer program may also produce unexpected or erroneous output, even if it is logically correct. This happens when the data on which the program operates are invalid. Consider, for example, the results of submitting the *erroneous* data in Figure 2.10 to the *valid* program in Figure 1.6. Neither Orville Wright nor John Roebling will be selected. Orville is an "engineer," whereas line 51 in the program is looking for "engineer*ing*" majors. John's credits are entered in the wrong column. Remember, a computer operates on the data as they are submitted, with no regard for their correctness. In other words, the output produced by a program is only as good as its input. (GIGO—"garbage in, garbage out"—states this principle rather well.)

```
JOHN ADAMS             090POLITICAL SCIENCE
ADAM SMITH             120ECONOMICS
ORVILLE WRIGHT         115ENGINEER             "Engineering" is spelled incorrectly.
FRANCIS KEY            080MUSIC
MERRIWEATHER LEWIS     115TRAVEL
JOHN KENNEDY           115POLITICAL SCIENCE
ALEX BELL              090ENGINEERING
GEORGE SAND            085LITERATURE
JOHN ROEBLING           115ENGINEERING         Data entered in wrong columns.
```

FIGURE 2.10 Erroneous Input Data

Summary

The single overriding objective of this chapter is to enable you to run the engineering senior problem at your installation. The presentation focused on the programming process, which detailed the various steps necessary to accomplish the objective. Specific topics included machine versus higher level languages, use of a text editor, preparation of JCL, and debugging both compilation and execution errors.

True/False Exercises

1. A compiler translates a machine-oriented language into a problem-oriented language.
2. A well-written program will always produce correct results, even with bad data.

3. A compiler is a computer program.
4. The COBOL compiler for a Univac computer is identical to the COBOL compiler for an IBM computer.
5. A single program, written in machine language, can run on a variety of computers.
6. A COBOL program can run on a variety of computers.
7. Division headers must begin in the A margin.
8. Division headers must begin in column 8.
9. Section headers must begin in column 12.
10. Paragraph names must begin in column 8.
11. PICTURE clauses may appear in column 12 or after.
12. If a program compiles correctly, then it must execute correctly.
13. Columns 1–6 are never used on the coding sheet.
14. The use of columns 73–80 is optional.
15. File names typically appear in three divisions.
16. Column 8 is used as a continuation column.
17. All text editors have identical commands.
18. All computers use the same job control language.

Problems

1. Figure 2.11*a* contains data for the COBOL program in Figure 2.11*b*. The latter is to process a file of employee records and print the names of all programmers under 30. Indicate the output that will be produced by the program, given the data in Figure 2.11*a*. In addition:
   (a) Are any potential problems introduced by checking age rather than date of birth?
   (b) Would processing be simplified if the employee records contained an abbreviated title code (e.g., 010) rather than an expanded title (e.g., programmer)? Are there any other advantages to storing codes rather than expanded values?

```
WALT BECHTEL             PRØGRAMMER34  39700
NELSØN KERBEL            PRØGRAMMER23  38000
MARGØT HUMMER            PRØGRAMMER30  45000
CATHY BENWAY             DATA DICT.23  50000
JUD MCDØNALD             DATA BASE 29  55000
JACKIE CLARK             PRØGRAMMER22  47500
LØUIS NØRIEGA            PRØGRAMER 24  42500
JEFF SHEESLEY            ANALYST   28  46400
```

FIGURE 2.11a Data

2. Modify the program in Figure 2.11*b* to accommodate all of the following:
   (a) Employee age is stored in positions 38 and 39 of the incoming record (positions 36 and 37 no longer contain useful data).
   (b) The report should list all employees under age 30 who earn at least $30,000, regardless of title.
   (c) The report should include the title of all selected employees in positions 41–52.
3. Figure 2.12 shows an initial attempt at creating the preamble to the U.S. Constitution. Enter Figure 2.12 *as is* on your computer; then use the text editor commands specific to your system to obtain a correct version.

```
00001                 IDENTIFICATION DIVISION.
00002                 PROGRAM-ID.      FIRSTTRY.
00003                 AUTHOR.          JACKIE CLARK.
00004
00005                 ENVIRONMENT DIVISION.
00006                 CONFIGURATION SECTION.
00007                 SOURCE-COMPUTER.   IBM-4341.
00008                 OBJECT-COMPUTER.   IBM-4341.
00009                 INPUT-OUTPUT SECTION.
00010                 FILE-CONTROL.
00011                     SELECT EMPLOYEE-FILE   ASSIGN TO UT-S-SYSIN.
00012                     SELECT PRINT-FILE      ASSIGN TO UT-S-SYSOUT.
00013
00014                 DATA DIVISION.
00015                 FILE SECTION.
00016                 FD  EMPLOYEE-FILE
00017                     LABEL RECORDS ARE OMITTED
00018                     RECORD CONTAINS 80 CHARACTERS
00019                     DATA RECORD IS EMPLOYEE-CARD.
00020                 01  EMPLOYEE-CARD.
00021                     05  EMP-NAME            PIC X(25).
00022                     05  EMP-TITLE           PIC X(10).
00023                     05  EMP-AGE             PIC 99.
00024                     05  FILLER              PIC XX.
00025                     05  EMP-SALARY          PIC 9(5).
00026                     05  FILLER              PIC X(36).
00027
00028                 FD  PRINT-FILE
00029                     LABEL RECORDS ARE OMITTED
00030                     RECORD CONTAINS 133 CHARACTERS
00031                     DATA RECORD IS PRINT-LINE.
00032                 01  PRINT-LINE.
00033                     05  FILLER              PIC X(1).
00034                     05  PRINT-NAME          PIC X(25).
00035                     05  FILLER              PIC X(2).
00036                     05  PRINT-AGE           PIC 99.
00037                     05  FILLER              PIC X(3).
00038                     05  PRINT-SALARY        PIC 9(5).
00039                     05  FILLER              PIC X(95).
00040
00041                 WORKING-STORAGE SECTION.
00042                 01  END-OF-DATA-FLAG        PIC X(3)       VALUE SPACES.
00043
00044                 PROCEDURE DIVISION.
00045                 MAINLINE-ROUTINE.
00046                     OPEN INPUT   EMPLOYEE-FILE
00047                          OUTPUT PRINT-FILE.
00048                     MOVE SPACES TO PRINT-LINE.
00049                     MOVE ' SALARY REPORT FOR PROGRAMMERS UNDER 30' TO PRINT-LINE.
00050                     WRITE PRINT-LINE AFTER ADVANCING 2 LINES.
00051                     READ EMPLOYEE-FILE
00052                         AT END MOVE 'YES' TO END-OF-DATA-FLAG.
00053
00054                     PERFORM PROCESS-EMPLOYEE-RECORDS
00055                         UNTIL END-OF-DATA-FLAG = 'YES'.
00056                     CLOSE EMPLOYEE-FILE
00057                           PRINT-FILE.
00058                     STOP RUN.
00059
00060                 PROCESS-EMPLOYEE-RECORDS.
00061                     IF EMP-TITLE = 'PROGRAMMER' AND EMP-AGE < 30
00062                         MOVE SPACES      TO PRINT-LINE
00063                         MOVE EMP-NAME    TO PRINT-NAME
00064                         MOVE EMP-AGE     TO PRINT-AGE
00065                         MOVE EMP-SALARY  TO PRINT-SALARY
00066                         WRITE PRINT-LINE AFTER ADVANCING 2 LINES.
00067
00068                     READ EMPLOYEE-FILE
00069                         AT END MOVE 'YES' TO END-OF-DATA-FLAG.
```

FIGURE 2.11b COBOL Listing for Problem 1

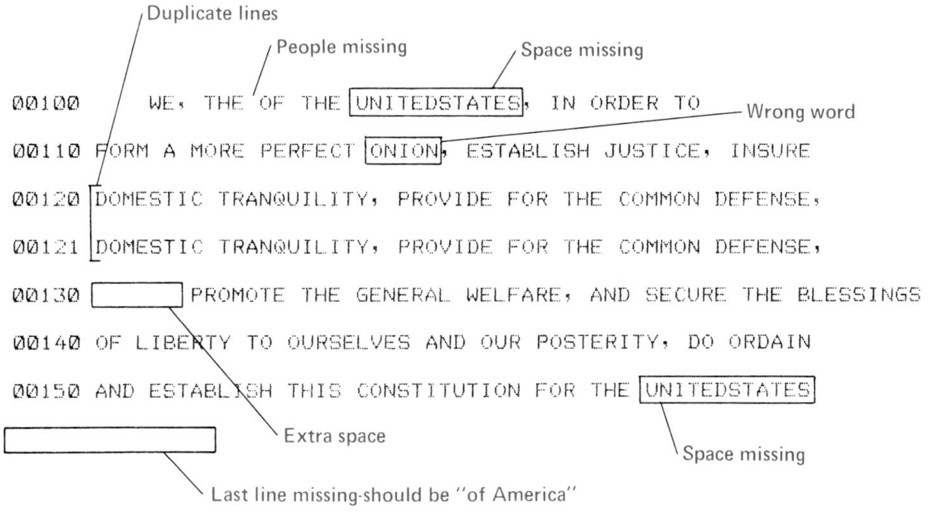

Duplicate lines
People missing
Space missing
00100 WE, THE OF THE UNITEDSTATES, IN ORDER TO
Wrong word
00110 FORM A MORE PERFECT ONION, ESTABLISH JUSTICE, INSURE
00120 DOMESTIC TRANQUILITY, PROVIDE FOR THE COMMON DEFENSE,
00121 DOMESTIC TRANQUILITY, PROVIDE FOR THE COMMON DEFENSE,
00130 PROMOTE THE GENERAL WELFARE, AND SECURE THE BLESSINGS
00140 OF LIBERTY TO OURSELVES AND OUR POSTERITY, DO ORDAIN
00150 AND ESTABLISH THIS CONSTITUTION FOR THE UNITEDSTATES
Extra space
Space missing
Last line missing-should be "of America"

FIGURE 2.12 Preamble Text

4. Match each item with its proper description:

___ 1. A Margin	(a) Denoted by an asterisk in column 7
___ 2. B Margin	(b) First line of any COBOL Program
___ 3. Comment	(c) Often appears in data names
___ 4. IDENTIFICATION DIVISION	(d) Columns 12 through 72
___ 5. PROCEDURE DIVISION	(e) Contains the logic of a program
___ 6. Hyphen	(f) Limited to 120 characters, and enclosed in quotes
___ 7. Nonnumeric literal	(g) Where division, section, and paragraph headers begin
___ 8. Reserved word	(h) Translates COBOL to machine language
___ 9. Compiler	(i) Preassigned meaning
___ 10. Literal	(j) A constant; may be numeric or nonnumeric

5. Indicate the starting column (or columns) for each of the following:

(a) Division headers
(b) Comments
(c) Paragraph names
(d) Statements in the Procedure Division (except paragraph names)
(e) WORKING-STORAGE SECTION
(f) FD
(g) 01 entries
(h) 05 entries
(i) PICTURE clauses
(j) OPEN statement
(k) WRITE statement
(l) SOURCE-COMPUTER
(m) SELECT statement

6. Explain how it is possible for a program to compile perfectly, be logically correct, and still produce invalid results. Provide three specific examples with your answer, in conjunction with the Engineering Senior Program.

Programming Specifications

Project 2–1

Program Name:

Employee Selection Program

Narrative:

Write a program to process a file of employee records. Print the name of every employee who earns $20,000 or more, works in New York, and is younger than 30.

Input File(s):

EMPLOYEE-FILE

Input Record Layout:

FIELD	POSITIONS	PICTURE
Employee Name	1–17	X(17)
Salary	18–23	9(6)
Location	25–36	X(12)
Age	39–40	99

Test Data:

```
DICK TRAUM        025000 NEW YORK     40
KEN ANDERSON      042000 NEW YORK     29
MARSHAL CRAWFORD  023000 MINNEAPOLIS  32
HARRY WICKS       019000 NEW YORK     28
DICK TRACY        034500 CHICAGO      26
FEARLESS FOSDICK  019500 NEW YORK     31
MARYANNE COULTER  022300 MIAMI        37
JOHN SMITH        025000 NEW YORK     30
PETER BROWN       022500 NEW YORK     26
ED BAKER          020000 NEW YORK     29
```

Report Format:

Use the following report layout:

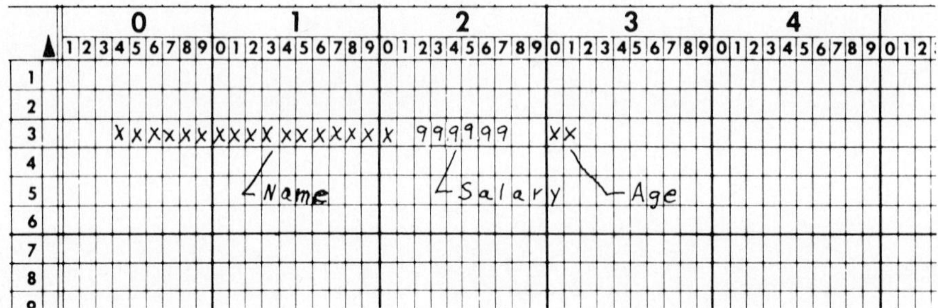

Processing Requirements:

1. Read a file of employee records.
2. For each record read, determine whether that employee earns $20,000 or more, works in New York, and is younger than 30.
3. Print the name and associated data of every employee who meets the requirements in item 2 above. Double-space detail lines.
4. Are any problems caused by using age as an input field? Are any problems caused by spelling out "New York" in the input data, rather than using an abbreviated code?

Programming Specifications

Project 2–2

Program Name:

Inter-City Piano Program

Narrative:

Write a program for the Inter-City Piano Company. The program is to process a file of customer records and produce a list of people eligible for a discount in buying a piano.

Input File(s):

CUSTOMER-LESSON-FILE

Input Record Layout:

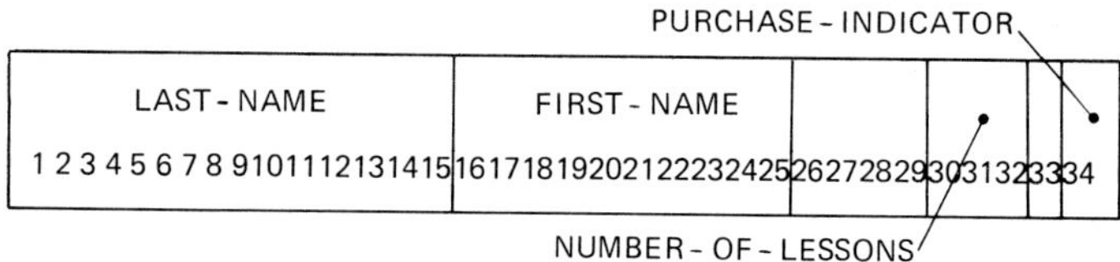

Test Data:

```
CRAWFORD    SHERRY    011 N
KARVAZY     KAREN     017 Y
MORSE       KENNETH   014 N
PLUMETREE   MICHELE   027 N
SLY         MATTHEW   019 N
POWERS      NANCY     024 Y
BLAKELY     KRISTEN   008 Y
```

Report Format:

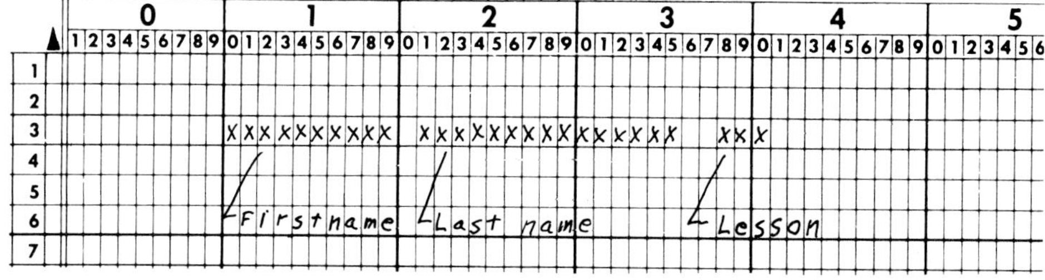

Processing Requirements:

1. Read a file of customer records.
2. For every record read, determine whether that person is eligible for a discount to buy a piano. Individuals who have taken 15 or more lessons and have not yet purchased a piano qualify. A "Y" in position 34 of the input record indicates that a piano has been purchased.
3. Print the names of all qualified individuals according to item 2 above. Single-space the output. Do *not* print the names of individuals who are not eligible.

Programming Specifications

Project 2–3

Program Name:

Delinquent Accounts

Narrative:

Write a program to process a corporation's account file to select a list of problem accounts. The generated list will then be brought to the attention of the comptroller.

Input File:

CUSTOMER-ACCOUNT-FILE

Input Record Layout:

FIELD NAME	*POSITIONS*	*PICTURE*
Customer Name	1–15	X(15)
Customer Number	17–22	9(6)
Amount Owed	24–28	9(5)
Days Overdue	30–32	9(3)

Test Data:

```
ACME ENTERPRISE 111111 01000 010
BAKER BROTHERS  222222 20000 030
BENJAMIN CO     333333 00500 015
FRANKEL CORP    444444 27500 045
CLARK PROGRESS  555555 32000 005
MARSHAK BOOKS   666666 03500 060
KARLSTROM INC   777777 00100 045
MILGROM THEATRE 888888 15000 014
SPRINGS WATER   999999 20000 007
```

Report Layout:

Design your own report layout in conjunction with the processing requirements.

Processing Requirements:

1. Read a file of customer account records.
2. Determine if the record is a problem account. An account is considered a problem if the amount owed is over 20,000 *or* the account is more than 30 days overdue.
3. Print the name and associated information (account number, amount owed, and days overdue) of all problem accounts. Space this information reasonably over a print line. Double-space the report. (Accounts that are not problem accounts will not appear on the report.)

The Identification, Environment, and Data Divisions

3

Overview

The overall approach of this book is to provide a rapid introduction to computer programming. To that end, we presented a complete COBOL program in Chapter 1. Our objective at that time was to put the reader on the computer immediately, without too much concern for the syntactical rules which you must eventually master.

We move now to a formal study of COBOL and begin with a notation to express the COBOL syntax fully. (The notation is subsequently used throughout the book to explain the nuances of COBOL.) This chapter focuses on elements in the Identification, Environment, and Data Divisions. It concludes with a second COBOL listing to illustrate the material in the chapter better. □

COBOL NOTATION

COBOL is an "English-like" language. As such, it has inherent flexibility in the way a particular entry may be expressed; there are a number of different but equally acceptable ways to say the same thing. Accordingly a standard notation is used to express permissible COBOL formats:

1. COBOL reserved words appear in upper-case (capital) letters.
2. Reserved words that are required are underlined; optional reserved words are not underlined.
3. Lower-case words denote programmer-supplied information.
4. Brackets ([ ]) indicate optional information.
5. Braces ({ }) indicate that one of the enclosed items must be chosen.
6. Three periods (...) mean that the previous entry can be repeated an arbitrary number of times.

This notation is clarified by example. Consider the condition portion in the IF statement:

```
            ⎧IS [NOT] GREATER THAN⎫
   ⎧identifier-1            ⎫ ⎪IS [NOT] LESS THAN   ⎪ ⎧identifier-2            ⎫
IF ⎨literal-1               ⎬ ⎨IS [NOT] EQUAL TO    ⎬ ⎨literal-2               ⎬
   ⎩arithmetic expression-1 ⎭ ⎪IS [NOT] >           ⎪ ⎩arithmetic expression-2 ⎭
                              ⎪IS [NOT] <           ⎪
                              ⎩IS [NOT] =           ⎭
```

The format for the IF statement has IF underlined in upper-case letters; thus IF is a required reserved word. The first set of braces means that a literal, identifier, or arithmetic expression must appear; all are in lower-case letters, indicating they are programmer supplied. The next set of braces requires a choice among one of three relationships: greater than, less than, or equal to. In each case IS appears in capital letters but is not underlined; hence its use is optional. Brackets denote NOT as an optional entry. THAN is an optional reserved word, which may be added to improve readability. Finally, a choice must be made among literal-2, identifier-2, and arithmetic expression-2.

Additional flexibility is supplied in that >, <, and = may be substituted for GREATER THAN, LESS THAN, and EQUAL, respectively. Returning to the engineering senior problem of Chapter 1, in which STU-MAJOR is compared to engineering, we see that all the following are acceptable as the condition portion of the IF statement:

```
IF STU-MAJOR IS EQUAL TO 'ENGINEERING'
IF STU-MAJOR EQUAL 'ENGINEERING'
IF 'ENGINEERING' IS EQUAL TO STU-MAJOR
IF STU-MAJOR = 'ENGINEERING'
```

IDENTIFICATION DIVISION

The Identification Division is the first of the four divisions in a COBOL program. Its function is to provide identifying information about the program, such as author, date written, and security. The division consists of a division header and up to six paragraphs:

```
IDENTIFICATION DIVISION.

PROGRAM-ID. program-name
[AUTHOR. [comment-entry] ...]
[INSTALLATION. [comment-entry] ...]
[DATE-WRITTEN. [comment-entry] ...]
[DATE-COMPILED. [comment-entry] ...]
[SECURITY. [comment-entry] ...]
```

The division header and PROGRAM-ID paragraph are required. The five remaining paragraphs are optional, as the COBOL notation shows. Only the DATE-COMPILED paragraph merits special mention. If it is used, then the compiler inserts the current date during program compilation. (This paragraph is redundant, since most compilers automatically print the date of compilation on the top of each page.) A completed Identification Division is shown:

```
IDENTIFICATION DIVISION.
PROGRAM-ID.      FIRSTTRY.
AUTHOR.          ROBERT T. GRAUER.
```

```
INSTALLATION.    UNIVERSITY OF MIAMI.
DATE-WRITTEN.    SEPTEMBER 1, 1985.
DATE-COMPILED.   The compiler supplies the compilation date.
SECURITY.        TOP SECRET-INSTRUCTORS ONLY.
```

Coding for the Identification Division follows the general rules described in Chapter 2. The division header and paragraph names begin in the A margin. All other entries begin in or past column 12 (B margin).

ENVIRONMENT DIVISION

The Environment Division serves two functions:

1. It identifies the computers to be used for compiling and executing the program (usually they are the same). This is done in the Configuration Section.
2. It relates the files used in the program to I/O devices. This is done in the Input-Output Section.

The nature of these functions makes the Environment Division heavily dependent on the computer on which one is working. Thus, the Environment Division for a COBOL program on a UNIVAC system is significantly different from that for a program for an IBM configuration. You should consult either your instructor or your computer center for the proper entries at your installation. The programs in this book use entries for an IBM OS system, because, like it or not, the Environment Division is installation dependent. *All* other COBOL entries follow the ANS Standard and hence are applicable to any compiler that adheres to the standard.

The Configuration Section has the format

```
CONFIGURATION SECTION.

SOURCE-COMPUTER. computer-name.

OBJECT-COMPUTER. computer-name.
```

The section header and paragraph names begin in the A margin. The computer-name entries begin in or past column 12. The source computer and object computer entries are usually the same.

The Input-Output Section relates the files known to the COBOL program to the files known to the operating system. Each file in a COBOL program has its own SELECT and ASSIGN clauses, which appear in the FILE-CONTROL paragraph of the Input-Output Section of the Environment Division. The format of the ASSIGN clause varies from compiler to compiler and from manufacturer to manufacturer. The following code is taken from lines 9 through 12 in the engineering senior problem and is for an IBM OS system.

```
INPUT-OUTPUT SECTION.
FILE-CONTROL.
    SELECT STUDENT-FILE ASSIGN TO UT-S-SYSIN.
    SELECT PRINT-FILE ASSIGN TO UT-S-SYSOUT.
```

As before, section headers and paragraph names begin in the A margin (columns 8 through 11). SELECT statements begin in or past column 12, with the format

```
SELECT file-name ASSIGN TO system-name
```

The system name varies from installation to installation depending on the physical I/O devices and/or the control statements. The dependence of the Environment Division on the individual computer installation bears repeating. You should consult either your instructor or your computer center for the proper statements to use in your program.

DATA DIVISION

The Data Division describes all data items that appear in a program. Most programs contain both a File Section and a Working-Storage Section in the Data Division.

File Section

The File Section is the first section in the Data Division. It describes every file mentioned in a SELECT statement in the Environment Division. (However, if there are no input/output files, there is no need for the File Section.)

The File Section contains both file description (FD) and record description entries. An *abbreviated* format for the file description (FD) entry is as follows:

```
FD file-name

    LABEL {RECORDS ARE} {OMITTED }
          {RECORD IS  } {STANDARD}

[RECORD CONTAINS integer-1 CHARACTERS]
[DATA RECORD IS data-name-1]
```

The FD provides information about the physical characteristics of a file. The LABEL RECORDS clause indicates whether standard, nonstandard, or no labels are to be processed. A label record is written at the beginning of a file stored on tape or disk. It contains information about the file such as date created and expiration date. Label records are not used for punched cards or printer files.

The RECORD CONTAINS clause indicates the number of characters per record. Although this clause is also optional, it is generally included for its value in documentation. In addition it causes the compiler to verify that the sizes of the individual data items do in fact sum to the stated value.

The DATA RECORD clause specifies the name of the 01 entry associated with the particular file. It has some value in documentation and is included for that reason. The record description itself is accomplished through the PICTURE clause and level numbers.

PICTURE Clause

All data names are described according to size and class. Size specifies the number of characters in a field. Class denotes the type of field. For the present we restrict type to numeric or alphanumeric, denoted by 9 or X, respectively. The size of a field is indicated by the number of times the 9 or X is repeated. Thus a data name with a picture of XXXX or X(4) is a four-position alphanumeric field. In similar fashion 999 or 9(3) denotes a three-position numeric field.

Level Numbers

Data items in COBOL are classified as either elementary or group items. A *group* item is one that is further divided, whereas an *elementary* item is not. As an example, consider Figure 3.1, depicting a student exam record.

In Figure 3.1 STUDENT-NAME is considered a group item, since it is divided into three fields: LAST-NAME, FIRST-NAME, and MID-INITIAL. LAST-NAME, FIRST-NAME, and MID-INITIAL are elementary items, since they are not further divided. SOC-SEC-NUM is an elementary item. EXAM-SCORES is a group item, as are MATH and ENGLISH. ALGEBRA, GEOMETRY, READING, etc., are elementary items.

Level numbers are used to describe the hierarchy among group and elementary items; they show which elementary items compose a group item. Level numbers within a record description can assume values of 01 to 49 inclusive. Level numbers and picture clauses are best described by example. Consider the Data Division statements in Figure 3.2, which correspond to the STUDENT-EXAM-RECORD in Figure 3.1.

The Data Division code in Figure 3.2 is in accordance with basic rules pertaining to level numbers:

1. 01 is used to denote the record as a whole.
2. 02–49 are used for subfields in the record.
3. Only elementary items have picture clauses.

Level numbers need not be consecutive as long as elementary items have a numerically higher level number than the group item to which they belong.

In Figure 3.2 STUDENT-EXAM-RECORD has a level number of 01. STUDENT-NAME is a subfield of STUDENT-EXAM-RECORD, and hence it has a higher level number (05). LAST-NAME, FIRST-NAME, and MID-INITIAL are subfields of STUDENT-NAME, and all have the level number 10. SOC-SEC-NUM and EXAM-SCORES are also subfields of STUDENT-EXAM-RECORD and have the same level number as STUDENT-NAME. EXAM-SCORES in turn is subdivided into two group items, MATH and ENGLISH, which in turn are further subdivided into elementary items.

Each elementary item *must* have a PICTURE clause to describe the data it contains. LAST-NAME has "PICTURE IS X(15)," denoting a 15-position alphanumeric field. (Names often have nonalphabetic characters, such as O'Brien, and are better classified as alphanumeric rather than alphabetic.) There is no picture entry for STUDENT-NAME, since that is a group item. The parentheses in a picture entry denote repetition; thus the entry 9(5) for ALGEBRA depicts a 5-position numeric field.

FILLER denotes a field that is not referenced by name. STUDENT-EXAM-RECORD in Figure 3.1 is arbitrarily assumed to contain 80 positions,

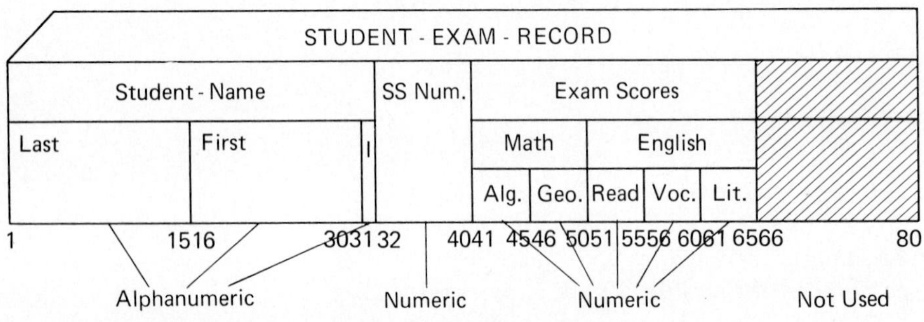

FIGURE 3.1 Student Exam Record

```
01  STUDENT-EXAM-RECORD.
    05  STUDENT-NAME.
        10  LAST-NAME         PICTURE IS X(15).
        10  FIRST-NAME        PICTURE IS X(15).
        10  MID-INITIAL       PICTURE IS X.
    05  SOC-SEC-NUM           PICTURE IS 9(9).
    05  EXAM-SCORES.
        10  MATH.
            15  ALGEBRA       PICTURE IS 9(5).
            15  GEOMETRY      PICTURE IS 9(5).
        10  ENGLISH.
            15  READING       PICTURE IS 9(5).
            15  VOCABULARY    PICTURE IS 9(5).
            15  LITERATURE    PICTURE IS 9(5).
    05  FILLER                PICTURE IS X(15).
```

FIGURE 3.2 Data Division Statements for Level Numbers and PICTURE Clauses

and all 80 positions must be accounted for. Since the last field (EXAM-SCORES, ENGLISH, or LITERATURE) ends in position 65, a FILLER entry is needed to account for the last 15 positions.

Considerable flexibility is permitted with level numbers and PICTURE clauses. Any level numbers from 02 to 49 are permitted in describing subfields as long as the basic rules are followed. Thus 04, 08, and 12 could be used in lieu of 05, 10, and 15. (However, the 01 level must be used to identify the record as a whole.) Next the PICTURE clause itself can assume any one of four forms: PICTURE IS, PICTURE, PIC IS, or PIC. Finally, parentheses may be used to signal repetition of a picture type; i.e., X(3) is equivalent to XXX. Figure 3.3 is an alternative way of coding Figure 3.2 with emphasis on the aforementioned flexibility.

Working-Storage Section

The Working-Storage Section is used for storing intermediate results and/or constants needed by the program, e.g., a switch used to control a performed paragraph or a counter for the number of engineering seniors. It is also used to define various print layouts, e.g., a heading, detail, or total line. An example of a Working-Storage Section appears in Figure 3.4.

```
01  STUDENT-EXAM-RECORD.
    04  STUDENT-NAME.
        08  LAST-NAME         PIC X(15).
        08  FIRST-NAME        PIC X(15).
        08  MID-INITIAL       PIC X.
    04  SOC-SEC-NUM           PIC 9(9).
    04  EXAM-SCORES.
        08  MATH.
            12  ALGEBRA       PIC 99999.
            12  GEOMETRY      PIC 99999.
        08  ENGLISH.
            12  READING       PIC 99999.
            12  VOCABULARY    PIC 99999.
            12  LITERATURE    PIC 99999.
    04  FILLER                PIC X(15).
```

FIGURE 3.3 Data Division Statements for Level Numbers and PICTURE Clauses: II

```
WORKING-STORAGE SECTION.
01  TOTAL-STUDENTS       PIC 9(3)     VALUE ZEROS.
01  DATA-REMAINS-SWITCH  PIC X(3)     VALUE SPACES.
01  HEADING-LINE.
    05  FILLER           PIC X(5)     VALUE SPACES.
    05  FILLER           PIC X(12)    VALUE 'STUDENT NAME'.
    05  FILLER           PIC X(5)     VALUE SPACES.
    05  FILLER           PIC X(5)     VALUE 'MAJOR'.
    05  FILLER           PIC X(106)   VALUE SPACES.
```

FIGURE 3.4 An Example of the Working-Storage Section

VALUE Clause

Figure 3.4 introduces the VALUE clause, which has the general form

```
VALUE IS literal
```

COBOL permits three types of constants: numeric literals (e.g., 80), nonnumeric literals (e.g., 'MAJOR'), and figurative constants (e.g., ZERO). Numeric and nonnumeric literals were discussed in Chapter 1 as basic COBOL elements. Figurative constants are COBOL reserved words with preassigned values. COBOL contains six of these constants, but only ZERO (equivalent forms are ZEROS and ZEROES) and SPACE (also SPACES) are discussed here.

The VALUE clause associated with a particular data name must be consistent with the corresponding PICTURE clause. It is *incorrect* to use a nonnumeric literal with a numeric picture or a numeric literal with a nonnumeric picture. Consider

```
(correct)     05  FIELD-A  PIC 9  VALUE 2.
(incorrect)   05  FIELD-B  PIC X  VALUE 2.
(incorrect)   05  FIELD-C  PIC 9  VALUE '2'.
(correct)     05  FIELD-D  PIC X  VALUE '2'.
```

Only the entries for FIELD-A and FIELD-D are correct. FIELD-B has a nonnumeric picture but a numeric value. FIELD-C has a numeric picture but a nonnumeric value (remember that anything enclosed in quotes is a nonnumeric literal).

Assumed Decimal Point

Incoming numeric data may not contain *actual* decimal points. On first reading, that statement may be somewhat hard to accept. How, for example, does one read a field containing dollars and cents? The answer is an *assumed* decimal point.

Consider the COBOL entry

```
05  HOURLY-RATE  PICTURE IS 9V99.
```

Everything is familiar except the "V" embedded in the PICTURE clause. The "V" means an *implied* decimal point; i.e., HOURLY-RATE is a three-digit (there are three 9's) numeric field, with two of the digits coming after the decimal point.

To check your understanding, assume that 9876543210 is found in positions 1–10 of an incoming record and that the following Data Division entries apply:

```
01  INCOMING-DATA-RECORD.
    05  FIELD-A   PIC 9V99.
    05  FIELD-B   PIC 99V9.
    05  FIELD-C   PIC 9.
    05  FIELD-D   PIC V999.
    05  FILLER    PIC X(40).
```

The values of FIELD-A, FIELD-B, FIELD-C, and FIELD-D are 9.87, 65.4, 3, and .210, respectively. FIELD-A is contained in the first three positions with two digits after the decimal point. FIELD-B is contained in the next three positions, i.e., 4, 5, and 6, with one digit after the decimal point. FIELD-C is contained in position 7 with no decimal places. Finally, FIELD-D is contained in positions 8, 9, and 10, with three decimal places. The last 40 positions do not contain data, as indicated by the FILLER entry.

THE ENGINEERING SENIOR PROGRAM EXTENDED

The report produced by the Engineering Senior Program in Chapter 1 was entirely too abbreviated to be of practical use. There was no *heading* line to identify the report, nor was there a *total* line at the end. Even the individual *detail* lines were lacking information. These problems are addressed in the next specification.

Programming Specifications

Program Name:

Extended Engineering Senior Program

Narrative:

This program illustrates many of the COBOL features covered in this chapter, with emphasis on the definition of multiple print line formats in Working-Storage.

Input File:

STUDENT-FILE

Input Record Layout:

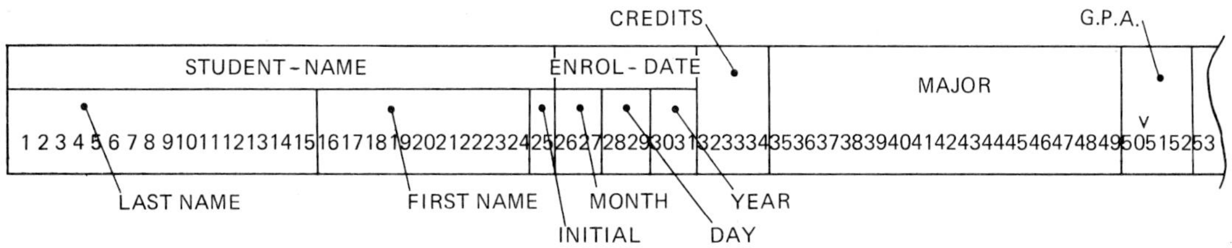

Report Layout:

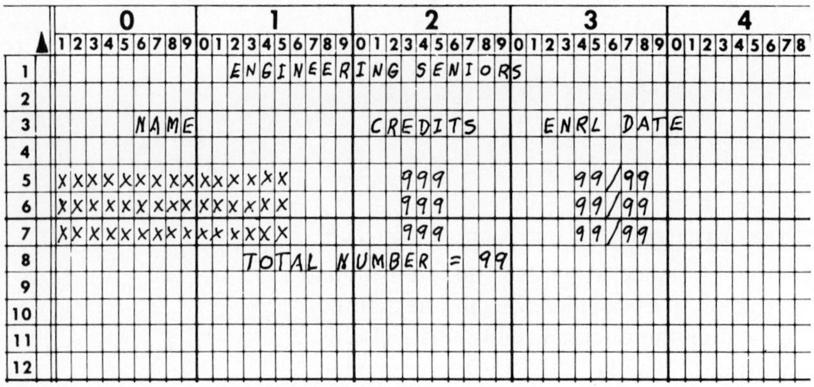

```
           ENGINEERING SENIORS

        NAME         CREDITS     ENRL DATE

XXXXXXXXXXXXXXXXX       999         99/99
XXXXXXXXXXXXXXXXX       999         99/99
XXXXXXXXXXXXXXXXX       999         99/99
            TOTAL NUMBER = 99
```

Processing Requirements:

1. Read a file of student records.
2. For every record read, determine whether that student has a major of engineering and has completed at least 110 credits.
3. Print a *detail* line for every student who meets the requirements of item 2 above. Detail lines are to be single-spaced and contain the student's last name, number of credits, and enrollment date.
4. When all records have been read, print a single *total* line at the conclusion of the report showing the number of qualified students.
5. Print a suitable heading at the beginning of the report, according to the report layout given earlier.

The COBOL Listing

Figure 3.5 contains only the Identification, Environment, and Data Divisions for the Extended Engineering Senior Program. (The completed program appears at the end of Chapter 4.) Our discussion focuses entirely on the Data Division, as the first two divisions are unchanged from the original version in Chapter 1.

The COBOL definition for the incoming student record appears in lines 20–32 and corresponds exactly to the record layout in the programming specifications. STU-NAME is a *group* item, consisting of the *elementary* items STU-LAST-NAME, STU-FIRST-NAME, and STU-MID-INIT (lines 21–24). In similar fashion, STU-ENROL-DATE contains three elementary items corresponding to the month, day, and year of enrollment. Note also that STU-GPA is defined as a three-position field with an *implied* decimal point (line 31).

The programming specifications called for several distinct print lines, each with its own format. This is best accomplished by defining *separate areas in Working-Storage* for heading, detail, and total lines. Hence the 01 entry PRINT-LINE, which is defined under the FD for PRINT-FILE, is *not* subdivided. Instead, individual 01 entries for HEADING-LINE-1, HEADING-LINE-2, DETAIL-LINE, and TOTAL-LINE are created in Working-Storage. Observe the ample use of FILLER and associated VALUE clauses to establish literal information for each of these print lines. Note also the exact correspondence between the COBOL statements and report layout in the original specifications; for example, the E in ENGINEERING SENIORS begins in column 12 of line 1, as can be seen in the print layout and matching FILLER entry.

Figure 3.6 contains test data and actual output, produced by the COBOL program. Check carefully the correspondence between the test data and record

```
IDENTIFICATION DIVISION.
PROGRAM-ID.     SECNTRY.
AUTHOR.         JACKIE CLARK.

ENVIRONMENT DIVISION.
CONFIGURATION SECTION.
SOURCE-COMPUTER.   IBM-4341.
OBJECT-COMPUTER.   IBM-4341.
INPUT-OUTPUT SECTION.
FILE-CONTROL.
    SELECT STUDENT-FILE ASSIGN TO UT-S-SYSIN.
    SELECT PRINT-FILE   ASSIGN TO UT-S-SYSOUT.

DATA DIVISION.
FILE SECTION.
FD  STUDENT-FILE
    LABEL RECORDS ARE OMITTED
    RECORD CONTAINS 80 CHARACTERS
    DATA RECORD IS STUDENT-IN.
01  STUDENT-IN.
    05  STU-NAME.
        10  STU-LAST-NAME       PIC X(15).
        10  STU-FIRST-NAME      PIC X(09).
        10  STU-MID-INIT        PIC X(01).
    05  STU-ENROL-DATE.
        10  STU-ENROL-MM        PIC 9(02).
        10  STU-ENROL-DD        PIC 9(02).
        10  STU-ENROL-YY        PIC 9(02).
    05  STU-CREDITS             PIC 9(3).
    05  STU-MAJOR               PIC X(15).
    05  STU-GPA                 PIC 9V99.
    05  FILLER                  PIC X(28).

FD  PRINT-FILE
    LABEL RECORDS ARE OMITTED
    RECORD CONTAINS 133 CHARACTERS
    DATA RECORD IS PRINT-LINE.
01  PRINT-LINE                  PIC X(133).

WORKING-STORAGE SECTION.
01  DATA-REMAINS-SWITCH         PIC X(02)   VALUE SPACES.

01  WS-STUDENT-COUNTER          PIC 9(02)   VALUE ZEROS.

01  HEADING-LINE-1.
    05  FILLER                  PIC X(11)   VALUE SPACES.
    05  FILLER                  PIC X(19)
            VALUE 'ENGINEERING SENIORS'.
    05  FILLER                  PIC X(103)  VALUE SPACES.

01  HEADING-LINE-2.
    05  FILLER                  PIC X(05)   VALUE SPACES.
    05  FILLER                  PIC X(04)   VALUE 'NAME'.
    05  FILLER                  PIC X(11)   VALUE SPACES.
    05  FILLER                  PIC X(07)   VALUE 'CREDITS'.
    05  FILLER                  PIC X(04)   VALUE SPACES.
    05  FILLER                  PIC X(09)   VALUE 'ENRL DATE'.
    05  FILLER                  PIC X(93)   VALUE SPACES.

01  DETAIL-LINE.
    05  DET-LAST-NAME           PIC X(15).
    05  FILLER                  PIC X(07)   VALUE SPACES.
    05  DET-CREDITS             PIC 9(03).
    05  FILLER                  PIC X(08)   VALUE SPACES.
    05  DET-MM                  PIC 9(02).
    05  FILLER                  PIC X(01)   VALUE '/'.
    05  DET-YY                  PIC 9(02).
    05  FILLER                  PIC X(95)   VALUE SPACES.

01  TOTAL-LINE.
    05  FILLER                  PIC X(12)   VALUE SPACES.
    05  FILLER                  PIC X(15)   VALUE 'TOTAL NUMBER = '.
    05  TOTAL-COUNT             PIC 99.
    05  FILLER                  PIC X(104)  VALUE SPACES.
```

STU-NAME is a group item with three elementary items.

Implied decimal point.

Each heading line has a separate 01 entry.

There are 4 spaces between the S in CREDITS and the E in ENRL.

FIGURE 3.5 Identification, Environment, and Data Divisions

description in the COBOL program. In addition, cross check the output with the heading, detail, and total line definitions in the COBOL program.

The Procedure Division for this program will be presented at the end of Chapter 4.

```
HUMMER         MARGOT     R010482115COMPUTER PROG.  389
KERBEL         NELSON      072382112ENGINEERING     357
CLARK          JACKIE     S051083060ACCOUNTING      367
MCDONALD       JUD         082482118ENGINEERING     325
FITZPATRICK    DAVID      T010482120ENGINEERING     376
BENWAY         CATHERINE 082583045LITERATURE        398
STUTZ          JOEL       D010583080MANAGEMENT      315
BEINHORN       CARIN      B072483054ECONOMICS       305
NORIEGA        LOUIS      A051183054ENGINEERING     278
```

Enrollment date is defined as a group item.

GPA does not contain an actual decimal point.

(a) Test Data

```
            ENGINEERING SENIORS

     NAME            CREDITS    ENRL DATE

KERBEL                  112        07/82
MCDONALD                118        08/82
FITZPATRICK             120        01/82
            TOTAL NUMBER = 03
```

(b) Associated Output

FIGURE 3.6 *Test Data and Associated Output*

COBOL 8X:

Changes and Enhancements

Three changes associated with the new compiler are mentioned here. First and foremost, COBOL 8X has made a significant improvement by allowing two additional relationships in the condition portion of an IF statement. The new conditions are

```
IS GREATER THAN OR EQUAL TO
IS LESS THAN OR EQUAL TO
```

This in turn permits one to eliminate a negative or compound condition. Applying this to the original Engineering Senior Program, we may now code

```
    IF STU-CREDITS > = 110
```

as opposed to the COBOL 74 requirement of

```
    IF STU-CREDITS NOT < 110
or  IF STU-CREDITS > 110 OR STU-CREDITS = 110
```

A second welcome change is that the Configuration Section and its associated source and object computer entries are optional. In other words, the 8X compiler includes brackets around these entries to indicate that they are not required. Thus we have the 8X syntax

```
    [CONFIGURATION SECTION.]
    [SOURCE-COMPUTER.    computer-name]
    [OBJECT-COMPUTER.    computer-name]
```

Finally, the LABEL RECORDS clause in the FD is optional in the new compiler (it was required in COBOL 74). Omission of the clause defaults to LABEL RECORDS ARE STANDARD.

Summary

The chapter covered the Identification, Environment, and Data Divisions. The first two divisions are very straightforward and vary only slightly from program to program (especially at the introductory level).

The bulk of the material centered on the Data Division. We began with the File Section, covering the FD and record description entries. Considerable attention was paid to level numbers, PICTURE clauses, and the Working-Storage Section.

True/False Exercises

1. The Identification Division may contain up to six paragraphs.
2. The PROGRAM-ID paragraph is the only required paragraph in the Identification Division.
3. Square brackets indicate a required entry.
4. Braces imply that one of the enclosed entries must be chosen.
5. A COBOL program that runs successfully on a UNIVAC system would also run successfully on an IBM system with no modification whatever.
6. Level numbers may go from 1 to 77 inclusive.
7. An 01-level entry cannot have a PICTURE clause.
8. All elementary items have a PICTURE clause.
9. A group item may have a PICTURE clause.
10. 01-level entries may appear in both the File and Working-Storage Sections of the Data Division.
11. A data name at the 10 level will always be an elementary item.
12. A data name at the 05 level may or may not have a PICTURE clause.
13. PICTURE, PICTURE IS, PIC, and PIC IS are *all* acceptable forms of the PICTURE clause.
14. "PICTURE IS 9(3)" and "PICTURE IS 999" are equivalent entries.
15. The Configuration Section is a required entry.
16. The File Section is required in every COBOL program.
17. An incoming numeric field may contain an actual decimal point.
18. The RECORD CONTAINS clause is required in an FD.

Problems

1. Consider the accompanying time card. Show an appropriate record description for this information in COBOL; use any PICTURE clauses you think appropriate.

TIME-RECORD							
NAME			NUMBER	DATE			HOURS
FIRST	MIDDLE	LAST		MO	DA	YR	

2. In which division(s) do we find

   (a) PROGRAM-ID paragraph?
   (b) FILE-CONTROL paragraph?
   (c) Configuration Section?
   (d) Working-Storage Section?
   (e) File Section?
   (f) FD's?
   (g) AUTHOR paragraph?
   (h) DATE-COMPILED paragraph?
   (i) Input-Output Section?
   (j) File names?
   (k) Level numbers?
   (l) SELECT statements?
   (m) VALUE clauses?
   (n) PICTURE clauses?

3. Given the following record layout:

```
01  EMPLOYEE-RECORD.
    05  SOC-SEC-NUMBER          PICTURE IS 9(9).
    05  EMPLOYEE-NAME.
        10  LAST-NAME           PICTURE IS X(12).
        10  FIRST-NAME          PICTURE IS X(10).
        10  MIDDLE-INIT         PICTURE IS X.
    05  FILLER                  PICTURE IS X.
    05  BIRTH-DATE.
        10  BIRTH-MONTH         PICTURE IS 99.
        10  BIRTH-DAY           PICTURE IS 99.
        10  BIRTH-YEAR          PICTURE IS 99.
    05  FILLER                  PICTURE IS X(3).
    05  EMPLOYEE-ADDRESS.
        10  NUMBER-AND-STREET.
            15  HOUSE-NUMBER    PICTURE IS X(6).
            15  STREET-NAME     PICTURE IS X(10).
        10  CITY-STATE-ZIP.
            15  CITY            PICTURE IS X(10).
            15  STATE           PICTURE IS X(4).
            15  ZIP             PICTURE IS 9(5).
    05  FILLER                  PICTURE IS X(3).
```

   (a) List all group items.
   (b) List all elementary items.
   (c) State the record positions in which the following fields are found:
      1. SOC-SEC-NUMBER
      2. EMPLOYEE-NAME
      3. LAST-NAME
      4. FIRST-NAME
      5. MIDDLE-INIT
      6. BIRTH-DATE
      7. BIRTH-MONTH
      8. BIRTH-DAY
      9. BIRTH-YEAR
      10. EMPLOYEE-ADDRESS
      11. NUMBER-AND-STREET
      12. HOUSE-NUMBER
      13. STREET-NAME

14. CITY-STATE-ZIP
15. CITY
16. STATE
17. ZIP

4. Given the following record layout (assume that FIELD-I is the last entry under FIELD-A),

```
01  FIELD-A
    05  FIELD-B
        10 FIELD-C
        10 FIELD-D
    05  FIELD-E
    05  FIELD-F
        10 FIELD-G
        10 FIELD-H
        10 FIELD-I
```

answer true or false:

(a) FIELD-C is an elementary item.
(b) FIELD-E is an elementary item.
(c) FIELD-E should have a picture.
(d) FIELD-F should have a picture.
(e) FIELD-B must be larger than FIELD-C.
(f) FIELD-C must be larger than FIELD-D.
(g) FIELD-C must be larger than FIELD-H.
(h) FIELD-B and FIELD-D end in the same column.
(i) FIELD-A and FIELD-I end in the same column.
(j) FIELD-E could be larger than FIELD-F.
(k) FIELD-D could be larger than FIELD-E.
(l) FIELD-F and FIELD-G start in the same column.

5. Use the COBOL notation introduced at the beginning of the chapter and the general format of the FD entry to determine whether the following are valid FD entries.

(a) FD EMPLOYEE-FILE
    LABEL RECORDS ARE OMITTED.
(b) FD EMPLOYEE-FILE
    LABEL RECORDS STANDARD
    RECORD CONTAINS 60 CHARACTERS.
(c) FD EMPLOYEE-FILE
    RECORD CONTAINS 60 CHARACTERS
    DATA RECORD IS EMPLOYEE-RECORD.
(d) FD EMPLOYEE-FILE
    LABEL RECORD STANDARD
    RECORD 60
    DATA RECORD EMPLOYEE-RECORD.
(e) FD EMPLOYEE-FILE
    LABEL RECORDS ARE OMITTED
    RECORDS CONTAIN 40 CHARACTERS.

6. Indicate whether each of the following entries is spelled correctly and whether it is syntactically valid:

(a) ENVIROMENT DIVISION.
(b) WORKING-STORAGE-SECTION.
(c) IDENTIFICATION-DIVISION.

(d) SOURCE COMPUTER.
(e) OBJECT-COMPUTER.
(f) FILE SECTION.
(g) PROGRAM ID.
(h) DATE-WRITTEN.
(i) DATE-EXECUTED.
(j) INPUT-OUTPUT SECTION.
(k) FILE-CONTROL SECTION.
(l) DATE DIVISION.
(m) COMMENTS.
(n) WRITTEN-BY.
(o) DATA-DIVISION.

Programming Specifications

Project 3–1

Program Name:

Grade Point Listing

Narrative:

The Identification, Environment, and Data Divisions for this project can be developed after the present chapter. Completion of the project requires you to finish Chapter 4 in order to do the Procedure Division.

Input File:

STUDENT-RECORD-FILE

Input Record Layout:

```
01  STUDENT-RECORD.
    05  STU-NAME-AND-INITIALS       PIC X(20).
    05  STU-GRADE-POINT-DATA.
        10  STU-CUMULATIVE-POINTS   PIC 999.
        10  STU-CUMULATIVE-CREDITS  PIC 999.
    05  STU-BIRTH-DATE.
        10  STU-BIRTH-MONTH         PIC 99.
        10  STU-BIRTH-YEAR          PIC 99.
```

Test Data:

```
ADAMS, J          1500500967
MILGROM, I        2000750768
LEE, B            0000000768
GROSSMAN, M       3501100467
GROSSMAN, I       2500800369
BOROW, J          0600500765
JOHNSON, L        0250180764
FRANKEL, L        0900280359
MARSHAK, K        1200850361
SUGRUE, P         3001151246
MILGROM, I        0000000720
```

Report Layout:

Use the following report layout:

```
            0         1         2         3         4
    1234567890123456789012345678901234567890123456789012345678901
 1
 2           STUDENT G.P.A. REPORT
 3
 4
 5     STUDENT NAME        DEAN'S LIST   PROBATION
 6
 7   XXXXXXXXXXXXXXXXXXXX      YES
 8
 9   XXXXXXXXXXXXXXXXXXXX                  YES
10
11
12         TOTAL STUDENTS ON DEAN'S LIST = 999
13
14         TOTAL STUDENTS ON PROBATION   = 999
15
```

Processing Requirements:

1. Print the indicated heading at the start of processing.
2. Read a file of student records, and for every record read:
   (a) Calculate the student's grade point average. The average is computed by dividing the cumulative points field by the cumulative credits field.
   (b) Determine whether the student is on the Dean's List; students with a grade point average of 3.00 or higher are on the Dean's List.
   (c) Determine whether the student is on academic probation; students with a grade point average of less than 1.50 are on probation. Incoming freshmen, with a grade point average of 0.00, are not to be considered on probation.
   (d) Print a detail line for every student containing the student's name, and whether or not the student is on the Dean's List or academic probation. (Print "yes" in the appropriate column on that student's detail line.) Follow the report layout for appropriate spacing. Double-space detail lines.
3. When all records have been read, print the total number of students on the Dean's List and the total number on probation. Two separate total lines are required.

Programming Specifications

Project 3–2

Program Name:

Inventory Parts List

Narrative:

The Identification, Environment, and Data Divisions for this project can be developed after this chapter. Completion of the project requires you to finish Chapter 4 in order to do the Procedure Division.

Input File:

MASTER-PART-FILE

Input Record Layout:

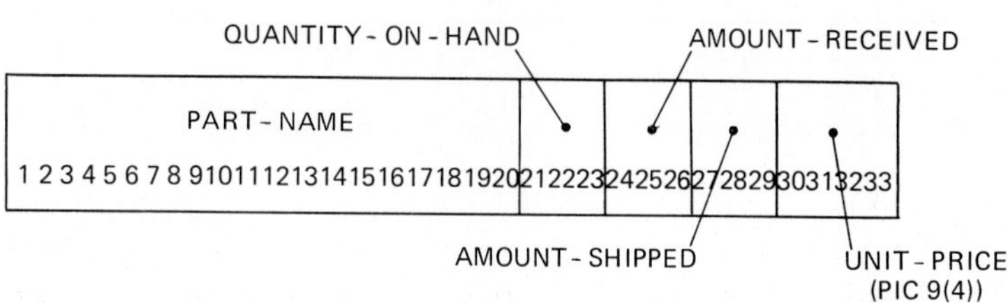

Test Data:

```
WIDGETS, SIZE S      1500500960070
WIDGETS, SIZE M      2000750760080
WIDGETS, SIZE L      0005004000090
WHOSIWHATSIS         3501100460100
GISMOS, TYPE A       2500800360200
GISMOS, TYPE B       0000500250300
GADGETS, SIZE S      0250180260015
GADGETS, SIZE L      0900280350025
```

Report Layout:

Use thc following report layout:

```
 1
 2                         *** INVENTORY REPORT ***
 3
 4
 5                        BEGINNING  RECEIVED   SHIPPED     ENDING   UNIT    TOTAL
 6       PART NAME         ON HAND                         ON HAND  PRICE    VALUE
 7
 8   XXXXXXXXXXXXXXXXXXX     XXX       XXX        XXX        XXX    XXXX   XXXXXXX
 9
10   XXXXXXXXXXXXXXXXXXX     XXX       XXX        XXX        XXX    XXXX   XXXXXXX
11
12                                                                         --------
13                                        TOTAL VALUE OF ALL INVENTORY    XXXXXXXX
14
15
16
```

Processing Requirements:

1. Read a file of inventory records, and for every record read:
   (a) Determine the quantity on hand at the end of the period. This is equal to the quantity on hand at the start of the period (contained in the input record), plus the amount received, minus the amount shipped.
   (b) Determine the value of the inventory on hand at the end of the period. This is equal to the unit price (contained in the input rec-

ord) multiplied by the quantity on hand at the end of the period [computed in part (a)].

(c) Print a detail line for every part containing the part name, quantity on hand at the beginning of the period, the amount shipped, the amount received, the quantity on hand at the end of the period, the unit price, and the value of the inventory at the end of the period. Double-space detail lines.

2. When all records have been read, print the total value of all inventory on hand at the end of the period.

Programming Specifications

Project 3–3

Program Name:

Money Changer

Narrative:

The ACME Widget Corporation has decided to pay its employees in cash rather than by check. This project is to read a file of payroll amounts and determine the required number of bills in each denomination.

The Identification, Environment, and Data Divisions for this project can be developed after this chapter. Completion of the project requires you to finish Chapter 4 in order to do the Procedure Division.

Input File:

PAYROLL-FILE

Input Record Layout:

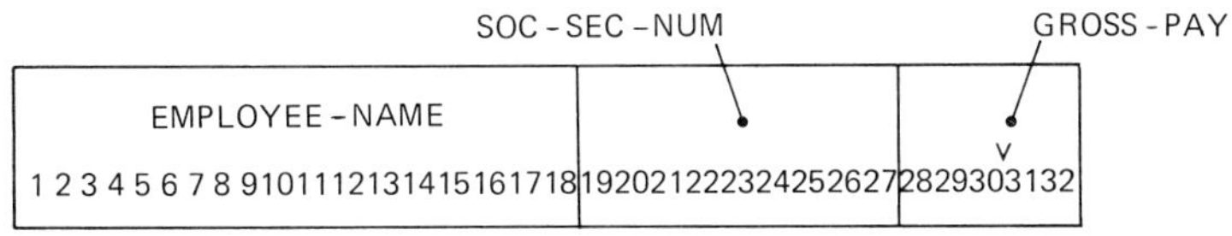

Test Data:

```
JOHN SMITH          12345678935000
JESSICA GRAUER      33344455547500
CHANDLER LAVOR      98765432117800
JEFFRY BOROW        77766888821900
MARION MILGROM      99988777734100
LYNN FRANKEL        49233678949200
KARL KARLSTROM      33322888831400
KATHY MARSHAK       24534787836800
RHODA HAAS          11111111130500
JIM FEGEN           22222222252200
```

Report Layout:

Use the following report layout:

```
         0         1         2         3         4         5         6
123456789012345678901234567890123456789012345678901234567890123456789012
 1
 2
 3
 4
 5   EMPLOYEE NAME                      $100    $50   $20   $10   $5   $1     PAY
 6
 7  XXXXXXXXXXXXXXXXXXXXXX     XXX-XX-XXXX      X      X     X     X    X    X     XXX
 8
 9  XXXXXXXXXXXXXXXXXXXXXX     XXX-XX-XXXX      X      X     X     X    X    X     XXX
10                                          ---    ---   ---   ---  ---  ---   ----
11        TOTALS                            XX     XX    XX    XX   XX   XX    XXXX
12
13
```

Processing Requirements:

1. Read a file of employee pay records.
2. For each record read:
   (a) Determine the number of bills of each denomination required to pay the employee in cash, rather than by check. (Do not include cents in your computation.)
   (b) Use denominations of $100, $50, $20, $10, $5, and $1. Pay employees in the highest denominations possible; e.g., an employee with a gross pay of $300 should be paid with three $100 bills rather than six $50 bills.
   (c) Maintain a running total of the total payroll as well as the number of bills in each denomination for the company as a whole.
   (d) Print a detail line for each employee according to the report format. Double-space detail lines.
3. When all records have been read, print a total line for the company according to specification 2(c) above.

The Procedure Division

4

Overview

The Procedure Division is the portion of a COBOL program that contains the logic; it is the part of the program that "actually does something." This chapter covers several of the basic COBOL verbs, beginning with those which do arithmetic: ADD, SUBTRACT, MULTIPLY, DIVIDE, and COMPUTE. We look at the READ, WRITE, OPEN, and CLOSE verbs for use in I/O (input/output) operations. We study the MOVE verb, which transfers data from one area of memory to another. We learn about the IF statement to enable choice, the PERFORM verb to implement a loop, and the STOP RUN statement to terminate program execution.

The chapter concludes with a complete COBOL listing, the Extended Engineering Senior Program, which was introduced in Chapter 3. □

ARITHMETIC VERBS

We shall use the standard COBOL notation to study the COBOL verbs for arithmetic: ADD, SUBTRACT, MULTIPLY, DIVIDE, and COMPUTE. You may be well advised to temporarily skip the material on ADD, SUBTRACT, MULTIPLY, and DIVIDE and concentrate instead on the COMPUTE statement.

ADD

The ADD verb has two basic formats:

```
ADD {identifier-1} ... TO {identifier-2 [ROUNDED]} ...
    {literal-1   }
```

and

```
ADD {identifier-1} ... {identifier-2}
    {literal-1   }     {literal-2   }

    GIVING {identifier-3 [ROUNDED]} ...
```

Recall from the COBOL notation that three dots implies the last syntactical unit may be repeated; hence, one or several identifiers (literals) may precede identifier-2. In the first format, or "TO" option, the value(s) of identifier-1, etc., is (are) added to the initial contents of identifier-2. In the second format, or "GIVING" option, the sum does *not* include the initial value of identifier-3. Simply stated, the "TO" option includes the initial value of identifier-2 in the final sum, while the "GIVING" option ignores the initial value.

Examples 4.1 and 4.2 illustrate the ADD statement.

Example 4.1

ADD A B TO C.

```
Before execution:   A [5]  B [10]  C [20]

After execution:    A [5]  B [10]  C [35]
```

In Example 4.1 the initial values of A, B, and C are 5, 10, and 20, respectively. After execution the values are 5, 10, and 35. The instruction took the initial value of A (5), added the value of B (10), added the initial value of C (20), and put the sum (35) back into C.

Example 4.2

ADD A B GIVING C.

```
Before execution:   A [5]  B [10]  C [20]

After execution:    A [5]  B [10]  C [15]
```

In Example 4.2 the initial value of A (5) is added to the initial value of B (10), and the sum (15) replaces the initial value of C.

Table 4.1 contains additional examples of the ADD instruction. In each instance the instruction is assumed to operate on the initial values of A, B, and C (5, 10, and 30, respectively). Note that the last example changes the values of both B and C.

TABLE 4.1 *The ADD Instruction*

Data name	A	B	C
Value *before* execution	5	10	30
Value *after* execution of			
ADD A TO C.	5	10	35
ADD A B TO C.	5	10	45
ADD A 18 B GIVING C.	5	10	33
ADD A 18 B TO C.	5	10	63
ADD 1 TO B C.	5	11	31

SUBTRACT

The SUBTRACT verb also has two formats:

```
SUBTRACT {identifier-1} ... FROM {identifier-3 [ROUNDED]} ...
         {literal-1   }
```

and

```
SUBTRACT {identifier-1} ... FROM {identifier-2}
         {literal-1   }          {literal-2   }

    GIVING {identifier-3 [ROUNDED]} ...
```

In the first format the initial value of identifier-3 is replaced by the result of the subtraction. In the second format the initial value of either identifier-2 or literal-2 is unchanged as the result is stored in identifier-3 (and beyond).

Example 4.3

SUBTRACT A FROM B.

```
Before execution:   A [5]   B [15]

After execution:    A [5]   B [10]
```

In Example 4.3 the SUBTRACT verb causes the value of A (5) to be subtracted from the initial value of B (15) and the result (10) to be stored in B. Only the value of B was changed.

Example 4.4

SUBTRACT A FROM B GIVING C.

```
Before execution:   A [5]   B [15]   C [100]

After execution:    A [5]   B [15]   C [10]
```

In the "FROM ...GIVING" format of Example 4.4 the value of A (5) is subtracted from the value of B (15), and the result (10) is placed in C. The values of A and B are unchanged, and the initial value of C (100) is replaced by 10. Table 4.2 contains additional examples. In each example the instruction is assumed to operate on the initial contents of A, B, C, and D.

TABLE 4.2 *The SUBTRACT Instruction*

Data name	A	B	C	D
Value *before* execution	5	10	30	100
Value *after* execution of				
SUBTRACT A FROM C.	5	10	25	100
SUBTRACT A B FROM C.	5	10	15	100
SUBTRACT A B FROM C GIVING D.	5	10	30	15
SUBTRACT 10 FROM C, D.	5	10	20	90

MULTIPLY

The MULTIPLY verb has two formats:

```
MULTIPLY {identifier-1} BY {identifier-2 [ROUNDED]} ...
         {literal-1   }
```

and

```
MULTIPLY {identifier-1} BY {identifier-2}
         {literal-1   }    {literal-2   }

    GIVING {identifier-3 [ROUNDED]} ...
```

If GIVING is used, then the result of the multiplication is stored in identifier-3 (and beyond). If GIVING is omitted, then the result is stored in identifier-2 (and beyond).

Example 4.5

MULTIPLY A BY B.

```
Before execution:  A [10]  B [ 20]
After execution:   A [10]  B [200]
```

Example 4.6

MULTIPLY A BY B GIVING C.

```
Before execution:  A [10]  B [20]  C [345]
After execution:   A [10]  B [20]  C [200]
```

Table 4.3 contains additional examples of the MULTIPLY verb.

TABLE 4.3 *The MULTIPLY Instruction*

Data name	A	B	C
Value *before* execution	5	10	30
Value *after* execution of			
MULTIPLY B BY A GIVING C.	5	10	50
MULTIPLY A BY B GIVING C.	5	10	50
MULTIPLY A BY B.	5	50	30
MULTIPLY B BY A.	50	10	30
MULTIPLY A BY 3 GIVING B, C.	5	15	15

DIVIDE

The DIVIDE statement has five formats. The primary distinction is between the words BY and INTO, which determine whether identifier-2 is the divisor or the dividend. As with the other arithmetic verbs, the presence of GIVING means that the initial value of identifier-2 or literal-2 is unchanged. Observe also that only the last two formats make explicit provision for storing the remainder.

```
DIVIDE {identifier-1} INTO {identifier-2 [ROUNDED]} ...
       {literal-1   }
```

```
DIVIDE {identifier-1} INTO {identifier-2}
       {literal-1   }      {literal-2   }

    GIVING {identifier-3 [ROUNDED]} ...
```

```
DIVIDE {identifier-1} BY {identifier-2}
       {literal-1   }    {literal-2   }
    GIVING {identifier-3 [ROUNDED]} ...

DIVIDE {identifier-1} INTO {identifier-2} GIVING identifier-3 [ROUNDED]
       {literal-1   }      {literal-2   }
    REMAINDER identifier-4

DIVIDE {identifier-1} BY {identifier-2} GIVING identifier-3 [ROUNDED]
       {literal-1   }    {literal-2   }
    REMAINDER identifier-4
```

Example 4.7

DIVIDE A INTO B.

Before execution:	A	10	B	50
After execution:	A	10	B	5

Example 4.8

DIVIDE A INTO B GIVING C REMAINDER D.

Before execution:	A	10	B	51	C	13	D	17
After execution:	A	10	B	51	C	5	D	1

Example 4.9

DIVIDE A BY B GIVING C REMAINDER D.

Before execution:	A	10	B	51	C	13	D	17
After execution:	A	10	B	51	C	0	D	10

In Example 4.7 the initial value of B (50) is divided by the value of A (10), and the quotient (5) replaces the initial value of B. In Example 4.8, which uses the GIVING option, the quotient goes into C, the remainder into D, and the values of A and B are unaffected. Example 4.9 parallels 4.8 except that BY replaces INTO, resulting in a quotient of zero and a remainder of 10.

Table 4.4 contains additional examples of the DIVIDE verb.

TABLE 4.4 *The DIVIDE Instruction*

Data name	A	B	C
Value *before* execution	5	10	30
Value *after* execution of			
DIVIDE 2 INTO B.	5	5	30
DIVIDE 2 INTO B GIVING C.	5	10	5
DIVIDE B BY 5 GIVING A.	2	10	30
DIVIDE A INTO B, C.	5	2	6
DIVIDE A INTO B GIVING C.	5	10	2
DIVIDE 3 INTO A GIVING B REMAINDER C.	5	1	2

COMPUTE

Any operation that can be done in an ADD, SUBTRACT, MULTIPLY, or DIVIDE statement may also be done using the COMPUTE instruction. In addition, the COMPUTE statement can combine different arithmetic operations in the same statement. For example, in the algebraic statement

$$X = \frac{2(A + B)}{C}$$

A and B are first added together, the sum is multiplied by 2, and the product is divided by C. The single algebraic statement requires three COBOL arithmetic statements, with the true value of X obtained after the last statement is executed:

```
ADD A B GIVING X.
MULTIPLY 2 BY X.
DIVIDE C INTO X.
```

These three statements can be combined into a single COMPUTE with obvious benefits:

```
COMPUTE X = 2 * (A + B) / C.
```

The general format of the COMPUTE statement is

```
COMPUTE {identifier-1 [ROUNDED]} ... = arithmetic-expression-1
```

Expressions are formed according to the following rules:

1. The symbols +, −, *, /, and ** denote addition, subtraction, multiplication, division, and exponentiation, respectively.
2. An expression consists of data names, literals, arithmetic symbols, and parentheses. Spaces must precede and follow arithmetic symbols.
3. Parentheses are used to clarify and in some cases alter the sequence of operations within a COMPUTE. Anything contained within the parentheses must also be a valid expression. The left parenthesis is preceded by a space and the right parenthesis followed by a space.

The COMPUTE statement calculates the value on the right side of the equal sign and stores it in the data name to the left of the equal sign. Expressions are evaluated as follows:

1. Anything contained in parentheses is evaluated first as a separate expression.
2. Within the expression, exponentiation is done first, then multiplication or division, then addition or subtraction.
3. If rule 2 results in a tie (e.g., if both multiplication and division are present), then evaluation proceeds from left to right.

Table 4.5 contains examples to illustrate the formation and evaluation of expressions in a COMPUTE statement.

Table 4.6 should further clarify evaluation of the COBOL COMPUTE. This table contains several algebraic expressions and the corresponding COMPUTE statements to accomplish the intended logic. Note that parentheses are often required in the COMPUTE that are not present in the algebraic counterpart. Parentheses may also be optionally used to clarify the intent of a COMPUTE statement; however, their use in Table 4.6 is mandatory in all instances.

TABLE 4.5 *The COMPUTE Instruction*

Data name	A	B	C	Comments
Value *before* execution	2	3	10	Initial values
Value *after* execution of				
COMPUTE C = A + B.	2	3	5	Simple addition
COMPUTE C = A + B * 2.	2	3	8	Multiplication done *before* addition
COMPUTE C = (A + B) * 2.	2	3	10	Parentheses evaluated first
COMPUTE C = A ** B.	2	3	8	Algebraically, $c = a^b$
COMPUTE C = B ** A.	2	3	9	Algebraically, $c = b^a$

TABLE 4.6 *The COMPUTE Instruction Continued*

ALGEBRAIC EXPRESSION	COBOL COMPUTE
$x = a + b$	COMPUTE X = A + B.
$x = \frac{a + b}{2}$	COMPUTE X = (A + B) / 2.
$x = \frac{(a + b)c}{2}$	COMPUTE X = (A + B) * C / 2.
$x = \frac{a + b}{2c}$	COMPUTE X = (A + B) / (2 * C).
$x = \sqrt{a}$	COMPUTE X = A ** .5.
$x = \frac{a^2 + b^2}{c^2}$	COMPUTE X = (A ** 2 + B ** 2) / C ** 2.

Assumed Decimal Point

Arithmetic can be performed on decimal as well as integer fields. One must be very aware of the decimal point, and in particular, *be sure to define the field holding the result with a sufficient number of decimal places.* Consider Example 4.10, in which A and B have pictures of 99 and 99V9, respectively.

Example 4.10

ADD A TO B

```
                                        V
Before execution:  A  |1|2|   B  |3|4|5|

                                        V
After execution:   A  |1|2|   B  |4|6|5|
```

Programming Tip

Use the COMPUTE Verb for Multiple Arithmetic Operators

The COMPUTE verb should always be used when *multiple* arithmetic operators are involved. Consider two sets of equivalent code:

Poor Code:

```
MULTIPLY B BY B GIVING B-SQUARED.
MULTIPLY 4 BY A GIVING FOUR-A.
MULTIPLY FOUR-A BY C GIVING FOUR-A-C.
SUBTRACT FOUR-A-C FROM B-SQUARED GIVING RESULT-1.
COMPUTE RESULT-2 = RESULT-1 ** .5.
SUBTRACT B FROM RESULT-2 GIVING NUMERATOR.
MULTIPLY 2 BY A GIVING DENOMINATOR.
DIVIDE NUMERATOR BY DENOMINATOR GIVING X.
```

Improved Code:

```
COMPUTE X = (-B + (B ** 2 - (4 * A * C)) ** .5) / (2 * A).
```

Both sets of code apply to the quadratic formula,

$$X = \frac{-B + \sqrt{B^2 - 4AC.}}{2A}$$

It is fairly easy to determine what is happening from the single COMPUTE statement. It is next to impossible to realize the cumulative effect of the eight individual arithmetic statements. Interpretation of the unacceptable code is further clouded by the mandatory definition of data names for intermediate results, RESULT-1, RESULT-2, etc.

Parentheses are often required in COMPUTE statements to alter the normal hierarchy of operations. For example, parentheses are *required* around 2 * A in the denominator. If they had been omitted, the numerator would have been divided by 2 and then the quotient would have been multiplied by A. Sometimes the parentheses are optional to the compiler but should be used to clarify things for the programmer. The parentheses around 4 * A * C do not alter the normal order of operations and hence are optional.

On the other hand, individual arithmetic verbs are preferable to the COMPUTE statement when only a *single* operation is required. Hence, ADD 1 TO COUNTER is easier to code than COMPUTE COUNTER = COUNTER + 1.

Field-B is stored with an implied decimal point. The compiler generates instructions to add an integer number (12) to a number with one decimal place (34V5). It maintains decimal alignment, obtains 46V5 as an answer, and stores the result in Field-B.

Consider what happens if the operation is reversed, i.e., ADD B TO A. The result of the addition is still 46V5; however, the field which stores the sum, A, is defined without a decimal point; hence, the .5 will be truncated. *It is criti-*

TABLE 4.7 Arithmetic on Fields with Assumed Decimal Points

Data name	A	B	C	
Picture	99	99V9	99V99	
Value *before* execution	12	345	4712	The decimal value in B is lost, because the receiving field, A, does not contain an implied decimal point.
Value *after* execution of				
ADD A TO B	12	465	4712	
ADD B TO A	46	345	4712	
ADD B TO C	12	345	8162	
ADD C TO B	12	816	4712	
ADD C TO A	59	345	4712	
ADD A TO C	12	345	5912	

cal, therefore, to define the receiving field with a sufficient number of decimal places.

Table 4.7 contains additional examples. In each instance the instruction is assumed to operate on the initial values of A, B, and C.

The ROUNDED Clause

Close inspection of the arithmetic verbs ADD, SUBTRACT, MULTIPLY, DIVIDE, and COMPUTE reveals an *optional* ROUNDED clause for each statement. If the ROUNDED clause is specified, COBOL carries the calculation to one more place than is specified in the result field. Then if that extra decimal place is 5 or larger, the answer is rounded up; if it is 4 or less, the answer is unchanged. If the ROUNDED clause is omitted, COBOL truncates any extra decimal positions. Table 4.8 shows the effect of the ROUNDED option.

IF

The IF statement is one of the more powerful verbs in COBOL. Our present concern is with only a few of the available options, and additional consideration is deferred to Chapter 9. An abbreviated format of the IF statement is

```
IF condition statement-1 [ELSE statement-2]
```

The ELSE Clause

The IF statement may be used with or without the ELSE clause as implied by the square brackets in its syntax. Figure 4.1*a* depicts the ELSE option; Figure 4.1*b* omits it.

TABLE 4.8 The ROUNDED Clause

Data name	A	B	C
Picture	9V99	9V99	9V9
Value *before* execution	123	456	immaterial
Value *after* execution of			
ADD A B GIVING C	123	456	57
ADD A B GIVING C ROUNDED	123	456	58

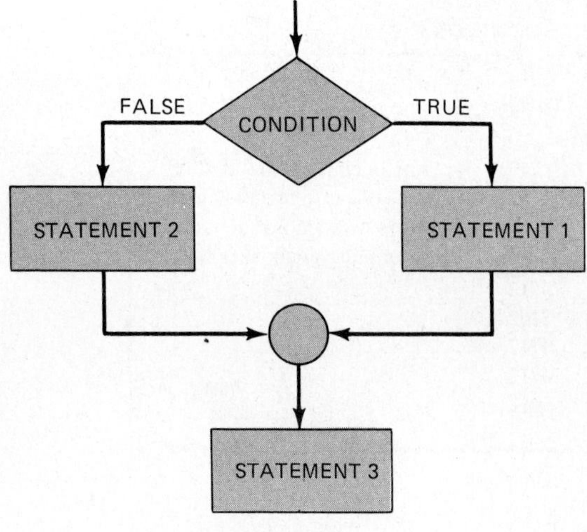

(a) with ELSE option

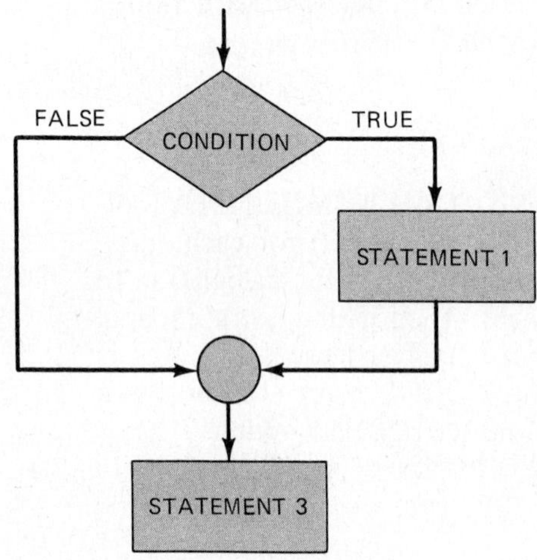

(b) without ELSE option

FIGURE 4.1 *Illustration of the IF Statement*

If the condition in Figure 4.1*a* is true, statement-1 is executed; if it is false, statement-2 is executed. In either case, after the IF statement is terminated execution continues with statement-3. A condition is also tested in Figure 4.1*b*. If true, statement-1 is executed, followed by statement-3. If false, the IF is terminated and statement-3 is executed.

Significance of the Period

Statement-1 following the condition portion in an IF statement is terminated by an ELSE clause or a period. Consider the following, which was extracted from the original program in Chapter 1:

```
IF STU-CREDITS NOT < 110 AND STU-MAJOR = 'ENGINEERING'
   [ MOVE SPACES TO PRINT-LINE
   [ MOVE STU-NAME TO PRINT-NAME
   [ WRITE PRINT-LINE.
                            Period terminates statement
  Executed collectively or not at all
```

If the condition is met, then *every* statement between the condition and the period will be executed. Hence, when an engineering senior is processed, two

MOVE statements and one WRITE are executed. If the condition is *not* met, then all three statements, i.e., two MOVES and a WRITE, are bypassed. (Indentation in an IF statement is for readability only and is not a COBOL requirement.)

Indentation in the IF Statement

Indentation in an IF statement is extremely important to enhance a programmer's understanding of a statement's intended effect. Consider Figure 4.2, which contains a flowchart and corresponding COBOL code.

The flowchart in Figure 4.2*a* implies that if the condition A = B is true, we are to ADD 1 TO C and ADD 1 TO D. If the condition is false, then SUBTRACT 1 FROM C and SUBTRACT 1 FROM D. In either case, i.e., whether the condition is true or false, we are to COMPUTE W = X + Y + Z. The latter is indicated by the IF and ELSE branches meeting in a *common* exit point, which leads to the COMPUTE statement.

The COBOL code in Figure 4.2*b* is carefully aligned to reflect this interpretation. Recall that the rules of COBOL require only that an IF statement appear in the B margin, i.e., in columns 12–72. Hence the indentation in Figure 4.2*b* is done solely for the purpose of making a program easier to read, rather than to satisfy a rule of COBOL. Nevertheless, proper *indentation* is essential and goes a long way to improve the quality of an individual's work. Accordingly, we suggest the following guidelines:

1. The word IF begins in column 12.
2. Put the word ELSE on a line by itself and directly under the IF.
3. Indent detail lines for both IF and ELSE four columns.

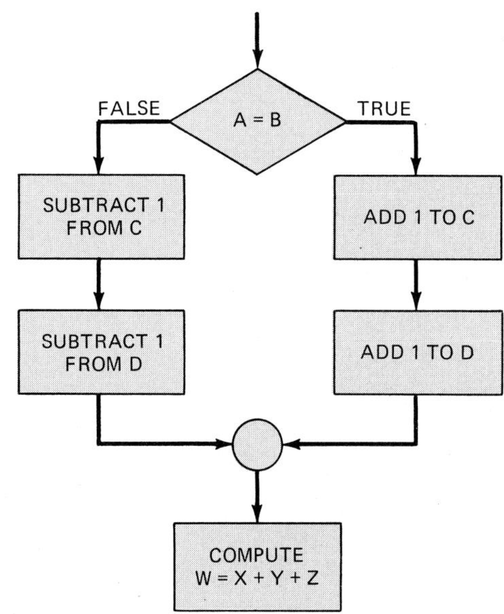

(a) IF/ELSE Flowchart

```
IF A = B
    ADD 1 TO C
    ADD 1 TO D
ELSE
    SUBTRACT 1 FROM C
    SUBTRACT 1 FROM D.
COMPUTE W = X + Y + Z.
```

(b) COBOL Code

FIGURE 4.2 The IF Statement (Flowchart and COBOL Code)

PERFORM

An abbreviated format of the PERFORM statement is

```
PERFORM procedure-name
   [UNTIL condition]
```

The PERFORM statement transfers control to and from a procedure (e.g., a paragraph) elsewhere in the program. This allows a complex program to be divided into a series of clear and straightforward routines.

Consider the simplest form of the PERFORM statement and the following code:

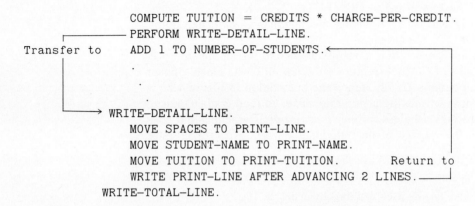

```
                 COMPUTE TUITION = CREDITS * CHARGE-PER-CREDIT.
         ┌────── PERFORM WRITE-DETAIL-LINE.
Transfer to      ADD 1 TO NUMBER-OF-STUDENTS.<─────────────────┐
         │       .                                             │
         │        .                                            │
         │         .                                           │
         └────> WRITE-DETAIL-LINE.                             │
                 MOVE SPACES TO PRINT-LINE.                    │
                 MOVE STUDENT-NAME TO PRINT-NAME.              │
                 MOVE TUITION TO PRINT-TUITION.       Return to
                 WRITE PRINT-LINE AFTER ADVANCING 2 LINES.─────┘
             WRITE-TOTAL-LINE.
```

The statement PERFORM WRITE-DETAIL-LINE transfers control to the first statement in the paragraph WRITE-DETAIL-LINE. When every statement in WRITE-DETAIL-LINE has been executed (i.e., when the next paragraph name is encountered), control returns to the statement immediately after the PERFORM, the ADD statement.

A PERFORM statement may also contain an UNTIL clause, which permits repeated execution of a paragraph. The condition in the UNTIL clause is tested *before* any transfer of control. The performed paragraph is executed repeatedly until the condition is met. Control passes to the statement following the PERFORM statement when the condition is eventually satisfied.

A loop is established by using the UNTIL clause, specifying a condition, and modifying that condition during execution of the performed paragraph. Consider:

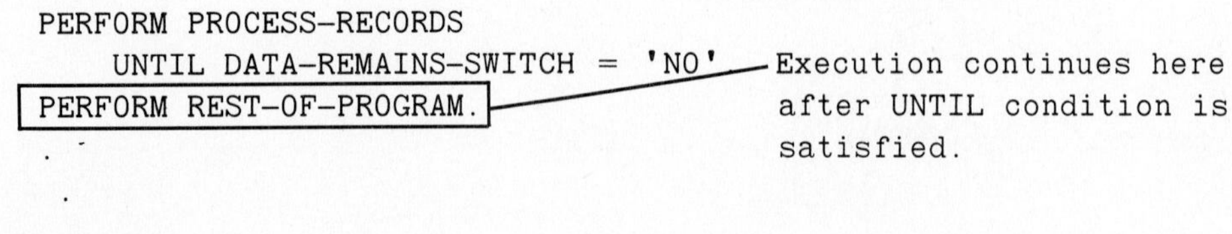

```
    PERFORM PROCESS-RECORDS
        UNTIL DATA-REMAINS-SWITCH = 'NO'   Execution continues here
    PERFORM REST-OF-PROGRAM.               after UNTIL condition is
    .                                      satisfied.
     .
      .

PROCESS-RECORDS.
    .
     .
      .
    READ STUDENT-FILE
        AT END MOVE 'NO' TO DATA-REMAINS-SWITCH.
```

The paragraph PROCESS-RECORDS is performed until DATA-REMAINS-SWITCH equals 'NO', i.e., until there are no more incoming records.

When the end of file is reached, the DATA-REMAINS-SWITCH is set to 'NO'. This causes the next test of the UNTIL condition to be met and prevents further execution of the PROCESS-RECORDS paragraph.

READ

An abbreviated format of the READ statement is

```
READ file-name AT END statement
```

As an example, consider lines 56 and 57 of the Engineering Senior Program in Figure 1.6.

```
READ STUDENT-FILE
    AT END MOVE 'NO' TO DATA-REMAINS-SWITCH.
```

This statement causes a record to be read into memory. However, if the end-of-file condition has been reached, i.e., there are no more records, then control passes to the statement(s) following the AT END clause. In this case, 'NO' will be moved to DATA-REMAINS-SWITCH when the end of file is sensed.

Placement of the READ Statement

The Engineering Senior Program in Figure 1.6 contained two distinct READ statements. There was an *initial* or *priming* READ in lines 42 and 43 and a second READ statement as the *last* instruction of the performed routine (lines 56 and 57). The necessity for *both* statements is best explained by considering Figure 4.3, which shows correct and incorrect ways to process a file of transactions.

Figure 4.3*a*, the *incorrect* implementation, causes *the last record of INPUT-FILE to be processed twice.* To understand better how this happens, consider a file with only two records, A and B. Recall that the PERFORM statement evaluates the UNTIL condition before branching. Further, a file with *two* records is read *three* times: once for each record and once to sense the end of file.

Record A is read the first time PROCESS-RECORDS is performed. Execution continues through the remainder of the PROCESS-RECORDS paragraph for record A. When the end of the paragraph is reached, DATA-REMAINS-SWITCH is still set to 'YES'. Hence PROCESS-RECORDS is executed a second time, during which it reads and processes record B. DATA-REMAINS-SWITCH remains set at 'YES', causing PROCESS-RECORDS to be executed a third time. The end-of-file condition is sensed immediately, but in the *middle* of the paragraph. Execution continues to the end of the paragraph, with the last record read processed a second time.

The alternative, and *correct,* structure in Figure 4.3*b* has an *initial* (or *priming*) READ, which is executed *only once*. It reads the first record and performs PROCESS-RECORDS for record A. The *last* statement of PROCESS-RECORDS is a second READ statement, which reads record B. PROCESS-RECORDS is executed a second time, this time with record B. Again the last statement of the performed routine is a READ, but this time it senses the end-of-file, terminating the PERFORM statement. (Note that PROCESS-RECORDS was executed twice, once for each record.)

```
MAINLINE.
      .
        .
          .
        MOVE 'YES' TO DATA-REMAINS-SWITCH.
        PERFORM PROCESS-RECORDS
            UNTIL DATA-REMAINS-SWITCH = 'NO'.
      .
        .
          .                                    First statement of performed routine is the
PROCESS-RECORDS.                               READ
    READ INPUT-FILE
        AT END MOVE 'NO' TO DATA-REMAINS-SWITCH.
  .
    .
      .
```

(a) Incorrect implementation

```
MAINLINE.
      .
        .
          .                                    Initial READ, executed once and
        MOVE 'YES' TO DATA-REMAINS-SWITCH.     only once
        READ INPUT-FILE
            AT END MOVE 'NO' TO DATA-REMAINS-SWITCH.
        PERFORM PROCESS-RECORDS
            UNTIL DATA-REMAINS-SWITCH = 'NO'.
  .
    .
      .
PROCESS-RECORDS.
      .
        .                                 Last statement of performed routine is
          .                               another READ.
```

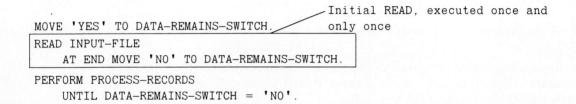

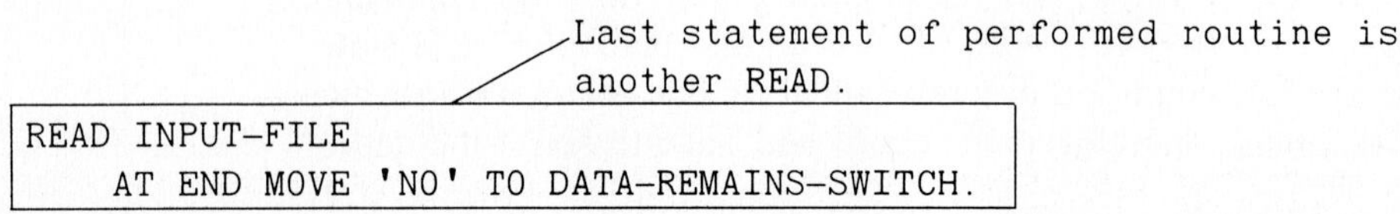

```
          READ INPUT-FILE
              AT END MOVE 'NO' TO DATA-REMAINS-SWITCH.
```

(b) Correct implementation

Figure 4.3 Placement of the READ Statement

WRITE

An abbreviated format of the WRITE statement is

```
WRITE record-name [{AFTER } ADVANCING {integer LINES}]
                  [{BEFORE}           {PAGE         }]
```

The WRITE statement transfers data from memory to an output device. The ADVANCING option controls line spacing on a printer; if omitted, single spacing occurs. If AFTER ADVANCING 3 LINES is used, the printer triple-spaces (i.e., skips two lines and writes on the third). Logically enough, the BEFORE option causes the line to be written first, after which the specified number of lines are skipped. Specification of PAGE, in lieu of LINES, will cause output to begin on top of a new page.

Note that the WRITE statement contains a *record* name, whereas the READ statement contains a *file* name. The record name in the WRITE will appear as an 01 entry in the File Section of the Data Division. The file in which it is contained will appear in SELECT, FD, OPEN, and CLOSE statements.

OPEN

Every file in a COBOL program must be "opened" before it can be accessed. The OPEN statement causes the operating system to initiate action to make a file available for processing. For example, it can ensure that the proper reel of tape has been mounted or that the proper diskette is available.

An abbreviated format of the OPEN statement is

```
OPEN { INPUT  } file-name-1 [,file-name-2 ...]
     { OUTPUT }
```

Notice that one must specify the type of file in an OPEN statement. INPUT is used for a file that is read, whereas OUTPUT is used for a file that is written to.

Lines 40 and 41 of the Engineering Senior Program contain an OPEN statement in which two files are opened in the same statement.

```
OPEN INPUT STUDENT-FILE
    OUTPUT PRINT-FILE.
```

One could also specify two OPEN statements, i.e.,

```
OPEN INPUT STUDENT-FILE.
OPEN OUTPUT PRINT-FILE.
```

However, a single statement is preferable.

CLOSE

All files must be closed before processing terminates. The format of the CLOSE is simply

```
CLOSE file-name-1 [, file-name-2...]
```

Several files may be closed in the same statement. The type of file, INPUT or OUTPUT, is not specified. Lines 46 and 47 in the Engineering Senior Program provide an example:

```
CLOSE STUDENT-FILE
      PRINT-FILE.
```

MOVE

The MOVE statement transfers data; that is, it moves data from one storage location to another. The statement MOVE A TO B moves the value stored in location A to location B. The initial value of A is in two places after the move has taken place; the initial value of B has been replaced by A. The general format of the MOVE statement is simply

```
MOVE {identifier-1} TO identifier-2 [identifier-3] ...
     {literal     }
```

Consider the following examples:

```
MOVE 127.50 TO PRICE-PER-CREDIT.
MOVE 'ABC UNIVERSITY' TO SCHOOL-NAME.
MOVE STU-NAME TO PRINT-NAME.
```

The first example moves a numeric literal, 127.50, to the data name PRICE-PER-CREDIT. The second moves a nonnumeric literal, 'ABC UNIVERSITY', to SCHOOL-NAME. The third example is taken from line 53 of the Engineering Senior Program and transfers data from an input area to an output area for subsequent printing.

The figurative constants, ZEROS and SPACES, are frequently used in a MOVE as shown:

```
MOVE SPACES TO PRINT-LINE.
MOVE ZEROS TO TOTAL-NUMBER.
```

The first statement moves spaces (i.e., blanks) to the data name PRINT-LINE. The second statement moves numeric zeros to TOTAL-NUMBER. In addition, a given quantity may be moved to several data names in the same statement. For example,

```
MOVE 10 TO FIELD-A FIELD-B FIELD-C.
```

is equivalent to

```
MOVE 10 TO FIELD-A.
MOVE 10 TO FIELD-B.
MOVE 10 TO FIELD-C.
```

Restrictions on the MOVE Statement

The results of a MOVE depend on the picture of the receiving field; whenever the receiving field has a picture different from that of the sending field, a conversion must take place. Further, certain moves are not permitted. Table 4.9

TABLE 4.9 *Rules of the MOVE Statement*

	RECEIVING FIELD				
SOURCE FIELD	Group	Alphabetic	Alpha-numeric	Numeric	Numeric Edited
Group	Valid	Valid	Valid	Valid	Valid
Alphabetic	Valid	Valid	Valid	Invalid	Invalid
Alphanumeric	Valid	Valid	Valid	Invalid	Invalid
Numeric	Valid	Invalid	Integers only	Valid	Valid
Numeric edited	Valid	Invalid	Valid	Invalid	Invalid

summarizes the rules of the MOVE. (It is not necessary to commit Table 4.9, or the discussion that follows, to memory. Instead be aware that certain restrictions exist and know where to turn when questions arise later.)

Inspection of Table 4.9 shows that an alphabetic field cannot be moved to a numeric field and vice versa.

Alphanumeric Sending Field to Alphanumeric Receiving Field

Data moved from an alphanumeric area to an alphanumeric area are moved one character at a time from left to right. If the receiving field is larger than the sending field, it is padded on the right with blanks; if the receiving field is smaller than the sending field, the rightmost characters are truncated.

Alphanumeric moves are illustrated in Table 4.10.

Example (a) is trivial in that the sending and receiving fields have the same picture clause. In example (b) the sending field is one byte longer than the receiving field; hence the rightmost byte is truncated. Data are moved from left to right one byte at a time; thus A, B, C, and D are moved in that order, and E is dropped.

In example (c), however, the receiving field is one byte longer than the sending field. A, B, C, D, and E are moved in that order, and a blank is added at the end.

TABLE 4.10 *Illustration of the MOVE Statement*

SOURCE FIELD		RECEIVING FIELD	
Picture	Contents	Picture	Contents
(a) X(5)	A B C D E	X(5)	A B C D E
(b) X(5)	A B C D E	X(4)	A B C D
(c) X(5)	A B C D E	X(6)	A B C D E

Numeric Sending Field to Numeric Receiving Field

All moves involving numeric fields maintain decimal alignment. If the receiving field is larger than the sending field, high-order zeros are added. If the receiving field is smaller than the sending field, the high-order positions are truncated. If the receiving field has more decimal places than the sending field, low-order zeros are added. These points are clarified in Table 4.11.

Example (a) is trivial. Example (b) attempts to move a five-position field to a four-position field. Since *decimal alignment is always maintained,* the leftmost digit (i.e., the *most significant* digit) is truncated. Example (c) moves a five-position sending field to a six-position receiving field, causing the addition of a leading (nonsignificant) zero. The sending field in example (d) has two digits after the decimal point, but the receiving field has none. Hence the 4 and 5 do not appear in the receiving field. Example (e) truncates the most significant digits. Example (f) adds two nonsignificant zeros to the receiving field.

One final point: The preceding discussion pertains to elementary items only. *If the receiving field is a group item, the move takes place as though the receiving field were an alphanumeric item, with padding or truncation on the right as necessary.*

TABLE 4.11 *Illustration of the MOVE Statement*

SOURCE FIELD		RECEIVING FIELD	
Picture	Contents	Picture	Contents
(a) 9(5)	1 2 3 4 5	9(5)	1 2 3 4 5
(b) 9(5)	1 2 3 4 5	9(4)	2 3 4 5
(c) 9(5)	1 2 3 4 5	9(6)	0 1 2 3 4 5
(d) 9(3)V99	1 2 3 4 5	9(3)	1 2 3
(e) 9(3)V99	1 2 3 4 5	9V99	3 4 5
(f) 9(3)	1 2 3	9(3)V99	1 2 3 0 0

STOP RUN

Every program must have at least one STOP RUN statement (or its equivalent, e.g., GOBACK on IBM systems); the format is

```
STOP RUN
```

When STOP RUN is encountered, execution of the COBOL program terminates and control passes back to the operating system. It is important to realize that STOP RUN is usually *not* the physically last statement in the Procedure Division. Further, there may be more than one of these statements in a program, but this is not recommended. STOP RUN means the programmer wants the job to cease execution because the program has come to a logical end.

ENGINEERING SENIOR PROGRAM CONTINUED

In Chapter 3 we presented specifications for the Extended Engineering Senior Program and developed the first three divisions. The completed program is shown in Figure 4.4. The logic in Figure 4.4 adheres to our usual program structure, namely an initial READ, in conjunction with a second READ as the last statement of a performed routine. Observe also that there are *separate* paragraphs to write the heading, detail, and total lines, just as the Data Division developed separate 01 records for the various print lines.

The condition in the IF statement (line 101) checks for engineering seniors. Any record that satisfies both conditions causes a detail line to be written and increments a counter. (The latter is initialized in Working-Storage, line 43, and written at the conclusion of processing.)

Of greatest significance, however, is the relationship of the paragraphs in the Procedure Division to one another. This is best expressed in a program's *hierarchy chart*.

THE HIERARCHY CHART AS A DOCUMENTATION TECHNIQUE

Figure 4.5 contains a *hierarchy chart* for the program in Figure 4.4. A program's hierarchy chart is analogous to a company's organization chart and shows the functions inherent in a program. A hierarchy chart is best explained by compar-

```
00001          IDENTIFICATION DIVISION.
00002          PROGRAM-ID.      SECNTRY.
00003          AUTHOR.          JACKIE CLARK.
00004
00005          ENVIRONMENT DIVISION.
00006          CONFIGURATION SECTION.
00007          SOURCE-COMPUTER.    IBM-4341.
00008          OBJECT-COMPUTER.    IBM-4341.
00009          INPUT-OUTPUT SECTION.
00010          FILE-CONTROL.
00011              SELECT STUDENT-FILE ASSIGN TO UT-S-SYSIN.
00012              SELECT PRINT-FILE    ASSIGN TO UT-S-SYSOUT.
00013
00014          DATA DIVISION.
00015          FILE SECTION.
00016          FD  STUDENT-FILE
00017              LABEL RECORDS ARE OMITTED
00018              RECORD CONTAINS 80 CHARACTERS
00019              DATA RECORD IS STUDENT-IN.
00020          01  STUDENT-IN.
00021              05  STU-NAME.
00022                  10   STU-LAST-NAME    PIC X(15).
00023                  10   STU-FIRST-NAME   PIC X(09).
00024                  10   STU-MID-INIT     PIC X(01).
00025              05  STU-ENROL-DATE.
00026                  10   STU-ENROL-MM     PIC 9(02).
00027                  10   STU-ENROL-DD     PIC 9(02).
00028                  10   STU-ENROL-YY     PIC 9(02).
00029              05  STU-CREDITS           PIC 9(3).
00030              05  STU-MAJOR             PIC X(15).
00031              05  STU-GPA               PIC 9V99.
00032              05  FILLER                PIC X(28).
00033
00034          FD  PRINT-FILE
00035              LABEL RECORDS ARE OMITTED
00036              RECORD CONTAINS 133 CHARACTERS
00037              DATA RECORD IS PRINT-LINE.
00038          01  PRINT-LINE                PIC X(133).
00039
00040          WORKING-STORAGE SECTION.
00041          01  DATA-REMAINS-SWITCH       PIC X(02)  VALUE SPACES.
00042
00043          01  WS-STUDENT-COUNTER        PIC 9(02)  VALUE ZEROS.     ── Counter for qualified students.
00044
00045          01  HEADING-LINE-1.
00046              05  FILLER                PIC X(11)  VALUE SPACES.
00047              05  FILLER                PIC X(19)
00048                       VALUE 'ENGINEERING SENIORS'.
00049              05  FILLER                PIC X(103) VALUE SPACES.
00050
00051          01  HEADING-LINE-2.
00052              05  FILLER                PIC X(05)  VALUE SPACES.
00053              05  FILLER                PIC X(04)  VALUE 'NAME'.
00054              05  FILLER                PIC X(11)  VALUE SPACES.
00055              05  FILLER                PIC X(07)  VALUE 'CREDITS'.
00056              05  FILLER                PIC X(04)  VALUE SPACES.
00057              05  FILLER                PIC X(09)  VALUE 'ENRL DATE'.
00058              05  FILLER                PIC X(93)  VALUE SPACES.
00059
00060          01  DETAIL-LINE.
00061              05  DET-LAST-NAME         PIC X(15).
00062              05  FILLER                PIC X(07)  VALUE SPACES.
00063              05  DET-CREDITS           PIC 9(03).
00064              05  FILLER                PIC X(08)  VALUE SPACES.
00065              05  DET-MM                PIC 9(02).
00066              05  FILLER                PIC X(01)  VALUE '/'.
00067              05  DET-YY                PIC 9(02).
00068              05  FILLER                PIC X(95)  VALUE SPACES.
00069
00070          01  TOTAL-LINE.
00071              05  FILLER                PIC X(12)  VALUE SPACES.
00072              05  FILLER                PIC X(15)  VALUE 'TOTAL NUMBER = '.
00073              05  TOTAL-COUNT           PIC 99.
00074              05  FILLER                PIC X(104) VALUE SPACES.
```

Heading, detail, and total lines are defined as separate 01 records.

FIGURE 4.4 *The Engineering Senior Program Extended*

```
       PROCEDURE DIVISION.
       MAINLINE.
           OPEN INPUT  STUDENT-FILE
                OUTPUT PRINT-FILE.
           PERFORM WRITE-HEADING-LINE.
           READ STUDENT-FILE
               AT END MOVE 'NO' TO DATA-REMAINS-SWITCH.
           PERFORM PROCESS-RECORDS
               UNTIL DATA-REMAINS-SWITCH = 'NO'.
           PERFORM WRITE-TOTAL-LINE.
           CLOSE STUDENT-FILE
                 PRINT-FILE.
           STOP RUN.

       WRITE-HEADING-LINE.
           MOVE HEADING-LINE-1 TO PRINT-LINE.
           WRITE PRINT-LINE
               AFTER ADVANCING PAGE.
           MOVE HEADING-LINE-2 TO PRINT-LINE.
           WRITE PRINT-LINE
               AFTER ADVANCING 2 LINES.
           MOVE SPACES TO PRINT-LINE.
           WRITE PRINT-LINE.

       PROCESS-RECORDS.
           IF STU-CREDITS NOT < 110 AND STU-MAJOR = 'ENGINEERING'
               PERFORM WRITE-DETAIL-LINE
               ADD 1 TO WS-STUDENT-COUNTER.
           READ STUDENT-FILE
               AT END MOVE 'NO' TO DATA-REMAINS-SWITCH.

       WRITE-DETAIL-LINE.
           MOVE STU-LAST-NAME TO DET-LAST-NAME.
           MOVE STU-CREDITS   TO DET-CREDITS.
           MOVE STU-ENROL-MM  TO DET-MM.
           MOVE STU-ENROL-YY  TO DET-YY.
           MOVE DETAIL-LINE TO PRINT-LINE.
           WRITE PRINT-LINE.

       WRITE-TOTAL-LINE.
           MOVE WS-STUDENT-COUNTER TO TOTAL-COUNT.
           MOVE TOTAL-LINE TO PRINT-LINE.
           WRITE PRINT-LINE.
```

Initial READ.

Last line of performed routine is a second READ.

FIGURE 4.4 (continued)

ing it to its associated program. Accordingly, observe the properties of the hierarchy chart in Figure 4.5 as they relate to the COBOL program in Figure 4.4.

- □ *Every box (module) in the hierarchy chart corresponds to a paragraph in the COBOL program.* There are five modules in the hierarchy chart, and five paragraphs in the program.
- □ *Each level in the hierarchy chart corresponds to a PERFORM statement in the COBOL program.* Thus the paragraph at the highest level, MAINLINE, contains three PERFORM statements for WRITE-HEADING-LINE, PROCESS-RECORDS, and WRITE-TOTAL-LINE. PROCESS-RECORDS in turn performs one lower level paragraph.
- □ *A paragraph can be entered only from the paragraph directly above it and must eventually return control to that paragraph.* Hence, PROCESS-RECORDS is entered via a PERFORM statement in MAINLINE. PROCESS-RECORDS invokes a lower level paragraph, which returns control to PROCESS-RECORDS, which eventually returns to MAINLINE.
- □ *Every module in a hierarchy chart (or paragraph within a program) should be dedicated to a single function.* The nature of that function should be apparent from the module's name and consist of a verb, one or two adjectives, and an object. (MAINLINE is the only exception to this rule.) If a module cannot be named in this fashion, it may be doing more than one job and some redesign may be advisable.

A hierarchy chart is very different from flowcharts or pseudocode. *A hierarchy chart shows what has to be done, but not when;* it contains no decision-making logic. Flowcharts and pseudocode, on the other hand, specify when and if a

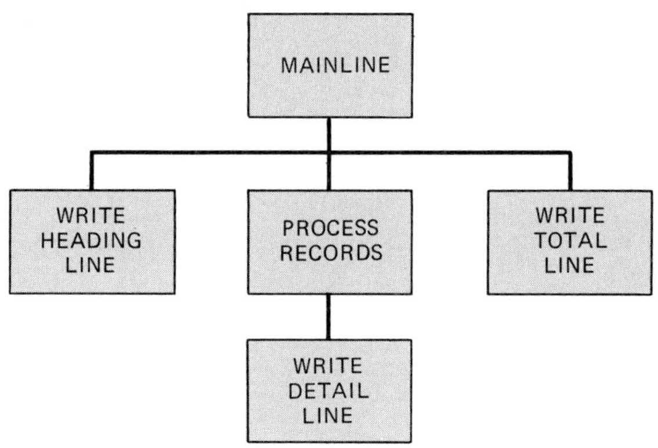

FIGURE 4.5 Hierarchy Chart of a COBOL Program

given block of code is executed. We say that hierarchy charts are *functional* in nature; they contain the tasks necessary to accomplish the specifications but do not indicate an order for execution. Flowcharts and pseudocode are *procedural* techniques and are read sequentially.

A hierarchy chart is useful as both a *design* aid, before a program is developed, and as a *documentation* technique after coding is completed. Its appearance in this chapter is solely for documentation purposes; it helps us understand the structure of a completed program. In Chapter 5 we will use the hierarchy chart as a tool for developing programs.

COBOL 8X:

Changes and Enhancements

By far the most significant change in COBOL 8X, as it relates to the material in this chapter, is the presence of the END-IF scope terminator. Simply stated, an IF statement is terminated by the new reserved word END-IF. Consider the 8X syntax

```
                                     { ELSE statement-2 [END-IF] }
IF condition THEN statement-1        {                           }
                                     { END-IF                    }
```

Lines 101–103 of the Extended Engineering Senior Program are rewritten to reflect use of END-IF:

```
IF STU-CREDITS NOT < 110 AND STU-MAJOR = 'ENGINEERING'
    PERFORM WRITE-DETAIL-LINE
    ADD 1 TO WS-STUDENT-COUNTER
END-IF.
```

The utility of the scope terminator is simply its prominence. Unlike a period, which can be easily missed or mistaken for a comma, END-IF is there for all to see. (You may want to peruse the discussion associated with the "missing period" in Figure B.1.)

Two other minor changes are worthy of mention. The 8X syntax for the IF statement permits optional use of the word THEN. In similar fashion, the GIVING format of the ADD statement accepts the word TO; i.e., one may say ADD A TO B GIVING C.

Summary

Several Procedure Division verbs were introduced.

Arithmetic:
- *ADD*
- *SUBTRACT*
- *MULTIPLY*
- *DIVIDE*
- *COMPUTE*

Input/Output:
- *READ*
- *WRITE*
- *OPEN*
- *CLOSE*

Selection:
- *IF*

Iteration:
- *PERFORM*

Data Transfer:
- *MOVE*

Program Termination:
- *STOP RUN*

IF and PERFORM were shown to be two of the more powerful COBOL statements. IF may be used with or without an ELSE clause. Indentation was stressed, as was the effect of a period.

The PERFORM UNTIL statement is used to implement a loop in COBOL, and care must be taken to place the READ statement correctly within the context of a PERFORM. The relationship of performed paragraphs within a program is best demonstrated through a hierarchy chart, *as seen in the Extended Engineering Senior Program.*

True/False Exercises

1. One ADD instruction can change the value of more than one data name.
2. Both GIVING and TO may be present in the same ADD instruction.
3. A valid ADD instruction may contain neither GIVING nor TO.
4. Both FROM and GIVING may appear in the same SUBTRACT instruction.
5. The use of GIVING is optional in the MULTIPLY verb.
6. The reserved word INTO must appear in a DIVIDE statement.
7. In the DIVIDE statement, the dividend is always identifier-1.
8. Multiplication and division can be performed in the same MULTIPLY statement.
9. Multiplication and addition can be performed in the same COMPUTE statement.
10. In a COMPUTE statement with no parentheses, multiplication is always done before subtraction.
11. In a COMPUTE statement with no parentheses, multiplication is always done before division.
12. Parentheses are sometimes required in a COMPUTE statement.
13. The COMPUTE statement changes the value of only one data name.
14. The IF statement must always contain the ELSE option.
15. The PERFORM statement transfers control to a paragraph elsewhere in the program and returns control to the statement immediately following when the paragraph has completed execution.

16. A program may contain more than one STOP RUN statement.
17. STOP RUN must be the last statement in the Procedure Division.
18. The ADVANCING option is mandatory in the WRITE statement.
19. The READ statement contains a record name.
20. The WRITE statement contains a record name.
21. The OPEN and CLOSE statements are optional.
22. The period has little effect in an IF statement.
23. An IF statement can cause the execution of several other statements.
24. If the ELSE clause is satisfied in an IF statement, it can cause execution of several statements.
25. An IF statement is terminated by END-IF.
26. The ROUNDED clause is required in the COMPUTE statement.

Problems

1. Some of the following arithmetic statements are invalid. Identify those which are invalid, and state why they are unacceptable to the COBOL compiler.

   (a) ADD A B C.
   (b) SUBTRACT 10 FROM A B.
   (c) SUBTRACT A FROM 10.
   (d) ADD A TO B GIVING C.
   (e) SUBTRACT A ROUNDED FROM B ROUNDED GIVING C.
   (f) MULTIPLY A BY 10.
   (g) MULTIPLY 10 BY A ROUNDED.
   (h) MULTIPLY A BY 10 GIVING B C.
   (i) DIVIDE A BY B.
   (j) DIVIDE A INTO B.
   (k) DIVIDE A INTO B GIVING C.
   (l) DIVIDE B BY A GIVING C.
   (m) COMPUTE X ROUNDED = A + B.
   (n) COMPUTE X = 2(A + B).
   (o) COMPUTE V = 20 / A − C.

2. Complete the table. In each instance, refer to the *initial* values of A, B, C, and D.

Data name	A	B	C	D
Value *before* execution	4	8	12	2
Value *after* execution of				
ADD 1 TO D B.				
ADD A B C GIVING D.				
ADD A B C TO D.				
SUBTRACT A B FROM C.				
SUBTRACT A B FROM C GIVING D.				
MULTIPLY A BY B C.				
MULTIPLY B BY A.				
DIVIDE A INTO C.				
DIVIDE C BY B GIVING D REMAINDER A.				
COMPUTE D = A + B / 2 * D.				
COMPUTE D = (A + B) / (2 * D).				

COMPUTE D = A + B / (2 * D).
COMPUTE D = (A + B) / 2 * D.
COMPUTE D = A + (B / 2) * D.

3. Indicate the logical errors inherent in the following COBOL fragment:

```
FILE SECTION.
FD  EMPLOYEE-FILE
 .
  .
   .
FD  PRINT-FILE
 .
  .
   .
WORKING-STORAGE SECTION.
 .
  .
   .
01  END-OF-FILE-SWITCH    PIC X(3)  VALUE 'YES'.
 .
  .
   .
PROCEDURE DIVISION.
    MOVE HEADING-LINE TO PRINT-LINE.
    WRITE PRINT-LINE
          AFTER ADVANCING PAGE.
    OPEN INPUT EMPLOYEE-FILE
        OUTPUT PRINT-FILE.
    READ EMPLOYEE-FILE
        AT END MOVE 'YES' TO END-OF-FILE-SWITCH
    PERFORM PROCESS-RECORDS
        UNTIL END-OF-FILE-SWITCH  =  'YES'
    CLOSE EMPLOYEE-FILE.
    STOP RUN.
PROCESS-RECORDS.
    .
     .
      .
```

4. Some of the following statements are invalid. Indicate those which are, and state why they are invalid. (Assume FILE-ONE and FILE-TWO are file names and RECORD-ONE is a record name.)

(a) OPEN INPUT RECORD-ONE.
(b) OPEN INPUT FILE-ONE OUTPUT FILE-TWO.
(c) OPEN INPUT FILE-ONE.
(d) CLOSE OUTPUT FILE-ONE.
(e) READ FILE-ONE.
(f) READ FILE-ONE AT END PERFORM END-OF-JOB-ROUTINE.
(g) READ RECORD-ONE AT END PERFORM END-OF-JOB.
(h) WRITE RECORD-ONE.
(i) WRITE RECORD-ONE AFTER ADVANCING TWO LINES.
(j) WRITE RECORD-ONE BEFORE ADVANCING TWO LINES.
(k) CLOSE FILE-ONE FILE-TWO.
(l) WRITE FILE-ONE.
(m) WRITE RECORD-ONE AFTER ADVANCING PAGE.

5. Write COBOL COMPUTE statements to accomplish the intended logic:

(a) $x = a + b + c$

(b) $x = \dfrac{a + bc}{2}$

(c) $x = a^2 + b^2 + c^2$

(d) $x = \dfrac{a + b}{2} - c$

(e) $x = a + b$

(f) $x = \sqrt{\dfrac{a + b}{2c}}$

(g) $x = \sqrt{\dfrac{a^2 + b^2}{c^2 - d^2}} + 2e$

6. Write Procedure Division code for the following:

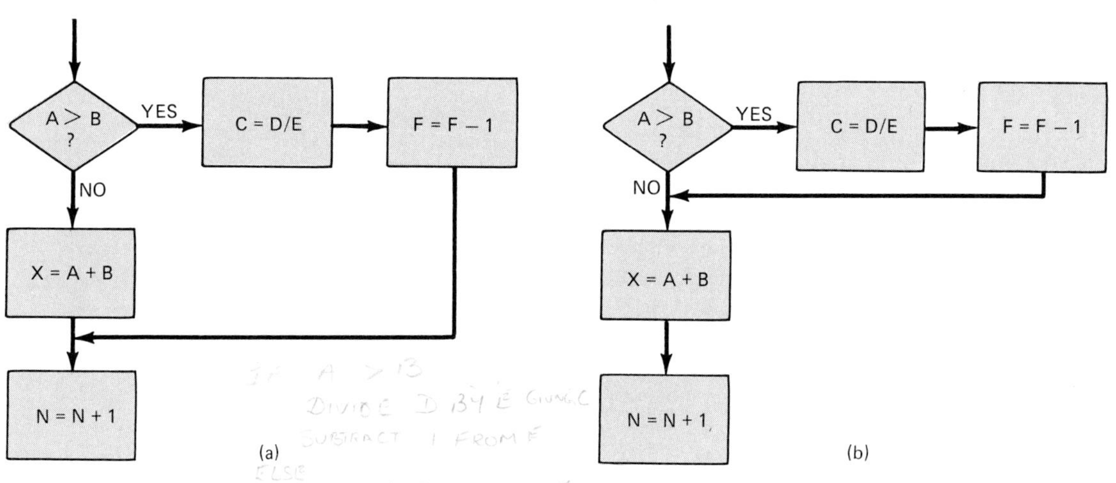

7. Given the following Procedure Division:

```
PROCEDURE DIVISION.
FIRST-PARAGRAPH.
    MOVE ZEROS TO FIELD-A FIELD-B.
    PERFORM SECOND-PARAGRAPH.
    PERFORM THIRD-PARAGRAPH.
    PERFORM SECOND-PARAGRAPH.
    STOP RUN.
SECOND-PARAGRAPH.
    ADD 10 TO FIELD-A.
    ADD 20 TO FIELD-B.
THIRD-PARAGRAPH.
    MULTIPLY FIELD-A BY FIELD-B GIVING FIELD-C.
    DIVIDE FIELD-A INTO FIELD-B GIVING FIELD-D.
```

(a) What are the final values for FIELD-A, FIELD-B, FIELD-C, and FIELD-D?

(b) How many times is each paragraph executed?

8. Complete the following table, showing the contents of the receiving field.

SENDING FIELD		RECEIVING FIELD	
Picture	Contents	Picture	Contents
(a) X(4)	H O P E	X(4)	
(b) X(4)	H O P E	9(4)	
(c) X(4)	H O P E	X(3)	
(d) X(4)	H O P E	X(5)	
(e) 9(4)	6 7 8 9	X(4)	
(f) 9(4)	6 7 8 9	9(3)	
(g) 9(4)	6 7 8 9	9(5)	
(h) 999V9	6 7 8 9	9(4)	
(i) 999V9	6 7 8 9	9(4)V9	
(j) 999V9	6 7 8 9	9(3)V99	
(k) 999V9	6 7 8 9	99V99	

9. Supply Procedure Division statements as indicated:

(a) Code two equivalent statements, an ADD and a COMPUTE, to add 1 to the counter NUMBER-QUALIFIED-EMPLOYEES.

(b) Code a COBOL statement to add the contents of five fields, MONDAY-SALES, TUESDAY-SALES, WEDNESDAY-SALES, THURSDAY-SALES, and FRIDAY-SALES, storing the result in WEEKLY-SALES.

(c) Code a COBOL statement to subtract the fields FED-TAX, STATE-TAX, FICA, and VOLUNTARY-DEDUCTIONS, from GROSS-PAY, and put the result in NET-PAY.

(d) Code a single COBOL statement to calculate NET-AMOUNT-DUE, which is equal to the GROSS-SALE minus a 2% discount.

(e) Recode part (d), using *two* statements (a MULTIPLY and a SUBTRACT).

(f) Code a COBOL statement to compute GROSS-PAY, which is equal to HOURS-WORKED times HOURLY-RATE.

(g) Code a *single* COBOL statement to compute GROSS-PAY, which is equal to REG-HOURS-WORKED times HOURLY-RATE plus OVERTIME-HOURS times HOURLY-RATE times 1.5.

(h) Code a COBOL statement to determine AVERAGE-SALARY by dividing TOTAL-SALARY by NUMBER-OF-EMPLOYEES.

(i) Code a COBOL COMPUTE equivalent to the algebraic statement

$$x = \frac{(a + b)c}{de}$$

(j) Code a COBOL COMPUTE equivalent to the algebraic statement

$$x = \frac{-b + \sqrt{b^2 - 4ac}}{2a}$$

Note that raising a number to the power .5 is equivalent to calculating its square root.

Programming Specifications

Projects 4–1, 4–2, and 4–3

Program Name:

Grade Point Listing, Inventory Parts List, and Money Changer

Narrative:

The specifications for these projects were introduced in Chapter 3, at which time you were to attempt the first three COBOL divisions. Complete the projects now.

a) COMPUTE NUMBER-QUALIFIED-EMPLOYEES = NUMBER-QUALIFIED-EMPLOYEES + 1

ADD 1 TO NUMBER-QUALIFIED-EMPLOYEES

b) COMPUTE WEEKLY-SALES = MON SALES + TUES SALES + WED-SALES + THURSDAY-SALES + FRIDAY-SALES

ADD MON ...... GIVING WEEKLY-SALES.

c) COMPUTE NET-PAY = GROSS-PAY − (FED-TAX + STATE-TAX + FICA + VOLUNTARY-DEDUCTIONS)

SUBTRACT FED-TAX STATE TAX FICA VOLUNTARY-DED FROM GROSS-PAY GIVING NET-PAY

d) COMPUTE NET-AMOUNT-DUE = GROSS-SALE − (GROSS-SALE * 2/100)

OR MULTIPLY GROSS-SALE * .98 GIVING NET-AMT-DUE

e) MULTIPLY GROSS-SALE BY .Ø2 GIVING DISCOUNT

SUBTRACT DISCOUNT FROM GROSS-SALE GIVING NET-AMT-DUE

f) COMPUTE GROSS-PAY = HOURS-WORKED * HOURLY-RATE

OR multiply Hours-worked by hourly-Rate giving gross-pay.

g) Compute Gross-pay = (Regular-hours-worked * hourly-rate) + (overtime-hours * hourly-rate * 1.5)

Writing a Report Program

5

Overview

This chapter begins with a discussion of COBOL's editing *facility, the ability to dress up printed reports by inserting dollar signs, decimal points, commas, etc. into numeric fields prior to printing. We introduce a new problem, the* Tuition Billing Program, *to illustrate editing. We also use this program to focus on the hierarchy chart as a design technique prior to actual coding. We examine test data and associated output and use all the COBOL elements from the first four chapters to write the completed program.*

The second half of the chapter develops the concept of coding standards, *a set of guidelines imposed by an installation to increase the readability (and maintainability) of COBOL programs.* □

EDITING

Incoming numeric fields may not contain anything other than digits or an implied decimal point. Nevertheless, it is highly desirable for dollar signs, commas, decimal points, etc. to appear in printed reports. The problem is resolved by the use of *editing symbols* and the *MOVE* statement.

This chapter presents the subject of editing, in which a *numeric* field (one defined with a PICTURE clause containing 9s and an optional implied decimal point) is moved to a *numeric*-edited field. As stated previously, *all moves involving numeric fields maintain decimal alignment*. Consider

```
05  FIELD-A           PIC 9V99.
05  FIELD-A-EDITED    PIC 9.99.
```

FIELD-A is a *three*-digit numeric field, with two digits after the decimal point. FIELD-A-EDITED is a *four*-position edit field containing an actual decimal point. All calculations are done using FIELD-A. Then, just prior to printing, FIELD-A is moved to FIELD-A-EDITED, and the latter field is printed. For example,

Before Move:

```
                 V
FIELD-A        |7|8|3|     FIELD-A-EDITED  |?|.|?|?|
```

After execution of MOVE FIELD-A TO FIELD-A-EDITED:

```
                 V
FIELD-A        |7|8|3|     FIELD-A-EDITED  |7|.|8|3|
```

The question marks that appear in FIELD-A-EDITED prior to the move imply that the initial values are immaterial. Notice also that the decimal point actually takes a position in FIELD-A-EDITED. However, it does not occupy a position in FIELD-A, as the decimal point is only implied.

The appearance of a single $ causes a dollar sign to be printed in the indicated position. Consider

```
05  FIELD-B              PIC 9(3)V99.
05  FIELD-B-EDITED       PIC $9(3).99.
```

Before Move:

```
                   V
FIELD-B   |6|5|4|3|2|     FIELD-B-EDITED  |$|?|?|?|.|?|?|
```

After execution of MOVE FIELD-B TO FIELD-B-EDITED:

```
                   V
FIELD-B   |6|5|4|3|2|     FIELD-B-EDITED  |$|6|5|4|.|3|2|
```

The dollar sign and decimal point both take up a position in FIELD-B-EDITED.

It is also possible to obtain a "floating" dollar sign by using multiple dollar signs in the edited field. In this instance *a single $ is printed immediately to the left of the first significant digit*. Thus

```
05  FIELD-C              PIC 9(3)V99.
05  FIELD-C-EDITED       PIC $$$$.99.
```

Before Move:

```
                   V
FIELD-C   |0|0|1|2|3|     FIELD-C-EDITED  |$|$|$|$|.|?|?|
```

After execution of MOVE FIELD-C TO FIELD-C-EDITED:

```
                   V
FIELD-C   |0|0|1|2|3|     FIELD-C-EDITED  | | |$|1|.|2|3|
```

A single dollar sign is printed immediately before the leftmost digit in the field. FIELD-C-EDITED is a seven-position field, but the first two positions hold blanks.

The presence of a comma as an editing symbol causes a comma to be printed if it is preceded by a significant digit. However, if a comma is preceded only by zeros, then it is supressed. Consider

```
05  FIELD-D              PIC 9(4).
05  FIELD-D-EDITED       PIC $$,$$9.
```

Before Move:

FIELD-D | 8 | 7 | 6 | 5 | FIELD-D-EDITED | $ | $ | , | $ | $ | ? |

After execution of MOVE FIELD-D TO FIELD-D-EDITED:

FIELD-D | 8 | 7 | 6 | 5 | FIELD-D-EDITED | $ | 8 | , | 7 | 6 | 5 |

The comma is printed in the indicated position. Suppose, however, that the contents of the sending field are less than 1,000, e.g.,

```
05  FIELD-E              PIC 9(4).
05  FIELD-E-EDITED       PIC $$,$$9.
```

Before Move:

FIELD-E | 0 | 0 | 8 | 7 | FIELD-E-EDITED | $ | $ | , | $ | $ | ? |

After execution of MOVE FIELD-E TO FIELD-E-EDITED:

FIELD-E | 0 | 0 | 8 | 7 | FIELD-E-EDITED | | | | $ | 8 | 7 |

The comma will be suppressed because it was not preceded by a significant digit. Observe also how the dollar sign floats to the left of the first significant digit.

A dollar sign can be made to print in a *fixed* position, with simultaneous suppression of nonsignificant (leading) zeros. Consider

```
05  FIELD-F              PIC 9(4).
05  FIELD-F-EDITED       PIC $Z,ZZZ.
```

Before Move:

FIELD-F | 0 | 0 | 8 | 7 | FIELD-F-EDITED | $ | Z | , | Z | Z | Z |

After execution of MOVE FIELD-F TO FIELD-F-EDITED:

FIELD-F | 0 | 0 | 8 | 7 | FIELD-F-EDITED | $ | | | | 8 | 7 |

The edit character Z prints only significant digits; that is, it suppresses high-order zeros. Hence a single dollar sign followed by a picture of Zs produces a fixed dollar sign in the leftmost position of the receiving field.

It is hardly prudent to leave blanks between a fixed dollar sign and a significant digit, especially when cutting checks. For this reason an asterisk is often used as a *fill character* in editing; e.g.,

Before Move:

FIELD-G	0	0	8	7	FIELD-G-EDITED	$	*	,	*	*	?

After execution of MOVE FIELD-G TO FIELD-G-EDITED:

FIELD-G	0	0	8	7	FIELD-G-EDITED	$	*	*	*	8	7

The dollar sign remains in its fixed position. An asterisk is printed in lieu of a leading (nonsignificant) zero; that is, the field is asterisk filled.

Information on editing is summarized in Table 5.1.

TABLE 5.1 *Use of Editing Symbols*

SOURCE FIELD		*RECEIVING FIELD*	
Picture	*Value*	*Picture*	*Edited Result*
(a) 9(4)	0678	Z(4)	_678
(b) 9(4)	0678	$9(4)	$0678
(c) 9(4)	0678	$Z(4)	$_678
(d) 9(4)V99	123456	9(4).99	1234.56
(e) 9(4)V99	123456	$9(4).99	$1234.56
(f) 9(4)V99	123456	$9,999.99	$1,234.56
(g) 9(4)	0008	$,$$$	______$8
(h) 9(4)V9	12345	9(4)	1234
(i) 9(4)V9	12345	9(4).99	1234.50
(j) 9(5)	00045	$****9	$***45

Numeric Versus Numeric-Edited Fields

Calculations in COBOL are performed on *numeric* fields, whereas *numeric-edited* fields are typically printed. The situation is shown in Figure 5.1, which illustrates a simple computation on a numeric field and a subsequent move to a numeric-edited field.

Incoming fields, such as EMP-HOURS or EMP-RATE, are defined with numeric picture clauses; so too are the intermediate work areas, such as WS-PAY. Any necessary calculations are done on these fields. Then, just prior to printing, the numeric fields are moved to numeric-edited fields as indicated. It is not unusual, therefore, for large commercial programs to have 10% or more of their Procedure Division consist of MOVE statements.

Additional Editing Characters

The complete set of editing characters is shown in Table 5.2.

Table 5.3 illustrates the use of *insertion characters,* symbols that are placed into the sending field at the indicated position. Examples (a), (b), and (c) show the use of slashes in a date field. Observe the difference in examples (b) and (c), between a picture of 9s and one of Zs. Example (d) puts blanks in a Social Security number. (The hyphen is not an insertion character in COBOL, as will be explained in Table 5.4.) Finally, example (e) shows how zeros may be inserted into a numeric field.

```
FD  EMPLOYEE-FILE
    .
     .
      .
01  EMPLOYEE-RECORD.
    .
     .        ——Numeric fields
      .
    05  EMP-HOURS              PIC 99.
    05  EMP-RATE               PIC 99V99.

FD  PRINT-FILE
    .
     .
      .
```

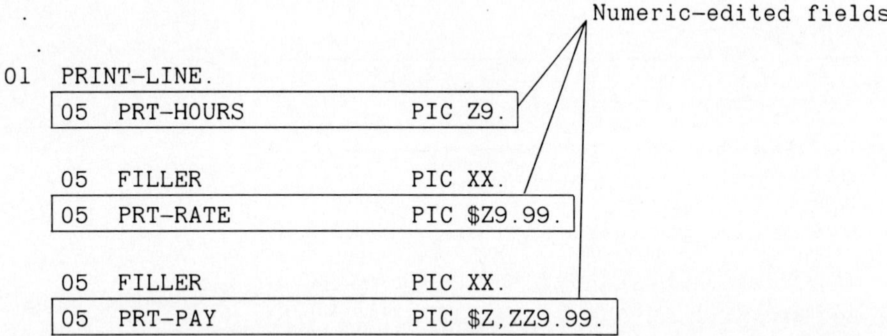


```
    .
     .
      .
WORKING-STORAGE SECTION.
    .
     .
      .
```

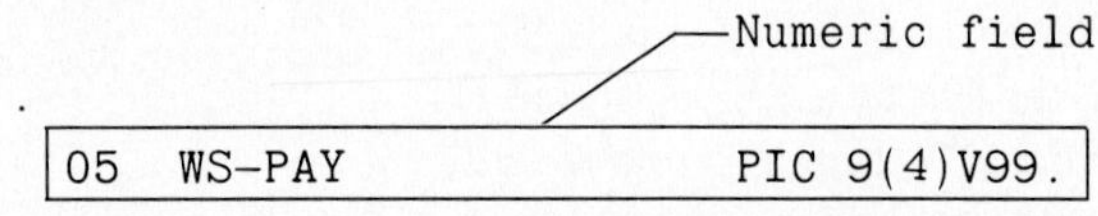


```
    .
     .
      .
PROCEDURE DIVISION.
    .
     .
      .
```

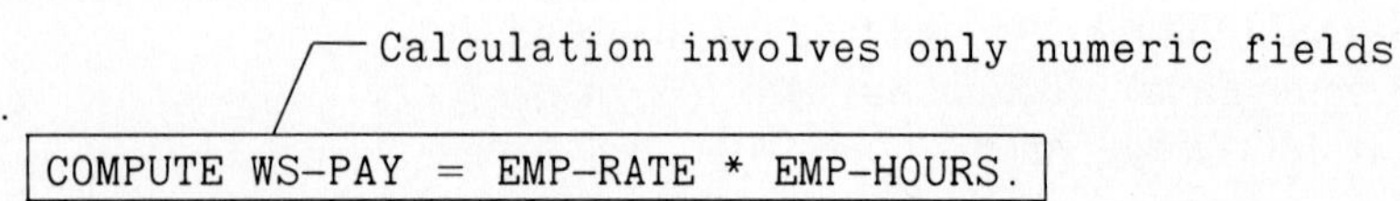

Calculation involves only numeric fields.
COMPUTE WS-PAY = EMP-RATE * EMP-HOURS.


```
    .
     .
      .
    MOVE EMP-HOURS TO PRT-HOURS.
    MOVE EMP-RATE TO PRT-RATE.      ——Numeric fields are moved to
    MOVE WS-PAY TO PRT-PAY.           numeric-edited fields.

    WRITE PRINT-LINE.
```

FIGURE 5.1 MOVE Statement with Numeric and Numeric-Edited Fields

TABLE 5.2 Editing Characters

SYMBOL	MEANING
.	Actual decimal point
Z	Zero suppress
*	Check protection
CR	Credit symbol
DB	Debit symbol
+	Plus sign
−	Minus sign
$	Dollar sign
,	Comma
0	Zero
B	Blank
/	Slash

TABLE 5.3 Insertion Characters: /, B, and 0

SOURCE FIELD		RECEIVING FIELD	
Picture	Value	Picture	Edited Result
(a) 9(6)	122586	99/99/99	12/25/86
(b) 9(6)	070485	99/99/99	07/04/85
(c) 9(6)	071085	Z9/99/99	7/10/85
(d) 9(9)	123456789	999B99B9999	123 45 6789
(e) 9(4)	1234	$$,$$9.00	$1,234.00

Signed Numbers

Frequently, the picture of a numeric source field is preceded by an S to indicate a signed field. The S is immaterial if only positive numbers can occur but absolutely essential any time a negative number results as the consquence of an arithmetic operation. *If the S is omitted, the result of the arithmetic operation will always assume a positive sign.* Consider

```
05  FIELD-A     PIC S99     VALUE -20.
05  FIELD-B     PIC 99      VALUE  15.
05  FIELD-C     PIC S99     VALUE -20.
05  FIELD-D     PIC 99      VALUE  15.

ADD FIELD-B TO FIELD-A.
ADD FIELD-C TO FIELD-D.
```

Numerically, we expect the sum of −20 and +15 to be −5. If the result is stored in FIELD-A, there is no problem. However, if the sum is stored in FIELD-D (an unsigned field), it will assume a value of +5. Many programmers adopt the habit of always using signed fields to avoid any difficulty.

Table 5.4 illustrates the use of floating plus and minus signs. If a plus sign is used, the sign of the edited field will appear if the number is either positive, negative, or zero [examples (a), (b), and (c)]. However, if a minus sign is used, the sign appears only when the edited result is negative. Note also that the receiving field must be at least one character longer than the sending field to accommodate the sign; otherwise, a compiler warning message results.

TABLE 5.4 Floating + and – Characters

SOURCE FIELD		RECEIVING FIELD	
Picture	*Value*	*Picture*	*Edited Result*
(a) S9(4)	1234	++,+++	+1,234
(b) S9(4)	0123	++,+++	+123
(c) S9(4)	–1234	++,+++	–1,234
(d) S9(4)	1234	––,–––	1,234
(e) S9(4)	0123	––,–––	123
(f) S9(4)	–1234	––,–––	–1,234

TABLE 5.5 CR and DB Symbols

SOURCE FIELD		RECEIVING FIELD	
Picture	*Value*	*Picture*	*Value*
(a) S9(5)	98765	$$$,999CR	$98,765
(b) S9(5)	–98765	$$$,999CR	$98,765CR
(c) S9(5)	98765	$$$,999DB	$98,765
(d) S9(5)	–98765	$$$,999DB	$98,765DB

Financial statements usually contain either the credit (CR) or debit (DB) symbol to indicate a negative number. The use of these characters is illustrated in Table 5.5.

CR and DB appear only when the sending field is negative [examples (b) and (d)]. If the field is positive or zero, the symbols are replaced by blanks. The choice of CR or DB depends on the accounting system. COBOL treats both identically; CR and/or DB appear if and only if the sending field is negative.

THE TUITION BILLING PROGRAM

The Tuition Billing Program is another example of a *heading, detail, and total line* problem. A file of records is to be processed requiring several calculations for *each* record. Every detail record is to be printed in an *edited* format. A heading line is to appear prior to the first detail line. (For simplicity, the heading line will appear only once, rather than at the top of every page; see Problem 4.) In addition, several fields in each record are to be summed for all records in the file, with a single total line appearing at the end of processing.

Detailed specifications are provided in the standard format in Figure 5.2.

Test Data

Figure 5.3*a* contains data used to test our program, and Figure 5.3*b* the desired output. Carefully check the correspondence between individual records in the input file and the associated lines in the printed report. Verification of the test data is an important step in reviewing program specifications.

Observe for example, that John Smith, John Part-Timer, and Peggy Jones each have a Y in column 32 of their input records, and that these are the only individuals who are charged a Union fee. In similar fashion, James, Baker, and Benway are the only students with scholarships in the incoming data and corresponding report. The student file has 12 records, and hence 12 students appear in the printed report.

Programming Specifications

Program Name:

Tuition Billing Program

Narrative:

This program processes a file of student records and computes and prints the tuition bill for each student and for the university as a whole.

Input File(s):

STUDENT-FILE

Input Record Layout:

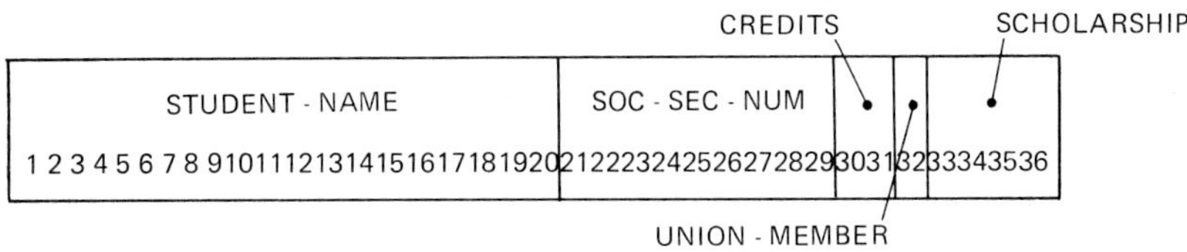

Test Data:

See Figure 5.3*a*.

Report Format:

See Figure 5.3*b*.

Processing Requirements:

1. Read a file of student records.
2. For every record read,
   (a) Calculate the tuition due, at the rate of $127.50 per credit.
   (b) Bill the student $25 for the union fee, if a "Y" is in record position 32; do not charge anything for union fee if column 32 does not contain a "Y."
   (c) Compute an activity fee based on the number of credits taken.

ACTIVITY FEE	CREDITS
$25	6 or less
$50	7–12
$75	more than 12

   (d) Compute the student's total bill, which is equal to the sum of tuition, union fee, and activity fee, minus a scholarship (if any).
   (e) Increment university totals for tuition, union fee, activity fee, scholarship, and student bill.
   (f) Print a detail line for each record read. Edit all fields as appropriate. Single-space detail lines.
3. Print a single heading line at the start of the report.
4. Print a total line at the end of the report.

FIGURE 5.2 *Program Specifications for Tuition Billing Program*

```
JOHN SMITH          12345678915Y0000
HENRY JAMES         98765432115 0500
SUSAN BAKER         11122333309 0500
JOHN PART-TIMER     45621345603Y0000
PEGGY JONES         45645645615Y0000
H. HEAVY-WORKER     78952123418 0000
BENJAMIN LEE        87687687618 0000
JACKIE CLARK        26480529806 0000
SHEILA GROSSMAN     22334436607 0000
LYNN FRANKEL        88999900010 0000
CATHY BENWAY        24511809503 0250
NELSON KERBEL       07235912304 0000
```

(a) Test Data

STUDENT NAME	SOC SEC NUM	CREDITS	TUITION	UNION FEE	ACT FEE	SCHOLARSHIP	TOTAL BILL
JOHN SMITH	123 45 6789	15	$1,912.50	$25	$75	$0	$2,012.50
HENRY JAMES	987 65 4321	15	$1,912.50	$0	$75	$500	$1,487.50
SUSAN BAKER	111 22 3333	09	$1,147.50	$0	$50	$500	$697.50
JOHN PART-TIMER	456 21 3456	03	$382.50	$25	$25	$0	$432.50
PEGGY JONES	456 45 6456	15	$1,912.50	$25	$75	$0	$2,012.50
H. HEAVY-WORKER	789 52 1234	18	$2,295.00	$0	$75	$0	$2,370.00
BENJAMIN LEE	876 87 6876	18	$2,295.00	$0	$75	$0	$2,370.00
JACKIE CLARK	264 80 5298	06	$765.00	$0	$25	$0	$790.00
SHEILA GROSSMAN	223 34 4366	07	$892.50	$0	$50	$0	$942.50
LYNN FRANKEL	889 99 9000	10	$1,275.00	$0	$50	$0	$1,325.00
CATHY BENWAY	245 11 8095	03	$382.50	$0	$25	$250	$157.50
NELSON KERBEL	072 35 9123	04	$510.00	$0	$25	$0	$535.00
UNIVERSITY TOTALS			$15,682.50	$75	$625	$1,250	$15,132.50

(b) Output

FIGURE 5.3 *Tuition Billing Program: Test Data and Output*

The Hierarchy Chart as a Design Aid

The first step in developing any program is to design its associated hierarchy chart. (The hierarchy chart was introduced in Chapter 4 as a means of documenting a COBOL program. It was shown that the paragraphs in a program corresponded one-to-one with the modules in a hierarchy chart, and consequently the chart provided a unique view of the Procedure Division.)

The main purpose of the hierarchy chart is not in documentation, however, but rather as a design aid. This in turn calls for one to list the functional modules required by the program, which are shown below:

Overall Program Function:

```
PREPARE-TUITION-REPORT
```

Functions Associated with Detail Records:

```
READ-STUDENT-FILE
PROCESS-A-RECORD
COMPUTE-INDIVIDUAL-BILL
INCREMENT-ALL-TOTALS
WRITE-DETAIL-LINE
```

Functions for Report Preparation:

```
WRITE-UNIVERSITY-TOTALS
WRITE-HEADING-LINE
```

One now attempts to develop the hierarchy chart, by incorporating the proper manager–subordinate relationships using these modules. We proceed in *top-down fashion,* beginning with the highest level function, PREPARE-TUITION-REPORT. This module will have four subordinates, WRITE-HEADING-LINE, READ-STUDENT-FILE, PROCESS-A-RECORD, and WRITE-UNIVERSITY-TOTALS. PROCESS-A-RECORD also has four subordinates: COMPUTE-INDIVIDUAL-BILL, INCREMENT-ALL-TOTALS, WRITE-DETAIL-LINE, and READ-STUDENT-FILE.

Figure 5.4 contains the hierarchy chart for the Tuition Billing Program. It consists of three levels, each of which corresponds to a COBOL PERFORM statement; that is, the module on level 1 performs the modules on level 2, and those on level 2 perform the modules on level 3. In other words, the only way a paragraph may be entered is via a PERFORM statement in the paragraph directly above it.

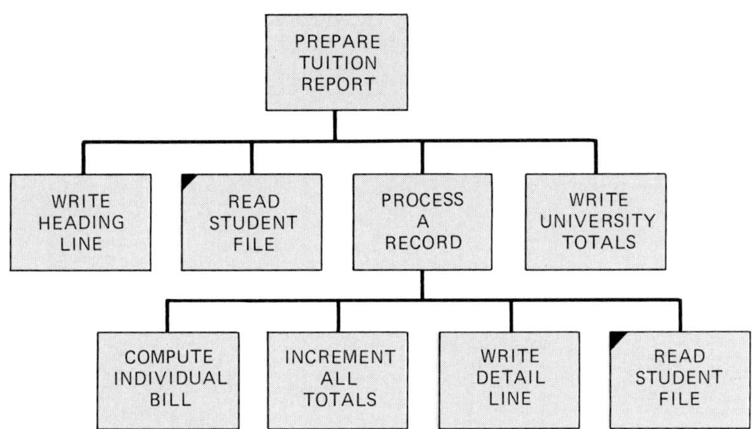

FIGURE 5.4 Hierarchy Chart for Tuition Billing Program

The module READ-STUDENT-FILE is shaded in its upper left corner, to indicate that it is called from two places in the program. (Our earlier programs did not put the READ statement in a separate paragraph but included two distinct READ statements: for the priming READ, and again as the last statement in a performed routine.) We choose now to recognize the READ statement as a separate and definable function; hence we put it in a paragraph by itself and invoke that paragraph from two places in the program. Either technique is acceptable.

The function of the individual paragraphs in Figure 5.4 should be apparent from the modules' names themselves. Nevertheless, the function of each paragraph is described in depth:

PREPARE-TUITION-REPORT	The "mainline" routine that drives the entire program. It opens the files, invokes the initial read, and performs PROCESS-A-RECORD until the input file is empty. It will close the files and terminate the run.
WRITE-HEADING-LINE	Writes a heading line at the beginning of the report. (In this program the heading routine will be called once, and only once for the sake of simplicity. Subsequently we will determine how to write a heading line on the top of each page, rather than just at the beginning.)

READ-STUDENT-FILE	Reads a record from STUDENT-FILE; sets a switch to indicate the end of data.
PROCESS-A-RECORD	This module is invoked repeatedly from PREPARE-TUITION-REPORT for each student record. It, in turn, controls the processing of a student record, by calling four subordinates in order.
WRITE-UNIVERSITY-TOTALS	Called once, at the conclusion of the program, this paragraph writes the university total line.
COMPUTE-INDIVIDUAL-BILL	Calculates an individual student bill from various fields contained within an input record.
INCREMENT-ALL-TOTALS	Increments the university totals for all values computed in COMPUTE-INDIVIDUAL-BILL.
WRITE-DETAIL-LINE	Writes a detail line for the record that was just processed.

Pseudocode

After the hierarchy chart has been completed, one develops the associated pseudocode, which depicts something very different. A hierarchy chart is *functional* in nature, and it shows what has to be done, but not necessarily when. Pseudocode, on the other hand, is *procedural;* it shows sequence and decision-making logic. In other words, pseudocode "connects" the modules in a hierarchy chart by including various loops and decision-making blocks. Pseudocode for the Tuition Billing Program is shown in Figure 5.5.

```
Open Files
Write heading-line(s)
Read STUDENT-FILE, at end indicate no more data
DO while data remains
    Compute individual bill
    Increment university totals
    Write detail record
    Read STUDENT-FILE, at end indicate no more data
ENDDO
Write university totals
Close files
Stop run
```

FIGURE 5.5 Pseudocode for Tuition Billing Program

An alternative to the pseudocode in Figure 5.5 is to express the required logic in a flowchart. The author chose not to do this, however, owing to the decreased use of the latter technique. Realize also that neither blocks in a flowchart nor statements in pseudocode correspond one-to-one with statements in a Procedure Division. Either technique depicts logic in a program, but at a higher level of aggregation. Indeed, if one insisted on one-to-one correspondence, one would in effect be writing the program twice.

The completed program is shown in Figure 5.6

```
IDENTIFICATION DIVISION.
PROGRAM-ID.    TUITION.
AUTHOR.        JACKIE CLARK.

ENVIRONMENT DIVISION.
CONFIGURATION SECTION.
SOURCE-COMPUTER.  IBM-4341.
OBJECT-COMPUTER.  IBM-4341.
INPUT-OUTPUT SECTION.
FILE-CONTROL.
    SELECT STUDENT-FILE
        ASSIGN TO UT-S-SYSIN.
    SELECT PRINT-FILE
        ASSIGN TO UT-S-SYSOUT.

DATA DIVISION.
FILE SECTION.
FD  STUDENT-FILE
    LABEL RECORDS ARE OMITTED
    RECORD CONTAINS 80 CHARACTERS
    DATA RECORD IS STUDENT-RECORD.
01  STUDENT-RECORD.
    05  STU-NAME              PIC X(20).
    05  STU-SOC-SEC-NO        PIC 9(9).
    05  STU-CREDITS           PIC 9(2).
    05  STU-UNION-MEMBER      PIC X.
    05  STU-SCHOLARSHIP       PIC 9(4).
    05  FILLER                PIC X(44).

FD  PRINT-FILE
    LABEL RECORDS ARE OMITTED
    RECORD CONTAINS 133 CHARACTERS
    DATA RECORD IS PRINT-LINE.
01  PRINT-LINE                PIC X(133).

WORKING-STORAGE SECTION.
01  DATA-REMAINS-SWITCH       PIC X(2)     VALUE SPACES.

01  INDIVIDUAL-CALCULATIONS.
    05  IND-TUITION           PIC 9(4)V99  VALUE ZEROS.
    05  IND-ACTIVITY-FEE      PIC 9(2)     VALUE ZEROS.
    05  IND-UNION-FEE         PIC 9(2)     VALUE ZEROS.
    05  IND-BILL              PIC 9(6)V99  VALUE ZEROS.

01  UNIVERSITY-TOTALS.
    05  TOTAL-TUITION         PIC 9(6)V99  VALUE ZEROS.
    05  TOTAL-SCHOLARSHIP     PIC 9(6)     VALUE ZEROS.
    05  TOTAL-ACTIVITY-FEE    PIC 9(6)     VALUE ZEROS.
    05  TOTAL-IND-BILL        PIC 9(6)V99  VALUE ZEROS.
    05  TOTAL-UNION-FEE       PIC 9(6)     VALUE ZEROS.

01  HEADING-LINE.
    05  FILLER                PIC X        VALUE SPACES.
    05  FILLER                PIC X(12)    VALUE 'STUDENT NAME'.
    05  FILLER                PIC X(10)    VALUE SPACES.
    05  FILLER                PIC X(11)    VALUE 'SOC SEC NUM'.
    05  FILLER                PIC X(2)     VALUE SPACES.
    05  FILLER                PIC X(7)     VALUE 'CREDITS'.
    05  FILLER                PIC X(2)     VALUE SPACES.
    05  FILLER                PIC X(7)     VALUE 'TUITION'.
    05  FILLER                PIC X(2)     VALUE SPACES.
    05  FILLER                PIC X(9)     VALUE 'UNION FEE'.
    05  FILLER                PIC X(2)     VALUE SPACES.
    05  FILLER                PIC X(7)     VALUE 'ACT FEE'.
    05  FILLER                PIC X(2)     VALUE SPACES.
    05  FILLER                PIC X(11)    VALUE 'SCHOLARSHIP'.
    05  FILLER                PIC X(2)     VALUE SPACES.
    05  FILLER                PIC X(10)    VALUE 'TOTAL BILL'.
    05  FILLER                PIC X(36)    VALUE SPACES.

01  DETAIL-LINE.
    05  FILLER                PIC X        VALUE SPACES.
    05  DET-STUDENT-NAME      PIC X(20).
    05  FILLER                PIC X(2)     VALUE SPACES.
    05  DET-SOC-SEC-NO        PIC 999B99B9999.
    05  FILLER                PIC X(4)     VALUE SPACES.
    05  DET-CREDITS           PIC 99.
    05  FILLER                PIC X(2)     VALUE SPACES.
    05  DET-TUITION           PIC $$$$,$$9.99.
    05  FILLER                PIC X        VALUE SPACES.
```

SELECT and FD statements refer to STUDENT-FILE.

Heading, detail, and total lines are defined in Working-Storage.

Use of implied decimal point.

VALUE clauses establish heading line.

FIGURE 5.6 Tuition Billing Program

```
           05  DET-UNION-FEE         PIC $$$$,$$9.
           05  FILLER                PIC X(3)    VALUE SPACES.
           05  DET-ACTIVITY-FEE      PIC $$$$,$$9.
           05  FILLER                PIC X(3)    VALUE SPACES.
           05  DET-SCHOLARSHIP       PIC $$$$,$$9.
           05  FILLER                PIC X(3)    VALUE SPACES.
           05  DET-IND-BILL          PIC $$$$,$$9.99.
           05  FILLER                PIC X(35)   VALUE SPACES.

       01  TOTAL-LINE.
           05  FILLER                PIC X(8)    VALUE SPACES.
           05  FILLER                PIC X(17) VALUE 'UNIVERSITY TOTALS'.
           05  FILLER                PIC X(17)   VALUE SPACES.
           05  PR-TOT-TUITION        PIC $$$$,$$9.99.
           05  FILLER                PIC X       VALUE SPACES.
           05  PR-TOT-UNION-FEE      PIC $$$$,$$9.
           05  FILLER                PIC X(3)    VALUE SPACES.
           05  PR-TOT-ACTIVITY-FEE   PIC $$$$,$$9.
           05  FILLER                PIC X(3)    VALUE SPACES.
           05  PR-TOT-SCHOLARSHIP    PIC $$$$,$$9.
           05  FILLER                PIC X(3)    VALUE SPACES.
           05  PR-TOT-IND-BILL       PIC $$$$,$$9.99.
           05  FILLER                PIC X(35)   VALUE SPACES.

       PROCEDURE DIVISION.
       0010-PREPARE-TUITION-REPORT.
           OPEN INPUT  STUDENT-FILE
                OUTPUT PRINT-FILE.
           PERFORM 0015-WRITE-HEADING-LINE.
           PERFORM 0017-READ-STUDENT-FILE.
           PERFORM 0020-PROCESS-A-RECORD
               UNTIL DATA-REMAINS-SWITCH = 'NO'.
           PERFORM 0060-WRITE-UNIVERSITY-TOTALS.
           CLOSE STUDENT-FILE
                 PRINT-FILE.
           STOP RUN.

       0015-WRITE-HEADING-LINE.
           MOVE HEADING-LINE TO PRINT-LINE.
           WRITE PRINT-LINE
               AFTER ADVANCING PAGE.

       0017-READ-STUDENT-FILE.
           READ STUDENT-FILE
               AT END MOVE 'NO' TO DATA-REMAINS-SWITCH.

       0020-PROCESS-A-RECORD.
           PERFORM 0030-COMPUTE-INDIVIDUAL-BILL.
           PERFORM 0040-INCREMENT-ALL-TOTALS
           PERFORM 0050-WRITE-DETAIL-LINE.
           PERFORM 0017-READ-STUDENT-FILE.

       0030-COMPUTE-INDIVIDUAL-BILL.
           COMPUTE IND-TUITION = 127.50 * STU-CREDITS.
           IF STU-UNION-MEMBER = 'Y'
               MOVE 25 TO IND-UNION-FEE
           ELSE
               MOVE ZERO TO IND-UNION-FEE.
           MOVE 25 TO IND-ACTIVITY-FEE.
           IF STU-CREDITS > 6
               MOVE 50 TO IND-ACTIVITY-FEE.
           IF STU-CREDITS > 12
               MOVE 75 TO IND-ACTIVITY-FEE.
           COMPUTE IND-BILL = IND-TUITION + IND-UNION-FEE +
               IND-ACTIVITY-FEE - STU-SCHOLARSHIP.

       0040-INCREMENT-ALL-TOTALS.
           ADD IND-TUITION TO TOTAL-TUITION.
           ADD IND-UNION-FEE TO TOTAL-UNION-FEE.
           ADD IND-ACTIVITY-FEE TO TOTAL-ACTIVITY-FEE.
           ADD IND-BILL TO TOTAL-IND-BILL.
           ADD STU-SCHOLARSHIP TO TOTAL-SCHOLARSHIP.

```

Initial (priming) READ.

Last statement of performed routine is a second READ.

IF statements with and without ELSE clause.

Computation is done on numeric fields with implied decimal point.

```
00154        0050-WRITE-DETAIL-LINE.
00155            MOVE STU-NAME TO DET-STUDENT-NAME.
00156            MOVE STU-SOC-SEC-NO TO DET-SOC-SEC-NO.
00157            MOVE STU-CREDITS TO DET-CREDITS.
00158            MOVE IND-TUITION TO DET-TUITION.
00159            MOVE IND-UNION-FEE TO DET-UNION-FEE.
00160            MOVE IND-ACTIVITY-FEE TO DET-ACTIVITY-FEE.
00161            MOVE STU-SCHOLARSHIP TO DET-SCHOLARSHIP.
00162            MOVE IND-BILL TO DET-IND-BILL.
00163            MOVE DETAIL-LINE TO PRINT-LINE.
00164            WRITE PRINT-LINE
00165                AFTER ADVANCING 1 LINE.
00166
00167        0060-WRITE-UNIVERSITY-TOTALS.
00168            MOVE TOTAL-TUITION TO PR-TOT-TUITION.
00169            MOVE TOTAL-UNION-FEE TO PR-TOT-UNION-FEE.
00170            MOVE TOTAL-ACTIVITY-FEE TO PR-TOT-ACTIVITY-FEE.
00171            MOVE TOTAL-SCHOLARSHIP TO PR-TOT-SCHOLARSHIP.
00172            MOVE TOTAL-IND-BILL TO PR-TOT-IND-BILL.
00173            MOVE TOTAL-LINE TO PRINT-LINE.
00174            WRITE PRINT-LINE
00175                AFTER ADVANCING 2 LINES.
```

Building a detail line.

Numeric field is moved to edited field (see lines 46, 94, 148).

FIGURE 5.6 (Continued)

The Completed Program

The completed program shown in Figure 5.6 encompasses all the material covered to date and indeed is somewhat formidable the first time you see it. We suggest you take it in pieces and review sections of the text as you need them. The following are some highlights:

1. The Identification Division: COBOL lines 1–3.
2. The Environment Division: COBOL lines 5–14. The two SELECT statements are applicable to our installation and may not be appropriate at yours.
3. The FD's for STUDENT-FILE and PRINT-FILE: COBOL lines 18–21, and 30–33.
4. The description for the incoming data: COBOL lines 22–28. Notice how this matches the problem description given earlier.
5. The presence of separate heading, detail, and total lines in Working-Storage (lines 52–69, 71–88, and 90–103, respectively); also note the use of VALUE clauses to initialize the heading line.
6. The definition of university counters in Working-Storage (lines 45–50) and the use of VALUE clauses to initialize them.
7. The initial READ is performed in line 110 of the Procedure Division. The PERFORM statement in lines 111 and 112 continually executes the paragraph PROCESS-A-RECORD (lines 127–131) as long as there are data. The *last* statement of this routine performs the paragraph READ-STUDENT-FILE; it is in effect a second READ statement.
8. The presence of separate paragraphs in the Procedure Division to compute an individual bill (lines 133–145), increment university totals (lines 147–152), and write a detail line (lines 154–165).
9. The use of *numeric* fields for calculations and *edited* fields for printing. Hence, the numeric field IND-TUITION, with PIC 9(4)V99, holds the result of the computation from line 134. It is moved to the edited field DET-TUITION, with PIC $$$$,$$9.99 prior to printing.

Bear in mind, however, that *programming is learned by doing,* and reading alone will not teach you COBOL. You *must write* programs for this material to have real meaning. The true learning experience comes when you pick up your own listings in the machine room.

Programming Tip

Avoid Literals

The constant (literal) portion of a print line should be defined in Working-Storage, rather than moved to the print line in the Procedure Division. Consider the following:

Poor Code:

Required to continue a nonnumeric literal

```
       MOVE 'STUDENT NAME          SOC SEC NUM     CREDITS     TUITION
      -    'SCHOLARSHIP    FEES' TO PRINT-LINE.
       WRITE PRINT-LINE.
```

Improved Code:

```
01  HEADING-LINE.
    05  FILLER      PIC X(12)     VALUE 'STUDENT NAME'.
    05  FILLER      PIC X(10)     VALUE SPACES.
    05  FILLER      PIC X(11)     VALUE 'SOC SEC NUM'.
    05  FILLER      PIC X(2)      VALUE SPACES.
    05  FILLER      PIC X(7)      VALUE 'CREDITS'.
    05  FILLER      PIC X(2)      VALUE SPACES.
    05  FILLER      PIC X(7)      VALUE 'TUITION'.
    05  FILLER      PIC X(3)      VALUE SPACES.
    05  FILLER      PIC X(11)     VALUE 'SCHOLARSHIP'.
    05  FILLER      PIC X(2)      VALUE SPACES.
    05  FILLER      PIC X(4)      VALUE 'FEES'.

    .
     .
      .

    WRITE PRINT-LINE FROM HEADING-LINE.
```

The poor code illustrates *continuation of a nonnumeric literal.* The first line begins with a quote before STUDENT NAME and ends *without* a closing quote in column 72. The continued line contains a hyphen in column 7, and both a beginning and ending quote.

The improved code may appear unnecessarily long in contrast to the poor code. However, it is an unwritten law that users will change column headings and/or spacing at least twice before being satisfied. Such changes are easily accommodated in the improved code but often tedious in the original solution. Assume, for example, that four spaces are required between CREDITS and TUITION, rather than the two that are there now. Modification of the poor code requires that *both* lines in the MOVE statement be completely rewritten, whereas only a picture clause changes in the improved version.

An alternative definition of HEADING-LINE is as follows:

```
01  HEADING-LINE.
    05  FILLER      PIC X(22)     VALUE 'STUDENT NAME'.
    05  FILLER      PIC X(13)     VALUE 'SOC SEC NUM'.
    05  FILLER      PIC X(9)      VALUE 'CREDITS'.
```

```
05  FILLER     PIC X(10)     VALUE 'TUITION'.
05  FILLER     PIC X(13)     VALUE 'SCHOLARSHIP'.
05  FILLER     PIC X(4)      VALUE 'FEES'.
```

In this example each VALUE clause contains fewer characters than the associated PICTURE clause. Accordingly, alignment is from left to right, with the extra (low-order) positions padded with blanks.

CODING STANDARDS

Figure 5.6 is a working program. As a beginning student your objective is exactly that. As an advanced student or professional your objective is enlarged: an efficient program that is easily read and maintained by someone other than yourself. Further, the professional's program should conform to his or her installation's standards. It must be tested under a variety of conditions, including obviously improper data, and should include programming checks to flag potentially invalid transactions. In short, while the beginner is concerned with merely translating a working flowchart or pseudocode into COBOL, the professional requires straightforward logic, easy-to-read COBOL code, and a well-tested program.

In a commercial installation it is absolutely essential that programs be well written, as the person who writes a program today may not be here tomorrow. Indeed, continuing success depends on someone other than the author being able to maintain a program. Accordingly, most installations impose a set of coding standards, such as those described here, which go beyond the requirements of COBOL. Such standards are optional for the student but typical of what is required in the real world.

This chapter suggests a series of *coding standards* for you to use. However there are no absolute truths, no right or wrong, insofar as programming style is concerned. Different programmers develop slightly or even radically different styles that are consistent within the rules of COBOL and within the programmer's objective. Accordingly, the discussion that follows reflects the viewpoint of the author and is necessarily subjective.

We begin with suggestions for the Data Division.

Data Division

Choose meaningful data names, specifically avoiding the easy way out with two- or three-character data names. It is impossible for the maintenance programmer, or even the original author, to determine the meaning of abbreviated data names. The usual student response is that this guideline adds unnecessarily to the burden of writer's cramp. Realize, however, that initial coding takes only 10–15% of the total time associated with a program. (Maintenance, testing, and debugging take the vast majority.) Hence the modest increase in initial coding is more than compensated by subsequent improvements in the latter activities.

Prefix all data names within the same FD or 01 with two or three characters unique to the FD; e.g., OM-LAST-NAME, OM-BIRTH-DATE. The utility of this guideline becomes apparent in the Procedure Division if it is necessary to refer back to the definition of a data name.

Begin all PICTURE clauses in the same column, usually in columns 36–48, but the choice is arbitrary. Do not be unduly disturbed if one or two entries stray from the designated column, because of long data names and/or indentation of level numbers.

Choose one form of the PICTURE clause (PIC, PIC IS, PICTURE, or PICTURE IS) and follow it consistently. PIC is the shortest and is as good as any.

Indent successive level numbers under an 01 by a consistent amount, e.g., two or four columns. Leave "gaps" between adjacent levels (e.g., 01, 05, 10, 15, or 01, 04, 08, 12) instead of using consecutive numbers; i.e., avoid 01, 02, 03. Use the *same* level numbers from FD to FD to maintain consistency within a program.

Avoid 77-level entries. 77-level entries have not been mentioned in the text, because *current* programming practice argues for their elimination. Nevertheless, they are apt to be found in existing programs and are discussed now for that reason.

A 77-level entry was originally defined as an *independent* data name with no relationship to any other data name in a program. (77-level entries are coded as elementary items in Working-Storage.) However, few if any data names are truly independent, and 77-level entries should be avoided for that reason. The author, for example, has gotten along quite nicely by grouping related entries under a common 01 description. Consider the following:

Poor Code:

```
77  TUITION                  PIC 9(4)V99     VALUE ZEROS.
77  ACTIVITY-FEE             PIC 9(2)        VALUE ZEROS.
77  UNION-FEE                PIC 9(2)        VALUE ZEROS.
```

Improved Code:

```
01  INDIVIDUAL-CALCULATIONS.
    05  IND-TUITION          PIC 9(4)V99     VALUE ZEROS.
    05  IND-ACTIVITY-FEE     PIC 9(2)        VALUE ZEROS.
    05  IND-UNION-FEE        PIC 9(2)        VALUE ZEROS.
```

The improved code also uses a common prefix, which reflects the similarities among the related items. There is simply no reason to use the older approach of "independent" data items.

Procedure Division

Develop functional paragraphs in which every statement in a paragraph is related to the overall task of that paragraph. A paragraph's function should be reflected in its name, which should consist of a verb, one or two adjectives, and an object: READ-STUDENT-FILE, WRITE-HEADING-LINE, and so on. If a paragraph cannot be named in this manner, it is probably not functional, and consideration should be given to redesigning the program and/or paragraph. (This concept is more fully developed in Chapter 7.)

Sequence paragraph names. Programmers and managers alike accept the utility of this guideline to locate paragraphs in the Procedure Division quickly. However, there is considerable disagreement on just what sequencing scheme to use—all numbers, a single letter followed by numbers, etc. We make no strong argument for one scheme over another, other than to insist that a consistent sequencing rule be followed. Some examples are A010-WRITE-NEW-MASTER-RECORD and 100-PRODUCE-ERROR-REPORT.

Avoid commas. The compiler treats a comma as noise; it has no effect on the generated object code. Many programmers have acquired the habit of inserting commas to increase readability. Though this works rather well with prose, it can have just the opposite effect in COBOL, because of blurred print chains, which make it difficult to distinguish a comma from a period. The best solution is to try to avoid commas altogether.

Indent—perhaps the most important standard of all, yet one that meets with unexplained resistance. Virtually no one argues against indenting successive level numbers in the Data Division, yet many individuals fail to apply a similar principle in the Procedure Division. The author maintains that the readability of a program is significantly enhanced by indenting subservient clauses under the main verbs. Some specific examples are

```
READ STUDENT-FILE
    AT END MOVE 'NO' TO DATA-REMAINS-SWITCH.

WRITE PRINT-LINE
    AFTER ADVANCING 2 LINES.

PERFORM 0020-PROCESS-A-RECORD
    UNTIL DATA-REMAINS-SWITCH = 'NO'.

IF STU-UNION-MEMBER = 'Y'
    MOVE 25 TO IND-UNION-FEE
ELSE
    MOVE ZERO TO IND-UNION-FEE.
```

Indentation should also be extended to continued lines; if a statement cannot fit on a single line, its continued portion should be indented. For example,

```
COMPUTE IND-BILL = IND-TUITION + IND-UNION-FEE +
    IND-ACTIVITY-FEE - STU-SCHOLARSHIP.
```

COBOL allows a statement to extend from line to line with no formal indication of continuation. (The exception is a nonnumeric literal, which was discussed in the preceding programming tip.) Indentation is especially important, therefore, to indicate continuation to the programmer.

Both Divisions

Space attractively. The adoption of various spacing conventions can go a long way toward improving the appearance of a program. The author believes very strongly in the insertion of *blank lines* throughout a program to highlight important statements. Specific suggestions include a blank line before all paragraphs, FDs, and 01 entries, and even before specific verbs.

You can also cause various portions of a listing to begin on a new page by putting a slash in column 7 of a separate statement.

Don't overcomment. Contrary to popular belief, the mere presence of comments does *not* ensure a well-documented program; indeed, poor comments are sometimes worse than no comments at all. The most common fault is *redundancy* with the source code. For example, in the code

```
*   CALCULATE NET PAY
    COMPUTE NET-PAY = GROSS-PAY - FED-TAX - VOL-DEDUCT
```

the comment does not add to the readability of the program. It might even be said to detract from legibility because it breaks the logical flow as one is reading. Worse than redundant, comments may be *obsolete, incorrect,* or *inconsistent with the associated code*. This happens if program statements are changed during debugging or maintenance and the comments are not correspondingly altered. *The compiler does not validate comments*. Comments may also be correct, but incomplete and hence misleading.

The author certainly does not advocate elimination of comments altogether. Comments are still essential, but great care, *more than is commonly exercised,* should be applied to developing and maintaining comments in a program.

Comments should be provided whenever you are doing something that is not immediately obvious to another person. When considering a comment, imagine you are turning the program over for maintenance, and insert comments whenever you would pause to explain a feature in your program. Do assume, however, that the maintenance programmer is as competent in COBOL as you are. Thus your comments should be directed to *why* you are doing something, rather than to what you are doing.

A WELL-WRITTEN PROGRAM

Figure 5.7 contains the Tuition Billing Program, which was discussed earlier in the chapter. This time, attention is drawn to the application of the coding standards that were just developed.

All data names within a 01 entry are given a common prefix: STU for entries in STUDENT-RECORD (lines 22–28), IND for data names under INDIVIDUAL-CALCULATIONS (lines 39–43), and so on. This guideline applies equally well to records in both the File and Working-Storage Sections.

Blank lines highlight 01 entries in the Data Division and paragraph headers in the Procedure Division. All PICTURE clauses are vertically aligned. Indentation is stressed in the Procedure Division with subservient clauses four columns under the associated verb. Continued lines (e.g., the COMPUTE statement in lines 144 and 145) are also indented.

Paragraph headers are *sequenced* and *functional* in nature. All statements within a paragraph pertain to the function of that paragraph, as indicated by its name.

COBOL 8X:

Changes and Enhancements

There are two changes in the new compiler that are associated with editing. First, a period or a comma is permitted as the last character in an edited picture, provided it is followed immediately by a separator period. Of greater import, *de-editing* is introduced in the new compiler; i.e., one may move an edited field to a field defined with a numeric picture. (This was *not* permitted in COBOL 74, as indicated by Table 4.9, which depicted rules of the MOVE statement.) This feature will most likely be used in on-line systems, enabling data to be accepted in a more user-friendly format.

```
00001              IDENTIFICATION DIVISION.
00002              PROGRAM-ID.    TUITION.
00003              AUTHOR.        JACKIE CLARK.
00004
00005              ENVIRONMENT DIVISION.
00006              CONFIGURATION SECTION.
00007              SOURCE-COMPUTER.  IBM-4341.
00008              OBJECT-COMPUTER.  IBM-4341.
00009              INPUT-OUTPUT SECTION.
00010              FILE-CONTROL.
00011                  SELECT STUDENT-FILE
00012                      ASSIGN TO UT-S-SYSIN.
00013                  SELECT PRINT-FILE
00014                      ASSIGN TO UT-S-SYSOUT.
00015
00016              DATA DIVISION.
00017              FILE SECTION.
00018              FD   STUDENT-FILE
00019                   LABEL RECORDS ARE OMITTED
00020                   RECORD CONTAINS 80 CHARACTERS
00021                   DATA RECORD IS STUDENT-RECORD.          ── Data names within 01 have a common prefix.
00022              01   STUDENT-RECORD.
00023                   05   STU-NAME             PIC X(20).
00024                   05   STU-SOC-SEC-NO       PIC 9(9).
00025                   05   STU-CREDITS          PIC 9(2).
00026                   05   STU-UNION-MEMBER     PIC X.
00027                   05   STU-SCHOLARSHIP      PIC 9(4).
00028                   05   FILLER               PIC X(44).
00029
00030              FD   PRINT-FILE
00031                   LABEL RECORDS ARE OMITTED
00032                   RECORD CONTAINS 133 CHARACTERS
00033                   DATA RECORD IS PRINT-LINE.
00034              01   PRINT-LINE               PIC X(133).
00035
00036              WORKING-STORAGE SECTION.
00037              01   DATA-REMAINS-SWITCH      PIC X(2)     VALUE SPACES.
00038
00039              01   INDIVIDUAL-CALCULATIONS.
00040                   05   IND-TUITION         PIC 9(4)V99 VALUE ZEROS.
00041                   05   IND-ACTIVITY-FEE    PIC 9(2)     VALUE ZEROS.
00042                   05   IND-UNION-FEE       PIC 9(2)     VALUE ZEROS.
00043                   05   IND-BILL            PIC 9(6)V99 VALUE ZEROS.
00044                                                                   ── Blank lines appear before 01 entries.
00045              01   UNIVERSITY-TOTALS.
00046                   05   TOTAL-TUITION       PIC 9(6)V99 VALUE ZEROS.
00047                   05   TOTAL-SCHOLARSHIP   PIC 9(6)     VALUE ZEROS.
00048                   05   TOTAL-ACTIVITY-FEE  PIC 9(6)     VALUE ZEROS.
00049                   05   TOTAL-IND-BILL      PIC 9(6)V99 VALUE ZEROS.
00050                   05   TOTAL-UNION-FEE     PIC 9(6)     VALUE ZEROS.
00051
00052              01   HEADING-LINE.
00053                   05   FILLER              PIC X        VALUE SPACES.
00054                   05   FILLER              PIC X(12)    VALUE 'STUDENT NAME'.
00055                   05   FILLER              PIC X(10)    VALUE SPACES.
00056                   05   FILLER              PIC X(11)    VALUE 'SOC SEC NUM'.
00057                   05   FILLER              PIC X(2)     VALUE SPACES.
00058                   05   FILLER              PIC X(7)     VALUE 'CREDITS'.
00059                   05   FILLER              PIC X(2)     VALUE SPACES.
00060                   05   FILLER              PIC X(7)     VALUE 'TUITION'.
00061                   05   FILLER              PIC X(2)     VALUE SPACES.
00062                   05   FILLER              PIC X(9)     VALUE 'UNION FEE'.
00063                   05   FILLER              PIC X(2)     VALUE SPACES.
00064                   05   FILLER              PIC X(7)     VALUE 'ACT FEE'.
00065                   05   FILLER              PIC X(2)     VALUE SPACES.
00066                   05   FILLER              PIC X(11)    VALUE 'SCHOLARSHIP'.
00067                   05   FILLER              PIC X(2)     VALUE SPACES.
00068                   05   FILLER              PIC X(10)    VALUE 'TOTAL BILL'.
00069                   05   FILLER              PIC X(36)    VALUE SPACES.
00070
00071              01   DETAIL-LINE.
00072                   05   FILLER              PIC X        VALUE SPACES.
00073                   05   DET-STUDENT-NAME    PIC X(20).
00074                   05   FILLER              PIC X(2)     VALUE SPACES.
00075                   05   DET-SOC-SEC-NO      PIC 999B99B9999.
00076                   05   FILLER              PIC X(4)     VALUE SPACES.
00077                   05   DET-CREDITS         PIC 99.
00078                   05   FILLER              PIC X(2)     VALUE SPACES.
00079                   05   DET-TUITION         PIC $$$,$$9.99.
00080                   05   FILLER              PIC X        VALUE SPACES.
```

FIGURE 5.7 Tuition Billing Program with Coding Standards

FIGURE 5.7 ***(Continued)***

```
           05  DET-UNION-FEE          PIC $$$$,$$9.
           05  FILLER                 PIC X(3)     VALUE SPACES.
           05  DET-ACTIVITY-FEE       PIC $$$$,$$9.
           05  FILLER                 PIC X(3)     VALUE SPACES.
           05  DET-SCHOLARSHIP        PIC $$$$,$$9.
           05  FILLER                 PIC X(3)     VALUE SPACES.
           05  DET-IND-BILL           PIC $$$$,$$9.99.
           05  FILLER                 PIC X(35)    VALUE SPACES.

       01  TOTAL-LINE.
           05  FILLER                 PIC X(8)     VALUE SPACES.
           05  FILLER                 PIC X(17) VALUE 'UNIVERSITY TOTALS'
           05  FILLER                 PIC X(17)    VALUE SPACES.
           05  PR-TOT-TUITION         PIC $$$$,$$9.99.
           05  FILLER                 PIC X        VALUE SPACES.
           05  PR-TOT-UNION-FEE       PIC $$$$,$$9.
           05  FILLER                 PIC X(3)     VALUE SPACES.
           05  PR-TOT-ACTIVITY-FEE    PIC $$$$,$$9.
           05  FILLER                 PIC X(3)     VALUE SPACES.
           05  PR-TOT-SCHOLARSHIP     PIC $$$$,$$9.
           05  FILLER                 PIC X(3)     VALUE SPACES.
           05  PR-TOT-IND-BILL        PIC $$$$,$$9.99.
           05  FILLER                 PIC X(35)    VALUE SPACES.

       PROCEDURE DIVISION.
       0010-PREPARE-TUITION-REPORT.
           OPEN INPUT  STUDENT-FILE
                OUTPUT PRINT-FILE.
           PERFORM 0015-WRITE-HEADING-LINE.
           PERFORM 0017-READ-STUDENT-FILE.
           PERFORM 0020-PROCESS-A-RECORD
               UNTIL DATA-REMAINS-SWITCH = 'NO'.
           PERFORM 0060-WRITE-UNIVERSITY-TOTALS.
           CLOSE STUDENT-FILE
                 PRINT-FILE.
           STOP RUN.

       0015-WRITE-HEADING-LINE.
           MOVE HEADING-LINE TO PRINT-LINE.
           WRITE PRINT-LINE
               AFTER ADVANCING PAGE.

       0017-READ-STUDENT-FILE.
           READ STUDENT-FILE
               AT END MOVE 'NO' TO DATA-REMAINS-SWITCH.

       0020-PROCESS-A-RECORD.
           PERFORM 0030-COMPUTE-INDIVIDUAL-BILL.
           PERFORM 0040-INCREMENT-ALL-TOTALS
           PERFORM 0050-WRITE-DETAIL-LINE.
           PERFORM 0017-READ-STUDENT-FILE.

       0030-COMPUTE-INDIVIDUAL-BILL.
           COMPUTE IND-TUITION = 127.50 * STU-CREDITS.
           IF STU-UNION-MEMBER = 'Y'
               MOVE 25 TO IND-UNION-FEE
           ELSE
               MOVE ZERO TO IND-UNION-FEE.
           MOVE 25 TO IND-ACTIVITY-FEE.
           IF STU-CREDITS > 6
               MOVE 50 TO IND-ACTIVITY-FEE.
           IF STU-CREDITS > 12
               MOVE 75 TO IND-ACTIVITY-FEE.
           COMPUTE IND-BILL = IND-TUITION + IND-UNION-FEE +
               IND-ACTIVITY-FEE - STU-SCHOLARSHIP.

       0040-INCREMENT-ALL-TOTALS.
           ADD IND-TUITION TO TOTAL-TUITION.
           ADD IND-UNION-FEE TO TOTAL-UNION-FEE.
           ADD IND-ACTIVITY-FEE TO TOTAL-ACTIVITY-FEE.
           ADD IND-BILL TO TOTAL-IND-BILL.
           ADD STU-SCHOLARSHIP TO TOTAL-SCHOLARSHIP.
```

Data names within 01 have common prefix.

Key Procedure Division verbs are indented.

Indentation in IF/ELSE statement.

Continued line is indented.

Paragraph names are functional, i.e., verb, adjective, object.

```
       0050-WRITE-DETAIL-LINE.
           MOVE STU-NAME TO DET-STUDENT-NAME.
           MOVE STU-SOC-SEC-NO TO DET-SOC-SEC-NO.
           MOVE STU-CREDITS TO DET-CREDITS.
           MOVE IND-TUITION TO DET-TUITION.
           MOVE IND-UNION-FEE TO DET-UNION-FEE.
           MOVE IND-ACTIVITY-FEE TO DET-ACTIVITY-FEE.
           MOVE STU-SCHOLARSHIP TO DET-SCHOLARSHIP.
           MOVE IND-BILL TO DET-IND-BILL.
           MOVE DETAIL-LINE TO PRINT-LINE.
           WRITE PRINT-LINE
               AFTER ADVANCING 1 LINE.

       0060-WRITE-UNIVERSITY-TOTALS.
           MOVE TOTAL-TUITION TO PR-TOT-TUITION.
           MOVE TOTAL-UNION-FEE TO PR-TOT-UNION-FEE.
           MOVE TOTAL-ACTIVITY-FEE TO PR-TOT-ACTIVITY-FEE.
           MOVE TOTAL-SCHOLARSHIP TO PR-TOT-SCHOLARSHIP.
           MOVE TOTAL-IND-BILL TO PR-TOT-IND-BILL.
           MOVE TOTAL-LINE TO PRINT-LINE.
           WRITE PRINT-LINE
               AFTER ADVANCING 2 LINES.
```

Paragraph names are sequenced with blank lines before paragraph headers.

FIGURE 5.7 ***(Continued)***

Summary

Our objective is for you to write meaningful COBOL programs, not to memorize what must appear to be an endless list of rules. You must eventually remember certain things, but we have found the best approach is to pattern your first few COBOL programs after existing examples. To that end, we have spent considerable time developing the Engineering Senior and Tuition Billing Programs. Everything you need to get started is contained in those listings (Figures 4.4 and 5.6) if you will look at them carefully. As a further aid, Figure 5.8 contains a skeleton outline of a COBOL program and some helpful hints.

Finally, we present a list of guidelines for writing COBOL programs:

1. *The four divisions must appear in specified order: Identification, Environment, Data, and Procedure. Division headers begin in the A margin and always appear on a line by themselves.*
2. *The Environment and Data Divisions contain sections with fixed names. The Identification Division does not contain any sections. (The Procedure Division may contain programmer-defined sections; however, this is usually not done in beginning programs.)*
3. *The Data Division is the only division without paragraph names. In the Identification and Environment Divisions the paragraph names are fixed. In the Procedure Division they are determined by the programmer. Paragraph names begin in the A margin.*
4. *Any entry not required to begin in the A margin may begin in or past column 12.*
5. *The COBOL program executes instructions sequentially as they appear in the Procedure Division, unless a transfer-of-control statement, such as PERFORM, is encountered.*
6. *Every file must be opened and closed. A file name will appear in at least four statements: SELECT, FD, OPEN, and CLOSE. In addition, the READ statement will contain the file name of an input file, whereas the WRITE statement contains the record name of an output file.*
7. *Commercial installations and/or your instructor will impose additional coding standards beyond the syntactical requirements of COBOL. The intent of these standards is to facilitate maintenance by making programs easier to read.*

```
IDENTIFICATION DIVISION.
PROGRAM-ID.    8-Character name.
AUTHOR.        Your name.

ENVIRONMENT DIVISION.
CONFIGURATION SECTION.
SOURCE-COMPUTER.      Computer name.
OBJECT-COMPUTER.      Computer name.
INPUT-OUTPUT SECTION.
FILE-CONTROL.
    SELECT INPUT-FILE ASSIGN TO ......
    SELECT PRINT-FILE ASSIGN TO ......

DATA DIVISION.
FILE SECTION.
FD  INPUT-FILE
    LABEL RECORDS ARE OMITTED                      ]
    RECORD CONTAINS 80 CHARACTERS                  ] Typical FD for an input file.
    DATA RECORD IS STUDENT-RECORD.                 ]
01  STUDENT-RECORD
    05  etc.
FD  PRINT-FILE
    LABEL RECORDS ARE OMITTED                      ]
    RECORD CONTAINS 133 CHARACTERS                 ] Typical FD for a print file.
    DATA RECORD IS PRINT-LINE.                     ]
01  PRINT-LINE      PIC X(133).

WORKING-STORAGE SECTION.
01  DATA-REMAINS-SWITCH  PIC XXX  VALUE SPACES.   ] Controls performed routine.
Other 01 entries for heading, detail, and total lines

PROCEDURE DIVISION.
MAINLINE.
    OPEN INPUT INPUT-FILE                          ] Housekeeping consists of
        OUTPUT PRINT-FILE.                         ] opening files and the
    READ INPUT-FILE                                ] initial READ.
        AT END MOVE 'NO' TO DATA-REMAINS-SWITCH.
    PERFORM PROCESS-RECORDS
        UNTIL DATA-REMAINS-SWITCH = 'NO'.
    CLOSE INPUT-FILE,                              ] Termination includes
        PRINT-FILE.                                ] closing files and
    STOP RUN.                                      ] STOP RUN.
PROCESS-RECORDS.

    your logic here

    READ INPUT-FILE                                ] Last line of performed routine
        AT END MOVE 'NO' TO DATA-REMAINS-SWITCH.   ] is a second READ statement.
```

FIGURE 5.8 Skeleton Outline of a COBOL Program

True/False Exercises

1. Programmer indentation within the B margin affects compiler interpretation.
2. Blank lines are not permitted within a COBOL program.
3. A COBOL program typically contains two distinct READ statements.
4. A PERFORM statement with an UNTIL clause causes the designated paragraph to be executed at least once.
5. The COBOL coding standards for AT&T and IBM are apt to be identical.
6. COBOL requires that paragraph names be sequenced.
7. A slash in column 7 causes the next line in a compiler listing to begin on a new page.
8. Data names should be as short as possible to cut down on the coding effort.
9. Indentation in COBOL is a waste of time.
10. A well-commented COBOL program should contain half as many comment lines as Procedure Division statements.
11. All continued statements require a hyphen in column 7.
12. A flowchart and pseudocode are equivalent ways of saying the same thing.
13. A flowchart and a hierarchy chart depict the same thing.
14. For reasons of efficiency a given paragraph should perform many functions.
15. COMPUTE-AND-WRITE is a good paragraph name.
16. A module in a hierarchy chart can be performed by another module at the same level.
17. A module in a hierarchy chart need not return control to the module that called it initially.
18. Paragraphs in a program and modules in a hierarchy chart have a one-to-one correspondence.
19. Heading, detail, and total lines may be established as separate 01 entries in Working-Storage.
20. Every PICTURE clause requires a corresponding VALUE clause.
21. Arithmetic may be done on numeric-edited fields.
22. A positive field should always be defined with a CR in its PICTURE clause, whereas a negative field requires DB.
23. A numeric-edited field may be moved to a numeric field.
24. A numeric field may be moved to a numeric-edited field.
25. A single numeric-edited field may contain a dollar sign, comma, decimal point, asterisk, and the character string CR in its PICTURE clause.
26. The same numeric-edited field may contain both CR and DB in its PICTURE clause.
27. Hyphens may be used as insertion characters in a social security number.
28. Slashes may be used as insertion characters in a date.
29. The presence of CR and/or DB in a numeric-edited field implies that the sending field is signed.
30. Zero is a valid insertion character.

Problems

1. Identify the syntactical errors in the COBOL fragment in Figure 5.9.

```
IDENTIFICATION DIVISION.
PROGRAM ID. ERRORS.
ENVIRONMENT DIVISION.
CONFIGURATION SECTION.
    SOURCE-COMPUTER.  IBM-4341.
    OBJECT-COMPUTER.  IBM-4341.
INPUT-OUTPUT SECTION.
    SELECT EMPLOYEE-FILE
        ASSIGN TO UT-S-EMPLOYEE.
DATA DIVISION.
FILE SECTION.
FD  EMPLOYEE-FILE
    LABEL RECORDS ARE OMITTED
    RECORD CONTAINS 50 CHARACTERS
    DATA RECORD IS EMPLOYEE-RECORD.
    EMPLOYEE-RECORD.
    05  EMP-NAME            PIC X(20).
    05  EMP-NUMBER          PIC X(9).
    05  FILLER              PIC X(20).
WORKING STORAGE SECTION.
10  END-OF-FILE-SWITCH      PIC X(3) VALUE BLANKS.
```

FIGURE 5.9 COBOL Fragment for Problem 1

2. Identify the logical errors in the COBOL fragment in Figure 5.10. (Assume there are no other READ statements in the program.)

```
WORKING-STORAGE SECTION.
01  END-OF-FILE-SWITCH      PIC X(3)   VALUE 'YES'.
.
.
.
PROCEDURE DIVISION.
MAINLINE.
.
.
.
   PERFORM PROCESS-RECORDS
       UNTIL END-OF-FILE-SWITCH = 'YES'.
.
.
.
PROCESS-RECORDS.
    READ EMPLOYEE-FILE
        AT END MOVE 'YES' TO END-OF-FILE-SWITCH.
.
.
.
```

FIGURE 5.10 COBOL Fragment for Problem 2

3. Can you suggest any improvements to the code in Figure 5.11?

```
FD  CARD-FILE
    LABEL RECORDS ARE OMITTED
    RECORD CONTAINS 80 CHARACTERS
    DATA RECORD IS STUDENT-RECORD.
01  STUDENT-RECORD.
    05  STUDENT-NAME       PICTURE IS A(20).
    05  SOC-SEC-NO         PICTURE IS 9(9).
    05  CREDITS            PICTURE IS 9(2).
    05  UNION-MEMBER       PICTURE IS A.
    05  SCHOLARSHIP        PICTURE IS 9(4).
    05  FILLER             PICTURE IS X(44).
```

FIGURE 5.11 COBOL Code for Problem 3

4. Modify the Tuition Billing Program so that the heading line will appear at the top of *every* page in the report. (As the program is now written, the heading line appears *once* at the beginning of the report.)

   Allow a maximum of ten students per page. Thus if there were 38 records in the file, a heading line would appear before the first, eleventh, twenty-first, and thirty-first records. There will still be only one total line. (*Hint:* A page heading routine requires a line counter in Working-Storage.)

   Does establishment of this routine require any additional modules in the hierarchy chart in Figure 5.4? Does it require a repositioning of existing modules?

5. Modify the Tuition Billing Program to account for *all* the following:

   (a) The grade point average (GPA) is contained in positions 33 to 36 of each input record as a 9V999 number. The scholarship amount is no longer present in the input record but is calculated according to the description in part (b).

   (b) The scholarship award is a function of grade point average rather than a flat amount:

GPA	SCHOLARSHIP
>3.500	20% reduction in tuition
3.001–3.500	15% reduction in tuition
2.500–3.000	10% reduction in tuition
<2.500	No scholarship

   (c) Calculate and print the total number of credits taken by all students.

   (d) Calculate and print the *average* GPA (weigh the GPAs of all students equally).

6. Supply PICTURE clauses for the receiving fields needed to accomplish the following:

   (a) A floating dollar sign, omission of cents, printing (or suppression) of commas as appropriate, and a maximum value of $9,999,999.

   (b) A fixed dollar sign, asterisk fill for insignificant leading zeros, printing (or suppression) of commas as appropriate, a maximum value of $9,999, and a trailing DB if the sending field is negative.

   (c) A fixed dollar sign, zero suppression of insignificant leading zeros, omission of commas in all instances, and a maximum value of $99,999.99.

   (d) A floating dollar sign, printing (or suppression) of commas as appropriate, a maximum value of $9,999.00, and a trailing CR if the sending field is negative.

7. Show the value of the edited result for each of the following entries:

SOURCE FIELD		RECEIVING FIELD	
Picture	Value	Picture	Edited Result
(a) 9(6)	123456	9(6)	
(b) 9(6)	123456	9(8)	
(c) 9(6)	123456	9(6).99	
(d) 9(4)V99	123456	9(6)	
(e) 9(4)V99	123456	9(4)	
(f) 9(4)V99	123456	$$$$$9.99	
(g) 9(4)V99	123456	$$$,$$9.99	
(h) 9(6)	123456	$$$$,$$9.99	
(i) 9(6)	123456	Z(8)	
(j) 9(4)V99	123456	$ZZZ,ZZZ.99	

8. Show the edited results for each entry:

SOURCE FIELD		RECEIVING FIELD	
Picture	Value	Picture	Edited Result
(a) S9(4)V99	45600	$$$$$.99CR	
(b) S9(4)V99	45600	$$,$$$.99DB	
(c) S9(4)	4567	$$,$$$.00	
(d) S9(6)	122577	99B99B99	
(e) S9(6)	123456	++++,+++	
(f) S9(6)	−123456	++++,+++	
(g) S9(6)	123456	----,---	
(h) S9(6)	−123456	----,---	
(i) 9(4)V99	567890	$$$$,$$$.99	
(j) 9(4)V99	567890	$ZZZ,ZZZ.99	
(k) 9(4)V99	567890	$***,***.99	

9. What, if anything, is wrong (either syntactically or logically) with the following PICTURE clauses?

(a) $,$$$,$$9.99
(b) 999-99-9999
(c) $$$$,$$$,$$$
(d) $ZZZ.ZZ
(e) $999V99
(f) $999,999,999.99
(g) $$$$$,$$9.99

10. Do you agree with all of the coding standards suggested by the author? Can you suggest any others? Do you think the imposition of coding standards within an installation impinges on the creativity of individual programmers? Are coding standards worth the extra time and trouble they require?

Programming Specifications

Project 5–1

Program Name:

Annual Compensation Report

Narrative:

Process a file of employee pay records to compute and print the annual earnings of each employee. In addition, compute and print the annual payroll and the average compensation of both monthly and hourly employees.

Input File(s):

EMPLOYEE-FILE

Input Record Layout:

```
01  EMPLOYEE-RECORD.
    05  EMP-SOC-SEC-NUMBER          PIC 9(9).
    05  EMP-NAME-AND-INITIALS.
        10  EMP-LAST-NAME           PIC X(13).
        10  EMP-INITIALS            PIC XX.
    05  EMP-COMPENSATION-RATE       PIC 9(5)V99.
    05  EMP-COMPENSATION-CODE       PIC X.
```

Test Data:

```
111111111GRAUER       RT0120000M
222222222JONES        JJ0000450H
333333333MILGROM      EA0000500H
444444444RICHARDS     IM0210000M
555555555JEFFRIES     JB0000550H
666666666STEVENS      SS0370000M
777777777BROWN        BB0000800H
888888888BAKER        ED0250000M
999999999SUGRUE       PK0150000M
```

Report Format:

```
                        ANNUAL COMPENSATION REPORT

               NAME              RATE       METHOD     ANNUAL AMT

          XXXXXXXXXXXXXXXX    $99,999.99      X       $99,999.99





                             AVERAGE ANNUAL WAGE FOR HOURLY EMPLOYEES  = $99,999.99

                             AVERAGE ANNUAL WAGE FOR MONTHLY EMPLOYEES = $99,999.99
```

Processing Requirements:

1. Print a suitable heading line at the beginning of the report.
2. Read a file of employee pay records.
3. For every record read,
   (a) Determine how the employee is paid, either hourly or monthly, according to the EMP-COMPENSATION-CODE of H and M, respectively. (The value in the EMP-COMPENSATION-RATE field is the employee's hourly or monthly compensation rate.)
   (b) Calculate the employee's annual compensation. Hourly employees work 40 hours per week, 52 weeks per year. Monthly employees receive their monthly salary for 12 months.
   (c) Print a detail line for each employee, showing his or her *annual* compensation. Single-space detail lines.
4. After all records have been read, compute the average annual compensation of all hourly employees; also compute the average of all monthly employees. Print these values at the conclusion of the report.

Programming Specifications

Project 5–2

Program Name:

Warehouse Shipments

Narrative:

Process a file of furniture shipment records from three distinct warehouses, to determine the anticipated revenue amount due to each warehouse.

Input File(s):

FURNITURE-SHIPMENT-FILE

Input Record Layout:

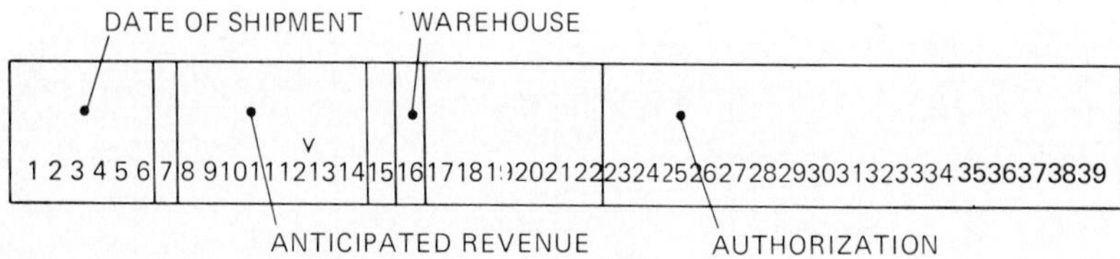

Test Data:

```
021285 0030000 C    RUSS FALLOWES
021485 0070000 C    RUSS FALLOWES
021985 0002500 B    DALE MANDRONA
022185 0044000 C    RAY DELODI
022885 0010700 A    PAUL ARON
030285 0000200 C    ART COOPER
030285 0004600 B    DALE MANDRONA
030985 0004800 B    DALE MANDRONA
030985 0092000 A    RAY DELODI
```

Report Format:

```
         0         1         2         3         4         5         6
123456789012345678901234567890123456789012345678901234567890123456789
1
2   SHIPMENT      ANTICIPATED      WAREHOUSE      PERSON WHO
3     DATE          REVENUE                       AUTHORIZED
4  ------------------------------------------------------------
5   99/99/99      $$$,$$9.99           X        XXXXXXXXXXXXXXXXXXXX
6
7   99/99/99      $$$,$$9.99           X        XXXXXXXXXXXXXXXXXXXX
8   .
9   .
10  -----------------------------------------------------------
11                     TOTAL REVENUE FOR WAREHOUSE A = $$$$,$$9.99
12                     TOTAL REVENUE FOR WAREHOUSE B = $$$$,$$9.99
13                     TOTAL REVENUE FOR WAREHOUSE C = $$$$,$$9.99
14
```

Processing Requirements:

1. Print a suitable heading line at the beginning of the report.
2. Read a file of furniture shipment records.
3. For each record read,
   (a) Determine which warehouse, A, B, or C, shipped the furniture and increment the appropriate warehouse total.
   (b) Print a detail line for that record, containing all input fields with appropriate editing. Double-space the detail lines.
4. After all records have been read, print the total revenue for each warehouse.

Programming Specifications

Project 5–3

Program Name:

Payroll

Narrative:

Process a file of employee pay records, compute and print individual payroll calculations, and compute and print company totals.

Input File(s):

EMPLOYEE-PAY-FILE

Input Record Layout:

FIELD	*COLUMNS*	*PICTURE*
Social Security Number	1–9	9(9)
Employee Last Name	10–22	X(13)
Employee Initials	23–24	X(2)
Hourly Rate	25–29	9(3)V99
Hours Worked Last Week	30–32	9(3)

Test Data:

```
111111111GRAUER      RT01000035
222222222JONES       JJ00450040
333333333MILGROM     EA00050045
444444444RICHARDS    IM01100050
555555555JEFFRIES    JB05500030
666666666STEVENS     SS00700035
777777777BROWN       BB00800250
888888888BAKER       ED02500030
999999999SUGRUE      PK01500025
```

Report Format:

```
         0         1         2         3         4         5         6         7         8
1234567890123456789012345678901234567890123456789012345678901234567890123456789012345678
 1
 2
 3                          HOURLY PAY REPORT - ABC WIDGETS
 4
 5         NAME             SOC SEC NUM    HOURS    RATE      GROSS PAY      FED TAX    NET PAY
 6
 7   XXXXXXXXXXXXXXXXXX     999-99-9999     99.9    ZZ9.99       $999.99      $999.99    $999.99
 8
 9   XXXXXXXXXXXXXXXXXX     999-99-9999     99.9    ZZ9.99       $999.99      $999.99    $999.99
10
11
12
13
14                                                       ------------------------------------
15            COMPANY TOTALS                         $999,999.99  $9,999.99  $9,999.99
16
17
18
```

Processing Requirements:

1. Print a suitable heading line at the beginning of the report. (As an extra assignment, limit the number of detail lines to four per page. Print a heading line at the start of every new page.)
2. For every record read,
   (a) Calculate the gross pay as follows:
      i. Straight time for the first 40 hours
      ii. Time and a half for the next 8 hours (between 40 and 48 hours)
      iii. Double time for anything over 48 hours
   (b) Calculate federal withholding tax as follows:
      i. 18% on first $200 of gross
      ii. 20% on amounts between $200 and $240
      iii. 22% on amounts between $240 and $280
      iv. 24% on amounts over $280
   (c) Calculate net pay as gross pay minus federal tax.
   (d) Print a detail line for each employee, with suitable editing in all fields. Double-space detail lines.
   (e) Increment company totals for gross pay, federal withholding, and net pay.
   (f) Does the Data seem reasonable? Can you suggest additional specifications for data validation?
3. When all records have been read, print the company total for all items in part 2(e).

Programming Specifications

Project 5–4

Program Name:

Consulting Profits

Narrative:

This project is a typical heading, detail, and total line program utilizing all features covered to date.

Input File:

CONSULTANT-BILLING-FILE

Input Record Layout:

```
01  CONSULTANT-RECORD.
    05  CONS-NAME-AND-INITIALS     PIC X(20).
    05  CONS-BILLING-DATA.
        10 CONS-BILLING-RATE       PIC 999.
        10 CONS-HOURS-BILLED       PIC 999V9.
    05  CONS-HOURLY-PAY-RATE       PIC 999.
```

Test Data:

```
JOHNSON, L       1500500035
MILGROM, I       2000750050
LEE, B           1000800040
FRANKEL, L       2000400075
GROSSMAN, I      2500800100
BOROW, J         1000500025
MARSHAK, K       1200850040
KARLSTROM, K     1001150025
```

Report Format:

Use the following report layout:

```
 1
 2                       CONSULTING PROFIT REPORT
 3
 4     CONSULTANT                AMOUNT BILLED   AMOUNT DUE   GROSS PROFIT
 5                                 TO CLIENT     CONSULTANT        TO FIRM
 6
 7   XXXXXXXXXXXXXXXXXXXX          $ZZZ,999.99   $ZZZ,999.99  $ZZZ,999.99
 8
 9
10
11                                 -----------   -----------  -----------
12    COMPANY TOTALS               $ZZZ,999.99   $ZZZ,999.99  $ZZZ,999.99
13
14
```

Processing Requirements:

1. Read a file of consultant billing records. For every record read:
   (a) Determine the amount to bill the client. The client bill is the consultant's billing rate times the number of hours billed.
   (b) Determine the amount to pay the consultant. The consultant is paid at the consultant's hourly rate times the number of hours billed.
   (c) Determine the gross profit earned for the firm by that consultant. The gross profit is the amount billed the client minus the amount paid to the consultant.
   (d) Print a detail line for every consultant containing the consultant's name, amount billed the client, amount due to the consultant, and the gross profit earned by the firm. Follow the report layout for appropriate spacing. Single-space detail lines.
2. When all records have been read, print the total value of all client billings, the total amount due to be paid to all consultants, and the total gross profit earned by the firm.

Debugging

6

Overview

Very few computer programs run successfully on the first attempt. Indeed the programmer is realistically expected to make errors, and an important "test" of a good programmer is not whether he or she makes mistakes but how quickly they are detected and corrected. Since this process is such an integral part of programming, an entire chapter is devoted to debugging. We consider errors in both compilation and execution.

Compilation errors *occur in the translation of COBOL to machine language and result from violation of a rule of the COBOL grammar, e.g., a missing period, a misspelled word, or an entry in a wrong column. If the program has been successfully translated to machine language, but the calculated results are different from those the programmer expected or intended,* execution errors *have occurred. Execution errors may be caused by an incorrect translation of proper pseudocode to the programming language or by a correct translation of incorrect logic.* □

ERRORS IN COMPILATION

There are four types of IBM COBOL compiler error messages or diagnostics, which are listed in order of increasing severity. Other compilers have similar classifications.

W *Warning diagnostic:* calls attention to what may cause a potential problem. A program can compile and execute with several W-level diagnostics present; however, ignoring these messages could lead to errors in execution.

C *Conditional diagnostic:* requires the compiler to make an assumption in order to complete the compilation. Execution is typically suppressed and, if not, usually inaccurate.

E *Error diagnostic:* a severe error in that the compiler cannot make corrections and therefore cannot generate object instructions. Execution will not take place. Any statement flagged as an E-level error is ignored and treated as if it were not present in the program.

D *Disaster diagnostic:* an error of such severity that the compiler does not know what to do and cannot continue. D-level diagnostics are extremely rare, and one practically has to submit a FORTRAN program to the COBOL compiler to cause a D-level message.

The COBOL compiler tends to rub salt in a wound in the sense that an error in one statement can cause error messages in other statements that appear correct. For example, should you have an E-level error in a SELECT statement, the compiler will flag the error, ignore the SELECT statement, and then flag any other statement which references that file even though those other statements are correct.

Often simple mistakes such as omitting a line or misspelling a reserved word can lead to a long and sometimes confusing set of error messages. The only consolation is that compiler errors can disappear as quickly as they occurred. Correction of the misspelled word or insertion of the missing statement will often eliminate several errors at once.

Proficiency in debugging comes from experience; the more programs you write, the better you become. To give you a better feel of what to expect in your own programs, we have taken the Tuition Billing Program from Chapter 5 and deliberately changed several of the statements to cause compilation errors.

Consider the COBOL listing and associated diagnostics in Figures 6.1 and 6.2. Each message in Figure 6.2 references a statement number and an IBM message number and contains a brief explanation of the error. Some of the errors will be immediately obvious; others may require you to seek help. As you progress through this book and gain practical experience, you will become increasingly self-sufficient.

Let us examine the errors:

Line 11 W LABEL RECORDS CLAUSE MISSING . . .
Line 11 is the SELECT statement for STUDENT-FILE. However, the diagnostic refers to the FD for this file in lines 18–20, and, sure enough, the LABEL RECORDS CLAUSE has been omitted. Since this is a W-level diagnostic, the compiler indicates what action it is taking; in this case it will extract the necessary information from the DD card, a JCL statement.
Correction: Insert a line LABEL RECORDS ARE OMITTED between lines 18 and 19.

Line 49 E 'UNION' INVALID IN DATA DESCRIPTION . . .
Note the occurrence of TOTAL UNION FEE in line 49; the hyphens between the parts of the name are missing. In COBOL a data name is followed by a blank, and the compiler does not know how to handle what it thinks are three data names in a row (TOTAL, UNION, and FEE) in line 49.
Correction: Insert hyphens to read TOTAL-UNION-FEE.

Line 55 W END OF SENTENCE SHOULD PRECEDE 05 . . .
Any level number must follow a completed statement, but the period ending line 54 has been removed. In this instance, the compiler assumes that the period is present, so no harm is done, but it is poor programming to permit such W-level diagnostics to remain. Moreover, there are situations in which a missing period can be very damaging.
Correction: Insert a period at the end of line 54.

Line 105 E 'START' SHOULD NOT BEGIN A-MARGIN.
A subtle error and one that typically sends the beginner for help. START is intended as a paragraph name, and paragraph names must begin in the A-MARGIN, so what's the problem? However, START is a reserved word in COBOL (see Appendix C), and its usage is severely restricted; it may not be used as a paragraph name.

```
00001          IDENTIFICATION DIVISION.
00002          PROGRAM-ID.     TUITION.
00003          AUTHOR.         JACKIE CLARK.
00004
00005          ENVIRONMENT DIVISION.
00006          CONFIGURATION SECTION.
00007          SOURCE-COMPUTER.    IBM-4341.
00008          OBJECT-COMPUTER.    IBM-4341.
00009          INPUT-OUTPUT SECTION.
00010          FILE-CONTROL.                         ─── LABEL RECORDS clause missing in this FD.
00011              SELECT STUDENT-FILE
00012                  ASSIGN TO UT-S-SYSIN.
00013              SELECT PRINT-FILE
00014                  ASSIGN TO UT-S-SYSOUT.
00015
00016          DATA DIVISION.
00017          FILE SECTION.
00018          FD  STUDENT-FILE
00019              RECORD CONTAINS 80 CHARACTERS
00020              DATA RECORD IS STUDENT-RECORD.
00021          01  STUDENT-RECORD.
00022              05  STU-NAME            PIC X(20).
00023              05  STU-SOC-SEC-NO      PIC 9(9).
00024              05  STU-CREDITS         PIC 9(2).
00025              05  STU-UNION-MEMBER    PIC X.
00026              05  STU-SCHOLARSHIP     PIC 9(4).
00027              05  FILLER              PIC X(44).
00028
00029          FD  PRINT-FILE
00030              LABEL RECORDS ARE OMITTED
00031              RECORD CONTAINS 133 CHARACTERS
00032              DATA RECORD IS PRINT-LINE.
00033          01  PRINT-LINE              PIC X(133).
00034
00035          WORKING-STORAGE SECTION.
00036          01  DATA-REMAINS-SWITCH     PIC X(2)      VALUE SPACES.
00037
00038          01  INDIVIDUAL-CALCULATIONS.
00039              05  IND-TUITION         PIC 9(4)V99 VALUE ZEROS.
00040              05  IND-ACTIVITY-FEE    PIC 9(2)    VALUE ZEROS.
00041              05  IND-UNION-FEE       PIC 9(2)    VALUE ZEROS.
00042              05  IND-BILL            PIC 9(6)V99 VALUE ZEROS.
00043                                                            ─── Alphanumeric picture
00044          01  UNIVERSITY-TOTALS.                                 not permitted for
00045              05  TOTAL-TUITION       PIC 9(6)V99 VALUE ZEROS.    numeric calculation.
00046              05  TOTAL-SCHOLARSHIP   PIC X(6)    VALUE ZEROS.
00047              05  TOTAL-ACTIVITY-FEE  PIC 9(6)    VALUE ZEROS.
00048              05  TOTAL-IND-BILL      PIC 9(6)V99 VALUE ZEROS.
00049              05  TOTAL UNION FEE     PIC 9(6)    VALUE ZEROS.
00050                                                            ─── Hyphens missing.
00051          01  HEADING-LINE.
00052              05  FILLER              PIC X       VALUE SPACES.
00053              05  FILLER              PIC X(12)   VALUE 'STUDENT NAME'.
00054              05  FILLER              PIC X(10)   VALUE SPACES □ ─── Period missing.
00055              05  FILLER              PIC X(11)   VALUE 'SOC SEC NUM'.
00056              05  FILLER              PIC X(2)    VALUE SPACES.
00057              05  FILLER              PIC X(7)    VALUE 'CREDITS'.
00058              05  FILLER              PIC X(.2)   VALUE SPACES.
00059              05  FILLER              PIC X(7)    VALUE 'TUITION'.
00060              05  FILLER              PIC X(2)    VALUE SPACES.
00061              05  FILLER              PIC X(9)    VALUE 'UNION FEE'.
00062              05  FILLER              PIC X(2)    VALUE SPACES.
00063              05  FILLER              PIC X(7)    VALUE 'ACT FEE'.
00064              05  FILLER              PIC X(2)    VALUE SPACES.
00065              05  FILLER              PIC X(11)   VALUE 'SCHOLARSHIP'.
00066              05  FILLER              PIC X(2)    VALUE SPACES.
00067              05  FILLER              PIC X(10)   VALUE 'TOTAL BILL'.
00068              05  FILLER              PIC X(36)   VALUE SPACES.
00069
00070          01  DETAIL-LINE.
00071              05  FILLER              PIC X       VALUE SPACES.
00072              05  DET-STUDENT-NAME    PIC X(20).
00073              05  FILLER              PIC X(2)    VALUE SPACES.
00074              05  DET-SOC-SEC-NO      PIC 999B99B9999.        ─── Should be DET-CREDITS.
00075              05  FILLER              PIC X(4)    VALUE SPACES.
00076              05  STU-CREDITS         PIC 99.
00077              05  FILLER              PIC X(2)    VALUE SPACES.
00078              05  DET-TUITION         PIC $$$$,$$9.99.
00079              05  FILLER              PIC X       VALUE SPACES.
00080              05  DET-UNION-FEE       PIC $$$$,$$9.
```

FIGURE 6.1 *Tuition Billing Program with Compilation Errors*

FIGURE 6.1 (Continued)

```
00081          05  FILLER                 PIC X(3)     VALUE SPACES.
00082          05  DET-ACTIVITY-FEE       PIC $$$$,$$9.
00083          05  FILLER                 PIC X(3)     VALUE SPACES.
00084          05  DET-SCHOLARSHIP        PIC $$$$,$$9.
00085          05  FILLER                 PIC X(3)     VALUE SPACES.
00086          05  DET-IND-BILL           PIC $$$$,$$9.99.
00087          05  FILLER                 PIC X(35)    VALUE SPACES.
00088
00089      01  TOTAL-LINE.
00090          05  FILLER                 PIC X(8)     VALUE SPACES.
00091          05  FILLER                 PIC X(17) VALUE 'UNIVERSITY TOTALS'.
00092          05  FILLER                 PIC X(17)    VALUE SPACES.
00093          05  PR-TOT-TUITION         PIC $$$$,$$9.99.
00094          05  FILLER                 PIC X        VALUE SPACES.
00095          05  PR-TOT-UNION-FEE       PIC $$$$,$$9.
00096          05  FILLER                 PIC X(3)     VALUE SPACES.
00097          05  PR-TOT-ACTIVITY-FEE    PIC $$$$,$$9.
00098          05  FILLER                 PIC X(3)     VALUE SPACES.
00099          05  PR-TOT-SCHOLARSHIP     PIC $$$$,$$9.
00100          05  FILLER                 PIC X(3)     VALUE SPACES.
00101          05  PR-TOT-IND-BILL        PIC $$$$,$$9.99.
00102          05  FILLER                 PIC X(35)    VALUE SPACES.
00103
00104      PROCEDURE DIVISION.
00105      START.                              Reserved word used as paragraph name.
00106          OPEN INPUT  STUDENT-FILE
00107               OUTPUT PRINT-FILE.
00108          PERFORM 0015-WRITE-HEADING-LINE.
00109          PERFORM 0017-READ-STUDENT-FILE.
00110          PERFORM 0020-PROCESS-A-RECORD
00111              UNTIL DATA-REMAINS-SWITCH = 'NO'.
00112          PERFORM 0060-WRITE-UNIVERSITY-TOTALS.
00113          CLOSE STUDENT-FILE
00114                PRINT-FILE.
00115          STOP RUN.
00116
00117      0015-WRITE-HEADING-LINE.
00118          MOVE HEADING-LINE TO PRINT-LINE.
00119          WRITE PRINT-LINE
00120              AFTER ADVANCING PAGE.
00121
00122      0017-READ-STUDENT-FILE.             Should be STUDENT-FILE.
00123          READ STUDNET-FILE
00124              AT END MOVE 'NO' TO DATA-REMAINS-SWITCH.
00125
00126      0020-PROCESS-A-RECORD.
00127          PERFORM 0030-COMPUTE-INDIVIDUAL-BILL.
00128          PERFORM 0040-INCREMENT-ALL-TOTALS
00129          PERFORM 0050-WRITE-DETAIL-LINE.
00130          PERFORM 0017-READ-STUDENT-FILE.
00131                                          Space missing after =
00132      0030-COMPUTE-INDIVIDUAL-BILL.
00133          COMPUTE IND-TUITION =127.50 * STU-CREDITS.
00134          IF STU-UNION-MEMBER = 'Y'
00135              MOVE 25 TO IND-UNION-FEE    Multiple definition in lines 24 and 76.
00136          ELSE
00137              MOVE ZERO TO IND-UNION-FEE.
00138          MOVE 25 TO IND-ACTIVITY-FEE.
00139          IF STU-CREDITS > 6
00140              MOVE 50 TO IND-ACTIVITY-FEE.
00141          IF STU-CREDITS > 12                     Extends past column 72.
00142              MOVE 75 TO IND-ACTIVITY-FEE.
00143          COMPUTE IND-BILL = IND-TUITION + IND-UNION-FEE + IND-ACTIVITY-FEE -
00144                             STU-SCHOLARSHIP.
00145                                          TO does not belong.
00146      0040-INCREMENT-ALL-TOTALS.
00147          ADD IND-TUITION TO TOTAL-TUITION GIVING TOTAL-TUITION.
00148          ADD IND-UNION-FEE TO TOTAL-UNION-FEE.
00149          ADD IND-ACTIVITY-FEE TO TOTAL-ACTIVITY-FEE.
00150          ADD IND-BILL TO TOTAL-IND-BILL.
00151          ADD STU-SCHOLARSHIP TO TOTAL-SCHOLARSHIP.   PIC X(6) is used in definition.
00152
00153      0050-WRITE-DETAIL-LINE.
00154          MOVE STU-NAME TO DET-STUDENT-NAME.   Multiple definition in lines 24 and 76.
00155          MOVE STU-SOC-SEC-NO TO DET-SOC-SEC-NO.
00156          MOVE STU-CREDITS TO DET-CREDITS.
00157          MOVE IND-TUITION TO DET-TUITION.
00158          MOVE IND-UNION-FEE TO DET-UNION-FEE.
00159          MOVE IND-ACTIVITY-FEE TO DET-ACTIVITY-FEE.
00160          MOVE STU-SCHOLARSHIP TO DET-SCHOLARSHIP.
00161          MOVE IND-BILL TO DET-IND-BILL.
```

```
00162           MOVE DETAIL-LINE TO PRINT-LINE.
00163           WRITE PRINT-FILE
00164               AFTER ADVANCING 1 LINE.
00165
00166       0060-WRITE-UNIVERSITY-TOTALS.
00167           MOVE TOTAL-TUITION TO PR-TOT-TUITION.
00168           MOVE TOTAL-UNION-FEE TO PR-TOT-UNION-FEE.
00169           MOVE TOTAL-ACTIVITY-FEE TO PR-TOT-ACTIVITY-FEE.
00170           MOVE TOTAL-SCHOLARSHIP TO PR-TOT-SCHOLARSHIP.
00171           MOVE TOTAL-IND-BILL TO PR-TOT-IND-BILL.
00172           MOVE TOTAL-LINE TO PRINT-LINE.
00173           WRITE PRINT-LINE
00174               AFTER ADVANCING 2 LINES.
```

Should be PRINT-LINE. (line 163, PRINT-FILE)

Put hyphens in Working-Storage definition in line 49. (line 168, TOTAL-UNION-FEE)

FIGURE 6.1 (Continued)

CARD	ERROR MESSAGE	
11	IKF2133I-W	LABEL RECORDS CLAUSE MISSING. DD CARD OPTION WILL BE TAKEN.
49	IKF1037I-E	UNION INVALID IN DATA DESCRIPTION. SKIPPING TO NEXT CLAUSE.
55	IKF1043I-W	END OF SENTENCE SHOULD PRECEDE 05 . ASSUMED PRESENT.
105	IKF1087I-W	' START ' SHOULD NOT BEGIN A-MARGIN.
105	IKF4050I-E	SYNTAX REQUIRES QISAM-FILE WITH NOMINAL KEY .
123	IKF3001I-E	STUDNET-FILE NOT DEFINED. STATEMENT DISCARDED.
133	IKF1007I-W	127.50 NOT PRECEDED BY A SPACE. ASSUME SPACE.
133	IKF3002I-E	STU-CREDITS NOT UNIQUE. DISCARDED.
139	IKF3002I-E	STU-CREDITS NOT UNIQUE. TEST DISCARDED.
141	IKF3002I-E	STU-CREDITS NOT UNIQUE. TEST DISCARDED.
143	IKF3001I-E	IND-ACTIVITY NOT DEFINED. DISCARDED.
147	IKF4008I-W	SUPERFLUOUS TO FOUND IN ADD STATEMENT. IGNORED.
148	IKF3001I-E	TOTAL-UNION-FEE NOT DEFINED. SUBSTITUTING TALLY .
151	IKF4019I-E	DNM=2-177 (AN) MAY NOT BE USED AS ARITHMETIC OPERAND.
156	IKF3002I-E	STU-CREDITS NOT UNIQUE. DISCARDED.
156	IKF3001I-E	DET-CREDITS NOT DEFINED.
163	IKF4050I-E	SYNTAX REQUIRES RECORD-NAME . FOUND DNM=1-431 .
168	IKF3001I-E	TOTAL-UNION-FEE NOT DEFINED. DISCARDED.

FIGURE 6.2 List of Compilation Messages

Correction: Choose another paragraph name, e.g., START-THE-PROGRAM.

Line 105 E SYNTAX REQUIRES QISAM-FILE WITH NOMINAL KEY . . . A most perplexing error and an example of how one mistake can cause several other diagnostics to appear. This error stems from the previous error concerning the word START.

Correction: None required beyond what was done for the previous error.

Line 123 E STUDNET-FILE NOT DEFINED. STATEMENT DISCARDED. Perhaps your initial reaction is that the compiler made a mistake. STUDENT-FILE is defined with a SELECT statement in line 11, and in an FD beginning in line 18. Take another look. Lines 11 and 18 define STUDENT-FILE, not STUDNET-FILE. You know they are the same, but the compiler does not.

Correction: Change to STUDENT-FILE in statement 123.

Line 133 W 127.50 NOT PRECEDED BY A SPACE. ASSUME SPACE. An easy error to fix; remember that all relational symbols, =, >, and <, as well as all arithmetic operators, +, −, *, /, and **, must be preceded and followed by a blank.

Correction: Insert a space after the =.

Line 133, 139, 141, 156 E STU-CREDITS NOT UNIQUE . . . A message of "not unique" means that there is more than one data item with the same name. In this case we find STU-CREDITS is defined in line 24 and again in line 76 (the latter should be DET-CREDITS), and the compiler does not know which is which.

Correction: Restore uniqueness to the data name, e.g., DET-CREDITS in line 76.

Line 143 E IND-ACTIVITY NOT DEFINED.

A rather strange error in that line 143 contains IND-ACTIVITY-FEE, rather than IND-ACTIVITY. However, line 143 extends *past* column 72; i.e., -FEE is in columns 73–76, which are not interpreted by the compiler.

Correction: Reformat the COMPUTE statement so that IND-ACTIVITY-FEE appears on the next line.

Line 147 W SUPERFLUOUS TO FOUND IN ADD STATEMENT. IGNORED.

Check the syntax of the COBOL ADD verb in Chapter 4 and observe that TO is not permitted with GIVING.

Correction: Eliminate TO in line 147.

Line 148 E TOTAL-UNION-FEE NOT DEFINED . . .
168

Another example of how one error can cause several others. In line 49 the hyphens were omitted in the definition of TOTAL-UNION-FEE; thus insofar as the compiler is concerned the data name TOTAL-UNION-FEE does not exist.

Correction: This diagnostic will disappear with the correction to line 49.

Line 151 E DNM-2-177 MAY NOT BE USED AS AN ARITHMETIC OPERAND.

This error becomes easy to understand once we guess that DNM-2-177 refers to TOTAL-SCHOLARSHIP. (DNM stands for Data NaMe; the 2-177 is the compiler's internal reference to the data name in question.) Observe that a picture of X(6) was specified in the definition of TOTAL-SCHOLARSHIP in line 46. This is not a numeric picture, which is required in arithmetic operations.

Correction: Change X(6) to 9(6) in line 46.

Line 156 E DET-CREDITS NOT DEFINED.

This diagnostic pertains to the nonunique message from lines 133, 139, 141, and 156.

Correction: If the earlier diagnostic is corrected by distinguishing between STU-CREDITS and DET-CREDITS, then this message will also disappear.

Line 163 E SYNTAX REQUIRES RECORD-NAME . . .

Statement 163 is WRITE PRINT-FILE. . . . The problem is that PRINT-FILE is a file name, not a record name. Remember that in COBOL one reads a file but writes a record.

Correction: Statement 163 should read WRITE PRINT-LINE. . . .

A SECOND EXAMPLE

We return to the original program in Figure 5.6 and make one very slight change; the word ENVIRONMENT is misspelled in line 5 of Figure 6.3. The remainder of the program is correct and *exactly* as it appeared originally. The result of this one error is devastating, as seen by the list of errors shown in Figure 6.4.

The single misspelling resulted in one W-level diagnostic and 26 E-level errors. Consider:

Line 16 W FOUND DATA. EXPECTING ENVIRONMENT.

The compiler is very precise in its message. It is saying that the Environment Division should be the next division after the Identification Division, but that the Data Division was found instead.

Correction: Spell ENVIRONMENT correctly.

```
IDENTIFICATION DIVISION.
PROGRAM-ID.    TUITION.
AUTHOR.        JACKIE CLARK.

ENVIROMENT DIVISION.
CONFIGURATION SECTION.
SOURCE-COMPUTER.  IBM-4341.
OBJECT-COMPUTER.  IBM-4341.
INPUT-OUTPUT SECTION.
FILE-CONTROL.
    SELECT STUDENT-FILE
        ASSIGN TO UT-S-SYSIN.
    SELECT PRINT-FILE
        ASSIGN TO UT-S-SYSOUT.

DATA DIVISION.
FILE SECTION.
FD  STUDENT-FILE
    LABEL RECORDS ARE OMITTED
    RECORD CONTAINS 80 CHARACTERS
    DATA RECORD IS STUDENT-RECORD.
01  STUDENT-RECORD.
    05  STU-NAME                PIC X(20).
    05  STU-SOC-SEC-NO          PIC 9(9).
    05  STU-CREDITS             PIC 9(2).
    05  STU-UNION-MEMBER        PIC X.
    05  STU-SCHOLARSHIP         PIC 9(4).
    05  FILLER                  PIC X(44).

FD  PRINT-FILE
    LABEL RECORDS ARE OMITTED
    RECORD CONTAINS 133 CHARACTERS
    DATA RECORD IS PRINT-LINE.
01  PRINT-LINE                  PIC X(133).

WORKING-STORAGE SECTION.
01  DATA-REMAINS-SWITCH         PIC X(2)     VALUE SPACES.

01  INDIVIDUAL-CALCULATIONS.
    05  IND-TUITION             PIC 9(4)V99  VALUE ZEROS.
    05  IND-ACTIVITY-FEE        PIC 9(2)     VALUE ZEROS.
    05  IND-UNION-FEE           PIC 9(2)     VALUE ZEROS.
    05  IND-BILL                PIC 9(6)V99  VALUE ZEROS.

01  UNIVERSITY-TOTALS.
    05  TOTAL-TUITION           PIC 9(6)V99  VALUE ZEROS.
    05  TOTAL-SCHOLARSHIP       PIC 9(6)     VALUE ZEROS.
    05  TOTAL-ACTIVITY-FEE      PIC 9(6)     VALUE ZEROS.
    05  TOTAL-IND-BILL          PIC 9(6)V99  VALUE ZEROS.
    05  TOTAL-UNION-FEE         PIC 9(6)     VALUE ZEROS.

01  HEADING-LINE.
    05  FILLER                  PIC X        VALUE SPACES.
    05  FILLER                  PIC X(12)    VALUE 'STUDENT NAME'.
    05  FILLER                  PIC X(10)    VALUE SPACES.
    05  FILLER                  PIC X(11)    VALUE 'SOC SEC NUM'.
    05  FILLER                  PIC X(2)     VALUE SPACES.
    05  FILLER                  PIC X(7)     VALUE 'CREDITS'.
    05  FILLER                  PIC X(2)     VALUE SPACES.
    05  FILLER                  PIC X(7)     VALUE 'TUITION'.
    05  FILLER                  PIC X(2)     VALUE SPACES.
    05  FILLER                  PIC X(9)     VALUE 'UNION FEE'.
    05  FILLER                  PIC X(2)     VALUE SPACES.
    05  FILLER                  PIC X(7)     VALUE 'ACT FEE'.
    05  FILLER                  PIC X(2)     VALUE SPACES.
    05  FILLER                  PIC X(11)    VALUE 'SCHOLARSHIP'.
    05  FILLER                  PIC X(2)     VALUE SPACES.
    05  FILLER                  PIC X(10)    VALUE 'TOTAL BILL'.
    05  FILLER                  PIC X(36)    VALUE SPACES.

01  DETAIL-LINE.
    05  FILLER                  PIC X        VALUE SPACES.
    05  DET-STUDENT-NAME        PIC X(20).
    05  FILLER                  PIC X(2)     VALUE SPACES.
    05  DET-SOC-SEC-NO          PIC 999B99B9999.
    05  FILLER                  PIC X(4)     VALUE SPACES.
    05  DET-CREDITS             PIC 99.
    05  FILLER                  PIC X(2)     VALUE SPACES.
    05  DET-TUITION             PIC $$$$,$$9.99.
    05  FILLER                  PIC X        VALUE SPACES.
```

Misspelling causes all errors.

FD is flagged because Environment Division was not recognized.

FIGURE 6.3 Tuition Billing Program with Environment Misspelled

```
           05  DET-UNION-FEE         PIC $$$$,$$9.
           05  FILLER                PIC X(3)     VALUE SPACES.
           05  DET-ACTIVITY-FEE      PIC $$$$,$$9.
           05  FILLER                PIC X(3)     VALUE SPACES.
           05  DET-SCHOLARSHIP       PIC $$$$,$$9.
           05  FILLER                PIC X(3)     VALUE SPACES.
           05  DET-IND-BILL          PIC $$$$,$$9.99.
           05  FILLER                PIC X(35)    VALUE SPACES.

       01  TOTAL-LINE.
           05  FILLER                PIC X(8)     VALUE SPACES.
           05  FILLER                PIC X(17) VALUE 'UNIVERSITY TOTALS'.
           05  FILLER                PIC X(17)    VALUE SPACES.
           05  PR-TOT-TUITION        PIC $$$$,$$9.99.
           05  FILLER                PIC X        VALUE SPACES.
           05  PR-TOT-UNION-FEE      PIC $$$$,$$9.
           05  FILLER                PIC X(3)     VALUE SPACES.
           05  PR-TOT-ACTIVITY-FEE   PIC $$$$,$$9.
           05  FILLER                PIC X(3)     VALUE SPACES.
           05  PR-TOT-SCHOLARSHIP    PIC $$$$,$$9.
           05  FILLER                PIC X(3)     VALUES SPACES.
           05  PR-TOT-IND-BILL       PIC $$$$,$$9.99.
           05  FILLER                PIC X(35)    VALUE SPACES.

       PROCEDURE DIVISION.
       0010-PREPARE-TUITION-REPORT.
           OPEN INPUT  STUDENT-FILE
               OUTPUT  PRINT-FILE.
```

File name is flagged because FD was rejected.

```
           PERFORM 0015-WRITE-HEADING-LINE.
           PERFORM 0017-READ-STUDENT-FILE.
           PERFORM 0020-PROCESS-A-RECORD
               UNTIL DATA-REMAINS-SWITCH = 'NO'.
           PERFORM 0060-WRITE-UNIVERSITY-TOTALS.
           CLOSE STUDENT-FILE
                 PRINT-FILE.
           STOP RUN.

       0015-WRITE-HEADING-LINE.
           MOVE HEADING-LINE TO PRINT-LINE.
           WRITE PRINT-LINE
               AFTER ADVANCING PAGE.

       0017-READ-STUDENT-FILE.
           READ STUDENT-FILE
               AT END MOVE 'NO' TO DATA-REMAINS-SWITCH.

       0020-PROCESS-A-RECORD.
           PERFORM 0030-COMPUTE-INDIVIDUAL-BILL.
           PERFORM 0040-INCREMENT-ALL-TOTALS
           PERFORM 0050-WRITE-DETAIL-LINE.
           PERFORM 0017-READ-STUDENT-FILE.

       0030-COMPUTE-INDIVIDUAL-BILL.
           COMPUTE IND-TUITION = 127.50 * STU-CREDITS.
           IF STU-UNION-MEMBER = 'Y'
               MOVE 25 TO IND-UNION-FEE
           ELSE
               MOVE ZERO TO IND-UNION-FEE.
           MOVE 25 TO IND-ACTIVITY-FEE.
           IF STU-CREDITS > 6
               MOVE 50 TO IND-ACTIVITY-FEE.
```

Data names are flagged because FD was rejected.

```
           IF STU-CREDITS > 12
               MOVE 75 TO IND-ACTIVITY-FEE.
           COMPUTE IND-BILL = IND-TUITION + IND-UNION-FEE +
               IND-ACTIVITY-FEE - STU-SCHOLARSHIP.

       0040-INCREMENT-ALL-TOTALS.
           ADD IND-TUITION TO TOTAL-TUITION.
           ADD IND-UNION-FEE TO TOTAL-UNION-FEE.
           ADD IND-ACTIVITY-FEE TO TOTAL-ACTIVITY-FEE.
           ADD IND-BILL TO TOTAL-IND-BILL.
           ADD STU-SCHOLARSHIP TO TOTAL-SCHOLARSHIP.

       0050-WRITE-DETAIL-LINE.
           MOVE STU-NAME TO DET-STUDENT-NAME.
           MOVE STU-SOC-SEC-NO TO DET-SOC-SEC-NO.
           MOVE STU-CREDITS TO DET-CREDITS.
           MOVE IND-TUITION TO DET-TUITION.
           MOVE IND-UNION-FEE TO DET-UNION-FEE.
           MOVE IND-ACTIVITY-FEE TO DET-ACTIVITY-FEE.
           MOVE STU-SCHOLARSHIP TO DET-SCHOLARSHIP.
```

```
00162           MOVE IND-BILL TO DET-IND-BILL.
00163           MOVE DETAIL-LINE TO PRINT-LINE.
00164           WRITE PRINT-LINE
00165               AFTER ADVANCING 1 LINE.
00166
00167       0060-WRITE-UNIVERSITY-TOTALS.
00168           MOVE TOTAL-TUITION TO PR-TOT-TUITION.
00169           MOVE TOTAL-UNION-FEE TO PR-TOT-UNION-FEE.
00170           MOVE TOTAL-ACTIVITY-FEE TO PR-TOT-ACTIVITY-FEE.
00171           MOVE TOTAL-SCHOLARSHIP TO PR-TOT-SCHOLARSHIP.
00172           MOVE TOTAL-IND-BILL TO PR-TOT-IND-BILL.
00173           MOVE TOTAL-LINE TO PRINT-LINE.
00174           WRITE PRINT-LINE
00175               AFTER ADVANCING 2 LINES.
```

FIGURE 6.3 ***(Continued)***

```
CARD   ERROR MESSAGE

16     IKF1128I-W    FOUND DATA . EXPECTING ENVIRONMENT.  ALL ENV. DIV. STATEMENTS IGNORED.
21     IKF1056I-E    FILE-NAME NOT DEFINED IN A SELECT. DESCRIPTION IGNORED.
33     IKF1056I-E    FILE-NAME NOT DEFINED IN A SELECT. DESCRIPTION IGNORED.
107    IKF3001I-E    STUDENT-FILE NOT DEFINED. DELETING TILL LEGAL ELEMENT FOUND.
107    IKF3001I-E    PRINT-FILE NOT DEFINED. DELETING TILL LEGAL ELEMENT FOUND.
107    IKF4002I-E    OPEN STATEMENT INCOMPLETE. STATEMENT DISCARDED.
114    IKF3001I-E    STUDENT-FILE NOT DEFINED. DELETING TILL LEGAL ELEMENT FOUND.
114    IKF3001I-E    PRINT-FILE NOT DEFINED.
114    IKF4002I-E    CLOSE STATEMENT INCOMPLETE. STATEMENT DISCARDED.
119    IKF3001I-E    PRINT-LINE NOT DEFINED. DISCARDED.
120    IKF3001I-E    PRINT-LINE NOT DEFINED. STATEMENT DISCARDED.
124    IKF3001I-E    STUDENT-FILE NOT DEFINED. STATEMENT DISCARDED.
134    IKF3001I-E    STU-CREDITS NOT DEFINED. DISCARDED.
135    IKF3001I-E    STU-UNION-MEMBER NOT DEFINED. TEST DISCARDED.
140    IKF3001I-E    STU-CREDITS NOT DEFINED. TEST DISCARDED.
142    IKF3001I-E    STU-CREDITS NOT DEFINED. TEST DISCARDED.
144    IKF3001I-E    STU-SCHOLARSHIP NOT DEFINED. DISCARDED.
152    IKF3001I-E    STU-SCHOLARSHIP NOT DEFINED. SUBSTITUTING TALLY .
155    IKF3001I-E    STU-NAME NOT DEFINED. DISCARDED.
156    IKF3001I-E    STU-SOC-SEC-NO NOT DEFINED. DISCARDED.
157    IKF3001I-E    STU-CREDITS NOT DEFINED. DISCARDED.
161    IKF3001I-E    STU-SCHOLARSHIP NOT DEFINED. DISCARDED.
163    IKF3001I-E    PRINT-LINE NOT DEFINED. DISCARDED.
164    IKF3001I-E    PRINT-LINE NOT DEFINED. STATEMENT DISCARDED.
173    IKF3001I-E    PRINT-LINE NOT DEFINED. DISCARDED.
174    IKF3001I-E    PRINT-LINE NOT DEFINED. STATEMENT DISCARDED.
```

FIGURE 6.4 *Errors Associated with Figure 6.3*

Line 21, 33 — E — FILE-NAME NOT DEFINED IN A SELECT.

The compiler is saying that the FDs for STUDENT-FILE and PRINT-FILE are inappropriate because there were no corresponding SELECT statements. There were, in fact, two valid SELECT statements, but these were ignored because the compiler did not perceive an Environment Division (see the previous error message). This error will reoccur on every reference to STUDENT-FILE or PRINT-FILE.

Correction: None required beyond correctly spelling ENVIRONMENT.

Line 134, 135, 140, etc. — STU-CREDITS, STU-UNION-MEMBER, STU-SCHOLARSHIP, etc. NOT DEFINED. DISCARDED.

These messages all refer to data names defined in valid record descriptions for STUDENT-FILE (lines 22–28) or PRINT-FILE (line 34). The problem is that the FDs were discarded because of the "missing" SELECTs. Hence, any reference to a data name defined under either file is invalid.

Correction: None required beyond correctly spelling ENVIRONMENT.

The point of this example is that a simple error in one statement can lead to a large number of errors in other, seemingly unrelated, statements. The latter will neatly disappear when the initial error is corrected. However, do not expect all errors you do not understand just to go away. There is always a logical explanation for everything the compiler does, although sometimes it may take quite a while to find it.

ERRORS IN EXECUTION

After a program has been successfully compiled, it proceeds to execution, and therein lie the strength and weakness of the computer. The primary attractiveness of the machine is its ability to perform its task quickly; its weakness stems from the fact that it does exactly what it has been instructed to do. The machine cannot think for itself; the programmer must think for the machine. If you were inadvertently to instruct the computer to compute tuition by charging $12 instead of $120 per credit, then that is what it would do.

To give you an idea of what can happen, we have deliberately altered the original Tuition Billing Program of Chapter 5 and created a new program, shown in Figure 6.5. That, in turn, created the output shown in Figure 6.6*a*, which at first glance resembles the original output shown in Figure 6.6*b* (which is reproduced from Chapter 5). However, there are subtle errors in Figure 6.6*a*:

1. The total of all individual bills in the total line appeared as $535 (the amount for the last record), rather than a running total.
2. The total for the individual union fees printed as 0, rather than $75.
3. The last record (for Nelson Kerbel) was processed twice.
4. The ACTIVITY FEE for John Smith and Henry James printed as $50 rather than $75.
5. The SCHOLARSHIP amount for Henry James and Susan Baker printed as $0 rather than $500, although their individual bills were reduced by $500.
6. The cents portion for the tuition amounts and individual bills is uniformly zero.

Figure 6.5, the program that produced the output in Figure 6.6*a*, compiled with a *warning* diagnostic relating to line 160. (This in turn created the difficulty in item 5, the scholarship amounts for Henry James and Susan Baker, as will be explained shortly.) Put another way, the errors inherent in Figure 6.5 are errors in execution, rather than compilation. The compiler successfully translated the COBOL program in Figure 6.5 into machine language because the program was *syntactically correct*. Unfortunately, the program was *logically incorrect*, and hence the errors in Figure 6.6. Each error is discussed in detail:

1. The sum of the individual bills is incorrect in the total line: TOTAL-IND-BILL is defined in line 49 and correctly incremented for each record in line 150; so far, so good. However, when the total line is built in lines 167–172, IND-BILL rather than TOTAL-IND-BILL is moved to PR-TOT-IND-BILL in line 171.
2. The total for UNION-FEE is wrong: TOTAL-UNION-FEE is defined and initialized in line 50. However, when the other counters are incremented in lines 147–151, an ADD statement for TOTAL-UNION-FEE is conspicuously absent. (Unlike the previous error, TOTAL-UNION-FEE is moved to PR-TOT-UNION-FEE in line 168, except that TOTAL-UNION-FEE never budged from its initial value of zero, because of the missing ADD statement.)
3. The last record was processed twice: Recall that when the program structure was first presented in Chapter 5, there was an initial READ statement in the PREPARE-TUITION-REPORT paragraph, and a second READ as the *last* statement in the performed routine. That structure was *correct*. In Figure 6.5 the initial READ statement was eliminated and the second READ *incorrectly* moved to the beginning of the performed routine.

   To understand the effect, consider a file with only a single record, which will be read as the performed routine of Figure 6.5 is entered for the first time. When

```
IDENTIFICATION DIVISION.
PROGRAM-ID.    TUITION.
AUTHOR.        JACKIE CLARK.
ENVIRONMENT DIVISION.
CONFIGURATION SECTION.
SOURCE-COMPUTER.  IBM-4341.
OBJECT-COMPUTER.  IBM-4341.
INPUT-OUTPUT SECTION.
FILE-CONTROL.
    SELECT STUDENT-FILE
        ASSIGN TO UT-S-SYSIN.
    SELECT PRINT-FILE
        ASSIGN TO UT-S-SYSOUT.
DATA DIVISION.
FILE SECTION.
FD  STUDENT-FILE
    LABEL RECORDS ARE OMITTED
    RECORD CONTAINS 80 CHARACTERS
    DATA RECORD IS STUDENT-RECORD.
01  STUDENT-RECORD.
    05  STU-NAME              PIC X(20).
    05  STU-SOC-SEC-NO        PIC 9(9).
    05  STU-CREDITS           PIC 9(2).
    05  STU-UNION-MEMBER      PIC X.
    05  STU-SCHOLARSHIP       PIC 9(4).
    05  FILLER                PIC X(44).
FD  PRINT-FILE
    LABEL RECORDS ARE OMITTED
    RECORD CONTAINS 133 CHARACTERS
    DATA RECORD IS PRINT-LINE.
01  PRINT-LINE                PIC X(133).
WORKING-STORAGE SECTION.
01  DATA-REMAINS-SWITCH       PIC X(2)     VALUE SPACES.
01  INDIVIDUAL-CALCULATIONS.
    05  IND-TUITION           PIC 9(6)     VALUE ZEROS.
    05  IND-ACTIVITY-FEE      PIC 9(2)     VALUE ZEROS.
    05  IND-UNION-FEE         PIC 9(2)     VALUE ZEROS.
    05  IND-BILL              PIC 9(8)     VALUE ZEROS.
01  UNIVERSITY-TOTALS.
    05  TOTAL-TUITION         PIC 9(6)V99  VALUE ZEROS.
    05  TOTAL-SCHOLARSHIP     PIC 9(6)     VALUE ZEROS.
    05  TOTAL-ACTIVITY-FEE    PIC 9(6)     VALUE ZEROS.
    05  TOTAL-IND-BILL        PIC 9(6)V99  VALUE ZEROS.
    05  TOTAL-UNION-FEE       PIC 9(6)     VALUE ZEROS.
01  HEADING-LINE.
    05  FILLER                PIC X        VALUE SPACES.
    05  FILLER                PIC X(12)    VALUE 'STUDENT NAME'.
    05  FILLER                PIC X(10)    VALUE SPACES.
    05  FILLER                PIC X(11)    VALUE 'SOC SEC NUM'.
    05  FILLER                PIC X(2)     VALUE SPACES.
    05  FILLER                PIC X(7)     VALUE 'CREDITS'.
    05  FILLER                PIC X(2)     VALUE SPACES.
    05  FILLER                PIC X(7)     VALUE 'TUITION'.
    05  FILLER                PIC X(2)     VALUE SPACES.
    05  FILLER                PIC X(9)     VALUE 'UNION FEE'.
    05  FILLER                PIC X(2)     VALUE SPACES.
    05  FILLER                PIC X(7)     VALUE 'ACT FEE'.
    05  FILLER                PIC X(2)     VALUE SPACES.
    05  FILLER                PIC X(11)    VALUE 'SCHOLARSHIP'.
    05  FILLER                PIC X(2)     VALUE SPACES.
    05  FILLER                PIC X(10)    VALUE 'TOTAL BILL'.
    05  FILLER                PIC X(36)    VALUE SPACES.
01  DETAIL-LINE.
    05  FILLER                PIC X        VALUE SPACES.
    05  DET-STUDENT-NAME      PIC X(20).
    05  FILLER                PIC X(2)     VALUE SPACES.
    05  DET-SOC-SEC-NO        PIC 999B99B9999.
    05  FILLER                PIC X(4)     VALUE SPACES.
    05  DET-CREDITS           PIC 99.
    05  FILLER                PIC X(2)     VALUE SPACES.
    05  DET-TUITION           PIC $$$$,$$9.99.
    05  FILLER                PIC X        VALUE SPACES.
```

Implied decimal point is missing.

FIGURE 6.5 *Errors in Execution*

FIGURE 6.5 (Continued)

```
               05  DET-UNION-FEE         PIC $$$$,$$9.
               05  FILLER                PIC X(3)     VALUE SPACES.
               05  DET-ACTIVITY-FEE      PIC $$$$,$$9.
               05  FILLER                PIC X(8)     VALUE SPACES.
               05  DET-SCHOLARSHIP       PIC $$9.
               05  FILLER                PIC X(3)     VALUE SPACES.
               05  DET-IND-BILL          PIC $$$$,$$9.99.
               05  FILLER                PIC X(35)    VALUE SPACES.

           01  TOTAL-LINE.
               05  FILLER                PIC X(8)     VALUE SPACES.
               05  FILLER                PIC X(17) VALUE 'UNIVERSITY TOTALS'.
               05  FILLER                PIC X(17)    VALUE SPACES.
               05  PR-TOT-TUITION        PIC $$$$,$$9.99.
               05  FILLER                PIC X        VALUE SPACES.
               05  PR-TOT-UNION-FEE      PIC $$$$,$$9.
               05  FILLER                PIC X(3)     VALUE SPACES.
               05  PR-TOT-ACTIVITY-FEE   PIC $$$$,$$9.
               05  FILLER                PIC X(3)     VALUE SPACES.
               05  PR-TOT-SCHOLARSHIP    PIC $$$$,$$9.
               05  FILLER                PIC X(3)     VALUE SPACES.
               05  PR-TOT-IND-BILL       PIC $$$$,$$9.99.
               05  FILLER                PIC X(35)    VALUE SPACES.

           PROCEDURE DIVISION.
           0010-PREPARE-TUITION-REPORT.
               OPEN INPUT  STUDENT-FILE
                    OUTPUT PRINT-FILE.
               PERFORM 0015-WRITE-HEADING-LINE.
               PERFORM 0020-PROCESS-A-RECORD
                   UNTIL DATA-REMAINS-SWITCH = 'NO'.
               PERFORM 0060-WRITE-UNIVERSITY-TOTALS.
               CLOSE STUDENT-FILE
                     PRINT-FILE.
               STOP RUN.

           0015-WRITE-HEADING-LINE.
               MOVE HEADING-LINE TO PRINT-LINE.
               WRITE PRINT-LINE
                   AFTER ADVANCING PAGE.

           0017-READ-STUDENT-FILE.
               READ STUDENT-FILE
                   AT END MOVE 'NO' TO DATA-REMAINS-SWITCH.

           0020-PROCESS-A-RECORD.
               PERFORM 0017-READ-STUDENT-FILE.
               PERFORM 0030-COMPUTE-INDIVIDUAL-BILL.
               PERFORM 0040-INCREMENT-ALL-TOTALS
               PERFORM 0050-WRITE-DETAIL-LINE.

           0030-COMPUTE-INDIVIDUAL-BILL.
               COMPUTE IND-TUITION = 127.50 * STU-CREDITS.
               IF STU-UNION-MEMBER = 'Y'
                   MOVE 25 TO IND-UNION-FEE
               ELSE
                   MOVE ZERO TO IND-UNION-FEE.
               MOVE 25 TO IND-ACTIVITY-FEE.
               IF STU-CREDITS > 12
                   MOVE 75 TO IND-ACTIVITY-FEE.
               IF STU-CREDITS > 6
                   MOVE 50 TO IND-ACTIVITY-FEE.
               COMPUTE IND-BILL = IND-TUITION + IND-UNION-FEE +
                   IND-ACTIVITY-FEE - STU-SCHOLARSHIP.

           0040-INCREMENT-ALL-TOTALS.
               ADD IND-TUITION TO TOTAL-TUITION.

               ADD IND-ACTIVITY-FEE TO TOTAL-ACTIVITY-FEE.
               ADD IND-BILL TO TOTAL-IND-BILL.
               ADD STU-SCHOLARSHIP TO TOTAL-SCHOLARSHIP.

           0050-WRITE-DETAIL-LINE.
               MOVE STU-NAME TO DET-STUDENT-NAME.
               MOVE STU-SOC-SEC-NO TO DET-SOC-SEC-NO.
               MOVE STU-CREDITS TO DET-CREDITS.
               MOVE IND-TUITION TO DET-TUITION.
               MOVE IND-UNION-FEE TO DET-UNION-FEE.
               MOVE IND-ACTIVITY-FEE TO DET-ACTIVITY-FEE.
               MOVE STU-SCHOLARSHIP TO DET-SCHOLARSHIP.
```

READ statement is incorrectly placed.

Order of IF statements is reversed.

ADD statement is missing for TOTAL-UNION-FEE.

```
00161              MOVE IND-BILL TO DET-IND-BILL.
00162              MOVE DETAIL-LINE TO PRINT-LINE.
00163              WRITE PRINT-LINE
00164                  AFTER ADVANCING 1 LINE.
00165
00166          0060-WRITE-UNIVERSITY-TOTALS.
00167              MOVE TOTAL-TUITION TO PR-TOT-TUITION.
00168              MOVE TOTAL-UNION-FEE TO PR-TOT-UNION-FEE.
00169              MOVE TOTAL-ACTIVITY-FEE TO PR-TOT-ACTIVITY-FEE.
00170              MOVE TOTAL-SCHOLARSHIP TO PR-TOT-SCHOLARSHIP.
00171              MOVE IND-BILL TO PR-TOT-IND-BILL.
00172              MOVE TOTAL-LINE TO PRINT-LINE.
00173              WRITE PRINT-LINE
00174                  AFTER ADVANCING 2 LINES.
```

Wrong field is moved to print line.

FIGURE 6.5 ***(Continued)***

the end of the routine is reached, the end of file has not yet been sensed; hence PROCESS-A-RECORD is entered a *second* time, even though there is only a single record. The end of file is sensed immediately in line 127, but the perform is not terminated until line 130. Consequently the intermediate statements are executed a second time for the previous record. The problem is corrected by restoring an initial READ between lines 109 and 110, and placing the existing READ statement of line 127 after line 130.

4. ACTIVITY-FEE computations are incorrect: Consider the case of John Smith and his 15 credits. The value of ACTIVITY-FEE is initially set to 25 in line 138. Since Smith has more than 12 credits, ACTIVITY-FEE is reset to 75 in line 140 and again reset to 50 in line 142. The problem is simply that the IF statements are reversed, causing anyone with 6 credits or more to be charged $50.
5. Individual SCHOLARSHIP is incorrect: This is the *only* error caught by the compiler, which flagged line 160 with the message AN INTERMEDIATE RESULT OR A SENDING FIELD MAY HAVE ITS HIGH ORDER DIGIT POSITION TRUNCATED. In line 160, STU-SCHOLARSHIP with picture 9(4) is moved to DET-SCHOLARSHIP with picture $$9. The largest value that can appear in the latter field is $99; hence any scholarship amounts in excess of $99 will have the higher-order digit eliminated.
6. Tuition charges are incorrect in that the cents portion is uniformly zero: The definition of IND-TUITION in line 40 specifies a picture clause of 9(6), omitting the implied decimal point. Hence any calculation involving IND-TUITION, i.e., line 133, will not include any decimals. Eventually IND-TUITION is moved to an edited field containing decimal points (line 157), but the cents portion has long been dropped. (A similar problem pertains to IND-BILL as well.)

We emphasize that these execution errors are not contrived but are typical of students and beginning programmers. Even the accomplished practitioner can be guilty of similar errors when rushed or careless. Realize also that execution errors occur without fanfare. There are no compiler diagnostics to warn of impending trouble. The program has compiled cleanly, and there is nothing to indicate a problem. A critical question, therefore, is how best to detect and prevent these errors.

ERROR DETECTION: THE STRUCTURED WALKTHROUGH

Although it is reasonable to expect errors, the programmer is also expected (reasonably) to find and correct them. Until recently, error detection and correction was a lonely activity. A programmer was encouraged to *desk check,* i.e., read and reread the code, in an attempt to discern logical errors *before* they occurred. Desk checking is still an important activity, but it is frequently supplemented by a newer technique, the *structured walkthrough.*

The walkthrough brings the evaluation into the open. It requires a programmer to have his or her work reviewed formally and periodically by a peer group.

Cents missing.
Activity fee should be $75.
Scholarship should be $500.

```
STUDENT NAME        SOC SEC NUM  CREDITS   TUITION  UNION FEE  ACT FEE  SCHOLARSHIP  TOTAL BILL
JOHN SMITH          123 45 6789    15    $1,912.00     $25       $50          $0     $1,987.00
HENRY JAMES         987 65 4321    15    $1,912.00      $0       $50          $0     $1,462.00
SUSAN BAKER         111 22 3333    09    $1,147.00      $0       $50          $0       $697.00
JOHN PART-TIMER     456 21 3456    03      $382.00     $25       $25          $0       $432.00
PEGGY JONES         456 45 6456    15    $1,912.00     $25       $50          $0     $1,987.00
H. HEAVY-WORKER     789 52 1234    18    $2,295.00      $0       $50          $0     $2,345.00
BENJAMIN LEE        876 87 6876    18    $2,295.00      $0       $50          $0     $2,345.00
JACKIE CLARK        264 80 5298    06      $765.00      $0       $25          $0       $790.00
SHEILA GROSSMAN     223 34 4366    07      $892.00      $0       $50          $0       $942.00
LYNN FRANKEL        889 99 9000    10    $1,275.00      $0       $50          $0     $1,325.00
CATHY BENWAY        245 11 8095    03      $382.00      $0       $25         $50       $157.00
NELSON KERBEL       072 35 9123    04      $510.00      $0       $25          $0       $535.00
NELSON KERBEL       072 35 9123    04      $510.00      $0       $25          $0       $535.00

      UNIVERSITY TOTALS                 $16,189.00      $0      $525      $1,250       $535.00
```

Last student appears twice.
Union fee was not summed.
Total is incorrect.

FIGURE 6.6a Invalid Output for Tuition Billing Program

```
STUDENT NAME        SOC SEC NUM  CREDITS   TUITION  UNION FEE  ACT FEE  SCHOLARSHIP  TOTAL BILL
JOHN SMITH          123 45 6789    15    $1,912.50     $25       $75          $0     $2,012.50
HENRY JAMES         987 65 4321    15    $1,912.50      $0       $75        $500     $1,487.50
SUSAN BAKER         111 22 3333    09    $1,147.50      $0       $50        $500       $697.50
JOHN PART-TIMER     456 21 3456    03      $382.50     $25       $25          $0       $432.50
PEGGY JONES         456 45 6456    15    $1,912.50     $25       $75          $0     $2,012.50
H. HEAVY-WORKER     789 52 1234    18    $2,295.00      $0       $75          $0     $2,370.00
BENJAMIN LEE        876 87 6876    18    $2,295.00      $0       $75          $0     $2,370.00
JACKIE CLARK        264 80 5298    06      $765.00      $0       $25          $0       $790.00
SHEILA GROSSMAN     223 34 4366    07      $892.50      $0       $50          $0       $942.50
LYNN FRANKEL        889 99 9000    10    $1,275.00      $0       $50          $0     $1,325.00
CATHY BENWAY        245 11 8095    03      $382.50      $0       $25        $250       $157.50
NELSON KERBEL       072 35 9123    04      $510.00      $0       $25          $0       $535.00

      UNIVERSITY TOTALS                 $15,682.50     $75      $625      $1,250    $15,132.50
```

FIGURE 6.6b Valid Output for Tuition Billing Program (Reproduced from Chapter 5)

The theory is simple: A programmer is too close to his or her work to see potential problems adequately and evaluate them objectively. The purpose of the walkthrough therefore is to ensure that all specifications are met, and that the logic and its COBOL implementation are correct.

The earlier an error is found, the easier it is to correct. Thus the single most important objective of a walkthrough is *early error detection.* Walkthroughs occur at several stages during a project, beginning in the *analysis* phase, where the purpose is to ensure that the systems analyst has understood the user's requirements. Walkthroughs occur again during the *design* phase, when the programmer has developed a hierarchy chart and/or associated pseudocode. Finally, walkthroughs occur during the *implementation* phase, during which the programmer presents actual code prior to testing.

Walkthroughs are scheduled by the person being reviewed, who also selects the reviewers. The reviewee distributes copies of the work (e.g., a hierarchy chart, pseudocode, or a COBOL program) prior to the session. Reviewers are supposed to study the material in advance so that they can discuss it intelligently. At the walkthrough itself, the reviewee presents the material objectively, concisely, and dispassionately. He or she should encourage discussion and be genuinely glad when (not if) errors are discovered.

One of the reviewers should function as a *moderator* to keep the discussion on track. Another should act as a *secretary* and maintain an *action list* of problems uncovered during the session. At the end of the walkthrough the action list is given to the reviewee, who in turn is expected to correct the errors and notify attendees accordingly. The objective of the walkthrough itself is to find errors, not to correct them. The latter is accomplished by the reviewee upon receipt of the action list.

The preceding discussion may read well in theory, but programmers often dislike the walkthrough concept. The probable reason is that they dislike having their work reviewed and regard criticism of code, intended or otherwise, as a personal affront. This attitude is natural and stems from years of working as individuals.

In addition, walkthroughs can and have become unpleasant and ego-deflating experiences. "Structured walkover" and "stompthrough" are terms that have been applied to less-than-successful sessions. Only if the atmosphere is kept open and nondefensive, only if the discussion is restricted to major problems rather than trivial errors, and only if personality clashes are avoided can the walkthrough be an effective technique. To have any chance of success, programmers who function as both reviewer and reviewee must adhere to the following guidelines:

1. *The program and not the programmer is reviewed.* Structured walkthroughs are intended to find programming problems; they will not be used by management as an evaluation tool. No one should keep count of how many errors are found in an individual's work or how many errors one finds in someone else's. It is quite logical, therefore, to *exclude* the project manager, i.e., the individual in charge of salaries and promotions, from review sessions.
2. *Emphasis is on error detection, not correction.* It is assumed that the individual being reviewed will take the necessary corrective action. Reviewers should not harp on errors by discussing how to correct them; indeed, *no* corrections whatever are made during a walkthrough.
3. *Everyone, from senior analyst to trainee, has his or her work reviewed.* This avoids singling out an individual and further removes any stigma from having one's work reviewed. It also promotes the give-and-take atmosphere that is so vital to making the concept work.
4. *A list of well-defined objectives for each session should be specified in advance.* Adherence to this guideline keeps the discussion on track and helps to guarantee productive discussions. A subsidiary guideline is to impose a predetermined time

limit, from half an hour to two hours. Walkthroughs will eventually cease to be productive and degenerate into a discussion of last night's ball game, the new manager, the latest rumor, or some other "hot" topic. The situation should be anticipated and avoided, perhap by scheduling walkthroughs an hour before lunch. If all of the walkthrough's objectives have not been met when the deadline is reached, schedule a second session.

5. *Participation must be encouraged and demanded from the reviewers.* A walkthrough will indeed become a waste of time if no one has anything to say. Let it be known that each reviewer will be expected to make at least two comments, one positive and one negative. Alternatively, require each reviewer to come to the session with a list of at least three questions.

Summary

This chapter focused on debugging, which remains a fact of life. Don't be discouraged if you have many compilation errors in your first few attempts, and don't be surprised if you have several pages of diagnostics. Remember that a single error in a COBOL program can result in many error messages and that the errors often can be made to disappear in bunches. (Recall the misspelling of ENVIRONMENT in Figure 6.3.)

Before leaving the subject of compilation errors, it is worthwhile to review a list of common errors and suggested ways to avoid them:

1. Nonunique data names. *Occurs because the same data name is defined in two different records or twice within the same record. For example, CREDITS might be specified as an input field in STUDENT-FILE and again as output in a detail line. To avoid the problem of nonunique data names, it is best to* prefix *every data name within a record by a unique prefix, as was suggested in Chapter 5. For example:*

```
01  STUDENT-RECORD.
    05  STU-NAME              PIC X(20).
    05  STU-SOC-SEC-NO        PIC 9(9).
    05  STU-CREDITS           PIC 9(2).
    05  STU-UNION-MEMBER      PIC X.
    05  STU-SCHOLARSHIP       PIC 9(4).
    05  FILLER                PIC X(44).
```

2. Omitted (or extra) periods. *Every COBOL sentence should have a period. Omission in the first three divisions often results in the compiler's assumption of a period where one belongs, and such errors are generally harmless.*

   The effect is far more serious in the Procedure Division, where missing and/or extra periods affect the generated logic. The IF statement, for example, is terminated by a period, and haphazard placement of periods will play havoc with the program's logic.

3. Omitted space before or after an arithmetic operator. *The arithmetic operators **, *, /, +, and − all require a blank before and after (a typical error for FORTRAN or PL/I programmers, since the space is not required in those languages).*

4. Invalid picture for numeric entry. *All data names used in arithmetic statements must have numeric pictures consisting of 9's and an optional sign or implied decimal point.*

5. Conflicting picture and value clause. *Numeric pictures must have numeric values (no quotes); nonnumeric data pictures must have nonnumeric values (must be enclosed in quotes). Both entries below are* invalid:

```
05  TOTAL          PIC 9(3)     VALUE '123'.
05  TITLE-WORD     PIC X(3)     VALUE 123.
```

6. Inadvertent use of COBOL reserved words. *COBOL has a list of some 300 reserved words that can only be used in their designated sense; any other use results in one or several diagnostics. Some reserved words are obvious, e.g., WORKING-STORAGE, IDENTIFICATION, ENVIRONMENT, DATA, and PROCEDURE. Others, such as CODE, DATE, START, and REPORT, are less obvious. Instead of memorizing the list or continually referring to it, we suggest this simple rule of thumb. Always use a hyphen in every data name you create. This will work more than 99% of the time.*
7. Conflicting RECORD CONTAINS clause and FD record description. *A recurrent error, even for established programmers. It stems from sometimes careless addition in that the sum of the pictures in an FD does not equal the number of characters in the RECORD CONTAINS clause. It can also result from other errors within the Data Division, e.g., when an entry containing a PICTURE clause is flagged. If an E-level diagnostic is present, that entry will be ignored, and the count is thrown off. This is often one of the last errors to disappear before a clean compile.*
8. Receiving field too small to accommodate sending field. *An extremely common error, often associated with edited pictures. Consider the entries*

```
05  PRINT-TOTAL-PAY    PIC $$,$$$.
 .
  .
   .
05  WS-TOTAL-PAY    PIC 9(5).
 .
  .
   .
MOVE WS-TOTAL-PAY TO PRINT-TOTAL-PAY.
```

The MOVE statement would generate the warning that the receiving field may be too small to accommodate the sending field. The greatest possible value for WS-TOTAL-PAY is 99,999; the largest possible value that could be printed by PRINT-TOTAL-PAY is $9,999. Even though the print field contains five $'s, one $ must always be printed and hence the warning.

9. Omitted (or extra) hyphens in a data name. *A careless error, but one that occurs too often. If in the Data Division we define PRINT-TOTAL-PAY and then reference PRINT TOTAL-PAY, the compiler objects violently. It doesn't state that a hyphen was omitted, but it flags both PRINT and TOTAL-PAY as undefined.*

   A related error is the insertion of extra *hyphens where they don't belong, e.g., WORKING-STORAGE-SECTION, or DATA-DIVISION.*
10. Misspelled data names or reserved words. *Too many COBOL students are poor spellers. Sound strange? How do you spell "environment"? One or many errors can result, depending on which word was spelled incorrectly.*
11. Reading a record name or writing a file name. *The COBOL rule is very simple. One is supposed to read a file and write a record; many people get it confused. Consider*

```
FD  STUDENT-FILE
     .
      .
       .
    DATA RECORD IS STUDENT-RECORD.
     .
      .
       .
FD  PRINT-FILE
     .
      .
       .
    DATA RECORD IS PRINT-RECORD.
```

Correct entries:

```
READ  STUDENT-FILE,.....
WRITE PRINT-RECORD....
```

Incorrect entries:

```
READ  STUDENT-RECORD....
WRITE PRINT-FILE...
```

12. Going past column 72. *This error can cause any of the preceding errors as well as a host of others. A COBOL statement must end in column 72 or before; columns 73–80 are left blank or used for program identification. If one goes past column 72 in a COBOL statement, it is very difficult to catch because the COBOL listing contains columns 1–80 although the compiler interprets only columns 1–72. (The 72-column restriction does not apply to data.)*

True/False Exercises

1. If a program compiles with no diagnostics, it must execute correctly.
2. If a program compiles with warning diagnostics, execution will be suppressed.
3. If a program contains logical errors but *not* syntactical errors, the compiler will print appropriate warnings.
4. A COBOL program is considered data by the COBOL compiler.
5. An error in one COBOL statement can cause errors in several other, apparently correct, statements.
6. There are four distinct levels of IBM compiler diagnostics.
7. A C-level diagnostic is more severe than a W-level diagnostic.
8. Paragraph names begin in the A margin.
9. Spaces are required before and after arithmetic symbols.
10. Spaces are required before and after punctuation symbols.
11. A data name that appears in a COMPUTE statement can be defined with a picture of Xs.
12. Data names may contain blanks.
13. The contents of columns 73–80 are ignored by the compiler.
14. In a COBOL program one reads a record name and writes a file name.
15. The emphasis in a structured walkthrough is on error detection rather than error correction.
16. Walkthroughs should be held for trainees only, as these are the individuals most likely to make mistakes.
17. Managers typically do *not* attend walkthroughs.
18. A walkthrough generally takes a minimum of two hours.
19. Walkthroughs should be restricted to the coding phase of a project.

Problems

1. Has your work ever been the subject of a structured walkthrough? Was the experience helpful or a waste of time, or worse? Are you looking forward to your next walkthrough?

2. Do you agree with banning managers from walkthroughs? Is it possible that the role of moderator in a walkthrough might best be filled by the project manager?

3. Do you agree with the author's suggestions for successful walkthroughs? Are there any guidelines you wish to add to the list? To remove from the list?

4. A COBOL program is required to compute a company payroll. Incoming data are in the following format:

COLUMNS	*FIELD*	*PICTURE*
1–25	EMP-NAME	X(25)
26–30	EMP-HOURS	9(3)V99
31–35	EMP-RATE	9(3)V99

An individual receives straight time for the first 40 hours worked, time and a half for the next 8 hours, and double time for each hour over 48. For example, an employee earning $7.00 per hour and working 49 hours would receive

Straight time	40 hours @ $7.00	$280
Time and a half	8 hours @ $10.50	84
Double time	1 hour @ $14.00	14
	Gross pay	$378

Federal income taxes are computed according to the following schedule:

GROSS PAY	*TAX*
$240 or less	16% of gross
More than $240, but less than $300	$38.40 + 20% of amount over $240
$300 or more	$50.40 + 22% of amount over $300

Thus individuals with gross wages of $200, $276, and $378 would pay $32.00, $45.60, and $67.56, respectively.

The completed program is to process a file of employee records and, for each employee, compute and print gross pay, federal tax, and net pay. Company totals are also required for these fields, as is a suitable heading line.

Figure 6.7 contains the first attempt at a COBOL program to solve the payroll program. Correct all compilation errors. Figure 6.8 contains the compilation errors themselves.

```
       IDENTIFICATION DIVISION.
       PROGRAM-ID.    PAYROLL.
       AUTHOR.        JACKIE CLARK.

       ENVIRONMENT DIVISION.
       CONFIGURATION SECTION.
       SOURCE-COMPUTER.   IBM-4341.
       OBJECT-COMPUTER.   IBM-4341.
       INPUT-OUTPUT SECTION.
       FILE-CONTROL.
           SELECT EMP-FILE ASSIGN TO UT-S-SYSIN.
           SELECT PRINT-FILE ASSIGN TO UT-S-SYSOUT.

       DATA DIVISION.
       FILE SECTION.
       FD  EMP-FILE
```

FIGURE 6.7 ***Payroll Problem with Compilation Errors***

FIGURE 6.7 (Continued)

```
    LABEL RECORDS ARE OMITTED
    RECORD CONTAINS 80 CHARACTERS
    DATA RECORD IS EMP-RECORD.
01  EMP-RECORD.
    05  EMP-NAME                 PIC X(25).
    05  EMP-HOURS                PIC 9(3)V99.
    05  EMP-RATE                 PIC 9(3)V99.
    05  FILLER                   PIC X(44).

FD  PRINT-FILE
    LABEL RECORDS ARE OMITTED
    RECORD CONTAINS 133 CHARACTERS
    DATA RECORD IS PRINT-LINE.
01  PRINT-LINE                   PIC X(132).

WORKING-STORAGE SECTION.
01  DATA-REMAINS-SWITCH          PIC X(03)  VALUE 'YES'.

01  INDIVIDUAL-COMPUTATIONS.
    05  IND-GROSS-PAY            PIC 9(4)V99.
    05  IND-FED-TAX              PIC 9(4)V99.
    05  IND-NET-PAY              PIC 9(4)V99.

01  COMPANY-TOTALS.
    05  COMP-GROSS-PAY           PIC 9(5)V99 VALUE ZEROS.
    05  COMP-FED-TAX             PIC 9(5)V99 VALUE ZEROS.
    05  COMP-NET-PAY             PIC 9(5)V99 VALUE ZEROS.

01  HEADING-LINE.
    05  FILLER                   PIC X(7)   VALUE SPACES.
    05  FILLER                   PIC X(4)   VALUE 'NAME'.
    05  FILLER                   PIC X(19)  VALUE SPACES.
    05  FILLER                   PIC X(5)   VALUE 'HOURS'.
    05  FILLER                   PIC X(5)   VALUE SPACES.
    05  FILLER                   PIC X(4)   VALUE 'RATE'.
    05  FILLER                   PIC X(6)   VALUE SPACES.
    05  FILLER                   PIC X(9)   VALUE 'GROSS PAY'.
    05  FILLER                   PIC X(5)   VALUE SPACES.
    05  FILLER                   PIC X(7)   VALUE 'FED TAX'.
    05  FILLER                   PIC X(5)   VALUE SPACES.
    05  FILLER                   PIC X(7)   VALUE 'NET PAY'.
    05  FILLER                   PIC X(51)  VALUE SPACES.

01  DETAIL-LINE.
    05  DET-NAME                 PIC X(25).
    05  FILLER                   PIC X(03)  VALUE SPACES.
    05  DET-HOURS                PIC ZZZZV99.
    05  FILLER                   PIC X(03)  VALUE SPACES.
    05  DET-RATE                 PIC $$$$.99.
    05  FILLER                   PIC X(03)  VALUE SPACES.
    05  DET-GROSS                PIC $$$$$.99
    05  FILLER                   PIC X(05)  VALUE SPACES.
    05  DET-FED-TAX              PIC $$$$$.99.
    05  FILLER                   PIC X(04)  VALUE SPACES.
    05  DET-NET                  PIC $$$$$.99.
    05  FILLER                   PIC X(51)  VALUE SPACES.

01  TOTAL-LINE.
    05  FILLER                   PIC X(33)  VALUE SPACES.
    05  FILLER                   PIC X(13)  VALUE 'TOTAL'.
    05  TOT-GROSS                PIC $$$,$$$.99.
    05  FILLER                   PIC X(03)  VALUE SPACES.
    05  TOT-FED-TAX              PIC $$$,$$$.99.
    05  FILLER                   PIC X(03)  VALUE SPACES.
    05  TOT-NET                  PIC $$$,$$$.99.
    05  FILLER                   PIC X(49)  VALUE SPACES.

PROCEDURE DIVISION.
MAINLINE.
    OPEN INPUT  EMP-FILE
         OUTPUT PRINT-FILE.
    PERFORM WRITE-HEADING-LINE.
    READ EMP-FILE
        AT END MOVE 'NO' TO DATA-REMAINS-SWITCH.
    PERFORM PROCESS-RECORD
        UNTIL DATA-REMAINS-SWITCH = 'NO'.
    PERFORM WRITE-TOTAL-LINE.
    CLOSE EMP-FILE
          PRINT-FILE.
    STOP RUN.
```

```
00097
00098          WRITE-HEADING-LINE.
00099              MOVE HEADNG-LINE TO PRINT-LINE.
00100              WRITE PRINT-LINE AFTER ADVANCING PAGE.
00101
00102          PROCESS-A-RECORD.
00103              PERFORM COMPUTE-IND-GROSS-PAY.
00104              PERFORM INCREMENT-COMPANY-TOTALS.
00105              PERFORM WRITE-DETAIL-LINE.
00106
00107              READ EMP-RECORD
00108                  AT END MOVE 'NO' TO DATA-REMAINS-SWITCH.
00109
00110          COMPUTE-IND-GROSS-PAY.
00111              COMPUTE IND-GROSS-PAY = EMP-HOURS * EMP-RATE.
00112              IF EMP-HOURS>40
00113                  COMPUTE IND-GROSS-PAY =
00114                      IND-GROSS-PAY + (EMP-HOURS - 40) * .5 * EMP-RATE.
00115              IF EMP-HOURS > 48
00116                  COMPUTE IND-GROSS-PAY =
00117                      IND-GROSS-PAY + (EMP-HOURS - 48) * .5 * EMP-RATE.
00118
00119              COMPUTE IND-FED-TAX = .16 * IND-GROSS-PAY.
00120              IF IND-GROSS-PAY > 240
00121                  COMPUTE IND-FED-TAX =
00122                      38.40 + .04 * (IND-GROSS-PAY - 240).
00123              IF IND-GROSS-PAY > 300
00124                  COMPUTE IND-FED-TAX =
00125                      50.40 + .02 * (IND-GROSS-PAY - 300).
00126              SUBTRACT IND-FED-TAX FROM IND-GROSS-PAY
00127                  GIVING IND-NET-PAY.
00128
00129          INCREMENT-COMPANY-TOTALS.
00130              ADD IND-GROSS-PAY TO COMP-GROSS-PAY.
00131              ADD IND-FED-TAX TO COMP-FED-TAX.
00132              ADD IND-NET-PAY TO COMP-NET-PAY.
00133
00134          WRITE-DETAIL-LINE.
00135              MOVE EMP-NAME  TO DET-NAME.
00136              MOVE EMP-HOURS TO DET-HOURS.
00137              MOVE EMP-RATE  TO DET-RATE.
00138              MOVE IND-GROSS-PAY TO DET-GROSS.
00139              MOVE IND-FED-TAX TO DET-FED-TAX.
00140              MOVE IND-NET-PAY TO DET-NET-PAY.
00141              MOVE DETAIL-LINE TO PRINT-LINE.
00142              WRITE PRINT-LINE
00143                  ADVANCING 2 LINES.
00144
00145          WRITE-TOTAL-LINE.
00146              MOVE COMP-GROSS-PAY TO TOT-GROSS.
00147              MOVE COMP-FED-TAX TO TOT-FED-TAX.
00148              MOVE COMP-NET-PAY TO TOT-NET.
00149              MOVE TOTAL-LINE TO PRINT-LINE.
00150              WRITE PRINT-FILE
00151                  AFTER ADVANCING 2 LINES.
```

FIGURE 6.7 (Continued)

```
CARD

11      RECORD SIZE IN RECORD-CONTAINS CLAUSE DISAGREES WITH COMPUTED RECORD SIZE. 00079
        ASSUMED.
12      RECORD SIZE IN RECORD-CONTAINS CLAUSE DISAGREES WITH COMPUTED RECORD SIZE. 00132
        ASSUMED.
68      END OF SENTENCE SHOULD PRECEDE 05 . ASSUMED PRESENT.
91      PROCESS-RECORD NOT DEFINED. STATEMENT DISCARDED.
99      HEADNG-LINE NOT DEFINED. DISCARDED.
107     SYNTAX REQUIRES FILE-NAME .
112     GREATER NOT PRECEDED BY A SPACE. ASSUME SPACE.
112     40 NOT PRECEDED BY A SPACE. ASSUME SPACE.
140     DET-NET-PAY NOT DEFINED. DISCARDED.
142     EXPECTING NEW STATEMENT. FOUND ADVANCING .
150     SYNTAX REQUIRES RECORD-NAME . FOUND DNM=1-312 . STATEMENT DISCARDED.
```

FIGURE 6.8 Compilation Errors for Payroll Program

5. A corrected listing for the payroll program is shown in Figure 6.9. It compiled cleanly but produced execution errors resulting in an incorrect report. Figure 6.10 contains the desired report followed by the erroneous report that was actually produced. Find and correct all logical errors.

```
       IDENTIFICATION DIVISION.
       PROGRAM-ID.    PAYROLL.
       AUTHOR.        JACKIE CLARK.
       ENVIRONMENT DIVISION.
       CONFIGURATION SECTION.
       SOURCE-COMPUTER.  IBM-4341.
       OBJECT-COMPUTER.  IBM-4341.
       INPUT-OUTPUT SECTION.
       FILE-CONTROL.
           SELECT EMP-FILE ASSIGN TO UT-S-SYSIN.
           SELECT PRINT-FILE ASSIGN TO UT-S-SYSOUT.
       DATA DIVISION.
       FILE SECTION.
       FD  EMP-FILE
           LABEL RECORDS ARE OMITTED
           RECORD CONTAINS 80 CHARACTERS
           DATA RECORD IS EMP-RECORD.
       01  EMP-RECORD.
           05  EMP-NAME                PIC X(25).
           05  EMP-HOURS               PIC 9(3)V99.
           05  EMP-RATE                PIC 9(3)V99.
           05  FILLER                  PIC X(45).
       FD  PRINT-FILE
           LABEL RECORDS ARE OMITTED
           RECORD CONTAINS 133 CHARACTERS
           DATA RECORD IS PRINT-LINE.
       01  PRINT-LINE                  PIC X(133).
       WORKING-STORAGE SECTION.
       01  DATA-REMAINS-SWITCH         PIC X(03)  VALUE 'YES'.
       01  INDIVIDUAL-COMPUTATIONS.
           05  IND-GROSS-PAY           PIC 9(4).
           05  IND-FED-TAX             PIC 9(4).
           05  IND-NET-PAY             PIC 9(4).
       01  COMPANY-TOTALS.
           05  COMP-GROSS-PAY          PIC 9(5)V99 VALUE ZEROS.
           05  COMP-FED-TAX            PIC 9(5)V99 VALUE ZEROS.
           05  COMP-NET-PAY            PIC 9(5)V99 VALUE ZEROS.
       01  HEADING-LINE.
           05  FILLER                  PIC X(7)   VALUE SPACES.
           05  FILLER                  PIC X(4)   VALUE 'NAME'.
           05  FILLER                  PIC X(19)  VALUE SPACES.
           05  FILLER                  PIC X(5)   VALUE 'HOURS'.
           05  FILLER                  PIC X(5)   VALUE SPACES.
           05  FILLER                  PIC X(4)   VALUE 'RATE'.
           05  FILLER                  PIC X(6)   VALUE SPACES.
           05  FILLER                  PIC X(9)   VALUE 'GROSS PAY'.
           05  FILLER                  PIC X(5)   VALUE SPACES.
           05  FILLER                  PIC X(7)   VALUE 'FED TAX'.
           05  FILLER                  PIC X(5)   VALUE SPACES.
           05  FILLER                  PIC X(7)   VALUE 'NET PAY'.
           05  FILLER                  PIC X(51)  VALUE SPACES.
       01  DETAIL-LINE.
           05  DET-NAME                PIC X(25).
           05  FILLER                  PIC X(03)  VALUE SPACES.
           05  DET-HOURS               PIC ZZZZ.99.
           05  FILLER                  PIC X(03)  VALUE SPACES.
           05  DET-RATE                PIC $$$$.99.
           05  FILLER                  PIC X(03)  VALUE SPACES.
           05  DET-GROSS               PIC $$$$$.99.
           05  FILLER                  PIC X(05)  VALUE SPACES.
           05  DET-FED-TAX             PIC $$$$$.99.
           05  FILLER                  PIC X(04)  VALUE SPACES.
```

FIGURE 6.9 Payroll Program with Logic Errors

FIGURE 6.9 *(Continued)*

```
           05  DET-NET               PIC $$$$$.99.
           05  FILLER                PIC X(51)   VALUE SPACES.

       01  TOTAL-LINE.
           05  FILLER                PIC X(33)   VALUE SPACES.
           05  FILLER                PIC X(13)   VALUE 'TOTAL'.
           05  TOT-GROSS             PIC $$$,$$$.99.
           05  FILLER                PIC X(03)   VALUE SPACES.
           05  TOT-FED-TAX           PIC $$$,$$$.99.
           05  FILLER                PIC X(03)   VALUE SPACES.
           05  TOT-NET               PIC $$$,$$$.99.
           05  FILLER                PIC X(49)   VALUE SPACES.

       PROCEDURE DIVISION.
       MAINLINE.
           OPEN INPUT  EMP-FILE
                OUTPUT PRINT-FILE.
           PERFORM WRITE-HEADING-LINE.
           READ EMP-FILE
               AT END MOVE 'NO' TO DATA-REMAINS-SWITCH.
           PERFORM PROCESS-A-RECORD
               UNTIL DATA-REMAINS-SWITCH = 'NO'.
           PERFORM WRITE-TOTAL-LINE.
           CLOSE EMP-FILE
                 PRINT-FILE.
           STOP RUN.

       WRITE-HEADING-LINE.
           MOVE HEADING-LINE TO PRINT-LINE
           WRITE PRINT-LINE AFTER ADVANCING PAGE.

       PROCESS-A-RECORD.
           PERFORM COMPUTE-IND-GROSS-PAY.
           PERFORM INCREMENT-COMPANY-TOTALS.
           PERFORM WRITE-DETAIL-LINE.

           READ EMP-FILE
               AT END MOVE 'NO' TO DATA-REMAINS-SWITCH.

       COMPUTE-IND-GROSS-PAY.
           COMPUTE IND-GROSS-PAY = EMP-HOURS * EMP-RATE.
           IF EMP-HOURS > 40
               COMPUTE IND-GROSS-PAY =
                   IND-GROSS-PAY + (EMP-HOURS - 40) * 1.5 * EMP-RATE.
           IF EMP-HOURS > 48
               COMPUTE IND-GROSS-PAY =
                   IND-GROSS-PAY + (EMP-HOURS - 48) * 2.0 * EMP-RATE.

           COMPUTE IND-FED-TAX = .16 * IND-GROSS-PAY.
           IF IND-GROSS-PAY > 240
               COMPUTE IND-FED-TAX =
                   38.40 + .20 * (IND-GROSS-PAY - 240).
           IF IND-GROSS-PAY > 300
               COMPUTE IND-FED-TAX =
                   50.40 + .22 * (IND-GROSS-PAY - 300).
           SUBTRACT IND-FED-TAX FROM IND-GROSS-PAY
               GIVING IND-NET-PAY.

       INCREMENT-COMPANY-TOTALS.
           ADD IND-GROSS-PAY COMP-GROSS-PAY GIVING COMP-GROSS-PAY.
           ADD IND-NET-PAY TO COMP-NET-PAY.

       WRITE-DETAIL-LINE.
           MOVE EMP-NAME  TO DET-NAME.
           MOVE EMP-RATE  TO DET-RATE.
           MOVE IND-GROSS-PAY TO DET-GROSS.
           MOVE IND-FED-TAX TO DET-FED-TAX.
           MOVE COMP-NET-PAY TO DET-NET.
           MOVE DETAIL-LINE TO PRINT-LINE.
           WRITE PRINT-LINE
               AFTER ADVANCING 2 LINES.

       WRITE-TOTAL-LINE.
           MOVE IND-GROSS-PAY TO  TOT-GROSS.
           MOVE COMP-FED-TAX TO TOT-FED-TAX.
           MOVE COMP-NET-PAY TO TOT-NET.
           MOVE TOTAL-LINE TO PRINT-LINE.
           WRITE PRINT-LINE
               AFTER ADVANCING 2 LINES.
```

NAME	HOURS	RATE	GROSS PAY	FED TAX	NET PAY
SMITH	40.00	$5.00	$200.00	$32.00	$168.00
JONES	44.00	$6.00	$276.00	$39.84	$236.16
PETERS	49.00	$7.00	$378.00	$51.96	$326.04
HANSEN	36.00	$5.55	$199.80	$31.96	$167.84
MILGROM	42.00	$10.14	$436.02	$53.12	$382.90
TATAR	40.00	$4.33	$173.20	$27.71	$145.49
	TOTAL		$1,663.02	$236.59	$1,426.43

FIGURE 6.10a *Desired Payroll Report*

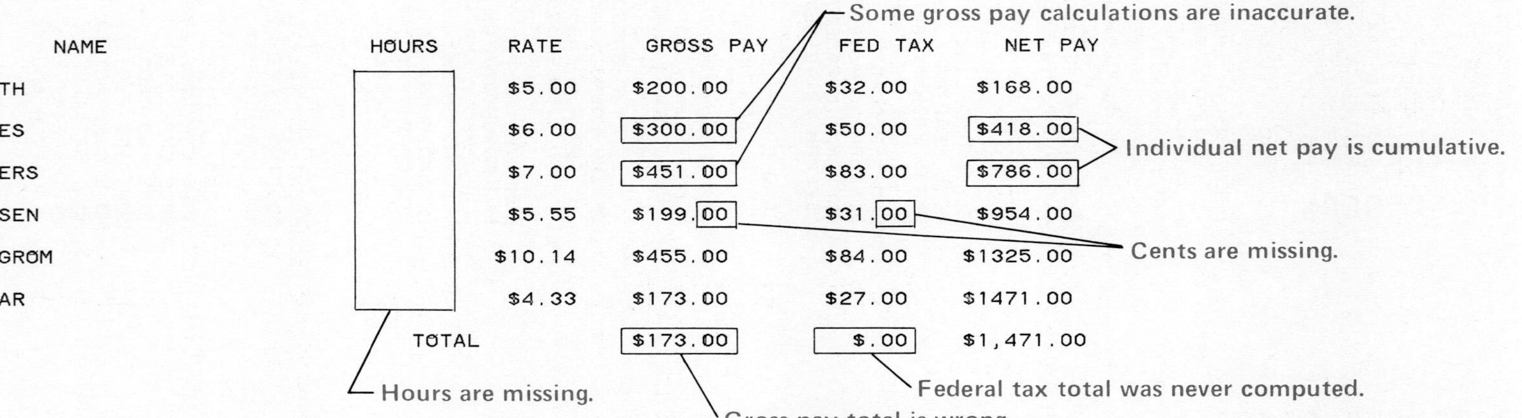

NAME	HOURS	RATE	GROSS PAY	FED TAX	NET PAY
SMITH		$5.00	$200.00	$32.00	$168.00
JONES		$6.00	$300.00	$50.00	$418.00
PETERS		$7.00	$451.00	$83.00	$786.00
HANSEN		$5.55	$199.00	$31.00	$954.00
MILGROM		$10.14	$455.00	$84.00	$1325.00
TATAR		$4.33	$173.00	$27.00	$1471.00
	TOTAL		$173.00	$.00	$1,471.00

Some gross pay calculations are inaccurate.
Individual net pay is cumulative.
Cents are missing.
Hours are missing.
Federal tax total was never computed.
Gross pay total is wrong.

FIGURE 6.10b *Erroneous Payroll Report*

Structured Programming and Design

7

Overview

This chapter formally defines structured programming *and* structured design. *These techniques are of special import to the practitioner who must produce programs that are easily read and maintained by someone other than the original author.*

We open with a pragmatic definition of structured programming, one that can be readily understood and applied by student and practitioner alike: The elementary building blocks of sequence, selection, *and* iteration *are introduced and shown to be sufficient to express any logic. The discussion is extended to include the* case construct *for a multibranch situation. An alternate form of the iteration structure (DO UNTIL in addition to DO WHILE) is also presented. Several documentation techniques are covered, with contrasts drawn between the traditional flowchart, and the more recent pseudocode and Nassi–Schneiderman charts.*

The chapter continues with a formal discussion of structured design. We cover the hierarchy chart and Yourdon stucture chart and touch on the concepts of coupling and cohesion. □

DEFINITION

The logic of any program can be developed entirely in terms of three types of logic structures: *sequence, selection,* and *iteration*. These elementary building blocks are depicted in Figure 7.1 and have one key feature in common, namely, a *single entry point* and a *single exit point*.

A *structured* program is one consisting entirely of these elementary building blocks. The fact that these structures are sufficient to express any desired logic was first postulated in a now-classic paper by Bohm and Jacopini.[1]

[1]Bohm and Jacopini, ''Flow Diagrams, Turing Machines and Languages with Only Two Formation Rules,'' *Communications of the ACM* (May 1966).

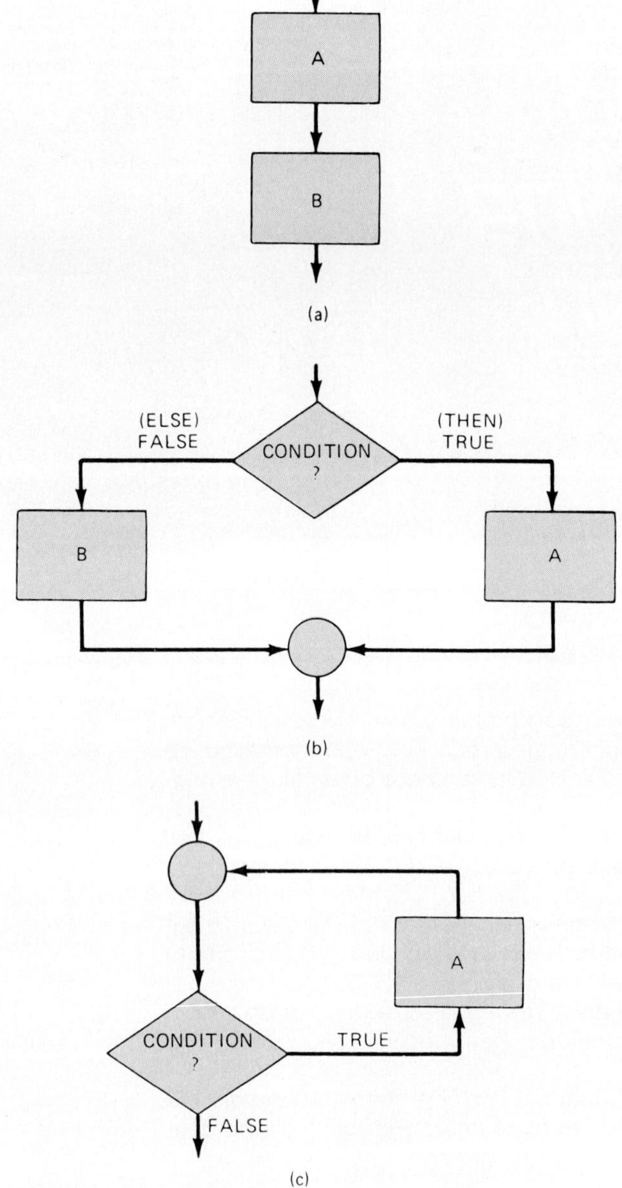

FIGURE 7.1 The Building Blocks of Structured Programming

The *sequence structure* shown in Figure 7.1 formally specifies that program statements are executed sequentially, in the order in which they appear. The two blocks, A and B, may denote anything from single statements to complete programs.

Selection (also known as IF THEN ELSE) is the choice between two actions. If the condition is true, block A is executed; if it is false, block B is executed. The condition is a *single entry* point to the structure, and both paths meet in a *single exit* point.

Iteration (also known as DO WHILE) calls for repeated execution of code while a condition is true. The condition is tested. If true, block A is executed; if false, the structure relinquishes control to the next sequential statement. Again, there is exactly *one entry* point and *one exit* point from the structure.

SUFFICIENCY OF THE BASIC STRUCTURES

Although the preceding definition of a structured program may seem somewhat limited, it is sufficient to produce any required logic. This is possible because an entire structure may be substituted anywhere block A or B appears. Figures 7.2 and 7.3 contain combinations of the basic structures.

The entry point to Figure 7.2 is a selection structure to evaluate $condition_1$. If $condition_1$ is true, an iteration structure is entered. If $condition_1$ is false, a sequence structure is executed instead. Both the iteration and sequence structures meet at a single point, which in turn becomes the exit point for the initial selection structure.

In Figure 7.3 the entry point is again a selection structure. If $condition_1$ is true, a second selection structure for $condition_2$ is entered. If this is also true, a third selection structure for $condition_3$ is entered. Note that the alternate paths for each selection structure always meet in a single exit point for that structure. Note also that the entire logic structure of Figure 7.3 has a single entry and a single exit point.

EXTENSION OF THE STRUCTURED THEOREM

Although any program can be developed using only the three basic building blocks of sequence, selection, and iteration, two additional structures are often included. These are the *case* construct for multibranch situations and the *DO UNTIL* construct (as opposed to DO WHILE). We discuss both extensions from a theoretical viewpoint.

The Case Construct

The *case* construct conveniently expresses a multibranch situation and is shown in Figure 7.4. As with the three fundamental structures in Figure 7.1, there is *one entry point and one exit point.*

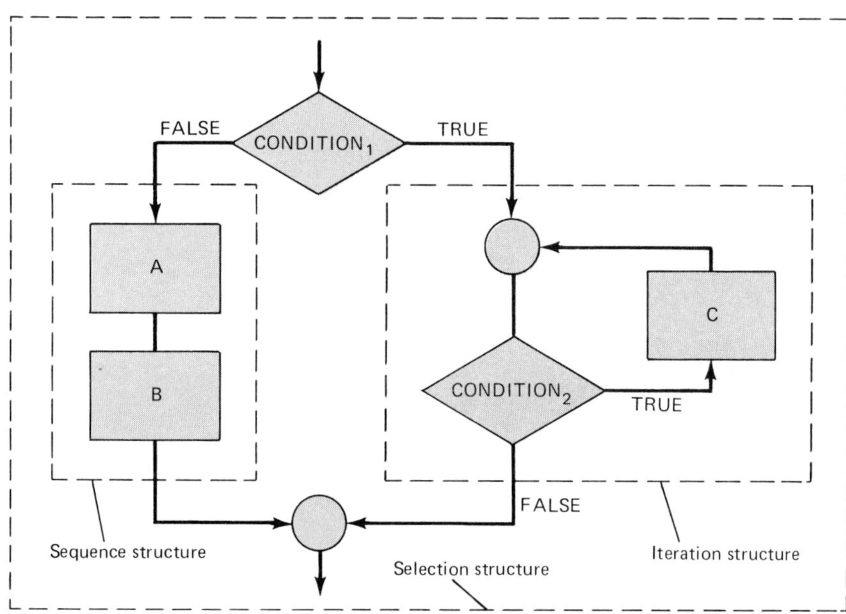

FIGURE 7.2 Combinations of Logic Structures

FALSE
CONDITION$_1$
TRUE
A
B
C
D
Sequence structure
FALSE
CONDITION$_2$
TRUE
E
FALSE
CONDITION$_3$
TRUE
F
G
Selection structure
Selection structure
Selection structure

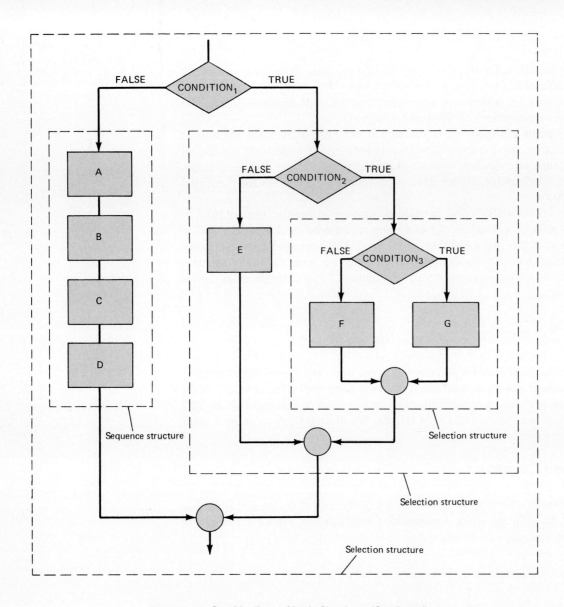

FIGURE 7.3 Combinations of Logic Structures (Continued)

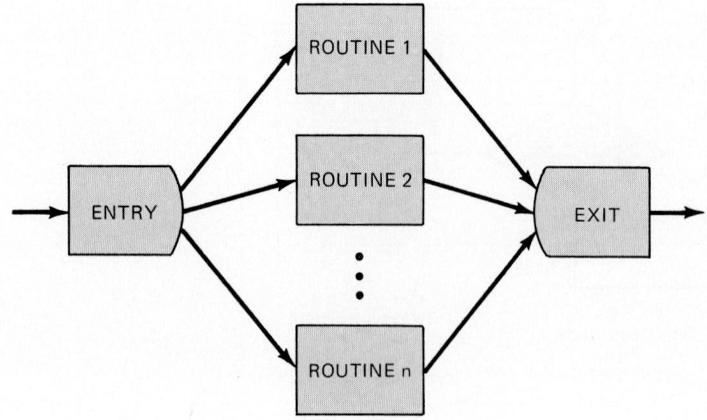

FIGURE 7.4 The Case Structure

At present, COBOL is limited in its ability to implement the case construct. One method is to use the GO TO DEPENDING statement, depicted in Figure 7.5.

The GO TO DEPENDING statement tests the value of a code, in this instance INCOMING-YEAR-CODE. If it is equal to 1, control passes to the first paragraph specified, FRESHMAN. If INCOMING-YEAR-CODE is equal to 2, control passes to the second paragraph, SOPHOMORE, and so on. If the code has any value other than 1, 2, 3, 4, or 5 (since five paragraphs were specified), control passes to the next statement immediately following the GO TO DEPENDING, which should be an error routine. Indentation in the GO TO DEPENDING is strictly for legibility; it is not required by COBOL.

Figure 7.5 contains several *forward* GO TO statements, which branch to a one-statement EXIT paragraph. *The EXIT statement does nothing per se;* it generates no object code but provides a destination for the GO TO statements. (What would be the effect of omitting the GO TO statements in Figure 7.5?)

Although a *forward* GO TO statement can be justified under certain conditions, one must still be extremely prudent in its use. If the GO TO statement is used, it must branch *forward* (i.e., down the page) to an EXIT paragraph, and the branch must occur *within* the range of a performed routine. (A common technique is to PERFORM PARAGRAPH-A THRU PARAGRAPH-A-EXIT, then GO TO PARAGRAPH-A-EXIT.) One may *never* branch out of a performed routine nor branch backward in a program. (The latter implies a loop, and loops are implemented via the iteration, or DO WHILE, construct.)

```
    PERFORM YEAR-IN-COLLEGE THROUGH YEAR-IN-COLLEGE-EXIT.
    .
     .
      .
YEAR-IN-COLLEGE.
    GO TO
        FRESHMAN
        SOPHOMORE
        JUNIOR
        SENIOR
        GRAD-SCHOOL
    DEPENDING ON INCOMING-YEAR-CODE.
    ...process error...
    GO TO YEAR-IN-COLLEGE-EXIT.
FRESHMAN.
    ...process...
    GO TO YEAR-IN-COLLEGE-EXIT.
SOPHOMORE.
    ...process...
    GO TO YEAR-IN-COLLEGE-EXIT.
JUNIOR.
    ...process...
    GO TO YEAR-IN-COLLEGE-EXIT.
SENIOR.
    ...process...
    GO TO YEAR-IN-COLLEGE-EXIT.
GRAD-SCHOOL.
    ...process...
YEAR-IN-COLLEGE-EXIT.
    EXIT.
```

FIGURE 7.5 COBOL Implementation of the Case Structure

DO UNTIL Construct

The DO UNTIL construct is an alternative way of implementing the iteration structure. Figure 7.6*a* depicts the DO WHILE construct and is reproduced from the iteration structure in Figure 7.1*c*. Note well that the condition is tested *prior* to executing block A. Hence if the condition is initially false, block A is never executed.

By contrast, the DO UNTIL structure in Figure 7.6*b* tests the condition *after* executing block A. Accordingly, block A will be executed once even if the condition is initially satisfied. Observe also the semantic differences and the contrasting placement of the True and False exits. The DO WHILE structure in Figure 7.6*a* executes block A repeatedly as long as the condition is true. However, the DO UNTIL construct executes block A only while the condition is false.

The DO WHILE construct is implemented by the PERFORM UNTIL statement as discussed earlier:

```
PERFORM PARAGRAPH-A
    UNTIL CONDITION IS MET.
```

Note that if the condition is satisfied immediately, PARAGRAPH-A is never executed. Hence a single PERFORM UNTIL statement corresponds directly to the logic in Figure 7.6*a*.

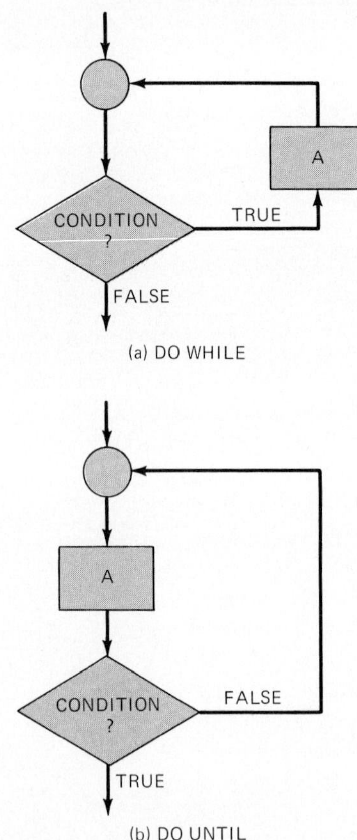

FIGURE 7.6 ***DO WHILE vs. DO UNTIL***

Implementation of DO UNTIL requires *two* PERFORM statements:

```
PERFORM PARAGRAPH-A.
PERFORM PARAGRAPH-A
    UNTIL CONDITION IS MET.
```

If the condition is satisfied initially, the PERFORM UNTIL statement will not cause execution of PARAGRAPH-A; however, PARAGRAPH-A is still executed once by the first PERFORM statement.

THE DEVELOPMENT OF STRUCTURED PROGRAMMING

Today's common acceptance of structured programming belies a rather shaky beginning. The original presentation of the structured theorem occurred at an International Colloquium in 1964, in Israel. The authors, Bohm and Jacopini, presented their work in Italian and were essentially ignored in the United States. The English translation of their paper, published in 1966 in *Communications of the ACM,* did not gain a great deal of attention either, because of its theoretical nature.

It was only after a 1968 letter to the editor,[2] by Edsger W. Dijkstra of the Netherlands, that the American data-processing community began to take notice. In his letter, entitled "GO TO Statement Considered Harmful," Dijkstra wrote that "the quality of programmers is a decreasing function of the density of GO TO statements in the programs they produce." He further suggested that "the GO TO statement should be abolished from all higher level programming languages . . . it is an invitation to make a mess of one's program."

At the time of Dijkstra's letters, most programmers could not even conceive of a program written without GO TO statements, nor did they have any inclination to try. Bohm and Jacopini had proved it theoretically possible, but it remained for two Americans, Harlan Mills and F. Terry Baker, to demonstrate the practical aspects of the then revolutionary technique. At the time Mills was a member of the IBM Corporate Technical Committee, and Baker was manager of the Newspaper System Development Group at IBM. Both became major advocates of structured programming and defined structured programming techniques for use throughout the IBM Federal Systems Division. They were instrumental in the first commercial application of the new methodology at *The New York Times.*

The New York Times project was an on-line information system, designed by IBM to provide access to past articles that had appeared in the newspaper. The project was large (83,000 lines of source code), practical (a real customer paid real money), successful (programmer productivity was 4 to 6 times normal), and relatively "bug free" (4 errors per 10,000 lines of code).[3] Much of the project's success was attributed to the new methodology.

Structured programming projects began to appear with greater frequency in the middle and late 1970s. The development was spurred considerably by the widespread introduction of Edward Yourdon's seminars on the subject; indeed, Yourdon is the individual most responsible for promoting the material in the United States. Today it is safe to say that virtually all practitioners at least acknowledge the merits of the discipline, and most practice it exclusively.

[2]Dijkstra, E. W., "GO TO Statement Considered Harmful," *Communications of the ACM* (March 1968).

[3]Baker, F. T., "Chief Programmer Team Management of Production Programming," *IBM Systems Journal* (January 1972), pp. 56–73.

SURVEY OF DOCUMENTATION TECHNIQUES

We now turn our attention to ways in which programmers express logic, to themselves and to others. We begin with the traditional flowchart and subsequently cover two newer techniques associated with structured programming, pseudocode and Nassi–Schneiderman diagrams.

The Traditional Flowchart

Every programmer is familiar with the traditional flowchart, a pictorial representation of the logic inherent in a computer program. In theory one is supposed to draw a flowchart before writing a program, so that it can be used as a development aid. In practice, the flowchart is often drawn *after* the program has been written, and then only because it is required as part of the documentation. (Proof of this phenomenon lies in the success of program products such as ADR's AUTOFLOW[4], which accept a program as input and produce a flowchart as output!)

To put it as gently as possible, use of the traditional flowchart as the primary means of communicating logic is on the way out and has been for many years (although the author will still, on occasion, flowchart a *small* portion of a complex program, perhaps 8 to 10 blocks). On the whole, however, flowcharts have given way to newer techniques, which are explained in a subsequent section.

Flowcharts have come into disfavor for many reasons. They are time consuming to draw and often stretch over several pages. They are difficult to follow and maintain. Of greater import is their natural affinity for expressing unconditional branches (i.e., GO TOs), which are anathema to current programming practice. Even when flowcharts are restricted to the three basic logic structures, the results are often awkward and not very helpful. For whatever the reason, many programmers and/or students avoid flowcharts unless compelled by a manager (or instructor) to submit a flowchart with the completed program.

However, individuals do, willingly and often, write notes to themselves prior to coding a program. A new technique, *pseudocode,* can be regarded as "*neat* notes to oneself," and since programmers tend to do this anyway, the technique is gaining favor.

Pseudocode

Pseudocode, also known as structured English or Program Development Language (PDL), uses statements similar to computer instructions to describe logic. Pseudocode is not bound by formal syntactical rules as is a programming language. Nor is it bound by rules of indentation, which are strictly at the discretion of the user.

The only real limitation is a restriction to the elementary logic structures of sequence, selection, and iteration, causing pseudocode to flow easily from the top down. Pseudocode has a very distinct block structure, which arises naturally and is extremely conducive to structured programming. An example of pseudocode to merge two sequential files is shown in Figure 7.7. (The specifications require the merged record to contain fields from records in both files and an appropriate error message to appear if matching records are not present.)

[4]AUTOFLOW is a trademark of Applied Data Research, a leading software house, and has sold several thousand copies.

```
OPEN files
Initial reads for FILE-1 and FILE-2
┌DO WHILE data remains on either file
│   ┌IF FILE-1 < FILE-2
│   │       WRITE error message 'FILE-2 record missing'
│   │       READ FILE-1 only
│   │ ELSE
│   │    ┌IF FILE-2 < FILE-1
│   │    │       WRITE error message 'FILE-1 record missing'
│   │    │       READ FILE-2 only
│   │    │ ELSE (if the files are equal)
│   │    │      Combine matching records
│   │    │      WRITE merged record
│   │    │      READ FILE-1 and FILE-2
│   │    └ENDIF
│   └ENDIF
└ENDDO
CLOSE files
STOP RUN
```

FIGURE 7.7 Pseudocode for a Two-File Merge

The example illustrates a desirable characteristic of pseudocode; *it is sufficiently precise to serve as a real aid in writing a program, while informal enough to be intelligible to nonprogrammers* (i.e., users). It can be written quickly and easily and hence is more likely to be maintained if modifications are necessary. The pseudocode in Figure 7.7 is an elegant example of how nontrivial logic can be expressed in clear and concise fashion.

Individuals often request precise rules to use in developing pseudocode. Unfortunately, the very nature of the technique prohibits such restrictions, as they imply a formalism which pseudocode does not possess. Nevertheless, the following guidelines may prove helpful:

- Indent for readability.
- Use ENDIF and ENDDO to indicate the end of a block of logic; use vertical lines to indicate the extent of a block.
- Minimize or avoid the use of adjectives and adverbs.
- Use strongly descriptive verbs; try to avoid innocuous ones such as "process" and "handle."
- Use parenthetical expressions to clarify conditions associated with the ELSE portion of an IF statement.
- Restrict the pseudocode for a given module to a single page; if it doesn't fit, divide the module into two or more subordinate modules.

Nassi–Schneiderman Charts

Nassi–Schneiderman (or simply N–S) charts are a third technique for depicting program logic. The diagrams are sometimes called structured flowcharts, because they depict only the three control structures of sequence, selection, and iteration and have no provision for the GO TO statement. (N–S charts are sometimes referred to as Chapin charts.)

A Nassi–Schneiderman diagram for a two-file merge is shown in Figure 7.8. It corresponds closely to the pseudocode in Figure 7.7; indeed, detractors of the technique have referred to it as "pseudocode with boxes around it."

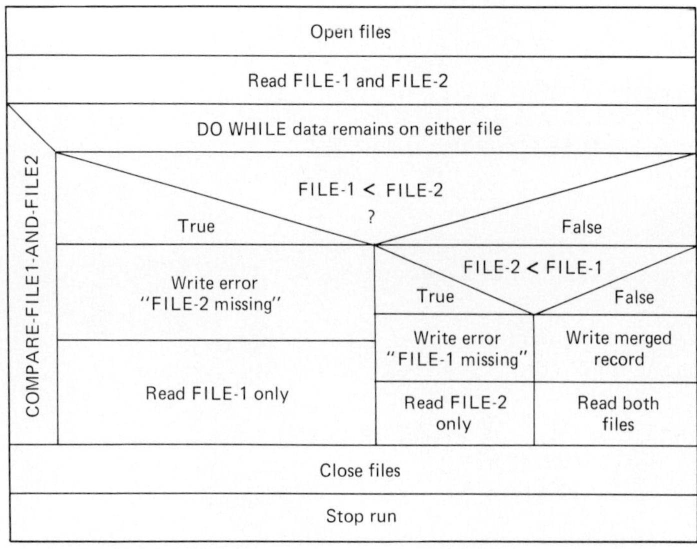

FIGURE 7.8 Nassi–Schneiderman Chart for Two-File Merge

An N–S chart is essentially a series of rectangles, which can be of any size to depict the necessary logic. Decisions are indicated by inverted triangles within a rectangle. The alternate logical paths are separated by a vertical line. Module names of the iteration structure are indicated vertically.

Both N–S charts and the traditional flowchart graphically depict the logic to be performed. An N–S diagram does not contain flow lines or arrowheads or have special shapes for different functions (e.g., a parallelogram for I/O). It is more compact and easier to draw than a flowchart and is readily translated to structured COBOL code. The author views it as distinctly superior to a flowchart but less desirable than pseudocode. The primary disadvantage of N–S diagrams is that they are cumbersome to maintain.

Comparison of Techniques

Let us consider an example contrasting pseudocode, flowcharts, and Nassi–Schneiderman charts. (The problem chosen is deliberately *not* related to data processing for the following reason. We are dealing with an exercise in logic and, further, with alternate means of communicating that logic. If the problem were data-processing oriented, you would already have encountered it, in one form or another. On the other hand, selection of an unrelated problem should eliminate any preexisting bias toward a particular solution.) Consider now the problem of the structured robot.

The objective of the exercise is to provide a series of commands to a robot, so that it can move through a maze to reach a goal. It is a simple maze in that there are no dead ends; the robot enters and makes steady progress to reach its objective.

The robot understands the following commands:

STEP:	Take one step forward
TURN RIGHT:	Turn 90° to the right
TURN LEFT:	Turn 90° to the left
STOP:	Stop

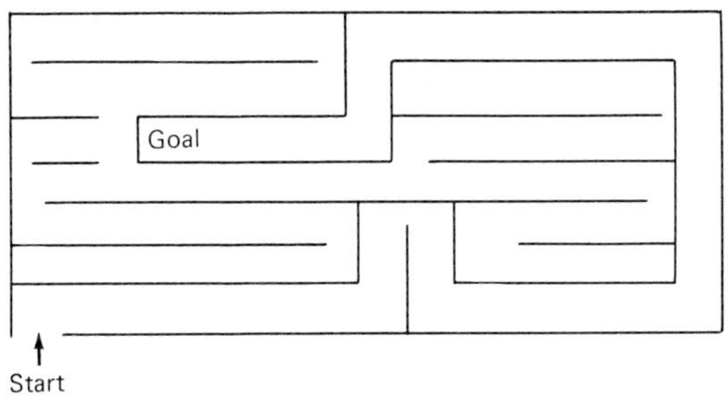

FIGURE 7.9 A Typical Maze

The first three commands return a condition code, AT WALL or NOT AT WALL. If AT WALL is returned, the robot is standing directly in front of a wall and cannot proceed further. If NOT AT WALL is given, the robot can take at least one step directly ahead.

A typical maze is shown in Figure 7.9. You may assume the robot is facing into the maze to start. The robot has reached the goal when it is confronted by a wall on three sides.

The problem is to develop the necessary logic to get the robot through *any* maze of the type shown in Figure 7.9 (i.e., a maze in which you never backtrack). The logic must be structured, i.e., must consist only of sequence, selection, and/or iteration blocks. The solution is expressed in flowchart, pseudocode, and Nassi–Schneiderman format for comparison purposes (Figures 7.10, 7.11, and 7.12, respectively, with Figure 7.10 divided into two parts). Observe also the dashed lines in Figure 7.10 to indicate the fundamental building blocks of sequence, selection, and iteration.

The author's personal preference is to use pseudocode in lieu of flowcharts and N–S diagrams. You are free, of course, to choose whatever method you like best.

STRUCTURED DESIGN

Unfortunately, adherence to the structured programming guidelines discussed in this chapter does not guarantee a ''good'' program. There are countless examples of structured programs that fail to work and are impossible to follow. Even an advocate as enthusiastic as Edward Yourdon has talked about the failure of the first structured revolution. However, the fault does not lie in structured programming per se. No discipline, structured or otherwise, can successfully implement systems of poor design or no design (as is often the case). Clearly something else is required prior to the implementation (or coding) phase.

Structured design is defined as a series of techniques that produce a *hierarchical* solution with the same components and relationships as the problem it is intended to solve. Our objective here is simply to present sufficient material, *of a practical nature,* so that the methodology can be used productively by the COBOL programmer. The author stresses *application* at the expense of theory. Individuals seeking a rigorous theoretical treatment are referred to the classic book by Yourdon and Constantine.[5]

We begin with a management analogy to structured design. A company's organization chart corresponds directly to a program's hierarchy chart, and various principles are shown to apply equally well to organizations *and* programs.

[5]Yourdon, E. and Constantine, L., *Structured Design* (Englewood Cliffs, N.J.: Prentice-Hall, 1979).

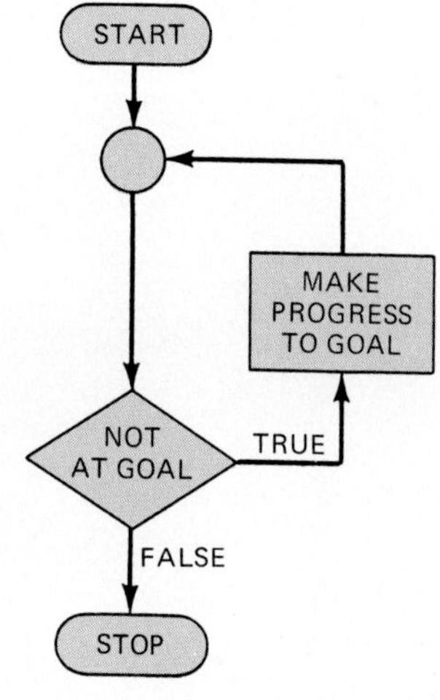

FIGURE 7.10a Overall Flowchart

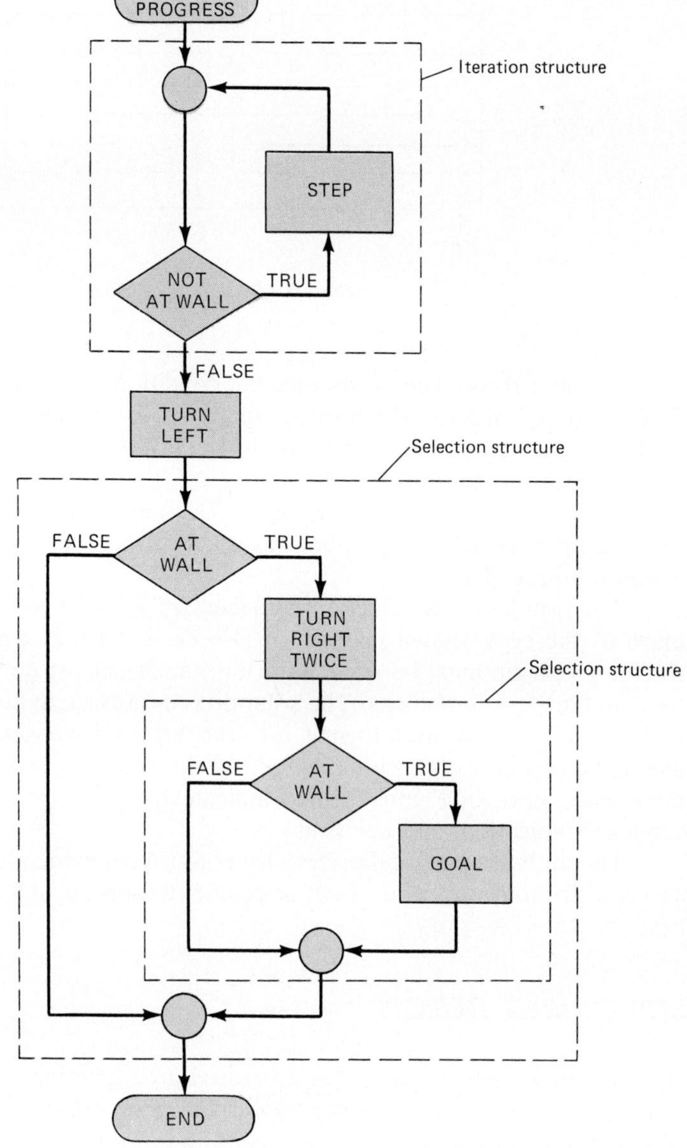

FIGURE 7.10b Details of the MAKE-PROGRESS-TOWARD-GOAL Module

```
┌DO WHILE not at goal
│   ┌DO WHILE not at wall
│   │   step
│   └ENDDO
│    Turn left
│   ┌IF at wall
│   │   Turn right twice
│   │  ┌IF at wall
│   │  │     Goal is reached
│   │  └ENDIF
│   └ENDIF
└ENDDO
 Stop
```

FIGURE 7.11 Pseudocode for Robot Problem

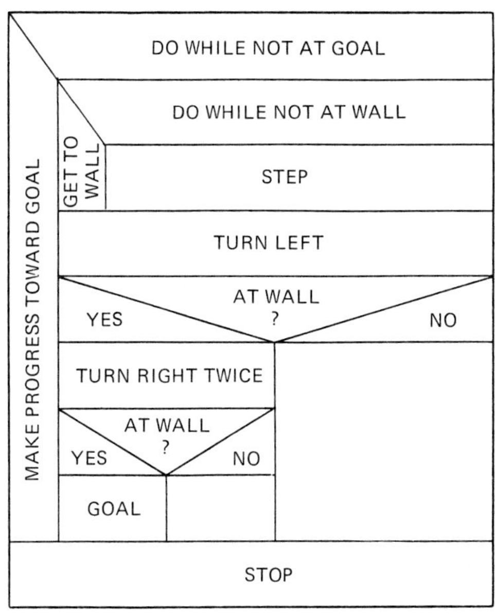

FIGURE 7.12 Nassi–Schneiderman Chart for Robot Problem

Management Analogy

A program's hierarchy chart shows the relationship of *paragraphs* within a program, just as an organization chart shows the relationship of people within a company.

Recall that the hierarchy chart was first introduced in Chapter 4 in connection with the Engineering Senior Program. Consider now Figure 7.13, representing a payroll program. *Each box in the hierarchy chart represents a paragraph in the program.* The box at the top, PREPARE-PAYROLL, is the "boss" of the

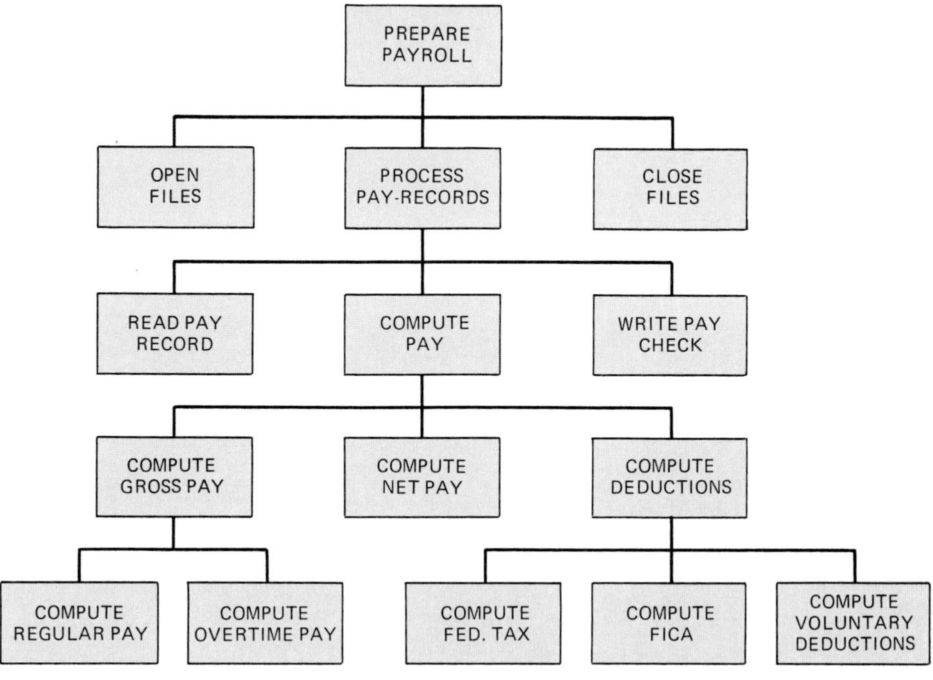

FIGURE 7.13 Hierarchy Chart of a Payroll Program

program. It in turn has three subordinates on the second level of the chart. One of these, PROCESS-PAY-RECORDS calls three lower level modules, which in turn call still lower level routines.

A company's organization chart clearly expresses manager–subordinate relationships. A program's hierarchy chart indicates the relationships between called and calling routines. *Each level in the hierarchy chart of a COBOL program corresponds to a PERFORM statement.* PREPARE-PAYROLL, for example, will contain three PERFORM statements, one for each subordinate routine. In a similar fashion, COMPUTE-PAY will perform COMPUTE-GROSS-PAY (as well as COMPUTE-NET-PAY and COMPUTE-DEDUCTIONS). COMPUTE-GROSS-PAY in turn performs COMPUTE-REGULAR-PAY and COMPUTE-OVERTIME-PAY, and so on.

An organization chart indicates the various *functions* inherent in running a company, just as a hierarchy chart establishes the functions necessary within a program. The overall function of a COBOL module can be inferred from the module name, just as a person's role can be deduced from his or her title, e.g., READ-PAY-RECORD, COMPUTE-VOLUNTARY-DEDUCTIONS. The exact nature of a person's job is fully described by a detailed job description. The logic within a module can be specified by pseudocode, flowchart, or Nassi–Schneiderman chart.

Additional principles of structured design can be drawn from the management analogy. These include span of control, top-down development, coupling, and cohesion.

Span of Control

The organization chart in Figure 7.14 depicts the Hatfield family business. The president, A. Hatfield, has been complaining of falling profits since he brought his sons, B. and C. Hatfield, into the company.

It doesn't take an extensive management background to realize that the company is top heavy. A. Hatfield does nothing other than manage B. Hatfield, who in turn controls C. Hatfield, whose role in life is to manage I. R. Milgrom. I. R. Milgrom, on the other hand, is overloaded in that 40 people report to him. The problems are related to *span of control,* i.e., the number of subordinates

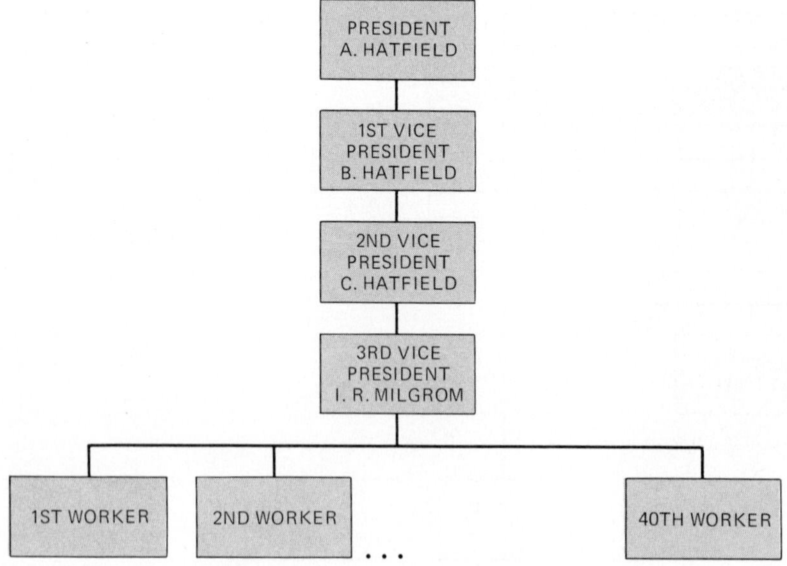

FIGURE 7.14 Hatfield Organization Chart

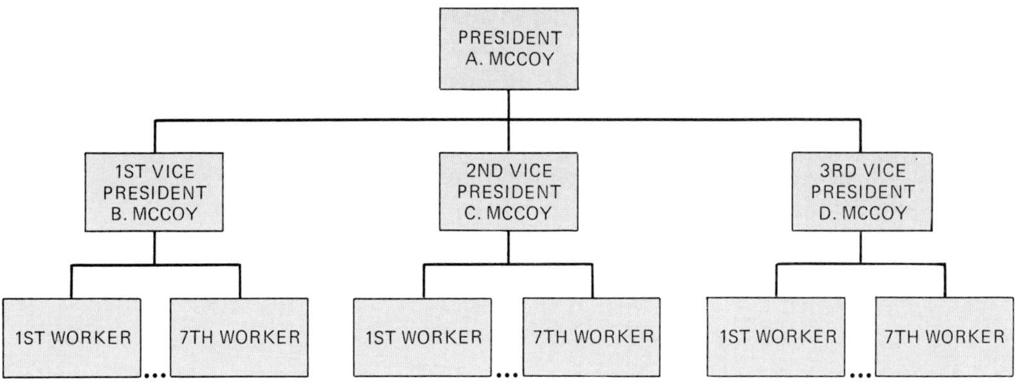

FIGURE 7.15 McCoy Organization Chart

reporting directly to a manager. I. R. Milgrom has too many, whereas each member of the Hatfield family has too few.

A better structure is exhibited by the McCoy family in Figure 7.15. Here the president manages three vice-presidents, who in turn each manage seven subordinates. Profits have continued to rise, even after the introduction of the McCoy offspring, and the company appears to be well run. This does not imply that every organization must have exactly three vice-presidents, nor must every vice-president have exactly seven subordinates. However, the McCoys are better organized than the Hatfields because there is a more effective span of control in their organization. The McCoys may, of course, have other problems that cannot be perceived from Figure 7.15. We do know, however, that the Hatfields exhibit structural problems not evidenced by the McCoys.

Similar conclusions can be drawn from a program's hierarchy chart. Have you ever written a COBOL program (structured or otherwise) in which PARAGRAPH-A did nothing but perform PARAGRAPH-B, which did nothing but perform PARAGRAPH-C, which in turn did all the work? Your program was fully structured in the sense that it contained only the fundamental building blocks of structured programming, yet it was difficult to follow. The problem was simply a poor design with inadequate span of control.

George Miller[6], a psychologist, wrote that the human ability to process information is limited to 7 ± 2 entries; that is, the average person can consider only 7 items simultaneously, after which there is a large increase in the number of errors. Accordingly, 9 may be established as the *maximum* desired value for span of control. This is not to say that a COBOL program is poorly designed if it contains spans outside the range from 5 to 9, because the nature of COBOL is such that lower spans are common, and acceptable. What we are saying is that span of control is an effective design criterion, and ideal spans will range from 2 or 3 to 9. If a span outside this range occurs, the designer should consider a modification.

Top-Down Development

The top-down approach is often confused with structured design, but the subjects are quite different. The term *top-down* simply refers to the *order* in which a system is tested and/or implemented. It has been practiced intuitively by some programmers for years, and certainly *prior* to the formal introduction of structured design in 1974. However, merely implementing a system in top-down fash-

[6]Miller, G. A., "The Magical Number Seven, Plus or Minus Two: Some Limits on Our Capacity for Processing Information," *Psychological Review*, vol. 63 (1956), pp. 81–97.

ion does not guarantee a good design. Indeed, truly horrible systems can, and have been, implemented from the top down.

Intuitive understanding of the top-down methodology can also be drawn from a corporate analogy. When an individual is sufficiently motivated to start a new company, he or she proceeds from the top of the organization down. More than likely, the entrepreneur installs himself as president, then hires vice-presidents for the various corporate functions of engineering, finance, and so on. Eventually, *when the top of the organization is in place,* assembly line workers, sales personnel, etc. are hired at the bottom of the organization to make and sell the product. Since this approach works rather well in the corporate world, it makes intuitive sense to try to develop systems and programs in the same way.

The top-down philosophy leads naturally to top-down testing, in which one implements a program from the top of its hierarchy chart (just as a new company originates with the president and not the janitor). The underlying premise is that the modules at or near the top of the chart are the most important (just as the people near the top of an organization chart have the biggest and most complex jobs). After all, the higher up a person appears on a company's organization chart, the more responsible his or her position, and the more money he or she earns. In much the same way paragraphs appearing toward the top of a hierarchy chart generally contain more complex logic than those near the bottom. The latter usually contain detailed but trivial logic and are least important with respect to the overall program flow.

Top-down testing suggests *that a program be tested even before it is completely coded.* This is accomplishd by initially coding lower level modules as program *stubs,* e.g., partially coded routines to indicate only that the module has been called. This approach results in several "working" versions of a program as more and more modules progress from mere stubs to completed code. The top-down approach is fully illustrated in Chapter 14 (see Figures 14.9–14.11).

Coupling

An individual in a company is not happy if others are constantly interfering with his or her job performance; an accountant does not want to hear from a purchasing agent how to do his or her job, and vice versa. Nor should the action of a purchasing agent have a direct effect on how the accountant balances the books. What we are saying is that people in a company (or paragraphs in a program) should be as autonomous as possible.

Adherents of structured design attempt to develop COBOL paragraphs that are *loosely coupled,* i.e., paragraphs that are *independent* of one another. If this is achieved, then a change in one COBOL paragraph (during maintenance) should *not* affect the inner workings of another. (Have you ever attempted to fix one part of your program and, in doing so, caused three other things to go wrong? Your trouble may have been due in part to tightly coupled [highly dependent] paragraphs.)

In the real world paragraphs in the same COBOL program cannot be completely independent of one another. Common sense dictates that there must be some connection between paragraphs; otherwise they would not be parts of the same program.

Coupling is present in COBOL when the same data name appears in more than one paragraph. Obviously this kind of coupling cannot be eliminated entirely, but it can and should be minimized.

Consider Figure 7.16, which illustrates the danger inherent in using the same data name in different paragraphs.

```
WORKING-STORAGE SECTION.
    .
    .
    .
```

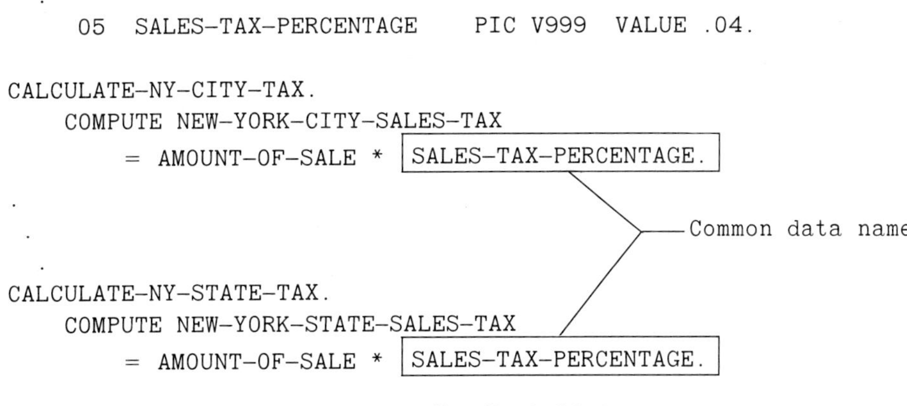

FIGURE 7.16 Coupling in COBOL

At one time the total sales tax on an item purchased in New York City was 8%. The city received 4% and the state 4%. There is no doubt that the code in Figure 7.16 will work as intended.

Now consider what happens if the state percentage increases to five percent. Chances are that the maintenance programmer will look only in the CALCULATE-NY-STATE-TAX module and will change the VALUE clause for SALES-TAX-PERCENTAGE. This is a straightforward change to the maintenance programmer. Further, it works when tested; NEW-YORK-STATE-SALES-TAX will be correct.

However, NEW-YORK-CITY-SALES-TAX is no longer correct because SALES-TAX-PERCENTAGE appeared in *two* paragraphs and was used for *two* purposes. Although this particular example is somewhat trivial, it effectively illustrates the dangers associated with coupling, namely, that a change in one paragraph causes changes in other apparently unrelated paragraphs. Accordingly one should take definite steps to minimize this problem. These include:

1. Restrict all data names to a single purpose; hence the example in Figure 7.16 requires two distinct data names, NY-STATE-SALES-TAX-PERCENTAGE and NY-CITY-SALES-TAX-PERCENTAGE.
2. Restrict all indicators and switches to a *single* purpose. Hence a given indicator reflects the answer to one and only one question.
3. Define a separate subscript for *every* table in a program. In addition, if a given table is referenced in more than one module, consider multiple subscripts for that table. In that way it is not possible to change a subscript in one module and have it affect another (see the Programming Tip in Chapter 11).

Cohesion

An additional design principle has to do with the *function* of the individual. Every organization has at least one person who tries to do too much, who voluntarily or otherwise does too many jobs at once. That individual is a strong candidate for burnout, and depending on his or her value, the organization may or may not develop serious problems when the person leaves. In analogous fashion, a COBOL paragraph that performs too many functions is also a cause for concern. Ideally, a paragraph should perform a *single* function. When every statement within a module is related to a common task, the module is said to be *highly cohesive*.

Every statement in a *functionally* cohesive COBOL paragraph is aimed at a *single* objective. One way of deciding whether a module is cohesive is to examine its name. A well-chosen name will *not* contain:

1. More than one verb, e.g., READ-AND-WRITE.
2. More than one object, e.g., EDIT-NAME-AND-ACCOUNT-DATA.
3. Nondescriptive or time-related terms, e.g., HOUSEKEEPING, TERMINATION-ROUTINE, INITIALIZATION, MAINLINE.

In other words, a module's function should be readily apparent from its name, which in turn should consist of a verb, one or two adjectives, and an object, e.g., READ-EMPLOYEE-RECORD, COMPUTE-SALES-TAX. If a module cannot be named in this fashion, it may not be properly cohesive, and redesign of the individual module and/or the hierarchy chart should be considered.

The Yourdon Structure Chart

In 1974 Stevens, Meyers, and Constantine[7] introduced the *structure chart,* which considerably expands the hierarchy chart shown earlier. (However, Edward Yourdon has done the most to publicize the technique, and so his name is generally associated with it.) Figure 7.17 illustrates the additional notation.

A structure chart indicates both decisions and loops, shown by a diamond and a semicircle, respectively. Module A calls module B, for example, on the basis of a decision in module A; modules E and F are called from B, on the basis of a decision made in B. Modules C and D are called repetitively from A, as implied from the semicircle notation. A structure chart should indicate only the *major* decisions and loops, to avoid unnecessary clutter.

A structure chart also contains the data and/or control information (i.e., switches) passed between modules. X is passed from A to B, Y from B to E, and Z from E to B. SWITCH-1 is passed from A to D. Names of the passed elements are written next to the arrow. A *data* element is indicated with an open circle on the end of the arrow. A *control* element (e.g., a switch or flag) is indicated by a closed circle at the end of the arrow.

The modules in a structure chart are connected by arrows that point from the calling to the called module. (It is understood that control is always returned to the calling module.)

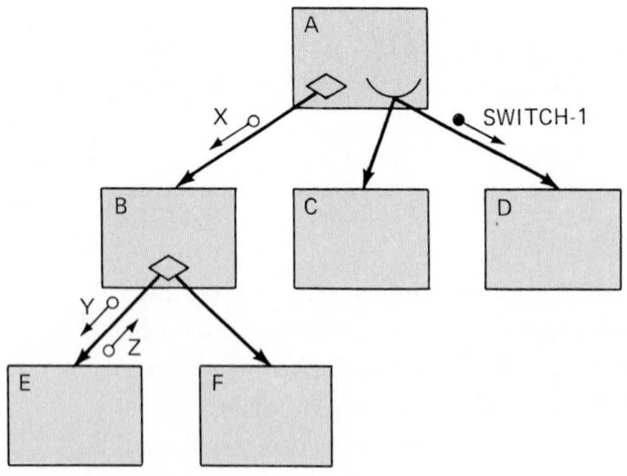

FIGURE 7.17 The Structure Chart

[7]Stevens, Wayne P., Meyers, G. J., and Constantine, Larry L., "Structured Design," *IBM Systems Journal,* Vol. 13, No. 2, pp. 115–139.

COBOL 8X:

Changes and Enhancements

A primary motivation, if not *the* primary motivation, behind the new compiler was the desire to make COBOL more conducive to the implementation of structured programming. COBOL-8X contains so many significant improvements which are related to structured programming, that an entire appendix, Appendix B, is included to present these changes in detail.

Summary

The chapter began with a pragmatic definition of structured programming, *namely, programming whose logic is expressed entirely in terms of three types of logic structures:* sequence, selection, *and* iteration. *These basic building blocks are sufficient to produce any required logic. The structured theorem was extended to include the* case *construct and a second type of iterative structure (DO UNTIL in addition to DO WHILE).*

Three distinct techiques for portraying the logic within a COBOL program were covered. We began with the traditional flowchart *and introduced two alternatives associated with structured methodology:* pseudocode *and* Nassi–Schneiderman *charts.*

The hierarchy (structure) chart was introduced as the primary tool of structured design. A hierarchy chart describes overall program structure and does not replace the flowchart, pseudocode, or N–S diagram. A hierarchy chart depicts function, *whereas a flowchart indicates sequence and decision-making logic. A hierarchy chart shows what has to be done, rather than when. It lists all the paragraphs in a program in a way that indicates their relative importance.*

True/False Exercises

1. A structured program is guaranteed not to contain logical errors.
2. Structured programming can be implemented in a variety of languages.
3. The DO UNTIL construct *cannot* be implemented in COBOL.
4. The COBOL PERFORM UNTIL corresponds exactly to the DO WHILE construct of structured programming.
5. The logic of any program can be expressed as a combination of only three types of logic structures.
6. The "one entry/one exit" philosophy is essential to structured programming.
7. Structured programming began in the United States.
8. Adoption of structured programming eliminates the need for coding standards.
9. A structured program should *never* contain a GO TO statement.
10. COBOL 74 is ideally suited to implement structured programming theory.
11. COBOL 8X contains several structured programming enhancements over COBOL 74.
12. The case construct is one of the basic logic structures.
13. A flowchart is probably the most popular way of communicating program logic.
14. Pseudocode has precise syntactical rules.

15. N–S charts are more easily modified than pseudocode.
16. Top-down design and structured design are synonymous.
17. Modules in a good design should be highly coupled.
18. A program must be completely coded before any testing can begin.
19. READ-WRITE-AND-COMPUTE is a good module name.
20. A single COBOL paragraph should accomplish many functions for optimal efficiency.
21. Program testing should be concentrated in the last 25% of the development phase.
22. A span of control from 15 to 25 COBOL paragraphs is desirable for the highest level modules.
23. The optimal number of modules in a system is equal to the number of programmers available for coding.
24. A module in a hierarchy chart can be called from another module on its own level.
25. Decision making should generally occur in higher, rather than lower, level modules.

Problems

1. Given the flowchart in Figure 7.18:
   (a) Write a COBOL IF statement to accomplish this logic.
   (b) Respond "true" or "false" to the following on the basis of the flowchart:
      i. If $X > Y$ and $W > Z$, then *always* add 1 to B.
      ii. If $X < Y$, then *always* add 1 to D.
      iii. If $Q > T$, then *always* add 1 to B.
      iv. If $X < Y$ and $W < Z$, then *always* add 1 to D.
      v. There are no conditions under which 1 will be added to both A and B simultaneously.
      vi. If $W > Z$ and $Q < T$, then *always* add 1 to C.

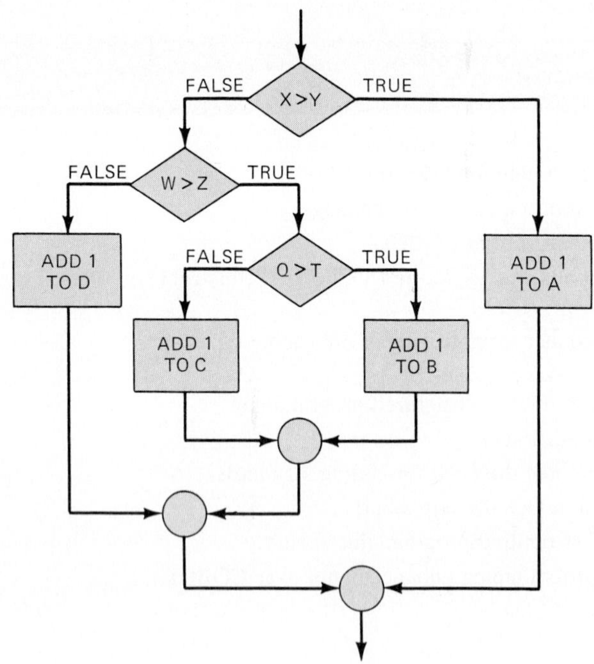

FIGURE 7.18 Flowchart for Problem 1

2. A robot is sitting on a chair, facing a wall a short distance away.

(a) Develop the logic necessary to have the robot walk to the wall and return to its initial position. The following commands are available:

STAND
SIT
TURN (turns right 90°)
STEP

In addition, the robot can raise its arms and sense the wall with its fingertips. (However, it cannot sense the chair on its return trip, since the chair is below arm level.) Accordingly the robot must count the number of steps to the wall or chair using the following commands:

ADD (increments counter by 1)
SUBTRACT (decrements counter by 1)
ZERO COUNTER (sets counter to zero)
ARMS UP
ARMS DOWN

The wall is assumed to be an integer number of steps away.

(b) Express your logic in the medium most convenient to you, flowchart, pseudocode, or N–S diagram. (You are, of course, restricted to the basic building blocks of structured programming.) Survey the class to determine the relative popularity of the different techniques.

(c) Present various solutions in class. *Select a volunteer to act as the robot,* and see whether the submitted solutions actually accomplish the objective.

3. Identify the elementary building blocks in Figure 7.19. Be sure you get all of them (the author can find eight).

4. This "non-data-processing" problem specifically avoids a business context. It was selected as one with which you probably are unfamiliar and consequently for which you have no preexisting bias toward a solution.

Develop a hierarchy chart to allow a user to play a series of tic-tac-toe games interactively against a computer. The following modules were used in the author's solution: PLAY-SERIES, PLAY-GAME, CLEAR-BOARD, GET-USER-MOVE, VALIDATE-USER-MOVE, CHECK-FOR-WINNER, UPDATE-BOARD, GET-COMPUTER-MOVE, DISPLAY-BOARD, DISPLAY-MESSAGE. (The last module, DISPLAY-MESSAGE, may be called from several places.) The module names should in themselves be indicative of the module functions.

5. (a) Redraw the hierarchy chart in Figure 7.13 as a Yourdon structure chart. Be sure to include:

i. An indication of which modules are likely to contain loops and/or decisions.
ii. Suitable names for data and control couples; indicate same on the structure chart.

(b) Which diagram do you prefer—the hierarchy chart in the text or the expanded Yourdon chart?

(c) What kind of information is included in the Yourdon chart that is not present on a plain hierarchy chart?

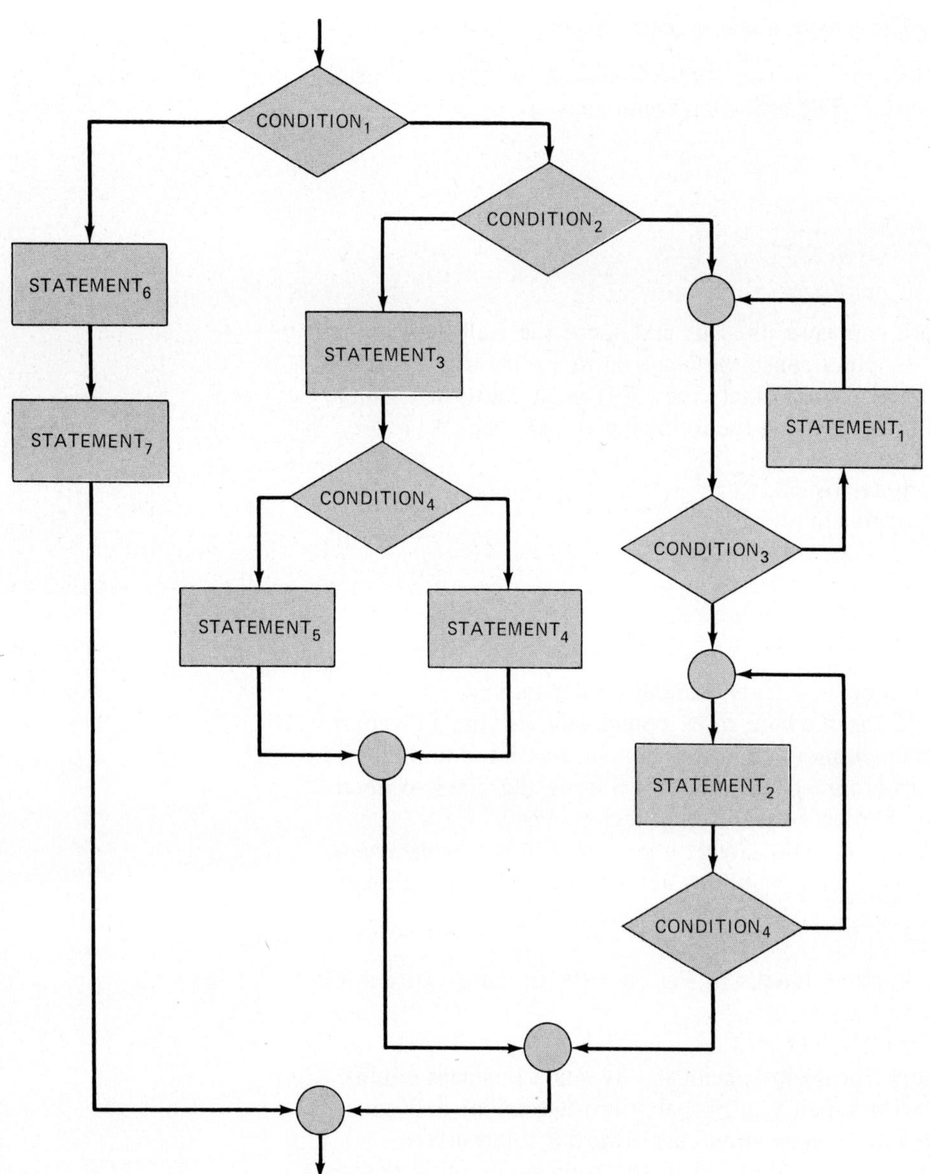

FIGURE 7.19 Flowchart for Problem 3

Control Breaks

8

Overview

This chapter does not present any new COBOL. Instead it uses the COBOL already covered to discuss one of the most common applications in data processing, control breaks.

Simply stated, a control break *is a change in a designated field. For example, if an incoming file has its records arranged by salesman, i.e., all transactions for the same salesman appear together, then a control break occurs from one salesman to the next.* Control totals *are usually required. Given that each incoming record has a transaction amount, a control total is the sum of all transactions for a given salesman.*

This chapter presents the control break application. It stresses the development of pseudocode and hierarchy charts. We begin with system concepts for both one- and two-level control breaks. □

SYSTEM CONCEPTS

Figure 8.1 depicts a single-level control break. In Figure 8.1 each record contains three fields: salesman name, account number, and amount. Salesman name has been designated as the *control field;* hence a control break on salesman occurs as we go from the last transaction for Benway to the first transaction for Hummer, and again from Hummer to Haas.

Figure 8.2 depicts a two-level application; there are *two* control fields, location and salesman. *All salesmen* in the *same location* appear together, as do all transactions for the *same salesman.*

A single-level control break occurs from Benway to Hummer; that is, salesman name changes, but location does not. A two-level control break occurs from Hummer to Haas in that the values of two control fields, name and location, change simultaneously.

DEVELOPING A SINGLE-LEVEL CONTROL BREAK PROGRAM

We are ready to develop the single control break application and begin with the Program Specifications in Figure 8.3.

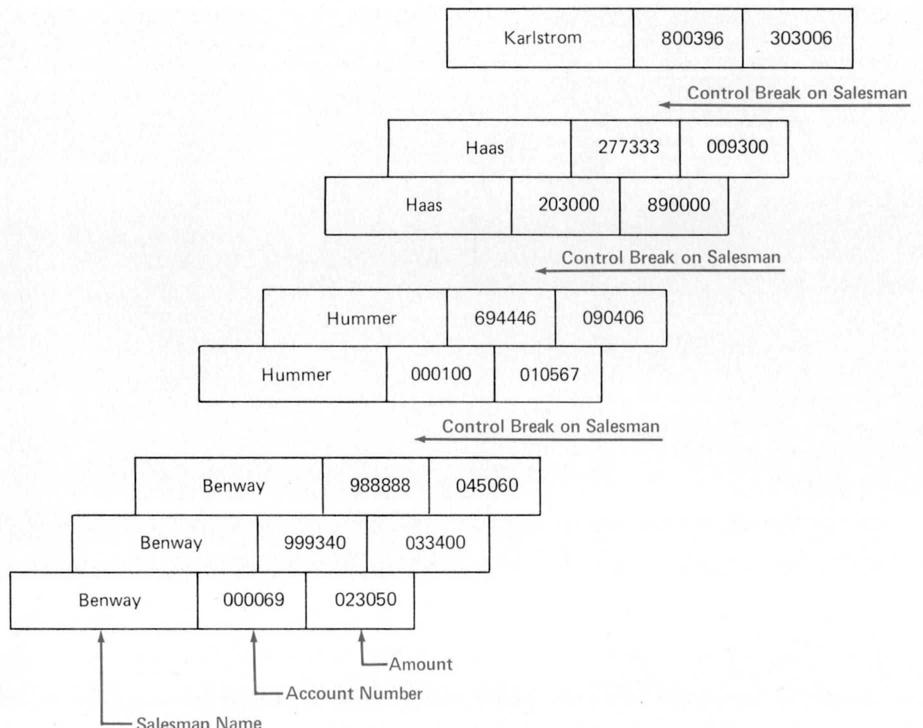

FIGURE 8.1 One Level Control Break

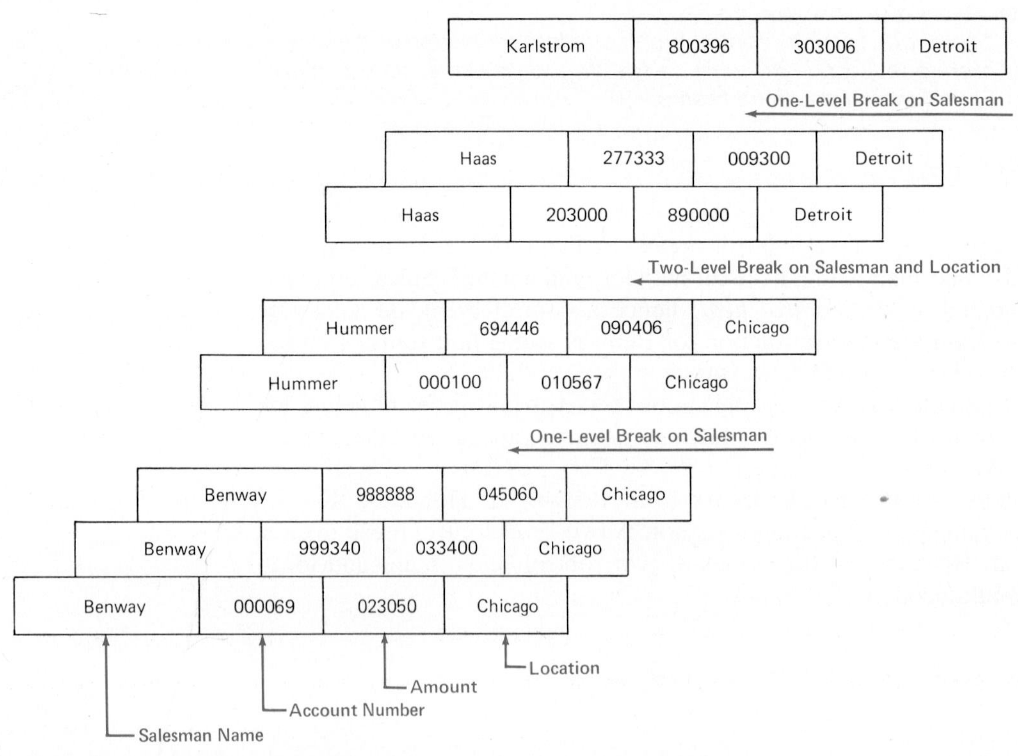

FIGURE 8.2 Two Level Control Break

Programming Specifications

Program Name:

One-Level Control Break

Narrative:

The management of XYZ Widgets, Inc., requires monthly information on the performance of its salesmen. This program processes a file of sales transactions for a given month. It computes and prints sales totals for each salesman, as well as for the company as a whole.

Input File(s):

SALES-FILE

Input Record Layout:

COLUMNS	FIELD	PICTURE
1–15	SALESMAN-NAME	X(15)
16–21	ACCOUNT-NUMBER	9(6)
22–27	AMOUNT	9(4)V99

Test Data:

```
BENWAY         000069023050
BENWAY         999340033400
BENWAY         988888045060
HUMMER         000100010567
HUMMER         694446090406
HAAS           203000890000
HAAS           277333009300
KARLSTROM      800396303006
MARCUS         700039093206
MARCUS         750020030500
MARSHAK        987654200540
MARSHAK        444333100450
MARSHAK        555666200350
FEGEN          444444010075
FEGEN          555555030400
FRANKEL        100000030350
FRANKEL        400000070650
FRANKEL        878787123556
CLARK          000104050078
CLARK          000101150044
CLARK          130101320009
```

Report Layout:

See Figure 8.4.

Processing Requirements:

1. Read a file of employee records.
2. For each record read:
   (a) Print the sales information in that record on a detail line.
   (b) Increment the salesman's total associated with the particular transaction by the transaction amount.
3. Print an appropriate heading prior to the first transaction for each salesman. Begin each salesman on a new page.
4. Print a total line for each salesman whenever salesman changes. Skip one line between the last detail line and the total line.
5. After all records have been read, print a total line for the company as a whole. Skip 5 lines prior to printing the company total line.

FIGURE 8.3 *Programming Specifications for One-Level Control Break Program*

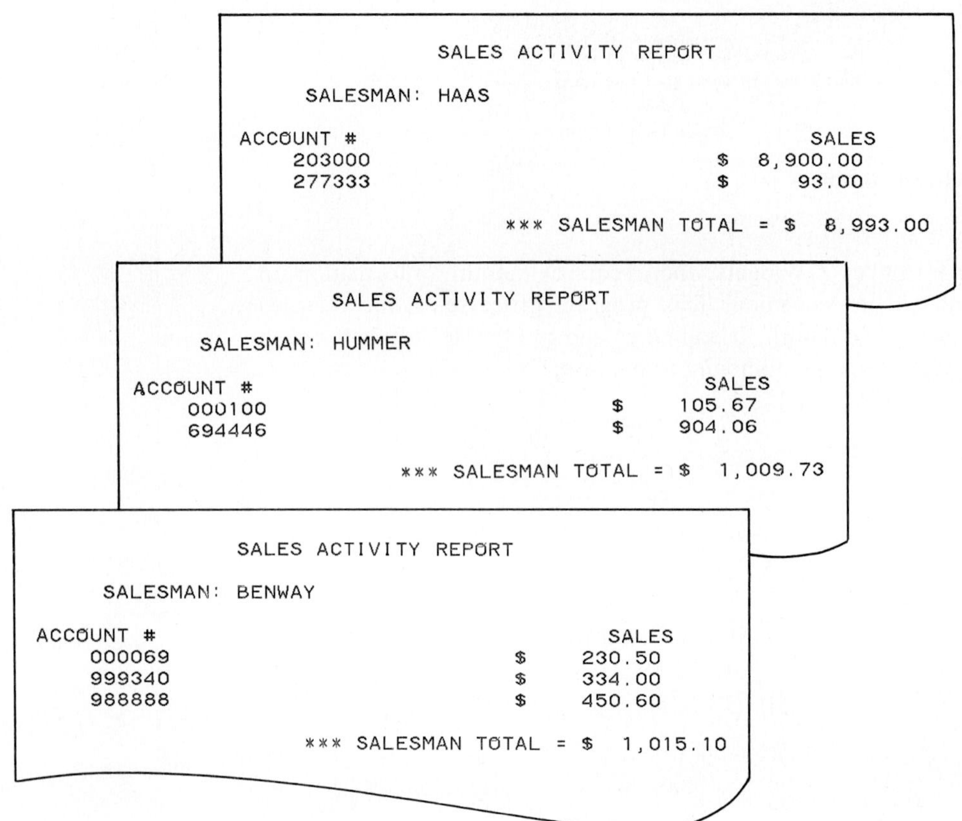

```
SALES ACTIVITY REPORT

SALESMAN: HAAS

ACCOUNT #                               SALES
    203000                         $ 8,900.00
    277333                         $     93.00

            *** SALESMAN TOTAL = $  8,993.00
```

```
SALES ACTIVITY REPORT

SALESMAN: HUMMER

ACCOUNT #                               SALES
    000100                         $   105.67
    694446                         $   904.06

            *** SALESMAN TOTAL = $  1,009.73
```

```
SALES ACTIVITY REPORT

SALESMAN: BENWAY

ACCOUNT #                               SALES
    000069                         $   230.50
    999340                         $   334.00
    988888                         $   450.60

            *** SALESMAN TOTAL = $  1,015.10
```

FIGURE 8.4 Report Format for One-Level Control Break Program

The logic associated with control break processing is difficult compared with what has previously been encountered. Students generally suffer more frustration in developing these programs than with any other assignment. Part of the problem stems from the fact that students, and indeed professional programmers, rush headlong into the coding phase of a project without giving suitable thought to the design phase, i.e., *how* to solve the problem.

One begins with a hierarchy chart.

The Hierarchy Chart

The design phase of a project starts with the hierarchy chart. Recall that this tool is *functional* rather than *procedural;* it shows what has to be done, but not when.

The development of a hierarchy chart begins at the top, with the highest level function. We proceed down, one level at a time, adding subservient functions at each level. We realize, for example, that an important function will be to PROCESS-ONE-SALESMAN. We must then evaluate which *subservient* functions are required to process a given salesman, namely WRITE-SALESMAN-HEADING, PROCESS-ONE-TRANSACTION, and WRITE-SALESMAN-TOTAL. Both the nature and the need for these various functions can be seen from the desired output of Figure 8.4. Figure 8.5 contains the resulting hierarchy chart.

A hierarchy chart is developed and critiqued *prior* to the actual writing of the program. Accordingly, we evaluate Figure 8.5 with respect to several design

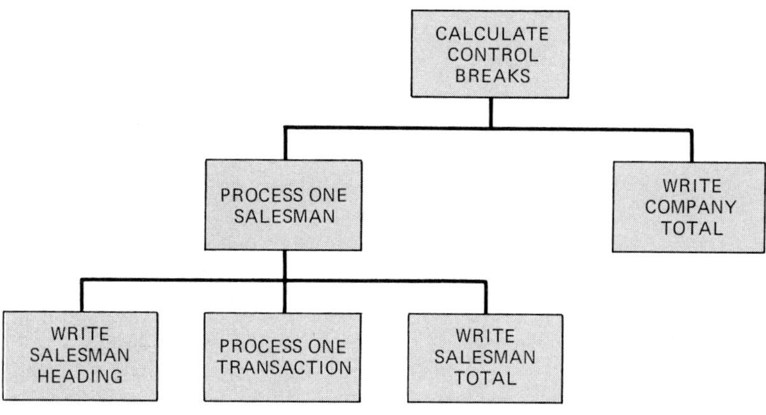

FIGURE 8.5 Hierarchy Chart for One-Level Control Break Program

criteria. First and foremost is *completeness;* does Figure 8.5 contain *all* necessary functions to accomplish the problem specifications, and further, are the *manager–subordinate* relationships correct? Apparently so. Observe, for example, that PROCESS-ONE-TRANSACTION is subordinate to PROCESS-ONE-SALESMAN, which in turn is subordinate to the mainline routine, CALCULATE-CONTROL-BREAKS. There is no other reasonable way to relate these functions. Moreover, PROCESS-ONE-SALESMAN has two additional subordinates, WRITE-SALESMAN-HEADING and WRITE-SALESMAN-TOTAL. Both of these are obviously required.

Next, check for *span of control,* which is reasonable at two or three throughout the chart. (The ''all chiefs and no Indians'' syndrome of the Hatfield organization in Figure 7.14 is clearly absent.) Observe also the *functional* nature of the paragraph names, which implies *cohesive* paragraphs, and the independence of the modules from each other, signifying a *loosely coupled* program. All told, the hierarchy chart in Figure 8.5 appears to be a reasonable base from which to develop the COBOL program.

The hierarchy chart does not show sequence or decision making, and it is not conducive to coding. A procedural tool, e.g. *pseudocode* is required before coding can begin. Pseudocode may be developed through the intermediate step of *stepwise refinement.*

Stepwise Refinement

Stepwise refinement divides a complex problem into smaller and smaller pieces until the lowest level results are easily translated into COBOL code. The major premise behind stepwise refinement is that most problems are too complex to code immediately. Accordingly, a problem is repeatedly divided into smaller units until coding is readily apparent. In applying this technique to the control break application, we can begin with three rather large pieces; initialization, processing, and termination. These are obviously still too general and are divided further. Figure 8.6*a* is the first real attempt at structuring the problem.

In Figure 8.6*a* initialization consists of opening files and general housekeeping. Processing involves a repetitive loop for each salesman. (Note that the instructions for each salesman also contain initialization, processing, and termination routines.) Finally, the termination routine for the whole program writes the company total, closes all files, and stops the run.

```
Initialization.......  [Open files
                       [Housekeeping (includes initial read)

                       [DO for each salesman
                       [    Initialize this salesman total
Processing...........  [    Process all transactions (for this salesman)
                       [    Write this salesman total
                       [    Increment company total
                       [ENDDO

                       [Write company total
Termination..........  [Close files
                       [Stop run
```

(a) Step 1

```
Initialization.......  [Open files
                       [Housekeeping (includes initial read)

                       [DO for each salesman                                        [DO for each transaction (for this salesman)
                       [    Initialize this salesman total                          [    Write detail line
Processing...........  [    Process all transactions (for this salesman)- - - - -  [    Increment salesman total
                       [    Write this salesman total                               [    Read next transaction
                       [    Increment company total                                 [ENDDO
                       [ENDDO

                       [Write company total
Termination..........  [Close files
                       [Stop run
```

(b) Step 2

FIGURE 8.6 ***Stepwise Refinement—Single-Level Control Break Program***

Figure 8.6*b* further expands the processing segment in Figure 8.6*a*. The statement "process all transactions for this salesman" is expanded into a second loop, with detail processing for each record. Figure 8.6*b* is the basis for our COBOL program. We go one step further, however, and translate that figure into the pseudocode in Figure 8.7. The latter resembles a COBOL program even more closely.

Pseudocode

The DO/ENDDO blocks of stepwise refinement are converted to PERFORM/ENDPERFORM statements in pseudocode. In addition, the pseudocode introduces actual COBOL data names, in particular SR-SALESMAN-NAME and WS-PREVIOUS-SALESMAN, which enable the program to detect a control break. In other words, COBOL cannot simply say "Do for each salesman." Instead it must specify explicitly how to determine when salesman changes. Hence, in order for a program to detect a control break, it compares the name on the record just read to the name on the previous record, i.e., SR-SALESMAN-NAME to WS-PREVIOUS-SALESMAN, as indicated in Figure 8.7.

It is now a simple matter to write the required program.

```
Open Files
Initial Read of SALES-FILE
PERFORM UNTIL no more data
    Zero salesman total
    Move SR-SALESMAN-NAME to WS-PREVIOUS-SALESMAN
    PERFORM UNTIL SR-SALESMAN-NAME ≠ WS-PREVIOUS-SALESMAN
      or no more data
        Write detail line
        Increment salesman total
        Read next record
    ENDPERFORM
    Write salesman total
    Increment company total
ENDPERFORM
Write company total
Close Files
Stop run
```

FIGURE 8.7 *Pseudocode for One-Level Control Break*

The Completed Program

Figure 8.8 is the COBOL program for the one-level control break program. It is straightforward and easy to follow, especially after the preceding discussion on hierarchy charts, stepwise refinement, and pseudocode.

Note especially the relationship of the hierarchy chart in Figure 8.5 to the paragraphs in the Procedure Division. The boxes in the chart correspond one to one with the paragraphs in the program. Observe also that each level in the hierarchy chart can be matched with a COBOL PERFORM statement.

The Working-Storage Section contains multiple 01 entries for the various print lines required by the program. There are three heading lines, one detail line (for each salesman), and two total lines. Working-Storage also contains separate counters for the salesman and company totals, as well as a switch, WS-PREVIOUS-SALESMAN, to detect the control break on salesman.

```
00001              IDENTIFICATION DIVISION.
00002              PROGRAM-ID.    ONELVL.
00003              AUTHOR.        JACKIE CLARK.
00004
00005              ENVIRONMENT DIVISION.
00006              CONFIGURATION SECTION.
00007              SOURCE-COMPUTER.     IBM-4341.
00008              OBJECT-COMPUTER.     IBM-4341.
00009
00010              INPUT-OUTPUT SECTION.
00011              FILE-CONTROL.
00012                  SELECT SALES-FILE
00013                      ASSIGN TO UT-S-SYSIN.
00014                  SELECT PRINT-FILE
00015                      ASSIGN TO UT-S-PRINT.
00016
00017              DATA DIVISION.
00018              FILE SECTION.
00019              FD  SALES-FILE
00020                  LABEL RECORDS ARE STANDARD
00021                  RECORD CONTAINS 80 CHARACTERS
00022                  DATA RECORD IS SALES-RECORD.
00023              01  SALES-RECORD.
00024                  05  SR-SALESMAN-NAME      PIC X(15).
00025                  05  SR-ACCOUNT-NUMBER     PIC 9(6).
00026                  05  SR-AMOUNT             PIC 9(4)V99.
00027                  05  SR-LOCATION           PIC X(15).
00028                  05  SR-REGION             PIC X(15).
00029                  05  FILLER                PIC X(23).
00030
00031              FD  PRINT-FILE
00032                  LABEL RECORDS ARE STANDARD
00033                  RECORD CONTAINS 133 CHARACTERS
00034                  DATA RECORD IS PRINT-LINE.
00035              01  PRINT-LINE                PIC X(133).
00036
00037              WORKING-STORAGE SECTION.
00038              01  PROGRAM-SWITCHES.
00039                  05  WS-DATA-REMAINS-SW    PIC X(3)      VALUE 'YES'.
00040                  05  WS-PREVIOUS-SALESMAN  PIC X(15)     VALUE SPACES.
00041
00042              01  CONTROL-BREAK-TOTALS.
00043                  05  THIS-SALESMAN-TOTAL   PIC 9(6)V99   VALUE ZEROS.
00044                  05  COMPANY-TOTAL         PIC 9(6)V99   VALUE ZEROS.
00045
00046              01  HDG-LINE-ONE.
00047                  05  FILLER                PIC X(25)     VALUE SPACES.
00048                  05  FILLER                PIC X(21)
00049                          VALUE 'SALES ACTIVITY REPORT'.
00050                  05  FILLER                PIC X(87)     VALUE SPACES.
00051
00052              01  HDG-LINE-TWO.
00053                  05  FILLER                PIC X(15)     VALUE SPACES.
00054                  05  FILLER                PIC X(10)     VALUE 'SALESMAN: '.
00055                  05  HDG-NAME              PIC X(15).
00056                  05  FILLER                PIC X(25)     VALUE SPACES.
00057                  05  FILLER                PIC X(78)     VALUE SPACES.
00058
00059              01  HDG-LINE-THREE.
00060                  05  FILLER                PIC X(10)     VALUE SPACES.
00061                  05  FILLER                PIC X(11)     VALUE 'ACCOUNT # '.
00062                  05  FILLER                PIC X(32)     VALUE SPACES.
00063                  05  FILLER                PIC X(5)      VALUE 'SALES'.
00064                  05  FILLER                PIC X(75)     VALUE SPACES.
00065
00066              01  DETAIL-LINE.
00067                  05  FILLER                PIC X(14)     VALUE SPACES.
00068                  05  DET-ACCOUNT-NUMBER    PIC 9(6).
00069                  05  FILLER                PIC X(26)     VALUE SPACES.
00070                  05  DET-SALES             PIC $Z(3),ZZ9.99.
00071                  05  FILLER                PIC X(77)     VALUE SPACES.
```

FIGURE 8.8 The One-Level Control Break Program

FIGURE 8.8 *(Continued)*

```
       01  SALESMAN-TOTAL-LINE.
           05  FILLER                  PIC X(30)      VALUE SPACES.
           05  FILLER                  PIC X(21)
               VALUE '*** SALESMAN TOTAL = '.
           05  PRT-SALESMAN-TOTAL      PIC $Z(3),ZZ9.99.
           05  FILLER                  PIC X(72)      VALUE SPACES.

       01  COMPANY-TOTAL-LINE.
           05  FILLER                  PIC X(40)      VALUE SPACES.
           05  FILLER                  PIC X(21)
               VALUE '*** COMPANY TOTAL = '.
           05  PRT-COMPANY-TOTAL       PIC $Z(3),ZZ9.99.
           05  FILLER                  PIC X(62)      VALUE SPACES.

       PROCEDURE DIVISION.
       005-CALCULATE-CONTROL-BREAKS.
           OPEN INPUT SALES-FILE
               OUTPUT PRINT-FILE.
           READ SALES-FILE
               AT END MOVE 'NO' TO WS-DATA-REMAINS-SW.
           PERFORM 020-PROCESS-ONE-SALESMAN
               UNTIL WS-DATA-REMAINS-SW = 'NO'.
           PERFORM 090-WRITE-COMPANY-TOTAL.
           CLOSE SALES-FILE
                 PRINT-FILE.
           STOP RUN.

       020-PROCESS-ONE-SALESMAN.
           MOVE SR-SALESMAN-NAME TO WS-PREVIOUS-SALESMAN.
           MOVE ZEROS TO THIS-SALESMAN-TOTAL.
           PERFORM 060-WRITE-SALESMAN-HEADING.
           PERFORM 030-PROCESS-ONE-TRANSACTION
               UNTIL SR-SALESMAN-NAME NOT EQUAL WS-PREVIOUS-SALESMAN
                 OR WS-DATA-REMAINS-SW = 'NO'.
           PERFORM 075-WRITE-SALESMAN-TOTAL.
           ADD THIS-SALESMAN-TOTAL TO COMPANY-TOTAL.

       030-PROCESS-ONE-TRANSACTION.
           MOVE SPACES TO DETAIL-LINE.
           MOVE SR-ACCOUNT-NUMBER TO DET-ACCOUNT-NUMBER.
           MOVE SR-AMOUNT TO DET-SALES
           ADD SR-AMOUNT TO THIS-SALESMAN-TOTAL.
           MOVE DETAIL-LINE TO PRINT-LINE.
           WRITE PRINT-LINE
               AFTER ADVANCING 1 LINE.
           READ SALES-FILE
               AT END MOVE 'NO' TO WS-DATA-REMAINS-SW.

       060-WRITE-SALESMAN-HEADING.
           MOVE HDG-LINE-ONE TO PRINT-LINE.
           WRITE PRINT-LINE
               AFTER ADVANCING PAGE.
           MOVE SR-SALESMAN-NAME TO HDG-NAME.
           MOVE HDG-LINE-TWO TO PRINT-LINE.
           WRITE PRINT-LINE
               AFTER ADVANCING 2 LINES.
           MOVE HDG-LINE-THREE TO PRINT-LINE.
           WRITE PRINT-LINE
               AFTER ADVANCING 2 LINES.

       075-WRITE-SALESMAN-TOTAL.
           MOVE THIS-SALESMAN-TOTAL TO PRT-SALESMAN-TOTAL.
           MOVE SALESMAN-TOTAL-LINE TO PRINT-LINE.
           WRITE PRINT-LINE
               AFTER ADVANCING 2 LINES.

       090-WRITE-COMPANY-TOTAL.
           MOVE COMPANY-TOTAL TO PRT-COMPANY-TOTAL.
           MOVE COMPANY-TOTAL-LINE TO PRINT-LINE.
           WRITE PRINT-LINE
               AFTER ADVANCING 5 LINES.
```

Highest level module in hierarchy chart. (005-CALCULATE-CONTROL-BREAKS)

Detects a control break. (SR-SALESMAN-NAME NOT EQUAL WS-PREVIOUS-SALESMAN)

Lowest level modules. (030-PROCESS-ONE-TRANSACTION, 060-WRITE-SALESMAN-HEADING, 075-WRITE-SALESMAN-TOTAL)

DEVELOPING A TWO-LEVEL CONTROL BREAK PROGRAM

The "System Concepts" section of this chapter presented two control breaks as an extension to the single-level problem. It is easy to envision the salesmen from the one-level example being grouped into various locations, with totals required for each location as well as each salesman. The situation is made clearer by examining the test data and partial report in Figures 8.9 and 8.10, respectively.

Figure 8.9 contains identical data as the original specifications in Figure 8.3, except that location has been appended as a fourth field. All salesmen in the same location appear together, as do all transactions for the same salesman. In other words, the data have been *arranged by location, and by salesman within location.*

```
BENWAY          000069023050CHICAGO
BENWAY          999340033400CHICAGO
BENWAY          988888045060CHICAGO
HUMMER          000100010567CHICAGO
HUMMER          694446090406CHICAGO
HAAS            203000890000DETROIT
HAAS            277333009300DETROIT
KARLSTROM       800396303006DETROIT
MARCUS          700039093206DETROIT
MARCUS          750020030500DETROIT
MARSHAK         987654200540NEW YORK
MARSHAK         444333100450NEW YORK
MARSHAK         555666200350NEW YORK
FEGEN           444444010075ST. PETERSBURG
FEGEN           555555030400ST. PETERSBURG
FRANKEL         100000030350ST. PETERSBURG
FRANKEL         400000070650ST. PETERSBURG
FRANKEL         878787123556ST. PETERSBURG
CLARK           000104050078TAMPA
CLARK           000101150044TAMPA
CLARK           130101320009TAMPA
```

Location is included as second control field.

FIGURE 8.9 Test Data for Two-Level Control Break Program

Figure 8.10 shows the desired output for the first two cities. This report resembles the earlier report in Figure 8.4, with two notable changes. First, all salesmen within the same city appear on the same page (as opposed to the earlier one page per salesman). Second, the location total for each city has been added as the second control total.

Hierarchy Chart

Let us begin by reviewing Figure 8.5, the hierarchy chart for the single-level break. In expanding this to two levels we must answer the following questions:

1. What functions have to be added?
2. What functions (if any) have to be deleted?
3. What functions have to be modified?

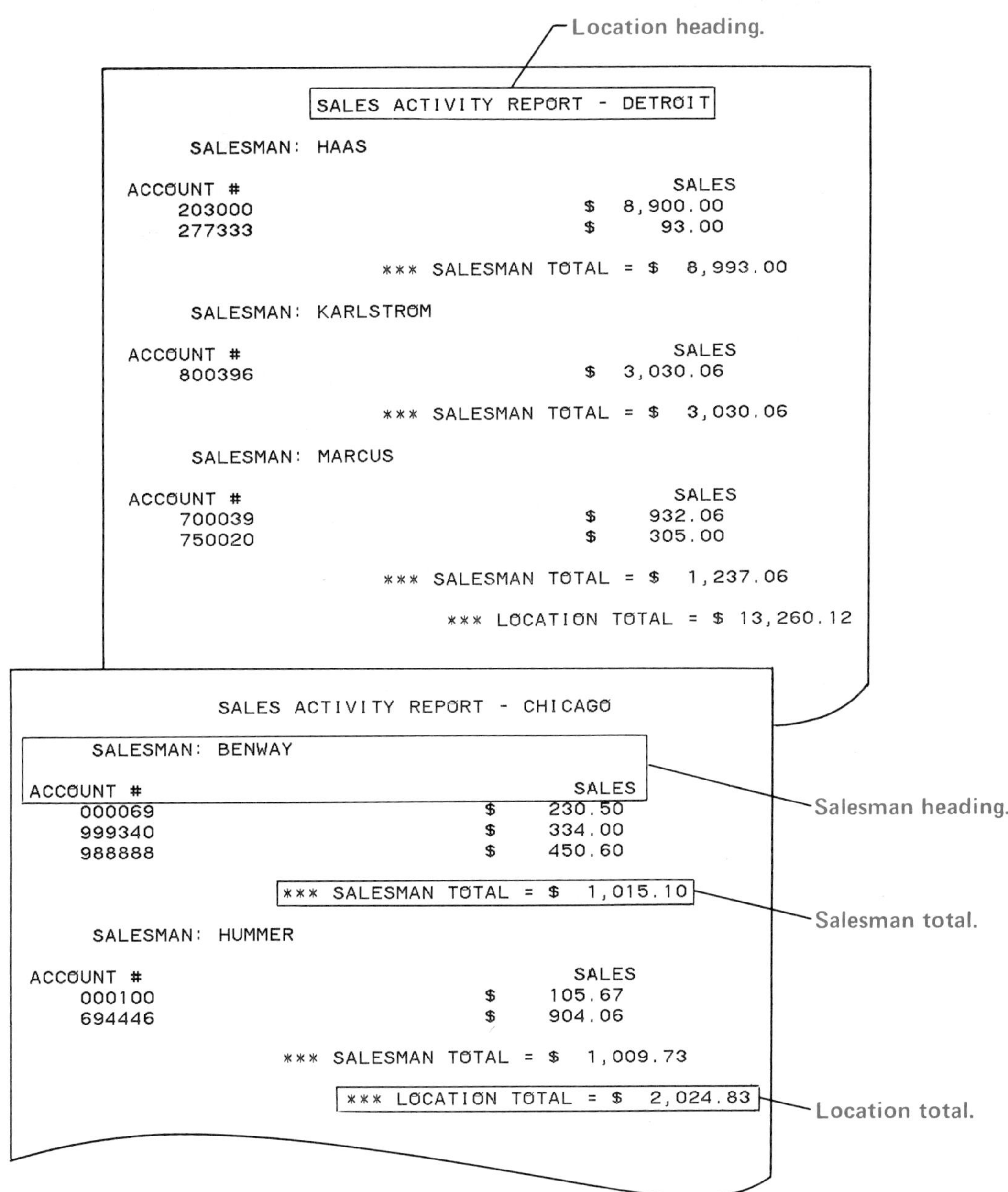

Location heading.
SALES ACTIVITY REPORT - DETROIT
SALESMAN: HAAS
ACCOUNT #
SALES
203000
$ 8,900.00
277333
$ 93.00
*** SALESMAN TOTAL = $ 8,993.00
SALESMAN: KARLSTROM
ACCOUNT #
SALES
800396
$ 3,030.06
*** SALESMAN TOTAL = $ 3,030.06
SALESMAN: MARCUS
ACCOUNT #
SALES
700039
$ 932.06
750020
$ 305.00
*** SALESMAN TOTAL = $ 1,237.06
*** LOCATION TOTAL = $ 13,260.12
SALES ACTIVITY REPORT - CHICAGO
SALESMAN: BENWAY
ACCOUNT #
SALES
000069
$ 230.50
999340
$ 334.00
988888
$ 450.60
*** SALESMAN TOTAL = $ 1,015.10
SALESMAN: HUMMER
ACCOUNT #
SALES
000100
$ 105.67
694446
$ 904.06
*** SALESMAN TOTAL = $ 1,009.73
*** LOCATION TOTAL = $ 2,024.83
Salesman heading.
Salesman total.
Location total.

FIGURE 8.10 Partial Output of Two-Level Control Break Program

It is fairly obvious that several new functions are necessary to accommodate the additional break on location. The question is really *where* these additional functions should go, i.e., what the manager-subordinate relationships are. Is PROCESS-ONE-SALESMAN subordinate or superior to PROCESS-ONE-LOCATION? A little thought will produce the correct solution.

Figure 8.11 contains the hierarchy chart for the two-level problem. New functions (those which were not present in the single-level example of Figure 8.5) are indicated by dashed lines. Figure 8.11 is subject to the same design considerations as its predecessor, namely, completeness, span of control, and proper manager–subordinate relationships. All design criteria appear satisfactory.

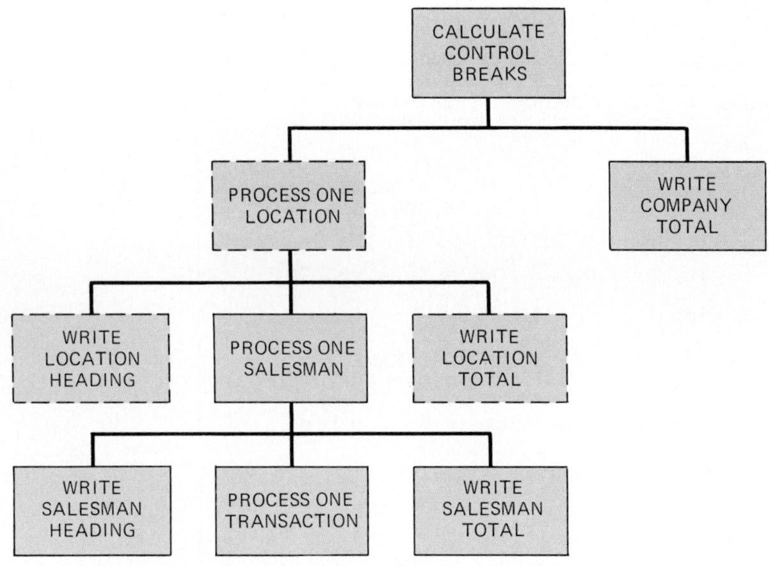

FIGURE 8.11 Hierarchy Chart for Two-Level Control Break Program

Figure 8.11 contains *every* module that was present in Figure 8.5; every function necessary for the one-level program is also required for the two-level program. However, the nature of the insides of some of the earlier functions may change.

In the one-level application, every salesman appeared on a separate page; hence the function WRITE-SALESMAN-HEADING contained the logic to jump to a new page for each new salesman. In the two-level problem all salesmen in the same location are to appear on the same page. The WRITE-SALESMAN-HEADING function is still required, but the "insides" of that module (COBOL paragraph) will change. Can you identify any other modules whose code will change?

The process of stepwise refinement works equally well with the two-level problem. An extra iteration is required as seen by comparing Figure 8.12 with its predecessor, Figure 8.6.

Figure 8.12 leads directly to the pseudocode in Figure 8.13. Recall that pseudocode is *procedural* in nature, whereas a hierarchy chart is *functional.* Unlike a hierarchy chart, pseudocode reflects the sequence and decision making; hence the introduction of the COBOL data names WS-PREVIOUS-LOCATION, WS-PREVIOUS-SALESMAN, etc., which indicate *how* and *when* to detect control breaks.

The Completed Program

Figure 8.14 is the completed program. It should present no problem whatever, given everything which preceded it. The utility of pseudocode and hierarchy chart as *design aids and documentation techniques* is readily appreciated. Both are useful *before* the program is written. A hierarchy chart indicates which paragraphs must be included. Pseudocode depicts how the paragraphs will be called as well as the "insides" of the various modules.

Both techniques are also helpful *after* the fact. Check the one-to-one correspondence between the blocks in the hierarchy chart and the paragraphs in the program. Note the levels in the hierarchy chart and the corresponding COBOL PERFORM statements.

```
Open files
Housekeeping (includes initial read)

DO for all locations
    Initialize this location total
    Process all salesmen in this location --
    Write this location total
    Increment company total
ENDDO

Write company total
Close files
Stop run
```

(a) **Step 1**

```
Open files
Housekeeping (includes initial read)

DO for all locations                          DO for each salesman (in this location)
    Initialize this location total                Initialize this salesman total
    Process all salesmen in this location --      Process all transactions (for this salesman) --
    Write this location total                     Write this salesman total
    Increment company total                       Increment location total
ENDDO                                         ENDDO

Write company total
Close files
Stop run
```

(b) **Step 2**

```
Open files
Housekeeping (includes initial read)

DO for all locations                          DO for each salesman (in this location)                DO for each transaction
    Initialize this location total                Initialize this salesman total                         Write detail line
    Process all salesmen in this location --      Process all transactions (for this salesman) --        Increment salesman total
    Write this location total                     Write this salesman total                              Read next transaction
    Increment company total                       Increment location total                           ENDO
    ENDDO                                     ENDDO

Write company total
Close files
Stop run
```

(c) **Step 3**

FIGURE 8.12 ***Stepwise Refinement—Two-Level Control Break Program***

```
          Open Files
          Initial Read of SALES-FILE
        ┌PERFORM UNTIL no more data
        │     Zero location total
        │     Move SR-LOCATION to WS-PREVIOUS-LOCATION
        │   ┌PERFORM UNTIL SR-LOCATION ≠ WS-PREVIOUS-LOCATION
        │   │   or no more data
        │   │     Zero salesman total
        │   │     Move SR-SALESMAN-NAME to WS-PREVIOUS-SALESMAN
        │   │   ┌PERFORM UNTIL SR-SALESMAN-NAME ≠ WS-PREVIOUS-SALESMAN
        │   │   │   or SR-LOCATION ≠ WS-PREVIOUS-LOCATION
        │   │   │   or no more data
        │   │   │     Write detail line
        │   │   │     Increment salesman total
        │   │   │     Read next record
        │   │   └ENDPERFORM
        │   │     Write salesman total
        │   │     Increment location total
        │   └ENDPERFORM
        │     Write location total
        │     Increment company total
        └ENDPERFORM
          Write company total
          Close Files
          Stop run
```

FIGURE 8.13 Pseudocode for Two-Level Control Break

```
00001              IDENTIFICATION DIVISION.
00002              PROGRAM-ID.    TWOLVL.
00003              AUTHOR.        JACKIE CLARK.
00004
00005              ENVIRONMENT DIVISION.
00006              CONFIGURATION SECTION.
00007              SOURCE-COMPUTER.      IBM-4341.
00008              OBJECT-COMPUTER.      IBM-4341.
00009
00010              INPUT-OUTPUT SECTION.
00011              FILE-CONTROL.
00012                  SELECT SALES-FILE
00013                      ASSIGN TO UT-S-SYSIN.
00014                  SELECT PRINT-FILE
00015                      ASSIGN TO UT-S-PRINT.
00016
00017              DATA DIVISION.
00018              FILE SECTION.
00019              FD  SALES-FILE
00020                  LABEL RECORDS ARE STANDARD
00021                  RECORD CONTAINS 80 CHARACTERS
00022                  DATA RECORD IS SALES-RECORD.
00023              01  SALES-RECORD.
00024                  05   SR-SALESMAN-NAME      PIC X(15).
00025                  05   SR-ACCOUNT-NUMBER     PIC 9(6).
00026                  05   SR-AMOUNT             PIC 9(4)V99.
00027                  05   SR-LOCATION           PIC X(15).
00028                  05   SR-REGION             PIC X(15).
00029                  05   FILLER                PIC X(23).
00030
00031              FD  PRINT-FILE
00032                  LABEL RECORDS ARE STANDARD
00033                  RECORD CONTAINS 133 CHARACTERS
00034                  DATA RECORD IS PRINT-LINE.
00035              01  PRINT-LINE                 PIC X(133).
00036
00037              WORKING-STORAGE SECTION.
```

FIGURE 8.14 Two-Level Control Break Program

FIGURE 8.14 *(Continued)*

```
       01  PROGRAM-SWITCHES.
           05  WS-DATA-REMAINS-SW      PIC X(3)       VALUE 'YES'.
           05  WS-PREVIOUS-SALESMAN    PIC X(15)      VALUE SPACES.
           05  WS-PREVIOUS-LOCATION    PIC X(15)      VALUE SPACES.

       01  CONTROL-BREAK-TOTALS.
           05  THIS-SALESMAN-TOTAL     PIC 9(6)V99    VALUE ZEROS.
           05  THIS-LOCATION-TOTAL     PIC 9(6)V99    VALUE ZEROS.
           05  COMPANY-TOTAL           PIC 9(6)V99    VALUE ZEROS.

       01  HDG-LINE-ONE.
           05  FILLER                  PIC X(25)      VALUE SPACES.
           05  FILLER                  PIC X(24)
                 VALUE 'SALES ACTIVITY REPORT - '.
           05  HDG-LOCATION            PIC X(15)      VALUE SPACES.
           05  FILLER                  PIC X(69)      VALUE SPACES.

       01  HDG-LINE-TWO.
           05  FILLER                  PIC X(15)      VALUE SPACES.
           05  FILLER                  PIC X(10)      VALUE 'SALESMAN: '.
           05  HDG-NAME                PIC X(15).
           05  FILLER                  PIC X(25)      VALUE SPACES.
           05  FILLER                  PIC X(78)      VALUE SPACES.

       01  HDG-LINE-THREE.
           05  FILLER                  PIC X(10)      VALUE SPACES.
           05  FILLER                  PIC X(11)      VALUE 'ACCOUNT # '.
           05  FILLER                  PIC X(32)      VALUE SPACES.
           05  FILLER                  PIC X(5)       VALUE 'SALES'.
           05  FILLER                  PIC X(75)      VALUE SPACES.

       01  DETAIL-LINE.
           05  FILLER                  PIC X(14)      VALUE SPACES.
           05  DET-ACCOUNT-NUMBER      PIC 9(6).
           05  FILLER                  PIC X(26)      VALUE SPACES.
           05  DET-SALES               PIC $Z(3),ZZ9.99.
           05  FILLER                  PIC X(77)      VALUE SPACES.

       01  SALESMAN-TOTAL-LINE.
           05  FILLER                  PIC X(30)      VALUE SPACES.
           05  FILLER                  PIC X(21)
               VALUE '*** SALESMAN TOTAL = '.
           05  PRT-SALESMAN-TOTAL      PIC $Z(3),ZZ9.99.
           05  FILLER                  PIC X(72)      VALUE SPACES.

       01  LOCATION-TOTAL-LINE.
           05  FILLER                  PIC X(35)      VALUE SPACES.
           05  FILLER                  PIC X(21)
               VALUE '*** LOCATION TOTAL = '.
           05  PRT-LOCATION-TOTAL      PIC $Z(3),ZZ9.99.
           05  FILLER                  PIC X(67)      VALUE SPACES.

       01  COMPANY-TOTAL-LINE.
           05  FILLER                  PIC X(40)      VALUE SPACES.
           05  FILLER                  PIC X(21)
               VALUE '*** COMPANY TOTAL = '.
           05  PRT-COMPANY-TOTAL       PIC $Z(3),ZZ9.99.
           05  FILLER                  PIC X(62)      VALUE SPACES.

       PROCEDURE DIVISION.
       005-CALCULATE-CONTROL-BREAKS.
           OPEN INPUT SALES-FILE
                OUTPUT PRINT-FILE.
           READ SALES-FILE
                AT END MOVE 'NO' TO WS-DATA-REMAINS-SW.
           PERFORM 015-PROCESS-ONE-LOCATION
                UNTIL WS-DATA-REMAINS-SW = 'NO'.
           PERFORM 090-WRITE-COMPANY-TOTAL.
           CLOSE SALES-FILE
                 PRINT-FILE.
           STOP RUN.

       015-PROCESS-ONE-LOCATION.
           PERFORM 065-WRITE-LOCATION-HEADING.
           MOVE SR-LOCATION TO WS-PREVIOUS-LOCATION.
           MOVE ZEROS TO THIS-LOCATION-TOTAL.
           PERFORM 020-PROCESS-ONE-SALESMAN
               UNTIL SR-LOCATION NOT EQUAL WS-PREVIOUS-LOCATION
                 OR WS-DATA-REMAINS-SW = 'NO'.
           PERFORM 080-WRITE-LOCATION-TOTAL.
```

New module is required for extra level of control break. (015-PROCESS-ONE-LOCATION.)

Test for location break. (UNTIL SR-LOCATION NOT EQUAL WS-PREVIOUS-LOCATION)

```
           ADD THIS-LOCATION-TOTAL TO COMPANY-TOTAL.

       020-PROCESS-ONE-SALESMAN.
           MOVE SR-SALESMAN-NAME TO WS-PREVIOUS-SALESMAN.
           MOVE ZEROS TO THIS-SALESMAN-TOTAL.
           PERFORM 060-WRITE-SALESMAN-HEADING.
           PERFORM 030-PROCESS-ONE-TRANSACTION
               UNTIL SR-SALESMAN-NAME NOT EQUAL WS-PREVIOUS-SALESMAN
                 OR SR-LOCATION NOT EQUAL WS-PREVIOUS-LOCATION
                 OR WS-DATA-REMAINS-SW = 'NO'.
           PERFORM 075-WRITE-SALESMAN-TOTAL.
           ADD THIS-SALESMAN-TOTAL TO THIS-LOCATION-TOTAL.

       030-PROCESS-ONE-TRANSACTION.
           MOVE SPACES TO DETAIL-LINE.
           MOVE SR-ACCOUNT-NUMBER TO DET-ACCOUNT-NUMBER.
           MOVE SR-AMOUNT TO DET-SALES
           ADD SR-AMOUNT TO THIS-SALESMAN-TOTAL
           MOVE DETAIL-LINE TO PRINT-LINE.
           WRITE PRINT-LINE
               AFTER ADVANCING 1 LINE.
           READ SALES-FILE
               AT END MOVE 'NO' TO WS-DATA-REMAINS-SW.

       060-WRITE-SALESMAN-HEADING.
           MOVE SR-SALESMAN-NAME TO HDG-NAME.
           MOVE HDG-LINE-TWO TO PRINT-LINE.
           WRITE PRINT-LINE
               AFTER ADVANCING 2 LINES.
           MOVE HDG-LINE-THREE TO PRINT-LINE.
           WRITE PRINT-LINE
               AFTER ADVANCING 2 LINES.

       065-WRITE-LOCATION-HEADING.
           MOVE SR-LOCATION TO HDG-LOCATION.
           MOVE HDG-LINE-ONE TO PRINT-LINE.
           WRITE PRINT-LINE
               AFTER ADVANCING PAGE.

       075-WRITE-SALESMAN-TOTAL.
           MOVE THIS-SALESMAN-TOTAL TO PRT-SALESMAN-TOTAL.
           MOVE SALESMAN-TOTAL-LINE TO PRINT-LINE.
           WRITE PRINT-LINE
               AFTER ADVANCING 2 LINES.

       080-WRITE-LOCATION-TOTAL.
           MOVE THIS-LOCATION-TOTAL TO PRT-LOCATION-TOTAL.
           MOVE LOCATION-TOTAL-LINE TO PRINT-LINE.
           WRITE PRINT-LINE
               AFTER ADVANCING 2 LINES.

       090-WRITE-COMPANY-TOTAL.
           MOVE COMPANY-TOTAL TO PRT-COMPANY-TOTAL.
           MOVE COMPANY-TOTAL-LINE TO PRINT-LINE.
           WRITE PRINT-LINE
               AFTER ADVANCING 5 LINES.
```

Test for salesman break.

The code inside this module is modified.

New modules are required to implement new functions.

FIGURE 8.14 ***(Continued)***

Summary

This chapter presented the control break *application. It covered no new COBOL per se, but focused instead on program development. Both hierarchy charts and pseudocode were found useful as design aids before a program is written, and as documentation techniques after the fact.*

The hierarchy chart is functional *in nature, showing what has to be done, but not when. It is the first step in the development process and is developed from the* top down. *Boxes in a hierarchy chart correspond one to one with paragraphs in a program.*

Pseudocode contains procedural *information and depicts a program's logic. It may be developed through a technique known as* stepwise refinement.

True/False Exercises

1. Control break processing is restricted to a single level.
2. Input to a control break program need not be in any special order.
3. Modules in a hierarchy chart and paragraphs in a COBOL program correspond one-to-one.
4. A hierarchy chart depicts decision-making logic.
5. Pseudocode can be used to depict the "insides" of a module in a hierarchy chart.
6. Hierarchy charts and pseudocode depict the same thing.
7. Each level in a hierarchy chart corresponds to a COBOL PERFORM statement.
8. Most problems are simple enough to begin coding immediately.
9. It is not possible for two control fields to change simultaneously.
10. Control break applications cannot extend beyond two levels.

Problems

1. Examine the COBOL code in Figure 8.14. In particular, note that the PERFORM statement to detect a break in salesman (lines 124–126) includes the clause SR-LOCATION NOT EQUAL WS-PREVIOUS-LOCATION. Why? (What would happen if this clause was not present and the last salesman in one location had the same name as the first salesman in the next location?) Can you state a generalized rule for the compound condition in PERFORM statements that is needed to detect control breaks?
2. Examine the COBOL code in Figure 8.14. An alternative way to compute the location total would be to insert the statement

```
ADD SR-AMOUNT TO THIS-LOCATION-TOTAL
```

after line 135 and simultaneously remove line 129. Although this modification would produce the correct result, it is less desirable than the original code. Why?

In similar fashion, line 118 would be removed in favor of inserting

```
ADD SR-AMOUNT TO COMPANY-TOTAL
```

after line 135. Is this change desirable?

Debugging Workshop

Figure 8.15 is an *invalid* version of the Two-Level Control Break Program presented in this chapter. It used the identical input as the original program but produced the erroneous output in Figure 8.16. Find and correct all errors.

```
IDENTIFICATION DIVISION.
PROGRAM-ID.  TWOLVL.
AUTHOR.      JACKIE CLARK.

ENVIRONMENT DIVISION.
CONFIGURATION SECTION.
SOURCE-COMPUTER.     IBM-4341.
OBJECT-COMPUTER.     IBM-4341.

INPUT-OUTPUT SECTION.
FILE-CONTROL.
    SELECT SALES-FILE
        ASSIGN TO UT-S-SYSIN.
    SELECT PRINT-FILE
        ASSIGN TO UT-S-PRINT.

DATA DIVISION.
FILE SECTION.
FD  SALES-FILE
    LABEL RECORDS ARE STANDARD
    RECORD CONTAINS 80 CHARACTERS
    DATA RECORD IS SALES-RECORD.
01  SALES-RECORD.
    05  SR-SALESMAN-NAME       PIC X(15).
    05  SR-ACCOUNT-NUMBER      PIC 9(6).
    05  SR-AMOUNT              PIC 9(4)V99.
    05  SR-LOCATION            PIC X(15).
    05  SR-REGION              PIC X(15).
    05  FILLER                 PIC X(23).

FD  PRINT-FILE
    LABEL RECORDS ARE STANDARD
    RECORD CONTAINS 133 CHARACTERS
    DATA RECORD IS PRINT-LINE.
01  PRINT-LINE                 PIC X(133).

WORKING-STORAGE SECTION.
01  PROGRAM-SWITCHES.
    05  WS-DATA-REMAINS-SW     PIC X(3)       VALUE 'YES'.
    05  WS-PREVIOUS-SALESMAN   PIC X(15)      VALUE SPACES.
    05  WS-PREVIOUS-LOCATION   PIC X(15)      VALUE SPACES.

01  CONTROL-BREAK-TOTALS.
    05  THIS-SALESMAN-TOTAL    PIC 9(6)V99    VALUE ZEROS.
    05  THIS-LOCATION-TOTAL    PIC 9(6)V99    VALUE ZEROS.
    05  COMPANY-TOTAL          PIC 9(6)V99    VALUE ZEROS.

01  HDG-LINE-ONE.
    05  FILLER                 PIC X(25)      VALUE SPACES.
    05  FILLER                 PIC X(24)
          VALUE 'SALES ACTIVITY REPORT - '.
    05  HDG-LOCATION           PIC X(15)      VALUE SPACES.
    05  FILLER                 PIC X(69)      VALUE SPACES.

01  HDG-LINE-TWO.
    05  FILLER                 PIC X(15)      VALUE SPACES.
    05  FILLER                 PIC X(10)      VALUE 'SALESMAN: '.
    05  HDG-NAME               PIC X(15).
    05  FILLER                 PIC X(25)      VALUE SPACES.
    05  FILLER                 PIC X(78)      VALUE SPACES.

01  HDG-LINE-THREE.
    05  FILLER                 PIC X(10)      VALUE SPACES.
    05  FILLER                 PIC X(11)      VALUE 'ACCOUNT # '.
    05  FILLER                 PIC X(32)      VALUE SPACES.
    05  FILLER                 PIC X(5)       VALUE 'SALES'.
    05  FILLER                 PIC X(75)      VALUE SPACES.

01  DETAIL-LINE.
    05  FILLER                 PIC X(14)      VALUE SPACES.
    05  DET-ACCOUNT-NUMBER     PIC 9(6).
    05  FILLER                 PIC X(26)      VALUE SPACES.
    05  DET-SALES              PIC $Z(3),ZZ9.99.
    05  FILLER                 PIC X(77)      VALUE SPACES.

01  SALESMAN-TOTAL-LINE.
    05  FILLER                 PIC X(30)      VALUE SPACES.
    05  FILLER                 PIC X(21)
       VALUE '*** SALESMAN TOTAL = '.
    05  PRT-SALESMAN-TOTAL     PIC $Z(3),ZZ9.99.
```

FIGURE 8.15 Erroneous Two Level Program

FIGURE 8.15 (Continued)

```
           05  FILLER                  PIC X(72)      VALUE SPACES.

       01  LOCATION-TOTAL-LINE.
           05  FILLER                  PIC X(35)      VALUE SPACES.
           05  FILLER                  PIC X(21)
               VALUE '*** LOCATION TOTAL = '.
           05  PRT-LOCATION-TOTAL      PIC $Z(3),ZZ9.99.
           05  FILLER                  PIC X(67)      VALUE SPACES.

       01  COMPANY-TOTAL-LINE.
           05  FILLER                  PIC X(40)      VALUE SPACES.
           05  FILLER                  PIC X(21)
               VALUE '*** COMPANY TOTAL = '.
           05  PRT-COMPANY-TOTAL       PIC $Z(3),ZZ9.99.
           05  FILLER                  PIC X(62)      VALUE SPACES.

       PROCEDURE DIVISION.
       005-CALCULATE-CONTROL-BREAKS.
           OPEN INPUT SALES-FILE
               OUTPUT PRINT-FILE.
           READ SALES-FILE
               AT END MOVE 'NO' TO WS-DATA-REMAINS-SW.
           PERFORM 015-PROCESS-ONE-LOCATION
               UNTIL WS-DATA-REMAINS-SW = 'NO'.
           PERFORM 090-WRITE-COMPANY-TOTAL.
           CLOSE SALES-FILE
                 PRINT-FILE.
           STOP RUN.

       015-PROCESS-ONE-LOCATION.
           MOVE SR-LOCATION TO WS-PREVIOUS-LOCATION.
           PERFORM 020-PROCESS-ONE-SALESMAN
               UNTIL SR-LOCATION NOT EQUAL WS-PREVIOUS-LOCATION
                 OR WS-DATA-REMAINS-SW = 'NO'.
           PERFORM 080-WRITE-LOCATION-TOTAL.
           ADD THIS-LOCATION-TOTAL TO COMPANY-TOTAL.

       020-PROCESS-ONE-SALESMAN.
           MOVE SR-SALESMAN-NAME TO WS-PREVIOUS-SALESMAN.
           MOVE ZEROS TO THIS-SALESMAN-TOTAL.
           PERFORM 060-WRITE-SALESMAN-HEADING.
           PERFORM 030-PROCESS-ONE-TRANSACTION
               UNTIL SR-SALESMAN-NAME NOT EQUAL WS-PREVIOUS-SALESMAN
                 OR SR-LOCATION NOT EQUAL WS-PREVIOUS-LOCATION
                 OR WS-DATA-REMAINS-SW = 'NO'.
           PERFORM 075-WRITE-SALESMAN-TOTAL.
           ADD THIS-SALESMAN-TOTAL TO THIS-LOCATION-TOTAL.

       030-PROCESS-ONE-TRANSACTION.
           MOVE SPACES TO DETAIL-LINE.
           MOVE SR-ACCOUNT-NUMBER TO DET-ACCOUNT-NUMBER.
           MOVE SR-AMOUNT TO DET-SALES
           ADD SR-AMOUNT TO THIS-SALESMAN-TOTAL
           MOVE DETAIL-LINE TO PRINT-LINE.
           WRITE PRINT-LINE
               AFTER ADVANCING 1 LINE.
           READ SALES-FILE
               AT END MOVE 'NO' TO WS-DATA-REMAINS-SW.

       060-WRITE-SALESMAN-HEADING.
           MOVE SR-SALESMAN-NAME TO HDG-NAME.
           MOVE HDG-LINE-TWO TO PRINT-LINE.
           WRITE PRINT-LINE
               AFTER ADVANCING 2 LINES.
           MOVE HDG-LINE-THREE TO PRINT-LINE.
      *    WRITE PRINT-LINE
      *        AFTER ADVANCING 2 LINES.

       065-WRITE-LOCATION-HEADING.
           MOVE SR-LOCATION TO HDG-LOCATION.
           MOVE HDG-LINE-ONE TO PRINT-LINE.
           WRITE PRINT-LINE
               AFTER ADVANCING PAGE.

       075-WRITE-SALESMAN-TOTAL.
           MOVE SR-AMOUNT TO PRT-SALESMAN-TOTAL.
           MOVE SALESMAN-TOTAL-LINE TO PRINT-LINE.
           WRITE PRINT-LINE
               AFTER ADVANCING 2 LINES.
```

```
       080-WRITE-LOCATION-TOTAL.
           MOVE THIS-LOCATION-TOTAL TO PRT-LOCATION-TOTAL.
           MOVE LOCATION-TOTAL-LINE TO PRINT-LINE.
           WRITE PRINT-LINE
               AFTER ADVANCING 2 LINES.

       090-WRITE-COMPANY-TOTAL.
           MOVE COMPANY-TOTAL TO PRT-COMPANY-TOTAL.
           MOVE COMPANY-TOTAL-LINE TO PRINT-LINE.
           WRITE PRINT-LINE
               AFTER ADVANCING 5 LINES.
```

FIGURE 8.15 (Continued)

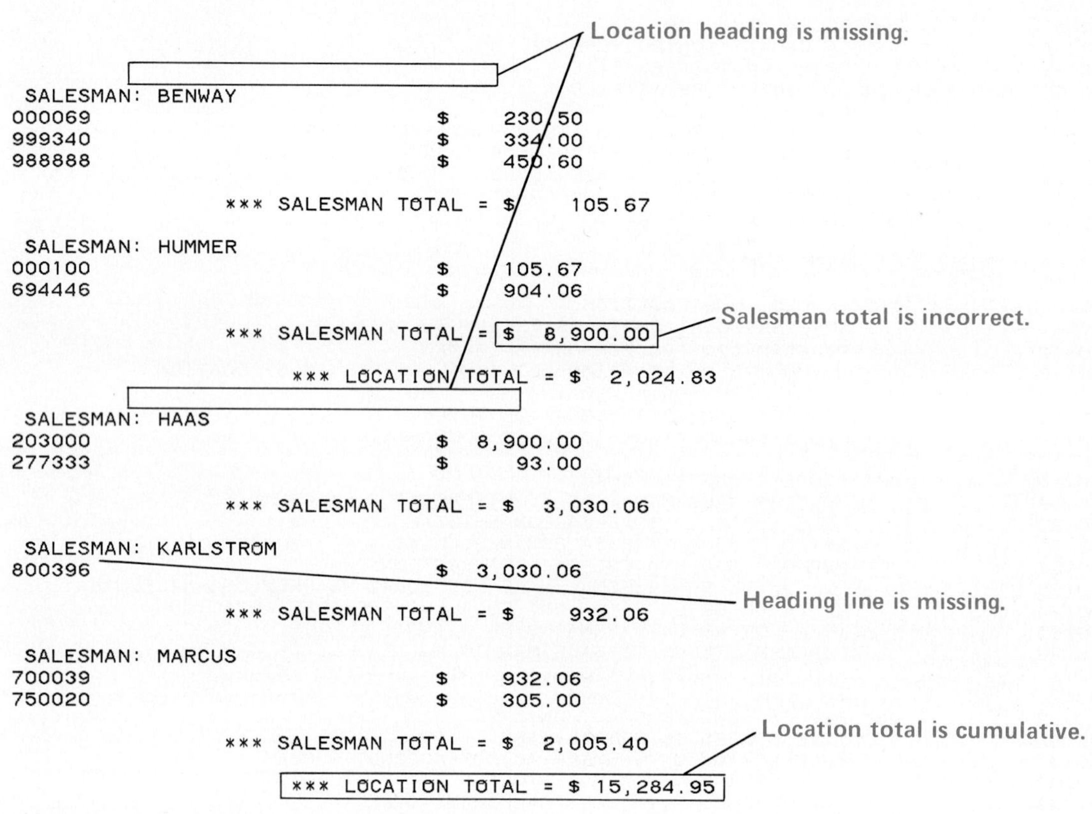
```
 SALESMAN: BENWAY
000069                                $     230.50
999340                                $     334.00
988888                                $     450.60

             *** SALESMAN TOTAL = $       105.67

 SALESMAN: HUMMER
000100                                $     105.67
694446                                $     904.06

             *** SALESMAN TOTAL = $   8,900.00

                  *** LOCATION TOTAL = $   2,024.83

 SALESMAN: HAAS
203000                                $   8,900.00
277333                                $      93.00

             *** SALESMAN TOTAL = $   3,030.06

 SALESMAN: KARLSTROM
800396                                $   3,030.06

             *** SALESMAN TOTAL = $      932.06

 SALESMAN: MARCUS
700039                                $     932.06
750020                                $     305.00

             *** SALESMAN TOTAL = $   2,005.40

                  *** LOCATION TOTAL = $  15,284.95
```


FIGURE 8.16 Erroneous Output of Two Level Program

Programming Specifications

Project 8–1

Program Name:

Three-Level Control Break

Narrative:

Management has requested that the sales information associated with the two-level program in this chapter be aggregated one level higher. Specifically, *regional* totals are required, in addition to salesman and location totals. Region is the highest level break; that is, one or more locations constitute a region.

Input File(s):

SALES-FILE

Input Record Layout:

Identical to the layout used in the example programs; for example, use lines 23–29 from the one-level program. (Observe that the field SR-REGION is present in the input record.)

Test Data:

```
BENWAY       000069023050CHICAGO          MIDWEST
BENWAY       999340033400CHICAGO          MIDWEST
BENWAY       988888045060CHICAGO          MIDWEST
HUMMER       000100010567CHICAGO          MIDWEST
HUMMER       694446090406CHICAGO          MIDWEST
HAAS         203000890000DETROIT          MIDWEST
HAAS         277333009300DETROIT          MIDWEST
KARLSTROM    800396303006DETROIT          MIDWEST
MARCUS       700039093206DETROIT          MIDWEST
MARCUS       750020030500DETROIT          MIDWEST
MARSHAK      987654200540NEW YORK         NORTHEAST
MARSHAK      444333100450NEW YORK         NORTHEAST
MARSHAK      555666200350NEW YORK         NORTHEAST
FEGEN        444444010075ST. PETERSBURG   SOUTHEAST
FEGEN        555555030400ST. PETERSBURG   SOUTHEAST
FRANKEL      100000030350ST. PETERSBURG   SOUTHEAST
FRANKEL      400000070650ST. PETERSBURG   SOUTHEAST
FRANKEL      878787123556ST. PETERSBURG   SOUTHEAST
CLARK        000104050078TAMPA            SOUTHEAST
CLARK        000101150044TAMPA            SOUTHEAST
CLARK        130101320009TAMPA            SOUTHEAST
```

Note that these are the same data used in the example programs, with the region field appended.

Record Layout:

Design the report layout as you see fit, subject to the processing requirements.

Processing Requirements:

1. Modify the two-level control break program in Figure 8.14 to accommodate a third, and highest, level break on region. Accommodate all of the following:
   (a) Begin every region on a new page, with the heading "SALES ACTIVITY REPORT- __________REGION." Include the regional total at the end of the page.
   (b) Omit the detailed information on every transaction; that is, include only a *single* line for every salesman showing the salesman's name and his or her total.
   (c) Omit the location heading; include the one-line location total.
2. Begin the project by modifying the hierarchy chart in Figure 8.11. Indicate the new modules that are required; show which modules can be deleted and those whose processing requirements are changed.

Programming Specifications

Project 8–2

Program Name:

Acme Electric Salary Report

Narrative:

Develop a program to process pay records for the Acme Electric Company to produce salary totals by city and department. This large corporation has offices in several cities. Its personnel are also grouped into functional departments, and a given department can appear in more than one city. The employee file has been sorted by location and by department within location.

Input File(s):

EMPLOYEE-SALARY-FILE

Input Record Layout:

EMPLOYEE NAME	SALARY	DEPARTMENT	LOCATION
1 2 3 4 5 6 7 8 9 10 11 12 13 14 15	16 17 18 19 20	21 22 23	24 25 26 27 28 29 30 31 32 33 34 35

Test Data:

```
ADAMS          15000100ATLANTA
BAKER          18000100ATLANTA
CHARLES        17000100ATLANTA
ALLEN          20000200ATLANTA
SMITH          14000200ATLANTA
JONES          25000100BOSTON
TYLER          26000250BOSTON
WEBER          18000300BOSTON
WHEELER        14000350BOSTON
GOODMAN        12000100CHICAGO
GORDON         12500100CHICAGO
DAVIS          15000150CHICAGO
ELSWORTH       18000150CHICAGO
HAYWARD        21000150CHICAGO
JACKSON        16000150CHICAGO
BABSON         14000150DETROIT
LEWIS          12000150DETROIT
HAYES          17000300DETROIT
JOHNSON        18000300DETROIT
KELLER         19000300DETROIT
```

Report Layout:

```
 1
 2                                                             PAGE ZZ9
 3          SALARY REPORT FOR LOCATION: XXXXXXXXXXXXXX
 4
 5               DEPT      EMPLOYEE          SALARY
 6
 7               999   XXXXXXXXXXXXXXXXXX  $$$,$$9
 8               999   XXXXXXXXXXXXXXXXXX  $$$,$$9
 9
10                  TOTAL SALARIES FOR DEPT 999 = $$,$$$,$$9
11
12
13               999   XXXXXXXXXXXXXXXXXX  $$$,$$9
14               999   XXXXXXXXXXXXXXXXXX  $$$,$$9
15               999   XXXXXXXXXXXXXXXXXX  $$$,$$9
16
17                  TOTAL SALARIES FOR DEPT 999 = $$,$$$,$$9
18
19                       TOTAL SALARIES FOR LOCATION XXXXXXXXXXXXXX = $$,$$$,$$9
20
21
```

Processing Requirements:

1. Read a file of employee records, and for every record:
   (a) Print a detail line containing the employee's name, department, and salary in edited format.
   (b) Increment the department, location, and company total as appropriate.
2. Print a department total whenever department changes. (See Report Format.)
3. Print a location total whenever location changes. (See Report Format.)
4. Begin every location on a new page with an appropriate heading containing the location name and page number of the report. (See Report Format.) The first location begins on page 1.
5. Print the company total on a separate page at the conclusion of the report.

Programming Specifications

Project 8–3

Program Name:

Brokerage Commissions

Narrative:

Write a program to process a brokerage firm's commission records in order to determine the amount earned by each salesman. Incoming records have been sorted by salesman; that is, all the commission records for the same salesman appear together.

Input File:

BROKER-COMMISSION-FILE

Input Record Layout:

FIELD NAME	*POSITIONS*	*PICTURE*
Broker's Name	1–14	X(14)
Social Security Number	15–23	9(9)
Branch Office	24–28	9(5)
Customer Number	29–33	9(5)
Commissions Earned	34–41	9(6)V99

Test Data:

```
MOLDOF, M      11111111101000001110100000
MOLDOF, M      11111111101000001500001005O
STEINMAN, H    33333333301000002220002000O
STEINMAN, H    33333333301000123450012345 6
STEINMAN, H    33333333301000678900067890 0
STEINMAN, G    44444444401000002220001200 0
FRIEDMAR, R    55555555502000004440002560 0
FRIEDMAR, R    55555555502000005550000432 1
ANTONIO, J     66666666602000006660002222 2
ANTONIO, J     66666666602000007770003333 3
ANTONIO, J     66666666602000008880004444 4
```

Report Layout:

Use the following report layout:

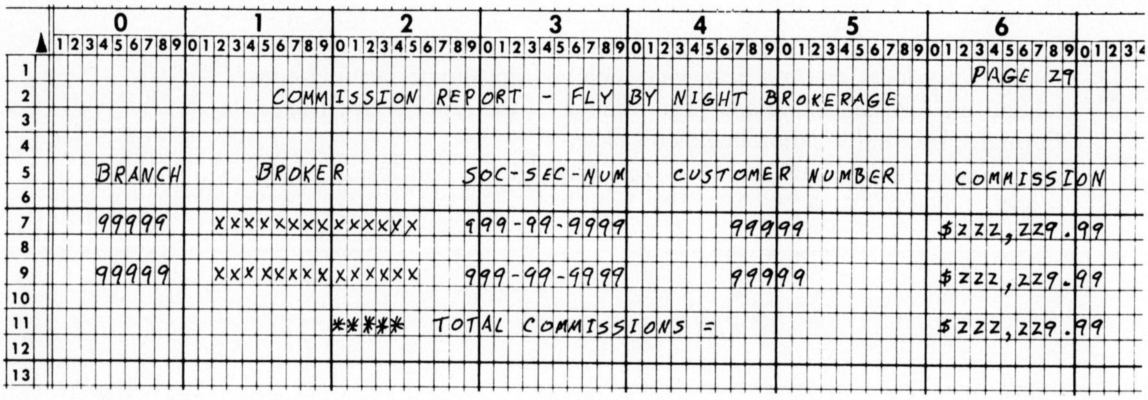

```
1                                                               PAGE Z9
2                COMMISSION REPORT - FLY BY NIGHT BROKERAGE
3
4
5    BRANCH        BROKER        SOC-SEC-NUM   CUSTOMER NUMBER   COMMISSION
6
7    99999   XXXXXXXXXXXXXX      999-99-9999       99999         $ZZZ,ZZ9.99
8
9    99999   XXXXXXXXXXXXXX      999-99-9999       99999         $ZZZ,ZZ9.99
10
11                  *****  TOTAL COMMISSIONS =                   $ZZZ,ZZ9.99
12
13
```

Processing Requirements:

1. Read a file of brokerage commission records.
2. For each record read:
   (a) Print the commission information in that record on a detail line.
   (b) Increment the broker's commission total associated with the particular record by the commission amount.
   (c) Increment the overall total by the commission amount.
3. Begin each broker on a new page.
4. Print a total line for each broker. Skip two lines between the last detail line and the overall total line.
5. After all records have been read, print a total line for the office as a whole. Skip three lines prior to printing the office total.

6. *Extra:* Print each broker's name, branch office, and Social Security number only once, on the detail line associated with the first record for each broker. (The present report repeats the information for each record.)
7. *Extra:* The incoming file is sorted by branch office, and by broker within branch office. Modify all requirements to develop a two-level control break program, with totals for each branch office in addition to each salesman.

More About the Procedure Division

9

Overview

This chapter is devoted entirely to the Procedure Division. Its objective is to introduce a somewhat disjoint set of Procedure Division elements to increase one's overall capability in COBOL. We shall study the IF and PERFORM statements in detail. We shall learn some new verbs to make life easier, e.g., ACCEPT, DISPLAY, and INSPECT. We shall learn new options for statements we already know something about, e.g., READ INTO, WRITE FROM, and MOVE CORRESPONDING. We also cover the SIZE ERROR option of the arithmetic verbs.

The "Systems Concepts" section of the chapter introduces data validation, i.e., checking incoming data prior to computation, to ensure correctness of the data. This is a critical and often underrated aspect of good programming practice.

There is so much material in this chapter that it is not possible to master it all in a first reading. We suggest you read initially for general content only and leave the details for later. Try to get a "feel" for the overall power of the material, but do not attempt to memorize all the options. Instead, return to specific portions of the chapter as you need the material in your projects. □

SYSTEMS CONCEPTS: DATA VALIDATION

Murphy's Law is only too prevalent in data processing. A well-written program, therefore, is not limited to computing answers but must first *validate the data* on which those answers are based. GIGO (Garbage In, Garbage Out) is the unfortunate result of programs (or systems) that fail to edit data.

The validation of incoming data is often done in a separate, stand-alone edit program. The essential point, however, is that incoming data must be checked; when and how this is done is of secondary importance. The following are typical error checks:

Numeric test: Ensures that a numeric field does in fact contain numeric data. Commas, decimal points, or numeric fields containing all blanks are not numeric and will cause problems in execution.

Alphabetic test: Analogous to a numeric test, except that it checks that alphabetic fields have been coded. Any errors detected here are typically less serious than for numeric fields.

Reasonableness check: Assures that a given number is within "normal" bounds. These tests often take the form of *limit* checks, that is, testing that a value does not exceed a designated upper or lower extreme. For example, a payroll program may check that no hourly worker's pay exceeds $500 per week. A weekly gross that exceeded this amount might be deemed unreasonable and the transaction flagged for further scrutiny. A *range* check ensures that a given value is within specified limits and is another form of reasonableness check.

Consistency check: Verifies that the values in two or more fields are consistent, for example, salary and job title. Since salary is partly a function of job title, there should be a correlation between the two. Other examples of consistency checks are an individual's credit rating and the amount of credit a bank is willing to extend, or an individual's reported income and the zip code, i.e., address.

Checking that a code exists: One of the most common, yet most important, tests. The author has seen countless errors compounded because this check was *not* implemented. For example, consider

```
IF SEX = 'M'
    ADD 1 TO NUMBER-OF-MEN
ELSE
    ADD 1 TO NUMBER-OF-WOMEN
```

It is decidedly *poor* practice to assume that an incoming record is female if it is not male. Rather, both codes should be explicitly checked, and if neither occurs, a suitable error should be printed.

Sequence check: Assures that incoming records are in proper order. It can also be used when one record comprises several lines to assure that the lines within a record are in proper sequence.

Completeness check: Verifies that all required fields are present. This check often occurs when records are added to a file.

Date check: Ensures that an incoming date is acceptable. This check is implemented in several ways. Birth dates can be checked to ensure that no one is hired who is younger than 16 or older than 65. Checks can be made on a date to test that the day falls between 1 and 31, the month between 1 and 12, and the year within a designated period, often just the current year.

Subscript check: Validates that a subscript or index is within a table's original definition. (Table processing is discussed fully in Chapter 11.)

Diligent application of data validation (sometimes referred to as defensive programming) minimizes the need for subsequent debugging. Realize that any debugging technique suffers from the fact that it is applied *after* a bug has occurred. Defensive programming assumes that errors will occur (they are, after all, inevitable) and takes steps to make them apparent to the programmer and/or user *before* a program terminates. Is it worth the extra time? Emphatically yes, especially if you have ever been called at two in the morning to hear that your program "bombed" because of invalid data.

Is it reasonable to impose the "burden" of defensive programming on the COBOL programmer? After all, the user is provided with a manual and instructions that "anyone" should be capable of following. Why should the programmer be held responsible for the sins of the user? The COBOL compiler itself yields the answer. Programmers are given manuals, yet the compiler assumes they will make errors and rejects incorrectly coded COBOL with appropriate messages. Since we as programmers depend on the compiler's ability to check our errors, we cannot object to the user's dependence on us to validate his or her transactions.

THE IF STATEMENT

The importance of the IF statement is obvious, yet the large number of options make it one of the more difficult statements to master. We cover class tests, sign tests, and condition names (88-level entries). We consider compound and implied IF's using AND and OR. Finally, we take a good look at NEXT SENTENCE, ELSE, and nested IF's.

Class Tests

A numeric field is limited to the digits 0 to 9 (a sign is optional). Blanks, decimal points, commas, etc. are *not* numeric characters.

An alphabetic field may contain the letters A to Z and/or blanks, whereas alphanumeric fields may contain letters, numbers, or special characters. (The use of alphabetic fields is discouraged, in favor of alphanumeric fields. Even "pure" alphabetic fields often contain alphanumeric characters; for example, an employee name may contain an apostrophe, as in O'Neil.)

Class tests are an excellent way to ensure that numeric data are in fact numeric, alphabetic data are alphabetic, etc. The general format is

```
                        { NUMERIC    }
IF identifier IS [NOT]  {            }
                        { ALPHABETIC }
```

The class test cannot be used indiscriminately. Specifically, a numeric test is used for data names defined with a numeric picture (i.e., a picture of 9's). An alphabetic test is valid for data names defined with a picture of A. However, either test may be performed on alphanumeric items. The validity of class tests is summarized in Table 9.1 and by examples in Figure 9.1.

TABLE 9.1 Valid Forms of Class Test

DATA TYPE AND PICTURE	VALID TESTS
Numeric (9)	NUMERIC, NOT NUMERIC
Alphabetic (A)	ALPHABETIC, NOT ALPHABETIC
Alphanumeric (X)	NUMERIC, NOT NUMERIC, ALPHABETIC, NOT ALPHABETIC

Sign Test

The sign test determines the sign of a numeric data field; the general format is

```
                                { IS [NOT] POSITIVE }
   { identifier            }    {                   }
IF {                       }    { IS [NOT] NEGATIVE }
   { arithmetic expression }    {                   }
                                { IS [NOT] ZERO     }
```

A value is positive if it is greater than zero and negative if it is less than zero. This test is frequently used to validate incoming data or to verify the results of a calculation. Consider these examples:

```
IF NET-PAY IS NOT POSITIVE PERFORM TOO-MUCH-TAXES.
IF CHECK-BALANCE IS NEGATIVE PERFORM OVERDRAWN.
```

```
            05  NUMERIC-FIELD          PIC 9(5).
            05  ALPHABETIC-FIELD       PIC A(5).
            05  ALPHANUMERIC-FIELD     PIC X(5).

(valid)     IF NUMERIC-FIELD IS NUMERIC. . . . .
(valid)     IF NUMERIC-FIELD IS NOT NUMERIC. . . . .
(invalid)   IF NUMERIC-FIELD IS NOT ALPHABETIC. . . . .
(invalid)   IF ALPHABETIC-FIELD IS NOT NUMERIC. . . . .
(valid)     IF ALPHANUMERIC-FIELD IS NOT NUMERIC. . . . .
(valid)     IF ALPHANUMERIC-FIELD IS NOT ALPHABETIC. . . . .
```

FIGURE 9.1 Examples of Class Test

Compound Tests

Any two "simple" tests may be combined to form a compound test through the logical operators AND and OR. AND means both; two conditions must be satisfied for the IF to be considered true. OR means either; only one of the two conditions need be satisfied for the IF to be considered true. A flowchart is shown in Figure 9.2*a* depicting the AND condition. It requires that *both* A be greater than B *and* C be greater than D in order to proceed to TRUE. If either of these tests fails, the compound condition is judged false.

Figure 9.2*b* contains a flowchart for a compound OR. As can be seen from Figure 9.2*b only* one of two conditions need be met for the IF to be considered true. If either A is greater than B *or* C is greater than D, processing is directed to TRUE. In other words, the OR provides a second chance in that the first test can fail but the IF can still be considered true.

Beginning programmers are often carried away with compound conditions. Consider the statement

```
IF X > Y OR X = Z AND X < W . . .
```

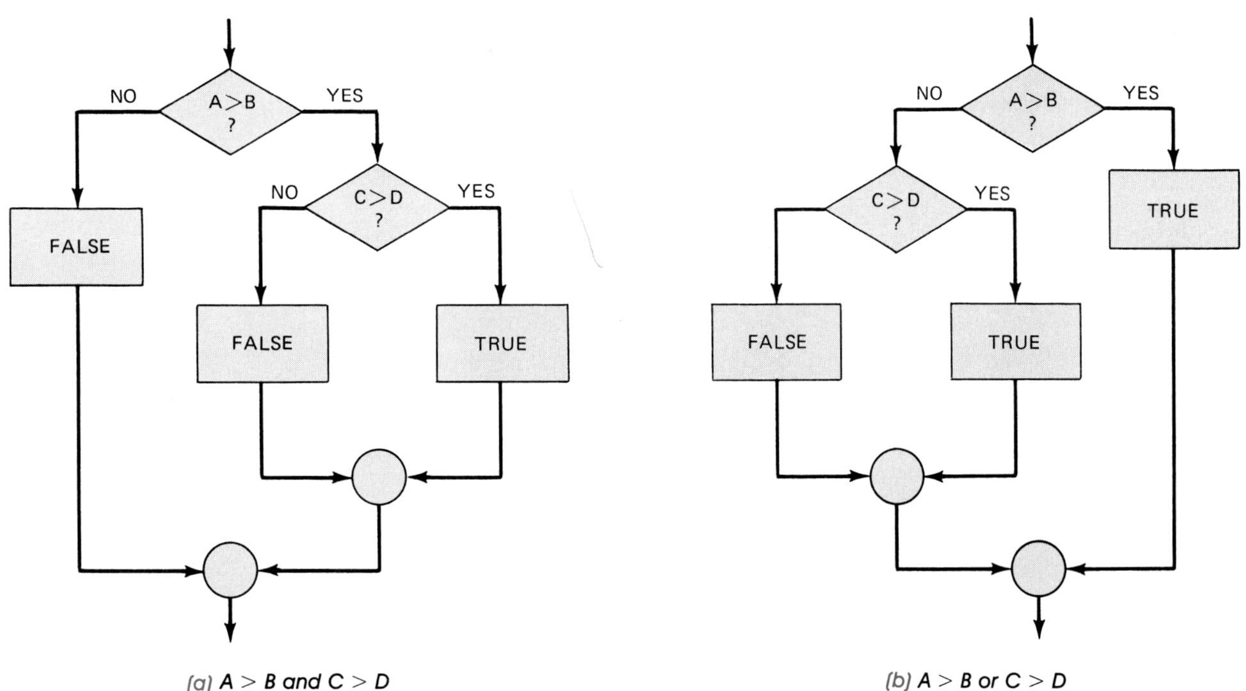

FIGURE 9.2 Compound Conditions

Surely the programmer knew what was intended at the time the statement was written. A day later, however, he or she is apt to stare at it and wonder what will happen first; which takes precedence, AND or OR? To provide an unequivocal evaluation of compound conditions, the following hierarchy is established by COBOL:

1. Arithmetic expressions
2. Relational operators
3. NOT condition
4. AND (from left to right if more than one)
5. OR (from left to right if more than one)

Thus, for the preceding statement to be true either

```
X > Y
```

or

```
X = Z and X < W
```

However, parentheses can and should be used to clarify the programmer's intent. The meaning of the preceding statement is made clearer if it is rewritten as

```
IF X > Y OR (X = Z AND X < W) . . .
```

Note well that parentheses can also *alter* meaning. Thus the following statement is *logically different* from the original code:

```
IF (X > Y OR X = Z) AND X < W . . .
```

Implied Conditions

The compound condition can be further clouded by the use of implied subjects; if a compound condition has the same subject immediately before each relation, only the first occurrence of the subject need be written. In other words;

```
IF SALARY > 30000 AND < 40000
```

is equivalent to

```
IF SALARY > 30000 AND SALARY < 40000
```

If both the subject and relational operator of the simple conditions within a compound condition are the same, then only the first occurrence of both needs to be written; that is,

```
IF DEPARTMENT = 10 OR 20
```

is equivalent to

```
IF DEPARTMENT = 10 OR DEPARTMENT = 20
```

Since implied conditions are often confusing, the following are provided as additional examples:

```
X = Y OR Z         is equivalent to  X = Y OR X = Z
A = B OR C OR D    is equivalent to  A = B OR A = C OR A = D
A = B AND > C      is equivalent to  A = B AND A > C
```

Condition Name Tests (88-Level Entries)

The condition in the IF statement often tests the value of an incoming code, e.g., IF YEAR-CODE = 1. . . . Though such coding is quite permissible and indeed commonplace, the meaning of the value 1 in YEAR-CODE may not be immediately apparent. Condition names (88-level entries) provide an alternate form of coding. 88-level entries are defined in the Data Division and can be applied only to elementary items. Consider

```
05  YEAR-IN-SCHOOL          PIC 9.
    88  FRESHMAN                       VALUE 1.
    88  SOPHOMORE                      VALUE 2.
    88  JUNIOR                         VALUE 3.
    88  SENIOR                         VALUE 4.
    88  GRAD-STUDENT                   VALUES ARE 5 THRU 8.
    88  UNDER-CLASSMAN                 VALUES ARE 1, 2.
    88  UPPER-CLASSMAN                 VALUES ARE 3, 4.
    88  VALID-CODES                    VALUES ARE 1 THRU 8.
```

If the preceding entries were made in the Data Division, one could code

```
IF FRESHMAN
```

as equivalent to

```
IF YEAR-IN-SCHOOL = 1
```

or

```
IF SOPHOMORE
```

as equivalent to

```
IF YEAR-IN-SCHOOL = 2
```

and so on.

There are several reasons for considering 88-level entries. Some would argue that they provide improved documentation in that IF FRESHMAN is inherently clearer than IF YEAR-IN-SCHOOL = 1. (The opposing argument is that the resulting page turning to the Data Division to find the definition of the condition name negates any advantage. The author is ambivalent on this point.)

One incontestable advantage, however, is that 88-level entries *reduce the need for compound conditions* because several codes may be defined under a single condition name. Consider the general format

```
              {VALUE IS  }
88 data-name  {VALUES ARE}  literal-1 [THRU literal-2]

    [literal-3 [THRU literal-4]] . . .
```

and the previous definition of GRAD-STUDENT,

```
88  GRAD-STUDENT    VALUES ARE 5 THRU 8.
```

Thus

```
IF GRAD-STUDENT . . .
```

is equivalent to

```
IF YEAR-IN-SCHOOL > 4 AND YEAR-IN-SCHOOL < 9 . . .
```

The VALUES ARE clause makes it very easy to test for error conditions by grouping all valid codes together as shown; i.e., IF VALID-CODES assures that an incoming year code is in the proper range.

Condition names also permit a given value to appear under more than one classification; e.g., records containing a 3 belong to JUNIOR, UPPER-CLASSMAN, and VALID-CODES.

Nested IFs

The general format of the IF statement is

$$\underline{\text{IF}}\ \text{condition} \begin{Bmatrix} \text{statement-1} \\ \underline{\text{NEXT}}\ \underline{\text{SENTENCE}} \end{Bmatrix} \left[\underline{\text{ELSE}} \begin{Bmatrix} \text{statement-2} \\ \underline{\text{NEXT}}\ \underline{\text{SENTENCE}} \end{Bmatrix} \right]$$

A *nested IF* results when either statement-1 or statement-2 is itself another IF statement, i.e., when there are two or more IF's in one sentence. For example, consider

```
IF A > B
    IF C > D
        MOVE S TO W
        MOVE X TO Y
    ELSE
        ADD 1 TO Z.
```

The ELSE clause is associated with the closest previous IF that is not already paired with another ELSE. Hence, in this example, Z is incremented by 1 if A is greater than B, but C is not greater than D. However, if A is not greater than B, control passes to the next sentence with no further action being taken.

Figure 9.3 shows a flowchart and corresponding COBOL code to determine the largest of three quantities A, B, and C. (They are assumed to be unequal numbers.) Observe how the true and false branches of each decision block meet in a single exit point and how this corresponds to the COBOL code. Notice also how the indentation in the COBOL statement facilitates interpretation of how the statement works. (The compiler pays no attention to the indentation, which is done strictly for programmer convenience.)

We strongly advocate careful attention to indentation and recommend the following guidelines:

1. Each nested IF should be indented four columns from the previous IF.
2. The word ELSE should appear on a line by itself and directly under its associated IF.
3. Detail lines should be indented four columns under both IF and ELSE.

These guidelines were used in Figure 9.3.

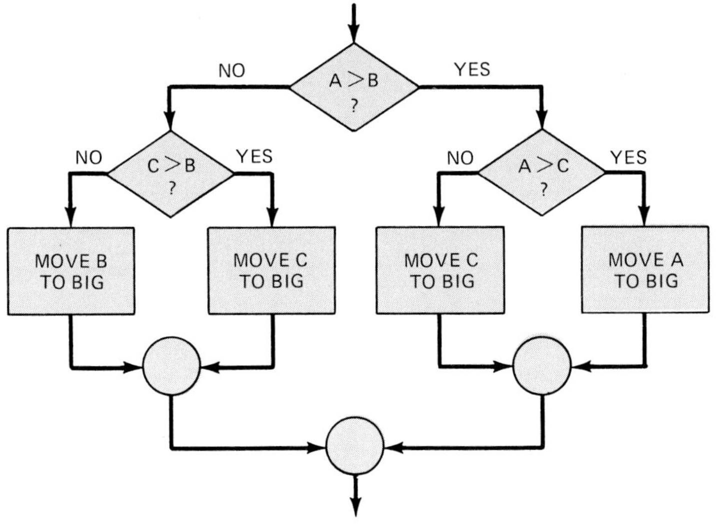

Illustrative Code:

```
IF A>B
    IF A>C
        MOVE A TO BIG
    ELSE
        MOVE C TO BIG
ELSE
    IF C>B
        MOVE C TO BIG
    ELSE
        MOVE B TO BIG.
```

FIGURE 9.3 Flowchart and COBOL Code for Nested IFs

NEXT SENTENCE

As indicated by the general syntax of the IF statement, both IF and ELSE may be followed immediately by NEXT SENTENCE. *This in turn directs control to the statement following the period in the original IF statement.* Use of the NEXT SENTENCE clause may at first appear obscure or superfluous, as most students visualize the situations depicted in Figure 9.4.

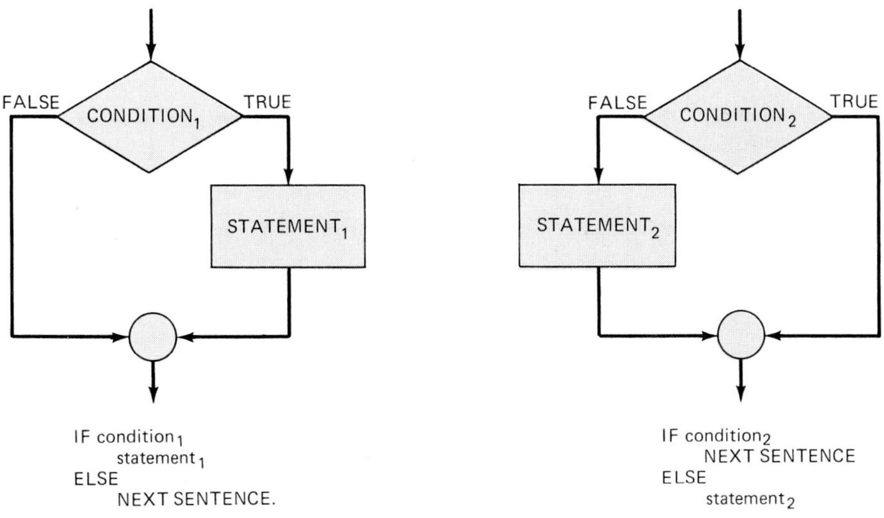


```
IF condition1
    statement1
ELSE
    NEXT SENTENCE.
```

```
IF condition2
    NEXT SENTENCE
ELSE
    statement2
```

FIGURE 9.4 "Trivial" Use of NEXT SENTENCE

The coding associated with Figure 9.4 may be easily rewritten to eliminate NEXT SENTENCE in both instances:

EXAMPLE 1

IF $condition_1$
    $statement_1$

EXAMPLE 2

IF NOT $condition_2$
    $statement_2$

Why, then, introduce the clause at all? The most important reason is that it eliminates the use of negative conditions in an IF statement. The use of NOT may appear innocuous in the rewritten version of Example 2, but programmers often miss the implications of negative conditions, especially when used in conjunction with AND or OR. A second reason for using NEXT SENTENCE is that it maintains symmetry within an IF (or nested IF) and consequently makes the program easier to read. Figure 9.5 illustrates the use of NEXT SENTENCE within a nested IF statement.

The NEXT SENTENCE clause is *required* in the code of Figure 9.5; i.e., the meaning of the IF statement would be different if ELSE NEXT SENTENCE were removed. (Remember, the ELSE clause is associated with the closest previous unpaired IF.)

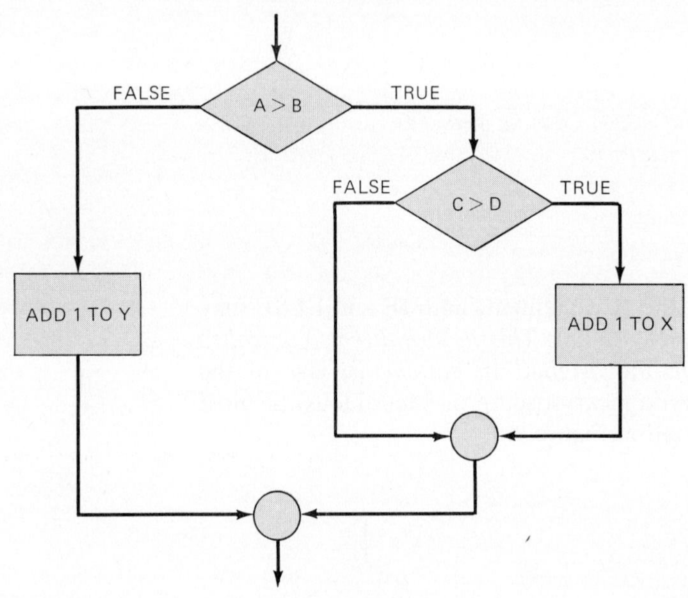


```
IF A > B
    IF C > D
        ADD 1 TO X
    ELSE
        NEXT SENTENCE
ELSE
    ADD 1 TO Y.
```

FIGURE 9.5 The NEXT SENTENCE Clause

Programming Tip

Downplay Efficiency, But Choose the Algorithm Carefully

Efficiency is not the primary criterion of a good program. *Correctness* is, and it is far easier to make a correct program efficient than an efficient program correct. Efficiency also takes a back seat to *maintainability*. A good program must be easily read and maintained by someone other than the original author. Nothing should be done, in the name of efficiency or anything else, to obscure program clarity.

However, efficiency need not be ignored completely, provided one concentrates on the "right" kind of efficiency. To that end, the *algorithm* chosen is often far more important than the generated object code. A case in point is testing the most likely condition first.

Consider a file of 10,000 records in which three types of transactions are possible: A (addition), C (correction), and D (deletion). Further assume that 7,000 records are corrections, 2,500 are additions, and 500 are deletions and that this distribution remains fairly constant from run to run. If the most likely condition, corrections, is tested first, a total of 13,500 comparisons are required, as shown:

```
IF IN-CODE = 'C' . . .              (executed 10,000 times)
ELSE IF IN-CODE = 'A' . . .         (executed  3,000 times)
ELSE IF IN-CODE = 'D' . . .         (executed    500 times)
```

On the other hand, if the least likely condition is tested first, then 26,500 comparisons are necessary:

```
IF IN-CODE = 'D' . . .              (executed 10,000 times)
ELSE IF IN-CODE = 'A' . . .         (executed  9,500 times)
ELSE IF IN-CODE = 'C' . . .         (executed  7,000 times)
```

Although this technique requires some knowledge of file characteristics, it can be used to great advantage when that information is available.

PERFORM

The PERFORM verb has been used all along to implement the iteration construct of structured programming. We now consider additional options that enable us to invoke more than one procedure with a single PERFORM or invoke the same procedure many times.

Performing Sections

The procedure name in the PERFORM statement can be either a *paragraph* name or a *section* name. We already know what a paragraph is. A section consists of one or more paragraphs. If the procedure name in the PERFORM refers to a section name, then *every* paragraph in the section will be executed prior to returning control. Consider

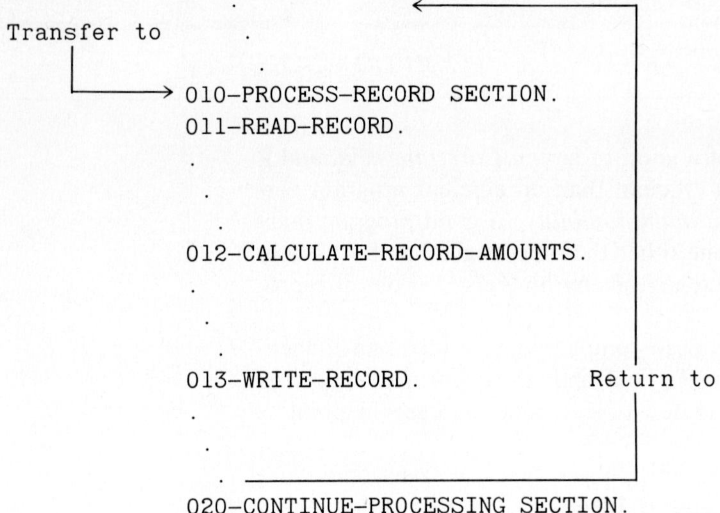
PERFORM 010-PROCESS-RECORD.
Transfer to
010-PROCESS-RECORD SECTION.
011-READ-RECORD.
012-CALCULATE-RECORD-AMOUNTS.
013-WRITE-RECORD.
Return to

```
020-CONTINUE-PROCESSING SECTION.
```

When the PERFORM statement references a section name, control is transferred to the first sentence in the section. Control will not return to the sentence after the PERFORM until the last statement in the section has been executed. Notice that this results in the execution of several paragraphs. How does the compiler know when the section ends? Simply when a new section name is encountered.

PERFORM THRU

An alternate format of PERFORM verb, the THROUGH (THRU) clause, also causes execution of many procedures:

```
PERFORM procedure-name-1 [{THRU   } procedure-name-2]
                          {THROUGH}
```

The THRU option causes all statements *between* the two procedure names to be executed. The procedures may be either paragraphs or sections, but procedure-name-1 must be physically before procedure-name-2 within the COBOL program. A common practice is to make procedure-name-2 a single-sentence paragraph consisting of the word EXIT. The EXIT statement causes no action to be taken; its function is to delineate the end of the PERFORM. Consider

```
    PERFORM PROCESS-RECORDS THRU PROCESS-RECORDS-EXIT.
     .
      .
       .
PROCESS-RECORDS.
      .
      .
      .
PROCESS-RECORDS-EXIT.
    EXIT.
```

The only practical reason to use a PERFORM . . . THRU with an EXIT paragraph is to enable downward branching to the exit depending on a condition in an IF statement within the paragraph. In certain limited instances, a good case may be made for this usage, but more generally the need for "GO TO PARAGRAPH-EXIT" reflects problems in program design. Beginning programmers should eschew this technique.

PERFORM UNTIL

The PERFORM UNTIL syntax invokes the designated procedure an indeterminate number of times, until a specified condition is met. Consider

```
PERFORM procedure-name-1 [{THRU   } procedure-name-2 [UNTIL condition]]
                          {THROUGH}
```

The specified procedure(s) are performed until the condition is satisfied. *The condition is tested prior to performing the procedure.* Thus, if the condition is satisfied initially, the procedure is never performed. For example,

```
MOVE 10 TO N.
PERFORM PAR-A UNTIL N = 10.
```

Since the condition is satisfied immediately (i.e., N = 10), PAR-A will never be performed. Consider this example:

```
    MOVE 1 TO N.
    PERFORM PAR-A UNTIL N = 5.
    .
     .
      .
 PAR-A.
    ADD 1 TO N.
```

PAR-A will be performed four times, not five. After the fourth time through PAR-A, N = 5. Thus, when the condition is next tested, N = 5, and PAR-A is not performed. (If the paragraph is to be performed five times, change the condition to N > 5.)

PERFORM VARYING

The PERFORM VARYING format also causes repeated execution of the designated procedure. Consider

```
PERFORM procedure-name-1 [{THRU   } procedure-name-2]
                          {THROUGH}

    VARYING identifier-1 FROM {literal-2   }
                              {identifier-2}

        BY {literal-3   } UNTIL condition-1
           {identifier-3}
```

The PERFORM VARYING format initializes identifier-1 to the value specified in the FROM clause, and evaluates condition-1. If the condition is *not* satisfied, it branches to the designated procedure, increments identifier-1 by the value in the BY clause, and re-evaluates condition-1. The perform is terminated when condition-1 is satisfied. In other words, a PERFORM VARYING statement first initializes, then loops through a sequence of testing, performing, and incrementing until a condition is satisfied.

Figure 9.6 illustrates this discussion.

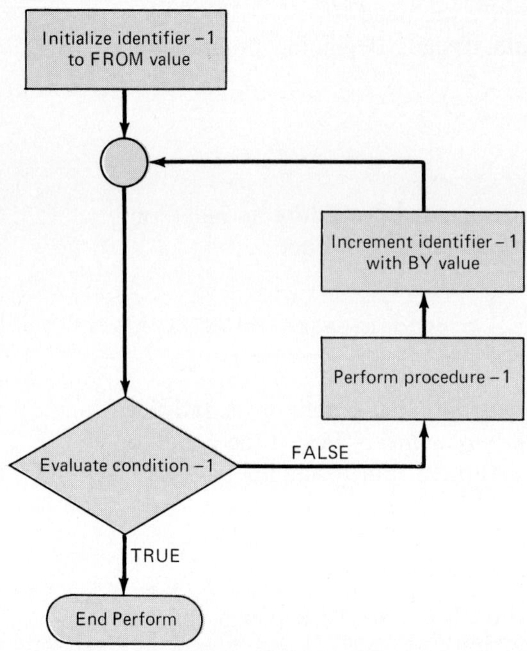

FIGURE 9.6 The PERFORM VARYING Statement

By way of illustration, the statement:

```
PERFORM COMPUTE-PAYMENT
    VARYING YEAR FROM 1 BY 1
        UNTIL YEAR > 3
```

will cause execution of the procedure COMPUTE-PAYMENT three times as follows:

YEAR is initially set to 1. The condition YEAR > 3 is not met, and so COMPUTE-PAYMENT is executed the first time. YEAR is now incremented to 2, the condition is again not met, and COMPUTE-PAYMENT is executed a second time. YEAR is now incremented to 3, but the condition is still *not* met; i.e., *3 is not greater than 3*. Hence COMPUTE-PAYMENT is executed the third, and last, time. Finally, YEAR is incremented to 4, the condition is satisfied, and the PERFORM is terminated. (Realize that if the condition had been specified as YEAR = 3, COMPUTE-PAYMENT would have been executed two times rather than three.)

Extending this reasoning to the general case of executing a paragraph N times, one specifies

```
PERFORM PARAGRAPH
    VARYING WS-COUNTER FROM 1 BY 1
        UNTIL WS-COUNTER > N.
```

The data name used to monitor execution, such as WS-COUNTER, must be explicitly defined in Working-Storage.

TIMES Option

This is the last means available to execute a procedure more than once. Consider

```
PERFORM procedure-name-1 [{THRU   } procedure-name-2]
                          {THROUGH}

    {identifier-1} TIMES
    {integer-1   }
```

as, for example,

```
PERFORM COMPUTE-TRANSCRIPT 5 TIMES
```

or

```
PERFORM COMPUTE-TRANSCRIPT NUMBER-OF-COURSE TIMES
```

The designated procedure is invoked the indicated number of times.

Programming Tip

Perform Paragraphs, not Sections

The motivation behind this guideline is best demonstrated by example. Given the following Procedure Division, what will be the final value of X?

```
PROCEDURE DIVISION.
MAINLINE SECTION.
    MOVE ZEROS TO X.
    PERFORM A.
    PERFORM B.
    PERFORM C.
    PERFORM D.
    STOP RUN.
A SECTION.
    ADD 1 TO X.
B.
    ADD 1 TO X.
C.
    ADD 1 TO X.
D.
    ADD 1 TO X.
```

The *correct* answer is 7, *not 4.* A common error made by many programmers is a misinterpretation of the statement PERFORM A. Since A is a *section* and not a *paragraph,* the statement PERFORM A invokes *every* paragraph in that section, namely, paragraphs B, C, and D, in addition to the unnamed paragraph immediately after the section header.

A PERFORM statement specifies a *procedure,* which is *either* a section *or* a paragraph. Unfortunately, there is no way of telling the nature of the procedure from the PERFORM statement itself. Consequently, when a section is specified as a procedure, the unfortunate result is too often execution of unintended code. Can't happen? Did you correctly compute the value of X?

DISPLAY

The DISPLAY verb is a convenient way of printing information without having to format a record description in the data division. The general form is

```
        ⎧identifier-1⎫ ⎡⎧identifier-2⎫⎤
DISPLAY ⎨            ⎬ ⎢⎨            ⎬⎥ . . . [UPON mnemonic-name]
        ⎩literal-1   ⎭ ⎣⎩literal-2   ⎭⎦
```

Some examples are

```
1. DISPLAY EMPLOYEE-NAME.
2. DISPLAY 'NAME =' EMPLOYEE-NAME.
3. DISPLAY EMPLOYEE-NAME, EMPLOYEE-NUMBER.
4. DISPLAY 'IDENTIFICATION', EMPLOYEE-NAME, EMPLOYEE-NUMBER.
```

Example 1 causes the value of the data name EMPLOYEE-NAME to print. Example 2 causes the literal 'NAME =' to print, prior to the value of EMPLOYEE-NAME. Example 3 prints the values of two data names, and example 4 prints one literal and two data names.

The clause "UPON mnemonic-name" is optional. If it is omitted, the information is displayed on the printer. If a mnemonic name is specified, then output goes to the referenced device, and the mnemonic name must have been defined in the SPECIAL-NAMES paragraph of the Environment Division. (Note, however, that IBM compilers establish CONSOLE and SYSOUT as reserved words, so that one may display directly on these devices *without* defining a mnemonic name.) Consider

```
SPECIAL-NAMES.
    SYSOUT IS LINE-PRINTER.
    CONSOLE IS KEYBOARD.
.
.
.
PROCEDURE DIVISION.
    DISPLAY FIELD-A.
    DISPLAY FIELD-B UPON LINE-PRINTER.
    DISPLAY FIELD-C UPON KEYBOARD.
    DISPLAY FIELD-D UPON CONSOLE.
```

Both FIELD-A and FIELD-B would appear on the printer. FIELD-C and FIELD-D would appear on the console typewriter. *It should be noted that many installations frown on sending messages to the operator. Indeed, within medium-sized and large configurations, the operator is apt to miss or ignore such messages.*

Use with Microcomputers

The DISPLAY statement has come into its own with vendor-supplied COBOL extensions, to facilitate input from terminal devices. Most, if not all, COBOL compilers available in microcomputers have significantly extended capabilities, including LINE and COLUMN positioning, reverse video, and flashing. You may read about them in an appropriate reference manual.

ACCEPT

The ACCEPT statement is a convenient way to "read" information without having to define the entire record. The general form is

```
ACCEPT identifier [FROM mnemonic-name]
```

As with the DISPLAY statement, the mnemonic name is optional. If the mnemonic name is omitted, then the input is taken from the card reader, an option that is rarely used today. If the mnemonic name is used, then it must be defined in the SPECIAL-NAMES paragraph in the Environment Division, e.g., to define the operator's console. However, taking input directly from the operator is discouraged, as the operator may not know the required response.

As with the DISPLAY statement, the ACCEPT statement has been significantly enhanced for microcomputers and screen formatting.

Obtaining Date and Time of Execution

A second form of the ACCEPT verb is used to obtain the date and/or time of program execution. Consider

```
                              {DATE}
ACCEPT identifier-1 FROM {DAY }
                              {TIME}
```

Identifier-1 is a programmer-defined work area to hold the information being accepted. If DATE is specified, then identifier-1 will receive a six-digit numeric field in the form yymmdd. The first two digits contain year, the next two month, and the last two day of the month; for example, 840316, denotes March 16, 1984. If DAY, rather than DATE, is specified, a five-digit numeric field is returned to the work area. The first two digits represent year and the last three the day of the year, numbered from 1 to 366. March 16, 1983, would be represented as 83075, but March 16, 1984, as 84076, since 1984 is a leap year.

TIME returns an eight-digit numeric field in a 24-hour system. It contains the number of elapsed hours, minutes, seconds, and hundredths of seconds after midnight, in that order, from left to right. 10:15 A.M. would return as 10150000, 10:15 P.M. as 22150000.

Calculations Involving Dates

Once the date of execution is obtained, it is often used in calculations, e.g., an employee's age, or accounts which haven't been paid in 30 days. Figure 9.7 illustrates how an employee's age may be calculated from the date of execution and the employee's birth date.

It is critical that you take the time to verify that the COMPUTE statement works as intended, and further that it works for all combinations of data. This is best accomplished by "playing computer" and plugging in numbers. Accordingly, consider two examples:

Example 1

Date of birth: 3/65
Date of execution: 6/85
Expected age: 20 ¼
Calculation: 85 − 65 + (6 − 3)/12 = 20 + 3/12 = 20 ¼

```
WORKING-STORAGE SECTION.
        .
        .
        .
01  EMPLOYEE-RECORD.
    .
    .
    .
    05  EMP-DATE-OF-BIRTH.
        10 EMP-BIRTH-MONTH      PIC 99.
        10 EMP-BIRTH-YEAR       PIC 99.

01  EMPLOYEE-AGE                PIC 99V9.

01  DATE-WORK-AREA.
    05  TODAYS-YEAR             PIC 99.
    05  TODAYS-MONTH            PIC 99.
    05  TODAYS-YEAR             PIC 99.
    .
    .
    .
PROCEDURE DIVISION.
    .
    .
    .
    ACCEPT DATE-WORK-AREA FROM DATE.
    .
    .
    .
    COMPUTE EMPLOYEE-AGE = TODAYS-YEAR - EMP-BIRTH-YEAR
        + (TODAYS-MONTH - EMP-BIRTH-MONTH) / 12.
```

FIGURE 9.7 Use of the Date of Execution in a Calculation

Example 2

Date of birth: 9/65
Date of execution: 6/85
Expected age: 19¾
Calculation: 85 − 65 + (6 − 9)/12 = 20 + −3/12 = 19¾

The calculations are correct, and they work for both combinations of data; it doesn't matter whether the month of execution is before or after the birth month. (For simplicity only month and year were used in the calculation.)

SIZE ERROR Option

The SIZE ERROR option is available for the five arithmetic verbs ADD, SUBTRACT, MULTIPLY, DIVIDE, and COMPUTE. Consider the general form of the COMPUTE statement:

```
COMPUTE identifier-1 [ROUNDED] = arithmetic expression . . .
    [ON SIZE ERROR imperative-statement]
```

The SIZE ERROR option is used to signal when the result of calculation is too large for the designated field; e.g.,

```
05  HOURLY-RATE        PIC 99.
05  HOURS-WORKED       PIC 99.
05  GROSS-PAY          PIC 999.
 .
  .
   .
    COMPUTE GROSS-PAY = HOURLY-RATE * HOURS-WORKED.
```

Assume that HOURLY-RATE and HOURS-WORKED are 25 and 40, respectively. The result of the multiplication should be 1,000. Unfortunately, GROSS-PAY is defined as a three-position numeric field. Only the three rightmost digits are retained, and GROSS-PAY becomes 000. The computer goes merrily on its way, for it does not sense any kind of error. Indeed, the director of data processing will first be made aware of this happening only when an irate employee pounds on his door asking about his check.

The situation is prevented by the inclusion of the SIZE ERROR option:

```
COMPUTE GROSS-PAY = HOURLY-RATE * HOURS-WORKED
   ON SIZE ERROR PERFORM ERROR-ROUTINE.
```

If the results of the computation are too large and exceed the allotted PICTURE clause, control passes to the statement(s) following the SIZE ERROR clause.

INSPECT

The INSPECT verb is used to accomplish two things:

1. To count the number of times a specified character appears within a field.
2. To replace one character by another within a field.

The INSPECT verb has several formats; consider first

```
INSPECT identifier-1 REPLACING
{ CHARACTERS BY {identifier-2} [ {BEFORE} INITIAL {identifier-3} ]
                {literal-1   }   {AFTER }         {literal-2   }
                                                                                    }
{ {ALL    } {identifier-4} BY {identifier-5} [ {BEFORE} INITIAL {identifier-6} ]  }
{ {LEADING} {literal-3   }    {literal-4   }   {AFTER }         {literal-5   }    }
{ {FIRST  }                                                                         }
```

This format is extremely useful for editing reports and is often used in conjunction with the edit characters of Chapter 5. Assume, for example, that the Social Security number is stored as a nine-position field (i.e., with no hyphens), but we wish it to appear with hyphens in a printed report. This is accomplished as follows:

```
01  RECORD-IN.
      .
       .
        .
    05  SOC-SEC-NUM         PIC 9(9).
```

```
01  PRINT-LINE.
     .
      .
     05  SOC-SEC-NUM-OUT     PIC 999B99B9999.

PROCEDURE DIVISION.
     .
      .
       .
     MOVE SOC-SEC-NUM TO SOC-SEC-NUM-OUT.
     INSPECT SOC-SEC-NUM-OUT REPLACING ALL ' ' BY '-'.
```

The MOVE statement transfers the incoming Social Security number to an 11-position field containing two blanks (denoted by B in the PICTURE clause). The INSPECT statement replaces every occurrence of a blank in SOC-SEC-NUM-OUT by the desired hyphen. (This technique is also used to insert slashes in date fields.)

Another frequent use of the INSPECT verb is the elimination of leading blanks in numeric fields. Numeric fields in COBOL should not contain anything other than the digits 0 to 9 and a sign over the rightmost (low-order) position, although the latter is infrequently used. Let us assume a lazy data-entry clerk did not enter the leading zeros but left blanks instead. One alternative is to reenter the data; our choice is to use the INSPECT verb as follows:

```
INSPECT FIELD-WITH-BLANKS REPLACING LEADING ' ' BY '0'.
```

If the CHARACTERS option is chosen instead, no comparison takes place. Instead, each character in identifier-1 is replaced by literal-1 or identifier-2.

A second format of the INSPECT verb includes the TALLYING option:

```
INSPECT identifier-1 TALLYING
                      { { ALL     } {identifier-3} } [ {BEFORE}          {identifier-4} ]
    identifier-2 FOR  { { LEADING } {literal-1   } } [ {AFTER }  INITIAL {literal-2   } ] . . .
                      {   CHARACTERS               }
```

TABLE 9.2 Use of the INSPECT Verb

INSPECT	*FIELD-A before execution*	*FIELD-A after execution*	*Value of COUNTER-1*
INSPECT FIELD-A REPLACING ALL ' ' BY '/'.	10 31 73	10/31/73	N/A
INSPECT FIELD-A TALLYING COUNTER-1 FOR ALL ' '.	10 31 73	10 31 73	2
INSPECT FIELD-A TALLYING COUNTER-1 FOR LEADING '1'.	32110	32110	0
INSPECT FIELD-A REPLACING LEADING ' ' BY '0'.	——— 123	000123	N/A
INSPECT FIELD-A TALLYING COUNTER-1 FOR CHARACTERS.	BENJAMIN	BENJAMIN	8
INSPECT FIELD-A REPLACING CHARACTERS BY 'A'.	BENJAMIN	AAAAAAAA	N/A

Notes: 1. N/A denotes not applicable.
Notes: 2. The programmer is responsible for initializing COUNTER-1 prior to each INSPECT statement.

The TALLYING option counts the number of times a designated character appears. The count is contained in the data name defined by the programmer as identifier-2. The programmer is responsible for defining identifier-2 in the data division and for *initializing* its value prior to using the INSPECT statement.

The INSPECT verb is summarized in Table 9.2.

READ INTO

The general form of the READ statement is

```
READ file-name RECORD [INTO identifier] AT END imperative statement.
```

The READ INTO option stores the input record in the specified area and, in addition, moves it to the designated identifier following INTO. Consider

```
FD  EMPLOYEE-FILE
 .
  .
   .
    DATA RECORD IS EMPLOYEE-RECORD.
01  EMPLOYEE-RECORD       PIC X(80).
 .
  .
   .
WORKING-STORAGE SECTION.
01  WS-EMPLOYEE-AREA     PIC X(80).
 .
  .
   .
PROCEDURE DIVISION.
    READ EMPLOYEE-FILE INTO WS-EMPLOYEE-AREA
       AT END PERFORM END-OF-JOB-ROUTINE.
```

The input data will be available in both EMPLOYEE-RECORD and WS-EMPLOYEE-AREA. Thus the single READ INTO statement is equivalent to both

```
READ EMPLOYEE-FILE
   AT END PERFORM END-OF-JOB-ROUTINE.
```

and

```
MOVE EMPLOYEE-RECORD TO WS-EMPLOYEE-AREA.
```

WRITE FROM

WRITE FROM is analogous to READ INTO in that it combines a MOVE and a WRITE statement into one. The general form of the WRITE statement is

```
WRITE record-name [FROM identifier-1]
                              ┌ ┌ identifier-2 ┐ ┌ LINE  ┐ ┐
      ┌ ┌ BEFORE ┐            │ └ integer      ┘ └ LINES ┘ │
      │ │        │ ADVANCING <                              >
      └ └ AFTER  ┘            │ ┌ mnemonic-name ┐           │
                              └ └ PAGE          ┘           ┘
```

Programming Tip

Use READ INTO, WRITE FROM, and WS BEGINS HERE

If a program terminates prematurely, the first task is to identify the record being processed at the instant the problem occurred. Unfortunately, I/O areas are difficult to find in a dump, whereas Working-Storage is far easier. The following technique is helpful:

```
WORKING-STORAGE SECTION.
01  FILLER                      PIC X(14)
        VALUE 'WS BEGINS HERE'.
01  WS-EMPLOYEE-RECORD.
    05  EMP-NAME                PIC X(25).
    05  EMP-SOC-SEC-NUMBER      PIC 9(9).
    .
     .
      .
01  WS-HDG-LINE-1.
    .
     .
      .
    READ EMPLOYEE-FILE INTO WS-EMPLOYEE-RECORD
        AT END . . .
    WRITE PRINT-LINE FROM WS-HDG-LINE-1
        AFTER ADVANCING . . .
```

The start of Working-Storage is found by scanning the alphabetic interpretation of the dump, searching for WS BEGINS HERE. The technique is not sophisticated, but it does work. Once the Working-Storage Section is found, one can easily identify the record in question as well as the values of all other data names defined in Working-Storage, e.g., switches and subscripts.

Several variations are common with this guideline. For example, when the Working-Storage Section is very large, several VALUE clauses may appear within the *same* program to indicate various areas of Working-Storage.

WRITE FROM is particularly useful when writing heading lines. Consider

```
FD  PRINT-FILE
.
 .
  .
    DATA RECORD IS PRINT-LINE.
01  PRINT-LINE                      PIC X(133).
.
 .
  .
WORKING-STORAGE SECTION.
01  HEADING-LINE.
    05  FILLER                      PIC X(20)
            VALUE SPACES.
```

```
       05  FILLER                    PIC X(12)
             VALUE 'ACME WIDGETS'.
   .
    .
     .
     WRITE PRINT-LINE FROM HEADING-LINE
       AFTER ADVANCING PAGE.
```

The single WRITE FROM statement is equivalent to

```
MOVE HEADING-LINE TO PRINT-LINE.
WRITE PRINT-LINE
    AFTER ADVANCING PAGE.
```

DUPLICATE DATA NAMES

Most programs require that the output contain some of the input, e.g., name and Social Security number. COBOL permits duplicate data names to be defined in the Data Division provided all Procedure Division references to duplicate data names use qualification. *We prefer not to use duplicate names in that they violate the prefix coding standard discussed in Chapter 5.* However, duplicate names are often used by others, since they are conducive to the CORRESPONDING option, which results in fewer statements in the Procedure Division. Both qualification and the CORRESPONDING option are discussed in accordance with Figure 9.8.

```
01  STUDENT-RECORD.
    05  STUDENT-NAME                PIC X(20).
    05  SOCIAL-SECURITY-NUM         PIC 9(9).
    05  STUDENT-ADDRESS.
        10  STREET                  PIC X(15).
        10  CITY-STATE              PIC X(15).
    05  ZIP-CODE                    PIC X(5).
    05  CREDITS                     PIC 999.
    05  MAJOR                       PIC X(10).
    05  FILLER                      PIC X(3).
     .
     .
01  PRINT-LINE.
    10  STUDENT-NAME                PIC X(20).
    10  FILLER                      PIC X(2).
    10  CREDITS                     PIC ZZ9.
    10  FILLER                      PIC X(2).
    10  TUITION                     PIC $$,$$9.99.
    10  FILLER                      PIC X(2).
    10  STUDENT-ADDRESS.
        15  STREET                  PIC X(15).
        15  CITY-STATE              PIC X(15).
        15  ZIP-CODE                PIC X(5).
    10  FILLER                      PIC X(2).
    10  SOCIAL-SECURITY-NUM         PIC 999B99B9999.
    10  FILLER                      PIC X(47).
```

FIGURE 9.8 Data Division Code for Duplicate Data Names

Qualification

The coding in Figure 9.8 has several data names contained in both STUDENT-RECORD and PRINT-LINE, e.g., CREDITS, and it is confusing to reference any of these data names in the Procedure Division.

Consider the statement

```
MULTIPLY CREDITS BY COST-PER-CREDIT GIVING CHARGE.
```

The use of CREDITS is ambiguous; the compiler does not know which CREDITS (in STUDENT-RECORD or PRINT-LINE) we are talking about. The solution is to qualify the data name, using OF or IN to clarify the reference. Thus the statement is rewritten as

```
MULTIPLY CREDITS OF STUDENT-RECORD BY COST-PER-CREDIT GIVING CHARGE.
```

Qualification may be required over several levels. For example, this statement is still ambiguous:

```
MOVE STREET OF STUDENT-ADDRESS TO OUTPUT-AREA.
```

Both STREET and STUDENT-ADDRESS are duplicate data names, so the qualification didn't help. We could use two levels to make our intent clear, e.g.,

```
MOVE STREET OF STUDENT-ADDRESS OF STUDENT-RECORD TO OUTPUT-AREA.
```

We could also skip the intermediate level and code

```
MOVE STREET IN STUDENT-RECORD TO OUTPUT-AREA.
```

Notice that OF and IN can be used interchangeably. Duplicate data names offer the advantage of not having to invent different names for the same item, e.g., an employee name appearing in both an input record and output report. They also permit the CORRESPONDING option.

CORRESPONDING Option

The general form of the CORRESPONDING option is

```
     {CORRESPONDING}
MOVE {CORR         } identifier-1 TO identifier-2.
```

Notice that CORR is the abbreviated form of CORRESPONDING (analogous to PIC and PICTURE). Consider the record description in Figure 9.8 and the statement

```
MOVE CORRESPONDING STUDENT-RECORD TO PRINT-LINE.
```

The MOVE CORRESPONDING statement is equivalent to several individual MOVEs. It takes every data name of STUDENT-RECORD and looks for a duplicate data name in PRINT-LINE. Whenever a match is found, an individual MOVE is generated. Thus the preceding MOVE CORRESPONDING is equivalent to

```
MOVE STUDENT-NAME OF STUDENT-RECORD          TO STUDENT-NAME OF PRINT-LINE.
MOVE SOCIAL-SECURITY-NUM OF STUDENT-RECORD   TO SOCIAL-SECURITY-NUM OF PRINT-LINE.
MOVE STREET OF STUDENT-RECORD                TO STREET OF PRINT-LINE.
MOVE CITY-STATE OF STUDENT-RECORD            TO CITY-STATE OF PRINT-LINE.
MOVE CREDITS OF STUDENT-RECORD               TO CREDITS OF PRINT-LINE.
```

Notice that the level numbers of the duplicate data names do not have to match; it is only the data names themselves that must be the same in each record. Further, notice that the order of the data names is immaterial; e.g., SOCIAL-SECURITY-NUM is the second field in STUDENT-RECORD and the next to last in PRINT-LINE.

There are several restrictions pertaining to the use of the CORRESPONDING option. In particular,

1. At least one item in each pair of CORRESPONDING items must be an elementary item for the MOVE to be effective. Thus, in the example, STUDENT-ADDRESS of STUDENT-RECORD is *not* moved to STUDENT-ADDRESS of PRINT-LINE. (The elementary items STREET and CITY-STATE are moved instead.)
2. Corresponding elementary items will be moved only if they have the same name and qualifications up to but not including identifier-1 and identifier-2. Thus ZIP-CODE will *not* be moved.
3. Any elementary item containing a REDEFINES, RENAMES, OCCURS, or USAGE IS INDEX clause is not moved.

A DATA-VALIDATION PROGRAM

While we hope the discussion on COBOL statements has been understandable, we readily admit it can make for dry reading. Our fundamental approach throughout the text is to learn by doing. To that end we have developed a complete COBOL program that incorporates most of the material in this chapter. In addition the program includes validation of incoming data, dating the report, and a page heading routine.

Specifications follow in the usual format.

Programming Specifications

Program Name:

Car Billing

Narrative:

This program illustrates data validation, as well as most of the Procedure Division features discussed in the chapter.

Input File:

RENTAL-RECORD-FILE

Input Record Layout:

```
01  RENTAL-RECORD.
    05  SOC-SEC-NUM                 PIC 9(9).
    05  NAME-FIELD                  PIC X(25).
```

```
05  DATE-RETURNED.
    10  DATE-RETURNED-YY             PIC 9(2).
    10  DATE-RETURNED-MM             PIC 9(2).
    10  DATE-RETURNED-DD             PIC 9(2).
05  CAR-TYPE                         PIC X.
    88  COMPACT                                     VALUE 'C'.
    88  INTERMEDIATE                                VALUE 'I'.
    88  FULL-SIZE                                   VALUE 'F'.
    88  VALID-CODES
            VALUES ARE 'C' 'I' 'F'.
05  DAYS-RENTED                      PIC 99.
05  MILES-DRIVEN                     PIC 9(4).
05  FILLER                           PIC X(33).
```

Test Data:

See Figure 9.9.

Report Layout:

See Figure 9.10*a* and *b*. Verify that the output in Figure 9.10 is consistent with the data in Figure 9.9 and the programming specifications.

Processing Requirements:

1. Read a file of car rental records.
2. Validate each input record for all of the following:
   (a) The presence of both Social Security number and customer name. Display the message "MISSING DATA" for any record missing in either field.
   (b) A valid car type code, i.e., C, I, or F. Display the message "INVALID CAR" for any record with an invalid car type.
   (c) A reasonable number of miles driven; i.e., flag any record where the number of miles driven is less than 10 times the number of days rented. Use the message "INVALID MILEAGE."
   (d) A reasonable number of rented days; i.e., the number of days rented cannot exceed 35. Flag these records with the message "REFER TO LONG-TERM LEASING."
   (e) Valid dates; month must be between 1 and 12, day cannot exceed 31, and year must be either the current year or the year before. Display a suitable message, i.e., "INVALID MONTH," "INVALID DAY," or "INVALID YEAR." Are these checks sufficient to validate a date field?
3. Any record that fails any validity test is to be rejected with no further processing, other than displaying the appropriate error message(s). It is quite possible that a given record may contain more than one error, and all errors are to be flagged.
4. Valid records are to have their bills calculated as follows:
   (a) The amount due is a function of car type, days rented, and miles driven. Compact cars are billed at $10.00 a day plus 18¢ a mile, intermediate cars at $12.00 a day and 20¢ a mile, and full size cars at $14.00 and 22¢ a mile.
   (b) The amount due is simply the mileage rate times the number of miles driven, plus the daily rate times the number of days rented.
5. Customer bills are to be double-spaced and limited to 5 per page. A suitable heading is required at the top of every page.

```
123456789BAKER,RG                   840430F050345
987654321BROWN,PG                   830112I102000
999999999JONES,PJ                   831309I450345
987654555BROWNING,PJ                841024 100898
999777666ELSINOR,TR                 821126F050345
655443366FITZPATRICK,DT             840432I070785
987654390SMITH,PG                   831213I030150
         PINNOCK                    841012F100345
093477777BUTLER,JH                  830619C050005
193456789SAMUELS,SH                 840221C050345
354679876KERBEL,NX                  830331I101259
264805298CLARK,JS                   841101F070524
233432454BEINHORN,CB                831122I020044
556564365HUMMER,MR                  830815C080225
677844338MCDONALD,J                 840123C050278
886222343VOGEL,JD                   840518F120413
008632212TOWER,DR                   840429I090376
```

FIGURE 9.9 *Test Data*

STACEY CAR RENTALS - REPORT DATE 03/21/84 — PAGE 3

ACCT #	NAME	TYPE	DAYS	MILES	AMOUNT
008-63-2212	TOWER,DR	I	9	376	$183.20

STACEY CAR RENTALS - REPORT DATE 03/21/84 — PAGE 2

ACCT #	NAME	TYPE	DAYS	MILES	AMOUNT
264-80-5298	CLARK,JS	F	7	524	$213.28
233-43-2454	BEINHORN,CB	I	2	44	$32.80
556-56-4365	HUMMER,MR	C	8	225	$120.50
677-84-4338	MCDONALD,J	C	5	278	$100.04
886-22-2343	VOGEL,JD	F	12	413	$258.86

STACEY CAR RENTALS - REPORT DATE 03/21/84 — PAGE 1

ACCT #	NAME	TYPE	DAYS	MILES	AMOUNT
123-45-6789	BAKER,RG	F	5	345	$145.90
987-65-4321	BROWN,PG	I	10	2000	$520.00
987-65-4390	SMITH,PG	I	3	150	$66.00
193-45-6789	SAMUELS,SH	C	5	345	$112.10
354-67-9876	KERBEL,NX	I	10	1259	$371.80

FIGURE 9.10a *Valid Output*

```
INVALID MILEAGE JONES,PJ

ERROR - REFER TO LONG-TERM LEASING JONES,PJ

INVALID MONTH JONES,PJ

INVALID CAR BROWNING,PJ

INVALID YEAR ELSINOR,TR

INVALID DAY FITZPATRICK,DT

MISSING DATA PINNOCK

INVALID MILEAGE BUTLER,JH
```

FIGURE 9.10b *Display Messages Caused by Invalid Input Data*

Pseudocode

One should always take the time to develop the logic of a program in pseudocode, prior to actual coding. Accordingly, Figure 9.11 contains the pseudocode for the data-validation program.

Since a working definition of pseudocode is "neat notes to oneself," pseudocode can be far less detailed than the actual program. Note for example, the single pseudocode statement "do all validity checks," which will correspond to several lines of COBOL code in the actual program. Nevertheless, the pseudocode is useful in that it contains sequence and decision-making logic and helps to ensure that the resulting COBOL program has its statements in the proper order. (The author sees little to be gained from excessively detailed pseudocode which is a duplication of the Procedure Division.)

```
Open Files
Obtain date of execution
Read first rental record
PERFORM UNTIL no more data
    Do all validity checks
    IF incoming record is valid
        Compute the car rental bill
        Write a detail line
    ENDIF
    Read next rental record
ENDPERFORM
Close files
Stop run
```

FIGURE 9.11 Pseudocode for Data-Validation Program

The Completed Program

The completed program is shown in Figure 9.12. The Identification and Environment Divisions are straightforward and contain no new material. The Working-Storage Section begins with a FILLER entry, 'WS BEGINS HERE', in conjunction with subsequent use of READ INTO and WRITE FROM in the Procedure Division. Consequently the input record layout is not defined in the File Section, but rather in Working-Storage (lines 61–76). Condition names (i.e., 88-level entries) are used to group valid codes (lines 72 and 73) and to define a value for the end-of-file condition (line 40).

As usual, the most useful description of the Procedure Division is provided by a hierarchy chart, as in Figure 9.13. It indicates that the driving paragraph, MAINLINE, has three subordinates: INITIALIZE-VALID-DATES, READ-RENTAL-RECORD, and PROCESS-CUSTOMER-RECORDS. The latter performs four lower-level paragraphs: VALIDATE-CUSTOMER-RECORD, COMPUTE-BILL, WRITE-RENTAL-LINE, and READ-RENTAL-RECORD. WRITE-RENTAL-LINE is seen to perform a lower-level paragraph WRITE-HEADING-LINES, which at first glance seems surprising. Recall, for example, that the hierarchy chart in Chapter 5 had the heading routine on a much higher level. However, the earlier program produced only a single heading, at the start of processing, whereas the current requirement is to produce a heading at the top of *every* page; hence the heading routine will be executed several times and is therefore subordinate to writing a detail line.

Establishment of a heading routine requires definition of two counters in Working-Storage, WS-LINE-COUNT and WS-PAGE-COUNT (lines 48 and 49).

```
         IDENTIFICATION DIVISION.
         PROGRAM-ID.
             CARS.
         AUTHOR.
             JACKIE CLARK.

         ENVIRONMENT DIVISION.
         CONFIGURATION SECTION.
         SOURCE-COMPUTER.
             IBM-4341.
         OBJECT-COMPUTER.
             IBM-4341.

         INPUT-OUTPUT SECTION.
         FILE-CONTROL.
             SELECT RENTAL-RECORD-FILE
                 ASSIGN TO UT-S-SYSIN.
             SELECT PRINT-FILE
                 ASSIGN TO UT-S-SYSPRT.

         DATA DIVISION.
         FILE SECTION.
         FD  RENTAL-RECORD-FILE
             LABEL RECORDS ARE OMITTED
             RECORD CONTAINS 80 CHARACTERS
             DATA RECORD IS RENTAL-RECORD.
         01  RENTAL-RECORD               PIC X(80).

         FD  PRINT-FILE
             LABEL RECORDS ARE OMITTED
             RECORD CONTAINS 133 CHARACTERS
             DATA RECORD IS PRINT-LINE.
         01  PRINT-LINE                  PIC X(133).

         WORKING-STORAGE SECTION.
         01  FILLER                      PIC X(14)
                 VALUE 'WS BEGINS HERE'.

         01  WS-END-OF-FILE-SWITCH       PIC XXX         VALUE 'NO '.
             88 WS-END-OF-FILE                           VALUE 'YES'.

         01  VALIDATION-AREA.
             05  VALID-RECORD-SW         PIC X(3).
             05  VALID-MILES             PIC 9(3).
             05  LAST-YEAR               PIC 99.

         01  PAGE-AND-LINE-COUNTERS.
             05  WS-LINE-COUNT           PIC 9(2)        VALUE 6.
             05  WS-PAGE-COUNT           PIC 9(2)        VALUE ZEROS.

         01  BILLING-CONSTANTS.
             05  WS-MILEAGE-RATE         PIC 9V99.
             05  WS-DAILY-RATE           PIC 99V99.
             05  WS-CUSTOMER-BILL        PIC 9999V99.

         01  DATE-WORK-AREA.
             05  TODAYS-YEAR             PIC 99.
             05  TODAYS-MONTH            PIC 99.
             05  TODAYS-DAY              PIC 99.

         01  WS-RECORD-IN.
             05  SOC-SEC-NUM             PIC 9(9).
             05  NAME-FIELD              PIC X(25).
             05  DATE-RETURNED.
                 10  DATE-RETURNED-YY    PIC 9(2).
                 10  DATE-RETURNED-MM    PIC 9(2).
                 10  DATE-RETURNED-DD    PIC 9(2).
             05  CAR-TYPE                PIC X.
                 88  COMPACT                             VALUE 'C'.
                 88  INTERMEDIATE                        VALUE 'I'.
                 88  FULL-SIZE                           VALUE 'F'.
                 88  VALID-CODES
                         VALUES ARE 'C' 'I' 'F'.
             05  DAYS-RENTED             PIC 99.
             05  MILES-DRIVEN            PIC 9(4).
             05  FILLER                  PIC X(33).

         01  WS-PRINT-LINE.
             05  FILLER                  PIC X(4).
             05  SOC-SEC-NUM             PIC 999B99B9999.
```

Literal used to facilitate debugging.

Definition of 88-level entry.

User-defined work area to hold date of execution.

A single 88-level entry can encompass multiple values.

FIGURE 9.12 Car Billing Program

```
           05  FILLER                  PIC X(4).
           05  NAME-FIELD              PIC X(25).
           05  FILLER                  PIC XX.
           05  CAR-TYPE                PIC X.
           05  FILLER                  PIC X(4).
           05  DAYS-RENTED             PIC Z9.
           05  FILLER                  PIC X(4).
           05  MILES-DRIVEN            PIC ZZZ9.
           05  FILLER                  PIC X(4).
           05  CUSTOMER-BILL           PIC $$,$$9.99.
           05  FILLER                  PIC X(59).

       01  WS-HEADING-LINE-ONE.
           05  FILLER                  PIC X(65)      VALUE SPACES.
           05  FILLER                  PIC X(5)       VALUE 'PAGE '.
           05  WS-PAGE-PRINT           PIC ZZ9.
           05  FILLER                  PIC X(60)      VALUE SPACES.

       01  WS-HEADING-LINE-TWO.
           05  FILLER                  PIC X(20)      VALUE SPACES.
           05  TITLE-INFO              PIC X(33).
           05  FILLER                  PIC XX         VALUE SPACES.
           05  TITLE-DATE.
               10  TITLE-MONTH         PIC 99.
               10  FILLER              PIC X          VALUE '/'.
               10  TITLE-DAY           PIC 99.
               10  FILLER              PIC X          VALUE '/'.
               10  TITLE-YEAR          PIC 99.
           05  FILLER                  PIC X(70)      VALUE SPACES.

       01  WS-HEADING-LINE-THREE.
           05  FILLER                  PIC X(8)       VALUE SPACES.
           05  FILLER                  PIC X(11)      VALUE ' ACCT #'.
           05  FILLER                  PIC XX         VALUE SPACES.
           05  FILLER                  PIC X(4)       VALUE 'NAME'.
           05  FILLER                  PIC X(19)      VALUE SPACES.
           05  FILLER                  PIC X(4)       VALUE 'TYPE'.
           05  FILLER                  PIC XX         VALUE SPACES.
           05  FILLER                  PIC X(4)       VALUE 'DAYS'.
           05  FILLER                  PIC XX         VALUE SPACES.
           05  FILLER                  PIC X(5)       VALUE 'MILES'.
           05  FILLER                  PIC X(4)       VALUE SPACES.
           05  FILLER                  PIC X(6)       VALUE 'AMOUNT'.
           05  FILLER                  PIC X(60)      VALUE SPACES.

       01  FILLER                      PIC X(12)
               VALUE 'WS ENDS HERE'.
       PROCEDURE DIVISION.
       010-MAINLINE.
           OPEN INPUT  RENTAL-RECORD-FILE
                OUTPUT PRINT-FILE.
           PERFORM 015-INITIALIZE-VALID-DATES.
           PERFORM 020-READ-RENTAL-RECORD.
           PERFORM 030-PROCESS-CUSTOMER-RECORDS
               UNTIL WS-END-OF-FILE.
           CLOSE RENTAL-RECORD-FILE
                 PRINT-FILE.
           STOP RUN.

       015-INITIALIZE-VALID-DATES.
           ACCEPT DATE-WORK-AREA FROM DATE.
           COMPUTE LAST-YEAR = TODAYS-YEAR - 1.

       020-READ-RENTAL-RECORD.
           READ RENTAL-RECORD-FILE INTO WS-RECORD-IN
               AT END MOVE 'YES' TO WS-END-OF-FILE-SWITCH.

       030-PROCESS-CUSTOMER-RECORDS.
           MOVE 'YES' TO VALID-RECORD-SW.
           PERFORM 040-VALIDATE-CUSTOMER-RECORD.
           IF VALID-RECORD-SW = 'YES'
               PERFORM 050-COMPUTE-BILL
               PERFORM 060-WRITE-RENTAL-LINE.
           PERFORM 020-READ-RENTAL-RECORD.

       040-VALIDATE-CUSTOMER-RECORD.
           IF NAME-FIELD OF WS-RECORD-IN = SPACES
               OR SOC-SEC-NUM OF WS-RECORD-IN NOT NUMERIC
                   MOVE 'NO ' TO VALID-RECORD-SW
                   DISPLAY 'MISSING DATA ' NAME-FIELD OF WS-RECORD-IN
                   DISPLAY ' '.
```

88-level entry used in UNTIL condition.

Obtains date of execution.

Use of READ INTO.

DISPLAY statements write all error messages.

FIGURE 9.12 (Continued)

```
           IF NOT VALID-CODES
               MOVE 'NO ' TO VALID-RECORD-SW
               DISPLAY 'INVALID CAR ' NAME-FIELD OF WS-RECORD-IN
               DISPLAY ' '.
           COMPUTE VALID-MILES = 10 * DAYS-RENTED OF WS-RECORD-IN.
           IF MILES-DRIVEN OF WS-RECORD-IN < VALID-MILES
               MOVE 'NO ' TO VALID-RECORD-SW
               DISPLAY 'INVALID MILEAGE ' NAME-FIELD OF WS-RECORD-IN
               DISPLAY ' '.
           IF DAYS-RENTED OF WS-RECORD-IN > 35
               MOVE 'NO ' TO VALID-RECORD-SW
               DISPLAY 'ERROR - REFER TO LONG-TERM LEASING '
                   NAME-FIELD OF WS-RECORD-IN
               DISPLAY ' '.
           IF DATE-RETURNED-MM < 1 OR DATE-RETURNED-MM > 12
               MOVE 'NO ' TO VALID-RECORD-SW
               DISPLAY 'INVALID MONTH ' NAME-FIELD OF WS-RECORD-IN
               DISPLAY ' '.
           IF DATE-RETURNED-DD > 31
               MOVE 'NO ' TO VALID-RECORD-SW
               DISPLAY 'INVALID DAY ' NAME-FIELD OF WS-RECORD-IN
               DISPLAY ' '.
           IF DATE-RETURNED-YY NOT = TODAYS-YEAR
               AND DATE-RETURNED-YY NOT = LAST-YEAR
                   MOVE 'NO ' TO VALID-RECORD-SW
                   DISPLAY 'INVALID YEAR ' NAME-FIELD OF WS-RECORD-IN
                   DISPLAY ' '.

       050-COMPUTE-BILL.
           IF COMPACT
               MOVE .18 TO WS-MILEAGE-RATE
               MOVE 10.00 TO WS-DAILY-RATE
           ELSE
               IF INTERMEDIATE
                   MOVE .20 TO WS-MILEAGE-RATE
                   MOVE 12.00 TO WS-DAILY-RATE
               ELSE
                   MOVE .22 TO WS-MILEAGE-RATE
                   MOVE 14.00 TO WS-DAILY-RATE.

           COMPUTE WS-CUSTOMER-BILL ROUNDED =
               MILES-DRIVEN OF WS-RECORD-IN * WS-MILEAGE-RATE
               + DAYS-RENTED OF WS-RECORD-IN * WS-DAILY-RATE
           ON SIZE ERROR
               DISPLAY 'RECEIVING FIELD TOO SMALL FOR BILL'
                   NAME-FIELD OF WS-RECORD-IN
               DISPLAY ' '.

       060-WRITE-RENTAL-LINE.
           IF WS-LINE-COUNT IS GREATER THAN 5
               PERFORM 070-WRITE-HEADING-LINES.
           MOVE SPACES TO WS-PRINT-LINE.
           MOVE CORRESPONDING WS-RECORD-IN TO WS-PRINT-LINE.
           INSPECT SOC-SEC-NUM OF WS-PRINT-LINE
               REPLACING ALL ' ' BY '-'.
           MOVE WS-CUSTOMER-BILL TO CUSTOMER-BILL.
           WRITE PRINT-LINE FROM WS-PRINT-LINE
               AFTER ADVANCING 2 LINES.
           ADD 1 TO WS-LINE-COUNT.

       070-WRITE-HEADING-LINES.
           MOVE 1 TO WS-LINE-COUNT.
           ADD 1 TO WS-PAGE-COUNT.
           MOVE WS-PAGE-COUNT TO WS-PAGE-PRINT.
           WRITE PRINT-LINE FROM WS-HEADING-LINE-ONE
               AFTER ADVANCING PAGE.
           MOVE ' STACEY CAR RENTALS - REPORT DATE ' TO TITLE-INFO.
           MOVE TODAYS-DAY TO TITLE-DAY.
           MOVE TODAYS-MONTH TO TITLE-MONTH.
           MOVE TODAYS-YEAR TO TITLE-YEAR.
           WRITE PRINT-LINE FROM WS-HEADING-LINE-TWO
               AFTER ADVANCING 1 LINES.
           WRITE PRINT-LINE FROM WS-HEADING-LINE-THREE
               AFTER ADVANCING 1 LINES.
```

Use of date of execution in validity check.

Nested IF statement.

COMPUTE statement has both ROUNDED and SIZE ERROR clauses.

MOVE CORRESPONDING requires nonunique data names.

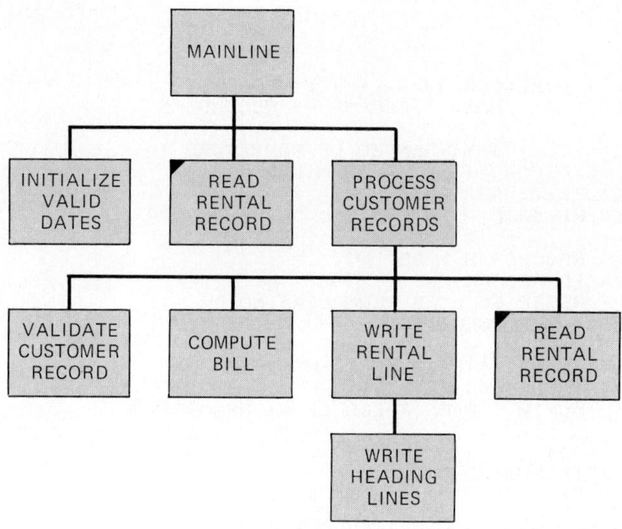

FIGURE 9.13 Hierarchy Chart for Car Billing Program

The value of the line counter, WS-LINE-COUNT, is tested prior to writing a detail line (lines 211–212). Since it was initialized to 6 (a value greater than the desired number of detail lines per page), a heading is written prior to the first detail record. The heading routine in turn resets the line counter (line 223), which is subsequently incremented after every detail line is written (line 220). The page counter is also incremented in the heading routine, so that the page number can appear on the top of every page in the report.

The paragraph PROCESS-CUSTOMER-RECORDS is performed as long as there are data records. Each incoming record is assumed to be valid (i.e., a validation switch is set to YES in line 149). The validation routine is invoked and contains several of the editing checks discussed earlier in the chapter. Observe that the validation switch is set to NO if any test fails; also that a given record can be flagged for more than one reason.

Any record that passes all validation checks invokes two additional paragraphs, COMPUTE-BILL and WRITE-RENTAL-LINE. Regardless of whether a record is valid or not, the next record is read so that processing may continue.

The date of execution is obtained by the ACCEPT statement in line 141. (The program contains a user-defined work area in lines 56–59 to accommodate the date in the form yymmdd.) The date is used in a validation check (lines 184 and 185) and also appears as part of the page heading (lines 229–231).

The author has tried to include as many Procedure Division features as possible in Figure 9.12. Accordingly, you will find condition names (in both IF and PERFORM statements), compound IF statements, and nested IF statements. Nonunique data names, qualification, and MOVE CORRESPONDING are also shown, although the author generally chooses not to use these features. The DISPLAY statement is illustrated, as are the ROUNDED and SIZE ERROR clauses of the COMPUTE statement.

Indentation of key words in the Procedure Division is very important to enhance readability. AT END is indented under READ, AFTER ADVANCING under WRITE, UNTIL under PERFORM, etc. Detail lines are indented 4 spaces under IF and ELSE statements, with special attention paid to indenting a nested IF statement. Continued lines, e.g. the COMPUTE statement in lines 202–208, are also indented.

Blank lines are used throughout the program to further aid its visual appearance. They appear before 01 entries in the Data Division and before paragraph headers in the Procedure Division.

COBOL 8X:

Changes and Enhancements

There are many enhancements to the Procedure Division statements discussed in this chapter. The most significant improvements were made to facilitate the use of structured programming constructs in COBOL; hence new features have been included in the IF and PERFORM statements. In addition, an entirely new statement, EVALUATE, has been introduced to implement the case construct (in lieu of the current implementation via a nested IF). A further change is the inclusion of a false condition branch in the READ statement. Collectively these changes are so significant that a separate appendix, Appendix B, is devoted to describing the structured programming improvements.

The ACCEPT statement has a DAY-OF-WEEK clause, which returns a number from 1 to 7, indicating the day, e.g., 1 for Monday, 2 for Tuesday.

Two changes were made to facilitate data entry via terminals. It is now possible to move an edited field to a numeric field; i.e., de-editing takes place. The intended use is to supply more user-friendly formats for inputting data on line. The DISPLAY statement has been amended to include a NO ADVANCING clause, which allows one to display and accept data from the same line on a CRT. DISPLAY ALL (e.g., DISPLAY ALL '*') is also permitted.

The ALPHABETIC-UPPER and ALPHABETIC-LOWER tests have been added to accept upper-and lower-case letters, respectively. The ALPHABETIC test is true for upper-case letters, lower-case letters, and the space character. (In COBOL 74 the ALPHABETIC test was true for upper-case letters only, in addition to the space character.)

Reference modification has been introduced to enhance the string processing capabilities. This feature allows one to address a string of characters within another string by specifying the leftmost character and length. For example, the statements

```
05  DATA-NAME     PIC X(19)     'UNIVERSITY OF MIAMI'.

MOVE DATA-NAME (15:5) TO OUTPUT-AREA.
```

will move MIAMI to OUTPUT-AREA. The reference modification of DATA-NAME begins in the fifteenth position and extends for a total length of 5 characters.

Summary

This chapter presented a wealth of information about the Procedure Division. It stressed the importance of the IF and PERFORM statements and covered all options associated with these verbs. Coverage of the IF statement included class, sign, and compound tests, implied conditions, 88-level entries, NEXT SENTENCE, and nested IFs. The PERFORM statement was expanded to include PERFORM THRU, PERFORM UNTIL, PERFORM VARYING, and PERFORM TIMES. A host of new verbs and clauses were also introduced. We discussed ACCEPT and DISPLAY, READ INTO and WRITE FROM, SIZE ERROR, and INSPECT.

The "Systems Concepts" section discussed data validation and is of critical importance. Several different kinds of validity checks were mentioned, including numeric tests, alphabetic tests, reasonableness checks, consistency checks, sequence checks, completeness checks, date checks, and subscript checks. These features were included in a complete program at the end of the chapter.

True/False Exercises

1. The INSPECT statement must contain the reserved word REPLACING.
2. The INSPECT statement has more than one format.
3. The numeric class test can be applied to alphanumeric data.
4. The alphabetic class test can be applied to alphanumeric data.
5. The numeric class test can be applied to alphabetic data.
6. The alphabetic class test can be applied to numeric data.
7. Several data names can appear in the same DISPLAY statement.
8. The ACCEPT statement has two distinct forms.
9. Both literals and data names can appear in a DISPLAY statement.
10. COBOL requires that the DISPLAY statement direct its output to the printer.
11. COBOL requires that the ACCEPT statement receive its input from the console typewriter.
12. Either OF or IN may be used to qualify data names.
13. Qualification over a single level will always remove ambiguity of duplicate data names.
14. The CORRESPONDING option is required if duplicate data names are used.
15. SIZE ERROR is allowed only in the COMPUTE statement.
16. SIZE ERROR is mandatory in the COMPUTE statement.
17. CORR is permitted instead of CORRESPONDING.
18. For the CORRESPONDING option to work, both duplicate names must be at the same level.
19. DATE is a COBOL reserved word, containing the date of execution in the form yymmdd.
20. DAY and DATE produce the same results.
21. TIME returns a six-digit numeric field, indicating the time of program execution.
22. The EXIT statement is required to delineate the end of a performed routine.
23. Every PERFORM statement must contain a paragraph name.
24. A paragraph consists of one or more sections.
25. It is permissible to "perform out of a perform."

Problems

1. Recode the following statements to show the ELSE indented under the relevant IF. Draw appropriate flowcharts, using the structures of Chapter 7.

   (a) IF A > B, IF C > D, MOVE E TO F,
   ELSE MOVE G TO H.

   (b) IF A > B, IF C > D, MOVE E TO F,
   ELSE MOVE G TO H, ELSE MOVE X TO Y.

   (c) IF A > B, IF C > D, MOVE E TO F,
   ADD 1 TO E, ELSE MOVE G TO H,
   ADD 1 TO G.

(d) IF A > B, MOVE X TO Y, MOVE Z TO W,
ELSE IF C > D MOVE 1 TO N,
ELSE MOVE 2 TO Y, ADD 3 TO Z.

2. Given the code

```
PROCEDURE DIVISION.
MAINLINE SECTION.
FIRST-PARAGRAPH.
    PERFORM SEC-A.
    PERFORM PAR-C THRU PAR-E.
    MOVE 1 TO N.
    PERFORM PAR-G UNTIL N > 3.
    STOP RUN.
SEC-A SECTION.
    ADD 1 TO X.
    ADD 1 TO Y.
    ADD 1 TO Z.
PAR-B.
    ADD 2 TO X.
PAR-C.
    ADD 10 TO X.
PAR-D.
    ADD 10 TO Y.
    ADD 20 TO Z.
PAR-E.
    EXIT.
PAR-F.
    MOVE 2 TO N.
PAR-G.
    ADD 1 TO N.
    ADD 5 TO X.
```

(a) How many times is each paragraph executed?
(b) What are the final values of X, Y, and Z? (Assume they were all initialized to 0.)
(c) What would happen if the statement ADD 1 TO N were removed from PAR-G?

3. Code COBOL statements to correspond to the accompanying flowcharts.

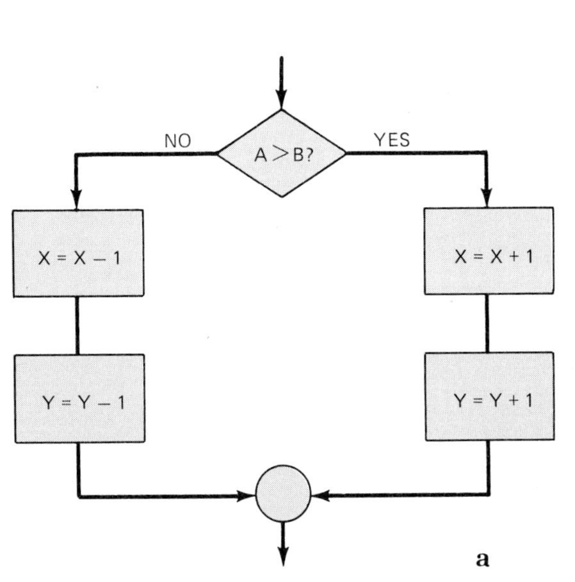

a

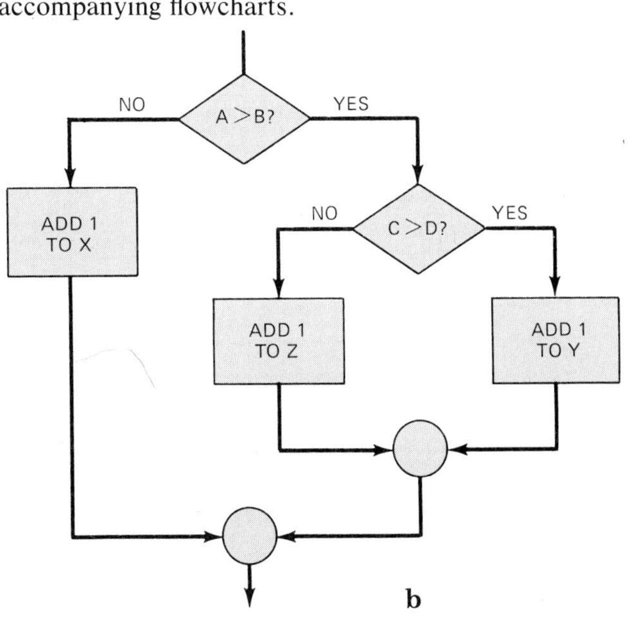

b

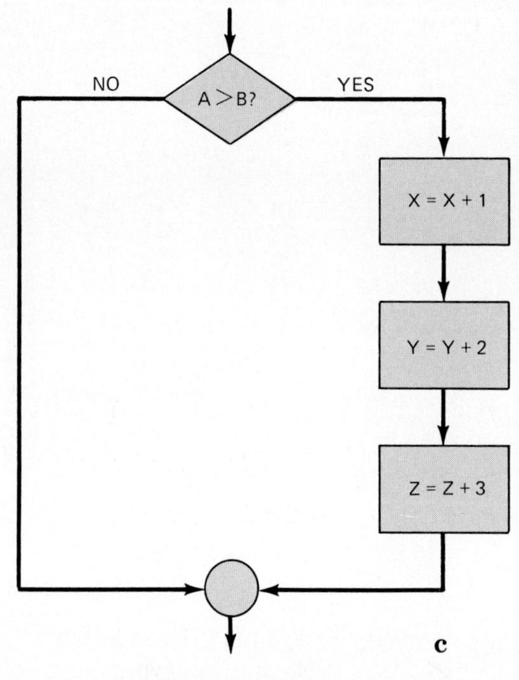

c

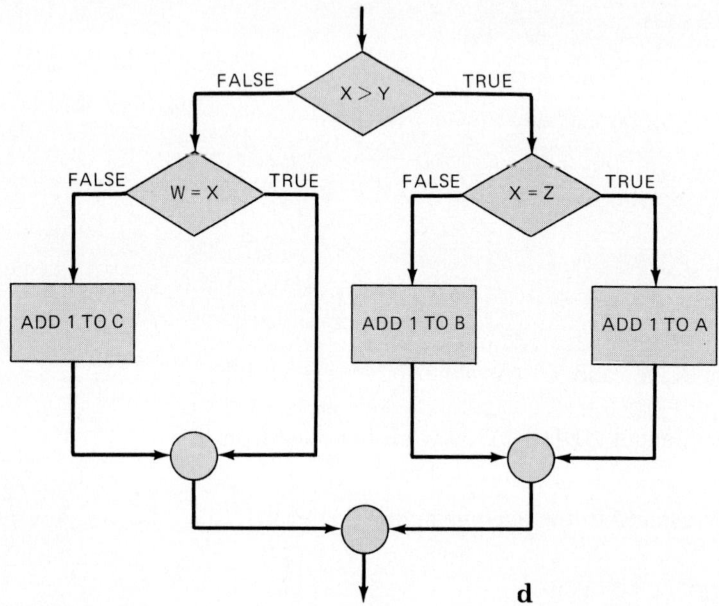

d

4. Given the following Data Division entries and the Procedure Division statement MOVE CORRESPONDING RECORD-ONE TO RECORD-TWO:

```
01  RECORD-ONE.
    05  FIELD-A         PIC X(4).
    05  FIELD-B         PIC X(4).
    05  FIELD-C.
        10  C-ONE       PIC X(4).
        10  C-TWO       PIC X(4).
    05  FIELD-D.
        10  D-ONE       PIC X(6).
        10  D-TWO       PIC X(6).
        10  D-THREE     PIC X(6).
```

```
01  RECORD-TWO.
    15  FIELD-E          PIC X(8).
    15  FIELD-D          PIC X(18).
    15  FIELD-C          PIC X(8).
    15  FIELD-B          PIC X(2).
    15  FIELD-A          PIC X(4).
    15  FIELD-F          PIC X(4).
    15  FIELD-G          PIC X(4).
    15  FIELD-H          PIC X(4).
```

Answer true or false (refer to the receiving field):

(a) The value of FIELD-E is unchanged.
(b) The value of FIELD-D is unchanged.
(c) No moves at all will take place, since the corresponding level numbers are different in both records.
(d) The value of FIELD-A will be unchanged, since it is the first entry in RECORD-ONE but the last entry in RECORD-TWO.
(e) The value of FIELD-B will be unchanged, since the length is different in both records.

5. The following code is used to keep a separate count of four different types of employees. Describe why it *won't* work. Recode the example with condition names to accomplish the intended effect.

```
IF EMPL-CODE = 'A'
    ADD 1 TO WS-CNT-OF-ACTIVE-EMP
ELSE
    IF EMPL-CODE = 'P'
        ADD 1 TO WS-CNT-OF-PART-TIME-EMP
    ELSE
        IF EMPL-CODE = 'R'
            ADD 1 TO WS-CNT-OF-RETIRED-EMP
            ADD 1 TO WS-CNT-OF-INACTIVE-EMP.
```

6. Given the nested IF statement

```
IF SEX = 'M'
    PERFORM PROCESS-MALE-RECORD
ELSE
    IF SEX = 'F'
        PERFORM PROCESS-FEMALE-RECORD
    ELSE
        PERFORM WRITE-ERROR-MESSAGE.
```

and the logically equivalent code

```
IF SEX = 'M'
    PERFORM PROCESS-MALE-RECORD.
IF SEX = 'F'
    PERFORM PROCESS-FEMALE-RECORD.
IF SEX NOT = 'M' AND SEX NOT = 'F'
    PERFORM WRITE-ERROR-MESSAGE.
```

(a) Discuss the relative efficiency of the two alternatives.
(b) What would be the effect of changing AND to OR in the third IF of the second set of statements?

(c) What would be the effect of removing the word ELSE wherever it occurs in the first set of IF statements?

7. Consider the following COBOL code and resulting output. The intent is to give customers with orders of $2,000 or more a 2% discount. (Customers with orders of less than $2,000 are *not* to receive any discount.) Explain the rather surprising output. (*Hint:* Count columns.)

COBOL code:

```
IF AMOUNT-ORDERED-THISWEEK < 2000
    MOVE ZEROS TO CUSTOMER-DISCOUNT
ELSE
    COMPUTE CUSTOMER-DISCOUNT = AMOUNT-ORDERED-THISWEEK * .02.
COMPUTE NET = AMOUNT-ORDERED-THISWEEK - CUSTOMER-DISCOUNT.
DISPLAY AMOUNT-ORDERED-THISWEEK CUSTOMER-DISCOUNT NET.
```

Output:

Amount Ordered	Discount	Net	
3000	60	2940	
4000	80	3920	Correct calculation
1000	0	3920	
5000	100	4900	
1500	0	4900	Net is incorrect and equal to value of previous order.

8. Are the two IF statements logically equivalent?

```
STATEMENT 1:    IF A > B
                    IF C > D
                        ADD 1 TO X
                    ELSE
                        ADD 1 TO Y.

STATEMENT 2:    IF A > B AND C > D
                    ADD 1 TO X
                ELSE
                    ADD 1 TO Y.
```

Try the following sets of values to aid in answering the question:

(a) A = 5, B = 1, C = 10, D = 15.
(b) A = 1, B = 5, C = 10, D = 15.

9. Consider the following code, intended to calculate an individual's age from a stored birth date and the date of execution.

```
01  EMPLOYEE-RECORD.
    05  EMP-BIRTH-DATE.
        10  BIRTH-MONTH    PIC 99.
        10  BIRTH-YEAR     PIC 99.
        .
        .
        .
```

```
01  DATE-WORK-AREA.
    05  TODAYS-MONTH        PIC 99.
    05  TODAYS-DAY          PIC 99.
    05  TODAYS-YEAR         PIC 99.
    .
     .
      .
PROCEDURE DIVISION.
    ACCEPT DATE-WORK-AREA FROM DATE.
    .
     .
      .
    COMPUTE EMPLOYEE-AGE = TODAYS-YEAR - BIRTH-YEAR
       + TODAYS-MONTH - BIRTH-MONTH.
```

There are *two* distinct reasons why the code will not work as intended. Find and correct the errors.

10. Company XYZ has four corporate functions: manufacturing, marketing, financial, and administrative. Each function in turn has several departments, as shown:

FUNCTION	*DEPARTMENTS*
MANUFACTURING	10, 12, 16–30, 41, 56
MARKETING	6–9, 15, 31–33
FINANCIAL	60–62, 75
ADMINISTRATIVE	1–4, 78

Establish condition name entries so that, given a value of EMPLOYEE-DEPARTMENT, we can determine the function. Include an 88-level entry, VALID-CODES, to verify that the incoming department is indeed a valid department (any department number not shown is invalid).

11. XYZ Corporation stocks four sizes of widgets: small (S), medium (M), large (L), and extra large (X). Sixty percent of all incoming orders are for medium widgets, 25% for large, 10% for small, and 5% for extra large.

(a) Rewrite the following COBOL code to reflect 88-level entries

```
DATA DIVISION.
  .
   .
    .
     05  IN-CODE    PICTURE IS X.
      .
       .
        .
PROCEDURE DIVISION.
        .
         .
          .
   IF IN-CODE IS EQUAL TO 'S', PERFORM SMALL-SIZE
   ELSE IF IN-CODE IS EQUAL TO 'M', PERFORM MEDIUM-SIZE
   ELSE IF IN-CODE IS EQUAL TO'L', PERFORM LARGE-SIZE
   ELSE IF IN-CODE IS EQUAL TO 'X', PERFORM EXTRA-LARGE-SIZE.
```

(b) In a file of 10,000 transactions, how many comparisons would be saved if the IF statements were reordered to check for transactions in the order M, L, S, and X?

12. Given the following COBOL definitions:

```
05  LOCATION-CODE       PIC 99.
    88  NEW-YORK            VALUE 10.
    88  BOSTON              VALUE 20.
    88  CHICAGO             VALUE 30.
    88  DETROIT             VALUE 40.
    88  NORTH-EAST          VALUES 10 20.
```

Are the following entries valid as the condition portion of an IF statement?

(a) IF LOCATION-CODE = '10'
(b) IF LOCATION-CODE = 40
(c) IF NEW-YORK
(d) IF LOCATION-CODE = 10 OR 20 OR 30
(e) IF NEW-YORK OR BOSTON OR CHICAGO
(f) IF DETROIT = 40

Would the following be valid examples of MOVE statements?

(g) MOVE 20 TO BOSTON.
(h) MOVE 20 TO LOCATION-CODE.
(i) MOVE '20' TO LOCATION-CODE.

13. Given the following pairs of IF statements, indicate whether the statements in each pair have the same effect:

(a) IF A > B OR C > D AND E = F
    IF A > B OR (C > D AND E = F)
(b) IF A > B OR C > D AND E = F
    IF (A > B OR C > D) AND E = F
(c) IF A > B OR A > C OR A > D
    IF A > B OR C OR D
(d) IF A > B
    IF A NOT < B OR A NOT = B

Debugging Workshop

Figure 9.14 is an *invalid* version of the Car Billing Program presented in this chapter. It used the identical input as the original program but produced the erroneous output shown in Figure 9.15. Find and correct all errors.

```
IDENTIFICATION DIVISION.
PROGRAM-ID.
    CARS.
AUTHOR.
    JACKIE CLARK.

ENVIRONMENT DIVISION.
CONFIGURATION SECTION.
SOURCE-COMPUTER.
    IBM-4341.
OBJECT-COMPUTER.
    IBM-4341.
```

FIGURE 9.14 Erroneous Car Billing Program

FIGURE 9.14 *(Continued)*

```
       INPUT-OUTPUT SECTION.
       FILE-CONTROL.
           SELECT RENTAL-RECORD-FILE
               ASSIGN TO UT-S-SYSIN.
           SELECT PRINT-FILE
               ASSIGN TO UT-S-SYSPRT.
       DATA DIVISION.
       FILE SECTION.
       FD  RENTAL-RECORD-FILE
           LABEL RECORDS ARE OMITTED
           RECORD CONTAINS 80 CHARACTERS
           DATA RECORD IS RENTAL-RECORD.
       01  RENTAL-RECORD               PIC X(80).
       FD  PRINT-FILE
           LABEL RECORDS ARE OMITTED
           RECORD CONTAINS 133 CHARACTERS
           DATA RECORD IS PRINT-LINE.
       01  PRINT-LINE                  PIC X(133).
       WORKING-STORAGE SECTION.
       01  FILLER                      PIC X(14)
               VALUE 'WS BEGINS HERE'.
       01  WS-END-OF-FILE-SWITCH       PIC XXX        VALUE 'NO '.
           88 WS-END-OF-FILE                          VALUE 'YES'.
       01  VALIDATION-AREA.
           05  VALID-RECORD-SW         PIC X(3).
           05  VALID-MILES             PIC 9(3).
           05  LAST-YEAR               PIC 99.
       01  PAGE-AND-LINE-COUNTERS.
           05  WS-LINE-COUNT           PIC 9(2)       VALUE 6.
           05  WS-PAGE-COUNT           PIC 9(2)       VALUE ZEROS.
       01  BILLING-CONSTANTS.
           05  WS-MILEAGE-RATE         PIC 9V99.
           05  WS-DAILY-RATE           PIC 99V99.
           05  WS-CUSTOMER-BILL        PIC 9999V99.
       01  DATE-WORK-AREA.
           05  TODAYS-YEAR             PIC 99.
           05  TODAYS-MONTH            PIC 99.
           05  TODAYS-DAY              PIC 99.
       01  WS-RECORD-IN.
           05  SOC-SEC-NUM             PIC 9(9).
           05  NAME-FIELD              PIC X(25).
           05  DATE-RETURNED.
               10  DATE-RETURNED-YY PIC 9(2).
               10  DATE-RETURNED-MM PIC 9(2).
               10  DATE-RETURNED-DD PIC 9(2).
           05  CAR-TYPE                PIC X.
               88  COMPACT                            VALUE 'C'.
               88  INTERMEDIATE                       VALUE 'I'.
               88  FULL-SIZE                          VALUE 'F'.
               88  VALID-CODES
                       VALUES ARE 'F' 'I'.
           05  CAR-USAGE-DATA.
               10  DAYS-RENTED         PIC 99.
               10  MILES-DRIVEN        PIC 9(4).
           05  FILLER                  PIC X(33).
       01  WS-PRINT-LINE.
           05  FILLER                  PIC X(4).
           05  SOC-SEC-NUM             PIC 999B99B9999.
           05  FILLER                  PIC X(4).
           05  NAME-FIELD              PIC X(25).
           05  FILLER                  PIC XX.
           05  CAR-TYPE                PIC X.
           05  FILLER                  PIC X(4).
           05  DAYS-RENTED             PIC Z9.
           05  FILLER                  PIC X(4).
           05  MILES-DRIVEN            PIC ZZZ9.
           05  FILLER                  PIC X(4).
           05  CUSTOMER-BILL           PIC $$,$$9.99.
           05  FILLER                  PIC X(59).
```

FIGURE 9.14 (Continued)

```
       01  WS-HEADING-LINE-ONE.
           05  FILLER                  PIC X(65)      VALUE SPACES.
           05  FILLER                  PIC X(5)       VALUE 'PAGE '.
           05  WS-PAGE-PRINT           PIC ZZ9.
           05  FILLER                  PIC X(60)      VALUE SPACES.

       01  WS-HEADING-LINE-TWO.
           05  FILLER                  PIC X(20)      VALUE SPACES.
           05  TITLE-INFO              PIC X(33).
           05  FILLER                  PIC XX         VALUE SPACES.
           05  TITLE-DATE.
               10  TITLE-MONTH         PIC 99.
               10  FILLER              PIC X          VALUE '/'.
               10  TITLE-DAY           PIC 99.
               10  FILLER              PIC X          VALUE '/'.
               10  TITLE-YEAR          PIC 99.
           05  FILLER                  PIC X(70)      VALUE SPACES.

       01  WS-HEADING-LINE-THREE.
           05  FILLER                  PIC X(8)       VALUE SPACES.
           05  FILLER                  PIC X(11)      VALUE ' ACCT #'.
           05  FILLER                  PIC XX         VALUE SPACES.
           05  FILLER                  PIC X(4)       VALUE 'NAME'.
           05  FILLER                  PIC X(19)      VALUE SPACES.
           05  FILLER                  PIC X(4)       VALUE 'TYPE'.
           05  FILLER                  PIC XX         VALUE SPACES.
           05  FILLER                  PIC X(4)       VALUE 'DAYS'.
           05  FILLER                  PIC XX         VALUE SPACES.
           05  FILLER                  PIC X(5)       VALUE 'MILES'.
           05  FILLER                  PIC X(4)       VALUE SPACES.
           05  FILLER                  PIC X(6)       VALUE 'AMOUNT'.
           05  FILLER                  PIC X(60)      VALUE SPACES.

       01  FILLER                      PIC X(12)
               VALUE 'WS ENDS HERE'.
       PROCEDURE DIVISION.
       010-MAINLINE.
           OPEN INPUT  RENTAL-RECORD-FILE
                OUTPUT PRINT-FILE.
           PERFORM 015-INITIALIZE-VALID-DATES.
           PERFORM 020-READ-RENTAL-RECORD.
           PERFORM 030-PROCESS-CUSTOMER-RECORDS
               UNTIL WS-END-OF-FILE.
           CLOSE RENTAL-RECORD-FILE
                 PRINT-FILE.
           STOP RUN.

       015-INITIALIZE-VALID-DATES.
           ACCEPT DATE-WORK-AREA FROM DATE.
           COMPUTE LAST-YEAR = TODAYS-YEAR - 1.

       020-READ-RENTAL-RECORD.
           READ RENTAL-RECORD-FILE INTO WS-RECORD-IN
               AT END MOVE 'YES' TO WS-END-OF-FILE-SWITCH.

       030-PROCESS-CUSTOMER-RECORDS.
           MOVE 'YES' TO VALID-RECORD-SW.
           PERFORM 040-VALIDATE-CUSTOMER-RECORD.
           IF VALID-RECORD-SW = 'YES'
               PERFORM 050-COMPUTE-BILL
               PERFORM 060-WRITE-RENTAL-LINE.
           PERFORM 020-READ-RENTAL-RECORD.

       040-VALIDATE-CUSTOMER-RECORD.
           IF NAME-FIELD OF WS-RECORD-IN = SPACES
               OR SOC-SEC-NUM OF WS-RECORD-IN NOT NUMERIC
                   MOVE 'NO ' TO VALID-RECORD-SW
                   DISPLAY 'MISSING DATA ' NAME-FIELD OF WS-RECORD-IN
                   DISPLAY ' '.
           IF NOT VALID-CODES
               MOVE 'NO ' TO VALID-RECORD-SW
               DISPLAY 'INVALID CAR ' NAME-FIELD OF WS-RECORD-IN
               DISPLAY ' '.
           COMPUTE VALID-MILES = 10 * DAYS-RENTED OF WS-RECORD-IN.
           IF MILES-DRIVEN OF WS-RECORD-IN < VALID-MILES
               MOVE 'NO ' TO VALID-RECORD-SW
               DISPLAY 'INVALID MILEAGE ' NAME-FIELD OF WS-RECORD-IN
               DISPLAY ' '.
           IF DAYS-RENTED OF WS-RECORD-IN > 35
```

```
            MOVE 'NO ' TO VALID-RECORD-SW
            DISPLAY 'ERROR - REFER TO LONG-TERM LEASING '
                NAME-FIELD OF WS-RECORD-IN
            DISPLAY ' '.
        IF DATE-RETURNED-MM < 1 OR DATE-RETURNED-MM > 12
            DISPLAY 'INVALID MONTH ' NAME-FIELD OF WS-RECORD-IN
            DISPLAY ' '.
        IF DATE-RETURNED-DD > 31
            MOVE 'NO ' TO VALID-RECORD-SW
            DISPLAY 'INVALID DAY ' NAME-FIELD OF WS-RECORD-IN
            DISPLAY ' '.
        IF DATE-RETURNED-YY NOT = TODAYS-YEAR
            AND DATE-RETURNED-YY NOT = LAST-YEAR
                MOVE 'NO ' TO VALID-RECORD-SW
                DISPLAY 'INVALID YEAR ' NAME-FIELD OF WS-RECORD-IN
                DISPLAY ' '.

    050-COMPUTE-BILL.
        IF FULL-SIZE
            MOVE .22 TO WS-MILEAGE-RATE
            MOVE 14.00 TO WS-DAILY-RATE.
            IF INTERMEDIATE
                MOVE .20 TO WS-MILEAGE-RATE
                MOVE 12.00 TO WS-DAILY-RATE
            ELSE
                MOVE .18 TO WS-MILEAGE-RATE
                MOVE 10.00 TO WS-DAILY-RATE

        COMPUTE WS-CUSTOMER-BILL ROUNDED =
            MILES-DRIVEN OF WS-RECORD-IN * WS-MILEAGE-RATE
            + DAYS-RENTED OF WS-RECORD-IN * WS-DAILY-RATE
        ON SIZE ERROR
            DISPLAY 'RECEIVING FIELD TOO SMALL FOR BILL'
                NAME-FIELD OF WS-RECORD-IN
            DISPLAY ' '.

    060-WRITE-RENTAL-LINE.
        IF WS-LINE-COUNT IS GREATER THAN 5
            PERFORM 070-WRITE-HEADING-LINES.
        MOVE SPACES TO WS-PRINT-LINE.
        MOVE CORRESPONDING WS-RECORD-IN TO WS-PRINT-LINE.
        INSPECT SOC-SEC-NUM OF WS-PRINT-LINE
            REPLACING ALL '-' BY ' '.
        MOVE WS-CUSTOMER-BILL TO CUSTOMER-BILL.
        WRITE PRINT-LINE FROM WS-PRINT-LINE
            AFTER ADVANCING 2 LINES.

    070-WRITE-HEADING-LINES.
        MOVE 1 TO WS-LINE-COUNT.
        ADD 1 TO WS-PAGE-COUNT.
        MOVE WS-PAGE-COUNT TO WS-PAGE-PRINT.
        WRITE PRINT-LINE FROM WS-HEADING-LINE-ONE
            AFTER ADVANCING PAGE.
        MOVE ' STACEY CAR RENTALS - REPORT DATE ' TO TITLE-INFO.
        MOVE TODAYS-DAY TO TITLE-DAY.
        MOVE TODAYS-MONTH TO TITLE-MONTH.
        MOVE TODAYS-YEAR TO TITLE-YEAR.
        WRITE PRINT-LINE FROM WS-HEADING-LINE-TWO
            AFTER ADVANCING 1 LINES.
        WRITE PRINT-LINE FROM WS-HEADING-LINE-THREE
            AFTER ADVANCING 1 LINES.
```

FIGURE 9.14 (Continued)

All records appear on the same page.

```
                                                                    PAGE    1
                            STACEY CAR RENTALS - REPORT DATE  04/09/84
      ACCT #                NAME                        TYPE  DAYS  MILES       AMOUNT

123 45 6789         BAKER,RG                        F                          $112.10
987 65 4321         BROWN,PG                        I                          $112.10
987 65 4390         SMITH,PG                        I                          $112.10
354 67 9876         KERBEL,NX                       I                          $112.10
264 80 5298         CLARK,JS                        F                          $164.32
233 43 2454         BEINHORN,CB                     I                          $164.32
886 22 2343         VOGEL,JD                        F                          $194.34
008 63 2212         TOWER,DR                        I                          $194.34
```

Hyphens missing in social security number.

Calculated amounts are wrong.

Information is missing from report.

FIGURE 9.15a Output Produced by Figure 9.14

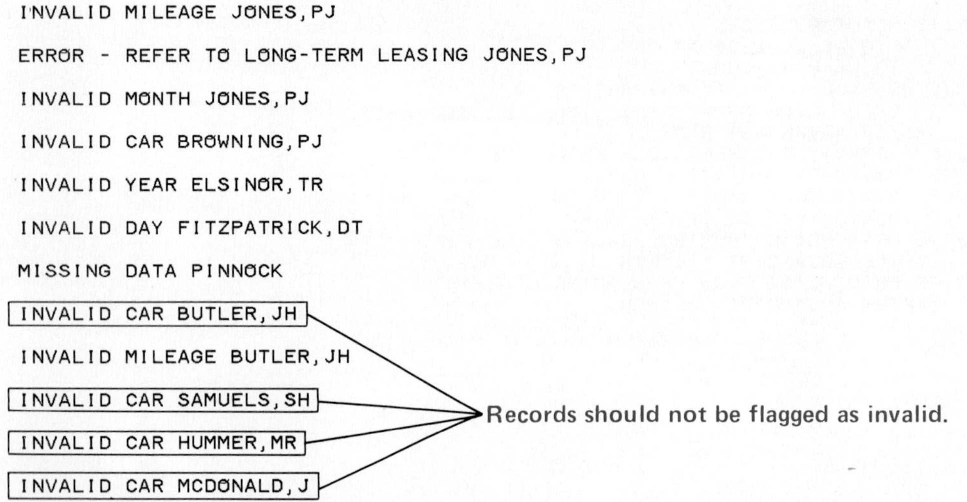

```
INVALID MILEAGE JONES,PJ
ERROR - REFER TO LONG-TERM LEASING JONES,PJ
INVALID MONTH JONES,PJ
INVALID CAR BROWNING,PJ
INVALID YEAR ELSINOR,TR
INVALID DAY FITZPATRICK,DT
MISSING DATA PINNOCK
INVALID CAR BUTLER,JH
INVALID MILEAGE BUTLER,JH
INVALID CAR SAMUELS,SH
INVALID CAR HUMMER,MR
INVALID CAR MCDONALD,J
```

Records should not be flagged as invalid.

FIGURE 9.15b Error Messages Produced by Figure 9.14

Programming Specifications

Project 9–1

Program Name:

Doctor Visits

Narrative:

This program illustrates data validation as well as most of the Procedure Division features discussed in this chapter.

Input File:

PATIENT-FILE

Input Record Layout:

COLUMNS	FIELD	PICTURE
1–15	LAST-NAME	X(15)
16–25	FIRST-NAME	X(10)
26–50	REASON-FOR-SEEING-DOCTOR	X(25)
51–55	AMOUNT-PAID	9(3)V99
56–80	FILLER	X(25)

Test Data (enter exactly as shown):

```
JONES         TOM                                      3600
KING          SARAH        EARACHE                     0100
WHITBECK      KENNETH      SORE SHOULDER               3600
DAY           BILL         UNEXPLAINED DIZZINESS       5000
POLLACK       MARY         HEADACHE
              LIZA         FOOT PROBLEMS               3075
SCHEUR        HELEN        PNEUMONIA REVISIT           3000
MCKEON        DICK         GENERAL PHYSICAL           1000A
GROSSMAN      IVY          BRONCHITIS                  0800
STACY         MEREDITH     NOSE BLEED                  2000
BASS          CAROL        NAUSEA                      3800
McGOVERN      JOHN         EYE INFECTION               1500
```

Report Layout:

Design your own report layout, subject to the problem specifications.

Processing Requirements:

1. Read a file of patient records.
2. Validate each patient record for all of the following:
   (a) The incoming field, AMOUNT-PAID, must be numeric. If not, display an appropriate error message that contains the entire input record. (Use the INSPECT statement with the REPLACING option prior to the numeric check to convert leading blanks to zeros).
   (b) The incoming record must contain data in all fields, i.e., LAST-NAME, FIRST-NAME, REASON-FOR-SEEING-DOCTOR, and AMOUNT-PAID. If any field is missing, display a single message, "INCOMING RECORD MISSING DATA," followed by the input record.

(c) Amount paid should be between $15.00 and $100.00; if not, display an error message and the input record.

3. No further processing is required for any records that are invalid according to specifications in item 2.
4. For each valid record (i.e., for each record passing the validity checks in item 2) do the following:
   (a) Print complete information for each valid record in a separate detail line. Double-space detail lines and limit each page to four detail lines.
   (b) Print a separate heading line at the top of each page. Include the date of execution in your heading; also include a page number.
5. When all patient records have been read and processed, compute and print the amount of the average visit. Include only valid patients in this total.
6. Use the following Procedure Division features in your program: READ INTO, WRITE FROM, DISPLAY (for error messages), ACCEPT (to obtain the date of execution), nonunique data names and MOVE CORRESPONDING, SIZE ERROR, and INSPECT REPLACING.

Programming Specifications

Project 9–2

Program Name:

Repayment Schedule

Narrative:

This program illustrates screen formatting and PERFORM VARYING. It is designed for those running on microcomputers with access to enhanced ACCEPT and DISPLAY statements. The program is to prompt the user for the amount he or she wishes to borrow, and other salient facts about the loan, i.e., interest rate and duration. The program is then to print a repayment schedule.

Input File:

None. All information is to be accepted from a terminal.

Input Record Layout:

No specific screen format is required, other than the general requirement of a user-friendly screen. Indeed, the screen design should be considered an integral part of the project.

Test Data:

You are to supply your own test data. Calculate the anticipated results independently and compare them to the computer's results.

Report Layout:

No specific screen format is given for the output of the program, other than the requirement of user-friendly screens.

Processing Requirements:

1. Prepare an opening screen, which will greet the user, then ask the user to input the amount he or she wishes to borrow, the annual interest rate, and the duration in years of the loan.
2. Your input module is to utilize as many features of the ACCEPT and DISPLAY statements as possible, in order to make the screen attractive and user oriented. Some features to include would be LINE and COLUMN positioning, reverse video, flashing, and left or right justification of an input field. The precise features you choose to use are a function of your compiler.
3. The annual payment is calculated according to the formula

$$\text{Annual Repayment} = \frac{i(1 + i)^n}{(1 + i)^n - 1}$$

   where n = the duration of the loan (in years)
   i = the annual rate as a decimal (e.g., 10% = .10)
4. Prepare a second screen, showing the variation in the annual repayment over several interest rates, which bracket the rate supplied by the user. Prepare a simple table (displayed attractively on a screen) showing the repayment as a function of interest rate. For example,

ANNUAL REPAYMENT	*INTEREST RATE*
____________	.08
____________	.09
____________	.10
____________	.11
____________	.12

   Calculate this table using a PERFORM VARYING statement over several interest rates. Use the user's originally supplied values for the number of years, and the borrowed amount.
5. Prepare a third screen, showing the variation in the annual repayment over several loan durations, which bracket the number of years supplied by the user. Prepare a simple table (displayed attractively on the screen) showing the repayment as a function of the length of the loan. Use a format similar to item 4 above.

   Calculate this table using a PERFORM VARYING statement over several different values of n. Use the originally supplied values for the interest rate and the borrowed amount.

Programming Specifications

Project 9–3

Program Name:

Stock Transactions

Narrative:

This project requires many of the advanced Procedure Division features that were covered in the chapter. These include data validation, calculations involving dates, READ INTO, WRITE FROM, DISPLAY, and INSPECT REPLACING.

Input File:

STOCK-TRANSACTION-FILE

Input Record Layout:

```
01  STOCK-RECORD.
    05  ST-TRANSACTION                  PIC X(24).
    05  ST-PURCHASE-INFORMATION.
        10  ST-PURCHASE-PRICE           PIC 9(5)V99.
        10  ST-PURCHASE-DATE.
            15  ST-PURCHASE-MONTH       PIC 99.
            15  ST-PURCHASE-YEAR        PIC 99.
    05  ST-SALE-INFORMATION.
        10  ST-SALE-PRICE               PIC 9(5)V99.
        10  ST-SALE-DATE.
            15  ST-SALE-MONTH           PIC 99.
            15  ST-SALE-YEAR            PIC 99.
```

Test Data:

```
100SHARES XYZ CORP       2000000184 3000000185
200SHARES ABC CORP      12000003852200000384
100SHARES ACME WIDGETS  11500000182 9500000385
100SHARES BOROW ASSOC   0050000    01000000486
300SHARES LEE ENTERPRISE45000001384900000000485
200SHARES NATL GADGET   0100A000058411000000684
100SHARES NATL GISMO    1000000068512000000685
400SHARES AMER WIDGETS  0900000078508000000985
350SHARES MILGROM POWER 1000000 4782500000 485
200SHARES PARKER INC    00300000783010000A0485
100SHARES SHELLY CO     0030000    0200000
200SHARES STEVENS INC   2000000088522000000985
```

Report Layout:

Design your own report layout. Be sure to comply with all the processing requirements.

Processing Requirements:

1. Read a file of stock records.
2. Validate each input record for all of the following:
   (a) The month and year of both the purchase and sale date must be numeric.
   (b) Month must be a valid value, i.e., between 1 and 12.
   (c) The date of sale cannot be earlier than the date of purchase.
   (d) The dollar amount of both purchase and sale must be numeric.
3. Several incoming fields were punched with leading blanks rather than leading zeros. Use the INSPECT REPLACING option to substitute leading zeros. Do this prior to any validity checks.
4. Display any transaction containing invalid data with an appropriate error message. If a given transaction contains more than one invalid field, multiple error messages are required. No further processing is required for invalid transactions.
5. Compute the gain or loss for each transaction.
6. Gains and losses are to be classified into short-term and long-term transactions. A short-term transaction is one where the elapsed time

between purchase and sale is less than one year. A long-term transaction has an elapsed time of one year or more. (Transaction dates are provided in the form mm/yy; i.e., the day of the month is not available. A transaction is to be considered long term if the number of months between dates is 12 or more; for example, if a purchase took place in 8/84 and the sale in 8/85, the transaction is long term.)

7. Design an appropriate report layout. Invalid transactions are to be displayed with an appropriate error message. Each valid transaction is to appear on a separate detail line and contain the following fields: the transaction, the amount and date of purchase, and the amount and date of sale. The computed gain (or loss) should also appear on the same line, together with an indication of whether the gain (or loss) is short or long term. Each detail line should contain space for four columns for short-term gain and loss and long-term gain and loss. A number will appear in only one of these columns for each transaction.
8. When all transactions have been processed, print a total line containing four totals: the short-term gain, the short-term loss, the long-term gain, and the long-term loss. These totals are to appear in the appropriate columns under the detail line.
9. Use READ INTO and WRITE FROM as appropriate.

More About the Data Division

10

Overview

We return to the Data Division to cover some of the finer points used by professional programmers. The "System Concepts" section reviews the terms character, field, record, *and* file *and introduces* logical *versus* physical *records. The COBOL portion discusses the use of tables, the OCCURS clause, subscripts, and indexes. The COPY statement is also presented, and subprograms are covered in detail.*

As in the preceding chapter, this chapter covers a lot of material. Again, we suggest you read initially for general content only and leave the details for later. Try to get a "feel" for the overall power of the material, but do not attempt to memorize all the options. Remember that the chapter will be effectively summarized by the illustrative program at its conclusion. □

SYSTEM CONCEPTS

You should be comfortable with the terms *character, field, record,* and *file,* which have been in constant use since Chapter 1. One or more *characters* constitute a *field;* a set of related *fields* compose a *record,* and a collection of *records* is known as a *file*.

Logical versus Physical Records

In Chapter 1 we defined a *record* as a set of facts (fields) about a logical entity, and that definition has been in constant use throughout the book. Strictly speaking, however, we have defined a *logical* record as opposed to a *physical* record.

To clarify the difference, let us envision a student directory, which for convenience exists as a printed book. The students are listed alphabetically in this book, with every page containing several students. If we need information on a particular student, e.g., Lynn Frankel, we thumb through the book, stopping at the appropriate page, then go down the students until we come to Ms. Frankel. The page in the directory that contains Lynn's record (as well as several other student records) is a *physical* record. The line on the page that con-

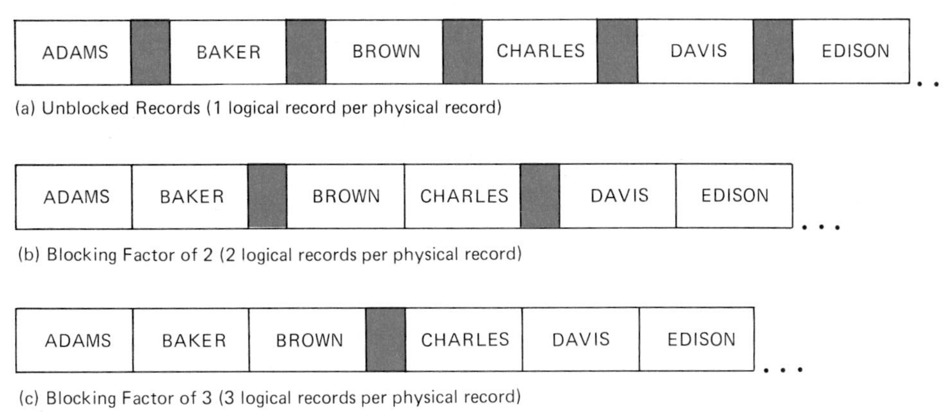

FIGURE 10.1 Blocked versus Unblocked Records

tains Lynn's data, and only Lynn's data, is her *logical* record. (If, by chance, the student records were printed one per page, then the logical record would correspond exactly to the physical record.) In other words, a physical record contains one or more logical records.

The number of logical records in a physical record is known as the *blocking factor*. Physical records are separated from each other on the storage medium by a *gap,* i.e., empty space, known as an *interrecord gap* (IRG) or *interblock gap* (IBG), as shown in Figure 10.1.

In Figure 10.1*a* the records are unblocked; there is one logical record per physical record. Figures 10.1*b* and *c* illustrate blocking factors of 2 and 3, respectively.

Why, you ask, must one bother with blocking and with the distinction between logical and physical records? The answer is simply that high-speed I/O devices, such as tape and disk, read (or write) physical rather than logical records.

Visualize a tape drive, concentrating on its operation. Is the movement uniform or uneven? It is *decidedly uneven,* and this peculiar motion is produced by the interrecord gaps between adjacent physical records. Interrecord gaps are required between adjacent records to enable the system to determine where one record ends and the next one begins. The uneven motion is caused by the constant deceleration (acceleration) as the drive passes over the IRG.

Passage over an IRG is time consuming; hence the fewer interrecord gaps within a file, the faster the file may be processed. Given that each IRG is associated with a single physical record, the fewer the number of physical records, the faster the I/O. The number of logical records in a file is constant, but *the number of physical records may be reduced by increasing the blocking factor.*

A file with 10,000 logical records and a blocking factor of 2 has 5,000 physical records. A blocking factor of 10 in the same file yields only 1,000 physical records. The higher the blocking factor, the smaller the number of physical records, and the faster the I/O time. (In both cases, however, the number of logical records is constant, i.e., 5,000 × 2 or 1,000 × 10.) The blocking factor should generally be as high as possible. Limitations on the maximum value depend in part on the physical characteristics of the device in question and are beyond the scope of this discussion.

COBOL Implementation

Implementation of blocking is straightforward in COBOL, as the programmer needs only to specify an additional clause in the FD entry. Consider

```
FD file-name

     [BLOCK CONTAINS [integer-1 TO] integer-2 {RECORDS   }]
                                              {CHARACTERS}

     [RECORD CONTAINS [integer-3 TO] integer-4 CHARACTERS]

     LABEL {RECORDS ARE} {STANDARD}
           {RECORD IS  } {OMITTED }

     [DATA RECORD IS record-name-1]
```

Let us assume a blocking factor of 5, with the associated entry BLOCK CONTAINS 5 RECORDS. *The operating system does all the necessary I/O for the programmer, including blocking and unblocking.* The first time a COBOL READ statement is executed, the entire block (i.e., physical record), consisting of 5 logical records, is brought into a storage area, but only the first record is made available to the program. The next time a COBOL READ is executed, the second record is made available to the program, but no physical I/O takes place. In similar fashion, no physical I/O occurs for the third, fourth, and fifth READs. The sixth, eleventh, sixteenth, etc., executions of the READ cause a new physical record to be brought into the I/O area, but there is no physical I/O for the seventh through tenth, twelfth through fifteenth, etc., executions of the READ. *All this is automatically done for the programmer by the operating system.*

TABLES

We move now to the major topic of this chapter, tables. A *table* is a grouping of similar data. The values in a table are stored in consecutive storage locations and assigned a single data name. Reference to individual items within a table is accomplished by *subscripts* that identify the location of the particular item.

Let us assume that company XYZ tabulates its sales on a monthly basis and that the sales of each month are to be referenced within a COBOL program. Without tables, 12 data names are required: SALES-FOR-JANUARY, SALES-FOR-FEBRUARY, etc. With tables, however, one may define only a single data name, such as SALES, and refer to individual months by an appropriate subscript. Thus SALES (2) would indicate sales for the second month, February.

A user's view of the sales table is shown in Figure 10.2.

MONTH	*SALES*
Jan.	$1,000
Feb.	$2,000
Mar.	$3,000
Apr.	$4,000
May	$5,000
June	$4,000
July	$3,000
Aug.	$2,000
Sept.	$1,000
Oct.	$2,000
Nov.	$3,000
Dec.	$6,000

Note: SALES (3) = sales for 3rd month = $3,000.

FIGURE 10.2 *Sales Table*

OCCURS Clause

The OCCURS clause specifies the number of entries in a table. An abbreviated format of the OCCURS clause is simply

```
OCCURS integer TIMES
```

Thus, for the one-dimension table in Figure 10.2, one might use

```
05  SALES    OCCURS 12 TIMES    PIC 9(6).
```

This entry would cause a 72-position table (12 entries × 6 positions per entry) to be established in the computer's memory, as shown:

SALES			
SALES (1)	SALES (2)		SALES (12)
		• • •	

Processing a Table

After a table has been established (via an OCCURS clause), we shall want to sum the 12 monthly totals and produce an annual total. There are several approaches, the first of which is brute force:

```
COMPUTE ANNUAL-SALES = SALES (1)  + SALES (2)  + SALES (3)
                     + SALES (4)  + SALES (5)  + SALES (6)
                     + SALES (7)  + SALES (8)  + SALES (9)
                     + SALES (10) + SALES (11) + SALES (12).
```

This technique is cumbersome to code, but it does explicitly illustrate the concept of table processing. A more elegant procedure is to establish a *loop* through the use of a variable subscript. This is best accomplished through the VARYING option of the PERFORM verb. Consider

```
    MOVE ZERO TO ANNUAL-SALES.
    PERFORM COMPUTE-ANNUAL-TOTALS
       VARYING SUBSCRIPT FROM 1 BY 1
          UNTIL SUBSCRIPT > 12.
    .
    .
    .
COMPUTE-ANNUAL-TOTALS.
    ADD SALES (SUBSCRIPT) TO ANNUAL-SALES.
```

The PERFORM VARYING statement initializes SUBSCRIPT to 1. It then loops through a sequence of testing, branching, and incrementing until the condition is satisfied. Hence in order to execute the paragraph COMPUTE-ANNUAL-TOTALS 12 times, the condition portion is SUBSCRIPT > 12, rather than SUBSCRIPT = 12. (You may wish to review the discussion of PERFORM VARYING in Chapter 9.)

A Second Example

Consider a personnel application, in which three sets of salary data are maintained for each employee. Specifically, each employee record contains the employee's present salary and date on which it became effective, the previous salary and date, and the second previous salary and date. (Not all employees have all three values.)

It is, of course, possible to develop unique data names for each occurrence of salary information, e.g.,

```
05  SALARY-DATA.
    10  PRESENT-SALARY                  PIC 9(6).
    10  PRESENT-SALARY-DATE             PIC 9(4).
    10  PREVIOUS-SALARY                 PIC 9(6).
    10  PREVIOUS-SALARY-DATE            PIC 9(4).
    10  SECOND-PREVIOUS-SALARY          PIC 9(6).
    10  SECOND-PREVIOUS-SALARY-DATE     PIC 9(4).
```

However, what if it were suddenly decided that four, five, or even ten levels of historical data were required? The situation is neatly circumvented by establishing a table that enables the programmer to define logically similar elements under a common name and to reference the desired entry subsequently by an appropriate subscript. Hence SALARY (1) denotes the present salary, SALARY (2) the previous salary, SALARY (3) the second previous salary, and so on. Figure 10.3 shows COBOL code and storage allocation for such a scheme.

Figure 10.3 depicts a total of 30 storage positions for the table SALARY-DATA, with the OCCURS clause at the *group* level. Positions 1–6 refer to SALARY (1), positions 7–10 refer to SAL-DATE (1), and positions 1–10 collectively to SALARY-DATA (1). In similar fashion, positions 11–16 refer to SALARY (2), positions 17–20 refer to SAL-DATE (2), and positions 11–20 collectively to SALARY-DATA (2). Whenever a subscript is used, it is enclosed in parentheses.

Figure 10.4 is a second illustration of the OCCURS clause, with two OCCURS clauses at the elementary level. A total of 30 storage positions is still assigned to the table. However, positions 1–6 refer to SALARY (1), positions 7–12 to SALARY (2), and positions 13–18 to SALARY (3). Positions 19–22 correspond to SAL-DATE (1), positions 23–26 to SAL-DATE (2), and positions 27–30 to SAL-DATE (3). Either arrangement, Figure 10.3 or Figure 10.4, is appropriate; the choice is up to the programmer.

COBOL Code:

```
05  SALARY-DATA OCCURS 3 TIMES.
    10  SALARY      PIC 9(6).
    10  SAL-DATE    PIC 9(4).
```

Storage Allocation:

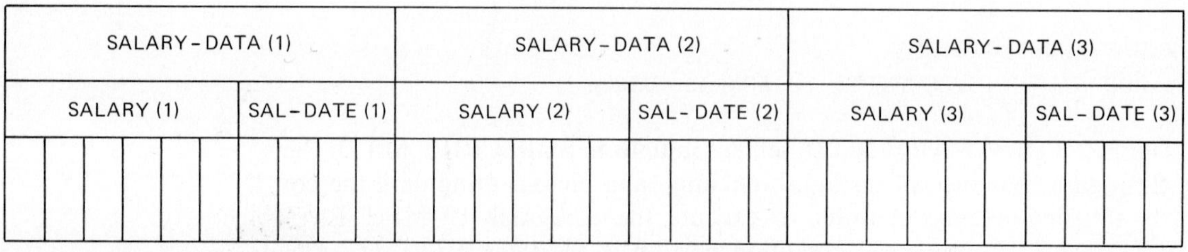

SALARY-DATA (1)		SALARY-DATA (2)		SALARY-DATA (3)	
SALARY (1)	SAL-DATE (1)	SALARY (2)	SAL-DATE (2)	SALARY (3)	SAL-DATE (3)

FIGURE 10.3 Illustration of OCCURS Clause

COBOL Code:

```
05 SALARY-DATA.
   10 SALARY      OCCURS 3 TIMES PIC 9(6).
   10 SAL-DATE    OCCURS 3 TIMES PIC 9(4).
```

Storage Allocation:

SALARY-DATA					
SALARY (1)	SALARY (2)	SALARY (3)	SAL-DATE (1)	SAL-DATE (2)	SAL-DATE (3)

FIGURE 10.4 Illustration of OCCURS Clause II

Problems with the OCCURS Clause

A common compilation error associated with tables is to use the wrong number of subscripts. Beginners often forget to specify a subscript where one is required, or they include a subscript when it is not permitted. The rule is very simple.

After a data name has been defined with an OCCURS clause, *or* if it is subservient to a group item with an OCCURS clause, it must always be referenced with a subscript. Failure to do so will result in a compilation error. Accordingly, given the table definition associated with Figure 10.3, all of the following are valid references: SALARY-DATA (2), SALARY (2), SAL-DATE (2). Since the OCCURS clause is at the group level, SALARY-DATA (2) refers collectively to the 10 bytes associated with SALARY (2) and SAL-DATE (2).

However, in the table definition associated with Figure 10.4, the OCCURS clauses are present at the elementary level. Hence SALARY-DATA is referenced *without* a subscript and refers collectively to the 30 bytes in the table.

Realize also that the compiler checks only for the presence (or absence) of a subscript but does not check for a proper value. SALARY (4) is valid syntactically in both Figures 10.3 and 10.4 and will *not* cause a compilation error. However, it will cause problems during *execution*. The compiler will treat the first six bytes *past* SALARY (3) as SALARY (4), which is not what the programmer intended.

Rules for Subscripts

COBOL subscripts may be either variable or constant. In either case subscripts *must* adhere to the following rules:

1. A space may not precede the right parenthesis nor follow the left parenthesis.

```
  VALID: SALES (SUB)
  VALID: SALES (2)
INVALID: SALES ( 2)
INVALID: SALES (2 )
```

2. At least one space is required between the data name and the left parenthesis.

```
INVALID: SALES(SUB)
  VALID: SALES (2)
INVALID: SALES(2)
```

3. Subscript values must be positive (nonzero) integers. Violation will not cause compilation errors but almost certainly will cause difficulty during execution.

The USAGE Clause

The USAGE clause does not affect the logic of a program. Instead it affects the generated object code and is used to make a program more efficient. (It is not required, however, and a program will run with or without the USAGE clause.) Ideally, a subscript should be defined as a binary value via any of the following:

```
05  SUBSCRIPT-1     PIC S9(4)     USAGE IS COMPUTATIONAL.
05  SUBSCRIPT-2     PIC S9(4)     COMPUTATIONAL.
05  SUBSCRIPT-3     PIC S9(4)     USAGE IS COMP.
05  SUBSCRIPT-4     PIC S9(4)     COMP.
```

Notice that each subscript was specified with a picture of S9(4). This should be standard practice under IBM, but this suggestion has to be taken on faith unless you have an appreciation for IBM assembler fundamentals.[1]

OCCURS DEPENDING ON

The general format of the OCCURS clause is

```
OCCURS { integer-1 TO integer-2 TIMES [DEPENDING ON data-name-1] }
       { integer-2 TIMES                                        }

       [ { ASCENDING  } KEY IS data-name-2 [data-name-3] . . . ]
       [ { DESCENDING }                                        ]

       [INDEXED BY index-name-1 [index-name-2] . . .]
```

The OCCURS DEPENDING ON option is used to implement a *variable-length table,* which in turn produces a *variable-length record.* Variable-length records are also reflected in the RECORD CONTAINS clause of the FD. Consider Figure 10.5.

```
FD  STUDENT-TRANSCRIPT-FILE
    RECORD CONTAINS 53 TO 1131 CHARACTERS
    LABEL RECORDS ARE STANDARD
    DATA RECORD IS STUDENT-RECORD.
01  STUDENT-RECORD.
    05  ST-NAME                                  PIC X(30).
    05  ST-YEAR-IN-SCHOOL                        PIC X(10).
    05  ST-COURSES-COMPLETED                     PIC 99.
    05  ST-COURSE-GRADE OCCURS 1 TO 99 TIMES
        DEPENDING ON ST-COURSES-COMPLETED.
        10  ST-COURSE-NUMBER                     PIC 9(6).
        10  ST-GRADE                             PIC X.
        10  ST-COURSE-DATE                       PIC 9(4).
```

FIGURE 10.5 Illustration of Variable-Length Record Description

[1]See, for example, Robert Grauer, *The IBM COBOL Environment* (Englewood Cliffs, N.J.: Prentice-Hall, 1984).

Every record contains a minimum of 53 characters (30 for name, 10 for year, 2 for the number of courses, and 11 for the first course). If the student is an entering freshman, the entire record consists of 53 characters. (An occurrence of 0 is *not* permitted; hence space for at least one course must be provided.) Records for upperclassmen contain an additional 11 bytes for every completed course. A maximum of 99 courses is permitted in a record.

Variable length records offer the advantage of allocating only as much space as necessary. Fixed length records, on the other hand, assign the same amount of storage space to every record in the file. Accordingly, in establishing the size of a fixed length record, one must determine the maximum number of courses a student could possibly take, and then allocate that amount of space for every student.

What, then, is the *maximum* number of courses? Is it five per semester, times 8 semesters, or 40 courses? What about the student who fails a course or the one with two majors, or the one who remains in the university to pursue a master's or doctoral degree? Perhaps we should allocate space for 100 courses, just to be safe. If we do, every student record will require 1,100 bytes (11 bytes per course times 100 courses). But at any given time the average student probably has completed twenty or fewer courses (i.e., there are freshmen, sophomores, juniors, and seniors in the file), and hence most records would require only 220 (20 × 11) bytes. In other words, approximately 900 bytes per record are wasted in the storage medium. If you multiply this by the number of students in the university, you can quickly see the inefficiency of fixed-length records in certain applications.

By contrast, *variable*-length records allow only as much space in each record as is actually required. There is a specific field in each record from which the length of the record is calculated. In our example that field would be the number of completed courses, and that value is reflected in the OCCURS DEPENDING ON clause.

Indexes versus Subscripts

The INDEXED BY clause in the OCCURS statement is used to define an *index* for use with the *particular* table. An index is conceptually the same as a subscript in that both reference an entry in a table. However, an index represents a *displacement* into the table and provides more efficient object code. The following example clarifies the difference:

```
05  MAJORS      OCCURS 10 TIMES
                INDEXED BY MAJOR-INDEX.
    10  MAJOR-CODE      PIC 9(4).
    10  MAJOR-NAME      PIC X(10).
```

A table with 10 entries is established and occupies a total of 140 positions. Valid *subscripts* for MAJOR-CODE are 1, 2, 3, . . ., 10; i.e., MAJOR-CODE can occur 10 times.

The concept of a displacement is best appreciated by those who know an assembler language. A *displacement* is the number of bytes (i.e., positions) one must go into a table to find the entry in question; hence valid *displacements* for MAJOR-CODE are 0, 14, 28, . . ., 126. In other words, the first value of MAJOR-CODE begins at position 1, a *displacement* of zero bytes into the table; the second value of MAJOR-CODE begins in position 15, a *displacement* of 14 positions into the table, etc. Thus the first entry in the table is referenced by a subscript of 1 or a displacement (an index) of 0, the second entry by a subscript of 2 or an index of 14, the last entry by a subscript of 10 or an index of 126.

Fortunately, the COBOL programmer need not be concerned with the actual value of an index and may regard it conceptually as a subscript. The COBOL programmer explicitly codes index values of 1, 2, etc., which are converted by the compiler to internal displacements of 0, 14, etc.

COBOL provides the capability to adjust an index to its proper value through the SET, SEARCH, and PERFORM verbs. Indeed, these are the *only* verbs that can be used to modify an index.

SET Statement

The SET statement is used solely to manipulate indexes. It has two formats:

Format 1

```
     identifier-1 [, identifier-2] . . .  }      { identifier-3 }
SET                                       }  TO  { index-name-3 }
     index-name-1 [, index-name-2] . . .  }      { integer-1    }
```

Format 2

```
SET index-name-4 [, index-name-5] . . . { UP BY   } { identifier-4 }
                                        { DOWN BY } { integer-2    }
```

Figure 10.6 illustrates the use of a SET verb to initialize and increment an index. A variable-length table is established, whose length depends on the number of checks written. It varies from 11 to 1,100 characters; that is, there are 11 characters per entry and the number of entries ranges from 1 to 100. In the

```
DATA DIVISION.
    .
    .
    .
```

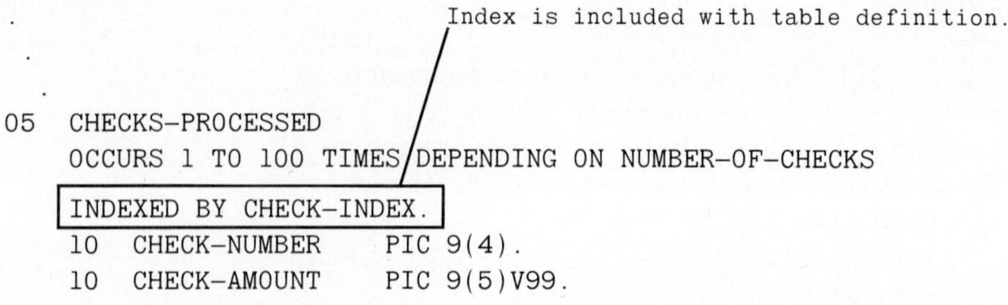

```
                              Index is included with table definition.
    05  CHECKS-PROCESSED
        OCCURS 1 TO 100 TIMES DEPENDING ON NUMBER-OF-CHECKS
        INDEXED BY CHECK-INDEX.
        10  CHECK-NUMBER     PIC 9(4).
        10  CHECK-AMOUNT     PIC 9(5)V99.
    .
    .
    .
PROCEDURE DIVISION.                    Index is initialized.
    SET CHECK-INDEX TO 1.
    PERFORM COMPUTE-CHECKBOOK-BALANCE NUMBER-OF-CHECKS TIMES.
    .
    .
COMPUTE-CHECKBOOK-BALANCE.
    SUBTRACT CHECK-AMOUNT (CHECK-INDEX) FROM INITIAL-BALANCE.

    SET CHECK-INDEX UP BY 1.
                              Index is incremented.
```

FIGURE 10.6 *Illustration of SET Verb with Variable Length Table*

Procedure Division the SET verb is used both to initialize and to increment the index, CHECK-INDEX.

Note well that indexing is *not* required in COBOL. Thus it is syntactically correct in Figure 10.6 to add a Working-Storage entry for CHECK-SUBSCRIPT, remove the INDEXED BY clause, substitute CHECK-SUBSCRIPT for CHECK-INDEX in the SUBTRACT statement, and change the two SET statements to MOVE 1 TO CHECK-SUBSCRIPT and ADD 1 TO CHECK-SUBSCRIPT, respectively. Such changes have no effect on the complexity of the source code. Indeed, their impact can be measured only by examining the generated object code.

Differences between indexes and subscripts are summarized in Table 10.1.

TABLE 10.1 *Indexes versus Subscripts*

INDEXES	*SUBSCRIPTS*
Defined with a specific table; can be used only with that table.	Defined in Working-Storage; the same subscript can be used with many tables, although this is not recommended (see Programming Tip in chapter 11.)
Initialized and incremented via the SET statement; can also be manipulated in PERFORM statements.	May not be used with SET statements (MOVE and ADD are used instead); can also be manipulated in PERFORM statements.
Provides more efficient object code; i.e., an index is a *displacement* within a table, whereas a subscript is merely an occurrence.	The USAGE clause, USAGE IS COMPUTATIONAL, helps to make subscripts more efficient, although indexes are still faster.
Arithmetic is permitted when an index is used to indicate an occurrence; i.e., TABLE-NAME (INDEX ± CONSTANT) is valid.	Arithmetic is not permitted; i.e., TABLE-NAME (SUBSCRIPT ± CONSTANT) is *invalid.*

COPY STATEMENT

Commercial applications are classified into systems (e.g., inventory, accounting, payroll), with each system consisting of several programs. The files of these programs are interrelated, and the same file may appear in several programs. The COPY clause enables an installation to build a library of record descriptions and offers the following advantages:

1. Individual programmers need not code the extensive Data Division entries that can make COBOL so tedious. (This is particularly helpful in commercial programs where record descriptions run into hundreds of lines.) Instead, a programmer merely codes a one-line COPY statement, and the compiler brings the proper entries into the COBOL program.
2. Changes are made only in one place, i.e., in the library version. Although changes in a file or record description occur infrequently, they do happen. However, only the library version need be altered explicitly, as individual programs will automatically bring in the corrected version during compilation.
3. Programming errors are reduced, and standardization is promoted. Since an individual is coding fewer lines, the program will contain fewer errors. More important, all fields are defined correctly. Further, there is no chance of omitting an existing field or erroneously creating a new one. Finally, all programmers will be using identical record descriptions.

Programmer codes only line 27.

```
00027                    COPY STUDREC.
00028 C           01     STUDENT-RECORD.
00029 C                  05   ST-NAME                        PIC X(19).
00030 C                  05   ST-NUMBER-OF-COURSES           PIC 9(2).
00031 C                  05   ST-COURSE-TABLE OCCURS 8       TIMES.
00032 C                       10   ST-COURSE-NUMBER          PIC X(3).
00033 C                       10   ST-COURSE-GRADE           PIC X.
00034 C                       10   ST-COURSE-CREDITS         PIC 9.
00035 C                  05   FILLER                         PIC X(19).
00036
00037             FD     PRINT-FILE
00038                    LABEL RECORDS ARE OMITTED
00039                    RECORD CONTAINS 133 CHARACTERS
00040                    DATA RECORD IS PRINT-LINE.
00041
```

Lines 28-35 are brought into the program by the compiler.

FIGURE 10.7 The COPY Statement

An abbreviated format of the COPY statement is simply

```
COPY text-name
```

where text-name is the name of a file (member, or element) that exists independently of the COBOL program elsewhere on disk. A COPY statement may be used *anywhere* within a COBOL program, except that the text being copied cannot contain another COPY. An example of the COPY statement is shown in Figure 10.7.

In Figure 10.7 the programmer codes COPY STUDREC. The COBOL compiler locates the file STUDREC and brings in lines 28–35 as though the programmer had coded them explicitly. IBM compilers insert a C after the compiler statement number to indicate a copied statement.

In a similar manner, standard segments of code for the Procedure Division can be inserted in the program using a COPY statement. For example, the code for a standard error routine might be stored on disk for use by all programmers in the organization.

SUBPROGRAMS

The PERFORM statement can be utilized to divide a program into a series of routines that are called by the mainline portion of the program. In effect the PERFORM invokes a subroutine in a COBOL program. As such, the called routine must be coded, compiled, and debugged *within* the main program. However, there is a way to make the subroutine an entirely separate entity from the main program. This technique requires the CALL and USING statements in the Procedure Division and the Linkage Section in the Data Division.

A subprogram (i.e., one that is independent of the main program) contains the four divisions of a regular program. In addition, it contains a Linkage Section in its Data Division that passes information to and from the main program. The same program may call several subprograms, and a subprogram may in turn call other subprograms.

Figure 10.8 contains code extracted from the listings at the end of the chapter to illustrate the use of subprograms. The main program contains a CALL statement somewhere in its Procedure Division. At that point control is transferred from the main program to the subroutine. The CALL statement contains a USING clause, which specifies the data on which the subprogram is to operate. The subprogram in turn contains a USING clause in its Procedure Division header indicating which data it is to receive from the calling program.

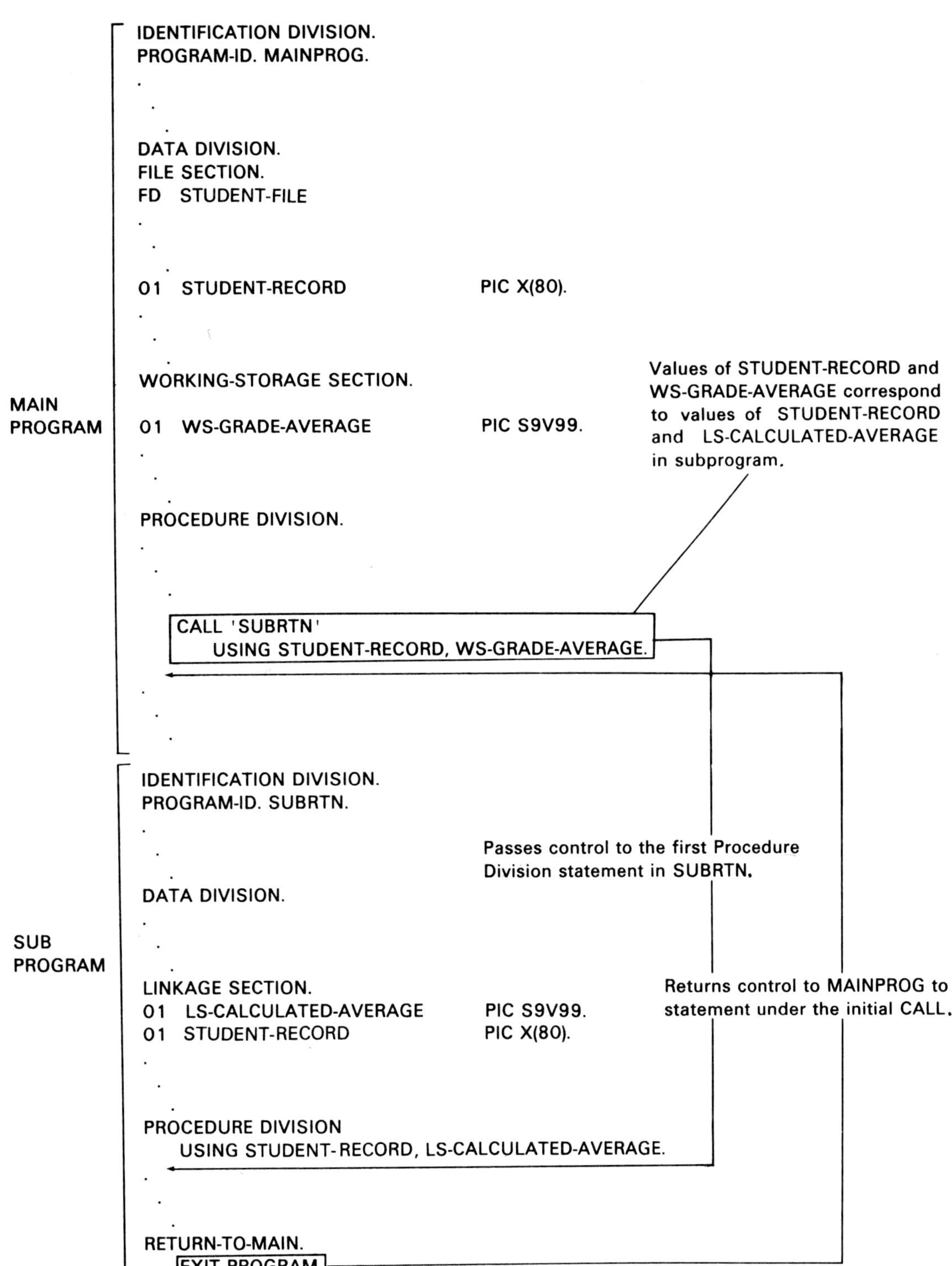
MAIN PROGRAM
IDENTIFICATION DIVISION.
PROGRAM-ID. MAINPROG.
DATA DIVISION.
FILE SECTION.
FD STUDENT-FILE
01 STUDENT-RECORD PIC X(80).
WORKING-STORAGE SECTION.
01 WS-GRADE-AVERAGE PIC S9V99.
PROCEDURE DIVISION.
CALL 'SUBRTN'
USING STUDENT-RECORD, WS-GRADE-AVERAGE.
Values of STUDENT-RECORD and WS-GRADE-AVERAGE correspond to values of STUDENT-RECORD and LS-CALCULATED-AVERAGE in subprogram.
SUB PROGRAM
IDENTIFICATION DIVISION.
PROGRAM-ID. SUBRTN.
Passes control to the first Procedure Division statement in SUBRTN.
DATA DIVISION.
LINKAGE SECTION.
01 LS-CALCULATED-AVERAGE PIC S9V99.
01 STUDENT-RECORD PIC X(80).
Returns control to MAINPROG to statement under the initial CALL.
PROCEDURE DIVISION
USING STUDENT-RECORD, LS-CALCULATED-AVERAGE.
RETURN-TO-MAIN.
EXIT PROGRAM.

FIGURE 10.8 Illustration of Subprogram

The data names in the two USING clauses can, but need not, be the same. However, the *order* and *structure* of data names within the USING clauses is absolutely critical. The first item in the USING clause of the main program (STUDENT-RECORD) corresponds to the first item in the USING clause of the subprogram (STUDENT-RECORD); both are 01 records with 80 characters and have the *same* name. The second item in the main program (WS-GRADE-AV-

ERAGE) matches the second item in the subroutine (LS-GRADE-AVERAGE). The picture clauses must be identical, but the data names are different.

Data names in the main program may be defined in either the File Section or Working-Storage, whereas data names in the subprogram (which are passed from the main program) are defined in the Linkage Section. In other words, the Linkage Section contains the definition of all arguments in the subprogram.

When the CALL statement in the main program is executed, the subprogram is entered at the beginning of its Procedure Division. It executes exactly as a regular COBOL program except that it contains an EXIT PROGRAM statement instead of a STOP RUN. EXIT PROGRAM terminates processing of the subprogram and returns control to the main program to the statement immediately after the CALL. (EXIT PROGRAM must be in a paragraph by itself.)

A SAMPLE PROGRAM

We are ready now to incorporate the material covered in this chapter into an example program, the specifications of which are provided in Figure 10.9. Test data and sample output are shown in Figure 10.10. The main program and its associated subroutine are shown in Figures 10.11 and 10.12, respectively.

Figures 10.11 and 10.12 contain the main (calling) program and subprogram (called), respectively. The main program calls the subprogram in COBOL lines

Programming Specifications

Program Name:

Student Transcript Program

Narrative:

This example consits of *two* programs, a main and a subprogram, which process a file of student records and print student transcripts. The main program reads a student record and passes information on the courses taken last semester to a subprogram. The subprogram calculates the student's GPA (Grade Point Average) and sends the value back to the main program, which prints the transcript.

Input File(s):

STUDENT-FILE

Input Record Layout:

```
01  STUDENT-RECORD.
    05  ST-NAME                     PIC X(19).
    05  ST-NUMBER-OF-COURSES        PIC 9(2).
    05  ST-COURSE-TABLE OCCURS 8 TIMES.
        10  ST-COURSE-NUMBER        PIC X(3).
        10  ST-COURSE-GRADE         PIC X.
        10  ST-COURSE-CREDITS       PIC 9.
    05  FILLER                      PIC X(19).
```

Test Data:

See Figure 10.10*a* on page 255.

FIGURE 10.9 Programming Specifications for Student Transcript Program

Report Format:

See Figure 10.10*b* on page 255.

Processing Requirements:

1. Read a file of student records.
2. For every record read,
   (a) Pass the input record to a subprogram in order for the subprogram to calculate the GPA according to item 3 below.
   (b) Accept the calculated GPA from the subprogram, and print a student transcript. Every transcript is to begin on a new page, according to the format in Figure 10.10*b*.
3. A four-point system is used in calculating the GPA; A, B, C, D, and F are worth 4, 3, 2, 1, and 0, respectively. Courses are weighted according to their credit value; the number of *quality points* for a given course is equal to number of credits for that course times the numeric value of that grade. The GPA is equal to the total number of quality points divided by the total number of credits.

   Assume, for example, that John Doe received an A in a 2-credit course and a B in a 4-credit course. The GPA is calculated as follows:

GRADE	*NUMERIC VALUE*	*CREDITS*	*QUALITY POINTS*
A	4	2	8
B	3	4	12
	Totals	6	20

GPA = 20/6 = 3.33

FIGURE 10.9 (Continued)

99–101 and passes two arguments, STUDENT-RECORD and WS-GRADE-AVERAGE. The subprogram in turn knows these arguments as STUDENT-RECORD and WS-CALCULATED-AVERAGE (subprogram lines 33–34). It defines these data names in its Linkage Section (subprogram lines 20–30). The data names in the main and subprogram can, but need not be, the same. It is good practice to use the same COPY clause in both programs for some or all of the passed parameters to ensure identical record descriptions. (See line 27 in the main program and line 22 in the subprogram.)

The subprogram is concerned exclusively with calculating the grade point average. Notice the four simple IF statements in lines 50–57. These could, of course, have been written as a single nested IF, but we have chosen to use the four statements for variety. Which is preferable? There is no unequivocal answer. Some installations discourage nested IFs on the grounds that they are too difficult to read. Other installations encourage their use. We use both techniques in the text to give the broadest exposure possible, but we do favor nested IFs.

The subprogram also illustrates table processing via the PERFORM VARYING option (lines 39–41). Each student record contains a variable number of courses (ST-NUMBER-OF-COURSES), and hence the routine to include each course in the overall average must be performed a variable number of times. The VARYING option increments WS-COURSE-SUB by 1 prior to entering 010-COMPUTE-QUALITY-POINTS. The UNTIL clause terminates the PERFORM when all courses have been processed. Finally, note the running total of quality points in 010-COMPUTE-QUALITY-POINTS and the use of subscripting in conjunction with the table of student courses.

After the subprogram has been executed, control returns to the main program (line 103), where generation of output begins.

Programming Tip

Use COPY to Pass Parameters

The *order* of arguments in the CALL USING and PROCEDURE DIVISION USING clauses of the calling and called programs is critical. One can *guarantee* that the order and PICTURE clauses will be identical in both calling and called programs by passing only a single 01 record, which is *copied* into both programs. Consider:

Poor Code:

```
CALL 'DECODER'
     USING TITLE-CODE, EXPANDED-TITLE,
          LOCATION-CODE, EXPANDED-LOCATION.
 .
  .
   .
PROCEDURE DIVISION
     USING LS-TITLE-CODE, LS-EXPANDED-TITLE,
          LS-LOCATION-CODE, LS-EXPANDED-LOCATION.
```

Improved Code:

```
         COPY ARGUMENTS.
C    01  PARAMETER-LIST.
C            05  TITLE-CODE             PIC 9(3).
C            05  EXPANDED-TITLE         PIC X(15).
C            05  LOCATION-CODE          PIC XX.
C            05  EXPANDED-LOCATION      PIC X(12).
         .
          .
           .
         CALL 'DECODER'
             USING PARAMETER-LIST.

     LINKAGE SECTION.
         COPY ARGUMENTS.
C    01  PARAMETER-LIST.
C            05  TITLE-CODE             PIC 9(3).
C            05  EXPANDED-TITLE         PIC X(15).
C            05  LOCATION-CODE          PIC XX.
C            05  EXPANDED-LOCATION      PIC X(12).
     PROCEDURE DIVISION
         USING PARAMETER-LIST.
```

Use of the single 01 parameter facilitates coding in the USING clauses and also makes them immune to change. Use of the same COPY member in both programs eliminates any problem with listing arguments in the wrong order or inconsistent definition through different pictures.

```
BENJAMIN, L        05111A3222A2333A3444A3555B3
BORROW, J          04666B3777B3888B3999B4
MILGROM, M         06123C4456C4789C4012C4345C3678C4
```

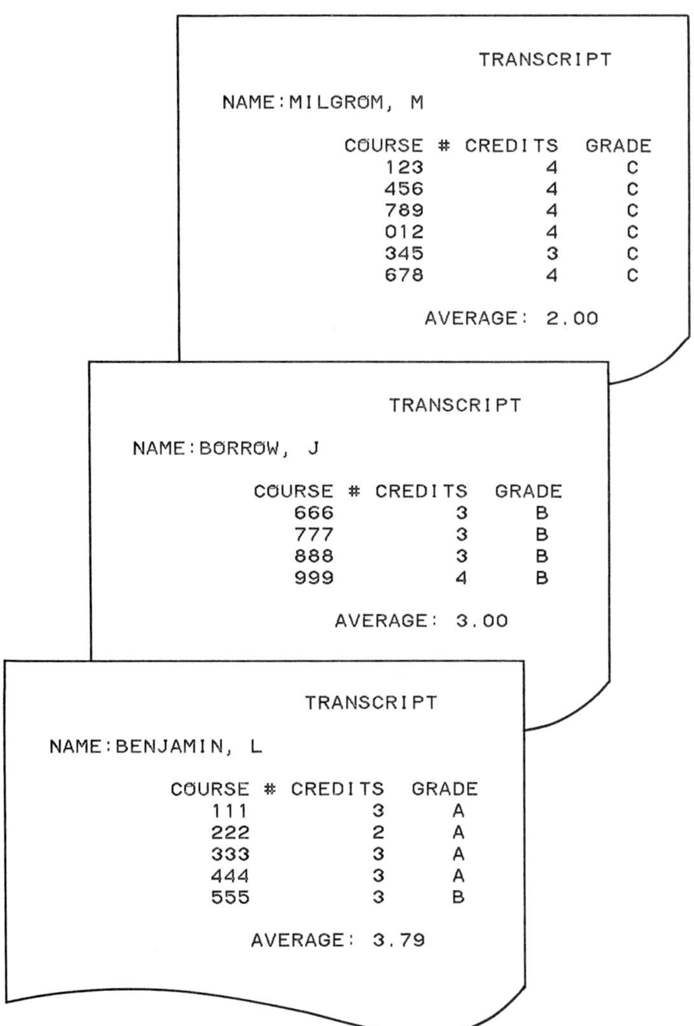

TRANSCRIPT
NAME:MILGROM, M
COURSE # CREDITS GRADE
123 4 C
456 4 C
789 4 C
012 4 C
345 3 C
678 4 C
AVERAGE: 2.00
TRANSCRIPT
NAME:BORROW, J
COURSE # CREDITS GRADE
666 3 B
777 3 B
888 3 B
999 4 B
AVERAGE: 3.00
TRANSCRIPT
NAME:BENJAMIN, L
COURSE # CREDITS GRADE
111 3 A
222 2 A
333 3 A
444 3 A
555 3 B
AVERAGE: 3.79

FIGURE 10.10 Test Data and Sample Output for Student Transcript Program

```
       IDENTIFICATION DIVISION.
       PROGRAM-ID.     MAINPROG.
       AUTHOR.         JACKIE CLARK.

       ENVIRONMENT DIVISION.
       CONFIGURATION SECTION.
       SOURCE-COMPUTER.
           IBM-4341.
       OBJECT-COMPUTER.
           IBM-4341.

       INPUT-OUTPUT SECTION.
       FILE-CONTROL.
           SELECT STUDENT-FILE
               ASSIGN TO UT-S-STUDENT.
           SELECT PRINT-FILE
               ASSIGN TO UT-S-PRINT.

       DATA DIVISION.
```

FIGURE 10.11 Main Program

FIGURE 10.11 (Continued)

```
       FILE SECTION.
       FD  STUDENT-FILE
           LABEL RECORDS ARE OMITTED
           RECORD CONTAINS 80 CHARACTERS
           BLOCK CONTAINS 0 RECORDS
           DATA RECORD IS STUDENT-RECORD.

           COPY STUDREC.
C      01  STUDENT-RECORD.
C          05  ST-NAME                    PIC X(19).
C          05  ST-NUMBER-OF-COURSES       PIC 9(2).
C          05  ST-COURSE-TABLE OCCURS 8 TIMES.
C              10  ST-COURSE-NUMBER       PIC X(3).
C              10  ST-COURSE-GRADE        PIC X.
C              10  ST-COURSE-CREDITS      PIC 9.
C          05  FILLER                     PIC X(19).

       FD  PRINT-FILE
           LABEL RECORDS ARE OMITTED
           RECORD CONTAINS 133 CHARACTERS
           DATA RECORD IS PRINT-LINE.

       01  PRINT-LINE                 PIC X(133).

       WORKING-STORAGE SECTION.
       01  WS-SUBSCRIPTS.
           05  WS-COURSE-SUB          PIC S9(4)    COMP.

       01  PROGRAM-SWITCHES.
           05 WS-END-OF-FILE-SWITCH PIC X(3)     VALUE 'NO '.

       01  WS-GRADE-AVERAGE           PIC S9V99.

       01  WS-HEADING-LINE-ONE.
           05  FILLER                 PIC X(20)      VALUE SPACES.
           05  FILLER                 PIC X(10)      VALUE 'TRANSCRIPT'.
           05  FILLER                 PIC X(103)     VALUE SPACES.

       01  WS-HEADING-LINE-TWO.
           05  FILLER                 PIC X(6)       VALUE ' NAME:'.
           05  HDG-NAME               PIC X(15).
           05  FILLER                 PIC X(112)     VALUE SPACES.

       01  WS-HEADING-LINE-THREE.
           05  FILLER                 PIC X(10)      VALUE SPACES.
           05  FILLER                 PIC X(9)       VALUE 'COURSE # '.
           05  FILLER                 PIC X(9)       VALUE 'CREDITS  '.
           05  FILLER                 PIC X(5)       VALUE 'GRADE'.
           05  FILLER                 PIC X(100)     VALUE SPACES.

       01  DETAIL-LINE.
           05  FILLER                 PIC X(13)      VALUE SPACES.
           05  DET-COURSE             PIC X(3).
           05  FILLER                 PIC X(9)       VALUE SPACES.
           05  DET-CREDITS            PIC 9.
           05  FILLER                 PIC X(5)       VALUE SPACES.
           05  DET-GRADE              PIC X.
           05  FILLER                 PIC X(101).

       01  TOTAL-LINE.
           05  FILLER                 PIC X(16)      VALUE SPACES.
           05  FILLER                 PIC X(9)       VALUE 'AVERAGE: '.
           05  TOT-GPA                PIC 9.99.
           05  FILLER                 PIC X(104)     VALUE SPACES.

       PROCEDURE DIVISION.

       010-MAINLINE.
           OPEN INPUT  STUDENT-FILE
                OUTPUT PRINT-FILE.
           READ STUDENT-FILE
               AT END MOVE 'YES' TO WS-END-OF-FILE-SWITCH.
           PERFORM 020-PROCESS-RECORDS
               UNTIL WS-END-OF-FILE-SWITCH = 'YES'.
           CLOSE STUDENT-FILE
                 PRINT-FILE.
           STOP RUN.

       020-PROCESS-RECORDS.
           CALL 'SUBRTN'
               USING STUDENT-RECORD
                     WS-GRADE-AVERAGE.
```

BLOCK CONTAINS clause indicates block size will be entered in JCL.

COPY statement.

Copied entries.

OCCURS clause establishes course table.

Subscript defined in Working-Storage.

Call to subprogram.

```
           WRITE PRINT-LINE FROM WS-HEADING-LINE-ONE
               AFTER ADVANCING PAGE.
           MOVE ST-NAME TO HDG-NAME.
           WRITE PRINT-LINE FROM WS-HEADING-LINE-TWO
               AFTER ADVANCING 2 LINES.
           WRITE PRINT-LINE FROM WS-HEADING-LINE-THREE
               AFTER ADVANCING 2 LINES.
           PERFORM 030-WRITE-DETAIL-LINE
               VARYING WS-COURSE-SUB FROM 1 BY 1
                   UNTIL WS-COURSE-SUB > ST-NUMBER-OF-COURSES.
           MOVE WS-GRADE-AVERAGE TO TOT-GPA.
           WRITE PRINT-LINE FROM TOTAL-LINE
               AFTER ADVANCING 2 LINES.
           READ STUDENT-FILE
               AT END MOVE 'YES' TO WS-END-OF-FILE-SWITCH.

       030-WRITE-DETAIL-LINE.      Paragraph is executed ST-NUMBER-OF-COURSES times.
           MOVE ST-COURSE-NUMBER (WS-COURSE-SUB) TO DET-COURSE.
           MOVE ST-COURSE-CREDITS (WS-COURSE-SUB) TO DET-CREDITS.
           MOVE ST-COURSE-GRADE (WS-COURSE-SUB) TO DET-GRADE.
           WRITE PRINT-LINE FROM DETAIL-LINE
               AFTER ADVANCING 1 LINES.
```

FIGURE 10.11 *(Continued)*

```
         IDENTIFICATION DIVISION.
         PROGRAM-ID.    SUBRTN.
         AUTHOR.        JACKIE CLARK.

         ENVIRONMENT DIVISION.
         CONFIGURATION SECTION.
         SOURCE-COMPUTER.
             IBM-4341.
         OBJECT-COMPUTER.
             IBM-4341.

         DATA DIVISION.
         WORKING-STORAGE SECTION.
         01  TRANSCRIPT-TOTALS.
             05  WS-TOTAL-CREDITS           PIC 999.
             05  WS-TOTAL-QUALITY-POINTS    PIC 999.
         01  WS-MULTIPLIER                  PIC 9.
         01  WS-COURSE-SUB                  PIC S9(4)     COMP.

         LINKAGE SECTION.      Linkage Section contains passed parameters.
         01  WS-CALCULATED-AVERAGE          PIC S9V99.
             COPY STUDREC.
C        01  STUDENT-RECORD.
C            05  ST-NAME                    PIC X(19).
C            05  ST-NUMBER-OF-COURSES       PIC 9(2).
C            05  ST-COURSE-TABLE OCCURS 8 TIMES.
C                10  ST-COURSE-NUMBER       PIC X(3).
C                10  ST-COURSE-GRADE        PIC X.
C                10  ST-COURSE-CREDITS      PIC 9.
C            05  FILLER                     PIC X(19).

         PROCEDURE DIVISION                 Procedure Division header contains USING clause.
             USING STUDENT-RECORD
                   WS-CALCULATED-AVERAGE.

         001-MAINLINE.
             MOVE ZERO TO WS-TOTAL-QUALITY-POINTS.
             MOVE ZERO TO WS-TOTAL-CREDITS.
             PERFORM 010-COMPUTE-QUALITY-POINTS
                 VARYING WS-COURSE-SUB FROM 1 BY 1
                     UNTIL WS-COURSE-SUB > ST-NUMBER-OF-COURSES.
             COMPUTE WS-CALCULATED-AVERAGE ROUNDED
                 = WS-TOTAL-QUALITY-POINTS / WS-TOTAL-CREDITS.

         005-RETURN-TO-MAIN.       Returns control to calling program.
             EXIT PROGRAM.

         010-COMPUTE-QUALITY-POINTS.
```

FIGURE 10.12 *Subroutine*

```
            MOVE ZERO TO WS-MULTIPLIER.
            IF ST-COURSE-GRADE (WS-COURSE-SUB) = 'A'
                MOVE 4 TO WS-MULTIPLIER.
            IF ST-COURSE-GRADE (WS-COURSE-SUB) = 'B'
                MOVE 3 TO WS-MULTIPLIER.
            IF ST-COURSE-GRADE (WS-COURSE-SUB) = 'C'
                MOVE 2 TO WS-MULTIPLIER.
            IF ST-COURSE-GRADE (WS-COURSE-SUB) = 'D'
                MOVE 1 TO WS-MULTIPLIER.

            COMPUTE WS-TOTAL-QUALITY-POINTS = WS-TOTAL-QUALITY-POINTS
                + ST-COURSE-CREDITS (WS-COURSE-SUB) * WS-MULTIPLIER.
            ADD ST-COURSE-CREDITS (WS-COURSE-SUB) TO WS-TOTAL-CREDITS.
```

FIGURE 10.12 *(Continued)*

COBOL 8X:

Changes and Enhancements

There are several changes in the new compiler affecting various elements covered in this chapter. Although most of the changes appear minor in nature, they do make life easier for the programmer.

The *OCCURS DEPENDING ON* clause may specify a value of zero; at least one occurrence was required in COBOL 74. (See Figure 10.5).

Relative subscripting is permitted in COBOL 8X, permitting one to code DATA-NAME (SUBSCRIPT ± INTEGER). Relative subscripting was not allowed in COBOL 74, although relative indexing was. You should come to appreciate the utility of this feature when you attempt Project 10–1.

EXIT PROGRAM (to return control to the calling program) need not be the only statement in a paragraph, as was required in COBOL 74. In addition, one may now *pass parameters at any level* provided the data name is an elementary item, as opposed to the previous restriction to 01- or 77-level entries. (The IBM OS/VS 74 compiler does in fact permit one to pass parameters at any level, but this was an extension to the ANS 74 standard.)

The PROGRAM-ID paragraph in the Identification Division has an optional clause that affects the way a subprogram is initialized, specifically:

```
PROGRAM-ID.    program-name [IS INITIAL PROGRAM]
```

If this clause is specified, then the program is restored to its *initial* state each time it is called. All data names are restored to their original values via any VALUE clauses that are present. (See the Debugging Workshop at the end of this chapter for an example of what can go wrong in COBOL 74.)

A calling program may also protect its data names from being changed by inclusion of the BY CONTENT clause in its CALL statement. Consider the syntax

```
                 ┌       ┌ [BY REFERENCE] {identifier-1} . . . ┐       ┐
CALL subprogram  │ USING │                                     │ . . . │
                 └       └ BY CONTENT {identifier-2} . . .     ┘       ┘
```

and an example:

```
CALL 'SUBRTN'
    USING BY CONTENT FIELD-A FIELD-B
        BY REFERENCE FIELD-C.
```

In the preceding code the called program may not modify the value of FIELD-A and FIELD-B as they exist in the calling program. However, a subprogram can change the value of the corresponding item in the USING phrase of its own Procedure Division header. The BY REFERENCE clause allows the data name to be modified in the calling program. Omission of both BY REFERENCE and BY CONTENT defaults to BY REFERENCE. Hence a CALL statement in the new compiler that omits both clauses is handled identically as its 74 counterpart.

Summary

The chapter dealt exclusively with the Data Division. The "System Concepts" section introduced logical *and* physical *records and the associated COBOL implementation. Additional COBOL elements discussed included the COPY statement, tables, and subprograms.*

Subprograms are a powerful concept and extremely useful in a commercial setting. They provide the capability to divide a large program into several smaller ones, which in turn are assigned to many programmers, who work independently according to common specifications.

Tables are very important, and this chapter has merely scratched the surface of this topic. The next chapter presents the SEARCH verb, in an extended discussion on table processing, and also covers multilevel tables.

The advantages of the COPY clause are obvious. This statement is permitted anywhere within a COBOL program, except within another COPY. A beneficial use of this feature is in establishing a parameter list for a subprogram as illustrated by the Programming Tip.

True/False Exercises

1. The COPY clause is permitted only in the Data Division.
2. Tables are established by a DIMENSION statement.
3. The same entry may not contain both an OCCURS clause and a PICTURE clause.
4. When using subscripts, a space is required between a data name and the left parenthesis.
5. The USAGE clause is required when defining a subscript in Working-Storage.
6. Subscripts can assume a zero value.
7. The same subscript can be used to reference many different tables.
8. The Linkage Section appears in the main program.
9. The Linkage Section appears in the called program.
10. Data names in CALL. . .USING and PROCEDURE DIVISION USING. . . must be the same.
11. A subprogram contains only the Data and Procedure Divisions.
12. The COPY clause can be used on an FD only.
13. Subscripts may be constant or variable.
14. A program can contain only one CALL statement.
15. The same program may be simultaneously considered a "called" and a "calling" program.
16. Data names that are passed to a subprogram must be defined as 01- or 77-level entries.
17. A logical record contains one or more physical records.

18. The use of blocking greatly complicates a Procedure Division.
19. In general, the higher the blocking factor, the less time will be required to read (or write) a file.
20. All records in the same file must be the same length.
21. An interrecord gap is required between adjacent logical records.
22. Variable-length records may be blocked or unblocked.
23. The SET statement is used to manipulate subscripts or indexes.
24. An index may be modified by either an ADD or a MOVE statement.
25. The PERFORM verb may manipulate both subscripts and indexes.

Problems

1. Indicate which entries are incorrectly subscripted. Assume SUB1 = 5 and that the following entry applies:

```
05  SALES-TABLE     OCCURS 12 TIMES    PIC 9(5).
```

(a) SALES-TABLE (1)
(b) SALES-TABLE (15)
(c) SALES-TABLE (0)
(d) SALES-TABLE (SUB1)
(e) SALES-TABLE(SUB1)
(f) SALES-TABLE (5)
(g) SALES-TABLE (SUB1, SUB2)
(h) SALES-TABLE (3)
(i) SALES-TABLE (3)
(j) SALES-TABLE (SUB1 + 1)

2. Recode the four simple IF statements in the program in Figure 10.12 as a single nested IF. Which would execute more efficiently? Could a knowledge of grade distributions be used to increase efficiency further?

3. Consider the subprogram in Figure 10.12, in which WS-TOTAL-QUALITY-POINTS and WS-TOTAL-CREDITS are initialized in the first two lines of the Procedure Division. What would be the effect (if any) of removing these statements and replacing them with VALUE ZERO clauses in the Data Division? What would be the effect (if any) of removing the periods in the IF statements in lines 51, 53, and 55?

4. Consider the following code:

```
01  AMOUNT-REMAINING        PIC 9(3)   VALUE 100.
01  WS-INPUT-AREA.
    05  QUANTITY-SHIPPED    PIC 99.
    05  REST-OF-A-RECORD    PIC X(50).
    .
    .
    .
    READ TRANSACTION-FILE INTO WS-INPUT-AREA
        AT END MOVE 'YES' TO EOF-SWITCH.
    PERFORM PROCESS-TRANSACTIONS
        UNTIL EOF-SWITCH = 'YES'.
    .
    .
    .
```

```
PROCESS-TRANSACTIONS.
    SUBTRACT QUANTITY-SHIPPED FROM AMOUNT-REMAINING.
    READ TRANSACTION-FILE INTO WS-INPUT-AREA
        AT END MOVE 'YES' TO EOF-SWITCH.
```

(a) Why will AMOUNT-REMAINING *never* be less than zero?
(b) What will be the final value of AMOUNT-REMAINING, given successive values of 30, 50, 25, and 15 for QUANTITY-SHIPPED?

5. How many times will PARAGRAPH-A be performed, given the following statements?

(a) PERFORM PARAGRAPH-A.
(b) PERFORM PARAGRAPH-A
        VARYING SUBSCRIPT FROM 1 BY 1
            UNTIL SUBSCRIPT > 5.
(c) PERFORM PARAGRAPH-A
        VARYING SUBSCRIPT FROM 1 BY 1
            UNTIL SUBSCRIPT = 5.
(d) PERFORM PARAGRAPH-A
        VARYING SUBSCRIPT FROM 1 BY 1
            UNTIL SUBSCRIPT < 5.
(e) PERFORM PARAGRAPH-A
        VARYING SUBSCRIPT FROM 1 BY 2
            UNTIL SUBSCRIPT > 10.
(f) PERFORM PARAGRAPH-A
        VARYING SUBSCRIPT FROM 3 BY 4
            UNTIL SUBSCRIPT > 20.
(g) PERFORM PARAGRAPH-A
        VARYING SUBSCRIPT FROM 1 BY 1
            UNTIL END-OF-FILE-SWITCH = 'YES'.

6. Given the following Working-Storage entries:

```
01  SAMPLE-TABLES.
    05  FIRST-TABLE OCCURS 10 TIMES
        INDEXED BY FIRST-INDEX.
        10  FIRST-TABLE-ENTRY         PIC X(5).
    05  SECOND-TABLE OCCURS 10 TIMES.
        10  SECOND-TABLE-ENTRY        PIC X(5).

01  SUBSCRIPT-ENTRIES.
    05  FIRST-TABLE-SUBSCRIPT     PIC 9(4).
    05  SECOND-TABLE-SUBSCRIPT    PIC 9(4).
```

Indicate whether the following table references are valid syntactically.

(a) FIRST-TABLE-ENTRY (FIRST-INDEX)
(b) FIRST-TABLE-ENTRY (FIRST-TABLE-SUBSCRIPT)
(c) SECOND-TABLE-ENTRY (FIRST-INDEX)
(d) SECOND-TABLE-ENTRY (SECOND-INDEX)
(e) SECOND-TABLE-ENTRY (FIRST-TABLE-SUBSCRIPT)
(f) SECOND-TABLE-ENTRY (SECOND-TABLE-SUBSCRIPT)
(g) FIRST-TABLE-ENTRY (FIRST-INDEX + 1)
(h) FIRST-TABLE-ENTRY (FIRST-TABLE-SUBSCRIPT + 1)

Indicate whether the following Procedure Division statements are valid syntactically.

(i) MOVE 1 TO FIRST-TABLE-SUBSCRIPT
(j) SET FIRST-TABLE-SUBSCRIPT TO 1
(k) MOVE 1 TO FIRST-INDEX
(l) SET FIRST-INDEX TO 1
(m) SET FIRST-INDEX UP BY 1
(n) ADD 1 TO FIRST-INDEX

7. Use the general format of the OCCURS clause to determine whether the following are valid entries (the level number has been omitted in each instance):

```
(a) TABLE-ENTRY OCCURS 4 TIMES.
(b) TABLE-ENTRY OCCURS 4.
(c) TABLE-ENTRY OCCURS 1 TIME.
(d) TABLE-ENTRY OCCURS 3 TO 30 TIMES
                DEPENDING ON NUMBER-OF-TRANS.
(e) TABLE-ENTRY OCCURS 5 TIMES
                INDEXED BY TABLE-INDEX.
(f) TABLE-ENTRY OCCURS 5 TIMES
                SUBSCRIPTED BY TABLE-SUBSCRIPT.
(g) TABLE-ENTRY OCCURS 5 TO 50 TIMES
                DEPENDING ON NUMBER-OF-TRANSACTIONS
                INDEXED BY TABLE-INDEX.
(h) TABLE-ENTRY OCCURS 6 TIMES
                ASCENDING KEY TABLE-CODE
                INDEXED TABLE-INDEX.
(i) TABLE-ENTRY OCCURS 6 TIMES
                ASCENDING KEY TABLE-CODE-1
                DESCENDING KEY TABLE-CODE-2
                INDEXED BY TABLE-INDEX.
(j) TABLE-ENTRY OCCURS 6 TIMES
                DEPENDING ON NUMBER-OF-TRANS
                INDEXED BY TABLE-INDEX.
```

Debugging Workshop

The test data in Figure 10.10*a* were rerun with the main program in Figure 10.11 and a *new* (erroneous) subprogram, producing the erroneous result shown in Figure 10.13. The erroneous subprogram is shown in Figure 10.14. Find and correct all errors. (*Note:* All three calculated averages are wrong, for three *different* reasons.)

```
                    TRANSCRIPT

NAME:MILGROM, M

          COURSE # CREDITS  GRADE
             123         4      C
             456         4      C
             789         4      C
             012         4      C
             345         3      C
             678         4      C

                 AVERAGE: 1.82
```

```
                    TRANSCRIPT

NAME:BORROW, J

          COURSE # CREDITS  GRADE
             666         3      B
             777         3      B
             888         3      B
             999         4      B

                 AVERAGE: 3.55
```

```
                    TRANSCRIPT

NAME:BENJAMIN, L

          COURSE # CREDITS  GRADE
             111         3      A
             222         2      A
             333         3      A
             444         3      A
             555         3      B

                 AVERAGE: 4.00
```

FIGURE 10.13 Erroneous Output for Debugging Workshop

```
    IDENTIFICATION DIVISION.
    PROGRAM-ID.     SUBRTN.
    AUTHOR.         JACKIE CLARK.

    ENVIRONMENT DIVISION.
    CONFIGURATION SECTION.
    SOURCE-COMPUTER.
        IBM-4341.
    OBJECT-COMPUTER.
        IBM-4341.

    DATA DIVISION.
    WORKING-STORAGE SECTION.
    01  TRANSCRIPT-TOTALS.
        05  WS-TOTAL-CREDITS          PIC 999         VALUE ZEROS.
        05  WS-TOTAL-QUALITY-POINTS   PIC 999         VALUE ZEROS.
    01  WS-MULTIPLIER                 PIC 9.
    01  WS-COURSE-SUB                 PIC S9(4)       COMP.

    LINKAGE SECTION.
    01  WS-CALCULATED-AVERAGE         PIC S9V99.
        COPY STUDREC.
C   01  STUDENT-RECORD.
C       05  ST-NAME                   PIC X(19).
C       05  ST-NUMBER-OF-COURSES      PIC 9(2).
C       05  ST-COURSE-TABLE OCCURS 8 TIMES.
```

FIGURE 10.14 Erroneous Subprogram

```
C                 10  ST-COURSE-NUMBER       PIC X(3).
C                 10  ST-COURSE-GRADE        PIC X.
C                 10  ST-COURSE-CREDITS      PIC 9.
C             05  FILLER                     PIC X(19).

          PROCEDURE DIVISION
              USING STUDENT-RECORD
                    WS-CALCULATED-AVERAGE.

          001-MAINLINE.
              PERFORM 010-COMPUTE-QUALITY-POINTS
                  VARYING WS-COURSE-SUB FROM 1 BY 1
                      UNTIL WS-COURSE-SUB = ST-NUMBER-OF-COURSES.
              COMPUTE WS-CALCULATED-AVERAGE ROUNDED
                  = WS-TOTAL-QUALITY-POINTS / WS-TOTAL-CREDITS.

          005-RETURN-TO-MAIN.
              EXIT PROGRAM.

          010-COMPUTE-QUALITY-POINTS.
              MOVE ZERO TO WS-MULTIPLIER.
              IF ST-COURSE-GRADE (WS-COURSE-SUB) = 'A'
                  MOVE 4 TO WS-MULTIPLIER.
              IF ST-COURSE-GRADE (WS-COURSE-SUB) = 'B'
                  MOVE 3 TO WS-MULTIPLIER
              IF ST-COURSE-GRADE (WS-COURSE-SUB) = 'C'
                  MOVE 2 TO WS-MULTIPLIER.
              IF ST-COURSE-GRADE (WS-COURSE-SUB) = 'D'
                  MOVE 1 TO WS-MULTIPLIER.

              COMPUTE WS-TOTAL-QUALITY-POINTS = WS-TOTAL-QUALITY-POINTS
                  + ST-COURSE-CREDITS (WS-COURSE-SUB) * WS-MULTIPLIER.
              ADD ST-COURSE-CREDITS (WS-COURSE-SUB) TO WS-TOTAL-CREDITS.
```

FIGURE 10.14 *(Continued)*

Programming Specifications

Project 10–1

Program Name:

Salary History

Narrative:

Large organizations typically do several analyses of employee compensation in order to see how individuals with similar skills are compensated with respect to each other. Develop a program to process a file of employee records and to compute and print various salary measures.

Input File:

EMPLOYEE-FILE

Input Record Layout:

```
01  EMPLOYEE-RECORD.
    05  EMP-SOC-SEC-NUMBER          PIC X(9).
    05  EMP-NAME-AND-INITIALS       PIC X(14).
    05  EMP-DATE-OF-BIRTH.
        10  EMP-BIRTH-MONTH         PIC 99.
        10  EMP-BIRTH-YEAR          PIC 99.
```

```
05  EMP-DATE-OF-HIRE.
    10  EMP-HIRE-MONTH          PIC 99.
    10  EMP-HIRE-YEAR           PIC 99.
05  EMP-SEX                     PIC X.
05  EMP-SALARY-DATA OCCURS 3 TIMES.
    10  EMP-SALARY              PIC 9(5).
    10  EMP-SALARY-TYPE         PIC X.
    10  EMP-SALARY-DATE.
        15  EMP-SALARY-MONTH    PIC 99.
        15  EMP-SALARY-YEAR     PIC 99.
    10  EMP-SALARY-GRADE        PIC 9.
```

Test Data:

```
100000000DOE          J 12441184M23000M1185321500M11843
200000000WILCOX       PA10481184M19000M1185217500H11842
400000000LEVINE       S 01500883F19000H08832
500000000SMITHERS     M 03460172M28000M0885426500M0584425000M05834
600000000SUPERPROG    S 04571084M39000H10846
700000000LEE          B 10530277F20000P0585310000M02842
800000000PERSNICKETY  P 08550385M19000H03853
900000000MILGROM      MB11550977F12000M1185210000M0584209000M09831
```

Report Layout:

The report below shows required information and illustrative calculations for A. B. Jones. Print your report according to these general specifications, but do not be concerned about exact line and column positions on a page. (See item 2b in the processing requirements for additional guidelines.)

```
                      PERSONNEL PROFILE
            NAME:  JONES A.B.    SOC-SEC-NO.:  123-45-6789
            AGE:   21.4 YEARS    HIRE DATE:    1/83

                        SALARY HISTORY
SALARY   DATE  TYPE  % INC.  MBI  RSI    GRADE  MIDPOINT  % MIDPOINT

$24,200  7/84   P     10.0     6  20.0%    4    $28,000       86.4
$22,000  1/84   M     10.0    12  10.0%    3    $21,000      104.7
$20,000  1/83   H                          3    $21,000       95.2
```

Processing Requirements:

1. Read a file of employee records.
2. For every record read,
   (a) Compute and print the employee's age, from the date of birth and date of execution. (The age calculation will be approximate, as the input birth date contains only the month and year.)
   (b) Print all indicated fields with appropriate editing. Print 3 employees per page; leave 6 blank lines between different employee reports.
   (c) Print all associated salary information as described in items 3–6.
3. Each employee has a salary history with 1, 2, or 3 levels of salary data, denoting present, previous, and second previous salary, respectively. Not every employee will have all three salaries indicated, but every employee *must* have a present salary.
4. Associated with every salary is a salary grade, indicative of the level of responsibility in the company (e.g., the janitor and president might have grade levels of 1 and 9, respectively). Each grade has an associ-

ated average salary, or midpoint. The salary midpoint is computed by multiplying the grade by $7,000. The percent of grade midpoint is found by dividing an individual's salary by grade midpoint and multiplying by 100.

5. Associated with every pair of salaries are three fields: percent salary increase, months between increase (MBI), and annual rate of salary increase (RSI).
   (a) Percent salary increase is found by subtracting the old salary from the new salary, dividing by the old salary, and multiplying by 100. For example, new and old salaries of $22,000 and $20,000 yield a percent increase of 10%.
   (b) Months between increase (MBI) is simply the number of months between the two salary dates.
   (c) Annual rate of salary increase (RSI) is computed by converting the percent salary increase to a 12-month basis; for example, 10% after 6 months is equivalent to an annual rate of 20%; 10% after 2 years is an annual rate of 5%.
6. Calculate percent salary increase, MBI, and RSI for each pair of salaries as appropriate. Realize, however, that not every employee will have all three salary levels, and hence the calculations cannot be made in every instance. Use an OCCURS clause, subscripts, and a PERFORM VARYING statement to do the calculations. Be sure to include a suitable test to avoid the computation if historical data are not present.

Programming Specifications

Project 10–2

Program Name:

Benefit Statement

Narrative:

Most employees do not realize the value of their fringe benefits, which often run to 30% of their annual salaries. Accordingly, benefit statements are often prepared to remind employees how well (their employer thinks) they are being treated. Develop a program to read a file of confidential employee data and to compute and print the fringe benefits for each employee.

Input File:

EMPLOYEE-FILE

Input Record Layout:

Use the same specifications as for Project 10–1.

Test Data:

Use the same test data as for Project 10–1.

Report Layout:

```
                               EMPLOYEE BENEFIT STATEMENT

    NAME:  XXXXXXXXXXXXXXXXXXXX                          BIRTH DATE: 99/99


    ANNUAL SALARY: $99,999                              HIRE DATE:  99/99

    ------------------------------------------------------------------------
                              SICK PAY BENEFIT

    WEEKS AT FULL PAY: 99       WEEKS AT HALF PAY: 99

    ------------------------------------------------------------------------
                             RETIREMENT BENEFIT

    COMPANY CONTRIBUTES: $99,999    INTEREST RATE: .99   AMT AT AGE 65:   $9,999,999

    ------------------------------------------------------------------------


                             LIFE INSURANCE = $$$$,$$$
```

Processing Requirements:

1. Read a file of employee records, preparing an individual benefit statement for every record.
2. Develop separate *subprograms* to calculate the sick pay, retirement, and life insurance benefits. Specifications for these programs are described in items 4–6.
3. The main program is to read the employee file, pass and receive control from the three subprograms, and print the benefit statements. Each individual statement is to appear on a separate page.
4. The *retirement* benefit is based on an annual company contribution for each employee. The contribution is equal to 5% of the first $15,000 of salary plus 3% on any salary in excess of $15,000. Hence the company would contribute $840 annually for an employee earning $18,000 (5% of 15,000 = 750, plus 3% of 3,000 = 90). The money is invested for the employees and assumed to earn 8% annually. Use the following formula:

$$\text{Amount at age 65} = \frac{((1 + i)^n - 1)}{i} * \text{Annual Contribution}$$

   where i = interest rate (for example, .08) and n = years until age 65 (specify the ROUNDED option of any arithmetic statement used in computing n).
5. The *life insurance* benefit is twice an employee's annual salary if the employee earns $23,000 or less; it is three times the annual salary for those earning more than $23,000.
6. The amount of *sick pay* is dependent on the individual's length of service. An employee is entitled to one week of full pay and an additional two weeks of half pay, for every year (or fraction thereof) of employment. The *maximum* benefit, however, is 10 weeks of full salary and 20 of half salary, which is reached after 10 years. (An employee with two years service, for example, is entitled to two weeks full pay and an additional four weeks of half pay.)
7. Use the individual's present salary, EMP-SALARY (1), in all benefit calculations.

Programming Specifications

Project 10–3

Program Name:

Check Register

Narrative:

The dollar amount of any check is written out in words, in addition to appearing as a number. This project is intended to accomplish that conversion.

The project is divided into a main program and a subprogram. The main program will accept the input dollar amount and print the result of the conversion. The conversion itself will be accomplished in a subroutine. Completion of the subprogram requires material from Chapter 11 on table lookups.

Input File:

CHECKING-ACCOUNT-FILE

Input Record Layout:

```
01  CHECKING-RECORD.
    05  CHECK-NUMBER     PIC 9(4).
    05  CHECK-AMOUNT     PIC 9(5).
```

Test Data:

```
111101234
222245000
333345200
444445986
666645906
777700689
888800089
999900008
100001000
200000100
300023000
```

Report Layout:

The resulting report need not be elaborate. All that is required is a single detail line for each input record, containing the dollar amount and associated conversion.

Processing Requirements:

1. Read a file of checking account records.
2. For each record read,
   (a) Pass the dollar amount to a subprogram.
   (b) Convert the dollar amount to a written amount, with the word "dollars" appended at the end; e.g., 234 should be converted to TWO HUNDRED THIRTY-FOUR DOLLARS.

(c) Cents are not included; that is, all incoming amounts are integer amounts. The maximum dollar amount to be converted is 99,999.
(d) After the conversion has been accomplished in the subprogram, control should return to the main program in order to print the results. The output report is to contain one line for each record, with the amount expressed in both numbers and words.

Table Processing

11

Overview

Tables are of paramount importance. The previous chapter introduced one-level tables, subscripts, and indexes; this chapter extends those concepts to two dimensions. The main accent, however, is on table lookups, *i.e., the conversion of incoming data from a* concise, coded *format to an expanded and more meaningful result.*

The "System Concepts" section begins with a discussion of codes, then proceeds to table organization and various techniques for table lookups. The body of the chapter discusses COBOL implementation via SEARCH and SEARCH ALL. Various means of table initialization are also presented. □

SYSTEM CONCEPTS

Figure 11.1 depicts a table of student major *codes* and the associated *expanded* majors. Records in the storage medium contain a two-position code, whereas printed reports display the expanded value. The conversion is accomplished through a *table lookup,* with the obvious advantage that less space is required

02	ART HISTORY
04	BIOLOGY
19	CHEMISTRY
21	CIVIL ENGINEERING
24	E.D.P.
32	ECONOMICS
39	FINANCE
43	MANAGEMENT
49	MARKETING
54	STATISTICS

FIGURE 11.1 *Table of Major Codes*

to store codes rather than expanded values. (Consider the implications for large files with thousands, perhaps millions of records.)

A second, perhaps more important reason for using codes is to assign records to consistent classes. It is a simple matter for a data-entry clerk to look up a *unique* code for a data-processing major (e.g., 24 in Figure 11.1), and different clerks will always obtain the same code for the same major. However, it is far less likely that different people will always use identical spellings for a given major; even the same individual is apt to use different spellings at different times, especially when one begins to abbreviate.

Types of Codes

The codes in a table may be *numeric, alphabetic,* or *alphanumeric*. A *numeric* code consists entirely of numbers; for example, the zipcode is a numeric code familiar to all Americans. A three-digit numeric code has 1,000 possible values (from 0 through 999). In similar fashion, four- and five-digit numeric codes have 10,000 and 100,000 values, respectively.

Alphabetic codes contain only letters, for example, state abbreviations. A two-position alphabetic code has 676 possible values. (Each character can assume one of 26 values, A through Z. Thus, a two-position alphabetic code has $26 \times 26 = 26^2 = 676$ possible values. In similar fashion, a three-position alphabetic code has $26^3 = 17{,}576$ possible values.)

Alphanumeric codes contain both letters and numbers, for example, license plates. Alphanumeric codes offer the advantage of providing a greater number of combinations than either pure numeric or pure alphabetic codes. For example, a three-digit numeric code has 1,000 (10^3) variations, a three-digit alphabetic code has 17,576 (26^3) possibilities, but a three-position alphanumeric code (in which each character can be either a letter or number) has 46,656 (36^3) choices.

Characteristics of Codes

A good coding system is *precise, mnemonic,* and *expandable*. A *precise* code is unique; that is, it should not be possible to select alternative choices from a table of codes for a given entry. Indeed, codes are often assigned because the original attribute is not unique. Universities, for example, may assign student numbers because it may have several students with the same name.

Good codes are *mnemonic,* that is, easy to remember. State abbreviations are alphabetic rather than numeric for this reason. Thus NY and TX are inherently easier to learn as abbreviations for New York and Texas than random two-digit numbers.

A coding system should be *expandable* so that future additions can be easily handled. It is poor design, for example, to allocate only two positions in a record for a numeric branch office code, if 98 unique branch offices already exist.

Sequential Table Lookup

A *table lookup* occurs when an incoming code is compared to entries in a table. In a *sequential* table lookup, the entries in the table are checked in order. This is shown in Figure 11.2.

Assume, for example, an incoming code of 39. A sequential lookup begins with the first entry, then the second entry, and so on until a match is found or the table is exhausted. In this instance, 7 "guesses" are required. In general, a sequential table lookup requires $N/2$ tries (where N is the number of entries in the table) to find a match, assuming that each entry is equally likely.

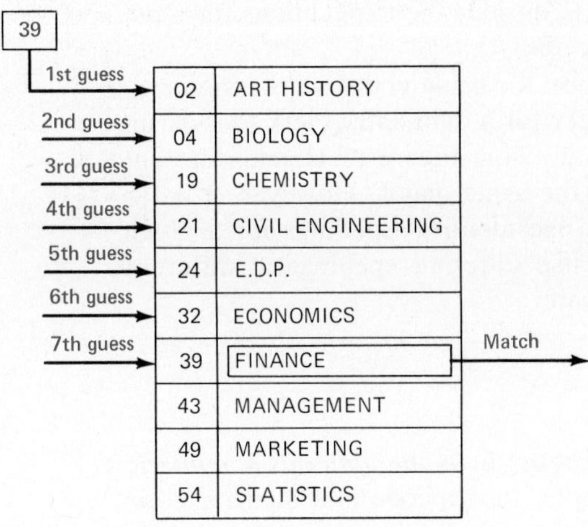

FIGURE 11.2 Sequential Table Lookup

The codes in Figure 11.2 were arranged sequentially. An alternative form of table organization, by *frequency of occurrence,* is sometimes used to reduce the number of trials needed to find a match in a sequential lookup. Assume, for example, that E.D.P. is the most common major, followed by management. It is reasonable to list these majors first and second in the table. In other words, *majors are listed according to the likelihood of finding a match, rather than by a strict numeric sequence.* The codes in the table are still examined in order, but the table itself has been rearranged.

Many tables follow a so-called 80/20 rule; i.e., 80% of the matches come from 20% of the entries. (For example, 80% of the questions raised in class may come from 20% of the students; 80% of the United States population lives in 20% of the states, etc. The numbers 80 and 20 are approximate, but the concept is valid over a surprising number of applications.)

Organization by frequency of occurrence requires a knowledge of code probabilities that is often unavailable. Sequential organization is therefore more common.

Binary Table Lookup

A binary lookup makes the number of comparisons relatively independent of where in the table the match occurs. *It requires, however, that the entries in the table be in sequence (either ascending or descending).* The action of a binary lookup is illustrated in Figure 11.3.

A binary search eliminates half the table with every comparison. One begins in the *middle* of Figure 11.3, at the fifth entry; the logic flow is as follows:

1. There are ten entries in the table; examine the middle (fifth) entry. Is the incoming entry (39) greater than the fifth entry (24)? Yes; therefore eliminate table entries 1–5.
2. There are five remaining entries (positions 6–10). Select the middle (eighth) entry. Is the incoming entry (39) greater than the eighth entry (43)? No; therefore eliminate table entries 9 and 10.
3. There are three remaining entries (positions 6–8). Select the middle (seventh) entry with a value of 39. A match is found, and the search is terminated.

A total of three comparisons was required to match the incoming code, 39. (If 32 had been the incoming entry, four comparisons would have been needed,

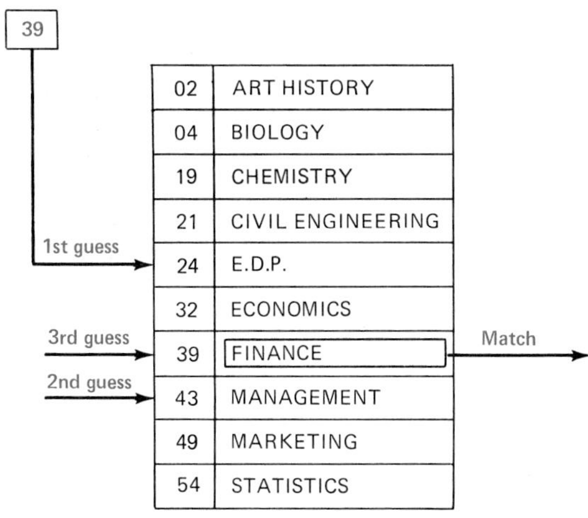

FIGURE 11.3 Binary Lookup

but this is the *maximum* number that would ever be required for a ten-position table.) A sequential lookup, on the other hand, required seven comparisons until a match was found on 39.

If all ten entries in a table have an equal chance of occurring, the *average* number of comparisons for a sequential search on a table of ten entries is five. This is greater than the *maximum* number for a binary search. Indeed, as table size increases, the advantage of the binary search increases dramatically. Table 11.1 shows the maximum number of comparisons for tables with 8 to 4,095 entries. (Although the number of comparisons is less for a binary search, additional machine time is required for individual comparisons. Thus, as a rule of thumb, the binary search should not be used for small tables, those with 25 elements or less.)

TABLE 11.1 Required Number of Comparisons for Binary Search

NUMBER OF ELEMENTS		MAXIMUM NUMBER OF COMPARISONS
8–15	(less than 2^4)	4
16–31	(less than 2^5)	5
32–63	(less than 2^6)	6
64–127	(less than 2^7)	7
128–255	(less than 2^8)	8
256–511	(less than 2^9)	9
512–1,023	(less than 2^{10})	10
1,024–2,047	(less than 2^{11})	11
2,048–4,095	(less than 2^{12})	12

Positional Organization and Direct Lookups

A *positional* table is a sequential table with a *consecutive* set of numeric codes. It permits immediate retrieval of an expanded value at the expense of unused storage space. Figure 11.4 depicts *positional* organization and the associated *direct lookup*.

The table in Figure 11.4 is considerably larger than the sequential table in Figures 11.2 and 11.3. Fifty-four entries are present in Figure 11.4, as opposed

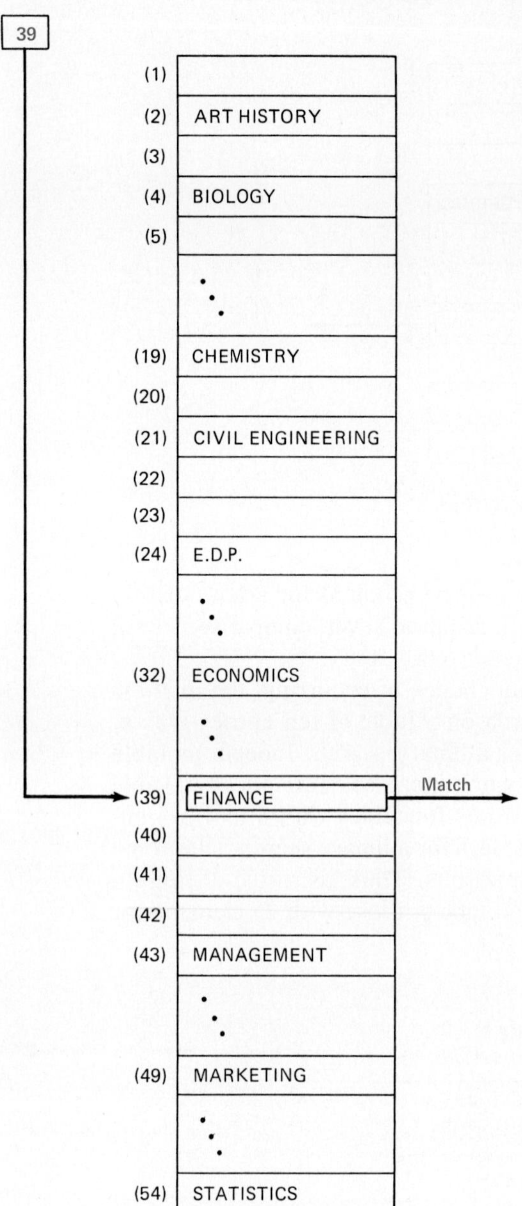

FIGURE 11.4 Positional Organization and Direct Lookup

to 10 in the earlier tables. Observe also that codes are *not* stored in a positional table; i.e., the value of the associated code is the position of the expanded value in the table. Hence, ART HISTORY is stored in the second position and has an associated code of 2; BIOLOGY is stored in the fourth position with an associated code of 4, etc. As can be seen, this arrangement results in considerable empty (i.e., wasted) space, as only 10 of the 54 table entries contain expanded values.

The advantage of a positional table occurs with the associated lookup in that a match is found immediately. Hence, in order to obtain the expanded value for an incoming code of 39, one goes *directly* to the 39th entry in the table. The match is found on the first "guess." (Prudent practice dictates that the programmer ensure the incoming code is valid, i.e., within the table's range, before attempting a direct lookup.)

COBOL IMPLEMENTATION

We move now to a discussion on implementation of table lookups. Realize, however, that in order to do a table lookup, the table must *first* be established.

Initialization by Hard Coding

A common way to initialize a table is to *hard-code* the table directly into a program. This requires the VALUE, OCCURS, and REDEFINES clauses as shown in Figure 11.5. (Figure 11.5 establishes the majors table in Figure 11.1.)

To understand Figure 11.5 better, let us consider the function of the various COBOL clauses, in particular:

VALUE	Assigns an initial value to a specified area in memory.
REDEFINES	Assigns another name to previously allocated memory locations.
OCCURS	Establishes a table, i.e., permits different locations to be referenced by the *same* data name, but with different subscripts.

COBOL does not permit a given entry to contain both an OCCURS clause and a VALUE clause, nor can a VALUE clause be subservient to a group item defined with an OCCURS clause; hence the need for a REDEFINES clause.

Consider now Figure 11.5. The ten successive VALUE clauses, which appear under MAJOR-VALUE, initialize 140 consecutive bytes with the table values. Bytes 1 and 2 contain 02, bytes 3–14 ART HISTORY, bytes 15 and 16 contain 04, bytes 17–28 BIOLOGY, etc.

The REDEFINES clause, in conjunction with the subservient OCCURS clause, assigns another name to these 140 bytes. The first two bytes are MAJOR-CODE (1) and contain 02, the first major code. Bytes 3–14 are known as EXP-MAJOR (1) and contain ART HISTORY, and so on. See Figure 11.6.

```
01  MAJOR-VALUE.
    05  FILLER              PIC X(14)    VALUE '02ART HISTORY'.
    05  FILLER              PIC X(14)    VALUE '04BIOLOGY'.
    05  FILLER              PIC X(14)    VALUE '19CHEMISTRY'.
    05  FILLER              PIC X(14)    VALUE '21CIVIL ENG'.
    05  FILLER              PIC X(14)    VALUE '24E.D.P.'.
    05  FILLER              PIC X(14)    VALUE '32ECONOMICS'.
    05  FILLER              PIC X(14)    VALUE '39FINANCE'.
    05  FILLER              PIC X(14)    VALUE '43MANAGEMENT'.
    05  FILLER              PIC X(14)    VALUE '49MARKETING'.
    05  FILLER              PIC X(14)    VALUE '54STATISTICS'.
01  MAJOR-TABLE REDEFINES MAJOR-VALUE.
    05  MAJORS OCCURS 10 TIMES.
        10  MAJOR-CODE      PIC 9(2).
        10  EXP-MAJOR       PIC X(12).
```

FIGURE 11.5 Table Initialization via Hard Coding

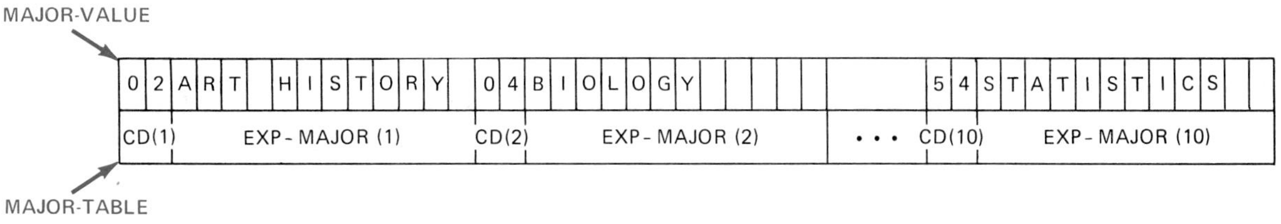

MAJOR-VALUE

0	2	A	R	T		H	I	S	T	O	R	Y		0	4	B	I	O	L	O	G	Y						...	5	4	S	T	A	T	I	S	T	I	C	S		
CD(1)		EXP-MAJOR (1)												CD(2)		EXP-MAJOR (2)												• • •	CD(10)		EXP-MAJOR (10)											

MAJOR-TABLE

FIGURE 11.6 Table Initialization (Storage Schematic)

Input-Loaded Tables

Although Figure 11.5 depicts a commonly used COBOL technique, it poses several problems in maintenance. Assume, for example, that the major table is used by three other programs and that the table changes. It is then necessary to alter all four programs that reference the table, a time-consuming and error-prone procedure.

A superior method would be to initialize the table via a COPY clause. This eliminates the need for multiple changes in that only the COPY clause is altered. However, even this technique is not without problems, because all four programs would have to be *recompiled,* even if they were not altered explicitly. (The COPY clause brings in elements during compilation rather than execution.) The ideal technique, therefore, is to *initialize a table dynamically,* by reading values from a file when the program is executed. This is known as an input-loaded table and is shown in Figure 11.7.

Figure 11.7 contains the COBOL code necessary to load a table dynamically at execution time. It contains Data Division entries to allocate space for the table, and Procedure Division code to initialize the table. Figure 11.8 depicts the actual physical process. Essentially records from an external file, containing the set of table codes and expanded values, are read one at a time and moved to the appropriate table entries.

```
01  MAJOR-TABLE.
    05  MAJORS OCCURS 10 TIMES
        INDEXED BY MAJOR-INDEX.
        10  MAJOR-CODE              PIC 9(2).
        10  EXP-MAJOR               PIC X(12).
 .
  .
   .
PROCEDURE DIVISION.
          .
           .
            .
    READ MAJOR-CODE-FILE
        AT END DISPLAY 'MAJOR-FILE EMPTY'
            MOVE 'YES' TO END-OF-MAJOR-FILE-SWITCH.
    PERFORM 010-INITIALIZE-MAJOR-TABLE
        VARYING MAJOR-INDEX FROM 1 BY 1
            UNTIL END-OF-MAJOR-FILE-SWITCH = 'YES'.
     .
      .
       .
010-INITIALIZE-MAJOR-TABLE.          Ensures that table size is not exceeded.

    IF MAJOR-INDEX > 10
        DISPLAY 'MAJOR TABLE TOO SMALL'
        MOVE 'YES' TO END-OF-MAJOR-FILE-SWITCH
    ELSE
        MOVE INCOMING-FILE-CODE TO MAJOR-CODE (MAJOR-INDEX)
        MOVE INCOMING-FILE-NAME TO EXP-MAJOR (MAJOR-INDEX).
    READ MAJOR-CODE-FILE
        AT END MOVE 'YES' TO END-OF-MAJOR-FILE-SWITCH.
```

FIGURE 11.7 Dynamic Table Initialization

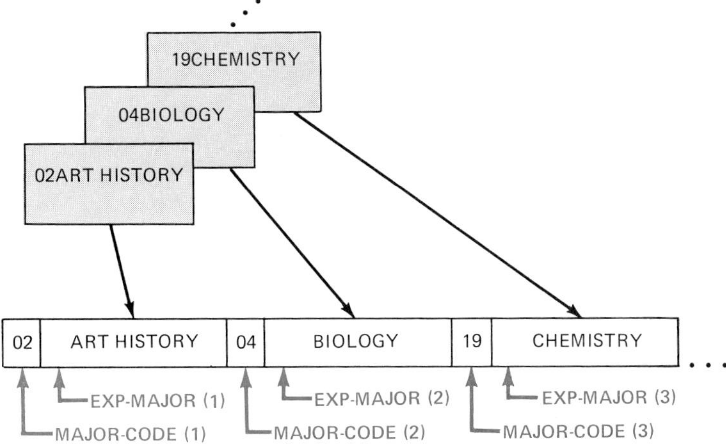

FIGURE 11.8 Dynamic Initialization

The Data Division entries in Figure 11.7 merely establish space for the major table *without* assigning values. The latter is accomplished at execution time in the Procedure Division. The first record in MAJOR-CODE-FILE contains the first code and expanded value, 02 and ART HISTORY. These are moved into MAJOR-CODE (1) and EXP-MAJOR (1), respectively. Subsequent table values are moved in similar fashion. The IF statement in the initialization procedure ensures that the table size is not exceeded. The process is depicted in Figure 11.8.

The advantage of an input-loaded table occurs during maintenance. When the table changes, all that is necessary is to modify the input file. The program itself remains unchanged.

TABLE LOOKUPS

Once a table has been established, the table lookup procedure itself is coded. We illustrate four alternative COBOL techniques: PERFORM VARYING, SEARCH, SEARCH ALL, and direct access to table entries.

Sequential Lookup via PERFORM VARYING Statement

Figure 11.9 contains COBOL code to implement the sequential table lookup in Figure 11.2. Entries in the table are compared sequentially to the incoming code, ST-MAJOR-CODE. If a match is found, then the corresponding expanded major is moved to the output area. However, if the incoming code is not in the major table, an appropriate message is written. Observe how WS-FOUND-MAJOR-SWITCH is initialized prior to the lookup and how the search is terminated after a match.

Notice also that the value of the subscript, WS-MAJOR-SUB, is tested against the number of entries in the table. If the entire table were checked without finding a match, an unknown major would be indicated and the loop terminated. This type of error processing is extremely important and is one way of distinguishing between professional work and sloppy coding. (What would happen if the check were not included and an unknown code did appear?)

```
WORKING-STORAGE SECTION.

01  TABLE-PROCESSING-ELEMENTS.
    05  WS-MAJOR-SUB             PIC S9(4)  USAGE IS COMPUTATIONAL.
    05  WS-FOUND-MAJOR-SWITCH    PIC X(3)   VALUE 'NO'.
01  MAJOR-VALUE.
    05  FILLER                   PIC X(14)  VALUE '02ACCOUNTING'.
    05  FILLER                   PIC X(14)  VALUE '04BIOLOGY'.
    05  FILLER                   PIC X(14)  VALUE '19CHEMISTRY'.
    05  FILLER                   PIC X(14)  VALUE '21CIVIL ENG'.
    05  FILLER                   PIC X(14)  VALUE '24E.D.P.'.
    05  FILLER                   PIC X(14)  VALUE '32ECONOMICS'.
    05  FILLER                   PIC X(14)  VALUE '39FINANCE'.
    05  FILLER                   PIC X(14)  VALUE '43MANAGEMENT'.
    05  FILLER                   PIC X(14)  VALUE '49MARKETING'.
    05  FILLER                   PIC X(14)  VALUE '54STATISTICS'.
01  MAJOR-TABLE REDEFINES MAJOR-VALUE.
    05  MAJORS    OCCURS 10 TIMES.
        10  MAJOR-CODE           PIC 9(2).
        10  EXP-MAJOR            PIC X(12).
.
.
.
PROCEDURE DIVISION.
    MOVE 'NO' TO WS-FOUND-MAJOR-SWITCH.
    PERFORM 030-FIND-MAJOR
        VARYING WS-MAJOR-SUB FROM 1 BY 1
            UNTIL WS-FOUND-MAJOR-SWITCH = 'YES'.
.
.
.
030-FIND-MAJOR.
    IF WS-MAJOR-SUB > 10         <- Check for invalid or unknown major
        MOVE 'YES' TO WS-FOUND MAJOR-SWITCH
        MOVE 'UNKNOWN' TO HDG-MAJOR
    ELSE
        IF ST-MAJOR-CODE = MAJOR-CODE (WS-MAJOR-SUB)
            MOVE 'YES' TO WS-FOUND-MAJOR-SWITCH
            MOVE EXP-MAJOR (WS-MAJOR-SUB) TO HDG-MAJOR.
```

FIGURE 11.9 Sequential Lookup with PERFORM VARYING

Sequential Table Lookup via the SEARCH Statement

COBOL contains a special SEARCH statement to facilitate table lookups. (There are two formats of the SEARCH verb, for sequential and binary searches.) The first format, for a *sequential* table lookup, is shown:

```
SEARCH identifier-1 [VARYING {index-name-1 }]
                             {identifier-2 }

    [AT END imperative-statement-1]
```

```
WHEN condition-1 {imperative-statement-2
                 {NEXT SENTENCE

[WHEN condition-2 {imperative-statement-3 ]
[                 {NEXT SENTENCE          ] . . .
```

Identifier-1 in the SEARCH statement designates a table defined in the Data Division containing both the OCCURS and INDEXED BY clauses. The AT END clause is optional *but highly recommended,* to detect invalid or unknown codes. The WHEN clause specifies a condition and imperative sentence. More than one of these clauses may be indicated, e.g., when a table is being searched for one of two keys and the required action depends on which key is matched. Control passes to the statement immediately following the SEARCH verb whenever the WHEN condition is satisfied. (A VARYING option is also possible but is not discussed.)

The SEARCH statement requires that the associated table be defined with an *index.* (Recall the discussion of indexes and the SET statement from Chapter 10.) Figure 11.10 illustrates how the SEARCH verb is used to implement a sequential lookup.

The Data Division portion of Figure 11.10 initialized the table by hard coding it directly into the program. The Procedure Division then accomplishes the sequential lookup. The table may also be initialized using other techniques such as a COPY statement or an input loaded table.

```
01  MAJOR-VALUE.
    05  FILLER              PIC X(14)  VALUE '02ACCOUNTING'.
    05  FILLER              PIC X(14)  VALUE '04BIOLOGY'.
    05  FILLER              PIC X(14)  VALUE '19CHEMISTRY'.
    05  FILLER              PIC X(14)  VALUE '21CIVIL ENG'.
    05  FILLER              PIC X(14)  VALUE '24E.D.P.'.
    05  FILLER              PIC X(14)  VALUE '32ECONOMICS'.
    05  FILLER              PIC X(14)  VALUE '39FINANCE'.
    05  FILLER              PIC X(14)  VALUE '43MANAGEMENT'.
    05  FILLER              PIC X(14)  VALUE '49MARKETING'.
    05  FILLER              PIC X(14)  VALUE '54STATISTICS'.
01  MAJOR-TABLE REDEFINES MAJOR-VALUE.
    05  MAJORS      OCCURS 10 TIMES               Index is required in table
                   [INDEXED BY MAJOR-INDEX.]
        10  MAJOR-CODE      PIC 9(2).
        10  EXP-MAJOR       PIC X(12).
 .
 .
 .
PROCEDURE DIVISION.
 .
 .
 .                                  Index is initialized.
[SET MAJOR-INDEX TO 1.]
 SEARCH MAJORS
     AT END
         MOVE 'UNKNOWN 'TO HDG-MAJOR
     WHEN ST-MAJOR-CODE = MAJOR-CODE (MAJOR-INDEX)
         MOVE EXP-MAJOR (MAJOR-INDEX) TO HDG-MAJOR.
```

FIGURE 11.10 SEARCH Verb (Sequential Lookup)

The statement SET MAJOR-INDEX TO 1 is analogous to MOVE 1 TO WS-MAJOR-SUB and initiates the point in the table where the search is to begin. The SET verb *must* be used to modify an index; i.e., it is *incorrect* to say MOVE 1 TO MAJOR-INDEX.

When the SEARCH verb is executed, it compares in sequence the entries in the MAJORS table to ST-MAJOR-CODE. If no match is found (i.e., if the AT END condition is reached), then UNKNOWN is moved to HDG-MAJOR. However, if a match does occur, [i.e., if ST-MAJOR-CODE = MAJOR-CODE (MAJOR-INDEX)], the appropriate major is moved to HDG-MAJOR. The search is terminated, and control passes to the statement following the SEARCH.

Binary Table Lookup via the SEARCH ALL Statement

A second format of the SEARCH statement is SEARCH ALL, which is used to implement a binary lookup. Its syntax is

```
SEARCH ALL identifier-1
    [AT END imperative-statement-1]
    WHEN condition-1 { imperative-statement-2 }
                     { NEXT SENTENCE          }
```

```
01  MAJOR-VALUE.
    05  FILLER              PIC X(14)  VALUE '02ACCOUNTING'.
    05  FILLER              PIC X(14)  VALUE '04BIOLOGY'.
    05  FILLER              PIC X(14)  VALUE '19CHEMISTRY'.
    05  FILLER              PIC X(14)  VALUE '21CIVIL ENG'.
    05  FILLER              PIC X(14)  VALUE '24E.D.P.'.
    05  FILLER              PIC X(14)  VALUE '32ECONOMICS'.
    05  FILLER              PIC X(14)  VALUE '39FINANCE'.
    05  FILLER              PIC X(14)  VALUE '43MANAGEMENT'.
    05  FILLER              PIC X(14)  VALUE '49MARKETING'.
    05  FILLER              PIC X(14)  VALUE '54STATISTICS'.
01  MAJOR-TABLE REDEFINES MAJOR-VALUE.
    05  MAJORS OCCURS 10 TIMES                  KEY clause is required in table
           ASCENDING KEY IS MAJOR-CODE          definition.
           INDEXED BY MAJOR-INDEX.
        10  MAJOR-CODE     PIC 9(2).
        10  EXP-MAJOR      PIC X(12).
 .
 .
 .
PROCEDURE DIVISION.
 .
 .
 .
    SEARCH ALL MAJORS
       AT END
          MOVE 'UNKNOWN 'TO HDG-MAJOR
       WHEN MAJOR-CODE (MAJOR-INDEX) = ST-MAJOR-CODE
          MOVE EXP-MAJOR (MAJOR-INDEX) TO HDG-MAJOR.
```

FIGURE 11.11 SEARCH ALL Verb (Binary Lookup)

SEARCH ALL also requires that the associated table be defined with an index. In addition, *the codes in the table must be in sequence.*

Figure 11.11 illustrates the implementation of a binary lookup and is quite similar in appearance to Figure 11.10. However, observe the KEY clause in the table definition, which is required for a binary search; codes must be in sequence (either ASCENDING or DESCENDING) for the algorithm to work. Note also the absence of a SET statement; SEARCH ALL calculates its own starting position in the table. The differences between SEARCH and SEARCH ALL are summarized in Table 11.2.

TABLE 11.2 SEARCH versus SEARCH ALL

SEARCH	SEARCH ALL
Implements a sequential lookup.	Implements a binary lookup.
Requires a SET statement prior to SEARCH, to establish the initial position in the table.	Does not require an initial SET statement, as it calculates its own starting position.
Does not require codes in a table to be in any special sequence.	Requires codes to be in sequence (either ascending or descending) and the associated KEY clause.
May specify more than one WHEN clause.	Restricted to a single WHEN clause.

Direct Lookup

The "System Concepts" section at the beginning of this chapter discusses both sequential and positional table organization. The latter technique results in wasted storage space but permits a far faster table lookup; one goes *directly* to the appropriate table entry, as shown in Figure 11.12.

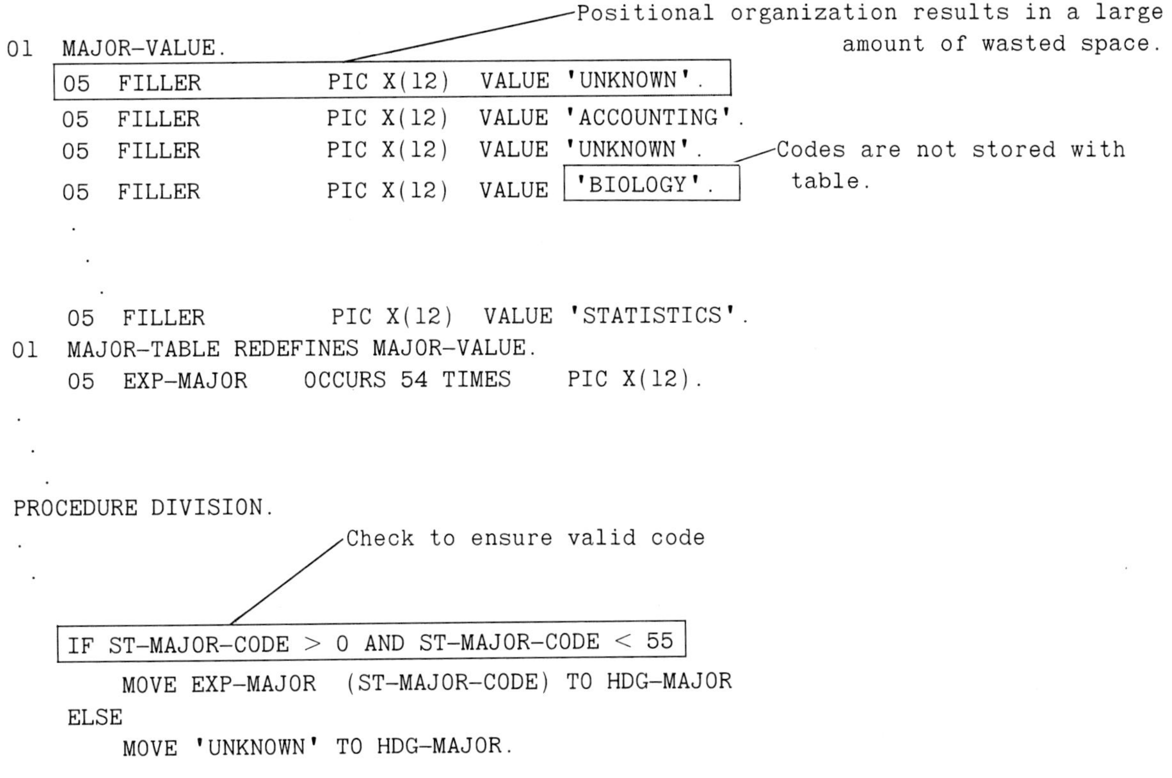

Positional organization results in a large amount of wasted space.
Codes are not stored with table.
Check to ensure valid code

```
01  MAJOR-VALUE.
    05  FILLER          PIC X(12)   VALUE 'UNKNOWN'.
    05  FILLER          PIC X(12)   VALUE 'ACCOUNTING'.
    05  FILLER          PIC X(12)   VALUE 'UNKNOWN'.
    05  FILLER          PIC X(12)   VALUE 'BIOLOGY'.
     .
      .
       .
    05  FILLER          PIC X(12)   VALUE 'STATISTICS'.
01  MAJOR-TABLE REDEFINES MAJOR-VALUE.
    05  EXP-MAJOR     OCCURS 54 TIMES     PIC X(12).
 .
  .
   .
PROCEDURE DIVISION.
 .
  .
    IF ST-MAJOR-CODE > 0 AND ST-MAJOR-CODE < 55
        MOVE EXP-MAJOR  (ST-MAJOR-CODE) TO HDG-MAJOR
    ELSE
        MOVE 'UNKNOWN' TO HDG-MAJOR.
```

FIGURE 11.12 Direct Access to Table Entries

The codes themselves are *not* stored in the table of expanded values; the *position* of an entry within the table corresponds to its associated code. The direct lookup is in essence a single MOVE statement; however, observe the associated IF statement, which ensures that the code to be expanded lies within the range of the table.

A COMPLETE EXAMPLE

We are ready now to incorporate the material on table lookups and initialization procedures into a complete example. Specifications are as follows:

Programming Specifications

Program Name:

Tables

Narrative:

This program fully illustrates table processing. Three distinct means for initialization (hard coding, use of a COPY statement, and dynamic loading) are shown, as are three techniques for table lookups (sequential, binary, and direct access to table entries).

Input File(s):

EMPLOYEE-FILE
TITLE-FILE

Input Record Layout(s):

Employee Record:

COLUMNS	FIELD	PICTURE
1–20	Name	X(20)
21–24	Title Code	X(4)
25–27	Location Code	X(3)
28	Education Code	9

Title Record:

COLUMNS	FIELD	PICTURE
1–4	Title Code	X(4)
5–19	Expanded Value	X(15)

Test Data:

See Figure 11.13*a* for TITLE-FILE. See Figure 11.13*b* for EMPLOYEE-FILE.

Report Layout:

See Figure 11.13*c*.

Processing Requirements:

1. Process an employee file, with each record containing *coded* data on an employee's location, education, and title.

2. Print a detail line for each employee with expanded information for location, education, and title. Double-space this report.
3. Three distinct table-lookup procedures are to be used: a *sequential search* for location, a *binary search* for title, and *direct access* for education.
4. Three distinct table-initialization procedures are to be used. The location table should be copied into the program, the education table hard-coded, and the title table read at execution time from the separate TITLE-FILE.

The Completed Program

Figure 11.14 contains the completed program depicting various techniques for table lookups and initialization.

The education table (lines 94–105) is hard-coded into the program via VALUE, REDEFINES, and OCCURS clauses. The education codes themselves (1, 2, . . ., 8) are not entered in the table, and the incoming employee education code is expanded via direct access to a table entry in the MOVE statement of line 160. Observe also the IF statement in line 157, which is executed prior to the MOVE to ensure a valid education code.

```
1000PROGRAMMER
1500DATA BASE
2000OPERATOR
2999SYSTEMS ANALYST
3499DATA DICTIONARY
```

(a) Title File

```
JACKIE CLARK        2999CHI4
MARGOT HUMMER       1000LA 6
PERCY GARCIA        2999IND3
CATHY BENWAY        3499ATL5
LOUIS NORIEGA       0100NC 9
JUD MCDONALD        1500ATL3
NELSON KERBEL       1000PHI3
```

(b) Employee File

```
JACKIE CLARK          CHICAGO        SYSTEMS ANALYST  4YR DEGREE

MARGOT HUMMER         LOSANGELES     PROGRAMMER       MASTERS

PERCY GARCIA          UNKNOWN        SYSTEMS ANALYST  2YR DEGREE

CATHY BENWAY          ATLANTA        DATA DICTIONARY  SOME GRAD

LOUIS NORIEGA         UNKNOWN        UNKNOWN          UNKNOWN

JUD MCDONALD          ATLANTA        DATA BASE        2YR DEGREE

NELSON KERBEL         PHILADELPHIA   PROGRAMMER       2YR DEGREE
```

(c) Output

FIGURE 11.13 Test Data and Output for Table Lookup Program

The location table is copied into the program in line 67. The resulting definition, lines 68–84, also uses the VALUE, REDEFINES, and OCCURS clauses. However, the COPY clause is preferred to hard coding in that subsequent changes to the table need only be made in the copy member, as opposed to every program that uses that table.

The title table is initialized in the best possible way, by reading values from a file. Space for the table is allocated by the OCCURS clause of line 87. (The INDEXED BY and ASCENDING KEY clauses are necessary for the subsequent binary search.) However, values are not assigned to the table until execution time when the paragraph 010-INITIALIZE-TITLES is performed.

```
00001          IDENTIFICATION DIVISION.
00002          PROGRAM-ID.    TABLES.
00003          AUTHOR.        JACKIE CLARK.
00004
00005          ENVIRONMENT DIVISION.
00006          CONFIGURATION SECTION.
00007          SOURCE-COMPUTER.    IBM-4341.
00008          OBJECT-COMPUTER.    IBM-4341.
00009
00010          INPUT-OUTPUT SECTION.
00011          FILE-CONTROL.
00012              SELECT EMPLOYEE-FILE
00013                  ASSIGN TO UT-S-SYSIN.
00014              SELECT PRINT-FILE
00015                  ASSIGN TO UT-S-PRINT.
00016              SELECT TITLE-FILE
00017                  ASSIGN TO UT-S-TITLES.
00018
00019          DATA DIVISION.
00020          FILE SECTION.
00021
00022          FD  TITLE-FILE
00023              LABEL RECORDS ARE OMITTED
00024              RECORD CONTAINS 19 CHARACTERS
00025              DATA RECORD IS TITLE-IN.
00026
00027          01  TITLE-IN.
00028              05  TITLE-IN-CODE          PIC X(4).
00029              05  TITLE-IN-NAME          PIC X(15).
00030
00031          FD  EMPLOYEE-FILE
00032              LABEL RECORDS ARE OMITTED
00033              RECORD CONTAINS 28 CHARACTERS
00034              DATA RECORD IS EMPLOYEE-RECORD.
00035
00036          01  EMPLOYEE-RECORD.
00037              05  EMP-NAME               PIC X(20).
00038              05  EMP-TITLE-CODE         PIC X(4).
00039              05  EMP-LOC-CODE           PIC X(3).
00040              05  EMP-EDUC-CODE          PIC 9.
00041
00042          FD  PRINT-FILE
00043              LABEL RECORDS ARE OMITTED
00044              RECORD CONTAINS 133 CHARACTERS
00045              DATA RECORD IS PRINT-LINE.
00046
00047          01  PRINT-LINE.
00048              05  FILLER                 PIC X.
00049              05  DET-NAME               PIC X(20).
00050              05  FILLER                 PIC XX.
00051              05  DET-LOCATION           PIC X(13).
00052              05  FILLER                 PIC XX.
00053              05  DET-TITLE              PIC X(15).
00054              05  FILLER                 PIC XX.
00055              05  DET-EDUCATION          PIC X(10).
00056              05  FILLER                 PIC X(68).
00057
00058          WORKING-STORAGE SECTION.
00059          01  WS-END-OF-FILE-SWITCHES.
00060              05  WS-END-OF-TITLE-FILE PIC X(3)       VALUE 'NO '.
00061              05  WS-END-OF-EMP-FILE   PIC X(3)       VALUE 'NO '.
00062
```

Separate file is used to initialize title table.

Different switches are defined for different files.

FIGURE 11.14 Table Lookup Program

FIGURE 11.14 (Continued)

```
       01  TITLE-TABLE-VARIABLES.
           05  WS-NUMBER-OF-TITLES    PIC 999        VALUE ZEROS.
           05  WS-TITLE-SUB           PIC 9(4)       VALUE ZEROS.
```

Location table is initialized via COPY clause.

```
           COPY LOCVAL.
C      01  LOCATION-VALUE.
C          05  FILLER                 PIC X(16) VALUE 'ATLATLANTA'.
C          05  FILLER                 PIC X(16) VALUE 'BOSBOSTON'.
C          05  FILLER                 PIC X(16) VALUE 'CHICHICAGO'.
C          05  FILLER                 PIC X(16) VALUE 'DETDETROIT'.
C          05  FILLER                 PIC X(16) VALUE 'KC KANSAS CITY'.
C          05  FILLER                 PIC X(16) VALUE 'LA LOSANGELES'.
C          05  FILLER                 PIC X(16) VALUE 'MINMINEAPOLIS'.
C          05  FILLER                 PIC X(16) VALUE 'NY NEW YORK'.
C          05  FILLER                 PIC X(16) VALUE 'PHIPHILADELPHIA'.
C          05  FILLER                 PIC X(16) VALUE 'SF SAN FRANCISCO'.
C
C      01  LOCATION-TABLE REDEFINES LOCATION-VALUE.
C          05  LOCATIONS OCCURS 10 TIMES
C              INDEXED BY LOCATION-INDEX.
C              10  LOCATION-CODE      PIC X(3).
C              10  LOCATION-NAME      PIC X(13).

       01  TITLE-TABLE.
           05  TITLES OCCURS 1 TO 999 TIMES
                 DEPENDING ON WS-NUMBER-OF-TITLES
                 ASCENDING KEY IS TITLE-CODE
                 INDEXED BY TITLE-INDEX.
               10  TITLE-CODE         PIC X(4).
               10  TITLE-NAME         PIC X(15).
```

Required for binary search.

```
       01  EDUCATION-TABLE.
           05  EDUCATION-VALUES.
               10  FILLER             PIC X(10)      VALUE 'SOME HS'.
               10  FILLER             PIC X(10)      VALUE 'HS DIPLOMA'.
               10  FILLER             PIC X(10)      VALUE '2YR DEGREE'.
               10  FILLER             PIC X(10)      VALUE '4YR DEGREE'.
               10  FILLER             PIC X(10)      VALUE 'SOME GRAD'.
               10  FILLER             PIC X(10)      VALUE 'MASTERS'.
               10  FILLER             PIC X(10)      VALUE 'PH. D.'.
               10  FILLER             PIC X(10)      VALUE 'OTHER'.
           05  EDU-NAME REDEFINES EDUCATION-VALUES
                  OCCURS 8 TIMES PIC X(10).

       PROCEDURE DIVISION.
       005-MAINLINE.
           PERFORM 010-INITIALIZE-TITLES.
```

Title table is initialized dynamically.

```
           OPEN INPUT  EMPLOYEE-FILE
                OUTPUT PRINT-FILE.
           READ EMPLOYEE-FILE
               AT END MOVE 'YES' TO WS-END-OF-EMP-FILE.
           PERFORM 020-PROCESS-EMPLOYEE-RECORDS
               UNTIL WS-END-OF-EMP-FILE = 'YES'.
           CLOSE EMPLOYEE-FILE
                 PRINT-FILE.
           STOP RUN.

       010-INITIALIZE-TITLES.
           OPEN INPUT TITLE-FILE.
           READ TITLE-FILE
               AT END MOVE 'YES' TO WS-END-OF-TITLE-FILE.
           PERFORM 015-READ-TITLE-FILE
               VARYING WS-TITLE-SUB FROM 1 BY 1
                   UNTIL WS-END-OF-TITLE-FILE = 'YES'.
           CLOSE TITLE-FILE.

       015-READ-TITLE-FILE.
           IF WS-TITLE-SUB > 999
```

Checks that table size is not exceeded.

```
               DISPLAY 'TITLE TABLE EXCEEDED'
               MOVE 'YES' TO WS-END-OF-TITLE-FILE
           ELSE
               ADD 1 TO WS-NUMBER-OF-TITLES
               MOVE TITLE-IN-CODE TO TITLE-CODE (WS-TITLE-SUB)
               MOVE TITLE-IN-NAME TO TITLE-NAME (WS-TITLE-SUB).


           READ TITLE-FILE
               AT END MOVE 'YES' TO WS-END-OF-TITLE-FILE.

       020-PROCESS-EMPLOYEE-RECORDS.
```

```
00143
00144          MOVE SPACES TO PRINT-LINE.
00145
00146          SEARCH ALL TITLES
00147              AT END MOVE 'UNKNOWN' TO DET-TITLE
00148              WHEN TITLE-CODE (TITLE-INDEX) = EMP-TITLE-CODE
00149                  MOVE TITLE-NAME (TITLE-INDEX) TO DET-TITLE.
00150
00151          SET LOCATION-INDEX TO 1.
00152          SEARCH LOCATIONS
00153              AT END MOVE 'UNKNOWN' TO DET-LOCATION
00154              WHEN EMP-LOC-CODE = LOCATION-CODE (LOCATION-INDEX)
00155                  MOVE LOCATION-NAME (LOCATION-INDEX) TO DET-LOCATION.
00156
00157          IF EMP-EDUC-CODE < 1 OR > 8
00158              MOVE 'UNKNOWN' TO DET-EDUCATION
00159          ELSE
00160              MOVE EDU-NAME (EMP-EDUC-CODE) TO DET-EDUCATION.
00161
00162
00163          MOVE EMP-NAME TO DET-NAME.
00164          WRITE PRINT-LINE AFTER ADVANCING 2 LINES.
00165
00166          READ EMPLOYEE-FILE
00167              AT END MOVE 'YES' TO WS-END-OF-EMP-FILE.
```

Binary table lookup.

Sequential table lookup.

Direct access to table entries.

FIGURE 11.14 (Continued)

The flow in the Procedure Division is simple and straightforward. Lines 112–113 contain the initial read for the EMPLOYEE-FILE. Lines 114–115 perform the paragraph 020-PROCESS-EMPLOYEE-RECORDS until the EMPLOYEE-FILE is empty; note that the last statement of the performed routine is a second READ.

Each incoming employee record has its title, location, and education codes expanded and a detail line written. SEARCH ALL is used in lines 146–149 to do a binary lookup on title. The location code is expanded via a sequential lookup in lines 152–155. Note the use of a SET statement prior to the SEARCH statement itself. Finally, education is expanded via a direct lookup in lines 157–160.

Programming Tip

Restrict Switches and Subscripts to a Single Use

Data names defined as switches and/or subscripts should be restricted to a single use. Consider the following:

Poor Code:

```
01  SUBSCRIPT      PIC S9(4).
01  EOF-SWITCH     PIC X(3)      VALUE SPACES.
 .
  .
   .
    PERFORM INITIALIZE-TITLE-FILE
      UNTIL EOF-SWITCH = 'YES'.

    MOVE SPACES TO EOF-SWITCH.
```

```
    PERFORM PROCESS-EMPLOYEE-RECORDS
      UNTIL EOF-SWITCH = 'YES'.

    PERFORM COMPUTE-SALARY-HISTORY
      VARYING SUBSCRIPT FROM 1 BY 1
        UNTIL SUBSCRIPT > 3.

    PERFORM FIND-MATCHING-TITLE
      VARYING SUBSCRIPT FROM 1 BY 1
        UNTIL SUBSCRIPT > 100.
```

Improved Code:

```
01  PROGRAM-SUBSCRIPTS.
    05  TITLE-SUBSCRIPT                PIC S9(4).
    05  SALARY-SUBSCRIPT               PIC S9(4).

01  END-OF-FILE-SWITCHES.
    05  END-OF-TITLE-FILE-SWITCH       PIC X(3)     VALUE SPACES.
    05  END-OF-EMPLOYEE-FILE-SWITCH    PIC X(3)     VALUE SPACES.
     .
      .
       .
    PERFORM INITIALIZE-TITLE-FILE
       UNTIL END-OF-TITLE-FILE-SWITCH = 'YES'.

    PERFORM PROCESS-EMPLOYEE-RECORDS
       UNTIL END-OF-EMPLOYEE-FILE-SWITCH = 'YES'.

    PERFORM COMPUTE-SALARY-HISTORY
       VARYING SALARY-SUBSCRIPT FROM 1 BY 1
         UNTIL SALARY-SUBSCRIPT > 3.

    PERFORM FIND-MATCHING-TITLE
       VARYING TITLE-SUBSCRIPT FROM 1 BY 1
         UNTIL TITLE-SUBSCRIPT > 100.
```

At the very least, the improved code offers superior documentation. By restricting data names to a single use, one automatically avoids such nondescript entries as EOF-SWITCH or SUBSCRIPT. Of greater impact, the improved code is more apt to be correct in that a given data name is modified or tested in fewer places within a program. Finally, if bugs do occur, the final values of the unique data names (TITLE-SUBSCRIPT and SALARY-SUBSCRIPT) will be of much greater use than the single value of SUBSCRIPT.

TWO-LEVEL TABLES

The material on tables is easily extended to two dimensions. A two-level table requires two subscripts to specify an entry. Consider Figure 11.15, which shows a two-dimensional table to determine entry-level salaries in Company X. The personnel department has established a policy that starting salary is a function of both responsibility level (values 1–10) and experience (values 1–5). For ex-

Experience

Responsibility	1	2	3	4	5
1	16,000	17,000	18,000	19,000	20,000
2	17,000	18,000	19,000	20,000	21,000
3	18,000	19,000	20,000	21,000	22,000
4	20,000	22,000	24,000	26,000	28,000
5	22,000	24,000	26,000	28,000	30,000
6	24,000	26,000	28,000	30,000	32,000
7	26,000	29,000	32,000	35,000	38,000
8	29,000	32,000	35,000	38,000	41,000
9	32,000	35,000	38,000	41,000	44,000
10	36,000	40,000	44,000	48,000	52,000

Responsibility level = 4
Experience level = 1

Responsibility level = 1
Experience level = 4

FIGURE 11.15 Entry-Level Salary (illustration of a two-dimension table)

ample, an employee with a responsibility level of 4 and an experience level of 1 receives $20,000. An employee with responsibility level 1 and experience level 4 would receive $19,000.

Multiple OCCURS Clauses

Establishment of space for the table in Figure 11.15 requires Data Division entries as follows:

```
01  SALARY-TABLE.
    05  SALARY-RESPONSIBILITY OCCURS 10 TIMES.
        10  SALARY-EXPERIENCE OCCURS 5 TIMES     PIC 9(5).
```

The preceding entries cause a total of 250 consecutive storage positions to be allocated (10 × 5 × 5) as shown in Figure 11.16.

The first 25 bytes in storage refer to the five experience levels for the first responsibility level. Bytes 1–5 refer to experience level 1, responsibility level 1; bytes 6–10 refer to experience level 2, responsibility level 1; and so on. In similar fashion, bytes 26–50 refer to the experience levels for responsibility level 2; bytes 51–75 to the experience levels for responsibility level 3; and so on.

SALARY-TABLE										
SALARY-RESPONSIBILITY (1)					SALARY-RESPONSIBILITY (2)					
Exp 1	Exp 2	Exp 3	Exp 4	Exp 5	Exp 1	Exp 2	Exp 3	Exp 4	Exp 5	
										. . .

FIGURE 11.16 Storage Schematic for Two-Level Table

```
01  SALARY-TABLE.
    05  FILLER PIC X(25)     VALUE '1600017000180001900020000'.
    05  FILLER PIC X(25)     VALUE '1700018000190002000021000'.
    05  FILLER PIC X(25)     VALUE '1800019000200002100022000'.
    05  FILLER PIC X(25)     VALUE '2000022000240002600028000'.
    05  FILLER PIC X(25)     VALUE '2200024000260002800030000'.
    05  FILLER PIC X(25)     VALUE '2400026000280003000032000'.
    05  FILLER PIC X(25)     VALUE '2600029000320003500038000'.
    05  FILLER PIC X(25)     VALUE '2900032000350003800041000'.
    05  FILLER PIC X(25)     VALUE '3200035000380004100044000'.
    05  FILLER PIC X(25)     VALUE '3600040000440004800052000'.

01  SALARY-MIDPOINTS REDEFINES SALARY-TABLE.
    05  SALARY-RESPONSIBILITY OCCURS 10 TIMES.
        10  SALARY-EXPERIENCE OCCURS 5 TIMES     PIC 9(5).
```

FIGURE 11.17 Initialization of a Two-Dimensional Table via the REDEFINES and VALUE Clauses.

Figure 11.17 illustrates the use of REDEFINES to initialize the two-dimensional table in Figure 11.15. This technique is made necessary because a COBOL entry that contains an OCCURS clause *cannot* also have a VALUE clause.

The statement SALARY-MIDPOINTS REDEFINES SALARY-TABLE gives another name to SALARY-TABLE and consequently places specified values in subscripted entries. The first VALUE clause fills the first 25 bytes in storage, the second VALUE clause fills bytes 26–50, and so on. The order of the VALUE clauses is critical and coincides with Figure 11.15.

The only problem students encounter in using two-level tables is in the proper specification of subscripts; a typical error is to specify too few or too many, or to specify subscripts in the wrong order. The problem is compounded because COBOL allows reference to data at different hierarchical levels; definition of a two-dimensional table automatically allows reference to other one-dimensional tables. Simply stated, the *number* of subscripts is equal to the number of OCCURS clauses used in defining the entry. Further, the *order* of subscripts corresponds to the order of the OCCURS clauses. Reference to the associated storage schematic (Figure 11.16) helps to clarify the issue. Some examples include the following:

SALARY-EXPERIENCE (10, 5)	Refers to salary responsibility level 10, experience level 5. SALARY-EXPERIENCE must always be referenced with two subscripts.
SALARY-EXPERIENCE (5, 10)	Syntactically correct in that SALARY-EXPERIENCE has two subscripts. The entry will compile cleanly but will cause problems in execution because it refers to responsibility and experience levels of 5 and 10, respectively, which are inconsistent with the table definition.
SALARY-TABLE	Refers to the entire table of 50 elements (250 bytes). SALARY-TABLE may *not* be used with any subscripts.
SALARY-RESPONSIBILITY (1)	Refers collectively to the five experience levels associated with the first level of salary responsibility; SALARY-RESPONSIBILITY must always appear with a single subscript.

PERFORM VARYING with Two Subscripts

Two-level tables are frequently processed with a PERFORM VARYING statement that manipulates two subscripts (indexes) simultaneously. (You would do well to review material from Chapter 10 on the use of PERFORM VARYING in one dimension, and the difference between an equal sign and a greater than sign in the relational condition.) Consider:

```
PERFORM PROCESS-TABLE
   VARYING SUB-1
      FROM 1 BY 1 UNTIL SUB-1 > 3
   AFTER SUB-2
      FROM 1 BY 1 UNTIL SUB-2 > 2.
```

The preceding statement will execute the paragraph PROCESS-TABLE *six* times. It will simultaneously vary SUB-1 from 1 to 3 and SUB-2 from 1 to 2. The *bottom* subscript (SUB-2 in this case) is always manipulated first. Hence the six pairs of SUB-1 and SUB-2 are

SUB-1	SUB-2
1	1
1	2
2	1
2	2
3	1
3	2

Extending this discussion to the table of Figure 11.15 would result in a PERFORM VARYING statement as follows:

```
PERFORM PROCESS-SALARY-TABLE
   VARYING RESPONSIBILITY-SUB FROM 1 BY 1
      UNTIL RESPONSIBILITY-SUB > 10
   AFTER EXPERIENCE-SUB FROM 1 BY 1
      UNTIL EXPERIENCE-SUB > 5.
```

A TWO-LEVEL TABLE PROGRAM

We will incorporate the material on two-level tables into a COBOL program. Specifications follow in the usual format.

Programming Specifications

Program Name:

Two-Level Tables

Narrative:

This program illustrates two-level tables and PERFORM VARYING in two dimensions. Incoming employee records are checked for one of three locations and one of two performance levels, producing 6 location–performance combinations. The average salary for each of these six combinations is computed.

Input File:

EMPLOYEE-FILE

Input Record Layout:

```
01  EMPLOYEE-RECORD.
    05  EMP-SOC-SEC-NUM            PIC X(9).
    05  EMP-NAME-AND-INITIALS      PIC X(15).
    05  EMP-DATE-OF-BIRTH.
        10  EMP-BIRTH-MONTH        PIC 9(2).
        10  EMP-BIRTH-YEAR         PIC 9(2).
    05  EMP-DATE-OF-HIRE.
        10  EMP-HIRE-MONTH         PIC 9(2).
        10  EMP-HIRE-YEAR          PIC 9(2).
    05  EMP-LOCATION-CODE          PIC 9(2).
            88  CHICAGO                VALUE 30.
            88  LOS-ANGELES            VALUE 60.
            88  NEW-YORK               VALUE 80.
    05  EMP-EDUCATION-CODE         PIC 9.
    05  EMP-TITLE-DATA.
        10  EMP-TITLE-CODE         PIC 9(3).
        10  EMP-TITLE-DATE         PIC 9(4).
        10  EMP-PERFORMANCE        PIC 9.
            88  HIGH-PERFORMANCE       VALUE 1.
            88  LOW-PERFORMANCE        VALUE 3.
    05  EMP-SALARY                 PIC 9(5).
    05  FILLER                     PIC X(32).
```

Test Data:

See Figure 11.18*a*.

Report Format:

See Figure 11.18*b*.

Processing Requirements:

1. Read a file of employee records.
2. For each record read, determine if the employee is in Chicago, Los Angeles, or New York *and* has a performance rating of 1 (high performance) or 3 (low performance). Any employee meeting *both* requirements, i.e., an employee with a valid location and performance rating, is a qualified employee. No further processing is necessary for nonqualified employees.
3. Establish a 2-by-3 table to compute salary statistics for the 6 performance–location combinations. Rows 1 and 2 designate high and low performance, respectively. Columns 1, 2, and 3 are for Chicago, Los Angeles, and New York.
4. For each qualified employee:
   (a) Determine the appropriate row–column (i.e., performance–location) combination.
   (b) Increment the total of all employee salaries for that row–column combination by this employee's salary.
   (c) Increment the number of employees in that row–column combination by 1.
5. When all employees have been processed, divide the total salaries for each combination by the number of employees in that combination, producing the average salary for that combination. Produce the required report shown in Figure 11.18*b*, showing the six values of average salary.

```
354679876KERBEL,NX         0759018080256406831 19500
264805298CLARK,JS          1160078130399901841 25300
223340090HUMMER,MR         075202828067340683123780
556667856BENWAY,CX         095911826059990184323554
667893343FITZPATRICK,DT    045706838038790184318550
433556767NORIEGA,LA        116004816024530683324200
455399829VOGEL,JD          036006838032330683116325
688773423BEINHORN,CB       098008823044550683121250
100334234GARCIA,PJ         075901806025640683312000
899843328TOWER,DR          056007803039990184119000
776338380MCDONALD,J        075311808067340683129080
```

(a) *Test Data*

	CHICAGO	LOS ANGELES	NEW YORK
HIGH PERFORMANCE	21,850.00	0.00	22,171.25
LOW PERFORMANCE	0.00	19,918.00	18,550.00

(b) *Associated Output*

FIGURE 11.18 *Test Data and Associated Output for Two-Level Program*

Program Design

This project is, in essence, a counting program. Each incoming record is checked to see in which of six performance–location combinations it falls. The salary total for the particular combination is incremented by the salary on the incoming record; in addition the number of employees in the particular combination is incremented by one. At the conclusion of processing, when all employee records have been read, the six salary totals are divided by the respective number of employees in each combination, producing the required averages.

The necessary logic is expressed in the pseudocode in Figure 11.19. The pseudocode itself is succinct, and flows from the top down. It is of course restricted to the basic building blocks of structured programming which were discussed in Chapter 7.

```
Open Files
Initialize salary totals table to zero
Initialize number of employees table to zero
Read first employee record
PERFORM UNTIL no more data
    Check for valid salary, location, and performance
    IF all values are valid
        Determine performance/location combination
        Increment salary total for the combination
        Increment number of employees in that combination
    ENDIF
    Read next employee record
ENDPERFORM
Compute average salary for all combinations
Print average salary for all combinations
Close files
Stop run
```

FIGURE 11.19 *Pseudocode for Two-Level Program*

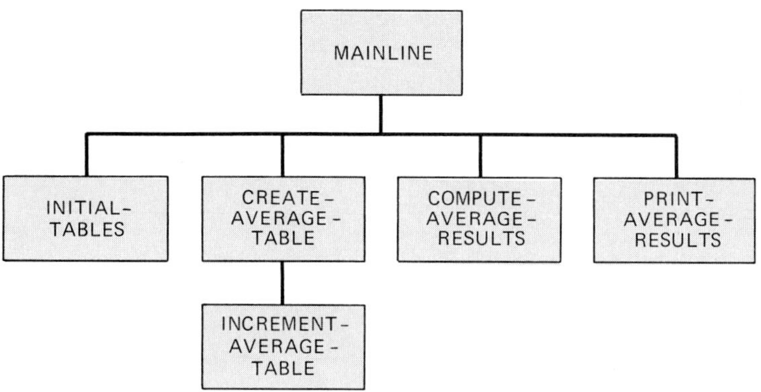

FIGURE 11.20 Hierarchy Chart for Two Level Program

The functions necessary to implement the logic in Figure 11.19 are contained in the hierarchy chart in Figure 11.20. The function of each module is as follows:

MAINLINE	This paragraph drives the entire program. It opens the files, initializes the table, reads the first record, and performs CREATE-AVERAGE-TABLE until the input file is empty. It invokes the modules to compute and print the averages, closes the files, and terminates the run.
INITIALIZE-TABLES	A straightforward paragraph that zeros out the salary and number of employees in each performance–location combination. This paragraph will be executed six times (once for each combination), via a PERFORM VARYING statement.
CREATE-AVERAGE-TABLE	This module validates an incoming record for a proper salary, performance, and location. If all conditions are met, it invokes a subordinate to update the salary and number of employees in the combination.
INCREMENT-AVERAGE-TABLE	This paragraph determines in which performance-location combination the employee falls, then increments the totals in the performance–location combination of the record just read.
COMPUTE-AVERAGE-RESULTS	This paragraph calculates the average salary in each combination by dividing the total salary for that combination by the number of employees. It is executed six times (once for each performance–location combination) via a PERFORM VARYING statement.
PRINT-AVERAGE-RESULTS	This module prints the answers.

The Completed Program

The completed program is shown in Figure 11.21. Observe that the incoming record description contains 88-level entries to define valid location and performance values (lines 31–33 and 39–40).

```
       IDENTIFICATION DIVISION.
       PROGRAM-ID.    TWOLEVEL.
       AUTHOR.        JACKIE CLARK.

       ENVIRONMENT DIVISION.
       CONFIGURATION SECTION.
       SOURCE-COMPUTER.  IBM-4341.
       OBJECT-COMPUTER.  IBM-4341.

       INPUT-OUTPUT SECTION.
       FILE-CONTROL.
           SELECT EMPLOYEE-FILE ASSIGN TO UT-S-SYSIN.
           SELECT PRINT-FILE    ASSIGN TO UT-S-SYSOUT.

       DATA DIVISION.
       FILE SECTION.
       FD  EMPLOYEE-FILE
           LABEL RECORDS ARE OMITTED
           RECORD CONTAINS 80 CHARACTERS
           DATA RECORD IS EMPLOYEE-RECORD.
       01  EMPLOYEE-RECORD.
           05  EMP-SOC-SEC-NUM          PIC X(9).
           05  EMP-NAME-AND-INITIALS    PIC X(15).
           05  EMP-DATE-OF-BIRTH.
               10  EMP-BIRTH-MONTH      PIC 9(2).
               10  EMP-BIRTH-YEAR       PIC 9(2).
           05  EMP-DATE-OF-HIRE.
               10  EMP-HIRE-MONTH       PIC 9(2).
               10  EMP-HIRE-YEAR        PIC 9(2).
           05  EMP-LOCATION-CODE        PIC 9(2).
               88  CHICAGO                  VALUE 30.
               88  LOS-ANGELES              VALUE 60.
               88  NEW-YORK                 VALUE 80.
           05  EMP-EDUCATION-CODE       PIC 9.
           05  EMP-TITLE-DATA.
               10  EMP-TITLE-CODE       PIC 9(3).
               10  EMP-TITLE-DATE       PIC 9(4).
               10  EMP-PERFORMANCE      PIC 9.
                   88  HIGH-PERFORMANCE     VALUE 1.
                   88  LOW-PERFORMANCE      VALUE 3.
           05  EMP-SALARY               PIC 9(5).
           05  FILLER                   PIC X(32).

       FD  PRINT-FILE
           LABEL RECORDS ARE OMITTED
           RECORD CONTAINS 133 CHARACTERS
           DATA RECORD IS PRINT-LINE.
       01  PRINT-LINE                   PIC X(133).

       WORKING-STORAGE SECTION.
       01  PROGRAM-SUBSCRIPTS.
           05  PERFORMANCE-SUB          PIC 9(4).
           05  LOCATION-SUB             PIC 9(4).

       01  WS-END-OF-DATA-SWITCH        PIC X(3)    VALUE SPACES.

       01  EMPLOYEE-SALARY-TABLE.
           05  PERFORMANCE  OCCURS 2 TIMES.
               10  LOCATION-DATA OCCURS 3 TIMES.
                   15  TOTAL-SAL        PIC 9(7)V99.
                   15  NUMBER-EMP       PIC 9(2).
                   15  AVG-SALARY       PIC 9(5)V99.

       01  REPORT-LINE-1.
           05  FILLER                   PIC X(28)   VALUE SPACES.
           05  FILLER                   PIC X(47)
                 VALUE '   CHICAGO            LOS ANGELES        NEW YORK'.
           05  FILLER                   PIC X(67)   VALUE SPACES.

       01  REPORT-LINE-2.
           05  FILLER                   PIC X(5)    VALUE SPACES.
           05  REP-PERFORMANCE          PIC X(16).
           05  REP-AVERAGE-VALUES OCCURS 3 TIMES.
               10  FILLER               PIC X(10).
               10  REP-AVG-SALARY       PIC ZZ,ZZ9.99.
           05  FILLER                   PIC X(67)    VALUE SPACES.

       PROCEDURE DIVISION.
       005-MAINLINE.
           OPEN INPUT  EMPLOYEE-FILE
```

88-level entries define valid location codes.

88-level entries define valid performance codes.

Subscripts are defined in Working-Storage.

Definition of 2-level table (see Figure 11.20).

FIGURE 11.21 Two-Level Program

FIGURE 11.21 (Continued)

```
           OUTPUT PRINT-FILE.
       PERFORM 015-INITIALIZE-TABLES
           VARYING PERFORMANCE-SUB FROM 1 BY 1
               UNTIL PERFORMANCE-SUB > 2
           AFTER LOCATION-SUB FROM 1 BY 1
               UNTIL LOCATION-SUB > 3.

       READ EMPLOYEE-FILE
           AT END MOVE 'YES' TO WS-END-OF-DATA-SWITCH.

       PERFORM 020-CREATE-AVERAGE-TABLE
           UNTIL WS-END-OF-DATA-SWITCH = 'YES'.

       PERFORM 040-COMPUTE-AVERAGE-RESULTS
           VARYING PERFORMANCE-SUB FROM 1 BY 1
               UNTIL PERFORMANCE-SUB > 2
           AFTER LOCATION-SUB FROM 1 BY 1
               UNTIL LOCATION-SUB > 3.

       PERFORM 050-PRINT-AVERAGE-RESULTS.
       CLOSE EMPLOYEE-FILE
             PRINT-FILE.
       STOP RUN.

   015-INITIALIZE-TABLES.
       MOVE ZEROS TO TOTAL-SAL (PERFORMANCE-SUB, LOCATION-SUB).
       MOVE ZEROS TO NUMBER-EMP (PERFORMANCE-SUB, LOCATION-SUB).
       MOVE ZEROS TO AVG-SALARY (PERFORMANCE-SUB, LOCATION-SUB).

   020-CREATE-AVERAGE-TABLE.
       IF EMP-SALARY > 0
           AND (HIGH-PERFORMANCE OR LOW-PERFORMANCE)
           AND (CHICAGO OR LOS-ANGELES OR NEW-YORK)
               PERFORM 025-INCREMENT-AVERAGE-TABLE.
       READ EMPLOYEE-FILE
           AT END MOVE 'YES' TO WS-END-OF-DATA-SWITCH.

   025-INCREMENT-AVERAGE-TABLE.
       IF HIGH-PERFORMANCE
           MOVE 1 TO PERFORMANCE-SUB
       ELSE
           IF LOW-PERFORMANCE
               MOVE 2 TO PERFORMANCE-SUB.

       IF CHICAGO
           MOVE 1 TO LOCATION-SUB
       ELSE
           IF LOS-ANGELES
               MOVE 2 TO LOCATION-SUB
           ELSE
               IF NEW-YORK
                   MOVE 3 TO LOCATION-SUB.

       ADD EMP-SALARY TO TOTAL-SAL (PERFORMANCE-SUB, LOCATION-SUB).
       ADD 1 TO NUMBER-EMP (PERFORMANCE-SUB, LOCATION-SUB).

   040-COMPUTE-AVERAGE-RESULTS.
       IF NUMBER-EMP (PERFORMANCE-SUB, LOCATION-SUB) > 0
           DIVIDE NUMBER-EMP (PERFORMANCE-SUB, LOCATION-SUB)
               INTO TOTAL-SAL (PERFORMANCE-SUB, LOCATION-SUB)
           GIVING AVG-SALARY (PERFORMANCE-SUB, LOCATION-SUB).

   050-PRINT-AVERAGE-RESULTS.
       WRITE PRINT-LINE FROM REPORT-LINE-1
           AFTER ADVANCING PAGE.

       MOVE 'HIGH PERFORMANCE' TO REP-PERFORMANCE.
       MOVE AVG-SALARY (1, 1) TO REP-AVG-SALARY (1).
       MOVE AVG-SALARY (1, 2) TO REP-AVG-SALARY (2).
       MOVE AVG-SALARY (1, 3) TO REP-AVG-SALARY (3).
       WRITE PRINT-LINE FROM REPORT-LINE-2
           AFTER ADVANCING 2 LINES.

       MOVE 'LOW PERFORMANCE' TO REP-PERFORMANCE.
       MOVE AVG-SALARY (2, 1) TO REP-AVG-SALARY (1).
       MOVE AVG-SALARY (2, 2) TO REP-AVG-SALARY (2).
       MOVE AVG-SALARY (2, 3) TO REP-AVG-SALARY (3).
       WRITE PRINT-LINE FROM REPORT-LINE-2
           AFTER ADVANCING 2 LINES.
```

PERFORM VARYING in two dimensions.

Determines row subscript.

Determines column subscript.

Prevents division by zero.

	(CHICAGO) LOCATION (1)			(LOS ANGELES) LOCATION (2)			(NEW YORK) LOCATION (3)		
	TOTAL SAL	NUM EMP	AVG SAL	TOTAL SAL	NUM EMP	AVG SAL	TOTAL SAL	NUM EMP	AVG SAL
(HIGH) PERFORMANCE (1)									
	TOTAL SAL	NUM EMP	AVG SAL	TOTAL SAL	NUM EMP	AVG SAL	TOTAL SAL	NUM EMP	AVG SAL
(LOW) PERFORMANCE (2)									

FIGURE 11.22 Conceptual View of Two-Level Table (See lines 57–62 in Figure 11.18)

Of greatest import is the definition of the two-level table for salary information (lines 57–62). The two OCCURS clauses are at the group level. The three elementary items, TOTAL-SAL, NUMBER-EMP, and AVG-SAL, are subservient to both OCCURS clauses and consequently require two subscripts in subsequent Procedure Division references. The situation is made clearer by examining Figure 11.22, which shows the associated storage schematic.

There are 6 (2 rows × 3 columns) performance–location combinations in Figure 11.22. Each of the six cells contains three elementary items for total salary, number of employees, and average salary. Rows 1 and 2 of the table refer to high and low performance, respectively. Columns 1, 2, and 3 denote Chicago, Los Angeles, and New York.

The Procedure Division of Figure 11.21 begins by opening files and initializing the two-level table. The PERFORM VARYING statement in lines 82–86 sets the number of employees, and salary counters in each combination, to zero. Verify that the paragraph 015-INITIALIZE-TABLES is performed six times, for all appropriate combinations of PERFORMANCE-SUB and LOCATION-SUB. The first EMPLOYEE-RECORD is read, and the paragraph 020-CREATE-AVERAGE-TABLE is executed until there is no more data.

Each incoming record has its salary, performance code, and location code validated (lines 111–113). *Only valid records* are used to increment the two-level table. Performance codes of high and low performance are assigned row subscripts of 1 and 2, respectively (lines 119–123). In similar fashion, a column subscript of 1, 2, or 3 is assigned to Chicago, Los Angeles, or New York in lines 125–132. The appropriate table entries are incremented in lines 134 and 135 for valid records.

When all records have been processed, the average salary is computed for each performance–location combination, by the PERFORM VARYING statement in lines 94–98, and the DIVIDE statement in lines 139–141. (The IF statement prior to the actual division precludes division by zero if there are no employees in the particular cell.) Finally, the averages are printed, and the report is terminated.

COBOL 8X:

Changes and Enhancements

Of greatest impact is the fact that initial values may be specified *without* redefining the table; i.e., the VALUE clause may be specified in a data entry that contains the OCCURS clause or in an entry that is subordinate to the OCCURS clause. Hence, in COBOL 8X one may code

```
5 TABLE-ENTRY    OCCURS 100 TIMES    PIC 9(4)    VALUE ZEROS.
```

as opposed to the COBOL 74 entries

```
05  TABLE-ENTRY OCCURS 100 TIMES    PIC 9(4).

05  TABLE-VALUE REDEFINES TABLE-ENTRY.
    10  FILLER        PIC X(400)  VALUE ZEROS.
```

COBOL 8X permits seven levels of subscripting (i.e., seven-level tables) as opposed to the earlier limit of 3. However, given that the typical programmer is hard-pressed to use three-level tables effectively, this extension seems to be of little benefit.

Finally, both SEARCH and SEARCH ALL may optionally include the END-SEARCH scope terminator to indicate better the end of the WHEN clause.

Summary

An entire chapter has been devoted to table processing. Individual elements are accessed by either subscripts or indexes. An index is conceptually the same as a subscript but results in more efficient machine code. If indexes are established, they can be referenced only by a SET, SEARCH, or PERFORM verb.

Three distinct methods for table lookups—sequential, binary, and direct—were covered with associated COBOL implementation. The SEARCH and SEARCH ALL verbs are available for sequential and binary searches, respectively.

Three distinct means of initializing a table were presented through the COBOL listing in Figure 11.14. These included use of the COPY clause, reading values from a file, and use of REDEFINES and VALUE clauses. Figure 11.14 also depicted three table-lookup procedures: sequential, binary, and direct access.

The material on table processing was extended to two levels. We saw how to define and initialize a multilevel table, stressed the importance of proper use of subscripts, and covered PERFORM VARYING in two dimensions.

True/False Exercises

1. A binary search over a table of 500 elements requires 9 or fewer comparisons.
2. A sequential search over a table of 500 elements could require 500 comparisons.
3. Direct access to table entries requires no comparisons.
4. The SEARCH verb requires an index.
5. SEARCH ALL denotes a binary search.
6. There are no additional requirements of table organization in order to implement a binary rather than a linear search.
7. An index (i.e., displacement) of zero refers to the first element in a table.
8. A subscript of zero refers to the first element in a table.
9. An index cannot be manipulated by a MOVE statement.
10. PERFORM VARYING can manipulate both indexes and subscripts.
11. A SEARCH verb can contain only a single WHEN clause.
12. The ASCENDING (DESCENDING) KEY clause is required whenever the SEARCH verb is applied to a table.

13. The INDEXED BY clause is required whenever the SEARCH verb is applied to a table.
14. The same index can be applied to many tables.
15. The same subscript can be applied to many tables.
16. An index and a subscript can be applied to the same table.
17. The same entry may not contain both an OCCURS clause and a VALUE clause.
18. The REDEFINES clause provides another name for previously allocated space.
19. The RENAMES clause *must* be used in initializing a table.
20. A binary search could be applied to a table if its elements were arranged in descending (rather than ascending) sequence.
21. A numeric code of *four* digits provides a greater number of possibilities than a *three*-digit alphabetic code.
22. Codes are used for reasons other than to conserve space.
23. Alphabetic codes are more likely to be mnemonic than numeric codes.
24. Numeric codes, such as Social Security numbers, should *not* be unique to accommodate individuals with the same last name.
25. Positionally organized tables require the first code to begin at 1.
26. Positionally organized tables require numeric codes.
27. Positionally organized tables often result in large amounts of wasted space.

Problems

1. Write out the 12 pairs of values that will be assumed by SUB-1 and SUB-2 as a result of the statement

```
PERFORM 10-PROCESS-TABLE
    VARYING SUB-1 FROM 1 BY 1
        UNTIL SUB-1 > 4
    AFTER SUB-2 FROM 1 BY 1
        UNTIL SUB-2 > 3.
```

2. Although three-level tables were not covered explicitly, you should be able to extend the concepts associated with PERFORM VARYING. Accordingly, write out the 24 pairs of values that will be assumed by SUB-1, SUB-2, and SUB-3 as a result of the following statement. Remember that the *bottom* subscript is varied first.

```
PERFORM 10-PROCESS-TABLE
  VARYING SUB-1 FROM 1 BY 1
      UNTIL SUB-1 > 3
  AFTER SUB-2 FROM 1 BY 1
      UNTIL SUB-2 > 2
  AFTER SUB-3 FROM 1 BY 1
      UNTIL SUB-3 > 4.
```

3. How many storage positions are allocated for each of the following table definitions? Show an appropriate schematic indicating storage assignment for each table. Are either of these two-level tables?

```
(a) 01  STATE-TABLE.
        05  STATE-NAME OCCURS 50 TIMES          PIC X(15).
        05  STATE-POPULATION OCCURS 50 TIMES    PIC 9(8).
```

(b)
```
01  STATE-TABLE.
    05  NAME-POPULATION OCCURS 50 TIMES.
        10  STATE-NAME                        PIC X(15).
        10  STATE-POPULATION                  PIC 9(8).
```

4. Given the following table definition:

```
01  SALARY-TABLE.
    05  SAL-RESPONSIBILITY OCCURS 8 TIMES.
        10  SAL-EXPERIENCE OCCURS 12 TIMES    PIC 9(5).
```

(a) Indicate an appropriate storage schematic.
(b) State whether the following are valid or invalid references, and if invalid indicate whether the problem occurs during compilation or execution:

i. SALARY-TABLE
ii. SAL-RESPONSIBILITY (3)
iii. SAL-EXPERIENCE (8, 12)
iv. SAL-EXPERIENCE (12, 8)
v. SAL-RESPONSIBILITY
vi. SAL-EXPERIENCE (SUB1, SUB2)
vii. SAL-EXPERIENCE (SUB2, SUB1)

5. Although three-level tables were not covered explicitly, you should be able to extend the discussion in the chapter. Accordingly, given the following table definition:

```
01  ENROLLMENTS.
    05  COLLEGE OCCURS 4 TIMES.
        10  SCHOOL OCCURS 5 TIMES.
            15  YEAR OCCURS 4 TIMES     PIC 9(4).
```

(a) Indicate an appropriate storage schematic.
(b) State whether the following are valid or invalid references, and if invalid indicate whether the problem occurs during compilation or execution:

i. ENROLLMENTS
ii. COLLEGE (1)
iii. SCHOOL (1)
iv. YEAR (1)
v. YEAR (1, 2)
vi. YEAR (1, 2, 3)
vii. YEAR (4, 5, 6)
viii. SCHOOL (1, 2)

6. Show Procedure Division code to determine the largest and smallest population in POPULATION-TABLE. (Assume the table has been initialized elsewhere.) Move these values to BIGGEST and SMALLEST, respectively. Move the state names to BIG-STATE and SMALL-STATE, respectively. POPULATION-TABLE is defined as follows:

```
01  POPULATION-TABLE.
    05  POPULATION-AND-NAME OCCURS 50 TIMES INDEXED BY POP-INDEX.
        10  POPULATION     PIC 9(8).
        10  STATE-NAME     PIC X(15).
```

7. Given the following table definition:

```
01  LOCATION-VALUE.
    05  FILLER     PIC X(16)  VALUE '010ATLANTA      '.
    05  FILLER     PIC X(16)  VALUE '020BOSTON       '.
    05  FILLER     PIC X(16)  VALUE '030CHICAGO      '.
    05  FILLER     PIC X(16)  VALUE '040DETROIT      '.
    05  FILLER     PIC X(16)  VALUE '050KANSAS CITY  '.
    05  FILLER     PIC X(16)  VALUE '060LOS ANGELES  '.
    05  FILLER     PIC X(16)  VALUE '070NEW YORK     '.
    05  FILLER     PIC X(16)  VALUE '080PHILADELPHIA '.
    05  FILLER     PIC X(16)  VALUE '090SAN FRANCISCO'.
    05  FILLER     PIC X(16)  VALUE '045DENVER       '.
01  LOCATION-TABLE REDEFINES LOCATION-VALUE.
    05  LOCATION OCCURS 10 TIMES
          ASCENDING KEY IS LOCATION-CODE
          INDEXED BY LOCATION-INDEX.
        10  LOCATION-CODE      PIC X(3).
        10  LOCATION-NAME      PIC X(13).
```

and the following procedure division code:

```
SET LOCATION-INDEX TO 1.
SEARCH LOCATION
   AT END DISPLAY '*ERROR IN LINEAR SEARCH FOR DENVER'
   WHEN LOCATION-CODE (LOCATION-INDEX)  =  '045'
   DISPLAY 'LINEAR SEARCH OK FOR DENVER'.
SEARCH LOCATION
   AT END DISPLAY '*ERROR IN LINEAR SEARCH FOR NEW YORK'
   WHEN LOCATION-CODE (LOCATION-INDEX)  =  '070'
   DISPLAY 'LINEAR SEARCH OK FOR NEW YORK'.
```

(a) Indicate the output that will be produced.

(b) Code a *binary* search statement to expand code 045 for Denver. Do you expect any trouble in the execution of that statement?

8. How many unique codes can be developed from a four-position *numeric* code? From a four-position *alphabetic* code? From a four-position *alphanumeric* code?

9. Ask a friend to pick a number from 1 to 2,000. What is the maximum number of guesses required to find the number if (a) a binary search is used; (b) a linear search is used? Answer parts (a) and (b), if the selected number is between 1 and 4,000.

Debugging Workshop

The test data in Figures 11.13*a* and 11.13*b* were run with a new (and erroneous) version of the table-lookup program, producing the *erroneous* report in Figure 11.23.

The erroneous program is shown in Figure 11.24. Find and correct all errors. *Note that in addition to the indicated errors, the program terminated improperly, with a statement "Attempted read past end of file."*

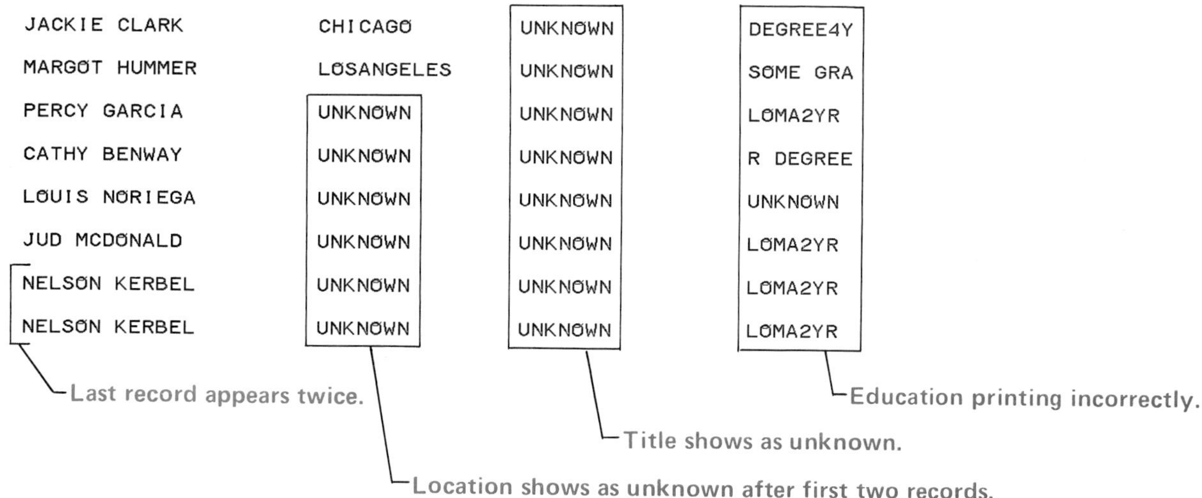

JACKIE CLARK CHICAGO UNKNOWN DEGREE4Y
MARGOT HUMMER LOSANGELES UNKNOWN SOME GRA
PERCY GARCIA UNKNOWN UNKNOWN LOMA2YR
CATHY BENWAY UNKNOWN UNKNOWN R DEGREE
LOUIS NORIEGA UNKNOWN UNKNOWN UNKNOWN
JUD MCDONALD UNKNOWN UNKNOWN LOMA2YR
NELSON KERBEL UNKNOWN UNKNOWN LOMA2YR
NELSON KERBEL UNKNOWN UNKNOWN LOMA2YR
Last record appears twice.
Education printing incorrectly.
Title shows as unknown.
Location shows as unknown after first two records.

FIGURE 11.23 Invalid Output (Produced by Figure 11.24)

```
       IDENTIFICATION DIVISION.
       PROGRAM-ID.    TABLES.
       AUTHOR.        JACKIE CLARK.

       ENVIRONMENT DIVISION.
       CONFIGURATION SECTION.
       SOURCE-COMPUTER.     IBM-4341.
       OBJECT-COMPUTER.     IBM-4341.

       INPUT-OUTPUT SECTION.
       FILE-CONTROL.
           SELECT EMPLOYEE-FILE
               ASSIGN TO UT-S-SYSIN.
           SELECT PRINT-FILE
               ASSIGN TO UT-S-PRINT.
           SELECT TITLE-FILE
               ASSIGN TO UT-S-TITLES.

       DATA DIVISION.
       FILE SECTION.

       FD  TITLE-FILE
           LABEL RECORDS ARE OMITTED
           RECORD CONTAINS 19 CHARACTERS
           DATA RECORD IS TITLE-IN.

       01  TITLE-IN.
           05  TITLE-IN-CODE          PIC X(4).
           05  TITLE-IN-NAME          PIC X(15).

       FD  EMPLOYEE-FILE
           LABEL RECORDS ARE OMITTED
           RECORD CONTAINS 28 CHARACTERS
           DATA RECORD IS EMPLOYEE-RECORD.

       01  EMPLOYEE-RECORD.
           05  EMP-NAME               PIC X(20).
           05  EMP-TITLE-CODE         PIC X(4).
           05  EMP-LOC-CODE           PIC X(3).
           05  EMP-EDUC-CODE          PIC 9.

       FD  PRINT-FILE
           LABEL RECORDS ARE OMITTED
           RECORD CONTAINS 133 CHARACTERS
           DATA RECORD IS PRINT-LINE.

       01  PRINT-LINE.
           05  FILLER                 PIC X.
           05  DET-NAME               PIC X(20).
           05  FILLER                 PIC XX.
           05  DET-LOCATION           PIC X(13).
```

FIGURE 11.24 Erroneous Table Lookup Program

```
           05  FILLER               PIC XX.
           05  DET-TITLE            PIC X(15).
           05  FILLER               PIC XX.
           05  DET-EDUCATION        PIC X(10).
           05  FILLER               PIC X(68).

       WORKING-STORAGE SECTION.
       01  WS-END-OF-FILE-SWITCHES.
           05  WS-END-OF-TITLE-FILE PIC X(3)       VALUE 'YES'.
           05  WS-END-OF-EMP-FILE   PIC X(3)       VALUE 'NO '.

       01  TITLE-TABLE-VARIABLES.
           05  WS-NUMBER-OF-TITLES  PIC 999        VALUE ZEROS.
           05  WS-TITLE-SUB         PIC 9(4)       VALUE ZEROS.

           COPY LOCVAL.
       01  LOCATION-VALUE.
           05  FILLER               PIC X(16) VALUE 'ATLATLANTA'.
           05  FILLER               PIC X(16) VALUE 'BOSBOSTON'.
           05  FILLER               PIC X(16) VALUE 'CHICHICAGO'.
           05  FILLER               PIC X(16) VALUE 'DETDETROIT'.
           05  FILLER               PIC X(16) VALUE 'KC KANSAS CITY'.
           05  FILLER               PIC X(16) VALUE 'LA LOSANGELES'.
           05  FILLER               PIC X(16) VALUE 'MINMINEAPOLIS'.
           05  FILLER               PIC X(16) VALUE 'NY NEW YORK'.
           05  FILLER               PIC X(16) VALUE 'PHIPHILADELPHIA'.
           05  FILLER               PIC X(16) VALUE 'SF SAN FRANCISCO'.

       01  LOCATION-TABLE REDEFINES LOCATION-VALUE.
           05  LOCATIONS OCCURS 10 TIMES
               INDEXED BY LOCATION-INDEX.
               10  LOCATION-CODE    PIC X(3).
               10  LOCATION-NAME    PIC X(13).

       01  TITLE-TABLE.
           05  TITLES OCCURS 1 TO 999 TIMES
                  DEPENDING ON WS-NUMBER-OF-TITLES
                  ASCENDING KEY IS TITLE-CODE
                  INDEXED BY TITLE-INDEX.
               10  TITLE-CODE       PIC X(4).
               10  TITLE-NAME       PIC X(15).

       01  EDUCATION-TABLE.
           05  EDUCATION-VALUES.
               10  FILLER           PIC X(10)      VALUE 'SOME HS'.
               10  FILLER           PIC X(10)      VALUE 'HS DIPLOMA'.
               10  FILLER           PIC X(10)      VALUE '2YR DEGREE'.
               10  FILLER           PIC X(10)      VALUE '4YR DEGREE'.
               10  FILLER           PIC X(10)      VALUE 'SOME GRAD'.
               10  FILLER           PIC X(10)      VALUE 'MASTERS'.
               10  FILLER           PIC X(10)      VALUE 'PH. D.'.
               10  FILLER           PIC X(10)      VALUE 'OTHER'.
           05  EDU-NAME REDEFINES EDUCATION-VALUES
                     OCCURS 10 TIMES PIC X(08).

       PROCEDURE DIVISION.
       005-MAINLINE.
           PERFORM 010-INITIALIZE-TITLES.
           OPEN INPUT  EMPLOYEE-FILE
                OUTPUT PRINT-FILE.
           READ EMPLOYEE-FILE
               AT END MOVE 'YES' TO WS-END-OF-EMP-FILE.
           PERFORM 020-PROCESS-EMPLOYEE-RECORDS
               UNTIL WS-END-OF-EMP-FILE = 'YES'.
           CLOSE EMPLOYEE-FILE
                 PRINT-FILE.
           STOP RUN.

       010-INITIALIZE-TITLES.
           OPEN INPUT TITLE-FILE.
           READ TITLE-FILE
               AT END MOVE 'YES' TO WS-END-OF-TITLE-FILE.
           PERFORM 015-READ-TITLE-FILE
               VARYING WS-TITLE-SUB FROM 1 BY 1
                   UNTIL WS-END-OF-TITLE-FILE = 'YES'.
           CLOSE TITLE-FILE.

       015-READ-TITLE-FILE.
           IF WS-TITLE-SUB > 999
               DISPLAY 'TITLE TABLE EXCEEDED'
```

```
                MOVE 'YES' TO WS-END-OF-TITLE-FILE
            ELSE
                ADD 1 TO WS-NUMBER-OF-TITLES
                MOVE TITLE-IN-CODE TO TITLE-CODE (WS-TITLE-SUB)
                MOVE TITLE-IN-NAME TO TITLE-NAME (WS-TITLE-SUB).


            READ TITLE-FILE
                AT END MOVE 'YES' TO WS-END-OF-TITLE-FILE.

        020-PROCESS-EMPLOYEE-RECORDS.

            MOVE SPACES TO PRINT-LINE.

            SEARCH ALL TITLES
                AT END MOVE 'UNKNOWN' TO DET-TITLE
                WHEN TITLE-CODE (TITLE-INDEX) = EMP-TITLE-CODE
                    MOVE TITLE-NAME (TITLE-INDEX) TO DET-TITLE.

            SEARCH LOCATIONS
                AT END MOVE 'UNKNOWN' TO DET-LOCATION
                WHEN EMP-LOC-CODE = LOCATION-CODE (LOCATION-INDEX)
                    MOVE LOCATION-NAME (LOCATION-INDEX) TO DET-LOCATION.

            IF EMP-EDUC-CODE < 1 OR > 8
                MOVE 'UNKNOWN' TO DET-EDUCATION
            ELSE
                MOVE EDU-NAME (EMP-EDUC-CODE) TO DET-EDUCATION.


            MOVE EMP-NAME TO DET-NAME.
            WRITE PRINT-LINE AFTER ADVANCING 2 LINES.

            READ EMPLOYEE-FILE
                AT END MOVE 'YE ' TO WS-END-OF-EMP-FILE.
```

FIGURE 11.24 ***(Continued)***

Programming Specifications

Project 11–1

Program Name:

Student Profile Program

Narrative:

Develop a program to print a set of student profiles, showing detailed information on each student. Among other functions, the program is to convert an incoming set of codes for each student to an expanded, and more readable, format.

Input File(s):

STUDENT-FILE
COURSE-FILE (see processing requirement 12)

Input Record Layout:

```
01  STUDENT-RECORD.
    05  STU-SOC-SEC-NUMBER          PIC 9(9).
    05  STU-NAME-AND-INITIALS.
        10  STU-LAST-NAME           PIC X(18).
        10  STU-INITIALS            PIC XX.
    05  STU-DATE-OF-BIRTH.
        10  STU-BIRTH-MONTH         PIC 99.
        10  STU-BIRTH-YEAR          PIC 99.
```

```
05  STU-SEX                    PIC X.
05  STU-MAJOR-CODE             PIC X(3).
05  STU-SCHOOL-CODE            PIC 9.
05  STU-CUMULATIVE-CREDITS     PIC 999.
05  STU-CUMULATIVE-POINTS      PIC 999.
05  STU-UNION-MEMBER-CODE      PIX X.
05  STU-SCHOLARSHIP            PIC 999.
05  STU-DATE-OF-ENROLLMENT     PIC 9(4).
05  STU-COURSES-THIS-SEMESTER OCCURS 7 TIMES.
    10  STU-COURSE-NUMBER      PIC XXX.
    10  STU-COURSE-CREDITS     PIC 9.
```

Test Data:

```
100000000ALBERT    A 0165MSTA1059118Y0150977100220033004400450136002601l
200000000BROWN     B 0264FSTA1089275N025097610022003300440O4
300000000CHARLES   CC0664MHIS2109286Y100097650135033504350535063
400000000SMITH     D 0764FXXX2090269N010097610022003300441 94
500000000BAKER     EF1060MCEN3032049Y000097822233333 4443
600000000GULFMAN   SF1166FELE4029059N0000978200333334443555366636752700l
700000000BOROW     JS1266MIEN3030090Y00009782223
800000000MILGROM   MB0359F    5015045Y0000979111313831503l603
900000000MILLER    K 0161MFRL2015054Y00009791113l4031503
999919999WAYNE     N 0466FHIS2090270Y000097650135033504350 53
```

Report Layout:

```
 1                                                              PAGE ZZ9
 2                    S T U D E N T   P R O F I L E S
 3
 4    ***********************************************************************
 5
 6     NAME: XXXXXXXXXXXXXXXXXXXXXXXXXX    AGE: 99.9    SOC SEC NUM: 999-99-9999
 7
 8     MAJOR: XXXXXXXXXXXXXXXXXXXXXX    ENROLLED: 99/99    SCHOOL: XXXXXXXXXXXX
 9
10                       (FRESHMAN )               (FULL TIME)          (MALE  )
11     YEAR IN SCHOOL:  (SOPHOMORE)     STATUS:   (PART TIME)     SEX: (FEMALE)
12                       (JUNIOR   )
13                       (SENIOR   )
14                     GRADE POINT AVERAGE: 9.99
15
16                        COURSES THIS SEMESTER
17
18                          COURSE      CREDITS
19                          ------      -------
20                     XXXXXXXXXXXXXXXX   ZZ
21                     XXXXXXXXXXXXXXXX   ZZ
22                     XXXXXXXXXXXXXXXX   ZZ
23
```

Processing Requirements:

1. Process a file of student records, printing a complete student profile for each record.
2. Student profiles are to appear two per page, with eight blank lines after the last line of the first profile on each page. The page number and literal heading "S T U D E N T   P R O F I L E S" are to appear only before the first profile on each page.
3. The detailed layout for each profile can be seen from the report layout. Additional specifications are given in items 4–11.

4. Student age is to be calculated from date of birth and date of program execution.
5. The Social Security number requires the insertion of hyphens; accomplish this by defining an output picture containing blanks in appropriate positions and then replace the blanks through the INSPECT verb.
6. Part-time students take fewer than 12 credits per semester.
7. Grade point average is defined as the cumulative points divided by the cumulative credits and does *not* include credits taken this semester. Calculate this field to two decimal places.
8. Year in school is a function of cumulative credits and again does not include credits taken this semester. Freshmen have completed fewer than 30, sophomores between 30 and 59, juniors between 60 and 89, and seniors 90 or more.
9. The incoming STU-SCHOOL-CODE is to be expanded via a *direct lookup*. *Hard-code* the following table in your program:

CODE	SCHOOL
1	BUSINESS
2	LIBERAL ARTS
3	ENGINEERING
4	EDUCATION

10. The incoming STU-MAJOR-CODE is to be expanded via a sequential search. Establish the following major table via a COPY statement.

CODE	MAJOR
STA	STATISTICS
FIN	FINANCE
MKT	MARKETING
MAN	MANAGEMENT
EDP	DATA PROCESSING
PHY	PHYSICS
ENG	ENGLISH
BIO	BIOLOGY
HIS	HISTORY
ECO	ECONOMICS
FRL	FOREIGN LANG
EEN	ELECTRICAL ENG
MEN	MECHANICAL ENG
CEN	CHEMICAL ENG
IEN	INDUSTRIAL ENG
ELE	ELEMENTARY EDUC
SEE	SECONDARY EDUC
SPE	SPECIAL EDUC

11. Convert each value of STU-COURSE-NUMBER to an expanded course name using a *binary* search. An incoming record contains up to seven courses; blanks (i.e., spaces) appear in an incoming record with fewer than seven courses.
12. The table of course codes is to be established by reading values from a separate COURSE-FILE, with the following format: course code in columns 1–3 and course name in columns 4–18. The maximum table length is 100 courses.

The table of course codes is shown:

COURSE CODE	COURSE NAME
100	ENGLISH 1
111	COMPUTER SCI
140	SPANISH I
150	MUSIC
160	ART APPREC
200	BIOLOGY
222	CHEMISTRY
300	CALCULUS
333	ELECT ENG 1
400	STAT INFERENCE
444	REGRESSION
501	AM HISTORY
503	EUR HISTORY
504	ECONOMICS
505	POL SCIENCE
506	CREATIVE WRIT
555	EDUC THEORY
600	FORTRAN
601	COBOL
666	PSYCHOLOGY
675	SPECIAL EDUC
700	THESIS

Programming Specifications

Project 11–2

Program Name:

Grade Distributions

Narrative:

The Registrar's office is trying to determine whether a student's GPA (grade point average) improves with age and/or year in school. Accordingly, develop a program to process a set of student records, and print the necessary information in tabular form.

Input File(s):

STUDENT-FILE

Input Record Layout:

Identical to that in Project 11–1.

Test Data:

Identical to that in Project 11–1.

Report Layout:

```
 2       GRADE DISTRIBUTIONS BY AGE AND YEAR
 4                         AVERAGE G.P.A.
 6                     UNDER 21      21 AND OVER
 8    FRESHMAN            9.99            9.99
10    SOPHOMORE           9.99            9.99
12    JUNIOR              9.99            9.99
14    SENIOR              9.99            9.99
```

Processing Requirements:

1. Process a file of student records, and for each record read:
   (a) Calculate the student's age from the date of execution and the student's birth date.
   (b) Compute the student's year in school, according to Project 11–1, item 8.
   (c) Compute the GPA, according to the specification in Project 11–1, item 7.
   (d) Determine the age and year classification as implied by the 4 × 2 table in the Report Layout; i.e., determine in which of the eight age–year combinations the record belongs, and increment an appropriate counter.
2. When all records have been read, print the required table. In order to compute the necessary statistics, you will have to maintain *two* 4 × 2 tables. The entries in one table will be a cumulative total of the GPA for each age–year combination. The entries in the second table will be number of students in the age–year combination. At the conclusion of processing, divide the eight entries in the first table by their corresponding entries in the second table.
3. Project 12–1, in the next chapter, requests a detail report to support the summary information provided by this project.

Programming Specifications

Project 11–3

Program Name:

Movies

Narrative:

Develop a program to compute the amount due the hundreds of movie extras who participated in the latest Hollywood extravaganza.

Input File(s):

MOVIE-EXTRA-FILE

Input Record Layout:

COLUMNS	FIELD	PICTURE
1–9	SOC-SEC-NUMBER	9(9)
10–34	NAME	X(25)
35–36	MOVIE-EXPERIENCE	99
38	TYPE-ROLE	X
40–43	HOURS-WORKED	999V9
45–46	EXPANDED-ROLE	XX

Test Data:

```
000000001JONES, J.                00 C  0800 CN
000000002JONES, ROY               02 F  0450 FA
000000003WILLIAMS, JOHN           01 E  0450 EA
000000004FOSTER, RAYMOND          11 B  0425 BN
000000005HIGH, LUCY               08 A  0450 AR
000000006HARDING, HOWARD          04 A  0450 AV
000000007ZHE, KEVEN               05 D  0450 DN
000000008JENNINGS, VIVIAN            D  0200 DA
000000009ROOSEVELT, TIMOTHY       07 E  0230 XX
000000010TRUELOVE, BILL           09 G  0450 EN
```

Report Layout:

```
                                                                                             PAGE ZZ9

  SOC SEC NUM       MOVIE EXTRA             EXP  ROLE  HOURLY-RATE  REG HOURS  EXTRA HOURS  PAY

  999-99-9999  XXXXXXXXXXXXXXXXXXXXXXXXX     99    X    $Z9.99       999.9        Z9      $$,$$9.99
```

Processing Requirements:

1. Process a file of pay records for movie extras, to determine the pay owed to each individual.
2. An hourly pay scale is used, with the individual's hourly rate a function of the type of role and his or her experience in previous movies. The following table contains the pay scale and is to be hard-coded in your program:

Previous experience (number of movies)

Type of Role	0	1	2	3	4	5–7	8-UP
A	20.00	25.00	30.00	32.00	34.00	38.00	40.00
B	14.00	17.00	18.00	19.00	21.00	23.00	24.00
C	7.00	7.50	8.00	8.00	8.50	8.50	9.00
D	4.00	5.00	5.50	5.50	5.50	6.00	6.00
E	3.75	4.50	5.00	5.00	5.25	5.50	5.50
F	3.50	3.50	3.50	3.75	3.75	3.75	4.00

The number of previous movies for an individual must be converted into a number from 1 to 7, so that it can be used as a subscript for access into the table.

3. Incoming pay records are to be checked for valid data; specifically:
   (a) Verify that the value in MOVIE-EXPERIENCE is numeric; if not, display an error message and do no further processing for that record.
   (b) Verify that the value in TYPE-ROLE is valid (i.e., A, B, C, D, E, or F); if not, display an error message and do no further processing for that record.
4. Each employee is to receive, as a bonus, a number of *extra* hours (not appearing on the employee's pay record), for which the employee will be paid at his or her regular hourly rate. The number of extra hours is a function of the EXPANDED-ROLE field in the incoming record as shown in the following table:

EXPANDED ROLE	*EXTRA HOURS*
AA	01
AV	01
BA	03
BN	05
CA	05
CN	04
DA	08
DN	08
DR	09
EA	14
EN	03
ER	03
FA	01
FN	06

5. The bonus table for extra hours is in *ascending* sequence by the expanded role field. Use a *binary search* to determine the number of extra hours an individual will receive; i.e., if a match is found, take the hours shown in the table and add it to the hours in the incoming record to determine pay. If no match is found, do not add any extra hours. An individual with no extra hours will be paid just for the number of hours on his or her incoming record.
6. The printed report should print no more than four valid records per page. (If possible, the employees with invalid data should be displayed in a separate error report.) Double-space between detail lines.

Programming Specifications

Project 11–4

Program Name:
Table Lookups and Subprograms

Narrative:

This project is a continuation of Project 8–2, page 188, on control breaks. It requires a one-level table lookup and is to be written as a subprogram.

Input File:

A separate input file is not required for the subprogram; instead data will be passed to it from the main program, Project 8–2.

Report Layout:

The report layout from the original program is to be modified slightly so that an *expanded* department name appears in the total line for department, rather than the department number.

Processing Requirements:

1. Develop a subprogram that will accept a three-position department code, and return a 15-position department name. The latter is to appear in the printed report.
2. Use the following table of department codes and expanded values:

DEPARTMENT CODE	*DEPARTMENT NAME*
100	DATA PROCESSING
150	LEGAL
200	FINANCIAL
250	MARKETING
300	MANUFACTURING
350	ACCOUNTING

3. The department table is to be hard-coded in the subprogram.
4. The department table is to be expanded using a SEARCH statement.
5. For the sake of efficiency the subprogram should not be called more often than necessary. In other words, it should not be called for each employee, but only before or after a control break on department has occurred.

Sorting

12

Overview

Sorting, the rearrangement of data, is one of the most frequent operations in data processing. Reports are presented in a variety of ways, depending on the analysis required. Transactions may be listed alphabetically, alphabetically within location, numerically, etc.

Sorting is typically accomplished in one of three ways:

1. *Internal sort, in which the programmer develops his or her own logic within the application program.*
2. *Utility sort, in which the sort program is called independently of the application program as a separate job step.*
3. *COBOL SORT verb, in which the utility sort program is called directly from a COBOL program.*

Regardless of which method is used, the objective is the same: to rearrange a file according to the requirements of a particular application. Our discussion deals exclusively with the third approach, the COBOL SORT verb.

We begin the chapter by developing system concepts. Next we consider COBOL requirements and present two complete programs to illustrate variations within the COBOL SORT verb. We conclude with a brief discussion of the MERGE statement. □

SYSTEM CONCEPTS

A sort *key* is a field within a record that determines how the file is to be arranged. Several keys may be specified in a single sort. For example, assume an unsorted file is to be used in preparing a department census in which employees are to appear alphabetically within department. In other words, the file is to be rearranged (i.e., sorted) so that all employees in the same department appear together, and further that employees in a given department appear alphabetically. Department is a more important key than employee name; thus department is considered the *major* key and employee name the *minor* key. (Other, equally correct, terminology refers to department as the *primary* key and name as the *secondary* key.)

Sorting is done in one of two sequences: *ascending* (low to high) or *descending* (high to low). If sequence is not specified, an ascending sort is assumed. Thus an alphabetic listing of employees represents an *ascending* sort on name. However, a listing of employees by age, with the oldest first, denotes a *descending* sort on age.

To be absolutely sure of this terminology, consider Figure 12.1. Figure 12.1*a* lists unsorted data for 12 students. Figure 12.1*b* sorts these records by name only; students with different majors and different years are mixed together in a single list. Figure 12.1*c* shows a primary sort on year (descending) and a secondary sort on name. Thus all students in year 4 are listed first (in alphabet-

NAME	YEAR	MAJOR
Smith	1	Liberal arts
Jones	4	Enginering
Adams	3	Business
Howe	2	Liberal arts
Frank	1	Engineering
Epstein	2	Engineering
Zev	4	Business
Benjamin	4	Business
Grauer	3	Liberal arts
Crawford	2	Engineering
Deutsch	4	Business
Makoske	1	Business

(a) *Unsorted data*

Primary Sort: Name (Ascending)

NAME	YEAR	MAJOR
Adams	3	Business
Benjamin	4	Business
Crawford	2	Engineering
Deutsch	4	Business
Epstein	2	Engineering
Frank	1	Engineering
Grauer	3	Liberal arts
Howe	2	Liberal arts
Jones	4	Engineering
Makoske	1	Business
Smith	1	Liberal arts
Zev	4	Business

(b) *Sorted data*

Primary Sort: Year (Descending)
Secondary Sort: Name (Ascending)

NAME	YEAR	MAJOR
Benjamin	4	Business
Deutsch	4	Business
Jones	4	Engineering
Zev	4	Business
Adams	3	Business
Grauer	3	Liberal arts
Crawford	2	Engineering
Epstein	2	Engineering
Howe	2	Liberal arts
Frank	1	Engineering
Makoske	1	Business
Smith	1	Liberal arts

(c) *Sorted data*

Primary Sort: Major (Ascending)
Secondary Sort: Year (Descending)
Tertiary Sort: Name (Ascending)

NAME	YEAR	MAJOR
Benjamin	4	Business
Deutsch	4	Business
Zev	4	Business
Adams	3	Business
Makoske	1	Business
Jones	4	Engineering
Crawford	2	Engineering
Epstein	2	Engineering
Frank	1	Engineering
Grauer	3	Liberal arts
Howe	2	Liberal arts
Smith	1	Liberal arts

(d) *Sorted data*

FIGURE 12.1

ical order), then all students in year 3, etc. Finally, Figure 12.1*d* illustrates primary, secondary, and tertiary sorts. All business majors are listed first, then all engineering majors, and finally all liberal arts majors. Within a major, students are listed by year in descending order and listed alphabetically within year.

Collating Sequence

The ordering of data during a sort is easily predictable when numeric quantities are involved. However, more explanation is required for alphabetic or alphanumeric items. Assume, for example, that BAKER is compared to BROWN. BAKER is considered smaller, since it is alphabetically before BROWN. *Comparison proceeds from left to right one letter at a time.* Both names begin with B, but the A in BAKER precedes the R in BROWN.

Now compare GREEN to GREENFIELD. GREEN is considered smaller. Comparison again proceeds from left to right. The first five characters, G, R, E, E, and N, are the same in both names. The shorter field, GREEN, is extended with blanks so that comparison may continue. A blank is always considered smaller than any other letter, so that GREEN is the smaller of the two names.

Comparison is possible on alphanumeric fields as well as alphabetic fields. In this instance determination of the smaller field depends on the *collating sequence* of the machine. Collating sequence is defined as the ordered list (from low to high) of all valid characters. Collating sequence is a function of manufacturer; IBM uses EBCDIC, while most others use ASCII. Both sequences are shown in Figure 12.2 for selected characters.

As can be seen from Figure 12.2, 1 is greater than A for EBCDIC. Under ASCII, however, 1 is less than A. In other words, in an alphanumeric sort, part number 111 *precedes* part number XYZ under the ASCII collating sequence, but *follows* it under EBCDIC. This poses potential problems in a multivendor

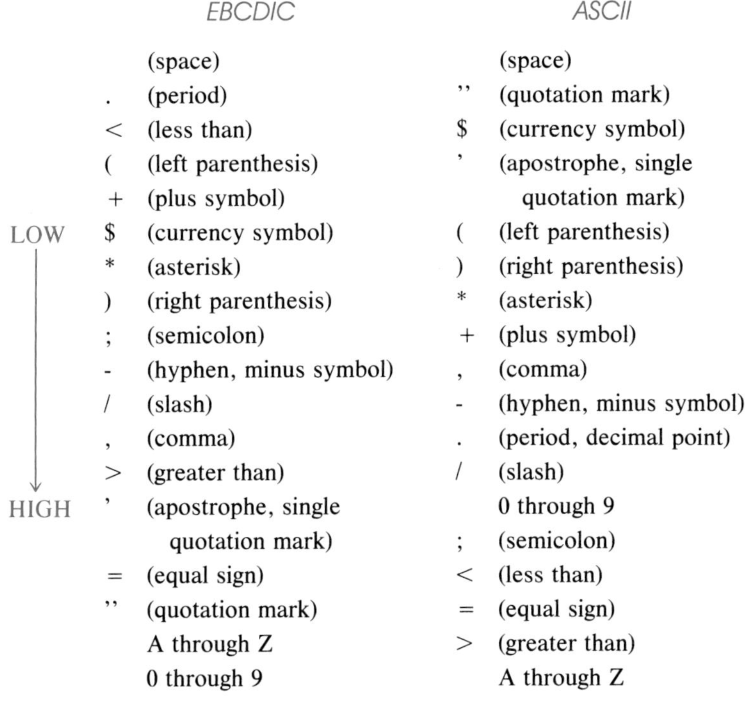

	EBCDIC		ASCII	
		(space)		(space)
	.	(period)	"	(quotation mark)
	<	(less than)	$	(currency symbol)
	(	(left parenthesis)	'	(apostrophe, single quotation mark)
	+	(plus symbol)	(	(left parenthesis)
LOW	$	(currency symbol)	)	(right parenthesis)
	*	(asterisk)	*	(asterisk)
	)	(right parenthesis)	+	(plus symbol)
	;	(semicolon)	,	(comma)
	-	(hyphen, minus symbol)	-	(hyphen, minus symbol)
	/	(slash)	.	(period, decimal point)
	,	(comma)	/	(slash)
	>	(greater than)		0 through 9
HIGH	'	(apostrophe, single quotation mark)	;	(semicolon)
	=	(equal sign)	<	(less than)
	"	(quotation mark)	=	(equal sign)
		A through Z	>	(greater than)
		0 through 9		A through Z

FIGURE 12.2 EBCDIC and ASCII Collating Sequences

environment, as when on-site mini- or microcomputers offload to an IBM mainframe. (You need not be concerned further about collating sequence, other than to know the situation exists.)

COBOL IMPLEMENTATION

The COBOL requirements for implementing a sort center on the SORT statement. In addition, you must be familiar with an SD (sort description) and with the RELEASE and RETURN statements.

SORT Verb

The complete syntax for the SORT statement is as follows:

```
SORT file-name-1

     ON {DESCENDING} KEY data-name-1 [data-name-2] . . .
        {ASCENDING }

    [ON {DESCENDING} KEY data-name-3 [data-name-4] . . .] . . .
        {ASCENDING }

    [COLLATING SEQUENCE IS alphabet-name]

    {INPUT PROCEDURE IS section-name-1 [{THRU   } section-name-2]}
    {USING file-name-2                  {THROUGH}                 }

    {OUTPUT PROCEDURE IS section-name-3 [{THRU   } section-name-4]}
    {GIVING file-name-3                  {THROUGH}                 }
```

Multiple sort keys are listed in the order of importance, with the *major* (primary) key listed first. Thus the statement

```
SORT STUDENT-FILE ASCENDING KEY STUDENT-MAJOR
                 DESCENDING KEY YEAR-IN-SCHOOL
                  ASCENDING KEY STUDENT-NAME
```

corresponds to the order of the keys in Figure 12.1*d*. (STUDENT-MAJOR is the primary sort, and STUDENT-NAME is the tertiary sort.) As can be seen from the general syntax, KEY is an optional reserved word, so that the preceding statement could have been recoded as

```
SORT STUDENT-FILE ASCENDING STUDENT-MAJOR
                 DESCENDING YEAR-IN-SCHOOL
                  ASCENDING STUDENT-NAME
```

When consecutive keys have the same sequence (both ascending or both descending), ASCENDING (or DESCENDING) need not be repeated. Hence, if it were desired to obtain a master list of students by year in school, and alphabetically within year, one could code

```
SORT STUDENT-FILE ASCENDING YEAR-IN-SCHOOL  STUDENT-NAME
```

The SORT statement contains an *optional* COLLATING SEQUENCE clause, making it possible to obtain different sequences for a given computer. In other words, one may obtain the ASCII sequence on an IBM mainframe and/or the EBCDIC sequence on a UNIVAC. One may also define a completely new sequence. However, implementation of an alternate collating sequence is less than straightforward, and you should consult an appropriate vendor manual if you wish to use one.

The general syntax indicates that one must choose between USING and INPUT PROCEDURE, and between GIVING and OUTPUT PROCEDURE. Hence there are *four* possible combinations of the SORT statement: USING/GIVING, USING/OUTPUT PROCEDURE, INPUT PROCEDURE/GIVING, and INPUT PROCEDURE/OUTPUT PROCEDURE. All four methods are valid and equally acceptable. (This chapter contains two listings for USING/GIVING and INPUT PROCEDURE/OUTPUT PROCEDURE; Figure 13.4 illustrates USING/OUTPUT PROCEDURE.)

We begin by distinguishing between USING and INPUT PROCEDURE. The latter is a more general technique in that it permits one to sort on a *calculated field,* a field not contained in an input record. For example, assume an incoming record has both an employee's present and previous salaries. The USING option permits a sort on either field, but not on percent of salary increase. Percent increase is a calculated field; it is not contained in the input record but is computed from two fields that are. The INPUT PROCEDURE option is required to sort on a calculated field.

INPUT PROCEDURE also allows one to *pass records selectively to the sort utility*. This is desirable in the many instances in which a *subset* of the input file is to appear in a subsequent report. Since sorting is a time-consuming process, one should not sort a file only to reject records subsequently. It is far more efficient to select records *prior* to the actual sort, and this is done using the INPUT PROCEDURE.

The difference between the two options is best summarized by the simple statement that the INPUT PROCEDURE requires the programmer to do his or her own I/O to and from the sort; i.e., the programmer decides which records are to be passed to the sort, and whether any additional fields need be added to the sort record. The USING option sorts an incoming file as is; the programmer does no I/O per se but is content to let the sort utility handle everything.

The difference between OUTPUT PROCEDURE and GIVING centers on the output of the sort utility. The GIVING option specifies a *permanent* file, which remains after the program has ended and which contains the sorted results. OUTPUT PROCEDURE uses a temporary work file, which does not exist after the program has terminated.

Related Statements

In addition to the SORT verb itself, three other statements are used in conjunction with sorting. These are the SD in the Data Division and the RELEASE and RETURN verbs in the Procedure Division.

The file name specified immediately after the word SORT is defined in an SD (rather than an FD) in the Data Division. The SD has the general syntax

```
SD file-name [RECORD CONTAINS [integer-1 TO] integer-2 CHARACTERS]

        [DATA {RECORD IS   } data-name-1 [data-name-2] . . .]
              {RECORDS ARE }
```

The RELEASE and RETURN verbs are required with the INPUT PROCEDURE/OUTPUT PROCEDURE option. RELEASE appears in the INPUT PROCEDURE and has the form

```
RELEASE record-name [FROM identifier]
```

RELEASE is analogous to WRITE; it writes a record to the sort work file (the file defined in the SD).

RETURN appears in the OUTPUT PROCEDURE and has the format

```
RETURN file-name [INTO identifier] AT END statement
```

RETURN is analogous to READ; it reads a record from the sort work file, the file defined in the SD.

The SORT verb and its related statements can be integrated into any COBOL program. We proceed now to develop a typical application, with specifications in the usual format. In actuality we present two separate programs, to illustrate both the INPUT PROCEDURE/OUTPUT PROCEDURE and USING/GIVING options of the SORT statement.

Programming Specifications

Program Name(s):
Sort Programs

Narrative:
These specifications provide for two programs to illustrate the USING/GIVING and INPUT PROCEDURE/OUTPUT PROCEDURE options of the SORT verb. Both programs are modified versions of the Car Billing Program from Chapter 9.

Input File:
RENTAL-RECORD-FILE

Input Record Layout:
See the original specifications on page 215.

Test Data:
See Figure 9.9.

Report Layout:
The report layout parallels the specifications of Figure 9.10a. However, the USING/GIVING option lists valid records in *alphabetical* order, whereas INPUT PROCEDURE/OUTPUT PROCEDURE lists them in *order of computed bill.*

Processing Requirements:

1. All processing requirements of the Car Billing Program from Chapter 9 (pages 215–216) pertain to these programs as well. In addition see items 2 and 3.
2. Implement the USING/GIVING option of the SORT verb to list valid records alphabetically.
3. Implement the INPUT PROCEDURE/OUTPUT PROCEDURE option to list valid records in order of computed bill. The INPUT PROCEDURE is to include the data validation, so that erroneous records are rejected prior to the actual sorting. This in turn makes this option more efficient, as significantly fewer records are sorted.

SORT VERB: INPUT PROCEDURE/OUTPUT PROCEDURE OPTION

Figure 12.3 is a modified version of the Car Billing Program from Chapter 9. It illustrates the INPUT PROCEDURE/OUTPUT PROCEDURE option of the SORT verb.

Explanation begins with the SORT statement itself, lines 149–152. The SORT verb references a sort work file, SORT-FILE, which is defined in an SD in the Data Division (lines 37–39), together with its associated record layout (lines 40–48). SORT-FILE is to be sorted on the field SORT-CUSTOMER-BILL, which is a calculated field (i.e., it is not contained in the incoming rental record). The INPUT PROCEDURE/OUTPUT PROCEDURE option involves several implicit transfers of control as follows:

1. Control passes from the SORT verb to the *section* designated as the INPUT PROCEDURE.
2. When the INPUT PROCEDURE is concluded, control passes to the sort utility, which orders the sort work file created by the INPUT PROCEDURE.
3. After the sort, control passes to the *section* designated as the OUTPUT PROCEDURE.
4. When the OUTPUT PROCEDURE is finished, control returns to the statement directly (physically) under the actual SORT statement.

The purpose of the INPUT PROCEDURE is to read records from an input file and build a sort work file. The INPUT PROCEDURE *must* be a section. A section contains one or more paragraphs and ends when the next section begins; hence the INPUT PROCEDURE ends with the EXIT statement in line 237.

```
00001          IDENTIFICATION DIVISION.
00002          PROGRAM-ID.
00003              CARSORT2.
00004          AUTHOR.
00005              JACKIE CLARK.
00006
00007          ENVIRONMENT DIVISION.
00008          CONFIGURATION SECTION.
00009          SOURCE-COMPUTER.
00010              IBM-4341.
00011          OBJECT-COMPUTER.
00012              IBM-4341.
00013
00014          INPUT-OUTPUT SECTION.
00015          FILE-CONTROL.
00016              SELECT RENTAL-RECORD-FILE
00017                  ASSIGN TO UT-S-SYSIN.
00018              SELECT PRINT-FILE
00019                  ASSIGN TO UT-S-SYSPRT.
00020              SELECT SORT-FILE
00021                  ASSIGN TO UT-S-SORTWK01.
00022
00023          DATA DIVISION.
00024          FILE SECTION.
00025          FD  RENTAL-RECORD-FILE
00026              LABEL RECORDS ARE OMITTED
00027              RECORD CONTAINS 80 CHARACTERS
00028              DATA RECORD IS RENTAL-RECORD.
00029          01  RENTAL-RECORD               PIC X(80).
00030
00031          FD  PRINT-FILE
00032              LABEL RECORDS ARE OMITTED
00033              RECORD CONTAINS 133 CHARACTERS
00034              DATA RECORD IS PRINT-LINE.
00035          01  PRINT-LINE                  PIC X(133).
00036
```

Sort work file is defined in SELECT and SD statements.

FIGURE 12.3 SORT Verb (INPUT PROCEDURE/OUTPUT PROCEDURE)

FIGURE 12.3 (Continued)

```
       SD  SORT-FILE
           RECORD CONTAINS 60 CHARACTERS
           DATA RECORD IS SORT-RECORD.
       01  SORT-RECORD.
           05  SORT-SOC-SEC-NUM        PIC 9(09).
           05  SORT-NAME-FIELD         PIC X(25).
           05  SORT-DATE-RETURNED      PIC X(06).
           05  SORT-CAR-TYPE           PIC X(01).
           05  SORT-DAYS-RENTED        PIC 9(02).
           05  SORT-MILES-DRIVEN       PIC 9(04).
           05  SORT-CUSTOMER-BILL      PIC 9(04)V99.
           05  FILLER                  PIC X(07).

       WORKING-STORAGE SECTION.
       01  FILLER                      PIC X(14)
               VALUE 'WS BEGINS HERE'.

       01  WS-END-SORT-FILE            PIC XXX        VALUE 'NO '.

       01  WS-END-OF-FILE-SWITCH       PIC XXX        VALUE 'NO '.
           88 WS-END-OF-FILE                          VALUE 'YES'.

       01  VALIDATION-AREA.
           05  VALID-RECORD-SW         PIC X(3).
           05  VALID-MILES             PIC 9(3).
           05  LAST-YEAR               PIC 99.

       01  PAGE-AND-LINE-COUNTERS.
           05  WS-LINE-COUNT           PIC 9(2)       VALUE 6.
           05  WS-PAGE-COUNT           PIC 9(2)       VALUE ZEROS.

       01  BILLING-CONSTANTS.
           05  WS-MILEAGE-RATE         PIC 9V99.
           05  WS-DAILY-RATE           PIC 99V99.
           05  WS-CUSTOMER-BILL        PIC 9999V99.

       01  DATE-WORK-AREA.
           05  TODAYS-YEAR             PIC 99.
           05  TODAYS-MONTH            PIC 99.
           05  TODAYS-DAY              PIC 99.

       01  WS-RECORD-IN.
           05  SOC-SEC-NUM             PIC 9(9).
           05  NAME-FIELD              PIC X(25).
           05  DATE-RETURNED.
               10  DATE-RETURNED-YY PIC 9(2).
               10  DATE-RETURNED-MM PIC 9(2).
               10  DATE-RETURNED-DD PIC 9(2).
           05  CAR-TYPE                PIC X.
               88  COMPACT                            VALUE 'C'.
               88  INTERMEDIATE                       VALUE 'I'.
               88  FULL-SIZE                          VALUE 'F'.
               88  VALID-CODES
                       VALUES ARE 'C' 'I' 'F'.
           05  DAYS-RENTED             PIC 99.
           05  MILES-DRIVEN            PIC 9(4).
           05  CUST-BILL               PIC 9(04)V99.
           05  FILLER                  PIC X(27).

       01  WS-PRINT-LINE.
           05  FILLER                  PIC X(4).
           05  PR-SOC-SEC-NUM          PIC 999B99B9999.
           05  FILLER                  PIC X(4).
           05  PR-NAME-FIELD           PIC X(25).
           05  FILLER                  PIC XX.
           05  PR-CAR-TYPE             PIC X.
           05  FILLER                  PIC X(4).
           05  PR-DAYS-RENTED          PIC Z9.
           05  FILLER                  PIC X(4).
           05  PR-MILES-DRIVEN         PIC ZZZ9.
           05  FILLER                  PIC X(4).
           05  PR-CUSTOMER-BILL        PIC $$,$$9.99.
           05  FILLER                  PIC X(59).

       01  WS-HEADING-LINE-ONE.
           05  FILLER                  PIC X(65)      VALUE SPACES.
           05  FILLER                  PIC X(5)       VALUE 'PAGE '
           05  WS-PAGE-PRINT           PIC ZZ9.
           05  FILLER                  PIC X(60)      VALUE SPACES.
```

Record length of sort work file is different from input file.

FIGURE 12.3 ***(Continued)***

```
       01  WS-HEADING-LINE-TWO.
           05  FILLER                 PIC X(20)      VALUE SPACES.
           05  TITLE-INFO             PIC X(33).
           05  FILLER                 PIC XX         VALUE SPACES.
           05  TITLE-DATE.
               10  TITLE-MONTH        PIC 99.
               10  FILLER             PIC X          VALUE '/'.
               10  TITLE-DAY          PIC 99.
               10  FILLER             PIC X          VALUE '/'.
               10  TITLE-YEAR         PIC 99.
           05  FILLER                 PIC X(70)      VALUE SPACES.

       01  WS-HEADING-LINE-THREE.
           05  FILLER                 PIC X(8)       VALUE SPACES.
           05  FILLER                 PIC X(11)      VALUE ' ACCT #'.
           05  FILLER                 PIC XX         VALUE SPACES.
           05  FILLER                 PIC X(4)       VALUE 'NAME'.
           05  FILLER                 PIC X(19)      VALUE SPACES.
           05  FILLER                 PIC X(4)       VALUE 'TYPE'.
           05  FILLER                 PIC XX         VALUE SPACES.
           05  FILLER                 PIC X(4)       VALUE 'DAYS'.
           05  FILLER                 PIC XX         VALUE SPACES.
           05  FILLER                 PIC X(5)       VALUE 'MILES'.
           05  FILLER                 PIC X(4)       VALUE SPACES.
           05  FILLER                 PIC X(6)       VALUE 'AMOUNT'.
           05  FILLER                 PIC X(60)      VALUE SPACES.

       01  FILLER                     PIC X(12)
               VALUE 'WS ENDS HERE'.
       PROCEDURE DIVISION.
       005-SORTING SECTION.
       010-MAINLINE.
           SORT SORT-FILE
               ASCENDING KEY SORT-CUSTOMER-BILL
                   INPUT  PROCEDURE 100-PROCESS-ALL-CUSTOMERS
                   OUTPUT PROCEDURE 200-PRODUCE-REPORT.
           STOP RUN.

       100-PROCESS-ALL-CUSTOMERS SECTION.
       110-PROCESS-VALID-CUSTOMERS.
           ACCEPT DATE-WORK-AREA FROM DATE.
           COMPUTE LAST-YEAR = TODAYS-YEAR - 1.
           OPEN INPUT RENTAL-RECORD-FILE.
           PERFORM 120-READ-RENTAL-RECORD.
           PERFORM 130-PROCESS-CUSTOMER-RECORDS
               UNTIL WS-END-OF-FILE.
           CLOSE RENTAL-RECORD-FILE.
           GO TO 190-EXIT.

       120-READ-RENTAL-RECORD.
           READ RENTAL-RECORD-FILE INTO WS-RECORD-IN
               AT END MOVE 'YES' TO WS-END-OF-FILE-SWITCH.

       130-PROCESS-CUSTOMER-RECORDS.
           MOVE 'YES' TO VALID-RECORD-SW.
           PERFORM 140-VALIDATE-CUSTOMER-RECORD.
           IF VALID-RECORD-SW = 'YES'
               PERFORM 150-COMPUTE-BILL
               PERFORM 160-WRITE-SORT-RECORD.
           PERFORM 120-READ-RENTAL-RECORD.

       140-VALIDATE-CUSTOMER-RECORD.
           IF NAME-FIELD OF WS-RECORD-IN = SPACES
               OR SOC-SEC-NUM OF WS-RECORD-IN NOT NUMERIC
                   MOVE 'NO ' TO VALID-RECORD-SW
                   DISPLAY 'MISSING DATA ' NAME-FIELD OF WS-RECORD-IN
                   DISPLAY ' '.
           IF NOT VALID-CODES
               MOVE 'NO ' TO VALID-RECORD-SW
               DISPLAY 'INVALID CAR ' NAME-FIELD OF WS-RECORD-IN
               DISPLAY ' '.
           COMPUTE VALID-MILES = 10 * DAYS-RENTED OF WS-RECORD-IN.
           IF MILES-DRIVEN OF WS-RECORD-IN < VALID-MILES
               MOVE 'NO ' TO VALID-RECORD-SW
               DISPLAY 'INVALID MILEAGE ' NAME-FIELD OF WS-RECORD-IN
               DISPLAY ' '.
           IF DAYS-RENTED OF WS-RECORD-IN > 35
               MOVE 'NO ' TO VALID-RECORD-SW
               DISPLAY 'ERROR - REFER TO LONG-TERM LEASING '
                   NAME-FIELD OF WS-RECORD-IN
```

Customers are listed by the amount of their bill.

INPUT PROCEDURE is a section.

Forward GO TO to EXIT paragraph.

Only valid records are written to sort work file.

```
            DISPLAY ' '.
        IF DATE-RETURNED-MM < 1 OR DATE-RETURNED-MM > 12
            MOVE 'NO ' TO VALID-RECORD-SW
            DISPLAY 'INVALID MONTH ' NAME-FIELD OF WS-RECORD-IN
            DISPLAY ' '.
        IF DATE-RETURNED-DD > 31
            MOVE 'NO ' TO VALID-RECORD-SW
            DISPLAY 'INVALID DAY ' NAME-FIELD OF WS-RECORD-IN
            DISPLAY ' '.
        IF DATE-RETURNED-YY NOT = TODAYS-YEAR
            AND DATE-RETURNED-YY NOT = LAST-YEAR
                MOVE 'NO ' TO VALID-RECORD-SW
                DISPLAY 'INVALID YEAR ' NAME-FIELD OF WS-RECORD-IN
                DISPLAY ' '.

    150-COMPUTE-BILL.
        IF COMPACT
            MOVE .18 TO WS-MILEAGE-RATE
            MOVE 10.00 TO WS-DAILY-RATE
        ELSE
            IF INTERMEDIATE
                MOVE .20 TO WS-MILEAGE-RATE
                MOVE 12.00 TO WS-DAILY-RATE
            ELSE
                MOVE .22 TO WS-MILEAGE-RATE
                MOVE 14.00 TO WS-DAILY-RATE.

        COMPUTE WS-CUSTOMER-BILL ROUNDED =
            MILES-DRIVEN OF WS-RECORD-IN * WS-MILEAGE-RATE
            + DAYS-RENTED OF WS-RECORD-IN * WS-DAILY-RATE
        ON SIZE ERROR
            DISPLAY 'RECEIVING FIELD TOO SMALL FOR BILL'
                NAME-FIELD OF WS-RECORD-IN
            DISPLAY ' '.
        MOVE WS-CUSTOMER-BILL TO CUST-BILL.

    160-WRITE-SORT-RECORD.
        RELEASE SORT-RECORD FROM WS-RECORD-IN.
```

RELEASE statement writes record to sort work file.

```
    190-EXIT.
        EXIT.

    200-PRODUCE-REPORT SECTION.
```

OUTPUT PROCEDURE is a section.

```
    210-PROCESS-SORTED-FILE.
        OPEN OUTPUT PRINT-FILE.
        PERFORM 220-RETURN-SORT-FILE.
        PERFORM 230-WRITE-REPORT
            UNTIL WS-END-SORT-FILE = 'YES'.
        CLOSE PRINT-FILE.
        GO TO 290-EXIT.

    220-RETURN-SORT-FILE.
        RETURN SORT-FILE INTO WS-RECORD-IN
            AT END MOVE 'YES' TO WS-END-SORT-FILE.
```

RETURN statement reads records from sort work file.

```
    230-WRITE-REPORT.
        IF WS-LINE-COUNT IS GREATER THAN 5
            PERFORM 240-WRITE-HEADING-LINES.
        MOVE SPACES TO WS-PRINT-LINE.
        MOVE SOC-SEC-NUM  TO PR-SOC-SEC-NUM.
        MOVE NAME-FIELD   TO PR-NAME-FIELD.
        MOVE CAR-TYPE     TO PR-CAR-TYPE.
        MOVE DAYS-RENTED  TO PR-DAYS-RENTED.
        MOVE MILES-DRIVEN TO PR-MILES-DRIVEN.
        INSPECT PR-SOC-SEC-NUM
            REPLACING ALL ' ' BY '-'.
        MOVE CUST-BILL TO PR-CUSTOMER-BILL.
        WRITE PRINT-LINE FROM WS-PRINT-LINE
            AFTER ADVANCING 2 LINES.
        ADD 1 TO WS-LINE-COUNT.
        PERFORM 220-RETURN-SORT-FILE.
```

Last line of the performed routine returns (reads) another record.

```
    240-WRITE-HEADING-LINES.
        MOVE 1 TO WS-LINE-COUNT.
        ADD 1 TO WS-PAGE-COUNT.
        MOVE WS-PAGE-COUNT TO WS-PAGE-PRINT.
        WRITE PRINT-LINE FROM WS-HEADING-LINE-ONE
            AFTER ADVANCING PAGE.
        MOVE ' STACEY CAR RENTALS - REPORT DATE ' TO TITLE-INFO.
        MOVE TODAYS-DAY TO TITLE-DAY.
```

```
00277              MOVE TODAYS-MONTH TO TITLE-MONTH.
00278              MOVE TODAYS-YEAR TO TITLE-YEAR.
00279              WRITE PRINT-LINE FROM WS-HEADING-LINE-TWO
00280                  AFTER ADVANCING 1 LINES.
00281              WRITE PRINT-LINE FROM WS-HEADING-LINE-THREE
00282                  AFTER ADVANCING 1 LINES.
00283
00284          290-EXIT.
00285              EXIT.
```

FIGURE 12.3 **(Continued)**

The INPUT PROCEDURE opens the input RENTAL-RECORD-FILE, does an initial read for this file, then performs a paragraph until the input file is empty. Each input record is validated in the paragraph 140-VALIDATE-CUSTOMER-RECORD, according to the validity checks from Chapter 9. *Only valid records are written to the sort work file* as provided by the check in line 173. (Records are written in a RELEASE statement in line 234.)

A *forward* GO TO statement is present in line 164 of the INPUT PROCEDURE and again in line 246 of the OUTPUT PROCEDURE. These are the *only* occurrences of the GO TO statement in the entire book, but they are quite necessary. Consider the effect of *omitting* the GO TO statement in the INPUT PROCEDURE, line 164. If this were done, control would fall through to READ-RENTAL-RECORD, after the end of file had been reached, causing rather obvious problems. It is necessary, therefore, to branch to the end of the INPUT PROCEDURE, and this is done using the GO TO statement.

The INPUT PROCEDURE must be a section. Hence the GO TO statement transfers control to the physical end of the INPUT PROCEDURE, i.e., to the one-statement EXIT paragraph. (EXIT does nothing per se; it merely sits at the end of the INPUT PROCEDURE.) It is not possible to avoid the GO TO statement in this instance, but its use should in no way be considered a catastrophe. (An alert reader may suggest that performing *sections* outside of the INPUT PROCEDURE would eliminate the GO TO. This is possible on the IBM OS/VS compiler, but it is a deviation from the ANS 74 standard and hence is not used.)

The OUTPUT PROCEDURE begins in line 239 and is also a section. Its purpose is to read records from the sorted file and prepare a report. (Observe that the sort work file, SORT-FILE, is neither opened nor closed explicitly by the programmer.) The initial read of the sorted file is accomplished by a RETURN statement, and the paragraph 230-WRITE-REPORT is performed until the sort file is empty. PRINT-FILE is closed, and a *forward* GO TO statement transfers control to the end of the OUTPUT PROCEDURE.

Control then passes to the statement under the SORT verb, STOP RUN in line 153, which terminates processing.

SORT VERB: USING/GIVING OPTION

The USING/GIVING option is illustrated in Figure 12.4. It simplifies the job of the programmer in that COBOL automatically does the I/O to and from the SORT. The option requires that the sort key be present in the incoming record.

The SORT statement in lines 148–151 references three files, *all of which must have identical record layouts*. The SORT verb opens RENTAL-RECORD-FILE, reads every record in that file, and releases every record to the sort work file. It rearranges the work file according to the sort key and writes the newly ordered file to SORTED-RENTAL-FILE. The programmer does not open or close SORT-FILE or RENTAL-RECORD-FILE.

```
IDENTIFICATION DIVISION.
PROGRAM-ID.
    CARSORT1.
AUTHOR.
    JACKIE CLARK.

ENVIRONMENT DIVISION.
CONFIGURATION SECTION.
SOURCE-COMPUTER.
    IBM-4341.
OBJECT-COMPUTER.
    IBM-4341.

INPUT-OUTPUT SECTION.
FILE-CONTROL.
    SELECT RENTAL-RECORD-FILE
        ASSIGN TO UT-S-SYSIN.
    SELECT PRINT-FILE
        ASSIGN TO UT-S-SYSPRT.
    SELECT SORT-FILE
        ASSIGN TO UT-S-SORTWK01.
    SELECT SORTED-RENTAL-FILE
        ASSIGN TO UT-S-SORTED.

DATA DIVISION.
FILE SECTION.
FD  RENTAL-RECORD-FILE
    LABEL RECORDS ARE OMITTED
    RECORD CONTAINS 80 CHARACTERS
    DATA RECORD IS RENTAL-RECORD.
01  RENTAL-RECORD                PIC X(80).

FD  PRINT-FILE
    LABEL RECORDS ARE OMITTED
    RECORD CONTAINS 133 CHARACTERS
    DATA RECORD IS PRINT-LINE.
01  PRINT-LINE                   PIC X(133).

SD  SORT-FILE
    RECORD CONTAINS 80 CHARACTERS
    DATA RECORD IS SORT-RECORD.
01  SORT-RECORD.
    05  FILLER                   PIC X(09).
    05  SORT-NAME                PIC X(25).
    05  FILLER                   PIC X(46).

FD  SORTED-RENTAL-FILE
    LABEL RECORDS ARE OMITTED
    RECORD CONTAINS 80 CHARACTERS
    DATA RECORD IS SORTED-RENTAL-RECORD.
01  SORTED-RENTAL-RECORD         PIC X(80).

WORKING-STORAGE SECTION.
01  FILLER                       PIC X(14)
        VALUE 'WS BEGINS HERE'.

01  WS-END-OF-FILE-SWITCH        PIC XXX        VALUE 'NO '.
    88 WS-END-OF-FILE                           VALUE 'YES'.

01  VALIDATION-AREA.
    05  VALID-RECORD-SW          PIC X(3).
    05  VALID-MILES              PIC 9(3).
    05  LAST-YEAR                PIC 99.

01  PAGE-AND-LINE-COUNTERS.
    05  WS-LINE-COUNT            PIC 9(2)       VALUE 6.
    05  WS-PAGE-COUNT            PIC 9(2)       VALUE ZEROS.

01  BILLING-CONSTANTS.
    05  WS-MILEAGE-RATE          PIC 9V99.
    05  WS-DAILY-RATE            PIC 99V99.
    05  WS-CUSTOMER-BILL         PIC 9999V99.

01  DATE-WORK-AREA.
    05  TODAYS-YEAR              PIC 99.
    05  TODAYS-MONTH             PIC 99.
    05  TODAYS-DAY               PIC 99.

01  WS-RECORD-IN.
```

Sort work file is defined in ordinary SELECT statement.

Sort work file is defined in an SD.

FIGURE 12.4 SORT Verb (USING/GIVING Option)

```
           05  SOC-SEC-NUM          PIC 9(9).
           05  NAME-FIELD           PIC X(25).
           05  DATE-RETURNED.
               10  DATE-RETURNED-YY PIC 9(2).
               10  DATE-RETURNED-MM PIC 9(2).
               10  DATE-RETURNED-DD PIC 9(2).
           05  CAR-TYPE             PIC X.
               88  COMPACT                        VALUE 'C'.
               88  INTERMEDIATE                   VALUE 'I'.
               88  FULL-SIZE                      VALUE 'F'.
               88  VALID-CODES
                       VALUES ARE 'C' 'I' 'F'.
           05  DAYS-RENTED          PIC 99.
           05  MILES-DRIVEN         PIC 9(4).
           05  FILLER               PIC X(33).

       01  WS-PRINT-LINE.
           05  FILLER               PIC X(4).
           05  PR-SOC-SEC-NUM       PIC 999B99B9999.
           05  FILLER               PIC X(4).
           05  PR-NAME-FIELD        PIC X(25).
           05  FILLER               PIC XX.
           05  PR-CAR-TYPE          PIC X.
           05  FILLER               PIC X(4).
           05  PR-DAYS-RENTED       PIC Z9.
           05  FILLER               PIC X(4).
           05  PR-MILES-DRIVEN      PIC ZZZ9.
           05  FILLER               PIC X(4).
           05  PR-CUSTOMER-BILL     PIC $$,$$9.99.
           05  FILLER               PIC X(59).

       01  WS-HEADING-LINE-ONE.
           05  FILLER               PIC X(65)     VALUE SPACES.
           05  FILLER               PIC X(5)      VALUE 'PAGE '.
           05  WS-PAGE-PRINT        PIC ZZ9.
           05  FILLER               PIC X(60)     VALUE SPACES.

       01  WS-HEADING-LINE-TWO.
           05  FILLER               PIC X(20)     VALUE SPACES.
           05  TITLE-INFO           PIC X(33).
           05  FILLER               PIC XX        VALUE SPACES.
           05  TITLE-DATE.
               10  TITLE-MONTH      PIC 99.
               10  FILLER           PIC X         VALUE '/'.
               10  TITLE-DAY        PIC 99.
               10  FILLER           PIC X         VALUE '/'.
               10  TITLE-YEAR       PIC 99.
           05  FILLER               PIC X(70)     VALUE SPACES.

       01  WS-HEADING-LINE-THREE.
           05  FILLER               PIC X(8)      VALUE SPACES.
           05  FILLER               PIC X(11)     VALUE ' ACCT #'.
           05  FILLER               PIC XX        VALUE SPACES.
           05  FILLER               PIC X(4)      VALUE 'NAME'.
           05  FILLER               PIC X(19)     VALUE SPACES.
           05  FILLER               PIC X(4)      VALUE 'TYPE'.
           05  FILLER               PIC XX        VALUE SPACES.
           05  FILLER               PIC X(4)      VALUE 'DAYS'.
           05  FILLER               PIC XX        VALUE SPACES.
           05  FILLER               PIC X(5)      VALUE 'MILES'.
           05  FILLER               PIC X(4)      VALUE SPACES.
           05  FILLER               PIC X(6)      VALUE 'AMOUNT'.
           05  FILLER               PIC X(60)     VALUE SPACES.

       01  FILLER                   PIC X(12)
               VALUE 'WS ENDS HERE'.
       PROCEDURE DIVISION.
       010-MAINLINE.
           SORT SORT-FILE
               ASCENDING KEY SORT-NAME
                   USING  RENTAL-RECORD-FILE
                   GIVING SORTED-RENTAL-FILE.
           OPEN INPUT  SORTED-RENTAL-FILE
                OUTPUT PRINT-FILE.
           PERFORM 015-INITIALIZE-VALID-DATES.
           PERFORM 020-READ-RENTAL-RECORD.
           PERFORM 030-PROCESS-CUSTOMER-RECORDS
               UNTIL WS-END-OF-FILE.
           CLOSE SORTED-RENTAL-FILE
                 PRINT-FILE.
```

All three files must have identical length and record layout.

FIGURE 12.4 (Continued)

```
    STOP RUN.

015-INITIALIZE-VALID-DATES.
    ACCEPT DATE-WORK-AREA FROM DATE.
    COMPUTE LAST-YEAR = TODAYS-YEAR - 1.

020-READ-RENTAL-RECORD.
    READ SORTED-RENTAL-FILE INTO WS-RECORD-IN
        AT END MOVE 'YES' TO WS-END-OF-FILE-SWITCH.

030-PROCESS-CUSTOMER-RECORDS.
    MOVE 'YES' TO VALID-RECORD-SW.
    PERFORM 040-VALIDATE-CUSTOMER-RECORD.
    IF VALID-RECORD-SW = 'YES'
        PERFORM 050-COMPUTE-BILL
        PERFORM 060-WRITE-RENTAL-LINE.
    PERFORM 020-READ-RENTAL-RECORD.

040-VALIDATE-CUSTOMER-RECORD.
    IF NAME-FIELD OF WS-RECORD-IN = SPACES
        OR SOC-SEC-NUM OF WS-RECORD-IN NOT NUMERIC
            MOVE 'NO ' TO VALID-RECORD-SW
            DISPLAY 'MISSING DATA ' NAME-FIELD OF WS-RECORD-IN
            DISPLAY ' '.
    IF NOT VALID-CODES
        MOVE 'NO ' TO VALID-RECORD-SW
        DISPLAY 'INVALID CAR ' NAME-FIELD OF WS-RECORD-IN
        DISPLAY ' '.
    COMPUTE VALID-MILES = 10 * DAYS-RENTED OF WS-RECORD-IN.
    IF MILES-DRIVEN OF WS-RECORD-IN < VALID-MILES
        MOVE 'NO ' TO VALID-RECORD-SW
        DISPLAY 'INVALID MILEAGE ' NAME-FIELD OF WS-RECORD-IN
        DISPLAY ' '.
    IF DAYS-RENTED OF WS-RECORD-IN > 35
        MOVE 'NO ' TO VALID-RECORD-SW
        DISPLAY 'ERROR - REFER TO LONG-TERM LEASING '
            NAME-FIELD OF WS-RECORD-IN
        DISPLAY ' '.
    IF DATE-RETURNED-MM < 1 OR DATE-RETURNED-MM > 12
        MOVE 'NO ' TO VALID-RECORD-SW
        DISPLAY 'INVALID MONTH ' NAME-FIELD OF WS-RECORD-IN
        DISPLAY ' '.
    IF DATE-RETURNED-DD > 31
        MOVE 'NO ' TO VALID-RECORD-SW
        DISPLAY 'INVALID DAY ' NAME-FIELD OF WS-RECORD-IN
        DISPLAY ' '.
    IF DATE-RETURNED-YY NOT = TODAYS-YEAR
        AND DATE-RETURNED-YY NOT = LAST-YEAR
            MOVE 'NO ' TO VALID-RECORD-SW
            DISPLAY 'INVALID YEAR ' NAME-FIELD OF WS-RECORD-IN
            DISPLAY ' '.

050-COMPUTE-BILL.
    IF COMPACT
        MOVE .18 TO WS-MILEAGE-RATE
        MOVE 10.00 TO WS-DAILY-RATE
    ELSE
        IF INTERMEDIATE
            MOVE .20 TO WS-MILEAGE-RATE
            MOVE 12.00 TO WS-DAILY-RATE
        ELSE
            MOVE .22 TO WS-MILEAGE-RATE
            MOVE 14.00 TO WS-DAILY-RATE.

    COMPUTE WS-CUSTOMER-BILL ROUNDED =
        MILES-DRIVEN OF WS-RECORD-IN * WS-MILEAGE-RATE
        + DAYS-RENTED OF WS-RECORD-IN * WS-DAILY-RATE
    ON SIZE ERROR
        DISPLAY 'RECEIVING FIELD TOO SMALL FOR BILL'
            NAME-FIELD OF WS-RECORD-IN
        DISPLAY ' '.

060-WRITE-RENTAL-LINE.
    IF WS-LINE-COUNT IS GREATER THAN 5
        PERFORM 070-WRITE-HEADING-LINES.
    MOVE SPACES TO WS-PRINT-LINE.
    MOVE SOC-SEC-NUM  TO PR-SOC-SEC-NUM.
    MOVE NAME-FIELD   TO PR-NAME-FIELD.
    MOVE CAR-TYPE     TO PR-CAR-TYPE.
    MOVE DAYS-RENTED  TO PR-DAYS-RENTED.
```

```
           MOVE MILES-DRIVEN TO PR-MILES-DRIVEN.
           INSPECT PR-SOC-SEC-NUM
               REPLACING ALL ' ' BY '-'.
           MOVE WS-CUSTOMER-BILL TO PR-CUSTOMER-BILL.
           WRITE PRINT-LINE FROM WS-PRINT-LINE
               AFTER ADVANCING 2 LINES.
           ADD 1 TO WS-LINE-COUNT.
       070-WRITE-HEADING-LINES.
           MOVE 1 TO WS-LINE-COUNT.
           ADD 1 TO WS-PAGE-COUNT.
           MOVE WS-PAGE-COUNT TO WS-PAGE-PRINT.
           WRITE PRINT-LINE FROM WS-HEADING-LINE-ONE
               AFTER ADVANCING PAGE.
           MOVE ' STACEY CAR RENTALS - REPORT DATE ' TO TITLE-INFO.
           MOVE TODAYS-DAY TO TITLE-DAY.
           MOVE TODAYS-MONTH TO TITLE-MONTH.
           MOVE TODAYS-YEAR TO TITLE-YEAR.
           WRITE PRINT-LINE FROM WS-HEADING-LINE-TWO
               AFTER ADVANCING 1 LINES.
           WRITE PRINT-LINE FROM WS-HEADING-LINE-THREE
               AFTER ADVANCING 1 LINES.
```

FIGURE 12.4 (Continued)

The remainder of the Procedure Division parallels exactly the original program in Chapter 9. The most significant difference is in the generated reports. In the original listing records were written in the order in which they came; in the report produced by this program the records appear in alphabetical order.

INPUT PROCEDURE/OUTPUT PROCEDURE VERSUS USING/GIVING

The differences between the two COBOL programs can be seen by comparing the generated reports. Figure 12.5 was produced by the INPUT PROCEDURE/OUTPUT PROCEDURE option and lists the records in order of the computed bill. Figure 12.6 was produced by the USING/GIVING option and lists the records in alphabetical order. The following are other differences:

1. Figure 12.3 sorts on SORT-CUSTOMER-BILL, a calculated field. Figure 12.4 sorts on SORT-NAME, which is contained in the incoming record.
2. Figure 12.3 requires the programmer to do his or her own I/O to and from the SORT. In Figure 12.4 the SORT verb causes RENTAL-RECORD-FILE to be opened, copied to SORT-FILE, and then closed.
3. Figure 12.3 uses the RELEASE and RETURN verbs to write to, and read from, SORT-FILE. These verbs are not used in Figure 12.4, since the USING/GIVING option does the I/O automatically.
4. Figure 12.3 requires only three files. Figure 12.4 uses four. (Compare SELECT statements.) The extra file is necessary because the sorted data are placed on a separate file (SORTED-RENTAL-FILE).
5. Record lengths in Figure 12.4 of RENTAL-RECORD-FILE, SORTED-RENTAL-FILE, and SORT-FILE must be the same (80 bytes). The record lengths of SORT-FILE and RENTAL-RECORD-FILE in Figure 12.3 are different.
6. Figure 12.3 *requires* section names for the INPUT PROCEDURE and OUTPUT PROCEDURE. Sections are optional in Figure 12.4.

MERGE

Merging files is a special case of sorting. The MERGE verb takes several input files, with identical record formats sorted in the same sequence, and combines them into a single output file (device type and blocking may differ for the various

```
                                                                  PAGE    3
                       STACEY CAR RENTALS - REPORT DATE  03/21/84
        ACCT #         NAME                       TYPE  DAYS  MILES     AMOUNT

   987-65-4321     BROWN,PG                        I     10    2000      $520.00
```

```
                                                                  PAGE    2
                       STACEY CAR RENTALS - REPORT DATE  03/21/84
        ACCT #         NAME                       TYPE  DAYS  MILES     AMOUNT

   123-45-6789     BAKER,RG                        F      5     345      $145.90

   008-63-2212     TOWER,DR                        I      9     376      $183.20

   264-80-5298     CLARK,JS                        F      7     524      $213.28

   886-22-2343     VOGEL,JD                        F     12     413      $258.86

   354-67-9876     KERBEL,NX                       I     10    1259      $371.80
```

```
                                                                  PAGE    1
                       STACEY CAR RENTALS - REPORT DATE  03/21/84
        ACCT #         NAME                       TYPE  DAYS  MILES     AMOUNT

   233-43-2454     BEINHORN,CB                     I      2      44       $32.80

   987-65-4390     SMITH,PG                        I      3     150       $66.00

   677-84-4338     MCDONALD,J                      C      5     278      $100.04

   193-45-6789     SAMUELS,SH                      C      5     345      $112.10

   556-56-4365     HUMMER,MR                       C      8     225      $120.50
```

FIGURE 12.5 Records in Order of Computed Bill

files). *A merge achieves the same results as sorting, but more efficiently*. In other words, the several input files to a merge could be concatenated as a single input file to a sort which would also produce a single output file. The advantage of the merge over a sort is in execution speed; a merge will execute faster because its logic realizes that the several input files are already in order.

The format of the MERGE statement is as follows:

```
MERGE file-name-1

   ON {ASCENDING }  KEY data-name-1   [data-name-2] . . .
      {DESCENDING}

  [ON {ASCENDING }  KEY data-name-3   [data-name-4] . . .] . . .
      {DESCENDING}

   [COLLATING SEQUENCE IS alphabet-name]
   USING file-name-2 file-name-3 [file-name-4] . . .
  {GIVING file-name-5
  {OUTPUT PROCEDURE

       IS section-name-1 [{THROUGH} section-name-2] }
                          {THRU   }
```

File-name-1 must be specified in an SD. Rules for ASCENDING/DESCENDING KEY, COLLATING SEQUENCE, USING/GIVING, and OUTPUT PROCEDURE are identical to the SORT verb.

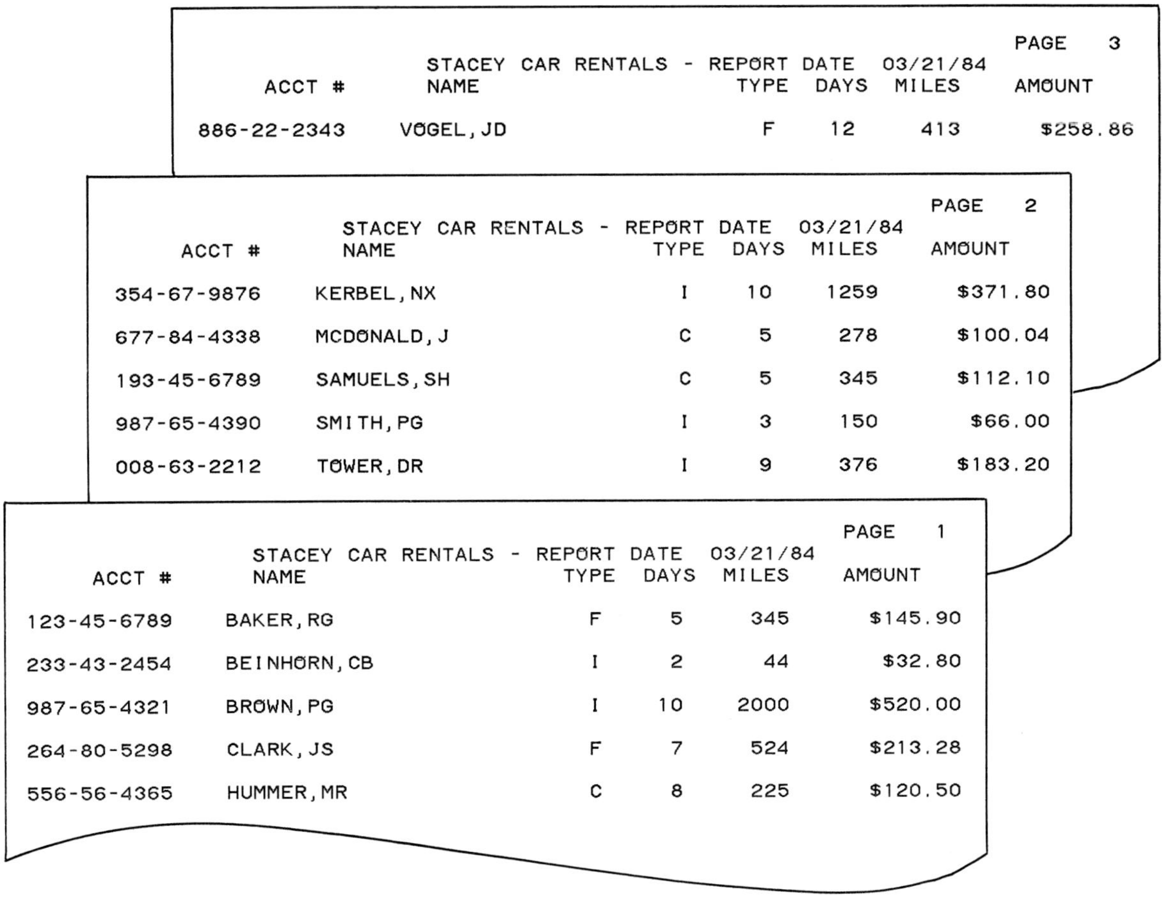

```
                                                                          PAGE   3
                        STACEY CAR RENTALS - REPORT DATE  03/21/84
     ACCT #             NAME                       TYPE  DAYS  MILES      AMOUNT

 886-22-2343       VOGEL,JD                          F     12     413      $258.86
```

```
                                                                          PAGE   2
                        STACEY CAR RENTALS - REPORT DATE  03/21/84
     ACCT #             NAME                       TYPE  DAYS  MILES      AMOUNT

 354-67-9876       KERBEL,NX                         I     10    1259      $371.80

 677-84-4338       MCDONALD,J                        C      5     278      $100.04

 193-45-6789       SAMUELS,SH                        C      5     345      $112.10

 987-65-4390       SMITH,PG                          I      3     150       $66.00

 008-63-2212       TOWER,DR                          I      9     376      $183.20
```

```
                                                                          PAGE   1
                        STACEY CAR RENTALS - REPORT DATE  03/21/84
     ACCT #             NAME                       TYPE  DAYS  MILES      AMOUNT

 123-45-6789       BAKER,RG                          F      5     345      $145.90

 233-43-2454       BEINHORN,CB                       I      2      44       $32.80

 987-65-4321       BROWN,PG                          I     10    2000      $520.00

 264-80-5298       CLARK,JS                          F      7     524      $213.28

 556-56-4365       HUMMER,MR                         C      8     225      $120.50
```

FIGURE 12.6 Records in Alphabetical Order

Unlike the SORT verb, there is no INPUT PROCEDURE option. The programmer must specify USING and list all files from which incoming records will be chosen. Hence *every* record in *every* file specified in USING will appear in the merged file. However, the user does have a choice between GIVING and OUTPUT PROCEDURE.

All files specified in a MERGE statement cannot be open when the statement is executed, as the MERGE operation implicitly opens them. In similar fashion, the files will be automatically closed by the MERGE.

An example of a MERGE statement follows:

```
MERGE WORK-FILE
   ON ASCENDING CUSTOMER-ACCOUNT-NUMBER
      DESCENDING AMOUNT-OF-SALE
   USING
      MONDAY-SALES-FILE
      TUESDAY-SALES-FILE
      WEDNESDAY-SALES-FILE
      THURSDAY-SALES-FILE
      FRIDAY-SALES-FILE
   GIVING
      WEEKLY-SALES-FILE.
```

WORK-FILE is defined in a COBOL SD. WEEKLY-SALES-FILE, MONDAY-SALES-FILE, TUESDAY-SALES-FILE, and so on are each specified in both FD and SELECT statements. These files must all be sequential and are both opened and closed by the merge operation.

The primary key is CUSTOMER-ACCOUNT-NUMBER (ascending), and the secondary key is AMOUNT-OF-SALE (descending). All records with the same account number will be grouped together with the highest sale for each account number listed first. Records with identical keys in one or more input files will be listed in the order in which the files appear in the MERGE statement itself. Hence, in the event of a tie on *both* account number and amount of sale, Monday's transactions will appear before Tuesday's, and so on.

COBOL 8X:

Changes and Enhancements

The most significant change pertaining to the SORT verb is that the INPUT and/or OUTPUT PROCEDURE may transfer control to points *outside* the procedure; for example, the INPUT PROCEDURE may perform a section outside the INPUT PROCEDURE. This in turn makes it possible to eliminate the forward GO TO statement when using INPUT or OUTPUT PROCEDURE. An additional change permits multiple file names to be mentioned in the GIVING phrase.

The RETURN verb has an optional scope terminator, END-RETURN, as well as a false condition branch, NOT AT END. (The significance of these features is explained in Appendix B, Structured Programming Enhancements in COBOL 8X.)

Summary

Sorting is an integral part of data processing. If the COBOL SORT verb is used to accomplish this task, four formats are possible. INPUT PROCEDURE/OUTPUT PROCEDURE and USING/GIVING were illustrated in Figures 12.3 and 12.4, respectively. INPUT PROCEDURE permits sorting on a calculated field; USING does not.

The chapter began with a definition of terms. Specifically, we discussed key, ascending *versus* descending *sorts, and* major *versus* minor *sorts. Next we covered the COBOL implementation of sorting to include the SORT, SD, RELEASE, and RETURN statements.*

We believe that you can readily adapt either Figure 12.3 or 12.4 to any problem with which you are confronted. As an additional aid, however, we list three basic rules associated with COBOL implementation. Should any of these points appear unclear, return to the examples in the chapter.

1. *File-name-1 of the SORT verb must be described in an SD. Further, each key (i.e., data name) appearing in the SORT verb must be described in the sort record.*
2. *If the USING/GIVING option is used, file-name-2 and file-name-3 each require an FD. The record sizes of file names 1, 2, and 3 must all be the same.*
3. *If INPUT PROCEDURE/OUTPUT PROCEDURE is used, both must be section names. The INPUT PROCEDURE must contain a RELEASE statement to transfer records to the sort; the OUTPUT PROCEDURE must contain a RETURN statement to read the sorted data.*

True/False Exercises

1. The SORT verb cannot be used on a calculated field.
2. If USING is specified in the SORT verb, then GIVING must also be specified.
3. If INPUT PROCEDURE is specified in the SORT verb, then OUTPUT PROCEDURE is also required.
4. Only one ascending and one descending key are permitted in the SORT verb.
5. *Major sort* and *primary sort* are synonymous.
6. *Minor sort* and *secondary sort* are synonymous.
7. RELEASE and RETURN are associated with the USING/GIVING option.
8. RELEASE is present in the INPUT PROCEDURE.
9. RETURN is specified in the OUTPUT PROCEDURE.
10. Both the INPUT and OUTPUT PROCEDURES must be paragraph names.
11. If a record is "released," it is written to the sort file.
12. If a record is "returned," it is read from the sort file.
13. If USING/GIVING is used, the sorted file *must* contain every record in the input file.
14. If INPUT PROCEDURE/OUTPUT PROCEDURE is used, the sorted file must contain *every* record in the input file.
15. XYZ will always come before 123 in an alphanumeric sort.
16. ADAMS will always appear before ADAMSON, regardless of collating sequence.
17. The file specified immediately after the word MERGE must be defined in an MD rather than an SD.
18. The MERGE verb can specify INPUT PROCEDURE/OUTPUT PROCEDURE.
19. The MERGE verb can specify USING/GIVING.
20. The MERGE verb can be applied to input files with different record layouts.

Problems

1. Given the following data:

NAME	*LOCATION*	*DEPARTMENT*
Milgrom	New York	1000
Samuel	Boston	2000
Isaac	Boston	2000
Chandler	Chicago	2000
Lavor	Los Angeles	1000
Elsinor	Chicago	1000
Tater	New York	2000
Craig	New York	2000
Borow	Boston	2000
Kenneth	Boston	2000
Renaldi	Boston	1000
Gulfman	Chicago	1000

rearrange the data according to the following sorts:

(a) Major field: department (descending); minor field: name (ascending).
(b) Primary field: department; secondary field: location; tertiary field: name.

Note: If neither ascending nor descending is specified, an ascending sequence should be used.

2. Given the statement

```
SORT SORT-FILE
    ASCENDING KEY STUDENT-MAJOR
    DESCENDING YEAR-IN-SCHOOL
    ASCENDING STUDENT-NAME
USING FILE-ONE
GIVING FILE-TWO.
```

   (a) What is the major key?
   (b) What is the minor key?
   (c) Which file will be specified in an SD?
   (d) Which file will contain the sorted output?
   (e) Which file(s) will be specified in a SELECT?
   (f) Which file contains the input data?
   (g) Which file must contain the data names STUDENT-NAME, YEAR-IN-SCHOOL, and STUDENT-MAJOR?

3. The following code is intended to sort a file of employee records in order of age, listing the oldest first:

```
FD  EMPLOYEE-FILE
     .
      .
       .
01  EMPLOYEE-RECORD.
    05  EMP-NAME                PIC X(25).
    05  EMP-BIRTH-DATE.
        10  EMP-BIRTH-MONTH     PIC 99.
        10  EMP-BIRTH-YEAR      PIC 99.
    05  FILLER                  PIC X(51).
SD  SORT-FILE
     .
      .
       .
01  SORT-RECORD.
    05  FILLER                  PIC X(20).
    05  SORT-BIRTH-DATE.
        10  SORT-BIRTH-MONTH    PIC 99.
        10  SORT-BIRTH-YEAR     PIC 99.
    05  FILLER                  PIC X(56).
     .
      .
       .
PROCEDURE DIVISION.
    SORT SORT-FILE
        DESCENDING KEY SORT-BIRTH-MONTH SORT-BIRTH-YEAR
        USING EMPLOYEE-FILE
        GIVING ORDERED-FILE.
```

   There are three distinct reasons why the intended code will not work. Find and correct the errors.

4. The registrar has asked for a simple report listing students by year, and alphabetically within year. Thus all freshmen are to appear first, followed by

all sophomores, juniors, seniors, and graduate students. The incoming record has the following layout:

```
01  STUDENT-RECORD.
    05  ST-NAME          PIC X(15).
    05  ST-MAJOR         PIC X(15).
    05  ST-YEAR          PIC XX.
    05  ST-CREDITS       PIC 99.
    05  ST-COLLEGE       PIC X(10).
```

The ST-YEAR field uses the following codes:

FR: Freshman
SO: Sophomore
JR: Junior
SR: Senior
GR: Graduate student

Develop the Procedure Division code to accomplish the desired sort. (It is not as easy as it looks.)

5. Given the statement

```
MERGE WORKFILE
   ASCENDING ACCOUNT-NUMBER
   DESCENDING AMOUNT-OF-SALE
USING
   JANUARY-SALES
   FEBRUARY-SALES
   MARCH-SALES
GIVING
   FIRST-QUARTER-SALES.
```

(a) Which file(s) are specified in an SD?
(b) Which file(s) are specified in an FD?
(c) Which file(s) contain the key ACCOUNT-NUMBER?
(d) What is the primary key?
(e) What is the secondary key?
(f) If a record on the JANUARY-SALES file has the identical ACCOUNT-NUMBER as a record on the FEBRUARY-SALES file, which record would come first on the merged file?
(g) If a record on the JANUARY-SALES file has the identical AMOUNT-OF-SALE as a record on the FEBRUARY-SALES file, which record would come first on the merged file?
(h) If a record on the JANUARY-SALES file has the identical AMOUNT-OF-SALE and ACCOUNT-NUMBER as a record on the FEBRUARY-SALES file, which record would come first on the merged file?

6. Indicate what is wrong with the following:

```
SD  SORT-WORK-FILE
    BLOCK CONTAINS 5 RECORDS
    RECORD CONTAINS 90 CHARACTERS
    LABEL RECORDS ARE STANDARD
    DATA RECORD IS SORT-RECORD.
01  SORT-RECORD     PIC X(90).
 .
  .
   .
PROCEDURE DIVISION.
```

```
MAINLINE SECTION.
    SORT SORT-WORK-FILE
        ON ASCENDING KEY SORT-LAST-NAME
    INPUT PROCEDURE PREPARE-SORT-RECORDS
    OUTPUT PROCEDURE PREPARE-REPORT.

PREPARE-SORT-RECORDS-SECTION.
    OPEN INPUT SORT-WORK-FILE.
.
 .
  .
PREPARE-REPORT SECTION.
.
 .
  .
    CLOSE SORT-WORK-FILE.
    STOP RUN.
```

7. Indicate the form of the SORT verb (USING, INPUT PROCEDURE, GIVING, OUTPUT PROCEDURE) that would most likely be used for the following applications:
   (a) Conversion of an incoming inventory file that has its part numbers in ASCII sequence to a new file, having its numbers in EBCDIC sequence.
   (b) Preparation of a report to select all graduating seniors (those with completed credits totaling 90 or more), listed in order of decreasing grade point average.
   (c) A data-validation program that reads unedited transactions, rejects those with invalid data, and prepares a sorted transaction file containing only valid records.
   (d) A program to prepare mailing labels in zipcode order from an incoming customer list.

8. Given the following COBOL definition:

```
05  TRANSACTION-DATE.
    05  TRANS-MONTH     PIC 99.
    05  TRANS-DAY       PIC 99.
    05  TRANS-YEAR      PIC 99.
```

   Write a portion of the SORT statement necessary to put transactions in sequence, with the earliest transaction listed first. Are there any problems in your solution when the century changes? Should you be concerned about those problems now?

9. The registrar of a major university requires an alphabetical list of graduating seniors. The report will be generated from the student master file which contains every student in the school, in social security number sequence.

   Two approaches have been suggested. The first uses the USING/GIVING option to sort the file alphabetically, after which the desired records are selected for inclusion in the report. The second selects the desired records in the INPUT PROCEDURE, after which the file is sorted and the report prepared in the OUTPUT PROCEDURE.

   Both approaches will produce a correct report. Is there any reason to choose one over the other?

Debugging Workshop

The program in Fig. 12.7 is intended to process a file of employee records and select all programmers, listing them in order of *decreasing* age. As can be seen from the output (Fig. 12.8), several errors occurred. In addition, the job was canceled by the operator because the program was in an infinite loop. Analyze and correct the errors.

1. Age is calculated incorrectly from the birth date, which prints correctly (the birth dates in Figure 12.8 are identical to those in the incoming data). Provide an explanation and a correction.

2. Employees are not listed by age, although the SORT attempted to list them by birth date. Provide an explanation and a correction.

3. The program went into an infinite loop the first time the employee being processed was *not* a programmer. Why?

```
00001          IDENTIFICATION DIVISION.
00002          PROGRAM-ID.     SORT1.
00003          AUTHOR.         JACKIE CLARK.
00004
00005          ENVIRONMENT DIVISION.
00006          CONFIGURATION SECTION.
00007          SOURCE-COMPUTER. IBM-4341.
00008          OBJECT-COMPUTER. IBM-4341.
00009
00010          INPUT-OUTPUT SECTION.
00011          FILE-CONTROL.
00012              SELECT EMPLOYEE-FILE
00013                  ASSIGN TO UT-S-SYSIN.
00014              SELECT PRINT-FILE
00015                  ASSIGN TO UT-S-SYSOUT.
00016              SELECT SORT-FILE
00017                  ASSIGN TO UT-S-SORTWK01.
00018              SELECT ORDERED-FILE
00019                  ASSIGN TO UT-S-SORTED.
00020
00021          DATA DIVISION.
00022          FILE SECTION.
00023          SD  SORT-FILE
00024              RECORD CONTAINS 80 CHARACTERS
00025              DATA RECORD IS SORT-RECORD.
00026          01  SORT-RECORD.
00027              05  FILLER          PIC X(35).
00028              05  SORT-MONTH      PIC 9(02).
00029              05  SORT-YEAR       PIC 9(02).
00030              05  FILLER          PIC X(41).
00031
00032          FD  EMPLOYEE-FILE
00033              LABEL RECORDS ARE OMITTED
00034              RECORD CONTAINS 80 CHARACTERS
00035              DATA RECORD IS EMPLOYEE-RECORD.
00036          01  EMPLOYEE-RECORD         PIC X(80).
00037
00038          FD  PRINT-FILE
00039              LABEL RECORDS ARE OMITTED
00040              RECORD CONTAINS 133 CHARACTERS
00041              DATA RECORD IS PRINT-LINE.
00042          01  PRINT-LINE             PIC X(133).
00043
00044          FD  ORDERED-FILE
00045              LABEL RECORDS ARE OMITTED
00046              RECORD CONTAINS 80 CHARACTERS
00047              DATA RECORD IS ORDERED-RECORD.
00048          01  SORTED-EMPLOYEE-RECORD  PIC X(80).
00049
00050          WORKING-STORAGE SECTION.
00051          01  WS-END-OF-DATA-FLAG    PIC XXX       VALUE SPACES.
00052          01  EMPLOYEE-AGE           PIC 99V9.
00053          01  PERCENT-SALARY-INCREASE PIC 99V9.
00054
```

FIGURE 12.7 Sort Program with Execution Errors

```
       01  WS-EMPLØYEE-RECØRD.
           05  WS-EMP-NAME.
               10  WS-LAST-NAME       PIC X(15).
               10  WS-FIRST-NAME      PIC X(09).
               10  WS-MIDDLE-INITIAL PIC X(1).
           05  WS-EMP-TITLE           PIC X(10).
           05  WS-DATE-ØF-BIRTH.
               10  WS-BIRTH-MØNTH     PIC 9(02).
               10  WS-BIRTH-YEAR      PIC 9(02).
           05  WS-PRESENT-SALARY      PIC 9(05).
           05  FILLER                 PIC X(04).
           05  WS-FØRMER-SALARY       PIC 9(05).
           05  FILLER                 PIC X(27).

       01  DATE-WØRK-AREA.
           05  TØDAYS-MØNTH           PIC 99.
           05  TØDAYS-DAY             PIC 99.
           05  TØDAYS-YEAR            PIC 99.

       01  DASHED-LINE.
           05  FILLER                 PIC X(69)     VALUE ALL '-'.
           05  FILLER                 PIC X(64)     VALUE SPACES.

       01  HEADING-LINE.
           05  FILLER                 PIC X(10)      VALUE SPACES.
           05  FILLER                 PIC X(04)      VALUE 'NAME'.
           05  FILLER                 PIC X(07)      VALUE SPACES.
           05  FILLER                 PIC X(03)      VALUE 'AGE'.
           05  FILLER                 PIC X(04)      VALUE SPACES.
           05  FILLER                 PIC X(09)      VALUE 'BIRTHDATE'.
           05  FILLER                 PIC X(03)      VALUE SPACES.
           05  FILLER                 PIC X(08)      VALUE 'PRES SAL'.
           05  FILLER                 PIC X(03)      VALUE SPACES.
           05  FILLER                 PIC X(07)      VALUE 'ØLD SAL'.
           05  FILLER                 PIC X(03)      VALUE SPACES.
           05  FILLER                 PIC X(06)      VALUE '% INCR'.
           05  FILLER                 PIC X(66)      VALUE SPACES.

       01  DETAIL-LINE.
           05  FILLER                 PIC X(01)      VALUE SPACES.
           05  PRINT-LAST-NAME        PIC X(15).
           05  FILLER                 PIC X(05)      VALUE SPACES.
           05  PRINT-AGE              PIC 99.9.
           05  FILLER                 PIC X(05)      VALUE SPACES.
           05  PRINT-BIRTH-DAY.
               10  PRINT-MØNTH        PIC 9(02).
               10  FILLER             PIC X          VALUE '/'.
               10  PRINT-YEAR         PIC 9(02).
           05  FILLER                 PIC X(05)      VALUE SPACES.
           05  PRINT-PRESENT-SALARY PIC $99,999.
           05  FILLER                 PIC X(03)      VALUE SPACES.
           05  PRINT-FØRMER-SALARY  PIC $99,999.
           05  FILLER                 PIC X(05)      VALUE SPACES.
           05  PRINT-PERCENT-INCREASE PIC ZZ.9.
           05  FILLER                 PIC X(69)      VALUE SPACES.

       PRØCEDURE DIVISIØN.
       0010-MAINLINE-RØUTINE.
           SØRT SØRT-FILE
               ASCENDING KEY SØRT-MØNTH SØRT-YEAR
                   USING  EMPLØYEE-FILE
                   GIVING ØRDERED-FILE.

           ØPEN INPUT  ØRDERED-FILE
                ØUTPUT PRINT-FILE.
           ACCEPT DATE-WØRK-AREA FRØM DATE.
           PERFØRM 0040-WRITE-HEADINGS.
           READ ØRDERED-FILE INTØ WS-EMPLØYEE-RECØRD
               AT END MØVE 'YES' TØ WS-END-ØF-DATA-FLAG.
           PERFØRM 0020-PRØCESS-EMPLØYEE-RECØRDS
               UNTIL WS-END-ØF-DATA-FLAG = 'YES'.
           CLØSE ØRDERED-FILE
                 PRINT-FILE.
           STØP RUN.

       0020-PRØCESS-EMPLØYEE-RECØRDS.
           CØMPUTE EMPLØYEE-AGE
               = TØDAYS-YEAR - WS-BIRTH-YEAR
               + (TØDAYS-MØNTH - WS-BIRTH-MØNTH) / 12.
           CØMPUTE PERCENT-SALARY-INCREASE
```

```
                 = 100 * (WS-PRESENT-SALARY - WS-FORMER-SALARY)
                     / WS-FORMER-SALARY.
             IF WS-EMP-TITLE = 'PROGRAMMER'
                 MOVE SPACES                    TO PRINT-LINE
                 MOVE WS-EMP-NAME               TO PRINT-LAST-NAME
                 MOVE EMPLOYEE-AGE              TO PRINT-AGE
                 MOVE WS-BIRTH-MONTH            TO PRINT-MONTH
                 MOVE WS-BIRTH-YEAR             TO PRINT-YEAR
                 MOVE WS-PRESENT-SALARY         TO PRINT-PRESENT-SALARY
                 MOVE WS-FORMER-SALARY          TO PRINT-FORMER-SALARY
                 MOVE PERCENT-SALARY-INCREASE TO PRINT-PERCENT-INCREASE
                 WRITE PRINT-LINE FROM DETAIL-LINE AFTER ADVANCING 2 LINES.
             READ ORDERED-FILE INTO WS-EMPLOYEE-RECORD
                 AT END MOVE 'YES' TO WS-END-OF-DATA-FLAG.

         0040-WRITE-HEADINGS.
             MOVE SPACES TO PRINT-LINE.
             MOVE '              SALARY REPORT FOR PROGRAMMERS'
                 TO PRINT-LINE.
             WRITE PRINT-LINE AFTER ADVANCING PAGE.
             MOVE HEADING-LINE TO PRINT-LINE.
             WRITE PRINT-LINE AFTER ADVANCING 3 LINES.
             WRITE PRINT-LINE FROM DASHED-LINE AFTER ADVANCING 1 LINE.
```

FIGURE 12.7 ***(Continued)***

SALARY REPORT FOR PROGRAMMERS

NAME	AGE	BIRTHDATE	PRES SAL	OLD SAL	% INCR
DOE	19.1	01/43	$23,000	$21,000	9.5
JOHNSON	23.1	01/47	$23,000	$22,000	4.5
SAMSON	30.4	04/54	$10,000	$08,500	17.6
PERSNICKETTY II	26.5	05/50	$19,000	$16,000	18.7
MILGROM	30.5	05/54	$10,000	$08,650	15.6
SMITH	30.5	05/54	$15,000	$14,100	6.3
ADAMSON	34.5	05/58	$10,000	$08,500	17.6
WILCOX	23.5	06/47	$19,000	$17,500	8.5
LEVINE	24.5	06/48	$19,000	$17,500	8.5
LEE	27.9	10/51	$12,000	$11,000	9.0
CRAWFORD	22.0	11/45	$28,000	$25,000	12.0

FIGURE 12.8 ***Incorrect Output Produced by the Program of Figure 12.7***

Programming Specifications

Project 12–1

Program Name:

Grade Distributions Detail Listing

Narrative:

Prepare a detail report, listing every student, to support the summary data of Project 11–2.

Input File(s):

See Project 11–2.

Input Record Layout:

See Project 11–2.

Report Layout:

```
         0         1         2         3         4         5
1234567890123456789012345678901234567890123456789012345678901234567890
1
2                   GRADE DISTRIBUTION DETAIL LISTING
3
4          YEAR IN SCHOOL           STUDENT NAME           AGE        G.P.A.
5          --------------           ------------           ---        ------
6
7            XXXXXXXXX          XXXXXXXXXXXXXXXXXXXXX       99.9        9.99
8            XXXXXXXXX          XXXXXXXXXXXXXXXXXXXXX       99.9        9.99
9
10
```

Processing Requirements:

1. Process a file of student records. For every record read:
   (a) Calculate the student's age, GPA, and year in school according to the specifications in Project 11–2.
   (b) Print a detail line for every student according to the report layout. Single space detail lines.
2. Students are to appear in the printed report by year in school (freshmen first) and by age within year (youngest first).

Programming Specifications

Project 12–2

Program Name:

Employee Census (Management versus Nonmanagement)

Narrative:

This project will develop a program to sort an incoming employee file and produce two lists, of management and nonmanagement employees.

Input File:

EMPLOYEE-FILE

Input Record Layout:

```
01  EMPLOYEE-RECORD.
    05  EMP-NAME-AND-INITIALS        PIC X(20).
    05  EMP-TYPE                     PIC X.
    05  EMP-BIRTH-DATE.
        10  EMP-BIRTH-MONTH          PIC 99.
        10  EMP-BIRTH-YEAR           PIC 99.
    05  EMP-SALARY-DATA.
        10  EMP-PRESENT-SALARY       PIC 9(5).
        10  EMP-PREVIOUS-SALARY      PIC 9(5).
```

Test Data:

```
ADAMS, J         209572300020500
MILGROM, I       207582200000000
LEE, B           107583900037500
GROSSMAN, M      204572650024000
GROSSMAN, I      103592200000000
BOROW, J         107652980028000
JOHNSON, L       107643400030000
FRANKEL, L       103593750035000
MARSHAK, K       203612600023000
SUGRUE, P        212461800013000
MILGROM, I       107202900027500
```

Report Layout:

```
 1
 2                   EMPLOYEE CENSUS - MANAGEMENT
 3
 4       EMPLOYEE NAME           BIRTH DATE       PRESENT SALARY
 5
 6  XXXXXXXXXXXXXXXXXXXXXXXXX       Z9/99                $Z9,999
 7  XXXXXXXXXXXXXXXXXXXXXXXXX       Z9/99                $Z9,999
 8
 9
10       **** TOTAL NUMBER OF MANAGEMENT PERSONNEL = ZZ9
11
```

Processing Requirements:

1. Sort a file of employee records according to the management/nonmanagement code contained on each record. Employees with a 1 in the EMP-TYPE field are managers; employees with a 2 in this field are nonmanagers. Employees are to be listed alphabetically within each classification. Use the USING/GIVING option of the SORT verb.
2. After the file has been sorted, prepare two separate reports for management and nonmanagement employees. Each report is to begin on a new page; detail lines are to be single-spaced.
3. Print a total at the end of each report indicating the numbers of management and nonmanagement employees.

Programming Specifications

Project 12–3

Program Name:

Alternate Employee Census

Narrative:

This project uses the test data and record layout of the preceding project to develop an alternate form of the SORT verb, namely, INPUT PROCEDURE/OUTPUT PROCEDURE.

Input File:

Same as for Project 12–2.

Input Record Layout:

Same as for Project 12–2.

Test Data:

Same as for Project 12–2.

Report Layout:

Develop your own report layout, consistent with the programming specifications. Use appropriate heading line(s), and print all incoming and calculated fields in the detail line. No total line is required.

Processing Requirements:

1. Sort a file of employee records according to the percent salary increase earned by each employee. The percent salary increase is calculated as follows:

$$\text{Percent increase} = \frac{(\text{Present salary} - \text{Previous salary})}{\text{Previous salary}} * 100$$

   Some employees do not have a previous salary, which makes it impossible to calculate the percent salary increase. (Assume a zero percent increase for these individuals.)
2. Only nonmanagers (those with an EMP-TYPE field of 2) are to appear in the final report. Hence, in order to make the sort as efficient as possible (i.e., to sort as few records as possible), only qualified records are to be passed to sort. Do not include individuals who do not have a previous salary.

Report Writer

13

Overview

Report Writer is paradoxically one of the most powerful yet least used facilities in COBOL. Practitioners list several reasons for its disfavor, including:

1. *"I find Report Writer statements difficult to code and modify. . . ."*
2. *"Maintenance is impossible because no one in the shop knows it. What will happen when you leave. . . ?"*
3. *"I tried it, and it didn't work; it seems that the Report Writer modules of most COBOL compilers contain one or more bugs. . . ."*
4. *"I never learned it in school; I tried to teach myself from the vendor's manual but couldn't follow the discussion. . . ."*
5. *"I used it successfully a few times until my program ABENDed in the middle of Report Writer; debugging was a joke. . . ."*
6. *"I would like to try it, but it's not available on the compiler we have. . . ."*
7. *"I can't use it because my manager has banned it from the shop. . . ."*

These comments were made to the author during seminars to some 1,000 programmers in 40 cities during 1980 and 1981. The groups he addressed ranged in experience from six months to 15 years, and they form the basis for a very informal survey. Prior to the seminar approximately one person in 10 used Report Writer on a regular basis. However, after a two-hour lecture, upwards of 75% expressed serious interest in using the facility.

For the time being let us refute the preceding arguments simply by stating that Report Writer works and works well; that it is no more difficult to code, debug, and maintain than other COBOL statements; and that there is no reason not to use it. A more elegant argument in favor of Report Writer will be the three COBOL listings in the chapter itself.

We begin with a definition of terms associated with Report Writer, then progress immediately to a program for processing two levels of control breaks. (The requirements of this program will parallel those of the two-level program in Chapter 8. It is always interesting to compare students' reactions to the two approaches used in solving the problem.) We modify the program to process a third-level control break and substitute summary for detail reporting. We conclude with a third Report Writer program containing many fine points of the module.

The overall approach is to teach Report Writer through example, and to avoid becoming bogged down with syntax and other technical considerations. However, we do conclude with a more formal discussion of how Report Writer works and end with rigid presentation of the syntax. You should consult a vendor's reference manual for additional information. □

SYSTEM CONCEPTS

Report Writer is best used for problems involving control breaks. A *control break* is defined as a change in a designated field. For example, if an incoming file is sorted by location, and location is the control field, a control break occurs every time location changes. If the file is sorted by location, and by department within location, it is possible to designate two control fields, department and location.

Let us assume a file has been sorted on location and on department within location. Hence all employees in department 100 in Atlanta precede the Atlanta employees in department 200, who precede those in department 300, etc. Next come the employees in department 100 in Boston, followed by department 200 in Boston, and so forth. A single control break occurs as departments change within the *same* location, e.g., from department 100 in Atlanta to department 200 in Atlanta. A double control break, on location and department, arises when we go from department 300 in Atlanta to department 100 in Boston.

Our second definition has to do with the way Report Writer generates output. Every line in every report belongs to one of seven kinds of *report groups*. It is not necessary that a given report contain all seven report groups. Moreover, control headings, control footings, and detail report groups may occur more than once. The seven categories are:

1. *Report heading:* one or more lines appearing once at the beginning (initiation) of a report.
2. *Report footing:* one or more lines appearing once at the conclusion (termination) of a report.
3. *Page heading:* one or more lines appearing at the beginning of each page after the report heading.
4. *Page footing:* one or more lines appearing at the end of each page.
5. *Control heading:* one or more lines appearing before a control break, i.e., when the contents of a designated field change.
6. *Control footing:* one or more lines appearing after a control break.
7. *Detail:* one or more lines for each selected record.

A given report may contain multiple *control headings, footings,* and/or *detail* report groups. A report may *not* contain more than one report heading or report footing, or more than one page heading or page footing.

Figure 13.1 contains the output produced by our first illustrative program and at the same time clarifies these definitions. Note, in particular, the presence of a *page heading, control heading* on a location change, and *control footings* on both salesman and location.

EXAMPLE 1: TWO CONTROL BREAKS

We proceed immediately to a complete program to illustrate Report Writer. Specifications follow in the usual format.

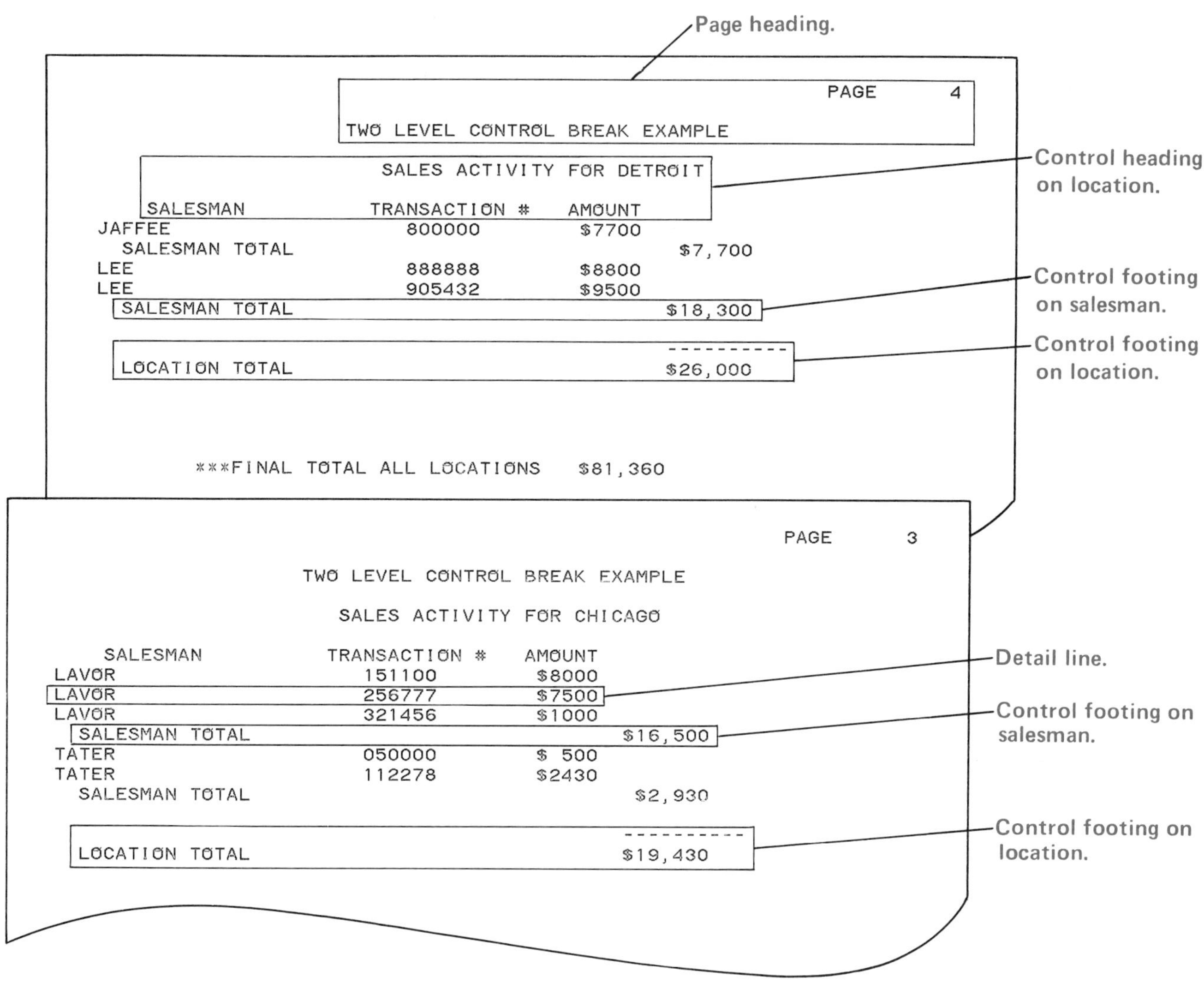

FIGURE 13.1 Output Produced by First Report Writer Program

Programming Specifications

Program Name:

Report Writer

Narrative:

This program introduces the salient features of Report Writer. It develops a two-level control break program with parallel requirements to the example in Chapter 8.

Input File:

SALES-FILE

Input Record Layout:

```
01  TRANSACTION-AREA.
    05  TR-SALESMAN-NAME          PIC X(20).
    05  TR-AMOUNT                 PIC S9(4).
```

```
05  FILLER                     PIC XX.
05  TR-NUMBER                  PIC X(6).
05  TR-TYPE                    PIC X.
05  TR-SALESMAN-REGION         PIC X(17).
05  TR-SALESMAN-LOCATION       PIC X(20).
05  FILLER                     PIC X(10).
```

Test Data:

```
ADAMS     8000  151100SATLANTIC     BOSTON
ADAMS     7500  256777SATLANTIC     BOSTON
BAKER     1000  321456SATLANTIC     NEW YORK
JONES     0500  050000SATLANTIC     NEW YORK
JONES     2430  112278SATLANTIC     NEW YORK
JONES     7700  800000SATLANTIC     NEW YORK
JONES     8800  888888SATLANTIC     NEW YORK
LAVOR     8000  151100SMIDWEST      CHICAGO
LAVOR     7500  256777SMIDWEST      CHICAGO
LAVOR     1000  321456SMIDWEST      CHICAGO
TATER     0500  050000SMIDWEST      CHICAGO
TATER     2430  112278SMIDWEST      CHICAGO
JAFFEE    7700  800000SMIDWEST      DETROIT
LEE       8800  888888SMIDWEST      DETROIT
LEE       9500  905432SMIDWEST      DETROIT
```

Report Layout:

See Figure 13.1.

Processing Requirements:

1. Process a file of sales records in order to obtain sales totals for each salesman, each location, and the company as a whole.
2. For each record read:
   (a) Print the sales information in that record on a detail line.
   (b) Increment the salesman total by the transaction amount.
3. Print an appropriate heading at the top of each page.
4. Whenever salesman changes, print the total sales figure for that salesman. Increment the location total by the salesman total. Reset the salesman total to zero.
5. Print an appropriate heading prior to the first transaction for each location. Begin each location on a new page.
6. Whenever location changes, print the total sales figure for that location. Increment the company total by the location total. Reset the location total to zero.
7. After all transactions have been read, print a total for the company as a whole.
8. The incoming data have been sorted by location and by salesman within location.

Data Division Requirements

The essence of Report Writer is to describe what a report should look like in the Data Division, rather than specify how it is generated in the Procedure Division. The happy consequence is that the latter is typically quite short, because much of the logic is generated automatically. The programmer is relieved of mundane tasks including page headings and footings, spacing, initializing, and reinitializing. Consider now Figure 13.2, the COBOL program that produced the output in Figure 13.1. At first its Data Division may appear unduly long and complex. In reality it is no longer than that of any meaningful COBOL program, with or without Report Writer.

A report is written to a file defined in a SELECT statement. The FD for this file contains an additional entry, REPORT IS (line 26 in Figure 13.2), which

```
00001          IDENTIFICATION DIVISION.
00002          PROGRAM-ID.  RWONE.
00003          AUTHOR.       JACKIE CLARK.
00004
00005          ENVIRONMENT DIVISION.
00006          CONFIGURATION SECTION.
00007          SOURCE-COMPUTER.     IBM-4341.
00008          OBJECT-COMPUTER.     IBM-4341.
00009          INPUT-OUTPUT SECTION.
00010          FILE-CONTROL.
00011              SELECT SALES-FILE
00012                  ASSIGN TO UT-S-SALES.
00013              SELECT PRINT-FILE
00014                  ASSIGN TO UT-S-REPORT.
00015
00016          DATA DIVISION.
00017          FILE SECTION.
00018          FD  SALES-FILE
00019              LABEL RECORDS ARE OMITTED
00020              BLOCK CONTAINS 0 RECORDS
00021              RECORD CONTAINS 80 CHARACTERS
00022              DATA RECORD IS SALES-RECORD.
00023          01  SALES-RECORD                     PIC X(80).
00024
00025          FD  PRINT-FILE
00026              REPORT IS CONTROL-BREAK
00027              LABEL RECORDS ARE OMITTED
00028              RECORD CONTAINS 133 CHARACTERS.
00029
00030          WORKING-STORAGE SECTION.
00031          01  FILLER                           PIC X(14)
00032                VALUE 'WS BEGINS HERE'.
00033          01  WS-DATA-FLAG                     PIC X(3)     VALUE SPACES.
00034
00035          01  TRANSACTION-AREA.
00036              05  TR-SALESMAN-NAME             PIC X(20).
00037              05  TR-AMOUNT                    PIC S9(4).
00038              05  FILLER                       PIC XX.
00039              05  TR-NUMBER                    PIC X(6).
00040              05  TR-TYPE                      PIC X.
00041              05  TR-SALESMAN-REGION           PIC X(17).
00042              05  TR-SALESMAN-LOCATION         PIC X(20).
00043              05  FILLER                       PIC X(10).
00044
00045          01  FILLER                           PIC X(12)
00046                VALUE 'WS ENDS HERE'.
00047
00048          REPORT SECTION.
00049          RD  CONTROL-BREAK
00050              CONTROLS ARE FINAL TR-SALESMAN-LOCATION TR-SALESMAN-NAME
00051              PAGE LIMIT 50 LINES
00052              HEADING 1
00053              FIRST DETAIL 5
00054              LAST DETAIL 45
00055              FOOTING 48.
00056
00057          01  TYPE IS PAGE HEADING.
00058              05  LINE NUMBER 1.
00059                  10  COLUMN NUMBER 61         PIC X(4)
00060                        VALUE 'PAGE'.
00061                  10  COLUMN NUMBER 66         PIC ZZZZZ9
00062                        SOURCE PAGE-COUNTER.
00063              05  LINE NUMBER PLUS 2.
00064                  10  COLUMN NUMBER 22         PIC X(31)
00065                        VALUE 'TWO LEVEL CONTROL BREAK EXAMPLE'.
00066
```

Identifies report name in subsequent RD.
Facilitates debugging in conjunction with READ INTO statements.
Fields designated as control breaks in Report Section.
Beginning of Report Section.
Report name matches entry in line 26.
Establishes control breaks.
Indicates absolute line number.

FIGURE 13.2 Report Writer Program

```
00067              01  TYPE IS CONTROL HEADING TR-SALESMAN-LOCATION.
00068                  05  LINE NUMBER 5.
00069                      10  COLUMN NUMBER 25         PIC X(18)
00070                          VALUE 'SALES ACTIVITY FOR'.
00071                      10  COLUMN NUMBER 44         PIC X(20)
00072                          SOURCE TR-SALESMAN-LOCATION.
00073                  05  LINE NUMBER 7.
00074                      10  COLUMN NUMBER 6          PIC X(8)
00075                          VALUE 'SALESMAN'.
00076                      10  COLUMN NUMBER 24         PIC X(13)
00077                          VALUE 'TRANSACTION #'.
00078                      10  COLUMN NUMBER 40         PIC X(7)
00079                          VALUE 'AMOUNT'.
00080
00081              01  TRANSACTION-LINE TYPE IS DETAIL.
00082                  05  LINE NUMBER PLUS 1.
00083                      10  COLUMN NUMBER 2          PIC X(20)
00084                          SOURCE TR-SALESMAN-NAME.
00085                      10  COLUMN NUMBER 27         PIC X(6)
00086                          SOURCE TR-NUMBER.
00087                      10  COLUMN NUMBER 41         PIC $ZZZ9
00088                          SOURCE TR-AMOUNT.
00089
00090              01  TYPE IS CONTROL FOOTING TR-SALESMAN-NAME.
00091                  05  LINE NUMBER PLUS 1.
00092                      10  COLUMN NUMBER 4          PIC X(15)
00093                          VALUE 'SALESMAN TOTAL'.
00094                      10  SALESMAN-TOTAL
00095                          COLUMN NUMBER 48         PIC $$$,$$9
00096                          SUM TR-AMOUNT.
00097
00098              01  TYPE IS CONTROL FOOTING TR-SALESMAN-LOCATION.
00099                  05  LINE NUMBER PLUS 2.
00100                      10  COLUMN NUMBER 48         PIC X(10)
00101                          VALUE ALL '-'.
00102                  05  LINE NUMBER PLUS 1.
00103                      10  COLUMN NUMBER 4          PIC X(14)
00104                          VALUE 'LOCATION TOTAL'.
00105                      10  LOCATION-TOTAL
00106                          COLUMN NUMBER 48         PIC $$$,$$9
00107                          SUM SALESMAN-TOTAL.
00108
00109              01  TYPE IS CONTROL FOOTING FINAL.
00110                  05  LINE NUMBER PLUS 5.
00111                      10  COLUMN NUMBER 10         PIC X(28)
00112                          VALUE '***FINAL TOTAL ALL LOCATIONS'.
00113                      10  COLUMN NUMBER 40         PIC $$$$,$$9
00114                          SUM LOCATION-TOTAL.
00115
00116              PROCEDURE DIVISION.
00117              0010-CREATE-REPORTS.
00118                  OPEN INPUT SALES-FILE
00119                       OUTPUT PRINT-FILE.
00120                  INITIATE CONTROL-BREAK.
00121                  READ SALES-FILE INTO TRANSACTION-AREA
00122                      AT END MOVE 'NO' TO WS-DATA-FLAG.
00123                  PERFORM 0020-PROCESS-ALL-TRANSACTIONS
00124                      UNTIL WS-DATA-FLAG = 'NO'.
00125                  TERMINATE CONTROL-BREAK.
00126                  CLOSE SALES-FILE
00127                        PRINT-FILE.
00128                  STOP RUN.
00129
00130              0020-PROCESS-ALL-TRANSACTIONS.
00131                  GENERATE TRANSACTION-LINE.
00132                  READ SALES-FILE INTO TRANSACTION-AREA
00133                      AT END MOVE 'NO' TO WS-DATA-FLAG.
```

Describes two fields on line 5.

Detail report group is referenced in GENERATE statement in line 131.

Control footing prints whenever a break occurs on TR-SALESMAN-NAME.

FINAL control footing prints at report termination.

INITIATE and TERMINATE reference report name in line 26.

GENERATE references detail report group of line 81.

FIGURE 13.2 (Continued)

specifies the name of the report. Note that there are no 01 entries for this FD, since the description of the file is handled in the Report Section. The entry in the REPORT IS clause has a corresponding RD (Report Description) in the Report Section (line 49) of the Data Division.

The CONTROLS clause (line 50 in Figure 13.2) identifies the control breaks as FINAL, TR-SALESMAN-LOCATION, and TR-SALESMAN-NAME. Subsequent specification of control headings and/or control footings will cause information to print before and/or after control breaks in these fields. Specification of CONTROL IS FINAL causes a control break at the end of the report. Note that the identifier(s) in the CONTROL clause, TR-SALESMAN-LOCATION and TR-SALESMAN-NAME, exist in each incoming record.

The remaining clauses of the RD physically describe the pages of the report. One can specify the maximum number of lines per page (PAGE LIMIT), the first line on which anything may be printed (HEADING), the first line for a detail (FIRST DETAIL), the last line for a control heading or detail (LAST DETAIL), and the last line for a footing (FOOTING).

The RD is followed by several 01 entries to describe report groups within that report (just as an FD is followed by 01 entries to describe records within a file). Recall that there are seven types of report groups. A given report need not contain all seven and can contain multiple entries for the same type report group. Figure 13.2, for example, does not contain either a page or report footing but does contain three control footings (lines 90, 98, and 109).

The most unusual aspect of Report Writer Data Division formats is that the *data name is optional*. Hence, when reading a Report Section for the first time, it is somewhat startling to find level numbers followed immediately by clauses other than data names. For example, there are six 01 entries in the Report Section of Figure 13.2, but only one includes a data name, TRANSACTION-LINE (line 81), and that is because of a requirement in a subsequent Procedure Division statement (GENERATE in line 131).

The TYPE clause is required for a 01 entry in the Report Section and cannot be specified at any other level. The program in Figure 13.2 contains six TYPE clauses, one for each report group. Consider, for example, the control heading for TR-SALESMAN-LOCATION (COBOL lines 67–79). It begins with a TYPE clause (line 67) to identify the nature of the report group. It in turn consists of two lines of output, which print every time there is a control break on TR-SALESMAN-LOCATION. The first line will appear on line 5 of the page. This in turn is a group entry, consisting of two fields beginning in columns 25 and 44. The second group item of the control heading specifies line 7 and in turn has 3 elementary items, beginning in columns 6, 24, and 40.

The value of an elementary item is obtained in one of three ways: by the SOURCE, VALUE, or SUM clauses. Specification of SOURCE, e.g., SOURCE IS TR-SALESMAN-LOCATION (in line 72), causes the current value of TR-SALESMAN-LOCATION to be moved to the output field. Specification of VALUE, e.g., VALUE 'SALESMAN' (in line 75), moves a literal to the output field. Finally, specification of SUM, e.g., SUM TR-AMOUNT (line 96), causes Report Writer to increment SALESMAN-TOTAL (line 94) by the value of TR-AMOUNT for each generated record (see Procedure Division requirements).

When a control break occurs on TR-SALESMAN-NAME, the salesman total is *rolled forward* into the next highest level counter, i.e., into LOCATION-TOTAL (line 105). The control footing for TR-SALESMAN-NAME is presented, after which SALESMAN-TOTAL is reset to zero.

In similar fashion, when a control break occurs on TR-SALESMAN-LOCATION, the value of LOCATION-TOTAL (line 105) is *rolled forward* into the next highest level total, i.e., into the FINAL total (line 114). The control footing for TR-SALESMAN-LOCATION is presented, and LOCATION-TOTAL is reset to zero.

Procedure Division Requirements

The Procedure Division of Figure 13.2 is remarkably short and contains three new verbs: INITIATE, GENERATE, and TERMINATE, all uniquely associated with Report Writer.

INITIATE is used to begin processing of a given report. Execution of this statement initializes counters, totals, etc. Its syntax is simply

```
INITIATE report-name-1 [report-name-2] ...
```

The report name, CONTROL-BREAK, appearing in the INITIATE statement in line 120 matches the entry in the REPORT clause of the FD for PRINT-FILE (line 26). The report name also appears in the RD entry in the Report Section (line 49) in the Data Division.

The GENERATE statement (line 131) causes Report Writer to produce automatically any of the seven report groups where and when they are needed. It has the general syntax

```
GENERATE {report-name}
         {data-name  }
```

Two types of reporting are possible: *summary reporting,* in which only heading and footing groups are produced, and *detail reporting,* in which the detail report group named in the GENERATE statement is produced each time the statement is executed.

The GENERATE statement in Figure 13.2 calls for detail reporting by specifying the data name of a report group, TRANSACTION-LINE. (The latter was designated as a DETAIL report group in line 81.) Figure 13.4, shown later in this chapter, illustrates summary reporting.

The TERMINATE statement (line 125) completes report processing as if a control break at the highest level occurred. All footing groups up to the highest level are produced, all counters are reset, and report processing is ended. The statement has the syntax

```
TERMINATE report-name-1 [report-name-2] ...
```

EXAMPLE 2: THREE CONTROL BREAKS

The program in Figure 13.2 provided a rapid introduction to Report Writer. We continue with a second example designed (1) to integrate SORT and Report Writer and (2) to show the ease with which a Report Writer program can be modified. Three control breaks (on region, location, and salesman) are now required rather than two. In addition, it is no longer necessary to show all transactions for a given salesman, but only his or her total. Figure 13.3 shows a page from the modified report. It contains output corresponding to Figure 13.1 except that Chicago and Detroit have been combined into the Midwest region.

Sorting is accomplished within the program in Figure 13.4 through the SORT statement in lines 147–150:

```
SORT SORT-FILE
    ASCENDING KEY SORT-REGION SORT-LOCATION SORT-NAME
    USING SALES-FILE
    OUTPUT PROCEDURE 0008-REPORT.
```

Three sort keys are indicated, with SORT-REGION as the major (most important) and SORT-NAME as the minor (least important). The clause USING SALES-FILE indicates that SALES-FILE contains the records to be sorted and causes the SORT verb to do the necessary I/O. Hence SALES-FILE is opened, its records are released to sort, and the file is closed, all without programmer action.

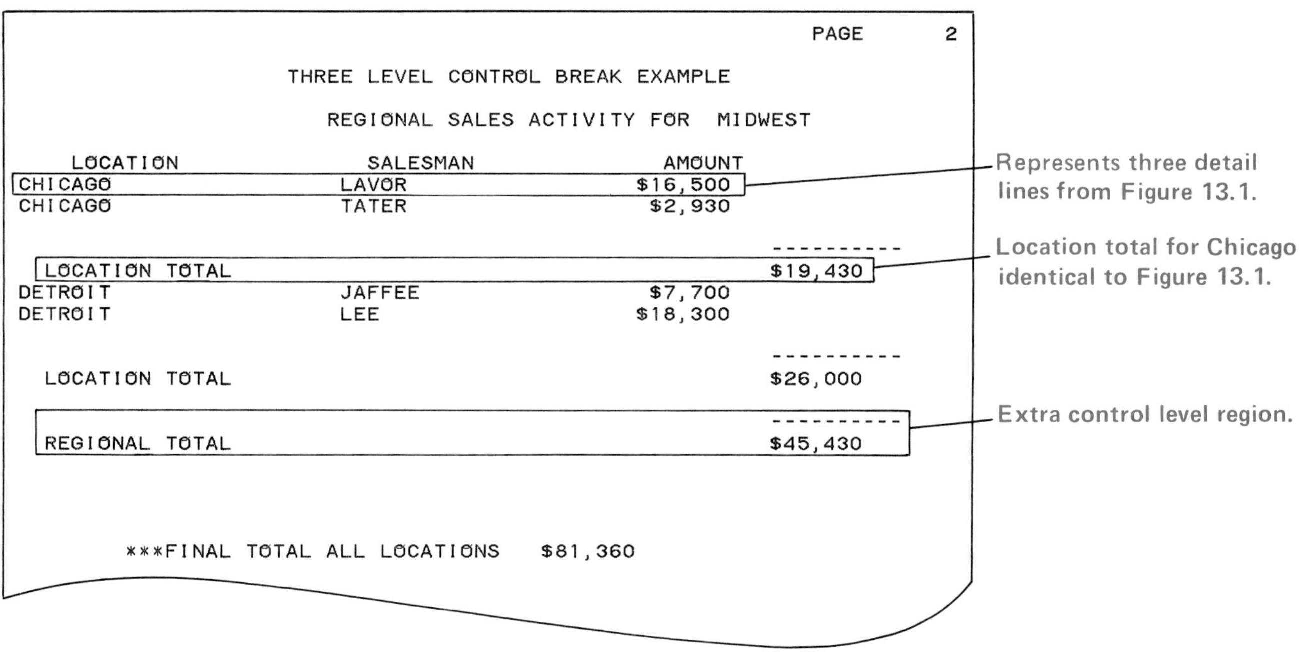

PAGE 2
THREE LEVEL CONTROL BREAK EXAMPLE
REGIONAL SALES ACTIVITY FOR MIDWEST
LOCATION SALESMAN AMOUNT
CHICAGO LAVOR $16,500
CHICAGO TATER $2,930

LOCATION TOTAL $19,430
DETROIT JAFFEE $7,700
DETROIT LEE $18,300

LOCATION TOTAL $26,000

REGIONAL TOTAL $45,430
***FINAL TOTAL ALL LOCATIONS $81,360
Represents three detail lines from Figure 13.1.
Location total for Chicago identical to Figure 13.1.
Extra control level region.

FIGURE 13.3 *Output from Three Level Control Break Program*

```
IDENTIFICATION DIVISION.
PROGRAM-ID.  RWTWO.
AUTHOR.       JACKIE CLARK.

ENVIRONMENT DIVISION.
CONFIGURATION SECTION.
SOURCE-COMPUTER.    IBM-4341.
OBJECT-COMPUTER.    IBM-4341.
INPUT-OUTPUT SECTION.
FILE-CONTROL.
    SELECT SORT-FILE
        ASSIGN TO UT-S-SORTWORK.
    SELECT SALES-FILE
        ASSIGN TO UT-S-SALES.
    SELECT PRINT-FILE
        ASSIGN TO UT-S-REPORT.

DATA DIVISION.
FILE SECTION.
FD  SALES-FILE
    LABEL RECORDS ARE OMITTED
    BLOCK CONTAINS 0 RECORDS
    RECORD CONTAINS 80 CHARACTERS
    DATA RECORD IS SALES-RECORD.
01  SALES-RECORD                      PIC X(80).

FD  PRINT-FILE
    REPORT IS CONTROL-BREAK
    LABEL RECORDS ARE OMITTED
    RECORD CONTAINS 133 CHARACTERS.

SD  SORT-FILE
    RECORD CONTAINS 80 CHARACTERS
    DATA RECORD IS SORT-RECORD.
01  SORT-RECORD.
    05  SORT-NAME                     PIC X(20).
    05  FILLER                        PIC X(13).
    05  SORT-REGION                   PIC X(17).
    05  SORT-LOCATION                 PIC X(20).
    05  FILLER                        PIC X(10).

WORKING-STORAGE SECTION.
01  FILLER                            PIC X(14)
      VALUE 'WS BEGINS HERE'.
01  WS-DATA-FLAG                      PIC X(3)    VALUE SPACES.
```

- SELECT statement required for sort work file.

FIGURE 13.4 *Modified Report Writer Program*

```
       01  TRANSACTION-AREA.
           05  TR-SALESMAN-NAME                PIC X(20).
           05  TR-AMOUNT                       PIC S9(4).
           05  FILLER                          PIC XX.
           05  TR-NUMBER                       PIC X(6).
           05  TR-TYPE                         PIC X.
           05  TR-SALESMAN-REGION              PIC X(17).
           05  TR-SALESMAN-LOCATION            PIC X(20).
           05  FILLER                          PIC X(10).
       01  FILLER                              PIC X(12)
             VALUE 'WS ENDS HERE'.
       REPORT SECTION.
       RD  CONTROL-BREAK
           CONTROLS ARE FINAL
                        TR-SALESMAN-REGION
                        TR-SALESMAN-LOCATION
                        TR-SALESMAN-NAME
           PAGE LIMIT 50 LINES
           HEADING 1
           FIRST DETAIL 5
           LAST DETAIL 45
           FOOTING 48.
       01  TYPE IS PAGE HEADING.
           05  LINE NUMBER 1.
               10  COLUMN NUMBER 61            PIC X(4)
                     VALUE 'PAGE'.
               10  COLUMN NUMBER 66            PIC ZZZZZ9
                     SOURCE PAGE-COUNTER.
           05  LINE NUMBER PLUS 2.
               10  COLUMN NUMBER 22            PIC X(33)
                     VALUE 'THREE LEVEL CONTROL BREAK EXAMPLE'.
       01  TYPE IS CONTROL HEADING TR-SALESMAN-REGION.
           05  LINE NUMBER 5.
               10  COLUMN NUMBER 25            PIC X(27)
                     VALUE 'REGIONAL SALES ACTIVITY FOR'.
               10  COLUMN NUMBER 54            PIC X(20)
                     SOURCE TR-SALESMAN-REGION.
           05  LINE NUMBER 7.
               10  COLUMN NUMBER 6             PIC X(8)
                     VALUE 'LOCATION'.
               10  COLUMN NUMBER 28            PIC X(15)
                     VALUE 'SALESMAN'.
               10  COLUMN NUMBER 50            PIC X(7)
                     VALUE 'AMOUNT'.
       01  TRANSACTION-LINE TYPE IS DETAIL.
           05  LINE NUMBER PLUS 1.
               10  COLUMN NUMBER 2             PIC X(20)
                     SOURCE TR-SALESMAN-NAME.
               10  COLUMN NUMBER 27            PIC X(6)
                     SOURCE TR-NUMBER.
               10  COLUMN NUMBER 41            PIC $ZZZ9
                     SOURCE TR-AMOUNT.
       01  TYPE IS CONTROL FOOTING TR-SALESMAN-NAME.
           05  LINE NUMBER PLUS 1.
               10  COLUMN NUMBER 2             PIC X(15)
                     SOURCE TR-SALESMAN-LOCATION.
               10  COLUMN NUMBER 26            PIC X(20)
                     SOURCE TR-SALESMAN-NAME.
               10  SALESMAN-TOTAL
                   COLUMN NUMBER 48            PIC $$$,$$9
                     SUM TR-AMOUNT.
       01  TYPE IS CONTROL FOOTING TR-SALESMAN-LOCATION.
           05  LINE NUMBER PLUS 2.
               10  COLUMN NUMBER 58            PIC X(10)
                     VALUE ALL '-'.
           05  LINE NUMBER PLUS 1.
               10  COLUMN NUMBER 4             PIC X(14)
                     VALUE 'LOCATION TOTAL'.
               10  LOCATION-TOTAL
                   COLUMN NUMBER 58            PIC $$$,$$9
                     SUM SALESMAN-TOTAL.
```

TR-SALESMAN-REGION has been added as a control field.

Control heading on region has been added.

```
00125
00126         01  TYPE IS CONTROL FOOTING TR-SALESMAN-REGION.
00127             05  LINE NUMBER PLUS 2.
00128                 10  COLUMN NUMBER 58           PIC X(10)
00129                     VALUE ALL '-'.
00130             05  LINE NUMBER PLUS 1.
00131                 10  COLUMN NUMBER 4            PIC X(14)
00132                     VALUE 'REGIONAL TOTAL'.
00133                 10  REGION-TOTAL
00134                     COLUMN NUMBER 58           PIC $$$,$$9
00135                     SUM LOCATION-TOTAL.
00136
00137         01  TYPE IS CONTROL FOOTING FINAL.
00138             05  LINE NUMBER PLUS 5.
00139                 10  COLUMN NUMBER 10           PIC X(28)
00140                     VALUE '***FINAL TOTAL ALL LOCATIONS'.
00141                 10  COLUMN NUMBER 40           PIC $$$$,$$9
00142                     SUM REGION-TOTAL.
00143
00144         PROCEDURE DIVISION.
00145         0000-SORT SECTION.
00146         0005-SORT.
00147             SORT SORT-FILE
00148                 ASCENDING KEY SORT-REGION SORT-LOCATION SORT-NAME
00149                 USING SALES-FILE
00150                 OUTPUT PROCEDURE 0008-REPORT.
00151                 STOP RUN.
00152
00153         0008-REPORT SECTION.
00154         0010-CREATE-REPORTS.
00155             OPEN OUTPUT PRINT-FILE.
00156             INITIATE CONTROL-BREAK.
00157             RETURN SORT-FILE INTO TRANSACTION-AREA
00158                 AT END MOVE 'NO' TO WS-DATA-FLAG.
00159             PERFORM 0020-PROCESS-ALL-TRANSACTIONS
00160                 UNTIL WS-DATA-FLAG = 'NO'.
00161             TERMINATE CONTROL-BREAK.
00162             CLOSE PRINT-FILE.
00163             GO TO 0030-SORT-EXIT.
00164
00165         0020-PROCESS-ALL-TRANSACTIONS.
00166             GENERATE CONTROL-BREAK.
00167             RETURN SORT-FILE INTO TRANSACTION-AREA
00168                 AT END MOVE 'NO' TO WS-DATA-FLAG.
00169
00170         0030-SORT-EXIT.
00171             EXIT.
```

Control footing on region has been added.
Sort keys are consistent with control breaks in lines 63-65.
Output procedure must be a section.
Report name implies summary reporting.

FIGURE 13.4 (Continued)

After the sort is completed, control passes to the *section* specified as the OUTPUT PROCEDURE. This in turn reads (i.e., returns) records from the sorted file and invokes Report Writer via INITIATE, GENERATE, and TERMINATE statements.

A second objective of Figure 13.4 is to demonstrate the ease with which changes can be made using Report Writer. The specifications have been amended to include a third control break on region. In addition, it is no longer necessary to show all transactions for a given salesman, but only his or her total.

The modifications in the program begin with specification of a control break on region (COBOL line 63). A control heading on region (line 82) is added to effect a page break on region, and the control heading on location from Figure 13.2 is eliminated. A control footing on region (line 126) is also added to achieve region totals. The GENERATE statement (line 166) reflects *summary* reporting by specifying the *report name,* CONTROL-BREAK, rather than a detail report group as was done in Figure 13.2. (The detail report group, lines 96–103, is *still required* even though summary reporting is performed.)

A single page of output was shown in Figure 13.3 for the MIDWEST region. The data reflected on this page are consistent with those in Figure 13.1. The three detail lines for LAVOR in Figure 13.1 have been replaced by a single summary line in Figure 13.3. The two location totals from Figure 13.1 have been grouped into a regional total in Figure 13.3. Finally, the page break is no longer on location (as in Figure 13.1) but on region.

EXAMPLE 3: FINER POINTS OF REPORT WRITER

We have seen two complete programs using Report Writer. The first was intended as an introduction, to demystify the subject, and to demonstrate that it could be learned easily. The second showed the ease of modifying existing Report Writer programs, and the parallel use of SORT. In this third and last example we illustrate some subtle features of the technique. Specifically, we include selective use of the GENERATE statement; the SUM UPON, GROUP INDICATE, NEXT GROUP, and RESET clauses; rolling totals forward; and the use of DECLARATIVES.

We return to the first program of the chapter and its associated output (Figure 13.1) and make the following changes:

1. The salesman's name is to appear *only once*, with the *first* transaction in the group. Detail lines are to be single-spaced, except for the first detail after a control footing, which is to be triple-spaced.
2. The *average* dollar amount per transaction is to be computed for each location. In addition, the number of transactions in each location is to be printed.
3. A *cumulative* total (within a location) is to appear every time a break on salesman occurs. (Individual salesman totals are no longer required.)
4. Only salesmen in Chicago and Detroit are to appear in the report.

A copy of the new output appears in Figure 13.5, and you may want to compare this figure to the previous report in Figure 13.1. Figure 13.6 contains the COBOL program that produced the modified report, and several items bear mention:

1. The GROUP INDICATE clause (line 88) specifies that an elementary item print only on the *first* occurrence after a control break. Hence the name LAVOR appeared only once in Figure 13.5, with the *first* of the three transactions associated with that salesman. GROUP INDICATE may appear only in a detail report group and must apply to an elementary item.
2. The NEXT GROUP clause (line 96) controls line spacing *after* the report group in which it is specified has been produced. In Figure 13.5 detail lines are single-spaced, *except for the first detail line after a control break on salesman, which is triple-spaced.* This is neatly accomplished by including NEXT GROUP in the control footing for salesman. The syntax of the NEXT GROUP clause is

```
                ⎧integer-1        ⎫
NEXT GROUP IS   ⎨PLUS integer-2   ⎬
                ⎩NEXT PAGE        ⎭
```

   indicating that the next group may begin on either a designated line or a new page.
3. The SUM UPON clause (line 111) is a convenient way to count the number of records in a file or within a control group. The SUM statement in line 111 specifies ONE, a data name that was defined and initialized to 1 in Working-Storage (line 46).

   The SUM UPON clause increments an internally defined counter by one (the value of ONE) every time the detail report group is generated.
4. The SUM RESET clause (line 102) prevents the automatic zeroing out of summation counters by telling Report Writer *when* the initialization is to take place. Recall

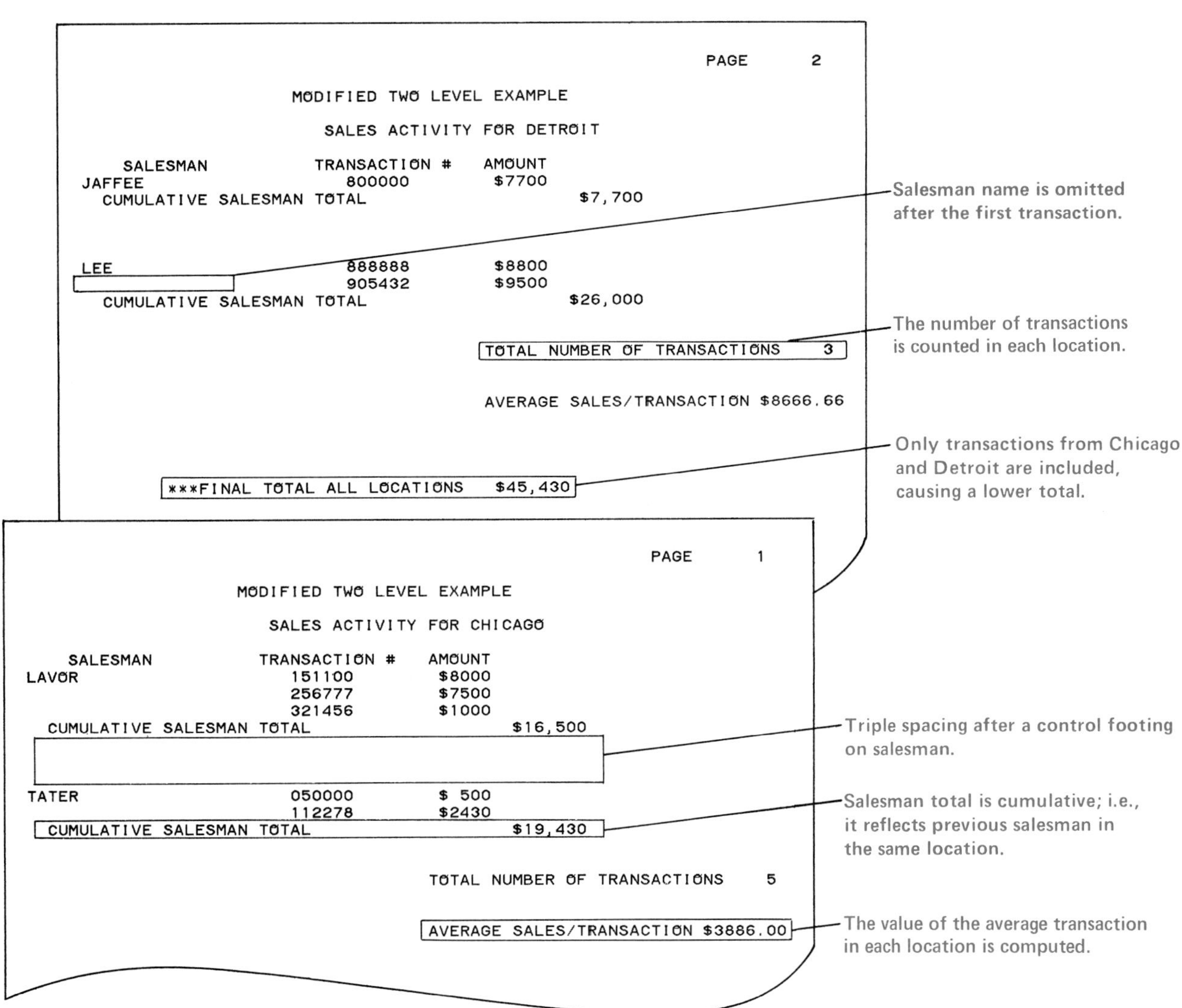

FIGURE 13.5 *Modified Output for Two Control Breaks*

```
IDENTIFICATION DIVISION.
PROGRAM-ID.  RWTHR.
AUTHOR.      JACKIE CLARK.

ENVIRONMENT DIVISION.
CONFIGURATION SECTION.
SOURCE-COMPUTER.    IBM-4341.
OBJECT-COMPUTER.    IBM-4341.
INPUT-OUTPUT SECTION.
FILE-CONTROL.
    SELECT SALES-FILE
        ASSIGN TO UT-S-SALES.
    SELECT PRINT-FILE
        ASSIGN TO UT-S-REPORT.

DATA DIVISION.
FILE SECTION.
FD  SALES-FILE
    LABEL RECORDS ARE OMITTED
    BLOCK CONTAINS 0 RECORDS
    RECORD CONTAINS 80 CHARACTERS
    DATA RECORD IS SALES-RECORD.
01  SALES-RECORD                     PIC X(80).

FD  PRINT-FILE
```

FIGURE 13.6 *Program Containing Finer Points of Report Writer*

```
00026              REPORT IS CONTROL-BREAK
00027              LABEL RECORDS ARE OMITTED
00028              RECORD CONTAINS 133 CHARACTERS.
00029
00030          WORKING-STORAGE SECTION.
00031          01  FILLER                              PIC X(14)
00032                VALUE 'WS BEGINS HERE'.
00033          01  WS-DATA-FLAG                        PIC X(3)     VALUE SPACES.
00034
00035          01  TRANSACTION-AREA.
00036              05  TR-SALESMAN-NAME                PIC X(20).
00037              05  TR-AMOUNT                       PIC S9(4).
00038              05  FILLER                          PIC XX.
00039              05  TR-NUMBER                       PIC X(6).
00040              05  TR-TYPE                         PIC X.
00041              05  TR-SALESMAN-REGION              PIC X(17).
00042              05  TR-SALESMAN-LOCATION            PIC X(20).
00043              05  FILLER                          PIC X(10).
00044
00045          01  PROGRAM-COUNTERS.
00046              05  ONE                             PIC 9(3)     VALUE 1.
00047              05  AVG-SALES-PER-TRANSACTION       PIC 9(4)V99.
00048
00049          01  FILLER                              PIC X(12)
00050                VALUE 'WS ENDS HERE'.
00051
00052          REPORT SECTION.
00053          RD  CONTROL-BREAK
00054              CONTROLS ARE FINAL TR-SALESMAN-LOCATION TR-SALESMAN-NAME
00055              PAGE LIMIT 50 LINES
00056              HEADING 1
00057              FIRST DETAIL 5
00058              LAST DETAIL 45
00059              FOOTING 48.
00060
00061          01  TYPE IS PAGE HEADING.
00062              05  LINE NUMBER 1.
00063                  10  COLUMN NUMBER 61            PIC X(4)
00064                         VALUE 'PAGE'.
00065                  10  COLUMN NUMBER 66            PIC ZZZZZ9
00066                         SOURCE PAGE-COUNTER.
00067              05  LINE NUMBER PLUS 2.
00068                  10  COLUMN NUMBER 22            PIC X(31)
00069                         VALUE 'MODIFIED TWO LEVEL EXAMPLE'.
00070
00071          01  TYPE IS CONTROL HEADING TR-SALESMAN-LOCATION.
00072              05  LINE NUMBER 5.
00073                  10  COLUMN NUMBER 25            PIC X(18)
00074                         VALUE 'SALES ACTIVITY FOR'.
00075                  10  COLUMN NUMBER 44            PIC X(20)
00076                         SOURCE TR-SALESMAN-LOCATION.
00077              05  LINE NUMBER 7.
00078                  10  COLUMN NUMBER 6             PIC X(8)
00079                         VALUE 'SALESMAN'.
00080                  10  COLUMN NUMBER 24            PIC X(13)
00081                         VALUE 'TRANSACTION #'.
00082                  10  COLUMN NUMBER 40            PIC X(7)
00083                         VALUE 'AMOUNT'.
00084
00085          01  TRANSACTION-LINE TYPE IS DETAIL.
00086              05  LINE NUMBER PLUS 1.
00087                  10  COLUMN NUMBER 2             PIC X(20)
00088                         GROUP INDICATE
00089                         SOURCE TR-SALESMAN-NAME.
00090                  10  COLUMN NUMBER 27            PIC X(6)
00091                         SOURCE TR-NUMBER.
00092                  10  COLUMN NUMBER 41            PIC $ZZZ9
00093                         SOURCE TR-AMOUNT.
00094
00095          01  TYPE IS CONTROL FOOTING TR-SALESMAN-NAME
00096              NEXT GROUP IS PLUS 3.
00097              05  LINE NUMBER PLUS 1.
00098                  10  COLUMN NUMBER 4             PIC X(27)
00099                         VALUE 'CUMULATIVE SALESMAN TOTAL'.
00100                  10  CUM-SALESMAN-TOTAL
00101                      COLUMN NUMBER 48            PIC $$$,$$9
00102                         SUM TR-AMOUNT RESET ON TR-SALESMAN-LOCATION.
00103
00104          01  LOCATION-TOTAL-LINE
00105              TYPE IS CONTROL FOOTING TR-SALESMAN-LOCATION.
```

Line 00046 (05 ONE … VALUE 1.): Used in SUM UPON clause in line 111.

Line 00088 (GROUP INDICATE): Suppresses printing of elementary item after the first detail line in a control group.

Line 00096 (NEXT GROUP IS PLUS 3.): Causes triple spacing after this report group.

Line 00102 (SUM TR-AMOUNT RESET ON TR-SALESMAN-LOCATION.): RESET clause produces cumulative totals.

```
00106            05  LINE NUMBER PLUS 3.
00107                10  COLUMN NUMBER 40          PIC X(29)
00108                      VALUE 'TOTAL NUMBER OF TRANSACTIONS'.
00109                10  TRANSACTIONS-IN-LOCATION
00110                    COLUMN NUMBER 70          PIC Z(3)
00111                      SUM ONE UPON TRANSACTION-LINE.
00112            05  LINE NUMBER PLUS 3.
00113                10  COLUMN NUMBER 40          PIC X(26)
00114                      VALUE 'AVERAGE SALES/TRANSACTION '.
00115                10  COLUMN NUMBER 66          PIC $$$$9.99
00116                      SOURCE AVG-SALES-PER-TRANSACTION.
00117
00118        01  TYPE IS CONTROL FOOTING FINAL.
00119            05  LINE NUMBER PLUS 5.
00120                10  COLUMN NUMBER 10          PIC X(28)
00121                      VALUE '***FINAL TOTAL ALL LOCATIONS'.
00122                10  COLUMN NUMBER 40          PIC $$$$,$$9
00123                      SUM TR-AMOUNT.
00124
00125        PROCEDURE DIVISION.
00126        DECLARATIVES.
00127        A-COMPUTE-LOCATION-AVERAGE SECTION.
00128            USE BEFORE REPORTING LOCATION-TOTAL-LINE.
00129
00130        A010-COMPUTE-LOCATION-AVERAGE.
00131            DIVIDE CUM-SALESMAN-TOTAL BY TRANSACTIONS-IN-LOCATION
00132                GIVING AVG-SALES-PER-TRANSACTION.
00133        END DECLARATIVES.
00134
00135        B-MAINLINE SECTION.
00136        B010-CREATE-REPORTS.
00137            OPEN INPUT SALES-FILE
00138                OUTPUT PRINT-FILE.
00139            INITIATE CONTROL-BREAK.
00140            READ SALES-FILE INTO TRANSACTION-AREA
00141                AT END MOVE 'NO' TO WS-DATA-FLAG.
00142            PERFORM B020-PROCESS-ALL-TRANSACTIONS
00143                UNTIL WS-DATA-FLAG = 'NO'.
00144            TERMINATE CONTROL-BREAK.
00145            CLOSE SALES-FILE
00146                  PRINT-FILE.
00147            STOP RUN.
00148
00149        B020-PROCESS-ALL-TRANSACTIONS.
00150            IF TR-SALESMAN-LOCATION = 'CHICAGO' OR 'DETROIT'
00151                GENERATE TRANSACTION-LINE.
00152            READ SALES-FILE INTO TRANSACTION-AREA
00153                AT END MOVE 'NO' TO WS-DATA-FLAG.
```

Adds 1 to the value of TRANSACTIONS-IN-LOCATION as defined in line 109.

DECLARATIVES comes at the beginning of the Procedure Division.

USE statement references a report group defined in line 104.

Terminates DECLARATIVE procedures.

FIGURE 13.6 (Continued)

that the original program in Figure 13.2 produced both salesman and location totals. Two SUM clauses were coded, and the associated counters were reset to zero at the appropriate time.

In this example a *cumulative* location total is required for a control break on salesman; in other words, the salesman total should print as a *running* total and not be continually reset to zero. The RESET clause indicates that the associated SUM counter is to be reinitialized to zero only when location changes. (RESET must reference a *higher* level of control than the control group in which it is coded, which is consistent with the concept of a cumulative total.)

5. DECLARATIVES (lines 126–133) are used to define procedures that are executed as a result of some condition that cannot be tested using regular language elements. If declarative procedures are used, they must be coded together at the beginning of the Procedure Division, be assigned *section* names, and appear between the headers DECLARATIVES and END DECLARATIVES.

   The USE BEFORE REPORTING statement in line 128 causes the *declarative section* to be executed before producing the control footing report group, LOCATION-TOTAL-LINE. It in turn contains the logic necessary to determine the average sale per transaction within a given location.

   A declaratives procedure may contain any COBOL verb except INITIATE, GENERATE, or TERMINATE. In addition, PERFORM statements within declaratives may not reference nondeclarative procedures; nor can declarative procedures be referenced in the nondeclarative portion of the Procedure Division.

Declarative procedures are discussed further in Chapter 15, in conjunction with indexed files.

6. GENERATE (lines 150 and 151) is used selectively. It is possible, and indeed commonplace, to include records in a report selectively. This is accomplished by making GENERATE the object of an IF statement, as was done in Figure 13.6.

HOW REPORT WRITER WORKS

The author believes that the programs in Figures 13.2, 13.4, and 13.6 are very effective in teaching fundamentals of Report Writer. Nevertheless, the practicing programmer or advanced student may feel a need for a better understanding of the internal workings of the module. To that end, we include a more technical discussion of the GENERATE statement. The user is referred to the vendor's reference manual (e.g., *VS COBOL for OS/VS,* GC26-3857) for additional information.

The GENERATE statement produces a report as specified in the Report Section. As was shown previously, one obtains *either detail or summary reporting* by specifying a data or report name, respectively. The action of the GEN-

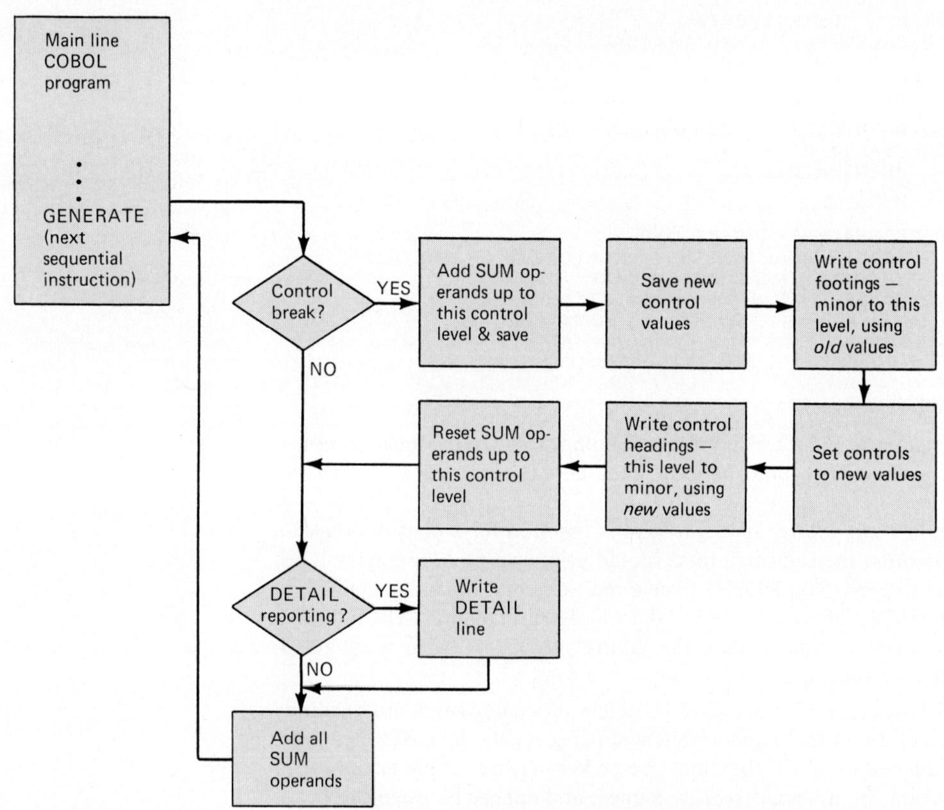

FIGURE 13.7 Action of Subsequent GENERATE Statements. (Courtesy of IBM Corporation.) Note: If a USE BEFORE REPORTING DECLARATIVE is specified, it is executed just before its associated control group is produced, whether or not a control break or page break occurred.

ERATE statement is the key to understanding how Report Writer works. Its *initial* execution causes the following events to occur in order:

1. REPORT HEADING report group (if specified) is produced.
2. PAGE HEADING report group (if specified) is produced.
3. CONTROL HEADINGs are produced in the order FINAL, major, intermediate, minor.
4. The DETAIL report group is produced, provided detail reporting was requested (i.e., a data name was specified in the GENERATE statement).

The action of *subsequent* GENERATE statements is described with the aid of Figure 13.7. The sequence of operations is as follows:

1. If a control break is detected, SUM counters are incremented, control footings are produced using *old* control values, new control values are stored, control headings are written with the *new* control values, and the SUM clauses are reset. (Any specified declarative procedures are executed before the associated report group is produced.)
2. Detail report groups are produced if necessary, i.e., if a data name was specified in the GENERATE statement.

Realize also that specification of the PAGE clause within the report RD causes additional processing to take place before each printable report group is produced. This is detailed in Figure 13.8 on page 356.

REPORT WRITER SYNTAX

The author's technique is to teach by example. Occasionally, however, questions arise that can only be answered by consulting the Reference Manual. To that end, various syntactical elements have been extracted to provide additional information.

TYPE Clause

The TYPE clause *must* be specified for a 01 entry in the Report Section. It has the following syntax:

```
            ⎧ {REPORT HEADING}                          ⎫
            ⎪ {RH            }                          ⎪
            ⎪                                           ⎪
            ⎪ {PAGE HEADING}                            ⎪
            ⎪ {PH          }                            ⎪
            ⎪                                           ⎪
            ⎪ {CONTROL HEADING} {FINAL       }          ⎪
            ⎪ {CH             } {identifier-n}          ⎪
            ⎪                                           ⎪
TYPE IS     ⎨ {DETAIL}                                  ⎬
            ⎪ {DE    }                                  ⎪
            ⎪                                           ⎪
            ⎪ {CONTROL FOOTING} {identifier-n}          ⎪
            ⎪ {CF             } {FINAL       }          ⎪
            ⎪                                           ⎪
            ⎪ {PAGE FOOTING}                            ⎪
            ⎪ {PF          }                            ⎪
            ⎪                                           ⎪
            ⎪ {REPORT FOOTING}                          ⎪
            ⎩ {RF            }                          ⎭
```

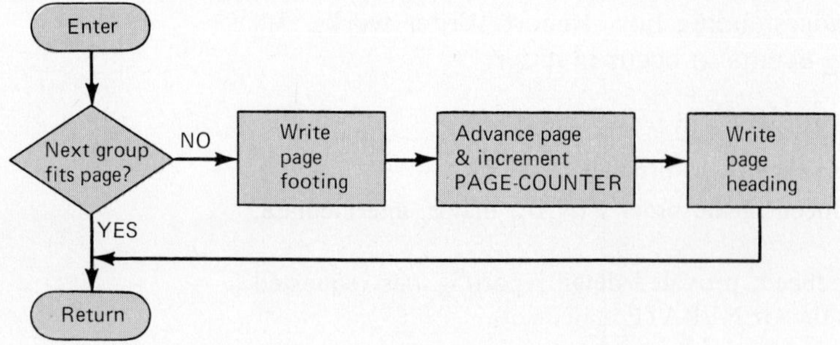

FIGURE 13.8 Effect of the PAGE Clause

Although the options are self-explanatory, Table 13.1 further summarizes the nature of each report group.

RD (Report Description)

The RD (Report Description) has the following format:

```
RD report-name
   [WITH CODE mnemonic-name]

   [{CONTROL IS  } [FINAL] identifier-1 [identifier-2] ...]
   [{CONTROLS ARE}                                        ]

   [{PAGE [LIMIT IS  ] integer-1 {LINE }
   [{     [LIMITS ARE]           {LINES}

        [HEADING        integer-2]
        [FIRST DETAIL   integer-3]
        [LAST DETAIL    integer-4]

        [FOOTING         integer-5]]
```

The CODE clause specifies an identifying character placed at the beginning of each report line and is meaningful only when multiple reports are written to the same file. It is not covered further. The CONTROL clause references the order of the control breaks and has been adequately discussed earlier in the chapter.

The PAGE LIMIT clause, described in Figure 13.9, establishes the physical characteristics of a report by specifying where each report group should appear. Although various defaults are assumed for integers 1 through 5, you are advised to code all entries explicitly.

Report Groups

A report group consists of one or more printable lines that are treated as a unit. Four general syntaxes are possible as shown by Figure 13.10. Examples of the various formats have appeared earlier in the illustrative programs.

TABLE 13.1 Report Group Types

TYPE	NUMBER OF GROUPS PER REPORT	CRITERIA FOR PRINTING
Report heading (RH)	Maximum of 1 per report	Printed once, before any other groups, at the beginning of the report
Page heading (PH)	Maximum of 1 per report	Printed at the beginning of each page before all other groups except the report heading group
Control heading (CH)	Maximum of 1 per identifier (including FINAL) named in the CONTROL clause	Printed at the beginning of a control group for a designated identifier or, in the case of FINAL, before the first control group
Detail (DE)	No limit, but each detail group must have a unique 01-level data name	Printed with each execution of the GENERATE statement, provided detail reporting was requested
Control footing (CF)	Maximum of 1 per identifier (including FINAL) named in the CONTROL clause	Printed at the end of a control group for a designated identifier
Page footing (PF)	Maximum of 1 per report	Printed at the end of each page after all other groups, except the report footing group
Report footing (RF)	Maximum of 1 per report	Printed at the termination of the report, after all other groups

- Format 1 specifies the beginning of a report group and is the first entry of any group.
- Format 2 establishes the line numbers of subordinate entries and groups subordinate elementary items together, e.g., listing several entries on a single line.
- Format 3 denotes an elementary item and is probably the most common. It has numerous options and subtleties, which have been depicted.
- Format 4 describes a report group consisting of a single elementary item.

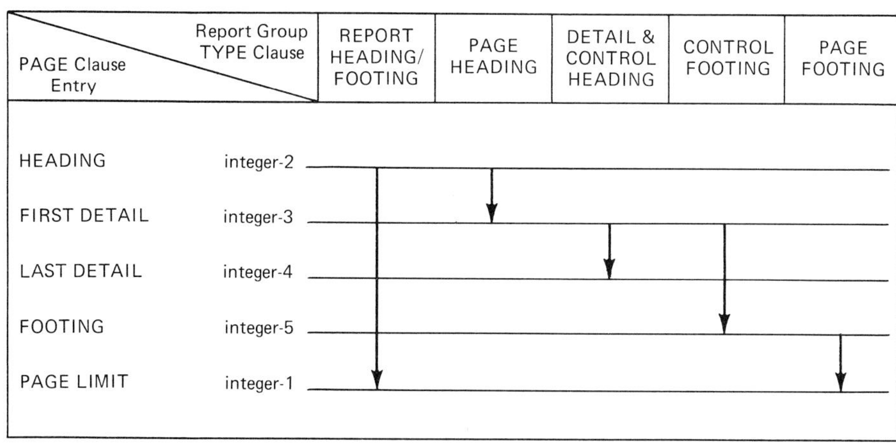

FIGURE 13.9 Effects of the PAGE Clause (Courtesy of IBM Corporation.)

General Format 1: level-01 Group Entry

```
01  [data-name]
    TYPE Clause
    [LINE Clause]
    [NEXT GROUP Clause]
    [USAGE Clause].
```

General Format 2: Group Entry

```
level-number [data-name]
    [LINE Clause]
    [USAGE Clause].
```

General Format 3: Elementary Entry

```
level-number [data-name]
    [COLUMN NUMBER IS integer]
    [GROUP INDICATE]
    [LINE Clause]
    { SOURCE IS identifier                                              }
    {                                                                   }
    { SUM identifier-1 [identifier-2] ... [UPON data-name-2]            }
    {                                                                   }
    {                   { FINAL        }                                }
    {     [RESET ON     {              } ]                              }
    {                   { identifier-3 }                                }
    {                                                                   }
    { VALUE IS literal                                                  }

     PICTURE Clause
    [USAGE Clause]
    [BLANK WHEN ZERO Clause]
    [JUSTIFIED Clause]
```

General Format 4: level-01 Elementary Entry

```
01  [data-name]
     TYPE Clause
     [LINE Clause]
     [NEXT GROUP Clause]
     [COLUMN Clause]
     [GROUP INDICATE Clause]
     { SOURCE Clause }
     { SUM Clause    }
     { VALUE Clause  }
     PICTURE Clause
     [USAGE Clause]
     [BLANK WHEN ZERO Clause]
     [JUSTIFIED Clause].
```

FIGURE 13.10 Report Group Syntax

COBOL 8X:

Changes and Enhancements

There are no significant changes in the new compiler concerning Report Writer. The conclusion to be drawn, therefore, is that the facility works well as is and that no changes were necessary. Try it!

Summary

Three programs were presented illustrating the use of Report Writer. In essence, Report Writer produces a report by describing its physical characteristics in the Data Division, rather than by specifying detailed instructions in the Procedure Division. This philosophy simplifies the involved logic in computing subtotals and rolling them forward. The Report Section is divided into distinct report groups for control headings, footings, etc. Hence modification of existing programs through the addition (or deletion) of report groups is easier than with ordinary COBOL programs.

The author is convinced of the merits of the facility and hopes that he has influenced you to some extent in its favor. To that end, let us review the opening arguments against Report Writer from the perspective of the completed chapter.

It is purely a matter of personal opinion as to whether Report Writer statements are more difficult to code than ordinary COBOL. The author certainly doesn't think so. In fact, a strong case could be made for the opposite argument, namely, that programs involving control breaks are developed more easily using Report Writer than conventional COBOL. For example, compare the programs in this chapter with those in Chapter 8.

The argument that no one else in a shop knows Report Writer, causing potential maintenance problems, is a case of Catch-22. No one will know Report Writer unless programmers take the initiative to learn it or enlightened managers insist that they do. Continued insistence on not using the facility, because few people know it, is self-defeating.

The lack of availability on some compilers cannot be denied, although Report Writer is part of the ANS 74 standard. The larger vendors have implemented the facility, but it doesn't yet exist on most minis and micros. (Ryan McFarland and Microsoft, for example, have fine COBOL compilers, but without Report Writer.) However, if the facility gains acceptance, then additional vendors may feel the need to make it available, in much the same way they were compelled to support COBOL in the first place.

The related argument of error-prone compilers originally had some validity, because the module had not been used sufficiently to have been thoroughly debugged. (This was especially true for those brave souls who used previous versions in the early 1970s.) However, the author has recently used both the IBM OS/VS and Univac compilers, without difficulty.

As to debugging, Report Writer will indeed "blow up" on invalid numeric data, but so does a conventional program. You may note inclusion of WS BEGINS HERE and READ INTO statements in the author's programs to pinpoint the invalid records. Use of this technique was described in Chapter 9 and pertains equally well to Report Writer programs.

In conclusion, Report Writer may not fit every application, nor is there a need to use it 100% of the time. However, it is ideally suited to programs with multiple control breaks and/or precisely aligned forms. *Report Writer is a powerful tool with a logic and beauty all its own, and it should be in the realm of any COBOL programmer.*

True/False Exercises

1. If Report Writer is used, the COBOL program must contain a minimum of seven report groups, i.e., at least one of all seven types.
2. Report Writer requires that control headings and control footings occur in pairs.
3. A report group is limited to a single print line.
4. Report Writer is not included in all ANS implementations.
5. A given COBOL program cannot contain both the SORT and Report Writer features.
6. The Procedure Division of a program containing Report Writer is typically quite short.
7. INITIATE, PROPAGATE, and TERMINATE are all associated with Report Writer.
8. Report Writer automatically sorts the incoming file if necessary.
9. A COBOL program that calls a subprogram cannot use Report Writer.
10. The Report Writer entries LINE NUMBER 2 and LINE NUMBER PLUS 2 are equivalent.
11. Data names are frequently omitted (following the level number) when using Report Writer.
12. It is possible for an FD not to have any 01 entries defined under it.
13. The GENERATE statement determines whether summary or detail reporting will result.
14. Report Writer computes *totals* only and is unsuitable if averages are required.
15. The SUM RESET clause prevents the automatic zeroing out of summation counters.
16. DECLARATIVES can be used with Report Writer.
17. Report Writer is an IBM extension to the ANS standard.
18. If an elementary item prints after the first occurrence of a control break, it must print for *all* occurrences.
19. A detail report group description may be omitted if summary reporting is performed.

Problems

1. Consider the SUM clauses in the program in Figure 13.2. Specifically, line 107, SUM SALESMAN-TOTAL, is used to compute a location total, and line 114, SUM LOCATION-TOTAL, is used to obtain the final total. Could either or both of these clauses have been replaced by SUM TR-AMOUNT? Is there any advantage in the original approach?

2. The report in Figure 13.11 is the result of a COBOL program utilizing Report Writer. The program processes a file which has been sorted by location and title within location. Salary totals are provided for all employees with similar titles. In addition, a salary total of all employees in each location is calculated.

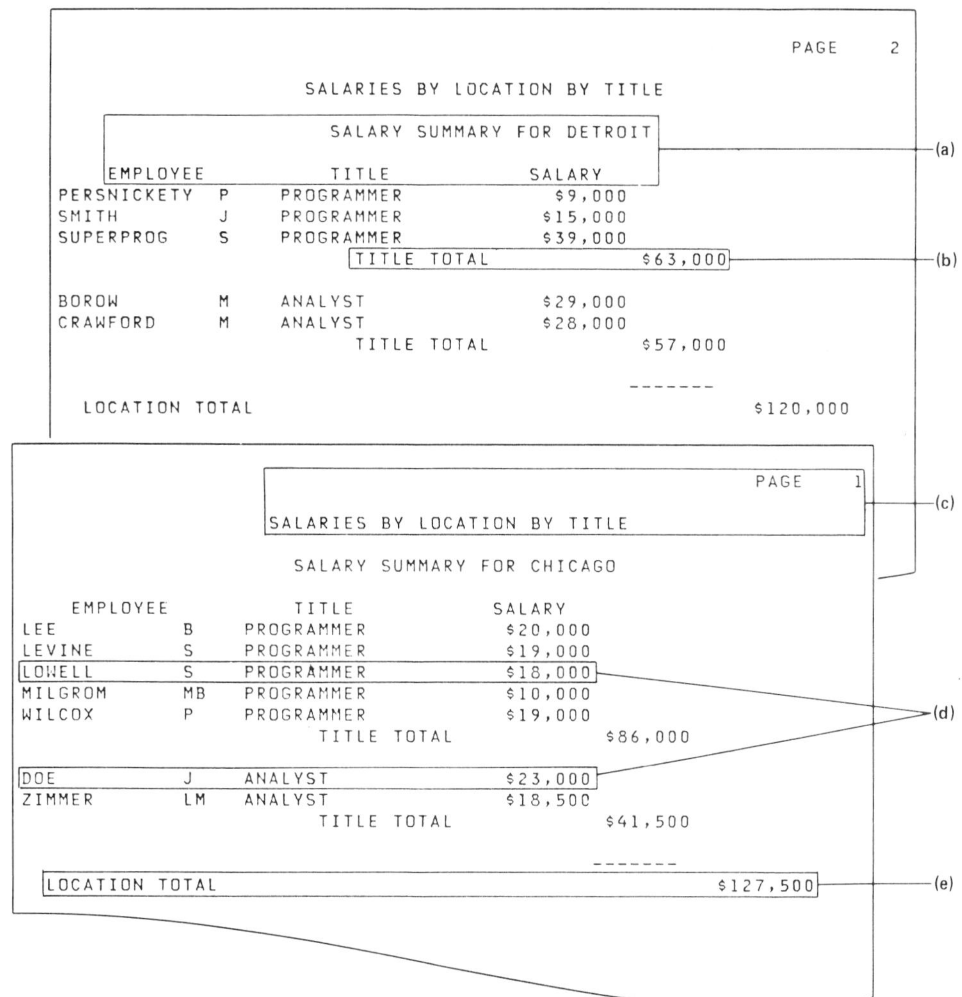

PAGE 2
SALARIES BY LOCATION BY TITLE
SALARY SUMMARY FOR DETROIT
EMPLOYEE TITLE SALARY
PERSNICKETY P PROGRAMMER $9,000
SMITH J PROGRAMMER $15,000
SUPERPROG S PROGRAMMER $39,000
TITLE TOTAL $63,000
BOROW M ANALYST $29,000
CRAWFORD M ANALYST $28,000
TITLE TOTAL $57,000

LOCATION TOTAL $120,000
PAGE 1
SALARIES BY LOCATION BY TITLE
SALARY SUMMARY FOR CHICAGO
EMPLOYEE TITLE SALARY
LEE B PROGRAMMER $20,000
LEVINE S PROGRAMMER $19,000
LOWELL S PROGRAMMER $18,000
MILGROM MB PROGRAMMER $10,000
WILCOX P PROGRAMMER $19,000
TITLE TOTAL $86,000
DOE J ANALYST $23,000
ZIMMER LM ANALYST $18,500
TITLE TOTAL $41,500

LOCATION TOTAL $127,500
(a)
(b)
(c)
(d)
(e)

FIGURE 13.11 Report for Problems 2, 3, and 4

Identify the boxed entries in the report of Figure 13.11 as to report group type; control heading, control footing, etc.

3. Complete the 01 entries in parts (a) through (e) to produce the report shown in problem 2. Use EMP-NAME, EMP-SALARY, EMP-TITLE, and EMP-LOCATION as data names in incoming records. Adhere to the horizontal and vertical spacing implied in the report of problem 2, and assume the first character of EMP-NAME appears in column 2.

   (a) 01 TYPE IS PAGE HEADING.
   (b) 01 TYPE IS CONTROL HEADING EMP-LOCATION.
   (c) 01 EMPLOYEE-LINE TYPE IS DETAIL.
   (d) 01 TYPE IS CONTROL FOOTING EMP-TITLE.
   (e) 01 TYPE IS CONTROL FOOTING EMP-LOCATION.

4. (a) With reference to the report of problem 2, code the FD for PRINT-FILE, the file to which the report SALARY-TOTALS will be written.
   (b) Code the associated RD for the report from part (a). Use appropriate controls consistent with your answers in problem 3.
   (c) Code the Procedure Division statements uniquely associated with Report Writer to correspond to previous answers in this problem, and problem 3.

Debugging Workshop

This exercise is based on the Report Writer listing in Figure 13.2. Input to the invalid program was identical to the test data in the Programming Specifications, with the intent of producing output identical to Figure 13.1. Instead, the *erroneous* output in Figure 13.12 resulted. Note the following errors:

1. Some, but not all, salesman totals are wrong; e.g., Tater is correct at $2,930, but Lavor should be $16,500 rather than the $6,500 shown.
2. Location totals are too high; e.g., Chicago's total should be $19,430 rather than the $25,360 shown.
3. The final total is also too high.
4. The transaction number prints only for the first transaction of every salesman; e.g., 888888 appears for Lee, but 905432 is missing.
5. The literal 'SALES ACTIVITY FOR' is missing in the location heading.

Find and correct all errors in the program in Figure 13.13.

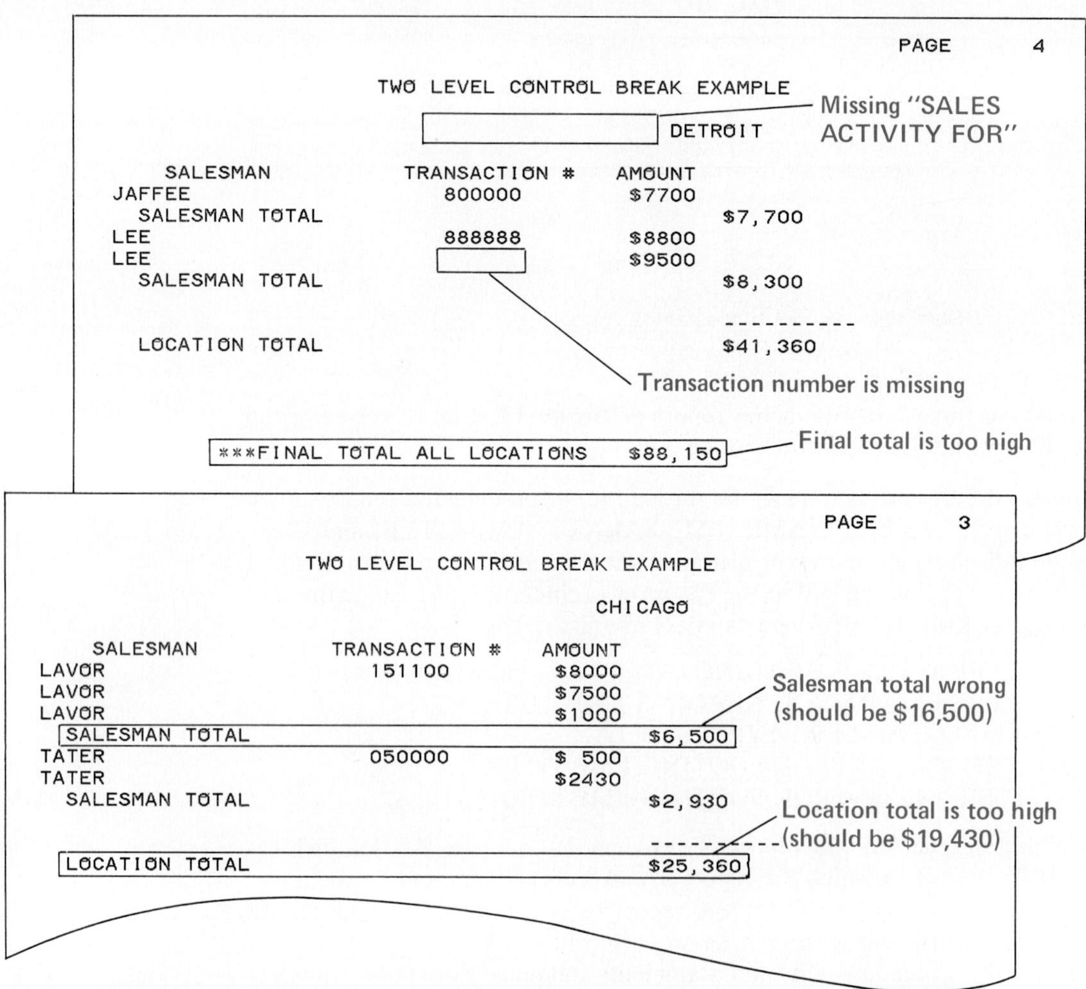

FIGURE 13.12 Erroneous Output

```
00001          IDENTIFICATION DIVISION.
00002          PROGRAM-ID.  ERWONE.
00003          AUTHOR.        JACKIE CLARK.
00004
00005          ENVIRONMENT DIVISION.
00006          CONFIGURATION SECTION.
00007          SOURCE-COMPUTER.    IBM-4341.
00008          OBJECT-COMPUTER.    IBM-4341.
00009          INPUT-OUTPUT SECTION.
00010          FILE-CONTROL.
00011              SELECT SALES-FILE
00012                  ASSIGN TO UT-S-SALES.
00013              SELECT PRINT-FILE
00014                  ASSIGN TO UT-S-REPORT.
00015
00016          DATA DIVISION.
00017          FILE SECTION.
00018          FD  SALES-FILE
00019              LABEL RECORDS ARE OMITTED
00021              RECORD CONTAINS 80 CHARACTERS
00022              DATA RECORD IS SALES-RECORD.
00023          01  SALES-RECORD                    PIC X(80).
00024
00025          FD  PRINT-FILE
00026              REPORT IS CONTROL-BREAK
00027              LABEL RECORDS ARE OMITTED
00028              RECORD CONTAINS 133 CHARACTERS.
00029
00030          WORKING-STORAGE SECTION.
00031          01  FILLER                          PIC X(14)
00032                  VALUE 'WS BEGINS HERE'.
00033          01  WS-DATA-FLAG                    PIC X(3)     VALUE SPACES.
00034
00035          01  TRANSACTION-AREA.
00036              05  TR-SALESMAN-NAME            PIC X(20).
00037              05  TR-AMOUNT                   PIC S9(4).
00038              05  FILLER                      PIC XX.
00039              05  TR-NUMBER                   PIC X(6).
00040              05  TR-TYPE                     PIC X.
00041              05  TR-SALESMAN-REGION          PIC X(17).
00042              05  TR-SALESMAN-LOCATION        PIC X(20).
00043              05  FILLER                      PIC X(10).
00044
00045          01  FILLER                          PIC X(12)
00046                  VALUE 'WS ENDS HERE'.
00047
00048          REPORT SECTION.
00049          RD  CONTROL-BREAK
00050              CONTROLS ARE FINAL TR-SALESMAN-LOCATION TR-SALESMAN-NAME
00051              PAGE LIMIT 50 LINES
00052              HEADING 1
00053              FIRST DETAIL 5
00054              LAST DETAIL 45
00055              FOOTING 48.
00056
00057          01  TYPE IS PAGE HEADING.
00058              05  LINE NUMBER 1.
00059                  10  COLUMN NUMBER 61        PIC X(4)
00060                      VALUE 'PAGE'.
00061                  10  COLUMN NUMBER 66        PIC ZZZZZ9
00062                      SOURCE PAGE-COUNTER.
00063              05  LINE NUMBER PLUS 2.
00064                  10  COLUMN NUMBER 22        PIC X(31)
00065                      VALUE 'TWO LEVEL CONTROL BREAK EXAMPLE'.
00066
00067          01  TYPE IS CONTROL HEADING TR-SALESMAN-LOCATION.
00068              05  LINE NUMBER 5.
00069                  10  COLUMN NUMBER 44        PIC X(18)
00070                      VALUE 'SALES ACTIVITY FOR'.
00071                  10  COLUMN NUMBER 44        PIC X(20)
00072                      SOURCE TR-SALESMAN-LOCATION.
00073              05  LINE NUMBER 7.
00074                  10  COLUMN NUMBER 6         PIC X(8)
00075                      VALUE 'SALESMAN'.
00076                  10  COLUMN NUMBER 24        PIC X(13)
00077                      VALUE 'TRANSACTION #'.
00078                  10  COLUMN NUMBER 40        PIC X(7)
00079                      VALUE 'AMOUNT'.
```

FIGURE 13.13 Erroneous Report Writer Program

```
       01  TRANSACTION-LINE TYPE IS DETAIL.
           05  LINE NUMBER PLUS 1.
               10  COLUMN NUMBER 2            PIC X(20)
                     SOURCE TR-SALESMAN-NAME.
               10  COLUMN NUMBER 27           PIC X(6)
                   GROUP INDICATE
                     SOURCE TR-NUMBER.
               10  COLUMN NUMBER 41           PIC $ZZZ9
                     SOURCE TR-AMOUNT.

       01  TYPE IS CONTROL FOOTING TR-SALESMAN-NAME.
           05  LINE NUMBER PLUS 1.
               10  COLUMN NUMBER 4            PIC X(15)
                     VALUE 'SALESMAN TOTAL'.
               10  SALESMAN-TOTAL
                   COLUMN NUMBER 48           PIC  $$,$$9
                     SUM TR-AMOUNT.

       01  TYPE IS CONTROL FOOTING TR-SALESMAN-LOCATION.
           05  LINE NUMBER PLUS 2.
               10  COLUMN NUMBER 48           PIC X(10)
                     VALUE ALL '-'.
           05  LINE NUMBER PLUS 1.
               10  COLUMN NUMBER 4            PIC X(14)
                     VALUE 'LOCATION TOTAL'.
               10  LOCATION-TOTAL
                   COLUMN NUMBER 48           PIC $$$,$$9
                     SUM SALESMAN-TOTAL RESET ON FINAL.

       01  TYPE IS CONTROL FOOTING FINAL.
           05  LINE NUMBER PLUS 5.
               10  COLUMN NUMBER 10           PIC X(28)
                     VALUE '***FINAL TOTAL ALL LOCATIONS'.
               10  COLUMN NUMBER 40           PIC $$$$,$$9
                     SUM LOCATION-TOTAL.

       PROCEDURE DIVISION.
       0010-CREATE-REPORTS.
           OPEN INPUT SALES-FILE
               OUTPUT PRINT-FILE.
           INITIATE CONTROL-BREAK.
           READ SALES-FILE INTO TRANSACTION-AREA
               AT END MOVE 'NO' TO WS-DATA-FLAG.
           PERFORM 0020-PROCESS-ALL-TRANSACTIONS
               UNTIL WS-DATA-FLAG = 'NO'.
           TERMINATE CONTROL-BREAK.
           CLOSE SALES-FILE
                 PRINT-FILE.
           STOP RUN.

       0020-PROCESS-ALL-TRANSACTIONS.
           GENERATE TRANSACTION-LINE.
           READ SALES-FILE INTO TRANSACTION-AREA
               AT END MOVE 'NO' TO WS-DATA-FLAG.
```

FIGURE 13.13 (Continued)

Programming Specifications

Projects 13–1 and 13–2

Program Name:

Control Breaks

Narrative:

It is strongly suggested that you use Report Writer to implement any or all of the projects at the end of Chapter 8. It may be quite revealing to contrast the alternate solutions obtained with Report Writer and "conventional" COBOL.

Programming Specifications

Project 13–3

Program Name:

Enrollment Totals

Narrative:

This project is designed to illustrate the major aspects of Report Writer and simultaneously review material on subprograms, sorting, DECLARATIVES, and table lookups. The latter aspects are optional, however, as can be seen from processing specifications.

Input File:

STUDENT-FILE

Input Record Layout:

```
01  STUDENT-RECORD.
    05  ST-NAME        PIC X(15).
    05  ST-MAJOR       PIC X(15).
    05  ST-YEAR        PIC XX.
    05  ST-CREDITS     PIC 99.
    05  ST-COLLEGE     PIC X(10).
```

Test Data:

```
ADAMS          ACCOUNTING     FR18BUSINESS
BAKER          ACCOUNTING     FR18BUSINESS
BROWN          ACCOUNTING     FR15BUSINESS
CALDWELL       ACCOUNTING     SO18BUSINESS
DAVIS          ACCOUNTING     SO17BUSINESS
FRANK          ACCOUNTING     JR16BUSINESS
GREENE         ACCOUNTING     JR16BUSINESS
HAINES         ACCOUNTING     SR19BUSINESS
MILLER         ACCOUNTING     SR15BUSINESS
NEWTON         ACCOUNTING     SR20BUSINESS
COULTER        INFO SYS       FR18BUSINESS
DREW           INFO SYS       FR18BUSINESS
ELLIOTT        INFO SYS       FR18BUSINESS
FORMAN         INFO SYS       FR18BUSINESS
GERBER         INFO SYS       SO18BUSINESS
HEWITT         INFO SYS       SO21BUSINESS
KENDALL        INFO SYS       SO21BUSINESS
LEVIN          INFO SYS       JR17BUSINESS
MOORE          INFO SYS       JR16BUSINESS
OBERMAN        INFO SYS       SR20BUSINESS
PRUITT         INFO SYS       SR18BUSINESS
CARSON         MANAGEMENT     FR15BUSINESS
DALTON         MANAGEMENT     FR15BUSINESS
ENGLAND        MANAGEMENT     SO15BUSINESS
FLANDERS       MANAGEMENT     JR12BUSINESS
TROOPER        MANAGEMENT     SR18BUSINESS
CRANDEL        MARKETING      FR15BUSINESS
CULVER         MARKETING      FR15BUSINESS
```

```
DAWSON      MARKETING     FR18BUSINESS
ECKERD      MARKETING     SO18BUSINESS
FRIENDLY    MARKETING     SO15BUSINESS
GANDY       MARKETING     SO15BUSINESS
HALPERN     MARKETING     JR20BUSINESS
ISAACS      MARKETING     JR18BUSINESS
JUMP        MARKETING     JR15BUSINESS
LACKLAND    MARKETING     SR12BUSINESS
MONROE      MARKETING     SR15BUSINESS
NEWLEY      MARKETING     SR15BUSINESS
```

Report Layout:

```
                                PAGE 1
MAJOR: ACCOUNTING

   NAME          YEAR        CREDITS
   ADAMS          FR            18
   BAKER          FR            18
   BROWN          FR            15

   TOTAL CREDITS FOR FRESHMEN = 51

   CALDWELL       SO            18
   DAVIS          SO            17

   TOTAL CREDITS FOR SOPHOMORES = 35
   .
   .
   .
   TOTAL CREDITS FOR SENIORS = 54

   TOTAL CREDITS FOR ACCOUNTING = 172

   NUMBER OF STUDENTS IN ACCOUNTING = 10
```

Processing Specifications:

1. Read a file of student records, and for every record read:
   (a) Print a detail line for that student, according to the report layout. Single-space detail lines.
   (b) Increment the total credits for the student's year by the number of credits that student is taking.
   (c) Increment the total credits for the student's major by the number of credits that student is taking.
   (d) Increment the total credits for the university by the number of credits that student is taking.
2. Print a heading, prior to the first student in each major. Begin each major on a new page. (Incoming student records have been sorted by major.)
3. Print total lines for each major whenever major changes, showing the total credits for that major and the number of students in that major.
4. Print a heading prior to the first student in each year, beginning two lines from the last line printed previously. (Incoming students have been sorted by major and by year within major.)
5. Print a total line for each year whenever year changes, showing the total credits for that year.
6. *Optional.* Add a report heading on a separate page, prior to the report. The general layout of the report heading is as follows:

```
XXXXXXXXXXXXXXXXXXXXXXXX

     SCHOOL OF BUSINESS
   CREDIT ANALYSIS REPORT

XXXXXXXXXXXXXXXXXXXXXXXX
```

7. *Optional.* At the conclusion of the report add a report footing that contains the number of credits for each major. This requires the use of DECLARATIVES and is more difficult than it may seem initially. Use the following general layout:

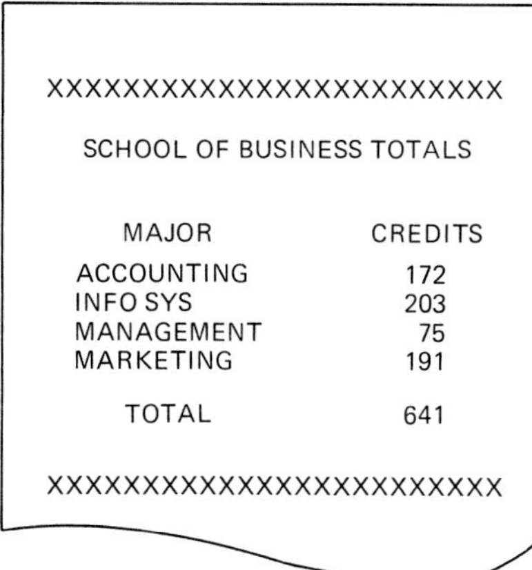

```
XXXXXXXXXXXXXXXXXXXXXXXX

 SCHOOL OF BUSINESS TOTALS

     MAJOR          CREDITS
  ACCOUNTING          172
  INFO SYS            203
  MANAGEMENT           75
  MARKETING           191

     TOTAL            641

XXXXXXXXXXXXXXXXXXXXXXXX
```

8. *Optional.* Assume the incoming data have not been sorted, and include the SORT verb in your program, prior to Report Writer.
9. *Optional.* Assume that incoming records contain a three-position major code, rather than a 15-position expanded major. Develop a *subprogram* that will be called prior to reporting a control heading on major to expand the major code. (The subprogram should be called from a DECLARATIVES section.) The test data are still applicable. However, the 15-byte field ST-MAJOR has to be redefined as a 3-position code, ST-MAJOR-CODE, and a 12-byte FILLER.

Sequential File Maintenance

14

Overview

A large proportion of data-processing activity is devoted to file maintenance. *Although printed reports are a more visible result of data processing, files must be maintained to reflect the changing nature of the physical environment. In a payroll system, for example, new employees can be added, while existing employees may be terminated or receive salary increases.*

This is the first of two chapters on file maintenance. It presents the balance line algorithm, *a* completely general *procedure to accomplish sequential file maintenance. The balance line approach should be readily appreciated by anyone who has had to develop or modify a COBOL program for a* sequential file update.

The algorithm is presented through pseudocode and associated hierarchy chart. It is implemented in stages through the top-down approach, *i.e., the philosophy of testing a program before it is completely coded. The requirements of a COBOL case study are presented, and two versions of a COBOL program are developed. The first contains several* program stubs *and tests the interaction among the higher level paragraphs in the hierarchy chart. The second, and completed, version fulfills the requirements of the case study.*

The chapter also considers the problem of program maintenance. *The requirements of the original case study are altered significantly to include a second transaction file. We show, however, that* nontrivial *modifications to a program's specifications can be easily implemented if the original program adhered to principles of sound design. Accordingly, the chapter is a good Illustration of how the structured theory of earlier chapters can be applied to a COBOL setting.* □

SYSTEM CONCEPTS

A sequential update is shown schematically in Figure 14.1.

A sequential update has two input files, an old master file and a transaction file. The latter contains information on whether a new record is to be *added* to the master file, an existing record *changed,* or an existing record *deleted.* In other words, there are three possible transaction types: additions, changes, and

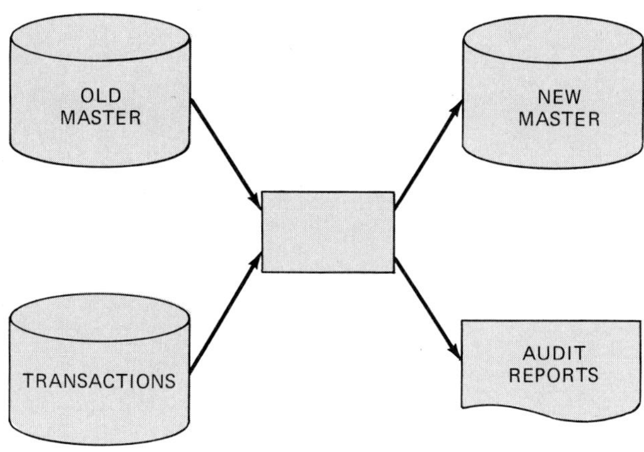

FIGURE 14.1 Sequential Update

deletions. Both the old master and transaction files are in *sequence,* e.g., by Social Security number or student number. Output from a sequential update consists of a new master file and various error (audit) reports indicating the success of the maintenance program.

A sequential update uses *two distinct master files,* an old master and a new master. *Every record in the old master has to be rewritten to the new master regardless of whether it changes.* Sequential processing is inefficient, therefore, if relatively few changes are made to the existing master file. It is a much better technique when there is substantial activity in the old master file. (A *nonsequential* update uses a single master file, which functions as both the old and new master. This method works very well with an "inactive" master file but less efficiently with "active" files. The decision whether to update a file sequentially or nonsequentially is beyond the scope of this discussion. Nonsequential file maintenance is discussed in Chapter 15.)

The Traditional Sequential Update

Figure 14.2 is an expanded version of Figure 14.1 with hypothetical data included. Each record in the old master contains four fields: Social Security number, name, salary, and location. Records in the old master are in *sequence* by Social Security number, the value of which must be *unique* for every record in the file.

Records in the transaction file are also in sequence by Social Security number. Three transaction types are permitted: *additions, changes,* and *deletions,* denoted by transaction codes of A, C, and D, respectively. There may be *multiple* transactions with the same Social Security number; e.g., employee 222222222 may have two corrections.

Records with a transaction type of A are to be added to the new master file in their entirety; e.g., NEW EMPLOYEE with Social Security number 400000000 does not appear on the old master but has been added to the new master. Records with a transaction type of D are to be deleted; e.g., SHERRY with Social Security number 666666666 appears in the old master but not the new master. Records with a transaction code of C are to change specific fields in the old master record. C-type transactions contain only the Social Security number and the field to be changed. The employee with Social Security number 222222222 has two transactions for salary and location, respectively. It is also possible to add a record and subsequently change a field; e.g., employee 610000000 has both an addition and a correction.

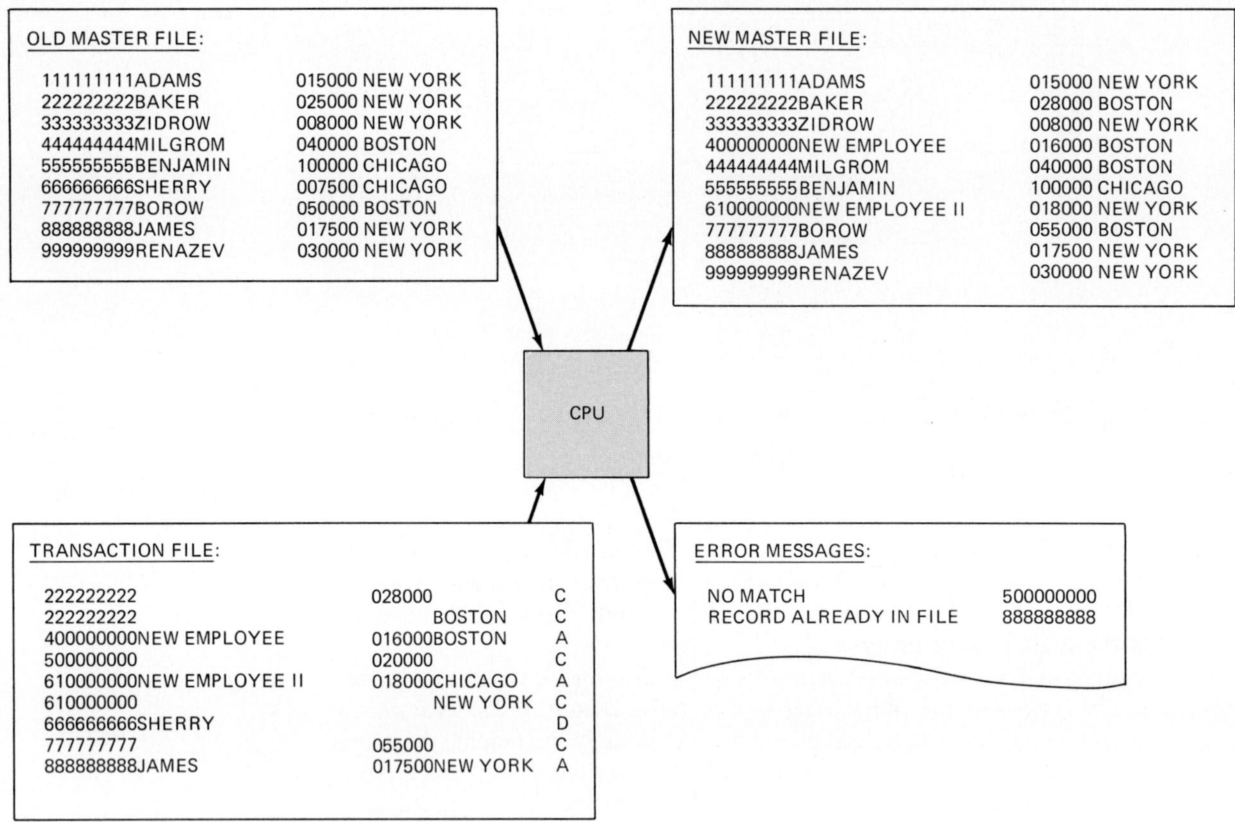

FIGURE 14.2 The Traditional Sequential Update

It is entirely possible that a record in the old master file will not have a corresponding transaction record; e.g., there are no transactions for the old master records whose Social Security numbers are 333333333 or 999999999. In this case the old master record is copied intact to the new master.

Despite our best intentions, Murphy's Law will prevail, and incoming transactions will contain errors. Hence a sequential update program must always check for two common mistakes. These are attempts to correct or delete a nonexistent record (i.e., a miscopied Social Security number) and addition of an already present record. These conditions are illustrated by transactions 500000000 and 888888888, respectively.

Periodic Maintenance

Sequential maintenance is done periodically, with frequency depending on the application. A file of student transcripts is updated only a few times a year; a bank's checking transactions are updated daily.

Assume, for example, a payroll system that is updated monthly, and begins with a current master file on January 1. Transactions are collected (batched) during the month of January. Then, on February 1, the master file of January 1 (now the old master) is processed with the transactions accrued during January, to produce a new master as of February 1. The process continues from month to month. Transactions are collected during February. On March 1 we take the file created February 1 as the old master, run it against the February transactions, and produce a new master as of March 1. Figure 14.3 illustrates this discussion.

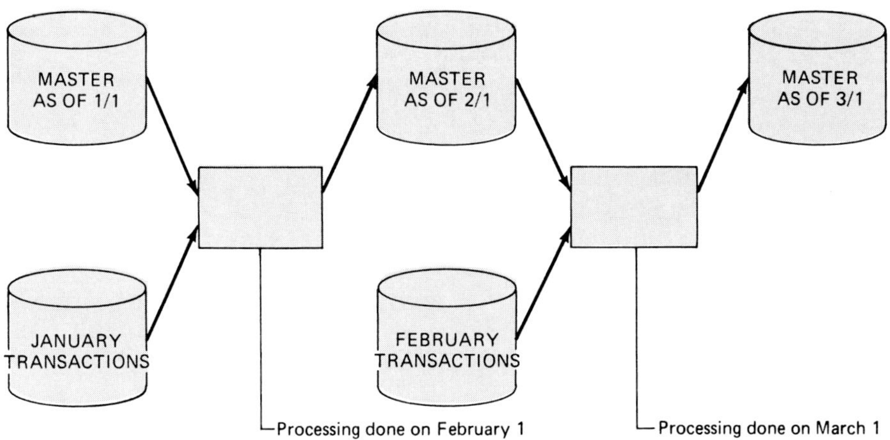

FIGURE 14.3 *Two Period Sequential Update*

Balance Line Algorithm

Although every COBOL book has confronted the problem of a sequential update, few, if any, have developed a truly general solution, with simultaneous simplicity of explanation. There is an impressive paper on the subject by Barry Dwyer,[1] which details a general solution to the problem. Dwyer's technique has been referred to as "the balance line algorithm" and is also described in a book by Johnson and Cooper.[2]

The logic in a sequential update is more difficult than what has been previously encountered because there are *multiple input* files; i.e., at a given point in the update process, one can read from the old master file, the transaction file, or both. The problem is handled in the *balance line algorithm* by the concept of an *active key*.

The active key is the smaller of the old master and transaction keys currently being processed. Thus, if the transaction key is less than the old master, the active key is equal to the transaction key; if the transaction and old master keys are equal, the active key is equal to either; finally, if the old master is less than the transaction key, then the active key is set to the old master. (Note how easily the technique is extended to multiple transaction files; *the active key is always defined as the smallest value of all keys currently processed.*)

The active key determines which records are admitted to the update process. For example, consider the data in Figure 14.2. When the program begins, the current old master and transaction records are 111111111 and 222222222, respectively, yielding an active key of 111111111. Hence the program will process only the old master record. It will then read the next record from the old master, 222222222, while simultaneously holding the transaction record 222222222. The active key will now be 222222222, and *both* old master and transaction records will be allowed in the updating process.

The balance line algorithm is best expressed in pseudocode. Consider, therefore, Figure 14.4, which contains pseudocode for the overall updating process.

[1]B. Dwyer, "One More Time—How to Update a Master File," *Communications of the ACM,* vol. 24, no. 1 (January 1981).

[2]L. F. Johnson and R. H. Cooper, *File Techniques for Data Base Organization in COBOL* (Englewood Cliffs, N.J.: Prentice-Hall, 1981).

```
OPEN FILES
READ TRANSACTION-FILE, AT END MOVE HIGH-VALUES TO TRANSACTION-KEY
READ OLD-MASTER-FILE, AT END MOVE HIGH-VALUES TO OLD-MASTER-KEY
CHOOSE FIRST ACTIVE-KEY
DO WHILE ACTIVE-KEY ≠ HIGH-VALUES
    IF OLD-MASTER-KEY = ACTIVE-KEY
        MOVE OLD-MASTER-RECORD TO NEW-MASTER-RECORD
        READ OLD-MASTER-FILE, AT END MOVE HIGH-VALUES TO OLD-MASTER-KEY
    ENDIF
    DO WHILE TRANSACTION-KEY = ACTIVE-KEY
        APPLY TRANSACTION TO NEW-MASTER-RECORD
        READ TRANSACTION-FILE, AT END MOVE HIGH-VALUES TO TRANSACTION-KEY
    ENDDO
    IF NO DELETION WAS PROCESSED
        WRITE NEW-MASTER-RECORD
    ENDIF
    CHOOSE NEXT ACTIVE-KEY
ENDDO
CLOSE FILES
STOP RUN
```

FIGURE 14.4 Balance Line Algorithm

Recall that the active key is the smallest value of all keys currently being processed. As can be seen from Figure 14.4, the initial records are read from each file, and the first active key is determined.

The major loop in Figure 14.4 executes repeatedly until both the old master and transaction files are out of data. (HIGH-VALUES is a COBOL reserved word and denotes the largest possible value. It is a convenient way of forcing end-of-file conditions, as will be seen when test data are examined later in the chapter.) If the key of the current old master record is equal to the active key, the old master record is moved to the new master and another record is read from the old master file. A second loop processes all transactions, whose key is equal to the active key. (The transaction file is read repeatedly in this inner loop after each transaction is processed.) When the transaction key no longer equals the active key, a check is made to see if a deletion was processed, and if not, the new master record is written. The next active key is chosen, and the outer loop continues.

Figure 14.4 does not include the logic necessary to accommodate error processing. Hence, although the transaction file is assumed to be valid in and of itself, there are additional errors that come to light only in the actual updating process. *Specifically, the update program must reject transactions which attempt to add records that already exist in the old master (i.e., duplicate additions). It should also reject transactions which attempt to change or delete records that do not exist (i.e., a miscopied transaction key).*

The easiest way to accomplish this error processing is through the assignment of an *allocation status* to every value of the active key; i.e., the value of the key is either allocated or it is not. If the allocation status is on, the record belongs in the file. If the allocation status is off, the record does not belong in the file. *Deletion of an existing record will change the status from on to off; addition of a new record alters the status from off to on.* An attempt to add a key whose status is already on signifies a duplicate addition. In similar fashion, attempting to change or delete a record whose allocation status is off also implies an error, as the transaction key is not present in the old master.

Figure 14.5 expands the pseudocode of Figure 14.4 to include RECORD-KEY-ALLOCATED-SWITCH to accommodate this discussion. A record is

```
OPEN FILES
READ TRANSACTION-FILE, AT END MOVE HIGH-VALUES TO TRANSACTION-KEY
READ OLD-MASTER-FILE, AT END MOVE HIGH-VALUES TO OLD-MASTER-KEY
CHOOSE FIRST ACTIVE-KEY
DO WHILE ACTIVE-KEY ≠ HIGH-VALUES
    IF OLD-MASTER-KEY = ACTIVE-KEY
        MOVE 'YES' TO RECORD-KEY-ALLOCATED-SWITCH
        MOVE OLD-MASTER-RECORD TO NEW-MASTER-RECORD
        READ OLD-MASTER-FILE, AT END MOVE HIGH-VALUES TO OLD-MASTER-KEY
    ELSE (ACTIVE-KEY IS NOT IN OLD-MASTER-FILE)
        MOVE 'NO' TO RECORD-KEY-ALLOCATED-SWITCH
    ENDIF
    DO WHILE TRANSACTION-KEY = ACTIVE-KEY
        IF ADDITION
            IF RECORD-KEY-ALLOCATED-SWITCH = 'YES'
                WRITE 'ERROR - DUPLICATE ADD'
            ELSE (ACTIVE-KEY IS NOT IN OLD-MASTER-FILE)
                MOVE TRANSACTION-RECORD TO NEW-MASTER-RECORD
                MOVE 'YES' TO RECORD-KEY-ALLOCATED-SWITCH
            ENDIF
        ELSE IF CORRECTION
            IF RECORD-KEY-ALLOCATED-SWITCH = 'YES'
                PROCESS CORRECTION
            ELSE (ACTIVE-KEY IS NOT IN OLD-MASTER-FILE)
                WRITE 'ERROR - NO MATCH'
            ENDIF
        ELSE IF DELETION
            IF RECORD-KEY-ALLOCATED-SWITCH = 'YES'
                MOVE 'NO' TO RECORD-KEY-ALLOCATED-SWITCH
                PROCESS DELETION
            ELSE (ACTIVE-KEY IS NOT IN OLD-MASTER-FILE)
                WRITE 'ERROR - NO MATCH'
            ENDIF
        ENDIF
        READ TRANSACTION-FILE, AT END MOVE HIGH-VALUES TO TRANSACTION-KEY
    ENDDO
    IF RECORD-KEY-ALLOCATED-SWITCH = 'YES'
        WRITE NEW-MASTER-RECORD
    ENDIF
    CHOOSE NEXT ACTIVE-KEY
ENDDO
CLOSE FILES
STOP RUN
```

FIGURE 14.5 Expanded Balance Line Algorithm

written to the new master file only when the RECORD-KEY-ALLOCATED-SWITCH is set to YES. In other words, deletions are accomplished simply by setting the switch to NO and not writing the record.

You should be convinced of the total generality of Figure 14.5 and, further, that *multiple transactions for the same key may be presented in any order.* For example, if an addition and correction are input in that order, the record will be added and corrected in the same run. However, if the correction precedes the addition, then the correction will be flagged as a no match, and only the addition will take effect. Two additions for the same key will result in adding the first and flagging the second as a duplicate add. An addition, correction, and deletion may be processed in that order for the same transaction. A deletion followed by an addition may also be processed. However, the latter combination will produce an error message, indicating an attempt to delete a record that is not in the old master. In other words, multiple transactions for the same key can be presented in any order, e.g., in *chronological* order, with no requirement for a secondary sort on transaction code.

COBOL CASE STUDY

Thus far we have postulated the general problem of a sequential update and alluded to a specific means of solution, the balance line algorithm. We continue with a specific problem statement, after which the COBOL solution will be developed completely.

Programming Specifications

Program Name:

Sequential Update

Narrative:

This program implements a traditional sequential update via the *balance line algorithm.*

Input File(s):

TRANSACTION-FILE
OLD-MASTER-FILE

Input Record Layout(s):

Old Master Record:

```
01  OLD-MASTER-RECORD.
    05  OLD-SOC-SEC-NUMBER      PIC X(9).
    05  OLD-NAME.
        10  OLD-LAST-NAME       PIC X(15).
        10  OLD-INITIALS        PIC XX.
    05  OLD-DATE-OF-BIRTH.
        10  OLD-BIRTH-MONTH     PIC 99.
        10  OLD-BIRTH-YEAR      PIC 99.
    05  OLD-DATE-OF-HIRE.
        10  OLD-HIRE-MONTH      PIC 99.
        10  OLD-HIRE-YEAR       PIC 99.
    05  OLD-LOCATION-CODE       PIC X(3).
    05  OLD-PERFORMANCE-CODE    PIC X.
    05  OLD-EDUCATION-CODE      PIC X.
    05  OLD-TITLE-DATA OCCURS 2 TIMES.
        10  OLD-TITLE-CODE      PIC 9(3).
        10  OLD-TITLE-DATE      PIC 9(4).
    05  OLD-SALARY-DATA OCCURS 3 TIMES.
        10  OLD-SALARY          PIC 9(5).
        10  OLD-SALARY-DATE     PIC 9(4).
```

Transaction Record:

```
01  TRANSACTION-RECORD.
    05  TR-SOC-SEC-NUMBER       PIC X(9).
    05  TR-NAME.
        10  TR-LAST-NAME        PIC X(15).
        10  TR-INITIALS         PIC XX.
    05  TR-DATE-OF-BIRTH.
        10  TR-BIRTH-MONTH      PIC 99.
        10  TR-BIRTH-YEAR       PIC 99.
    05  TR-DATE-OF-HIRE.
        10  TR-HIRE-MONTH       PIC 99.
        10  TR-HIRE-YEAR        PIC 99.
    05  TR-LOCATION-CODE        PIC X(3).
    05  TR-PERFORMANCE-CODE     PIC X.
    05  TR-EDUCATION-CODE       PIC X.
    05  TR-TITLE-DATA.
        10  TR-TITLE-CODE       PIC 9(3).
        10  TR-TITLE-DATE       PIC 9(4).
    05  TR-SALARY-DATA.
        10  TR-SALARY           PIC 9(5).
        10  TR-SALARY-DATE      PIC 9(4).
    05  TR-TRANSACTION-CODE     PIC X.
        88  ADDITION       VALUE 'A'.
        88  CORRECTION     VALUE 'C'.
        88  DELETION       VALUE 'D'.
    05  FILLER                  PIC X(24).
```

Output File:

NEW-MASTER-FILE

Output Record Layout:

Identical to old master layout.

Processing Requirements:

1. Develop a sequential update program to process an incoming transaction file and the associated old master file to produce a new master file.
2. Three transaction codes are permitted: A, C, and D, denoting additions, corrections, and deletions, respectively.
3. The transaction file is assumed to be valid in itself because it has been processed by a stand-alone edit program. Hence each transaction has a valid transaction code (A, C, or D), numeric fields are numeric, and so on. Nevertheless, the update program must check (and flag) two kinds of errors that could not be detected in the stand-alone edit, as they require interaction with the old master file. These are:
   (a) *Duplicate additions,* in which the Social Security number of transaction coded as an addition *already* exists in the old master,
   (b) *No matches,* in which the Social Security number of either a deletion or a correction transaction type does *not* exist in the old master.
4. Transactions coded as *additions* are added to the new master file in their entirety. These transactions require all fields in the transaction record to be present.

5. Transactions coded as *deletions* are removed from the master file. These transactions need contain only the Social Security number and transaction code.
6. Transactions coded as *corrections* contain only the Social Security number and the corrected value of any field(s) to be changed and are handled on a parameter-by-parameter basis. For example, if birth date and location are to be corrected, the incoming transaction will contain *only* the Social Security number and *corrected* values of birth date and location code in the *designated* positions on the transaction record.
7. Any old master record for which there is no corresponding transaction is to be copied intact to the new master.

Designing the Hierarchy Chart

The first step in writing a program is to develop its hierarchy chart. (Recall that pseudocode and a hierarchy chart depict different things. Pseudocode indicates sequence and decision-making logic, whereas a hierarchy chart depicts function. It indicates what has to be done, but not necessarily when.) Accordingly, we begin by listing the *functional* modules necessary to accomplish a sequential update using the balance line algorithm:

Overall Program Function	UPDATE-MASTER-FILE
Functional Modules	READ-TRANSACTION-FILE READ-OLD-MASTER-FILE CHOOSE-ACTIVE-KEY PROCESS-ACTIVE-KEY BUILD-NEW-MASTER WRITE-NEW-MASTER APPLY-TRANSACTIONS-TO-MASTER ADD-NEW-RECORD CORRECT-OLD-RECORD DELETE-OLD-RECORD

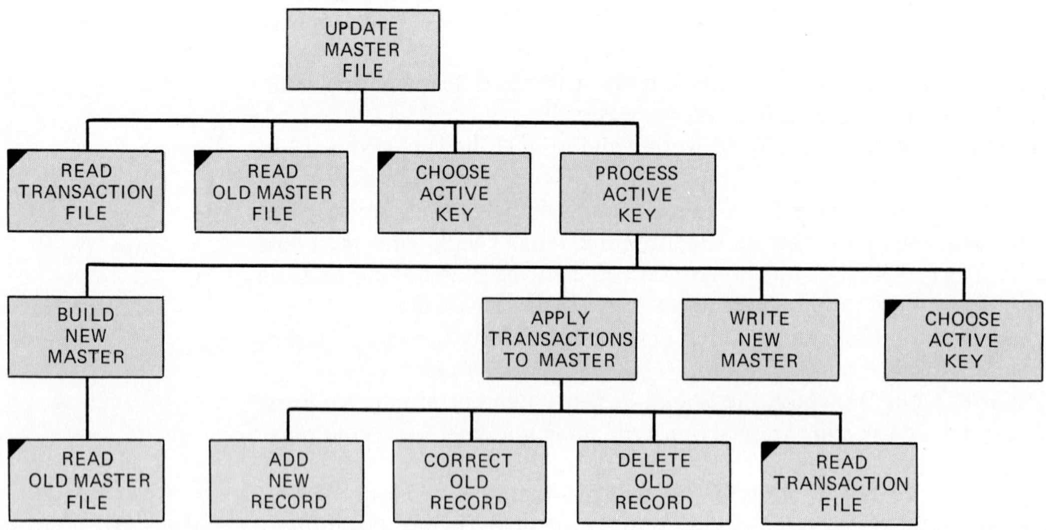

FIGURE 14.6 Hierarchy Chart for Balance Line Algorithm

The hierarchy chart in Figure 14.6 is developed in *top-down* fashion, beginning with the overall program function, UPDATE-MASTER-FILE. Development of a hierarchy chart requires explicit specification of the *function* of each module, which should be apparent from the module name, consisting of a verb, one or two adjectives and an object. Nevertheless, the module functions are described in depth:

UPDATE-MASTER-FILE	The mainline routine which drives the entire program. It opens the program files, invokes subordinate routines to do an initial read from each input file, and determines the first active key. It invokes PROCESS-ACTIVE-KEY until all files are out of data, closes the files, and terminates the run.
READ-TRANSACTION-FILE	Reads a record from the transaction file; moves HIGH-VALUES to the transaction key when the file is empty. This module is called from more than one place in the program as indicated by the shading in the upper left-hand corner.
READ-OLD-MASTER-FILE	Reads a record from the old master file; moves HIGH-VALUES to the old master key when the file is empty. This module is called from more than one place in the program as indicated by the shading in the upper left-hand corner.
CHOOSE-ACTIVE-KEY	Determines the active key for the balance line algorithm from the current values of the old master and transaction records. This module is also called from more than one place.
PROCESS-ACTIVE-KEY	A module that will call up to four subordinates, on the basis of the value of active key; e.g., all four subordinates are invoked when the keys on the old master and transaction files equal the active key, and no deletions were processed.
BUILD-NEW-MASTER	Moves the current old master record to a corresponding new master. This paragraph is mandated by the nature of a sequential update, which requires that every record in the old master file be copied to the new master file, regardless of whether it changes.
WRITE-NEW-MASTER	Writes a new master record, and is called only after all transactions for that record have been processed.
APPLY-TRANS-TO-MASTER	Calls one of three subordinates to add, correct, or delete a record according to the current transaction code. Regardless of the transaction type, it invokes READ-TRANSACTION-FILE to obtain the next transaction and executes repeatedly as long as the transaction key equals the active key.
ADD-NEW-RECORD	Lowest level module to add a new record. Addition of a new record requires that

	RECORD-KEY-ALLOCATED-SWITCH be set to "YES".
CORRECT-OLD-RECORD	Lowest level module to correct one or more fields in an existing record.
DELETE-OLD-RECORD	Lowest level module to delete an existing record. Deletion of an existing record requires that RECORD-KEY-ALLOCATED-SWITCH be set to "NO".

TOP-DOWN TESTING

Top-down testing demands that *the highest (and most difficult) modules in a hierarchy chart be tested earlier, and more often, than the lower level (and often trivial) routines*. It requires that testing begin *as soon as possible, and well before the program is finished.* Testing a program before it is completed can be accomplished by coding lower level modules as *program stubs,* i.e., *abbreviated* versions of completed modules.

The major advantage in this approach is that testing begins sooner in the development cycle. Errors that do exist are found earlier and consequently are easier to correct. Later versions can still contain bugs, but these will be in *lower* level modules, where fixing them is easier. The more difficult problems will already have been resolved in the initial tests.

A second advantage of top-down testing is that programmer morale is improved as testing and coding become parallel activities. Consider Figure 14.7, which contrasts testing patterns. Figure 14.7*a* depicts the traditional panic mode. No testing is done for the first 11 months of the project, until the weekend before the system goes live. Last-minute panic sets in with abundant overtime and chaos. By contrast, Figure 14.7*b* indicates a more uniform pattern of testing, which begins almost immediately and continues throughout the project's duration.

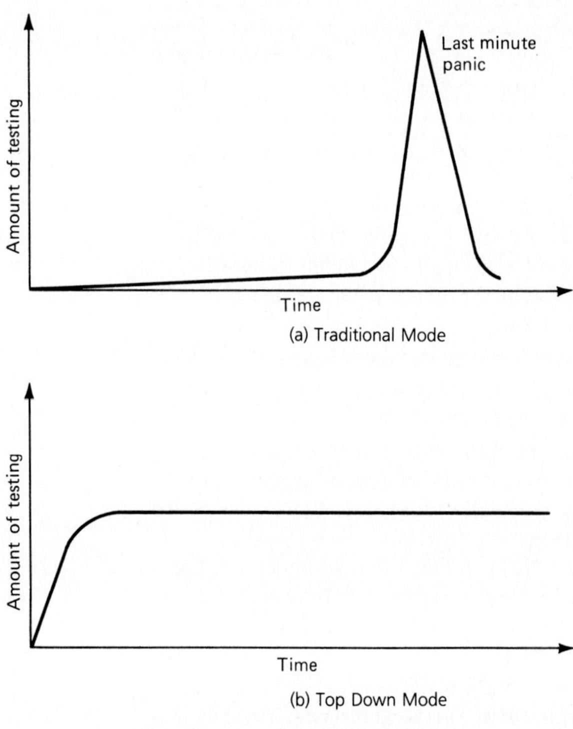

FIGURE 14.7 Testing Patterns

```
100000000SUGRUE        P 12450879100E533308802220879280001081260000980
200000000CRAWFØRD      MA09430678100E64440678       420000680360000678
300000000MILGRØM       IR06130580200E65551081400068148000580
400000000BENJAMIN      BL10531073100E73331073       300001081280001080
500000000TATER         JS02500779200P43330779       310001081270000779
600000000GRAUER        RT11450877200E590011818001180500001181450001180
700000000JØNES         A 09500778100G644407793330778390000881360000779
800000000SMITH         BB08520681300P84440681       385000681
900000000BAKER         E 06490879100G99870879       650000881550000879
```

(a) ***Old Master File***

Multiple transactions are permitted for the same old master record.

```
000000000BØRØW         JS03431281100 99871281550001281A
000000000BØRØW         JS            X                C
200000000CRAWFØRD      MA09430678100E64440680420000680A
400000000BENJAMIN      BL                             C
400000000BENJAMIN      BL1054                         C
400000000BENJAMIN      BL    1074                     C
400000001BENJAMIN      BL        200                  C
500000000TATER         C                              D
555555555NEW EMPLØYEE  RT1145                         C
555555555NEW EMPLØYEE  RT11440681100E64440681390000681A
555555555NEW EMPLØYEE  RT             555             C
700000000JØNES         A                     385000781C
800000000SMITH         BB             400             C
```

(b) ***Transaction File***

FIGURE 14.8 ***Test Data***

In order to appreciate the significance of top-down testing fully, we develop a "stubs" program for the sequential update. This in turn requires preparation of test data as shown in Figure 14.8.

You should be convinced that Figure 14.8 contains sufficient data to test the eventual update program adequately. All transaction types are present. Multiple transactions have the same key (000000000, 400000000, and 555555555). There is a duplicate addition (200000000), which should be flagged as an error, as well as attempted corrections on erroneous Social Security numbers (400000001 and the first correction for 555555555).

While on the subject of test data, it is desirable that a person other than the programmer, *preferably the user,* supply the data. The latter individual does not know how the program actually works and thus is in a better position to make up *objective* data. In addition, the user knows the *original* specification and is not subject to distortions from the analysis phase. The programmer, on the other hand, is biased, either consciously or subconsciously, and will generate data to accommodate his or her program or interpretation of the specifications.

We should also mention that anticipated results are best computed *before* testing begins. Otherwise, it is too easy to assume the program works, because the output "looks right." Indeed, trainees are often so overjoyed merely to get output that they conclude the testing phase upon receiving their first printout.

Given the need for adequate test data, consider now the stubs program in Figure 14.9 and its associated output in Figure 14.10.

Stubs Program

Figure 14.9 shows the stubs program for a sequential update implemented according to the balance line algorithm. It is "complete" in that it contains a paragraph for every module in the hierarchy chart of Figure 14.6. It is "incomplete" because several of the lower level modules exist only as program stubs, i.e., abbreviated paragraphs.

Upon closer examination, Figure 14.9 is seen to contain only two files, the old master and transaction, with record descriptions corresponding to the programming specifications. (These files are accessed through READ INTO statements and are described in Working-Storage according to the guidelines in Chapter 9.) The new master file is not referenced explicitly in Figure 14.9. Instead, the paragraphs 0060-BUILD-NEW-MASTER and 0080-WRITE-NEW-MASTER contain DISPLAY statements to indicate only that they have been called.

```
IDENTIFICATION DIVISION.
PROGRAM-ID.    SEQSTUB.
AUTHOR.        JACKIE CLARK.

ENVIRONMENT DIVISION.
CONFIGURATION SECTION.
SOURCE-COMPUTER.       IBM-4341.
OBJECT-COMPUTER.       IBM-4341.

INPUT-OUTPUT SECTION.
FILE-CONTROL.
    SELECT TRANSACTION-FILE
        ASSIGN TO UT-S-TRANS.
    SELECT OLD-MASTER-FILE
        ASSIGN TO UT-S-MASTER.

DATA DIVISION.
FILE SECTION.
FD  TRANSACTION-FILE
    LABEL RECORDS ARE STANDARD
    BLOCK CONTAINS 0 RECORDS
    RECORD CONTAINS 80 CHARACTERS
    DATA RECORD IS TRANSACTION-RECORD.
01  TRANSACTION-RECORD                          PIC X(80).

FD  OLD-MASTER-FILE
    LABEL RECORDS ARE STANDARD
    BLOCK CONTAINS 0 RECORDS
    RECORD CONTAINS 80 CHARACTERS
    DATA RECORD IS OLD-MAST-RECORD.
01  OLD-MAST-RECORD                             PIC X(80).

WORKING-STORAGE SECTION.
01  FILLER                                      PIC X(14)
        VALUE 'WS BEGINS HERE'.

01  WS-TRANS-RECORD.
    05  TR-SOC-SEC-NUMBER                       PIC X(9).
    05  TR-NAME.
        10  TR-LAST-NAME                        PIC X(15).
        10  TR-INITIALS                         PIC XX.
    05  TR-DATE-OF-BIRTH.
        10  TR-BIRTH-MONTH                      PIC 99.
        10  TR-BIRTH-YEAR                       PIC 99.
    05  TR-DATE-OF-HIRE.
        10  TR-HIRE-MONTH                       PIC 99.
        10  TR-HIRE-YEAR                        PIC 99.
    05  TR-LOCATION-CODE                        PIC X(3).
    05  TR-PERFORMANCE-CODE                     PIC X.
    05  TR-EDUCATION-CODE                       PIC X.
    05  TR-TITLE-DATA.
        10  TR-TITLE-CODE                       PIC 9(3).
        10  TR-TITLE-DATE                       PIC 9(4).
    05  TR-SALARY-DATA.
        10  TR-SALARY                           PIC 9(5).
        10  TR-SALARY-DATE                      PIC 9(4).
    05  TR-TRANSACTION-CODE                     PIC X.
        88  ADDITION         VALUE 'A'.
        88  CORRECTION       VALUE 'C'.
        88  DELETION         VALUE 'D'.
    05  FILLER                                  PIC X(24).
```

Two input files are required.

Facilitates debugging.

Three transaction types are permitted.

FIGURE 14.9 Stubs Program

FIGURE 14.9 (Continued)

```
       01  WS-OLD-MAST-RECORD.
           05  OLD-SOC-SEC-NUMBER                PIC X(9).
           05  OLD-NAME.
               10  OLD-LAST-NAME                 PIC X(15).
               10  OLD-INITIALS                  PIC XX.
           05  OLD-DATE-OF-BIRTH.
               10  OLD-BIRTH-MONTH               PIC 99.
               10  OLD-BIRTH-YEAR                PIC 99.
           05  OLD-DATE-OF-HIRE.
               10  OLD-HIRE-MONTH                PIC 99.
               10  OLD-HIRE-YEAR                 PIC 99.
           05  OLD-LOCATION-CODE                 PIC X(3).
           05  OLD-PERFORMANCE-CODE              PIC X.
           05  OLD-EDUCATION-CODE                PIC X.
           05  OLD-TITLE-DATA OCCURS 2 TIMES.
               10  OLD-TITLE-CODE                PIC 9(3).
               10  OLD-TITLE-DATE                PIC 9(4).
           05  OLD-SALARY-DATA OCCURS 3 TIMES.
               10  OLD-SALARY                    PIC 9(5).
               10  OLD-SALARY-DATE               PIC 9(4).

       01  WS-BALANCE-LINE-SWITCHES.
           05  WS-ACTIVE-KEY                     PIC X(9).
           05  WS-RECORD-KEY-ALLOCATED-SWITCH    PIC X(3).

       PROCEDURE DIVISION.
       0010-UPDATE-MASTER-FILE.
           OPEN INPUT TRANSACTION-FILE
                      OLD-MASTER-FILE.
           PERFORM 0020-READ-TRANSACTION-FILE.
           PERFORM 0030-READ-OLD-MASTER-FILE.
```

Initial reads.

```
           PERFORM 0040-CHOOSE-ACTIVE-KEY.
           PERFORM 0050-PROCESS-ACTIVE-KEY
               UNTIL WS-ACTIVE-KEY = HIGH-VALUES.
           CLOSE TRANSACTION-FILE
                 OLD-MASTER-FILE.
           STOP RUN.

       0020-READ-TRANSACTION-FILE.
           READ TRANSACTION-FILE INTO WS-TRANS-RECORD
               AT END MOVE HIGH-VALUES TO TR-SOC-SEC-NUMBER.

       0030-READ-OLD-MASTER-FILE.
           READ OLD-MASTER-FILE INTO WS-OLD-MAST-RECORD
               AT END MOVE HIGH-VALUE TO OLD-SOC-SEC-NUMBER.

       0040-CHOOSE-ACTIVE-KEY.
           IF TR-SOC-SEC-NUMBER LESS THAN OLD-SOC-SEC-NUMBER
               MOVE TR-SOC-SEC-NUMBER TO WS-ACTIVE-KEY
           ELSE
               MOVE OLD-SOC-SEC-NUMBER TO WS-ACTIVE-KEY.
```

Determines active key.

DISPLAY statements to facilitate testing.

```
       0050-PROCESS-ACTIVE-KEY.
           DISPLAY '     '.
           DISPLAY '     '.
           DISPLAY 'RECORDS BEING PROCESSED'.
           DISPLAY '  TRANSACTION SOC SEC #: ' TR-SOC-SEC-NUMBER.
           DISPLAY '  OLD MASTER SOC SEC #:  ' OLD-SOC-SEC-NUMBER.
           DISPLAY '  ACTIVE KEY:            ' WS-ACTIVE-KEY.
           DISPLAY '     '

           IF OLD-SOC-SEC-NUMBER = WS-ACTIVE-KEY
               MOVE 'YES' TO WS-RECORD-KEY-ALLOCATED-SWITCH
               PERFORM 0060-BUILD-NEW-MASTER
           ELSE
               MOVE 'NO' TO WS-RECORD-KEY-ALLOCATED-SWITCH.

           PERFORM 0070-APPLY-TRANS-TO-MASTER
               UNTIL WS-ACTIVE-KEY NOT EQUAL TR-SOC-SEC-NUMBER.

           IF WS-RECORD-KEY-ALLOCATED-SWITCH = 'YES'
               PERFORM 0080-WRITE-NEW-MASTER.

           PERFORM 0040-CHOOSE-ACTIVE-KEY.

       0060-BUILD-NEW-MASTER.
           DISPLAY '0060-BUILD-NEW-MASTER ENTERED'.
           PERFORM 0030-READ-OLD-MASTER-FILE.

       0070-APPLY-TRANS-TO-MASTER.
```

```
         DISPLAY '0070-APPLY-TRANS-TO-MASTER ENTERED'
                 '    TRANSACTION CODE: '  TR-TRANSACTION-CODE.
         IF ADDITION
             PERFORM 0090-ADD-NEW-RECORD
         ELSE
             IF CORRECTION
                 PERFORM 0100-CORRECT-OLD-RECORD
             ELSE
                 IF DELETION
                     PERFORM 0110-DELETE-OLD-RECORD.

         PERFORM 0020-READ-TRANSACTION-FILE.

     0080-WRITE-NEW-MASTER.
         DISPLAY '0080-WRITE-NEW-MASTER ENTERED'.

     0090-ADD-NEW-RECORD.
         DISPLAY '0090-ADD-NEW-RECORD ENTERED'.
         IF WS-RECORD-KEY-ALLOCATED-SWITCH = 'YES'
             DISPLAY '  ERROR-DUPLICATE ADDITION: ' TR-SOC-SEC-NUMBER
         ELSE
             MOVE 'YES' TO WS-RECORD-KEY-ALLOCATED-SWITCH.

     0100-CORRECT-OLD-RECORD.
         DISPLAY '0100-CORRECT-OLD-RECORD ENTERED'.
         IF WS-RECORD-KEY-ALLOCATED-SWITCH = 'YES'
             NEXT SENTENCE
         ELSE
             DISPLAY '  ERROR-NO MATCHING RECORD: ' TR-SOC-SEC-NUMBER.

     0110-DELETE-OLD-RECORD.
         DISPLAY '0110-DELETE-OLD-RECORD ENTERED'.
         IF WS-RECORD-KEY-ALLOCATED-SWITCH = 'YES'
             MOVE 'NO' TO WS-RECORD-KEY-ALLOCATED-SWITCH
         ELSE
             DISPLAY '  ERROR-NO MATCHING RECORD: ' TR-SOC-SEC-NUMBER.
```

Determines which lower level module to execute.

Partially coded paragraphs.

Error check.

FIGURE 14.9 ***(Continued)***

```
RECORDS BEING PROCESSED
  TRANSACTION SOC SEC #:  000000000
  OLD MASTER SOC SEC #:   100000000
  ACTIVE KEY:             000000000

0070-APPLY-TRANS-TO-MASTER ENTERED      TRANSACTION CODE: A
0090-ADD-NEW-RECORD ENTERED
0070-APPLY-TRANS-TO-MASTER ENTERED      TRANSACTION CODE: C
0100-CORRECT-OLD-RECORD ENTERED
0080-WRITE-NEW-MASTER ENTERED


RECORDS BEING PROCESSED
  TRANSACTION SOC SEC #:  200000000
  OLD MASTER SOC SEC #:   100000000
  ACTIVE KEY:             100000000

0060-BUILD-NEW-MASTER ENTERED
0080-WRITE-NEW-MASTER ENTERED


RECORDS BEING PROCESSED
  TRANSACTION SOC SEC #:  200000000
  OLD MASTER SOC SEC #:   200000000
  ACTIVE KEY:             200000000

0060-BUILD-NEW-MASTER ENTERED
0070-APPLY-TRANS-TO-MASTER ENTERED      TRANSACTION CODE: A
0090-ADD-NEW-RECORD ENTERED
  ERROR-DUPLICATE ADDITION: 200000000
0080-WRITE-NEW-MASTER ENTERED
```

Active key is the smaller of old master and transaction keys.

Existing old master with no activity is copied to new master.

Duplicate addition is flagged.

FIGURE 14.10 ***Output of Stubs Program***

FIGURE 14.10 (Continued)

```
RECORDS BEING PROCESSED
   TRANSACTION SOC SEC #:  400000000
   OLD MASTER SOC SEC #:   300000000
   ACTIVE KEY:             300000000

0060-BUILD-NEW-MASTER ENTERED
0080-WRITE-NEW-MASTER ENTERED


RECORDS BEING PROCESSED
   TRANSACTION SOC SEC #:  400000000
   OLD MASTER SOC SEC #:   400000000
   ACTIVE KEY:             400000000

0060-BUILD-NEW-MASTER ENTERED
0070-APPLY-TRANS-TO-MASTER ENTERED      TRANSACTION CODE: C
0100-CORRECT-OLD-RECORD ENTERED
0070-APPLY-TRANS-TO-MASTER ENTERED      TRANSACTION CODE: C
0100-CORRECT-OLD-RECORD ENTERED
0070-APPLY-TRANS-TO-MASTER ENTERED      TRANSACTION CODE: C
0100-CORRECT-OLD-RECORD ENTERED
0080-WRITE-NEW-MASTER ENTERED
```

Three transactions are applied to same master record.

```
RECORDS BEING PROCESSED
   TRANSACTION SOC SEC #:  400000001
   OLD MASTER SOC SEC #:   500000000
   ACTIVE KEY:             400000001

0070-APPLY-TRANS-TO-MASTER ENTERED      TRANSACTION CODE: C
0100-CORRECT-OLD-RECORD ENTERED
   ERROR-NO MATCHING RECORD: 400000001
```

Error message indicating a miscopied Social Security number.

```
RECORDS BEING PROCESSED
   TRANSACTION SOC SEC #:  500000000
   OLD MASTER SOC SEC #:   500000000
   ACTIVE KEY:             500000000

0060-BUILD-NEW-MASTER ENTERED
0070-APPLY-TRANS-TO-MASTER ENTERED      TRANSACTION CODE: D
0110-DELETE-OLD-RECORD ENTERED


RECORDS BEING PROCESSED
   TRANSACTION SOC SEC #:  555555555
   OLD MASTER SOC SEC #:   600000000
   ACTIVE KEY:             555555555

0070-APPLY-TRANS-TO-MASTER ENTERED      TRANSACTION CODE: C
0100-CORRECT-OLD-RECORD ENTERED
   ERROR-NO MATCHING RECORD: 555555555
0070-APPLY-TRANS-TO-MASTER ENTERED      TRANSACTION CODE: A
0090-ADD-NEW-RECORD ENTERED
0070-APPLY-TRANS-TO-MASTER ENTERED      TRANSACTION CODE: C
0100-CORRECT-OLD-RECORD ENTERED
0080-WRITE-NEW-MASTER ENTERED
```

Attempted correction is flagged before addition is accomplished.

Correction successfully applied <u>after</u> addition.

```
RECORDS BEING PROCESSED
   TRANSACTION SOC SEC #:  700000000
   OLD MASTER SOC SEC #:   600000000
   ACTIVE KEY:             600000000

0060-BUILD-NEW-MASTER ENTERED
0080-WRITE-NEW-MASTER ENTERED


RECORDS BEING PROCESSED
   TRANSACTION SOC SEC #:  700000000
   OLD MASTER SOC SEC #:   700000000
   ACTIVE KEY:             700000000

0060-BUILD-NEW-MASTER ENTERED
0070-APPLY-TRANS-TO-MASTER ENTERED      TRANSACTION CODE: C
0100-CORRECT-OLD-RECORD ENTERED
0080-WRITE-NEW-MASTER ENTERED
```

```
RECORDS BEING PROCESSED
  TRANSACTION SOC SEC #:  800000000
  OLD MASTER SOC SEC #:   800000000
  ACTIVE KEY:             800000000

0060-BUILD-NEW-MASTER ENTERED
0070-APPLY-TRANS-TO-MASTER ENTERED      TRANSACTION CODE: C
0100-CORRECT-OLD-RECORD ENTERED
0080-WRITE-NEW-MASTER ENTERED

RECORDS BEING PROCESSED
  TRANSACTION SOC SEC #:  ▒▒▒▒▒▒▒▒▒
  OLD MASTER SOC SEC #:   900000000
  ACTIVE KEY:             900000000

0060-BUILD-NEW-MASTER ENTERED
0080-WRITE-NEW-MASTER ENTERED
```

Transaction key has been set to HIGH-VALUES and does not print.

FIGURE 14.10 (Continued)

Indeed, Figure 14.9 is seen to contain many such DISPLAY statements to *facilitate testing by indicating program flow*. It will be shown that significant testing can take place without providing full details of the lower level modules such as 0090-ADD-NEW-RECORD or 0100-CORRECT-OLD-RECORD.

Consider the test data in Figure 14.8, in conjunction with the program in Figure 14.9 and its associated output (Figure 14.10). We begin by reading the first record from each file, Social Security numbers 000000000 and 100000000 for the transaction and old master, respectively. The active key is the *smaller* of the two, Social Security number 000000000, and corresponds to the transaction value. The paragraph 0070-APPLY-TRANS-TO-MASTER is entered for the first transaction, after which the lower level paragraph 0090-ADD-NEW-RECORD is invoked. The second transaction in the test data also has Social Security number 000000000, so that 0070-APPLY-TRANS-TO-MASTER is executed a second time, followed by 0100-CORRECT-OLD-RECORD. When the transaction key no longer equals the active key, i.e., when the third transaction (CRAWFORD, Social Security number 200000000) is read from Figure 14.8, the paragraph 0080-WRITE-NEW-MASTER is invoked, and this implies that a new master record will be written.

The second determination of the active key compares transaction and old master Social Security numbers of 200000000 and 100000000, producing an active key of 100000000. There is no activity for the existing old master, so that it is copied to the new master, as implied by the paragraphs 0060-BUILD-NEW-MASTER and 0080-WRITE-NEW-MASTER.

The third determination of the active key finds the *same* Social Security number in both files, producing an error message for a duplicate addition. The fourth active key, 300000000, indicates a second inactive master record with appropriate action as previously discussed. Multiple corrections are processed for the next active key 400000000, followed by an error message for the miscopied transaction Social Security number of 400000001.

By this time you should have the feeling *that the program in Figure 14.9 appears to be working*. In other words, paragraphs are executed in the correct sequence for the test data in Figure 14.8. A critical analysis of the output in Figure 14.10 can be construed as initial program testing. A successful conclusion, i.e., correspondence between the output in Figure 14.10 and the anticipated output for the test data, leads one to believe that the overall logic of the update program is correct. (The remainder of Figure 14.10 is left to you as an exercise.)

COMPLETED PROGRAM

Once the stubs program has been tested and debugged, it is relatively easy to "fill in the blanks" and complete the program. In other words, the most difficult portion of the program is the *interaction* between modules: whether to read from the old master or transaction file or both, how to hold the current old master record to apply multiple transactions, which lower level module to call (add, correct or delete), and so on.

Figure 14.11 is the completed version of Figure 14.9. The most obvious difference between the two programs is the increased length of Figure 14.11, which has been achieved by expanding the earlier program stubs. The completed program contains an added paragraph, 0105-CORRECT-INDIVIDUAL-FIELDS, which is called from 0100-CORRECT-OLD-RECORD. This extra paragraph is necessary because COBOL does not have an "in-line" perform capability. The completed program references NEW-MASTER-FILE explicitly and contains the requisite COBOL entries; SELECT, FD, etc.

```
IDENTIFICATION DIVISION.
PROGRAM-ID.    SEQUPDT.
AUTHOR.        JACKIE CLARK.

ENVIRONMENT DIVISION.
CONFIGURATION SECTION.
SOURCE-COMPUTER.      IBM-4341.
OBJECT-COMPUTER.      IBM-4341.

INPUT-OUTPUT SECTION.
FILE-CONTROL.
    SELECT TRANSACTION-FILE
        ASSIGN TO UT-S-TRANS.
    SELECT OLD-MASTER-FILE
        ASSIGN TO UT-S-MASTER.
    SELECT NEW-MASTER-FILE
        ASSIGN TO UT-S-NEWMAST.

DATA DIVISION.
FILE SECTION.
FD  TRANSACTION-FILE
    LABEL RECORDS ARE STANDARD
    BLOCK CONTAINS 0 RECORDS
    RECORD CONTAINS 80 CHARACTERS
    DATA RECORD IS TRANSACTION-RECORD.
01  TRANSACTION-RECORD                       PIC X(80).

FD  OLD-MASTER-FILE
    LABEL RECORDS ARE STANDARD
    BLOCK CONTAINS 0 RECORDS
    RECORD CONTAINS 80 CHARACTERS
    DATA RECORD IS OLD-MAST-RECORD.
01  OLD-MAST-RECORD                          PIC X(80).

FD  NEW-MASTER-FILE
    LABEL RECORDS ARE STANDARD
    BLOCK CONTAINS 0 RECORDS
    RECORD CONTAINS 80 CHARACTERS
    DATA RECORD IS NEW-MAST-RECORD.
01  NEW-MAST-RECORD                          PIC X(80).

WORKING-STORAGE SECTION.
01  FILLER                                   PIC X(14)
        VALUE 'WS BEGINS HERE'.

01  WS-TRANS-RECORD.
    05  TR-SOC-SEC-NUMBER                    PIC X(9).
    05  TR-NAME.
        10  TR-LAST-NAME                     PIC X(15).
        10  TR-INITIALS                      PIC XX.
    05  TR-DATE-OF-BIRTH.
```

Output file has been added. (boxed: SELECT NEW-MASTER-FILE / ASSIGN TO UT-S-NEWMAST.)

IBM OS feature to indicate block size is entered in JCL. (boxed: BLOCK CONTAINS 0 RECORDS in NEW-MASTER-FILE)

FIGURE 14.11 Completed Sequential Update

FIGURE 14.11 (Continued)

```
                10  TR-BIRTH-MONTH                     PIC 99.
                10  TR-BIRTH-YEAR                      PIC 99.
            05  TR-DATE-OF-HIRE.
                10  TR-HIRE-MONTH                      PIC 99.
                10  TR-HIRE-YEAR                       PIC 99.
            05  TR-LOCATION-CODE                       PIC X(3).
            05  TR-PERFORMANCE-CODE                    PIC X.
            05  TR-EDUCATION-CODE                      PIC X.
            05  TR-TITLE-DATA.
                10  TR-TITLE-CODE                      PIC 9(3).
                10  TR-TITLE-DATE                      PIC 9(4).
            05  TR-SALARY-DATA.
                10  TR-SALARY                          PIC 9(5).
                10  TR-SALARY-DATE                     PIC 9(4).
            05  TR-TRANSACTION-CODE                    PIC X.
                88  ADDITION           VALUE 'A'.
                88  CORRECTION         VALUE 'C'.
                88  DELETION           VALUE 'D'.
            05  FILLER                                 PIC X(24).

        01  WS-OLD-MAST-RECORD.
            05  OLD-SOC-SEC-NUMBER                     PIC X(9).
            05  OLD-NAME.
                10  OLD-LAST-NAME                      PIC X(15).
                10  OLD-INITIALS                       PIC XX.
            05  OLD-DATE-OF-BIRTH.
                10  OLD-BIRTH-MONTH                    PIC 99.
                10  OLD-BIRTH-YEAR                     PIC 99.
            05  OLD-DATE-OF-HIRE.
                10  OLD-HIRE-MONTH                     PIC 99.
                10  OLD-HIRE-YEAR                      PIC 99.
            05  OLD-LOCATION-CODE                      PIC X(3).
            05  OLD-PERFORMANCE-CODE                   PIC X.
            05  OLD-EDUCATION-CODE                     PIC X.
            05  OLD-TITLE-DATA OCCURS 2 TIMES.
                10  OLD-TITLE-CODE                     PIC 9(3).
                10  OLD-TITLE-DATE                     PIC 9(4).
            05  OLD-SALARY-DATA OCCURS 3 TIMES.
                10  OLD-SALARY                         PIC 9(5).
                10  OLD-SALARY-DATE                    PIC 9(4).

        01  WS-NEW-MAST-RECORD.
            05  NEW-SOC-SEC-NUMBER                     PIC X(9).
            05  NEW-NAME.
                10  NEW-LAST-NAME                      PIC X(15).
                10  NEW-INITIALS                       PIC XX.
            05  NEW-DATE-OF-BIRTH.
                10  NEW-BIRTH-MONTH                    PIC 99.
                10  NEW-BIRTH-YEAR                     PIC 99.
            05  NEW-DATE-OF-HIRE.
                10  NEW-HIRE-MONTH                     PIC 99.
                10  NEW-HIRE-YEAR                      PIC 99.
            05  NEW-LOCATION-CODE                      PIC X(3).
            05  NEW-PERFORMANCE-CODE                   PIC X.
            05  NEW-EDUCATION-CODE                     PIC X.
            05  NEW-TITLE-DATA OCCURS 2 TIMES.
                10  NEW-TITLE-CODE                     PIC 9(3).
                10  NEW-TITLE-DATE                     PIC 9(4).
            05  NEW-SALARY-DATA OCCURS 3 TIMES.
                10  NEW-SALARY                         PIC 9(5).
                10  NEW-SALARY-DATE                    PIC 9(4).

        01  WS-BALANCE-LINE-SWITCHES.
            05  WS-ACTIVE-KEY                          PIC X(9).
            05  WS-RECORD-KEY-ALLOCATED-SWITCH         PIC X(3).

        PROCEDURE DIVISION.
        0010-UPDATE-MASTER-FILE.
            OPEN INPUT  TRANSACTION-FILE
                        OLD-MASTER-FILE
                OUTPUT  NEW-MASTER-FILE.
            PERFORM 0020-READ-TRANSACTION-FILE.
            PERFORM 0030-READ-OLD-MASTER-FILE.
            PERFORM 0040-CHOOSE-ACTIVE-KEY.
            PERFORM 0050-PROCESS-ACTIVE-KEY
                UNTIL WS-ACTIVE-KEY = HIGH-VALUES.
            CLOSE TRANSACTION-FILE
                  OLD-MASTER-FILE
                  NEW-MASTER-FILE.
            STCP RUN.
```

Three transaction types.

Record layouts are identical.

Processing terminates when the active key is HIGH-VALUE; i.e., when both files are empty.

FIGURE 14.11 **(Continued)**

```
       0020-READ-TRANSACTION-FILE.
           READ TRANSACTION-FILE INTO WS-TRANS-RECORD
               AT END MOVE HIGH-VALUES TO TR-SOC-SEC-NUMBER.

       0030-READ-OLD-MASTER-FILE.
           READ OLD-MASTER-FILE INTO WS-OLD-MAST-RECORD
               AT END MOVE HIGH-VALUE TO OLD-SOC-SEC-NUMBER.

       0040-CHOOSE-ACTIVE-KEY.
           IF TR-SOC-SEC-NUMBER LESS THAN OLD-SOC-SEC-NUMBER
               MOVE TR-SOC-SEC-NUMBER TO WS-ACTIVE-KEY
           ELSE
               MOVE OLD-SOC-SEC-NUMBER TO WS-ACTIVE-KEY.

       0050-PROCESS-ACTIVE-KEY.
           IF OLD-SOC-SEC-NUMBER = WS-ACTIVE-KEY
               MOVE 'YES' TO WS-RECORD-KEY-ALLOCATED-SWITCH
               PERFORM 0060-BUILD-NEW-MASTER
           ELSE
               MOVE 'NO' TO WS-RECORD-KEY-ALLOCATED-SWITCH.

           PERFORM 0070-APPLY-TRANS-TO-MASTER
               UNTIL WS-ACTIVE-KEY NOT EQUAL TR-SOC-SEC-NUMBER.

           IF WS-RECORD-KEY-ALLOCATED-SWITCH = 'YES'
               PERFORM 0080-WRITE-NEW-MASTER.

           PERFORM 0040-CHOOSE-ACTIVE-KEY.

       0060-BUILD-NEW-MASTER.
           MOVE WS-OLD-MAST-RECORD TO WS-NEW-MAST-RECORD.
           PERFORM 0030-READ-OLD-MASTER-FILE.

       0070-APPLY-TRANS-TO-MASTER.
           IF ADDITION
               PERFORM 0090-ADD-NEW-RECORD
           ELSE
               IF CORRECTION
                   PERFORM 0100-CORRECT-OLD-RECORD
               ELSE
                   IF DELETION
                       PERFORM 0110-DELETE-OLD-RECORD.

           PERFORM 0020-READ-TRANSACTION-FILE.

       0080-WRITE-NEW-MASTER.
           WRITE NEW-MAST-RECORD FROM WS-NEW-MAST-RECORD.

       0090-ADD-NEW-RECORD.
           IF WS-RECORD-KEY-ALLOCATED-SWITCH = 'YES'
               DISPLAY '  ERROR-DUPLICATE ADDITION: ' TR-SOC-SEC-NUMBER
           ELSE
               MOVE 'YES' TO WS-RECORD-KEY-ALLOCATED-SWITCH
               MOVE SPACES TO WS-NEW-MAST-RECORD
               MOVE TR-SOC-SEC-NUMBER TO NEW-SOC-SEC-NUMBER
               MOVE TR-NAME TO NEW-NAME
               MOVE TR-DATE-OF-BIRTH TO NEW-DATE-OF-BIRTH
               MOVE TR-DATE-OF-HIRE TO NEW-DATE-OF-HIRE
               MOVE TR-LOCATION-CODE TO NEW-LOCATION-CODE
               MOVE TR-PERFORMANCE-CODE TO NEW-PERFORMANCE-CODE
               MOVE TR-EDUCATION-CODE TO NEW-EDUCATION-CODE
               MOVE TR-TITLE-DATA TO NEW-TITLE-DATA (1)
               MOVE TR-SALARY-DATA TO NEW-SALARY-DATA (1).

       0100-CORRECT-OLD-RECORD.
           IF WS-RECORD-KEY-ALLOCATED-SWITCH = 'YES'
               PERFORM 0105-CORRECT-INDIVIDUAL-FIELDS
           ELSE
               DISPLAY '  ERROR-NO MATCHING RECORD: ' TR-SOC-SEC-NUMBER.

       0105-CORRECT-INDIVIDUAL-FIELDS.
           IF TR-NAME NOT EQUAL SPACES
               MOVE TR-NAME TO NEW-NAME.
           IF TR-DATE-OF-BIRTH NOT EQUAL SPACES
               MOVE TR-DATE-OF-BIRTH TO NEW-DATE-OF-BIRTH.
           IF TR-DATE-OF-HIRE NOT EQUAL SPACES
               MOVE TR-DATE-OF-HIRE TO NEW-DATE-OF-HIRE.
           IF TR-LOCATION-CODE NOT EQUAL SPACES
               MOVE TR-LOCATION-CODE TO NEW-LOCATION-CODE.
```

Applies multiple transactions to a single master record.

Expanded from a program stub.

```
00212          IF  TR-PERFORMANCE-CODE NOT EQUAL SPACES
00213              MOVE TR-PERFORMANCE-CODE TO NEW-PERFORMANCE-CODE.
00214          IF TR-EDUCATION-CODE NOT EQUAL SPACES
00215              MOVE TR-EDUCATION-CODE TO NEW-EDUCATION-CODE.
00216          IF TR-TITLE-CODE IS NUMERIC
00217              MOVE TR-TITLE-CODE TO NEW-TITLE-CODE (1).
00218          IF TR-TITLE-DATE IS NUMERIC
00219              MOVE TR-TITLE-DATE TO NEW-TITLE-DATE (1).
00220          IF TR-SALARY IS NUMERIC
00221              MOVE TR-SALARY TO NEW-SALARY (1).
00222          IF TR-SALARY-DATE IS NUMERIC
00223              MOVE TR-SALARY-DATE TO NEW-SALARY-DATE (1).
00224
00225      0110-DELETE-OLD-RECORD.
00226          IF WS-RECORD-KEY-ALLOCATED-SWITCH = 'YES'
00227              MOVE 'NO' TO WS-RECORD-KEY-ALLOCATED-SWITCH
00228          ELSE
00229              DISPLAY '  ERROR-NO MATCHING RECORD: ' TR-SOC-SEC-NUMBER.
```

Precludes writing new master and deletes record (see lines 157-158).

FIGURE 14.11 **(Continued)**

Output produced by the program in Figure 14.11 using the test data in Figure 14.8 is shown in Figure 14.12. You should carefully verify the correctness of the output with respect to the original test data. Observe in particular how multiple transactions were applied to a single old master record (BENJAMIN), how BOROW was successfully added to the new master, and how TATER was deleted. The error messages successfully reflect both erroneous conditions, a duplicate addition and a miscopied Social Security number.

The error message associated with employee 555555555 further illustrates the power of the balance line algorithm. The first transaction is correctly flagged as an error because the Social Security number is not present in the old master. The second transaction adds the record, and the third and last transaction changes title from 444 to 555.

This record has been added. Two fields have been corrected from two different transactions.

```
000000000BOROW         JS0343128110OX99871281         550001281
100000000SUGRUE        P 124508791OOE5333088022208792800010812600O0980
200000000CRAWFORD      MA0943067810OE64440678         420000680360000678
300000000MILGROM       IR0613058O200E6555108140006814800O0580
400000000BENJAMIN      BL1054107410OE73331073         300001081280001080
555555555NEW EMPLOYEE  RT1144068110OE65550681         390000681
600000000GRAUER        RT1145087720OE590011818001180500001181450001180
700000000JONES         A 09500778100G644407793330778385000781360000779
800000000SMITH         BB0852068130OP84000681         385000681
900000000BAKER         E 06490879100G99870879         650000881550000879
```

Social Security number 500000000 has been deleted.

(a) New Master

```
ERROR-DUPLICATE ADDITION: 200000000
ERROR-NO MATCHING RECORD: 400000001
ERROR-NO MATCHING RECORD: 555555555
```

Pertains to first transaction for this record.

(b) Error Messages

FIGURE 14.12 Output of Sequential Update (see test data of Figure 14.8)

PROGRAM MAINTENANCE

We have stated repeatedly that a well-written program must be easily read and maintained and have argued that adherence to the structured methodology brings this goal closer. This section puts the theory to the acid test of program maintenance. Specifically, we consider a number of nontrivial changes to the completed program in Figure 14.11. These are:

1. Inclusion of a *second* transaction (i.e., a promotion) file to accommodate promotions and/or salary increases. The record layout for this file is shown in Figure 14.13.
2. Salary increases are to be handled in the following manner: the transaction salary becomes the present salary in the new master, causing the present salary in the old master to become the previous salary in the new master. In similar fashion, the previous salary in the old master becomes the second previous salary in the new master. (The record layout of the master file in the programming specifications allowed three salary levels.) The situation is shown schematically in Figure 14.14. Each occurrence of salary is accompanied by a salary date in both the old master and promotion record layouts. Accordingly, the salary dates and the salaries are to be adjusted simultaneously.
3. Promotions (i.e., title changes in the new file) are to be handled in a manner analogous to salary increases. Hence the transaction title, PR-TITLE-CODE, becomes the present title in the new master, causing the present title in the old master to

```
01  PROMOTION-RECORD.
    05  PR-SOC-SEC-NUMBER               PIC X(9).
    05  PR-NAME.
        10  PR-LAST-NAME                PIC X(15).
        10  PR-INITIALS                 PIC XX.
    05  PR-SALARY-DATA.
        10  PR-SALARY                   PIC 9(5).
        10  PR-SALARY-DATE              PIC 9(4).
    05  PR-TITLE-DATA.
        10  PR-TITLE-CODE               PIC 9(3).
        10  PR-TITLE-DATE               PIC 9(4).
    05  PR-PROMOTION-CODE               PIC X.
        88  SALARY-RAISE          VALUE 'R'.
        88  PROMOTION             VALUE 'P'.
    05  FILLER                          PIC X(37).
```

FIGURE 14.13 **Promotion Record**

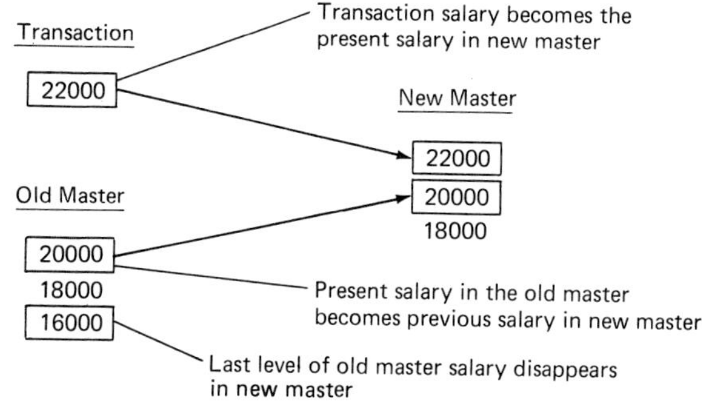

FIGURE 14.14 **Salary Increases**

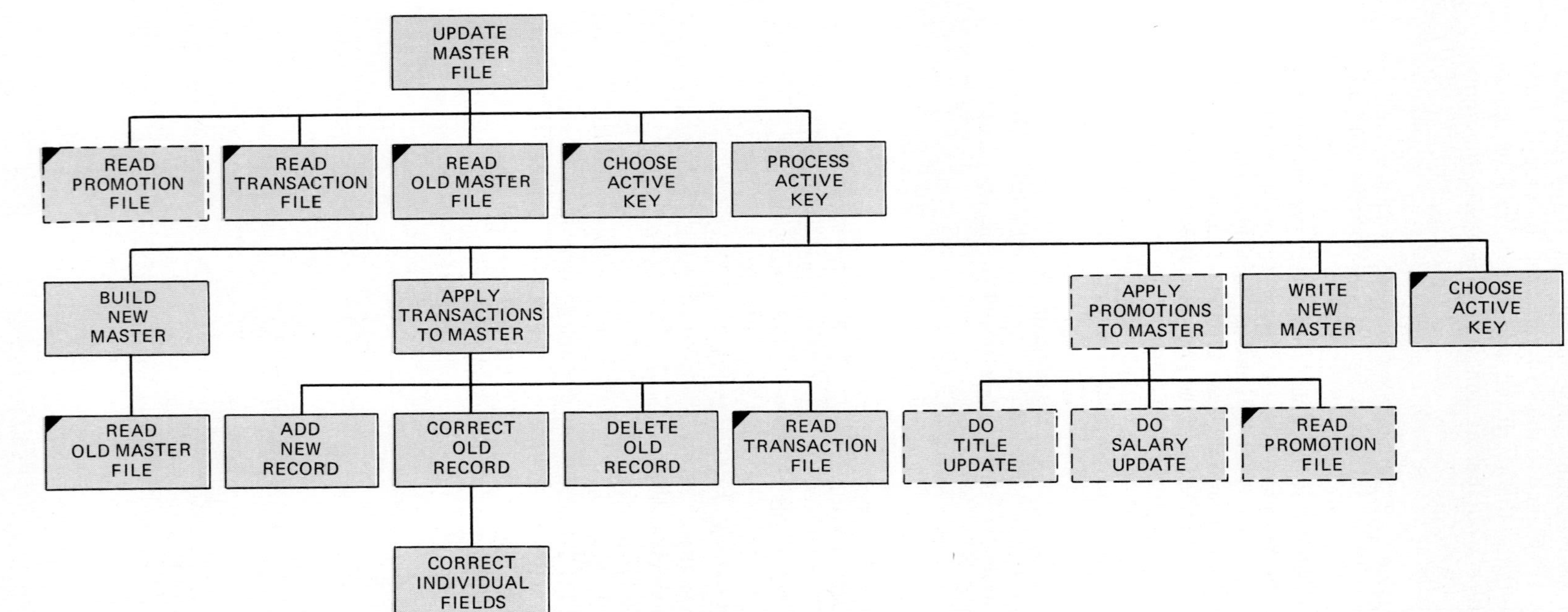

FIGURE 14.15 Expanded Hierarchy Chart. Notes: 1. Dotted lines indicate new modules which must be added as a consequence of the modification requirements. 2. The internal logic of CHOOSE-ACTIVE-KEY, and DELETE-OLD-RECORD will change. 3. Shading in upper left corner indicates a module which is called from more than one place.

become the previous title in the new master. The associated dates are to be adjusted simultaneously.

4. Deletions (in the original transaction file) are to be written in their entirety to a new file, DELETED-RECORD-FILE, for possible recall at a future date.
5. All error messages are to be expanded to print the entire transaction that is in error.

The implementation of these modifications is best accomplished by considering the necessary changes in the program's hierarchy chart. Figure 14.6 contained the chart for the original problem, and Figure 14.15 depicts the expanded version. Dashed lines in Figure 14.15 denote additional modules mandated by the required changes.

It should be apparent that a new module, APPLY-PROMOTIONS-TO-MASTER, is necessary to process the additional file. It in turn has three subordinates, DO-TITLE-UPDATE, DO-SALARY-UPDATE, and READ-PROMOTION-FILE. The latter is called from two places: in UPDATE-MASTER-FILE to provide the priming read for the promotion file, and from APPLY-PROMOTIONS-TO-MASTER to read the next promotion record.

The true generality of the balance line algorithm is appreciated from the expanded chart in Figure 14.15. Even though a new input file has been added, there are no new modules required for the algorithm per se. It is, of course, necessary to change the logic of CHOOSE-ACTIVE-KEY, in that active key is now the smallest of *three* values (old master, transaction, and promotion Social Security numbers), rather than two as before. However, it is relatively simple to make this change, and further, we are confident it will work. (Could the same degree of confidence be achieved if you were suddenly asked to modify the last maintenance program you wrote?)

It is also necessary to change the internal code of DELETE-OLD-RECORD in order to write deleted transactions to a special file. Again, we are confident that the change will work and, further, that *the change will not affect any other modules in the program*. This is because the modules in the hierarchy chart were carefully developed to be *highly cohesive,* but *loosely coupled,* COBOL paragraphs. In other words, each paragraph in the maintenance program accomplishes a *single* function, and further, the paragraphs are relatively independent of one another. We are able to make changes easily and avoid the almost universal condition of fixing one problem but creating two new ones in its stead.

The modified program is shown in Figure 14.16. The program should be self-explanatory, and we say nothing further. Test data and associated output are shown in Figure 14.17. (The transaction and old master files in Figure 14.17 are the same as in Figure 14.8.)

COBOL EXTENSIONS

The illustrations of Figures 14.9, 14.11, and 14.16 were well-written and complete COBOL programs. They served to demonstrate the balance line algorithm, top-down testing, and program maintenance. Nevertheless, there are additional COBOL constructs in the SELECT statement that are useful in processing sequential files in a commercial setting. You are referred to the discussion on page 397 and to the 1974 ANS COBOL language summary[3] for additional information.

[3]*American National Standard Programming Language COBOL,* X3.23-1974 (New York: American National Standards Institute, 1974).

```
IDENTIFICATION DIVISION.
PROGRAM-ID.    SEQUPEX.
AUTHOR.        JACKIE CLARK.

ENVIRONMENT DIVISION.
CONFIGURATION SECTION.
SOURCE-COMPUTER.       IBM-4341.
OBJECT-COMPUTER.       IBM-4341.

INPUT-OUTPUT SECTION.
FILE-CONTROL.
    SELECT TRANSACTION-FILE
        ASSIGN TO UT-S-TRANS.
    SELECT OLD-MASTER-FILE
        ASSIGN TO UT-S-MASTER.
    SELECT PROMOTION-FILE
        ASSIGN TO UT-S-PROMOTE.
    SELECT DELETED-RECORD-FILE
        ASSIGN TO UT-S-DELETE.
    SELECT NEW-MASTER-FILE
        ASSIGN TO UT-S-NEWMAST.

DATA DIVISION.
FILE SECTION.
FD  TRANSACTION-FILE
    LABEL RECORDS ARE STANDARD
    BLOCK CONTAINS 0 RECORDS
    RECORD CONTAINS 80 CHARACTERS
    DATA RECORD IS TRANSACTION-RECORD.
01  TRANSACTION-RECORD                       PIC X(80).

FD  OLD-MASTER-FILE
    LABEL RECORDS ARE STANDARD
    BLOCK CONTAINS 0 RECORDS
    RECORD CONTAINS 80 CHARACTERS
    DATA RECORD IS OLD-MAST-RECORD.
01  OLD-MAST-RECORD                          PIC X(80).

FD  PROMOTION-FILE
    LABEL RECORDS ARE STANDARD
    BLOCK CONTAINS 0 RECORDS
    RECORD CONTAINS 80 CHARACTERS
    DATA RECORD IS PROMOTION-RECORD.
01  PROMOTION-RECORD                         PIC X(80).

FD  DELETED-RECORD-FILE
    LABEL RECORDS ARE STANDARD
    BLOCK CONTAINS 0 RECORDS
    RECORD CONTAINS 80 CHARACTERS
    DATA RECORD IS DELETED-RECORD.
01  DELETED-RECORD                           PIC X(80).

FD  NEW-MASTER-FILE
    LABEL RECORDS ARE STANDARD
    BLOCK CONTAINS 0 RECORDS
    RECORD CONTAINS 80 CHARACTERS
    DATA RECORD IS NEW-MAST-RECORD.
01  NEW-MAST-RECORD                          PIC X(80).

WORKING-STORAGE SECTION.
01  FILLER                                   PIC X(14)
        VALUE 'WS BEGINS HERE'.

01  WS-TRANS-RECORD.
    05  TR-SOC-SEC-NUMBER                    PIC X(9).
    05  TR-NAME.
        10  TR-LAST-NAME                     PIC X(15).
        10  TR-INITIALS                      PIC XX.
    05  TR-DATE-OF-BIRTH.
        10  TR-BIRTH-MONTH                   PIC 99.
        10  TR-BIRTH-YEAR                    PIC 99.
    05  TR-DATE-OF-HIRE.
        10  TR-HIRE-MONTH                    PIC 99.
        10  TR-HIRE-YEAR                     PIC 99.
    05  TR-LOCATION-CODE                     PIC X(3).
    05  TR-PERFORMANCE-CODE                  PIC X.
    05  TR-EDUCATION-CODE                    PIC X.
    05  TR-TITLE-DATA.
        10  TR-TITLE-CODE                    PIC 9(3).
        10  TR-TITLE-DATE                    PIC 9(4).
```

PROMOTION-FILE has been added

FIGURE 14.16 Modified Sequential Update

```
               05  TR-SALARY-DATA.
                   10  TR-SALARY                       PIC 9(5).
                   10  TR-SALARY-DATE                  PIC 9(4).
               05  TR-TRANSACTION-CODE                 PIC X.
                   88  ADDITION         VALUE 'A'.
                   88  CORRECTION       VALUE 'C'.
                   88  DELETION         VALUE 'D'.
               05  FILLER                              PIC X(24).

           01  WS-PROMOTION-RECORD.
               05  PR-SOC-SEC-NUMBER                   PIC X(9).
               05  PR-NAME.
                   10  PR-LAST-NAME                    PIC X(15).
                   10  PR-INITIALS                     PIC XX.
               05  PR-SALARY-DATA.
                   10  PR-SALARY                       PIC 9(5).
                   10  PR-SALARY-DATE                  PIC 9(4).
               05  PR-TITLE-DATA.
                   10  PR-TITLE-CODE                   PIC 9(3).
                   10  PR-TITLE-DATE                   PIC 9(4).
               05  PR-PROMOTION-CODE                   PIC X.
                   88  SALARY-RAISE     VALUE 'R'.
                   88  PROMOTION        VALUE 'P'.
               05  FILLER                              PIC X(37).

           01  WS-OLD-MAST-RECORD.
               05  OLD-SOC-SEC-NUMBER                  PIC X(9).
               05  OLD-NAME.
                   10  OLD-LAST-NAME                   PIC X(15).
                   10  OLD-INITIALS                    PIC XX.
               05  OLD-DATE-OF-BIRTH.
                   10  OLD-BIRTH-MONTH                 PIC 99.
                   10  OLD-BIRTH-YEAR                  PIC 99.
               05  OLD-DATE-OF-HIRE.
                   10  OLD-HIRE-MONTH                  PIC 99.
                   10  OLD-HIRE-YEAR                   PIC 99.
               05  OLD-LOCATION-CODE                   PIC X(3).
               05  OLD-PERFORMANCE-CODE                PIC X.
               05  OLD-EDUCATION-CODE                  PIC X.
               05  OLD-TITLE-DATA OCCURS 2 TIMES.      <-- Two levels of title data.
                   10  OLD-TITLE-CODE                  PIC 9(3).
                   10  OLD-TITLE-DATE                  PIC 9(4).
               05  OLD-SALARY-DATA OCCURS 3 TIMES.     <-- Three levels of salary data.
                   10  OLD-SALARY                      PIC 9(5).
                   10  OLD-SALARY-DATE                 PIC 9(4).

           01  WS-NEW-MAST-RECORD.
               05  NEW-SOC-SEC-NUMBER                  PIC X(9).
               05  NEW-NAME.
                   10  NEW-LAST-NAME                   PIC X(15).
                   10  NEW-INITIALS                    PIC XX.
               05  NEW-DATE-OF-BIRTH.
                   10  NEW-BIRTH-MONTH                 PIC 99.
                   10  NEW-BIRTH-YEAR                  PIC 99.
               05  NEW-DATE-OF-HIRE.
                   10  NEW-HIRE-MONTH                  PIC 99.
                   10  NEW-HIRE-YEAR                   PIC 99.
               05  NEW-LOCATION-CODE                   PIC X(3).
               05  NEW-PERFORMANCE-CODE                PIC X.
               05  NEW-EDUCATION-CODE                  PIC X.
               05  NEW-TITLE-DATA OCCURS 2 TIMES.
                   10  NEW-TITLE-CODE                  PIC 9(3).
                   10  NEW-TITLE-DATE                  PIC 9(4).
               05  NEW-SALARY-DATA OCCURS 3 TIMES.
                   10  NEW-SALARY                      PIC 9(5).
                   10  NEW-SALARY-DATE                 PIC 9(4).

           01  WS-BALANCE-LINE-SWITCHES.
               05  WS-ACTIVE-KEY                       PIC X(9).
               05  WS-RECORD-KEY-ALLOCATED-SWITCH      PIC X(3).

           PROCEDURE DIVISION.
           0010-UPDATE-MASTER-FILE.
               OPEN INPUT  TRANSACTION-FILE
                           PROMOTION-FILE
                           OLD-MASTER-FILE
                    OUTPUT NEW-MASTER-FILE
                           DELETED-RECORD-FILE.
               PERFORM 0015-READ-PROMOTION-FILE.
               PERFORM 0020-READ-TRANSACTION-FILE.
```

```
           PERFORM 0030-READ-OLD-MASTER-FILE.
           PERFORM 0040-CHOOSE-ACTIVE-KEY.
           PERFORM 0050-PROCESS-ACTIVE-KEY
               UNTIL WS-ACTIVE-KEY = HIGH-VALUES.
           CLOSE TRANSACTION-FILE
                 PROMOTION-FILE
                 OLD-MASTER-FILE
                 NEW-MASTER-FILE
                 DELETED-RECORD-FILE.
           STOP RUN.

       0015-READ-PROMOTION-FILE.
           READ PROMOTION-FILE INTO WS-PROMOTION-RECORD
               AT END MOVE HIGH-VALUES TO PR-SOC-SEC-NUMBER.

       0020-READ-TRANSACTION-FILE.
           READ TRANSACTION-FILE INTO WS-TRANS-RECORD
               AT END MOVE HIGH-VALUES TO TR-SOC-SEC-NUMBER.

       0030-READ-OLD-MASTER-FILE.
           READ OLD-MASTER-FILE INTO WS-OLD-MAST-RECORD
               AT END MOVE HIGH-VALUE TO OLD-SOC-SEC-NUMBER.

       0040-CHOOSE-ACTIVE-KEY.
           IF TR-SOC-SEC-NUMBER LESS THAN OLD-SOC-SEC-NUMBER
               IF TR-SOC-SEC-NUMBER LESS THAN PR-SOC-SEC-NUMBER
                   MOVE TR-SOC-SEC-NUMBER TO WS-ACTIVE-KEY
               ELSE
                   MOVE PR-SOC-SEC-NUMBER TO WS-ACTIVE-KEY
           ELSE
               IF PR-SOC-SEC-NUMBER LESS THAN OLD-SOC-SEC-NUMBER
                   MOVE PR-SOC-SEC-NUMBER TO WS-ACTIVE-KEY
               ELSE
                   MOVE OLD-SOC-SEC-NUMBER TO WS-ACTIVE-KEY.

       0050-PROCESS-ACTIVE-KEY.
           IF OLD-SOC-SEC-NUMBER = WS-ACTIVE-KEY
               MOVE 'YES' TO WS-RECORD-KEY-ALLOCATED-SWITCH
               PERFORM 0060-BUILD-NEW-MASTER
           ELSE
               MOVE 'NO' TO WS-RECORD-KEY-ALLOCATED-SWITCH.

           PERFORM 0070-APPLY-TRANS-TO-MASTER
               UNTIL WS-ACTIVE-KEY NOT EQUAL TR-SOC-SEC-NUMBER.

           PERFORM 0075-APPLY-PROMO-TO-MASTER
               UNTIL WS-ACTIVE-KEY NOT EQUAL PR-SOC-SEC-NUMBER.

           IF WS-RECORD-KEY-ALLOCATED-SWITCH = 'YES'
               PERFORM 0080-WRITE-NEW-MASTER.

           PERFORM 0040-CHOOSE-ACTIVE-KEY.

       0060-BUILD-NEW-MASTER.
           MOVE WS-OLD-MAST-RECORD TO WS-NEW-MAST-RECORD.
           PERFORM 0030-READ-OLD-MASTER-FILE.

       0070-APPLY-TRANS-TO-MASTER.
           IF ADDITION
               PERFORM 0090-ADD-NEW-RECORD
           ELSE
               IF CORRECTION
                   PERFORM 0100-CORRECT-OLD-RECORD
               ELSE
                   IF DELETION
                       PERFORM 0110-DELETE-OLD-RECORD.

           PERFORM 0020-READ-TRANSACTION-FILE.

       0075-APPLY-PROMO-TO-MASTER.
           IF PROMOTION
               PERFORM 0120-DO-TITLE-UPDATE
           ELSE
               IF SALARY-RAISE
                   PERFORM 0130-DO-SALARY-RAISE.

           PERFORM 0015-READ-PROMOTION-FILE.

       0080-WRITE-NEW-MASTER.
           WRITE NEW-MAST-RECORD FROM WS-NEW-MAST-RECORD.
```

00241
Logic expanded to include PROMOTION-FILE.

Intermediate-level module has been added.

FIGURE 14.16 *(Continued)*

```
00242          0090-ADD-NEW-RECORD.
00243             IF WS-RECORD-KEY-ALLOCATED-SWITCH = 'YES'
00244                 DISPLAY '    '
00245                 DISPLAY '    ERROR DUPLICATE ADDITION: '
00246                 DISPLAY '       TRANSACTION IN ERROR: ' WS-TRANS-RECORD
00247             ELSE
00248                 MOVE 'YES' TO WS-RECORD-KEY-ALLOCATED-SWITCH
00249                 MOVE SPACES TO WS-NEW-MAST-RECORD
00250                 MOVE TR-SOC-SEC-NUMBER TO NEW-SOC-SEC-NUMBER
00251                 MOVE TR-NAME TO NEW-NAME
00252                 MOVE TR-DATE-OF-BIRTH TO NEW-DATE-OF-BIRTH
00253                 MOVE TR-DATE-OF-HIRE TO NEW-DATE-OF-HIRE
00254                 MOVE TR-LOCATION-CODE TO NEW-LOCATION-CODE
00255                 MOVE TR-PERFORMANCE-CODE TO NEW-PERFORMANCE-CODE
00256                 MOVE TR-EDUCATION-CODE TO NEW-EDUCATION-CODE
00257                 MOVE TR-TITLE-DATA TO NEW-TITLE-DATA (1)
00258                 MOVE TR-SALARY-DATA TO NEW-SALARY-DATA (1).
00259
00260          0100-CORRECT-OLD-RECORD.
00261             IF WS-RECORD-KEY-ALLOCATED-SWITCH = 'YES'
00262                 PERFORM 0105-CORRECT-INDIVIDUAL-FIELDS
00263             ELSE
00264                 DISPLAY '    '
00265                 DISPLAY '  ERROR-NO MATCHING RECORD: '
00266                 DISPLAY '      TRANSACTION IN ERROR: ' WS-TRANS-RECORD.
00267
00268          0105-CORRECT-INDIVIDUAL-FIELDS.
00269             IF TR-NAME NOT EQUAL SPACES
00270                 MOVE TR-NAME TO NEW-NAME.
00271             IF TR-DATE-OF-BIRTH NOT EQUAL SPACES
00272                 MOVE TR-DATE-OF-BIRTH TO NEW-DATE-OF-BIRTH.
00273             IF TR-DATE-OF-HIRE NOT EQUAL SPACES
00274                 MOVE TR-DATE-OF-HIRE TO NEW-DATE-OF-HIRE.
00275             IF TR-LOCATION-CODE NOT EQUAL SPACES
00276                 MOVE TR-LOCATION-CODE TO NEW-LOCATION-CODE.
00277             IF TR-PERFORMANCE-CODE NOT EQUAL SPACES
00278                 MOVE TR-PERFORMANCE-CODE TO NEW-PERFORMANCE-CODE.
00279             IF TR-EDUCATION-CODE NOT EQUAL SPACES
00280                 MOVE TR-EDUCATION-CODE TO NEW-EDUCATION-CODE.
00281             IF TR-TITLE-CODE IS NUMERIC
00282                 MOVE TR-TITLE-CODE TO NEW-TITLE-CODE (1).
00283             IF TR-TITLE-DATE IS NUMERIC
00284                 MOVE TR-TITLE-DATE TO NEW-TITLE-DATE (1).
00285             IF TR-SALARY IS NUMERIC
00286                 MOVE TR-SALARY TO NEW-SALARY (1).
00287             IF TR-SALARY-DATE IS NUMERIC
00288                 MOVE TR-SALARY-DATE TO NEW-SALARY-DATE (1).
00289
00290          0110-DELETE-OLD-RECORD.
00291             IF WS-RECORD-KEY-ALLOCATED-SWITCH = 'YES'
00292                 MOVE 'NO' TO WS-RECORD-KEY-ALLOCATED-SWITCH
00293                 WRITE DELETED-RECORD FROM WS-NEW-MAST-RECORD
00294             ELSE
00295                 DISPLAY '    '
00296                 DISPLAY '  ERROR-NO MATCHING RECORD: '
00297                 DISPLAY '      TRANSACTION IN ERROR: ' WS-TRANS-RECORD.
00298
00299          0120-DO-TITLE-UPDATE.
00300             IF WS-RECORD-KEY-ALLOCATED-SWITCH = 'YES'
00301                 MOVE NEW-TITLE-CODE (1) TO NEW-TITLE-CODE (2)
00302                 MOVE NEW-TITLE-DATE (1) TO NEW-TITLE-DATE (2)
00303                 MOVE PR-TITLE-CODE TO NEW-TITLE-CODE (1)
00304                 MOVE PR-TITLE-DATE TO NEW-TITLE-DATE (1)
00305             ELSE
00306                 DISPLAY '    '
00307                 DISPLAY '  ERROR-NO MATCHING RECORD: '
00308                 DISPLAY '     PROMOTION IN ERROR: ' WS-PROMOTION-RECORD.
00309
00310          0130-DO-SALARY-RAISE.
00311             IF WS-RECORD-KEY-ALLOCATED-SWITCH = 'YES'
00312                 MOVE NEW-SALARY (2) TO NEW-SALARY (3)
00313                 MOVE NEW-SALARY-DATE (2) TO NEW-SALARY-DATE (3)
00314                 MOVE NEW-SALARY (1) TO NEW-SALARY (2)
00315                 MOVE NEW-SALARY-DATE (1) TO NEW-SALARY-DATE (2)
00316                 MOVE PR-SALARY TO NEW-SALARY (1)
00317                 MOVE PR-SALARY-DATE TO NEW-SALARY-DATE (1)
00318             ELSE
00319                 DISPLAY '    '
00320                 DISPLAY '  ERROR-NO MATCHING RECORD: '
00321                 DISPLAY '     PROMOTION IN ERROR: ' WS-PROMOTION-RECORD.
```

Error messages are better formatted.

Deleted records are written to a new file.

Low-level modules have been added.

```
000000000BOROW        JS03431281100 99871281550001281A
000000000BOROW        JS            X                C
200000000CRAWFORD     MA09430678100E6444068042000068 0A
400000000BENJAMIN     BL                             C
400000000BENJAMIN     BL1054                         C
400000000BENJAMIN     BL     1074                    C
400000001BENJAMIN     BL          200                C
500000000TATER        C                              D
555555555NEW EMPLOYEE RT1145                         C
555555555NEW EMPLOYEE RT11440681100E64440681390000681A
555555555NEW EMPLOYEE RT                555          C
700000000JONES        A                     385000781C
800000000SMITH        BB                400          C
```

FIGURE 14.17a *Transaction File (repeated from Figure 14.8b)*

Benjamin's salary will be updated in the new master.

```
400000000BENJAMIN      350000182       R
400000000BENJAMIN             4440182P
500000000TATER         330000182       R
600000000GRAUER               9990182P
800000000SMITH         900000182       R
888888888JOHNSON       400000182       R
```

FIGURE 14.17b *Promotion File*

```
100000000SUGRUE       P 12450879100E5333088022208792800010812600000980
200000000CRAWFORD     MA09430678100E64440678        420000680360000678
300000000MILGROM      IR06130580200E655510814000681480000580
400000000BENJAMIN     BL10531073100E73331073        300001081280001080
500000000TATER        JS02500779200P43330779        310001081270000779
600000000GRAUER       RT11450877200E590011818001180500001181450001180
700000000JONES        A 09500778100G644407793330778390000881360000779
800000000SMITH        BB08520681300P84440681        385000681
900000000BAKER        E 06490879100G99870879        650000881550000879
```

FIGURE 14.17c *Old Master File (repeated from Figure 14.8a)*

Benjamin now has three salary levels to indicate that a salary update has taken place.

```
000000000BOROW        JS03431281100X99871281        550001281
100000000SUGRUE       P 12450879100E5333088022208792800010812600000980
200000000CRAWFORD     MA09430678100E64440678        420000680360000678
300000000MILGROM      IR06130580200E655510814000681480000580
400000000BENJAMIN     BL10541074100E74440182333107335000018230000108128000 1080
555555555NEW EMPLOYEE RT11440681100E65550681        390000681
600000000GRAUER       RT11450877200E599901829001181500001181450001180
700000000JONES        A 09500778100G644407793330778385000781360000779
800000000SMITH        BB08520681300P84000681        900000182385000681    0   0
900000000BAKER        E 06490879100G99870879        650000881550000879
```

FIGURE 14.17d *New Master File*

Deleted records are now written to a separate file.

```
500000000TATER          JS02500779200P43330779          310001081270000779
```

FIGURE 14.17e Deleted Record File

Error message is better formatted than in Figure 6.10b.

```
ERROR DUPLICATE ADDITION:
  TRANSACTION IN ERROR: 200000000CRAWFORD        MA094306781OOE64440680420000680A

ERROR-NO MATCHING RECORD:
  TRANSACTION IN ERROR: 400000001BENJAMIN        BL          200                   C

ERROR-NO MATCHING RECORD:
  PROMOTION IN ERROR: 500000000TATER             330000182           R

ERROR-NO MATCHING RECORD:
  TRANSACTION IN ERROR: 555555555NEW EMPLOYEE    RT1145                            C

ERROR-NO MATCHING RECORD:
  PROMOTION IN ERROR: 888888888JOHNSON           400000182           R
```

FIGURE 14.17f Error Messages

SELECT Statement

The 1974 standard recognizes three types of file organization (sequential, relative, and indexed), with three distinct SELECT statements. The complete SELECT statement for sequential files has the format

```
SELECT [OPTIONAL] file-name
    ASSIGN TO implementor-name-1 [, implementor-name-2] ...
   [RESERVE integer-1 {AREA | AREAS}]
   [ORGANIZATION IS SEQUENTIAL]
   [ACCESS MODE IS SEQUENTIAL]
   [FILE STATUS IS data-name-1]
```

The OPTIONAL clause means that the file need not be present when the program is run, e.g., during the first cycle of sequential maintenance during which the old master file does not exist. The RESERVE clause increases processing efficiency by providing alternate I/O areas (buffers), and unless otherwise instructed, most compilers reserve at least one alternate area. The ORGANIZATION and ACCESS MODE clauses default to sequential, and consequently these clauses are often omitted for sequential files. They are required, however, for other types of file organization, such as indexed files. The FILE STATUS clause allows one to monitor the execution of each I/O request and is further discussed in Chapter 15.

COBOL 8X:

Changes and Enhancements

As indicated previously, a major motivation behind the new compiler was to make COBOL more conducive to structured programming theory. Consequently many features have been added which, if included, can further improve the readability and structure of the sequential update programs in this chapter.

Appendix B contains a complete discussion of the following enhancements: END-IF scope terminator, in-line PERFORM, false condition branch on a READ statement (i.e., NOT AT END), and the EVALUATE statement for expressing the case construct. Collectively, these elements can be applied to the sequential update program in a manner analogous to Figure B.3.

Summary

The chapter began with discussion of the balance line algorithm, a truly general approach to sequential file maintenance. The algorithm allows multiple transactions to reference a single master record, as well as multiple transaction files. The flexibility of the approach was further demonstrated by the example on program maintenance in which the original specifications were significantly altered.

The author made a point of the ease with which he was able to modify the program in Figure 14.11 to accommodate revised specifications. Attention was drawn to the expanded hierarchy chart in which new modules were added and existing modules enlarged. Program maintenance was also facilitated by the attention paid to programming style, in particular the use of meaningful data names and indentation, which is present in all illustrative programs.

The concept of top-down testing was demonstrated through the stubs program in Figure 14.9 and its associated output in Figure 14.10. Early testing ensures that modules are called in proper sequence and facilitates the correction of any errors detected. The preparation of test data was discussed. It was suggested that anyone but the programmer *provide the data and that the anticipated results be calculated* before *the program is actually run.*

The chapter concluded with a discussion of advanced syntactical features in the SELECT statement for sequential files.

True/False Exercises

1. The balance line algorithm requires a unique key for every record in the old master file.
2. Transactions to the balance line algorithm must be presented in the following order: additions, changes, deletions.
3. The balance line algorithm permits multiple transactions for the same master record and can be generalized to any number of transaction files.
4. A program must be completely coded before any testing can begin.

5. The highest level modules in a hierarchy chart should be tested first.
6. One can logically assume that input to a maintenance program will be valid.
7. One need not check for duplicate additions if the transaction file has been run through a stand-alone edit program.
8. A module in a hierarchy chart can be called from more than one place.
9. Pseudocode and hierarchy charts depict the same thing.
10. A program stub may consist of a one-line DISPLAY paragraph.
11. Test data should be designed by the programmer writing the program.
12. Top-down testing can be applied to complete systems as well as individual programs.
13. All records in a sequential file must be of the same length.
14. Variable-length records may be blocked.
15. "Physical record" and "logical record" are synonymous.
16. A blocking factor of 3 implies that 3 buffers will be used to process the file.
17. The ORGANIZATION and ACCESS MODE clauses are optional in the SELECT statement for sequential files.
18. BLOCK CONTAINS 0 RECORDS is a valid entry under IBM's OS operating system.
19. Use of FILE STATUS and DECLARATIVES is not permitted with sequential files.
20. Sequential files may be stored on either tape or disk.
21. The balance line algorithm is restricted to a single transaction file.
22. A hierachy chart contains decision making logic.

Problems

1. Modify the pseudocode in Figure 14.5 to accommodate the change in specifications associated with the additional file. Does the additional pseudocode make the overall figure unwieldy? Do you think the resulting pseudocode should be subdivided into more than one page? If so, how?

2. Redraw the hierarchy chart in Figure 14.15 as a Yourdon structure chart by including control couples and indicating the major loops and decisions. Which do you find easier to read—the original figure or its Yourdon counterpart?

3. The transaction file in Figure 14.8*b* has both name and initials entered on C-type transactions in addition to the Social Security number. Is this necessary according to the specifications and subsequent COBOL implementation (Figure 14.11)? Describe both an advantage and a disadvantage of entering the name and initials.

4. The specifications of the update program do not discuss how to change (i.e., correct) the Social Security number of an *existing* record. With respect to Figure 14.8*a*, for example, how could the Social Security number of Sugrue, who already exists in the old master file, be changed to 100000001? Discuss two different approaches, with an advantage and a disadvantage for each. (See processing requirement 1(f) in Project 14-1 for one suggestion.)

5. Use Figure 14.18 as test data for the program in Figure 14.9. Indicate the expected output.

```
100000000HUMMER           MR12450879100E533308802220879280001081260000980
200000000BENWAY           C 09430678100E64440678       420000680360000678
300000000KERBEL           N 06130580200E655510814000681480000580
400000000NØRIEGA          LA10531073100E73331073       300001081280001080
500000000FITZPATRICK      DT02500779200P43330779       310001081270000779
600000000VØGEL            JD11450877200E590011818001180500001181450001180
700000000GARCIA           PJ09500778100G644407793330778390000881360000779
800000000PINNØCK          JØ08520681300P84440681       385000681
900000000CLARK            JS06490879100G99870879       650000881550000879
```

(a) Old master file

```
000000000BEINHØRN     CB03431281100 99871281550001281A
000000000BEINHØRN     CB           X                  C
200000000BENWAY       C 09430678100E64440680420000680A
400000000NØRIEGA      LA                              C
400000000NØRIEGA      LA1054                          C
400000000NØRIEGA      LA    1074                      C
400000001NØRIEGA      LA        200                   C
500000000FITZPATRICK  TD                              D
555555555MCDØNALD     J 1145                          C
555555555MCDØNALD     J 11440681100E64440681390000681A
555555555MCDØNALD     J              555              C
700000000GARCIA       PJ                      385000781C
800000000PINNØCK      JØ             400              C
```

(b) Transaction file

FIGURE 14.18 Data for Problem 5

6. Use the general format of the SELECT statement to indicate whether the following are valid entries for sequential files. (The entries in the ASSIGN clause are for an IBM OS system; substitute any entry which applies to your compiler for this clause).

   (a)
   ```
   SELECT OLD-MASTER-FILE
       ASSIGN TO UT-S-OLDMAST.
   ```

   (b)
   ```
   SELECT OLD-MASTER-FILE
       ASSIGN TO UT-S-OLDMAST
       RESERVE 3 AREAS
       ORGANIZATION IS SEQUENTIAL
       ACCESS MODE IS SEQUENTIAL
       FILE STATUS IS WS-FILE-STATUS-BYTES.
   ```

   (c)
   ```
   SELECT OLD-MASTER-FILE
       RESERVE 3 AREAS
       ORGANIZATION IS SEQUENTIAL
       ACCESS MODE IS SEQUENTIAL
       FILE STATUS IS WS-FILE-STATUS-BYTES.
   ```

   (d)
   ```
   SELECT OLD-MASTER-FILE
       ASSIGN UT-S-OLDMAST
       ORGANIZATION IS SUCCESSFUL
       ACCESS MODE IS NON-SEQUENTIAL.
   ```

   (e)
   ```
   SELECT OLD-MASTER-FILE
       ASSIGN TO UT-S-OLDMAST
       RESERVE 0 AREAS
       ORGANIZATION SEQUENTIAL
       MODE SEQUENTIAL
       FILE IS OLD-MASTER-FILE.
   ```

Debugging Workshop

This exercise is based on the specifications associated with the program in Figure 14.16. There are three input files: a transaction, promotion, and old master, as shown in Figure 14.17*a, b,* and *c,* respectively. Desired output is to consist of a new master file, a deleted record file, and a set of error messages, shown in Figure 14.17*d, e,* and *f.* The invalid output is displayed in Figure 14.19. Note the following errors:

1. All salary raises in the promotion file are ignored; hence the new master record for Benjamin does not reflect the new salary of $35,000. Error messages associated with salary raises for Tater and Johnson are also missing.
2. Title updates (i.e., promotions) do take effect but erase historical information. Benjamin, for example, shows 444 as both the present and previous title code.
3. Tater was correctly written to the deleted record file but *incorrectly* remained in the new master.
4. NEW EMPLOYEE is missing a location code in the new master, although the transaction to add this record contained a location code of 100.
5. NEW EMPLOYEE failed to have his title code corrected to 555, although there was a valid transaction to this effect.

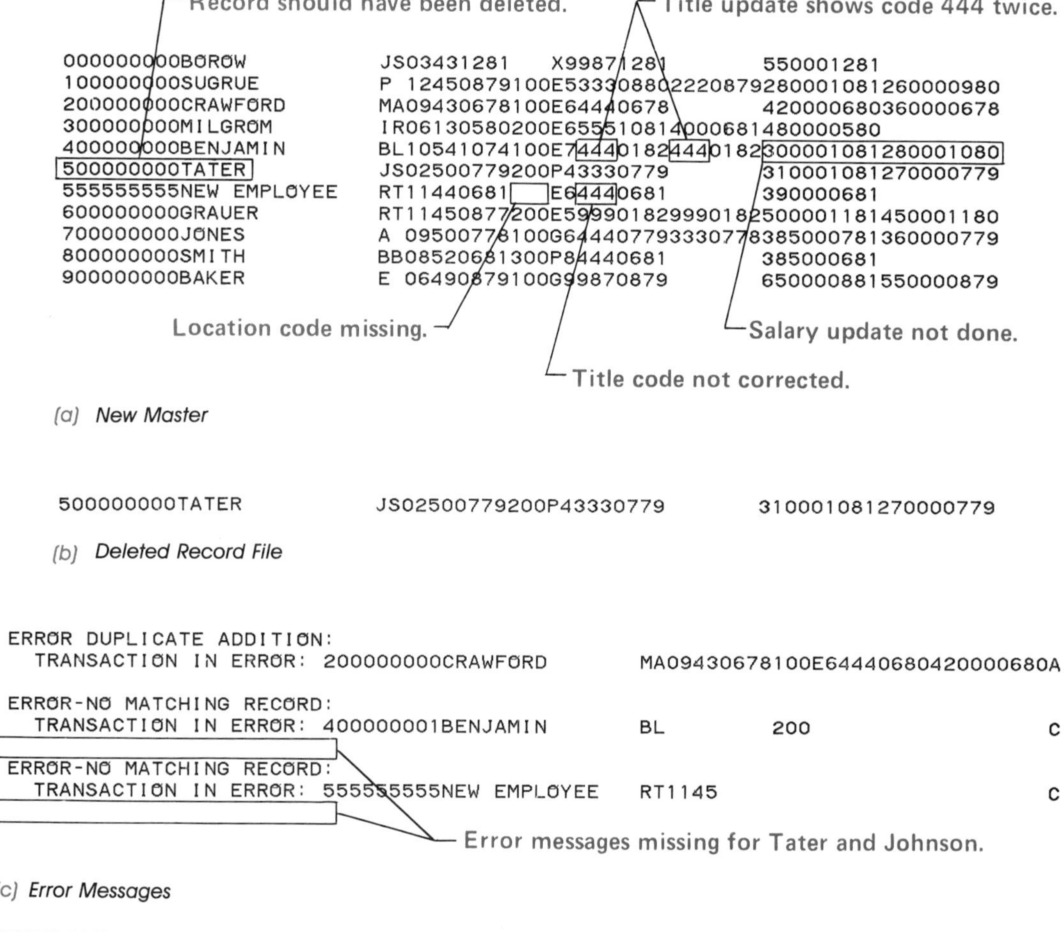


```
000000000BOROW           JS03431281    X9987128           550001281
100000000SUGRUE          P 12450879100E533308802220879280001081260000980
200000000CRAWFORD        MA09430678100E64440678           420000680360000678
300000000MILGROM         IR06130580200E655510814000681480000580
400000000BENJAMIN        BL10541074100E744401824440182300001081280001080
500000000TATER           JS02500779200P43330779           310001081270000779
555555555NEW EMPLOYEE    RT11440681     E6444 0681        390000681
600000000GRAUER          RT11450877200E599901829990182500001181450001180
700000000JONES           A 09500778100G644407793330778385000781360000779
800000000SMITH           BB08520681300P84440681           385000681
900000000BAKER           E 06490879100G99870879           650000881550000879
```

(a) New Master

```
500000000TATER           JS02500779200P43330779           310001081270000779
```

(b) Deleted Record File

```
ERROR DUPLICATE ADDITION:
  TRANSACTION IN ERROR: 200000000CRAWFORD        MA09430678100E64440680420000680A

ERROR-NO MATCHING RECORD:
  TRANSACTION IN ERROR: 400000001BENJAMIN        BL        200                C

ERROR-NO MATCHING RECORD:
  TRANSACTION IN ERROR: 555555555NEW EMPLOYEE    RT1145                       C
```

(c) Error Messages

FIGURE 14.19 Erroneous Output from Sequential Update

Find and correct all errors in the program in Figure 14.20.

```
IDENTIFICATION DIVISION.
PROGRAM-ID.    ESEQUP.
AUTHOR.        JACKIE CLARK.
ENVIRONMENT DIVISION.
CONFIGURATION SECTION.
SOURCE-COMPUTER.       IBM-4341.
OBJECT-COMPUTER.       IBM-4341.
INPUT-OUTPUT SECTION.
FILE-CONTROL.
    SELECT TRANSACTION-FILE
        ASSIGN TO UT-S-TRANS.
    SELECT OLD-MASTER-FILE
        ASSIGN TO UT-S-MASTER.
    SELECT PROMOTION-FILE
        ASSIGN TO UT-S-PROMOTE.
    SELECT DELETED-RECORD-FILE
        ASSIGN TO UT-S-DELETE.
    SELECT NEW-MASTER-FILE
        ASSIGN TO UT-S-NEWMAST.
DATA DIVISION.
FILE SECTION.
FD  TRANSACTION-FILE
    LABEL RECORDS ARE STANDARD
    BLOCK CONTAINS 0 RECORDS
    RECORD CONTAINS 80 CHARACTERS
    DATA RECORD IS TRANSACTION-RECORD.
01  TRANSACTION-RECORD                          PIC X(80).
FD  OLD-MASTER-FILE
    LABEL RECORDS ARE STANDARD
    BLOCK CONTAINS 0 RECORDS
    RECORD CONTAINS 80 CHARACTERS
    DATA RECORD IS OLD-MAST-RECORD.
01  OLD-MAST-RECORD                             PIC X(80).
FD  PROMOTION-FILE
    LABEL RECORDS ARE STANDARD
    BLOCK CONTAINS 0 RECORDS
    RECORD CONTAINS 80 CHARACTERS
    DATA RECORD IS PROMOTION-RECORD.
01  PROMOTION-RECORD                            PIC X(80).
FD  DELETED-RECORD-FILE
    LABEL RECORDS ARE STANDARD
    BLOCK CONTAINS 0 RECORDS
    RECORD CONTAINS 80 CHARACTERS
    DATA RECORD IS DELETED-RECORD.
01  DELETED-RECORD                              PIC X(80).
FD  NEW-MASTER-FILE
    LABEL RECORDS ARE STANDARD
    BLOCK CONTAINS 0 RECORDS
    RECORD CONTAINS 80 CHARACTERS
    DATA RECORD IS NEW-MAST-RECORD.
01  NEW-MAST-RECORD                             PIC X(80).
WORKING-STORAGE SECTION.
01  FILLER                                      PIC X(14)
        VALUE 'WS BEGINS HERE'.
01  WS-TRANS-RECORD.
    05  TR-SOC-SEC-NUMBER                       PIC X(9).
    05  TR-NAME.
        10  TR-LAST-NAME                        PIC X(15).
        10  TR-INITIALS                         PIC XX.
    05  TR-DATE-OF-BIRTH.
        10  TR-BIRTH-MONTH                      PIC 99.
        10  TR-BIRTH-YEAR                       PIC 99.
    05  TR-DATE-OF-HIRE.
        10  TR-HIRE-MONTH                       PIC 99.
        10  TR-HIRE-YEAR                        PIC 99.
    05  TR-LOCATION-CODE                        PIC X(3).
    05  TR-PERFORMANCE-CODE                     PIC X.
    05  TR-EDUCATION-CODE                       PIC X.
```

FIGURE 14.20 Erroneous Sequential Update

FIGURE 14.20 (Continued)

```
           05  TR-TITLE-DATA.
               10  TR-TITLE-CODE                    PIC 9(3).
               10  TR-TITLE-DATE                    PIC 9(4).
           05  TR-SALARY-DATA.
               10  TR-SALARY                        PIC 9(5).
               10  TR-SALARY-DATE                   PIC 9(4).
           05  TR-TRANSACTION-CODE                  PIC X.
               88  ADDITION         VALUE 'A'.
               88  CORRECTION       VALUE 'C'.
               88  DELETION         VALUE 'D'.
           05  FILLER                               PIC X(24).

       01  WS-PROMOTION-RECORD.
           05  PR-SOC-SEC-NUMBER                    PIC X(9).
           05  PR-NAME.
               10  PR-LAST-NAME                     PIC X(15).
               10  PR-INITIALS                      PIC XX.
           05  PR-SALARY-DATA.
               10  PR-SALARY                        PIC 9(5).
               10  PR-SALARY-DATE                   PIC 9(4).
           05  PR-TITLE-DATA.
               10  PR-TITLE-CODE                    PIC 9(3).
               10  PR-TITLE-DATE                    PIC 9(4).
           05  PR-PROMOTION-CODE                    PIC X.
               88  SALARY-RAISE     VALUE 'S'.
               88  PROMOTION        VALUE 'P'.
           05  FILLER                               PIC X(37).

       01  WS-OLD-MAST-RECORD.
           05  OLD-SOC-SEC-NUMBER                   PIC X(9).
           05  OLD-NAME.
               10  OLD-LAST-NAME                    PIC X(15).
               10  OLD-INITIALS                     PIC XX.
           05  OLD-DATE-OF-BIRTH.
               10  OLD-BIRTH-MONTH                  PIC 99.
               10  OLD-BIRTH-YEAR                   PIC 99.
           05  OLD-DATE-OF-HIRE.
               10  OLD-HIRE-MONTH                   PIC 99.
               10  OLD-HIRE-YEAR                    PIC 99.
           05  OLD-LOCATION-CODE                    PIC X(3).
           05  OLD-PERFORMANCE-CODE                 PIC X.
           05  OLD-EDUCATION-CODE                   PIC X.
           05  OLD-TITLE-DATA OCCURS 2 TIMES.
               10  OLD-TITLE-CODE                   PIC 9(3).
               10  OLD-TITLE-DATE                   PIC 9(4).
           05  OLD-SALARY-DATA OCCURS 3 TIMES.
               10  OLD-SALARY                       PIC 9(5).
               10  OLD-SALARY-DATE                  PIC 9(4).

       01  WS-NEW-MAST-RECORD.
           05  NEW-SOC-SEC-NUMBER                   PIC X(9).
           05  NEW-NAME.
               10  NEW-LAST-NAME                    PIC X(15).
               10  NEW-INITIALS                     PIC XX.
           05  NEW-DATE-OF-BIRTH.
               10  NEW-BIRTH-MONTH                  PIC 99.
               10  NEW-BIRTH-YEAR                   PIC 99.
           05  NEW-DATE-OF-HIRE.
               10  NEW-HIRE-MONTH                   PIC 99.
               10  NEW-HIRE-YEAR                    PIC 99.
           05  NEW-LOCATION-CODE                    PIC X(3).
           05  NEW-PERFORMANCE-CODE                 PIC X.
           05  NEW-EDUCATION-CODE                   PIC X.
           05  NEW-TITLE-DATA OCCURS 2 TIMES.
               10  NEW-TITLE-CODE                   PIC 9(3).
               10  NEW-TITLE-DATE                   PIC 9(4).
           05  NEW-SALARY-DATA OCCURS 3 TIMES.
               10  NEW-SALARY                       PIC 9(5).
               10  NEW-SALARY-DATE                  PIC 9(4).

       01  WS-BALANCE-LINE-SWITCHES.
           05  WS-ACTIVE-KEY                        PIC X(9).
           05  WS-RECORD-KEY-ALLOCATED-SWITCH       PIC X(3).

       PROCEDURE DIVISION.
       0010-UPDATE-MASTER-FILE.
           OPEN INPUT TRANSACTION-FILE
                      PROMOTION-FILE
                      OLD-MASTER-FILE
               OUTPUT NEW-MASTER-FILE
```

FIGURE 14.20 *(Continued)*

```
                DELETED-RECORD-FILE.
    PERFORM 0015-READ-PROMOTION-FILE.
    PERFORM 0020-READ-TRANSACTION-FILE.
    PERFORM 0030-READ-OLD-MASTER-FILE.
    PERFORM 0040-CHOOSE-ACTIVE-KEY.
    PERFORM 0050-PROCESS-ACTIVE-KEY
        UNTIL WS-ACTIVE-KEY = HIGH-VALUES.
    CLOSE TRANSACTION-FILE
          PROMOTION-FILE
          OLD-MASTER-FILE
          NEW-MASTER-FILE
          DELETED-RECORD-FILE.
    STOP RUN.

0015-READ-PROMOTION-FILE.
    READ PROMOTION-FILE INTO WS-PROMOTION-RECORD
        AT END MOVE HIGH-VALUES TO PR-SOC-SEC-NUMBER.

0020-READ-TRANSACTION-FILE.
    READ TRANSACTION-FILE INTO WS-TRANS-RECORD
        AT END MOVE HIGH-VALUES TO TR-SOC-SEC-NUMBER.

0030-READ-OLD-MASTER-FILE.
    READ OLD-MASTER-FILE INTO WS-OLD-MAST-RECORD
        AT END MOVE HIGH-VALUE TO OLD-SOC-SEC-NUMBER.

0040-CHOOSE-ACTIVE-KEY.
    IF TR-SOC-SEC-NUMBER LESS THAN OLD-SOC-SEC-NUMBER
        IF TR-SOC-SEC-NUMBER LESS THAN PR-SOC-SEC-NUMBER
            MOVE TR-SOC-SEC-NUMBER TO WS-ACTIVE-KEY
        ELSE
            MOVE PR-SOC-SEC-NUMBER TO WS-ACTIVE-KEY
    ELSE
        IF PR-SOC-SEC-NUMBER LESS THAN OLD-SOC-SEC-NUMBER
            MOVE PR-SOC-SEC-NUMBER TO WS-ACTIVE-KEY
        ELSE
            MOVE OLD-SOC-SEC-NUMBER TO WS-ACTIVE-KEY.

0050-PROCESS-ACTIVE-KEY.
    IF OLD-SOC-SEC-NUMBER = WS-ACTIVE-KEY
        MOVE 'YES' TO WS-RECORD-KEY-ALLOCATED-SWITCH
        PERFORM 0060-BUILD-NEW-MASTER
    ELSE
        MOVE 'NO' TO WS-RECORD-KEY-ALLOCATED-SWITCH.

    PERFORM 0070-APPLY-TRANS-TO-MASTER
        UNTIL WS-ACTIVE-KEY NOT EQUAL TR-SOC-SEC-NUMBER.

    PERFORM 0075-APPLY-PROMO-TO-MASTER
        UNTIL WS-ACTIVE-KEY NOT EQUAL PR-SOC-SEC-NUMBER.

    IF WS-RECORD-KEY-ALLOCATED-SWITCH = 'YES'
        PERFORM 0080-WRITE-NEW-MASTER.

    PERFORM 0040-CHOOSE-ACTIVE-KEY.

0060-BUILD-NEW-MASTER.
    MOVE WS-OLD-MAST-RECORD TO WS-NEW-MAST-RECORD.
    PERFORM 0030-READ-OLD-MASTER-FILE.

0070-APPLY-TRANS-TO-MASTER.
    IF ADDITION
        PERFORM 0090-ADD-NEW-RECORD
    ELSE
        IF CORRECTION
            PERFORM 0100-CORRECT-OLD-RECORD
        ELSE
            IF DELETION
                PERFORM 0110-DELETE-OLD-RECORD.

    PERFORM 0020-READ-TRANSACTION-FILE.

0075-APPLY-PROMO-TO-MASTER.
    IF PROMOTION
        PERFORM 0120-DO-TITLE-UPDATE
    ELSE
        IF SALARY-RAISE
            PERFORM 0130-DO-SALARY-RAISE.

    PERFORM 0015-READ-PROMOTION-FILE.
```

FIGURE 14.20 (Continued)

```
00239            0080-WRITE-NEW-MASTER.
00240               WRITE NEW-MAST-RECORD FROM WS-NEW-MAST-RECORD.
00241

00242            0090-ADD-NEW-RECORD.
00243               IF WS-RECORD-KEY-ALLOCATED-SWITCH = 'YES'
00244                   DISPLAY '     '
00245                   DISPLAY '   ERROR DUPLICATE ADDITION: '
00246                   DISPLAY '     TRANSACTION IN ERROR: ' WS-TRANS-RECORD
00247               ELSE
00248                   MOVE 'YES' TO WS-RECORD-KEY-ALLOCATED-SWITCH
00249                   MOVE SPACES TO WS-NEW-MAST-RECORD
00250                   MOVE TR-SOC-SEC-NUMBER TO NEW-SOC-SEC-NUMBER
00251                   MOVE TR-NAME TO NEW-NAME
00252                   MOVE TR-DATE-OF-BIRTH TO NEW-DATE-OF-BIRTH
00253                   MOVE TR-DATE-OF-HIRE TO NEW-DATE-OF-HIRE
00254                   MOVE TR-PERFORMANCE-CODE TO NEW-PERFORMANCE-CODE
00255                   MOVE TR-EDUCATION-CODE TO NEW-EDUCATION-CODE
00256                   MOVE TR-TITLE-DATA TO NEW-TITLE-DATA (1)
00257                   MOVE TR-SALARY-DATA TO NEW-SALARY-DATA (1).
00258

00259            0100-CORRECT-OLD-RECORD.
00260               IF WS-RECORD-KEY-ALLOCATED-SWITCH = 'YES'
00261                   PERFORM 0105-CORRECT-INDIVIDUAL-FIELDS
00262               ELSE
00263                   DISPLAY '     '
00264                   DISPLAY '   ERROR-NO MATCHING RECORD: '
00265                   DISPLAY '     TRANSACTION IN ERROR: ' WS-TRANS-RECORD.
00266

00267            0105-CORRECT-INDIVIDUAL-FIELDS.
00268               IF TR-NAME NOT EQUAL SPACES
00269                   MOVE TR-NAME TO NEW-NAME.
00270               IF TR-DATE-OF-BIRTH NOT EQUAL SPACES
00271                   MOVE TR-DATE-OF-BIRTH TO NEW-DATE-OF-BIRTH.
00272               IF TR-DATE-OF-HIRE NOT EQUAL SPACES
00273                   MOVE TR-DATE-OF-HIRE TO NEW-DATE-OF-HIRE.
00274               IF TR-LOCATION-CODE NOT EQUAL SPACES
00275                   MOVE TR-LOCATION-CODE TO NEW-LOCATION-CODE.
00276               IF  TR-PERFORMANCE-CODE NOT EQUAL SPACES
00277                   MOVE TR-PERFORMANCE-CODE TO NEW-PERFORMANCE-CODE.
00278               IF TR-EDUCATION-CODE NOT EQUAL SPACES
00279                   MOVE TR-EDUCATION-CODE TO NEW-EDUCATION-CODE
00280               IF TR-TITLE-CODE IS NUMERIC
00281                   MOVE TR-TITLE-CODE TO NEW-TITLE-CODE (1).
00282               IF TR-TITLE-DATE IS NUMERIC
00283                   MOVE TR-TITLE-DATE TO NEW-TITLE-DATE (1).
00284               IF TR-SALARY IS NUMERIC
00285                   MOVE TR-SALARY TO NEW-SALARY (1).
00286               IF TR-SALARY-DATE IS NUMERIC
00287                   MOVE TR-SALARY-DATE TO NEW-SALARY-DATE (1).
00288

00289            0110-DELETE-OLD-RECORD.
00290               IF WS-RECORD-KEY-ALLOCATED-SWITCH = 'YES'
00291                   WRITE DELETED-RECORD FROM WS-NEW-MAST-RECORD
00292               ELSE
00293                   DISPLAY '     '
00294                   DISPLAY '   ERROR-NO MATCHING RECORD: '
00295                   DISPLAY '     TRANSACTION IN ERROR: ' WS-TRANS-RECORD.
00296

00297            0120-DO-TITLE-UPDATE.
00298               IF WS-RECORD-KEY-ALLOCATED-SWITCH = 'YES'
00299                   MOVE PR-TITLE-CODE TO NEW-TITLE-CODE (1)
00300                   MOVE PR-TITLE-DATE TO NEW-TITLE-DATE (1)
00301                   MOVE NEW-TITLE-CODE (1) TO NEW-TITLE-CODE (2)
00302                   MOVE NEW-TITLE-DATE (1) TO NEW-TITLE-DATE (2)
00303               ELSE
00304                   DISPLAY '     '
00305                   DISPLAY '   ERROR-NO MATCHING RECORD: '
00306                   DISPLAY '     PROMOTION IN ERROR: ' WS-PROMOTION-RECORD.
00307

00308            0130-DO-SALARY-RAISE.
00309               IF WS-RECORD-KEY-ALLOCATED-SWITCH = 'YES'
00310                   MOVE NEW-SALARY (2) TO NEW-SALARY (3)
00311                   MOVE NEW-SALARY-DATE (2) TO NEW-SALARY-DATE (3)
00312                   MOVE NEW-SALARY (1) TO NEW-SALARY (2)
00313                   MOVE NEW-SALARY-DATE (1) TO NEW-SALARY-DATE (2)
00314                   MOVE PR-SALARY TO NEW-SALARY (1)
00315                   MOVE PR-SALARY-DATE TO NEW-SALARY-DATE (1)
00316               ELSE
00317                   DISPLAY '     '
00318                   DISPLAY '   ERROR-NO MATCHING RECORD: '
00319                   DISPLAY '     PROMOTION IN ERROR: ' WS-PROMOTION-RECORD.
```

Programming Specifications

Project 14–1

Program Name:

Program Maintenance

Narrative:

This rather substantial project involves *maintenance,* i.e., changes to an existing program, and as such is typical of what entry-level programmers are apt to encounter in the "real world." You are asked to implement a number of changes to the sequential update program in Figure 14.16.

Input File(s):

TRANSACTION-FILE
OLD-MASTER-FILE
PROMOTION-FILE

Input Record Layout(s):

See Figure 14.16 as follows:
  Transaction record: lines 64–88
  Old Master record: lines 106–125
  Promotion record: lines 90–104
In addition, individual processing requirements require changes to the transaction record layout as indicated.

Test Data:

Old Master File:

```
123456789JACKSON     MA09430678120E64440678       420000681360000678
244567899JARREAU     E 06490882120G99870882       640000881440000882
355355600BENSON      P 12440882120E433308812220882281001281260000981
398765000JONES       IR06130481200E6444128140006814810000481
400040000BASIL       BL12431273120E73331273       300001281281001281
543212345LENNOX      JS02400782200P43330782       312001281270000782
666660000ADAMS       RT09440877200E490009818100981400000981440000981
767676767MILLER      A 09400778120G644407823330778390000883360000782
810000000WESTWOOD    BB08420681300G84440681       384000681
```

Promotion File:

```
123456789JACKSON                4440678P
123456789JACKSON     MA420000681       R
123456789JACKSON     MA440000681       R
400040000BASIL       BL340000182       R
400040000BASIL       BL         4440182P
543212345LENNOX      JS330000182       R
666660000ADAMS                  9990182P
810000000WESTWOOD      900000182       R
810000000WESTWOOD
888888888GAYNOR        400000182       R
888888888                       8881182
```

Transaction File:

```
111111111TYLER        JS03431281920 99871281454321281A
111111111                          X                C
111111111TYLER                      899
123456789JACKSON                                    D
244567899                                           D
400040000                          G                C
400040000               1244                        C
400040000                   1274                    C
444444441                       200                 C
444444444NEWTON       RT09440681920E64440681390000681A
444444444                       666                 C
444444444               0945                        C
444444444                            3330681        C1
543212345LENNOX       JS             9990782        D
543212345LENNOX       C              9990782        D
767676767                                   330000778C3
767676767                                   384000781C
767676767MILLER                                     S 123456789
810000000WESTWOOD     BB             400            C
810000000                            660            C4
810000000                                           S 000000008
```

Output File(s):

NEW-MASTER-FILE
DELETED-RECORD-FILE

Output Record Layout(s):

See Figure 14.16 as follows:
New Master record: lines 127–146
Deleted record: identical to new master record

Processing Requirements:

1. The powers that be have decided to amend the specifications associated with the sequential update program in Figure 14.16. Accordingly, modify Figure 14.16 to accommodate all of the following:
   (a) Salary increases are to be *rejected* with an appropriate error message if any of the following conditions occur:
      i. The new salary matches the present salary in the old master.
      ii. The new salary date matches the present salary date in the old master.
      iii. The performance code in the old master is P.
      iv. The name and initials on the salary increase record do *not* match the name and initials in the old master.

   (b) Promotions (i.e., title changes) are to be *rejected* if any of the following conditions occur:
      i. The new title matches the present title in the old master.
      ii. The new title date matches the present title date in the old master.
      iii. The name and initials in the promotion record do not match the name and initials in the old master.

   (c) Any transaction coded as an addition must contain every field in the record layout in Figure 14.6; otherwise, the transaction is to be rejected with an appropriate message. (A single error message, ATTEMPTED ADDITION HAS INCOMPLETE DATA, is acceptable.)

(d) Transactions coded as deletions are to contain a date in the TR-TITLE-DATE field and should be rejected if the date is missing. Records deleted from the old master file are still to be written to DELETED-RECORD-FILE. However, the deleted record should contain the transaction date as its present title date and the title code 999 as its present title. (This in turn causes the present title data from the old master to become the previous title data in the deleted record.)

(e) A new one-position numeric field is to be included at the end of the transaction record (in column 57) to permit historical corrections on title or salary data. Specifically, a 1 indicates that the present level is to be corrected, a 2 the previous level, and so on. (Valid values are 1, 2, and 3, since 3 levels of salary data are defined in Figure 14.5. Valid levels for a title correction are 1 and 2.) Corrections to either title or salary data must have a valid level entered, or else the transaction is to be rejected, with an appropriate error message.

(f) A new transaction type, S, is to be permitted to accommodate a change in Social Security number to an existing record. The existing (but incorrect) Social Security number is to appear in columns 1–9 of the transaction record, while the corrected Social Security number appears in columns 58–66. The change is *not* to take place, however, if it would produce two records in the new master with the same Social Security number. Realize also that *if* any Social Security number is changed, the new master file will be out of sequence and must be resorted. Sorting is not to take place, however, if no Social Security numbers are changed. Finally, if multiple transactions are included, all transactions should reference the *old* Social Security number. (The Social Security modification is *by far the most difficult* portion of the assignment.)

(g) Incoming transactions can no longer be assumed to have valid transaction codes, i.e., A, C, D, or S (as in the Social Security modification). Reject any transactions containing an invalid code through an appropriate error message.

(h) Incoming promotions can no longer be assumed to have a valid code, i.e., P or R. Reject invalid transactions with an appropriate message.

(i) Separate counts are to be maintained for the number of old master records, for the number of *valid* additions processed, and for the number of *valid* deletions processed. Display the anticipated number of new master records (equal to the number of records in the old master, plus the number of additions, minus the number of deletions) at the end of the update.

2. In spite of the substantial nature and number of changes, the author is convinced you will be able to make the necessary modifications. However, it is critical that you follow the admonition, *think first and code later*. To that end, it is strongly suggested that the following activities be done *before* actual coding takes place.

(a) Expand the hierarchy chart in Figure 14.15 to include any new modules that are necessary. In addition, indicate the existing modules that must be altered. *Present the results to the class in a structured walkthrough.*

(b) Determine in advance the anticipated results for the test data provided in these specifications. This should help to clarify any ambiguity in the specifications. *Present the results to the class in a structured walkthrough.*

(c) Develop pseudocode for some of the more involved modules, e.g., DO-SALARY-UPDATE, APPLY-TRANSACTIONS-TO-MASTER. *Again, present the results in a structured walkthrough.*

3. You may recognize that some of the modifications could better be implemented in a stand-alone edit, e.g., checking for a valid transaction code in part (g) or (h), checking for a deletion date in part (d). Nevertheless, *all* changes are to be done in the maintenance program in Figure 14.16. Good luck.

Programming Specifications

Project 14–2

Program Name:

Two File Merge

Narrative:

This project merges two sequential files to produce a third file; all three files have different record layouts. Strictly speaking, it is not an "update" program per se. Nevertheless, it is not a simple problem, in that the program is reading from multiple input files. The balance line approach is applicable as well.

Input Files:

EMPLOYEE-DATA-FILE
SALARY-FILE

Input Record Layouts:

```
01  EMPLOYEE-DATA-RECORD.
    05  EMP-SOC-SEC-NUMBER      PIC X(9).
    05  EMP-NAME.
        10  EMP-LAST-NAME       PIC X(15).
        10  EMP-INITIALS        PIC XX.
    05  EMP-BIRTH-DATE          PIC 9(4).
    05  EMP-HIRE-DATE           PIC 9(4).
    05  EMP-LOC-CODE            PIC X(3).
    05  EMP-TITLE-CODE          PIC 9(3).

01  SALARY-RECORD.
    05  SAL-SOC-SEC-NUMBER      PIC X(9).
    05  SAL-ANNUAL-SALARY       PIC 9(6).
```

Test Data:

Employee Data File:

```
111111111ADAMS         J010521082ATL111
222222222MOLDOF        MI10590484FLA222
333333333FRANKEL       LY06560579NJ 111
```

```
555555555BOROW        JE01430670NY 222
666666666MILGROM      IR03480180NY 222
888888888JONES        JJ09600684NY 222
```

Salary File:

```
111111111050000
222222222100000
444444444075000
555555555040000
777777777043500
888888888035000
999999999042000
```

Output File:

MERGED-FILE

Output Record Layout:

```
01  MERGED-DATA-RECORD.
    05  MGD-SOC-SEC-NUMBER      PIC X(9).
    05  MGD-NAME.
        10  MGD-LAST-NAME       PIC X(15).
        10  MGD-INITIALS        PIC XX.
    05  MGD-BIRTH-DATE          PIC 9(4).
    05  MGD-HIRE-DATE           PIC 9(4).
    05  MGD-LOC-CODE            PIC X(3).
    05  MGD-TITLE-CODE          PIC 9(3).
    05  MGD-ANNUAL-SALARY       PIC 9(6).
```

Report Layout:

There is no report produced by this program, other than the error messages indicated in the processing requirements. The latter may be produced using DISPLAY statements with programmer discretion as to the precise layout.

Processing Requirements:

1. Write a program to merge two input files, in sequence by social security number, to produce a third file as output.
2. In order to produce an output record with a given key, that key must be present on *both* input files. With respect to the test data, records 111111111 and 222222222 should both appear on the merged file. A record is written to the MERGED-FILE by combining fields on the two input records as per the record layouts.
3. If a key appears on only one input file, that record key is not to appear in the MERGED-FILE. With respect to the test data, record 333333333 should not appear on the MERGED-FILE, as it is not present in the SALARY-FILE. Nor should record key 444444444 as it is not present in the EMPLOYEE-DATA-FILE.
4. Any key appearing in only one file should be flagged with an appropriate error message, for example:
   ERROR – RECORD 333333333 NOT IN SALARY-FILE
   ERROR – RECORD 444444444 NOT IN EMPLOYEE-DATA-FILE

Nonsequential File Maintenance

15

Overview

This chapter continues the discussion of file maintenance begun in Chapter 14. It opens with a conceptual view of indexed files and covers all COBOL elements necessary for this type of file organization. It includes two programs to illustrate the use of indexed files. The first shows the use of alternate keys, and the second is a nonsequential update with parallel requirements to the program of Chapter 14.

The opening section provides an intuitive discussion of how an indexed file works. The example chosen is IBM's VSAM implementation, and the terminology and physical characteristics are unique to VSAM. Different vendors have different vocabulary or other means of implementation, but the underlying concepts are the same, namely, a series of indexes that access individual records on a sequential or random basis. Of greater import, the COBOL syntax is identical for all vendors who adhere to the ANS 74 standard.

The opening section is followed by complete coverage of COBOL syntax. Material is included on SEQUENTIAL, RANDOM, and DYNAMIC ACCESS; FILE STATUS bytes and DECLARATIVES; ALTERNATE RECORD KEY; and the DELETE, START, READ, WRITE, and REWRITE statements. □

SYSTEM CONCEPTS

As stated in the overview, different vendors have different *physical* implementations of indexed files, and consequently different terminology. Nevertheless, the principles are the same, namely, a series of indexes that allow individual records to be accessed either sequentially or nonsequentially. This section provides an intuitive discussion of how an indexed file actually works.

In reality, the physical implementation of an indexed file is of little or no concern to the programmer. The operating system automatically establishes and maintains the indexes, and the programmer is concerned primarily with accessing the file through the appropriate COBOL elements. Nevertheless, a conceptual understanding is of benefit in developing a more competent and better-rounded individual. Accordingly, we consider IBM's VSAM implementation.

A VSAM file or data set is divided into *control areas* and *control intervals*. A control interval is a continuous area of auxiliary storage. A control area contains one or more control intervals. A control interval is independent of the physical device on which it resides (i.e., a control interval that takes exactly one track of a given direct access device may require more or less than one track if the file were moved to another type of device).

The length of a control interval is fixed, either by VSAM or by the user. VSAM will determine an optimum length based on record size, type of device, and the amount of space required for an I/O buffer. All control intervals in a given file are of the same length and cannot be changed without creating an entirely new data set.

A VSAM file is defined with an index so that individual records may be located on a random basis. (In actuality, there are two kinds of VSAM data sets, *key-sequenced* and *entry-sequenced*. This discussion concerns only the former, and entry-sequenced data sets are not mentioned further.) Entries in the index are known as index records. The lowest level index is called the *sequence set*. Records in all higher levels are collectively called the *index set*.

An entry in a sequence set contains the *highest* key in a control interval and a vertical pointer to that interval. An entry in an index set contains the *highest* key in the index record at the next lower level and a vertical pointer to that index record. These concepts are made clearer by examination of Figure 15.1.

Figure 15.1 shows 28 records hypothetically distributed in a VSAM data set. The entire file consists of three control areas; each area in turn contains three control intervals. The shaded areas shown at the end of each control interval contain information required by VSAM. The index set has only one level of indexing. There are three entries in the index set, one for each control area. Each entry in the index set contains the highest key in the corresponding control area; thus 377, 619, and 800 are the highest keys in the first, second, and third control areas, respectively. Each control area has its own sequence set. The

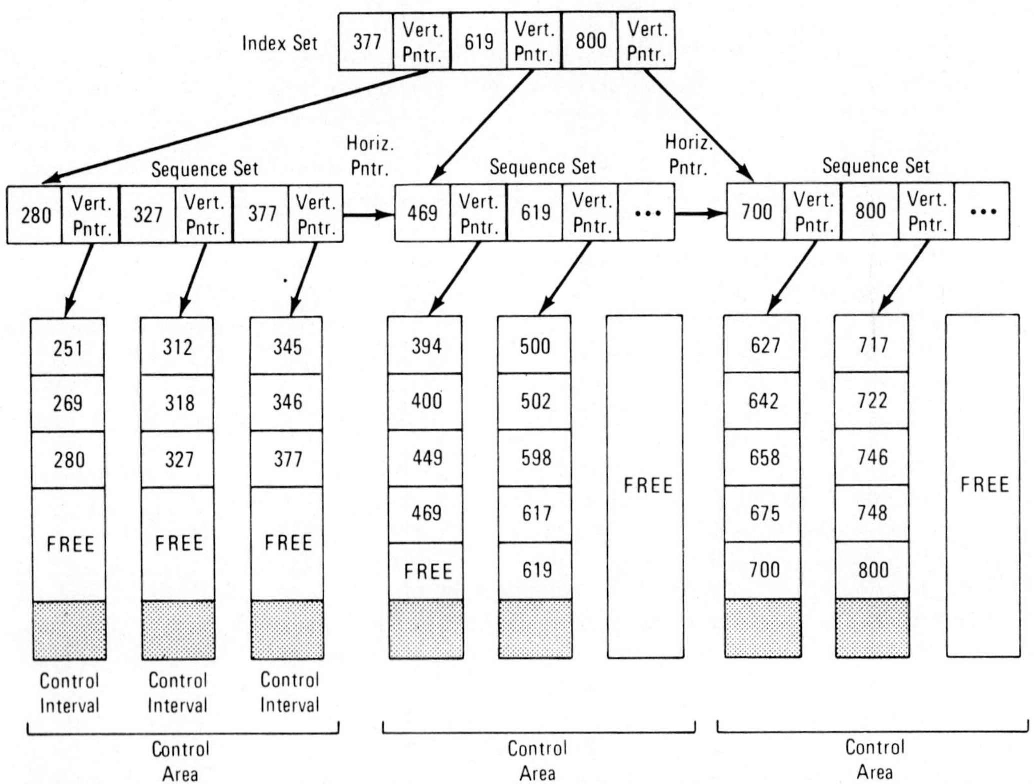

FIGURE 15.1 Initial VSAM Data Set

entries in the first sequence set show the highest keys of the control intervals in the first control area to be 280, 327, and 377, respectively. Note that the highest entry in the third control interval, 377, corresponds to the highest entry in the first control area of the index set.

Figure 15.1 illustrates two kinds of pointers, vertical and horizontal. Vertical pointers are used for direct access to an individual record. For example, assume that the record with a key of 449 is to be retrieved. VSAM begins at the highest level of index (i.e., at the index set). It concludes that record key 449, *if it is present,* is in the second control area (377 is the highest key in the first area, whereas 619 is the highest key in the second control area). VSAM follows the vertical pointer to the sequence set for the second control area and draws its final conclusion: record key 449, if it exists, will be in the first control interval of the second control area.

Horizontal pointers are used for sequential access only. In this instance, VSAM begins at the first sequence set and uses the horizontal pointer to get from that sequence set record to the one containing the next highest key. Put another way, the vertical pointer in a sequence set points to data; the horizontal pointer indicates the sequence set containing the next highest record.

Figure 15.1 contains several allocations of *free space,* which is distributed in one of two ways: as free space within a control interval or as a free control interval within a control area. In other words, as VSAM loads a file, empty space is deliberately left throughout the file. This is done to facilitate subsequent insertion of new records.

Figure 15.2 shows the changes brought about by the addition of two new records, with keys of 410 and 730, to the file of Figure 15.1. Addition of the first record, key 410, poses no problem, as free space is available in the control interval where the record belongs. Record 410 is inserted into its proper place and the other records in that control interval are moved down.

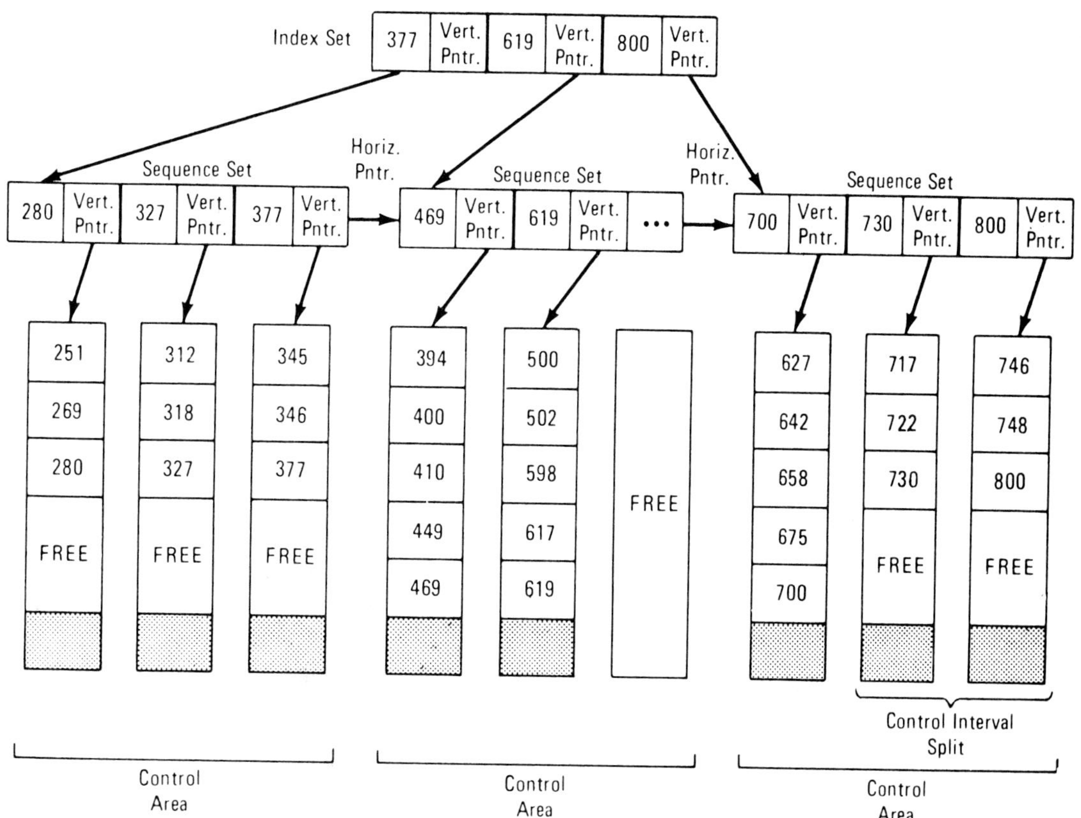

FIGURE 15.2 Control Interval Split

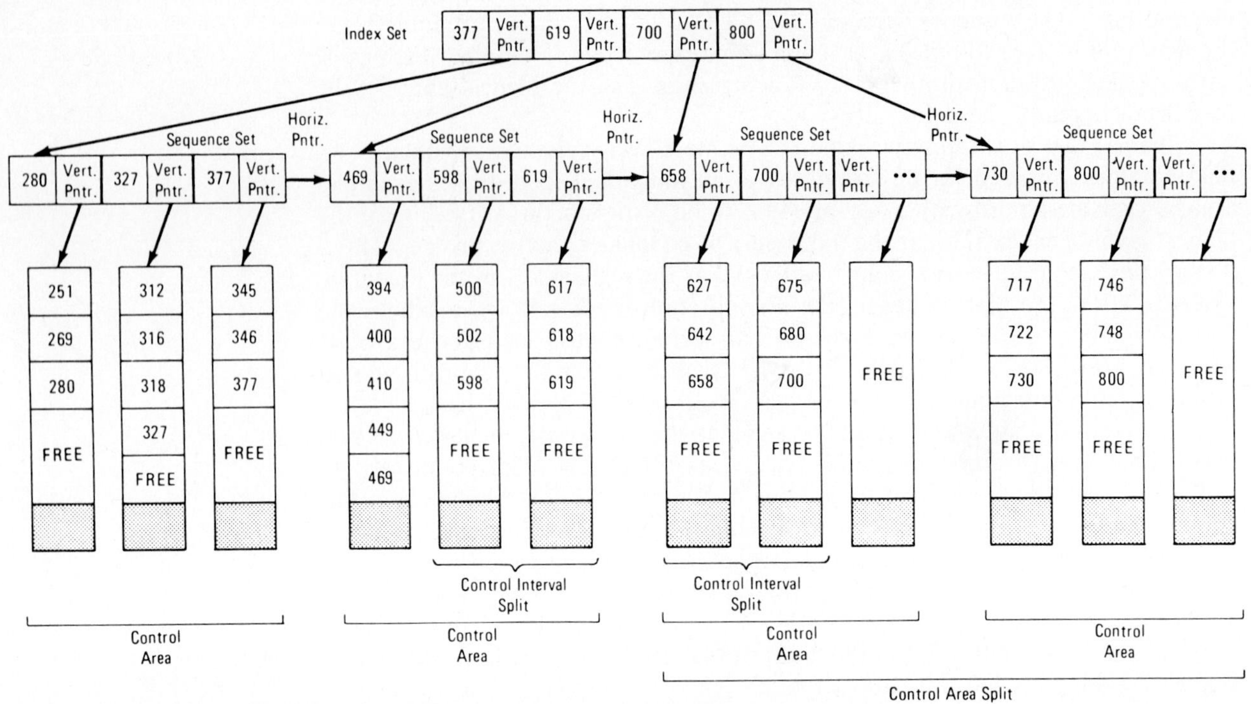

FIGURE 15.3 *Control Area Split*

The addition of record key 730 requires different action. The control interval that should contain this record is full in Figure 15.1. Consequently VSAM causes a *control interval split,* in which some of the records in the previously filled control interval are moved to an empty control interval in the same control area. Entries in the sequence set for the third control area will change, as shown in Figure 15.2. This makes considerable sense when we realize that each record in a sequence set contains the key of the highest record in the corresponding control interval. Thus the records in the sequence set must reflect the control interval split. Note that after a control interval split, subsequent additions are facilitated, as free space is again readily available.

Figure 15.3 shows the results of including three additional records, with keys of 316, 618, and 680. Record 316 is inserted into free space in the second control interval of the first control area, with the other records initially in this interval shifted down. Record 618 causes a control interval split in the second control area.

Record 680 also requires a control interval split except that there are no longer any free control intervals in the third control area. Accordingly, a *control area split* is initiated, in which some of the records in the old control area are moved into a new control area at the end of the data set. Both the old and the new control areas will have free control intervals as a result of the split. In addition, the index set has a fourth entry, indicating the presence of a new control area. The sequence set is also expanded to allow for the fourth control area.

COBOL REQUIREMENTS

Indexed files have additional COBOL requirements that center on the Environment and Procedure Divisions. The former uses an expanded SELECT statement, while the latter employs new forms of the OPEN, READ, and WRITE and introduces the START, REWRITE, and DELETE verbs. In addition, DECLARATIVES are frequently coded to monitor the result of I/O operations. (DECLARATIVES can also be used with sequential files.) This section presents the COBOL syntax in detail.

Environment Division

The COBOL requirements for indexed files in the Environment Division are concerned exclusively with the SELECT statement.

SELECT

The complete syntax of the SELECT statement for ANS 74 indexed files is shown:

```
SELECT file-name
    ASSIGN TO implementor-name-1 [, implementor-name-2] ...

    [RESERVE integer-1 [AREA ]]
                       [AREAS]
    ORGANIZATION IS INDEXED

    [              {SEQUENTIAL}]
    [ACCESS MODE IS {RANDOM    }]
    [              {DYNAMIC   }]

    RECORD KEY IS data-name-1

    [ALTERNATE RECORD KEY IS data-name-2 [WITH DUPLICATES]] ...

    [FILE STATUS IS data-name-3]
```

Three clauses, ASSIGN, ORGANIZATION IS INDEXED, and RECORD KEY, are *required* for indexed files. Two other clauses, RESERVE AREA and FILE STATUS, may be specified for sequential as well as indexed files.

The ASSIGN clause ties a programmer-chosen file name to a system (i.e., implementor) name. The control language links the system name to a physical device. (On IBM OS systems, for example, the ASSIGN clause references a DDname, which is repeated on a JCL DD statement to specify the actual file.)

The RESERVE AREA clause increases processing efficiency by allocating alternate I/O areas (or buffers) for the file. If the clause is omitted, the number of alternate areas defaults to the vendor's implementation. Specification of RESERVE 0 AREAS will slow processing but will save an amount of storage equal to the buffer size. This is generally done only on smaller systems when the amount of main memory is limited.

ORGANIZATION IS INDEXED is mandatory for indexed files and requires no further explanation.

The meaning of ACCESS MODE is readily apparent when either SEQUENTIAL or RANDOM is specified. ACCESS IS DYNAMIC allows a file to be read either sequentially or nonsequentially in the *same* program. The format of the READ statement determines the access method and is further discussed in that section.

The RECORD KEY clause references a field *defined in the indexed record whose value must be unique for each record in the file*. The value of the RECORD KEY is used by the operating system to establish the necessary indexes for the file.

ALTERNATE RECORD KEY provides a *second* path for random access. Unlike the RECORD KEY, which must be unique for every record, the ALTERNATE KEY may contain duplicate values. This capability is extremely powerful and gives COBOL some limited facility for data base management. A common application is to specify Social Security or account number as the RECORD KEY and name as the ALTERNATE KEY. This is useful in on-line applications where a customer, e.g., Grauer, doesn't know his account number. A *random* read on name would locate the first Grauer followed by a series of *sequential* reads to locate the proper record (ACCESS IS DYNAMIC is required to allow both sequential and random access in the same program). Realize also that while the ALTERNATE KEY is powerful, it is quite *expensive* in that a second set of indexes must be maintained by the operating system. Consequently the feature should *not* be used indiscriminately but only when absolutely required by the application.

The FILE STATUS clause defines a two-byte area to indicate the success or failure of every I/O operation. It is used in conjunction with DECLARATIVES and is explained in that section.

Procedure Division

Several verbs in the Procedure Division are uniquely associated with indexed files or have extended formats for indexed files. These include OPEN, READ, WRITE, REWRITE, DELETE, and START. In addition, DECLARATIVE procedures are used frequently with such files.

OPEN

A new option of the OPEN verb, OPEN I-O, is required when updating indexed files. Consider first the syntax of the OPEN statement:

```
     {INPUT }
OPEN {OUTPUT} file-name
     {I-O   }
```

INPUT and OUTPUT are used when an indexed file is accessed or created, respectively. However, when only a single master file is specified, as for nonsequential maintenance, OPEN I-O is necessary. In other words, the single master file functions as both an input and an output file.

READ

The READ statement has two distinct syntaxes, for sequential and nonsequential access, respectively. These are:

Format 1 (Sequential Access):

```
READ file-name [NEXT] RECORD [INTO identifier-1]
    [AT END imperative-statement-1]
```

Format 2 (Random Access):

```
READ file-name RECORD [INTO identifier-1]
    [KEY IS data-name-1]
    [INVALID KEY imperative-statement-1]
```

Format 1, for sequential access, has been used throughout the text and should present no difficulty. The NEXT phrase is required if a sequential read is called for, and ACCESS IS DYNAMIC was specified. Use of READ INTO is strongly suggested to simplify debugging as recommended in Chapter 9.

A *random* READ is preceded by a MOVE statement, in which the key of the desired record is moved to the data name designated as the RECORD KEY in the SELECT statement. *The INVALID KEY clause is activated if the specified key cannot be found in the indexed file.* For example,

```
MOVE 888888888 TO SOC-SEC-NUMBER.
READ INDEXED-FILE INTO WS-WORK-AREA
   INVALID KEY DISPLAY 'RECORD NOT FOUND'.
```

The indexed file is randomly accessed for the record with Social Security number 888888888 (assuming SOC-SEC-NUMBER was designated as the RECORD KEY in the file's SELECT statement). If record 888888888 does not exist in the indexed file, the INVALID KEY condition is raised.

If ALTERNATE RECORD KEY was specified in the SELECT statement, the KEY IS clause is used in the READ statement to indicate which field will be used to retrieve the record. For example,

```
MOVE 'SMITH' TO EMP-NAME.
READ INDEXED-FILE INTO WS-WORK-AREA
   KEY IS EMP-NAME
   INVALID KEY DISPLAY 'RECORD NOT FOUND'.
```

The indexed file is randomly accessed for the *first* record with EMP-NAME of Smith (assuming EMP-NAME was designated as the ALTERNATE RECORD KEY). If no Smith can be found, the INVALID KEY condition is raised.

WRITE

The WRITE statement includes an additional clause for indexed files. Consider

```
WRITE record-name [FROM identifier-1]
   [INVALID KEY imperative statement]
```

If ACCESS IS SEQUENTIAL is specified when an indexed file is created, then incoming records are required to be in sequential order, and further, each record is required to have a unique key. The INVALID KEY condition is raised if either of these requirements is violated.

REWRITE

The REWRITE verb replaces existing records when a file has been opened as an I-O file. Its syntax is similar to that of the WRITE verb:

```
REWRITE record-name [FROM identifier-1]
   [INVALID KEY imperative statement]
```

The INVALID KEY condition is raised if the record key of the last record read does not match the key of the record to be replaced.

DELETE

The DELETE statement removes a record from an indexed file. Its syntax is simply

```
DELETE file-name RECORD
    [INVALID KEY imperative statement]
```

When a DELETE statement is successfully executed, the record that was deleted is logically removed from the file and can no longer be accessed. The DELETE statement can be used only on a file that was opened in the I-O mode.

START

The START statement causes the file to be positioned to the first record whose value is equal to, greater than, or not less than the value contained in the identifier. INVALID KEY is raised if no record that meets the specified criterion is found. Syntactically, the START statement has the form

```
                             { EQUAL TO        }
                             { =               }
START file-name [KEY IS      { GREATER THAN    }  identifier]
                             { >               }
                             { NOT LESS THAN   }
                             { NOT <           }
    [INVALID KEY imperative statement]
```

The START verb is more useful than may be thought initially. (See Problem 3.)

A COBOL EXAMPLE

Continued focus on COBOL syntax, without specific examples, can make for rather dry reading. Accordingly, consider the following program specifications.

Programming Specifications

Program Name:

Alternate Indexes

Narrative:

This program illustrates primary and alternate indexes, as well as nonsequential retrieval on either type of key. It does no useful processing per se, other than to illustrate COBOL syntax.

Input File:

INDEXED-FILE

Input Record Layout:

COLUMNS	FIELD	PICTURE
1–9	SOC-SEC-NUMBER	X(9)
10–24	EMPLOYEE-LAST-NAME	X(15)
25–80	REST-OF-RECORD	X(56)

Note: Social Security number is established as the *unique primary* key. The employee's last name is established as a *nonunique* secondary key.

Test Data:

The data file is listed two ways, by Social Security number and by name.

By Social Security Number:

```
050555500GRAUER             RT
264805298CLARK              JS
300000000MILGROM            IR
400000000BENJAMIN           BL
638972393GRAUER             J
800000000SMITH              BB
900000000BAKER              E
955000000GRAUER             B
```

By Employee Name:

```
900000000BAKER              E
400000000BENJAMIN           BL
264805298CLARK              JS
050555500GRAUER             RT
638972393GRAUER             J
955000000GRAUER             B
300000000MILGROM            IR
800000000SMITH              BB
```

Report Layout:

There is no formal report produced by this program; instead, DISPLAY statements are used to indicate the results.

Processing Requirements:

The processing requirements are designed to illustrate random access (successful and unsuccessful), on both the primary and secondary key. Accordingly, the following reads are executed with respect to the test data:

(a) *Successful read on primary key:* Execute a random read for Social Security number 955000000.
(b) *Unsuccessful read on primary key:* Execute a random read for Social Security number 245118095.
(c) *Successful read on secondary key:* Execute a random read for the first occurrence of GRAUER.
(d) *Sequential read on duplicate occurrences of secondary key:* Retrieve all occurrences of GRAUER.
(e) *Unsuccessful read on secondary key:* Execute a random read for HUMMER.

Figure 15.4 contains a complete COBOL program to illustrate the use of *alternate* indexes. Figure 15.5 displays the output produced by Figure 15.4, given the test data in the program specifications.

The SELECT statement in lines 12–18 identifies RECORD KEY as INDEX-SOC-SEC-NUMBER and ALTERNATE RECORD KEY as INDEX-NAME. Both are defined within the FD for INDEXED-FILE. The former field is unique, but the latter is not, as indicated by the WITH DUPLICATES clause of the SELECT statement.

The Procedure Division contains several forms of the READ statement. COBOL lines 58–72 illustrate a *random read on the primary key*. The first

```
00001          IDENTIFICATION DIVISION.
00002          PROGRAM-ID.   ALTINDEX.
00003          AUTHOR.       JACKIE CLARK.
00004
00005          ENVIRONMENT DIVISION.
00006          CONFIGURATION SECTION.
00007          SOURCE-COMPUTER.     IBM-4341.
00008          OBJECT-COMPUTER.     IBM-4341.
00009
00010          INPUT-OUTPUT SECTION.
00011          FILE-CONTROL.
00012              SELECT INDEXED-FILE
00013                  ASSIGN TO DA-VSAMMAST
00014                  ORGANIZATION IS INDEXED
00015                  ACCESS IS DYNAMIC
00016                  RECORD KEY IS INDEX-SOC-SEC-NUMBER
00017                  ALTERNATE RECORD KEY IS INDEX-NAME
00018                      WITH DUPLICATES.
00019
00020          DATA DIVISION.
00021          FILE SECTION.
00022          FD  INDEXED-FILE
00023              LABEL RECORDS ARE STANDARD
00024              RECORD CONTAINS 80 CHARACTERS
00025              DATA RECORD IS INDEXED-RECORD.
00026
00027          01  INDEXED-RECORD.
00028              05  INDEX-SOC-SEC-NUMBER                 PIC X(9).
00029              05  INDEX-NAME                           PIC X(15).
00030              05  REST-OF-INDEXED-RECORD               PIC X(56).
00031
00032
00033          WORKING-STORAGE SECTION.
00034          01  FILLER                                   PIC X(14)
00035                  VALUE 'WS BEGINS HERE'.
00036
00037          01  WS-NDX-MAST-RECORD.
00038              05  NDX-SOC-SEC-NUMBER                   PIC X(9).
00039              05  NDX-NAME.
00040                  10  NDX-LAST-NAME                    PIC X(15).
00041                  10  NDX-INITIALS                     PIC XX.
00042              05  FILLER                               PIC X(54).
00043
00044          01  WS-ACTIVE-NAME                           PIC X(15).
00045
00046          01  WS-BALANCE-LINE-SWITCHES.
00047              05  WS-RECORD-KEY-ALLOCATED-SWITCH       PIC X(3).
00048              05  WS-END-INDEX-FILE                    PIC X(3).
00049
00050          PROCEDURE DIVISION.
00051          0010-PROCESS-NAME-FILE.
00052              OPEN INPUT INDEXED-FILE.
00053
00054         ***************************************************************
00055         *        RETRIEVE RECORDS BY SOCIAL SECURITY NUMBER           *
00056         ***************************************************************
00057
00058              MOVE '955000000'  TO  INDEX-SOC-SEC-NUMBER.
00059              PERFORM 0040-READ-INDEX-FILE-BY-NUMBER.
00060              IF WS-RECORD-KEY-ALLOCATED-SWITCH = 'YES'
00061                  DISPLAY WS-NDX-MAST-RECORD
00062              ELSE
00063                  DISPLAY '    '
00064                  DISPLAY 'NO MATCH FOUND FOR:  955000000'.
00065
00066              MOVE '245118095'  TO  INDEX-SOC-SEC-NUMBER.
00067              PERFORM 0040-READ-INDEX-FILE-BY-NUMBER.
00068              IF WS-RECORD-KEY-ALLOCATED-SWITCH = 'YES'
00069                  DISPLAY WS-NDX-MAST-RECORD
00070              ELSE
00071                  DISPLAY '    '
00072                  DISPLAY 'NO MATCH FOUND FOR:  245118095'.
00073
00074         ***************************************************************
00075         *     RETRIEVE RECORDS BY NAME - THE ALTERNATE RECORD KEY     *
00076         ***************************************************************
00077
00078              MOVE 'GRAUER          '  TO  INDEX-NAME
00079                                           WS-ACTIVE-NAME.
00080              PERFORM 0020-READ-INDEX-FILE-BY-NAME.
00081              IF WS-RECORD-KEY-ALLOCATED-SWITCH = 'NO'
```

Annotations:

- Line 00015 (ACCESS IS DYNAMIC): **Permits both sequential and nonsequential access.**
- Lines 00017–00018: **Alternate key need not be unique.**
- Line 00028: **RECORD KEY defined in line 16.**
- Line 00029: **ALTERNATE KEY defined in line 17.**
- Line 00066: **Desired value is moved to RECORD KEY.**
- Line 00078: **Desired value is moved to ALTERNATE KEY.**

FIGURE 15.4 COBOL Program with Alternate Indexes

```
00082                DISPLAY '      '
00083                DISPLAY 'NO MATCH FOUND FOR:   ' WS-ACTIVE-NAME
00084            ELSE
00085                PERFORM 0030-READ-DUPLICATES
00086                    UNTIL WS-ACTIVE-NAME NOT = NDX-LAST-NAME
00087                        OR  WS-END-INDEX-FILE = 'YES'.
00088
00089            MOVE 'HUMMER            '  TO   INDEX-NAME
00090                                            WS-ACTIVE-NAME.
00091            PERFORM 0020-READ-INDEX-FILE-BY-NAME.
00092            IF WS-RECORD-KEY-ALLOCATED-SWITCH = 'YES'
00093                DISPLAY WS-NDX-MAST-RECORD
00094            ELSE
00095                DISPLAY '      '
00096                DISPLAY 'NO MATCH FOUND FOR:   ' WS-ACTIVE-NAME
00097
00098            CLOSE INDEXED-FILE.
00099            STOP RUN.
00100
00101        0020-READ-INDEX-FILE-BY-NAME.
00102            MOVE 'YES' TO WS-RECORD-KEY-ALLOCATED-SWITCH.
00103            READ INDEXED-FILE INTO WS-NDX-MAST-RECORD
00104                KEY IS INDEX-NAME
00105                INVALID KEY
00106                    MOVE 'NO' TO WS-RECORD-KEY-ALLOCATED-SWITCH.
00107
00108        0030-READ-DUPLICATES.
00109            DISPLAY WS-NDX-MAST-RECORD.
00110            READ INDEXED-FILE NEXT RECORD
00111                INTO WS-NDX-MAST-RECORD
00112                    AT END
00113                        MOVE 'YES'  TO  WS-END-INDEX-FILE.
00114
00115        0040-READ-INDEX-FILE-BY-NUMBER.
00116            MOVE 'YES' TO WS-RECORD-KEY-ALLOCATED-SWITCH.
00117            READ INDEXED-FILE INTO WS-NDX-MAST-RECORD
00118                INVALID KEY
00119                    MOVE 'NO' TO WS-RECORD-KEY-ALLOCATED-SWITCH.
```

KEY clause is required if READ is on ALTERNATE KEY.

NEXT clause is required for sequential access.

FIGURE 15.4 (Continued)

READ statement is successful (as seen by the output in Figure 15.5); the second is not. Both READ statements are preceded by a MOVE statement, in which the desired Social Security number is moved to the field defined as the RECORD KEY.

COBOL lines 78–87 retrieve records on the *secondary* key. The desired value, GRAUER, is moved to the field defined as the ALTERNATE RECORD KEY in line 78. The random READ statement for INDEXED-FILE contains the KEY IS clause (line 104), to indicate that retrieval is based on the *secondary* key. If retrieval is successful, the paragraph 0030-READ-DUPLICATES is executed repeatedly to retrieve all occurrences of GRAUER. The NEXT clause in the READ statement of line 110 indicates the file is read *sequentially* after the first occurrence of GRAUER was located. (This in turn requires that ACCESS IS DYNAMIC be specified in the SELECT statement, as was done in line 15.) The necessary JCL is described in Robert Grauer's, *The IBM COBOL Environment.*[1]

```
955000000GRAUER          B

NO MATCH FOUND FOR:   245118095
050555500GRAUER          RT
638972393GRAUER          J
955000000GRAUER          B

NO MATCH FOUND FOR:   HUMMER
```

Alternate key may have duplicate values.

FIGURE 15.5 Output of Figure 15.4

[1] Grauer, Robert T., *The IBM COBOL Environment* (Englewood Cliffs, N.J.: Prentice Hall, 1984)

DECLARATIVES

DECLARATIVES consist of one or more special-purpose *sections,* which appear at the *beginning* of the Procedure Division, before the first executable statement. The purpose of DECLARATIVES is to expand the normal error-handling procedures of the operating system or to aid in debugging. (DECLARATIVES can also be used in conjunction with Report Writer, as was discussed in Chapter 13.)

Declarative sections contain a USE verb to specify when the procedure is to take effect. Consider the first format, which enables the programmer to specify his or her own error-handling procedure for indexed files:

```
                                                  {file-name-1} . . .
                                                  INPUT
USE AFTER STANDARD {EXCEPTION} PROCEDURE ON      { OUTPUT            }
                   {ERROR    }                    I-O
                                                  EXTEND
```

The user's error procedure generally interrogates the two-byte area designated in the FILE STATUS clause of the SELECT statement. The operating system automatically updates the value of the FILE STATUS bytes after *every* I/O operation, according to Table 15.1.

The entries in Table 15.1 correspond to the ANS 74 standard for key-1 equal to 0, 1, 2, or 3. The standard also allows the vendor to define additional codes when key-1 equals 9, and the entries in Table 15.1 match IBM's VSAM implementation. The advantage of DECLARATIVES is that the user can gain more information than with the standard error routine. Consider, for example, Figure 15.6, and assume that there is an error associated with the statement WRITE VSAM-RECORD.

If the programmer had specified the INVALID KEY clause in the WRITE statement, then the associated imperative statement would execute when the error occurred. The programmer would know that there was a problem in the attempted WRITE but would *not* know the reason. However, if a declarative procedure is established, as in Figure 15.6, then the file status bytes can be examined to determine *why* the error occurred.

TABLE 15.1 *File Status Codes*

KEY-1	KEY-2	CAUSE
0	0	Successful completion
1	0	End of file
2	1	Invalid key: Sequence error
	2	Duplicate key
	3	No record found
	4	Boundary violation
3	0	Permanent I/O error: No further information
	4	Boundary violation
9	1	Other error: Password failure
	2	Logical error
	3	Resource not available
	4	Sequential record not available
	5	Invalid or incomplete file information
	6	No DD statement

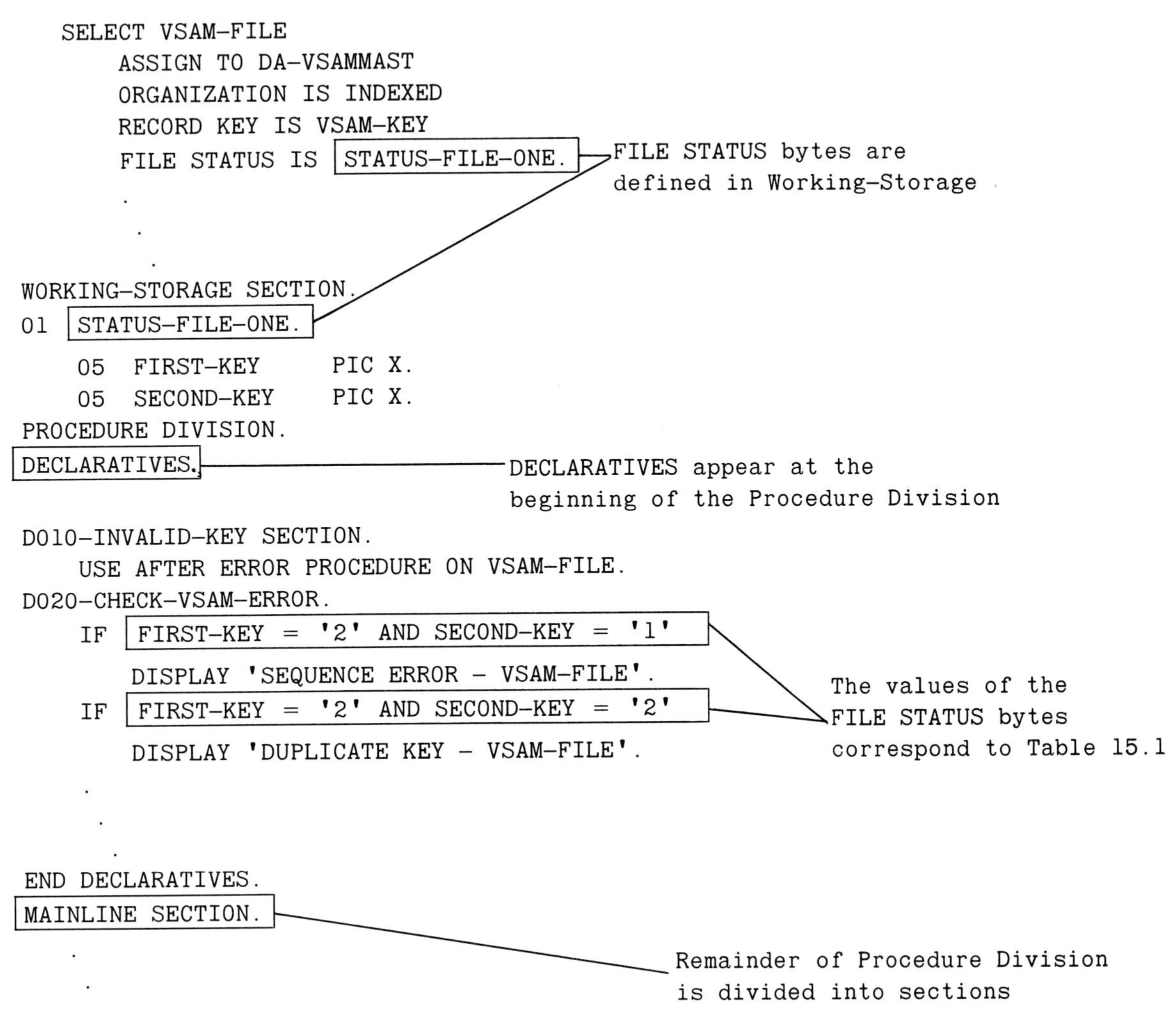

SELECT VSAM-FILE
ASSIGN TO DA-VSAMMAST
ORGANIZATION IS INDEXED
RECORD KEY IS VSAM-KEY
FILE STATUS IS STATUS-FILE-ONE.
FILE STATUS bytes are defined in Working-Storage
WORKING-STORAGE SECTION.
01 STATUS-FILE-ONE.
05 FIRST-KEY PIC X.
05 SECOND-KEY PIC X.
PROCEDURE DIVISION.
DECLARATIVES.
DECLARATIVES appear at the beginning of the Procedure Division
D010-INVALID-KEY SECTION.
USE AFTER ERROR PROCEDURE ON VSAM-FILE.
D020-CHECK-VSAM-ERROR.
IF FIRST-KEY = '2' AND SECOND-KEY = '1'
DISPLAY 'SEQUENCE ERROR - VSAM-FILE'.
IF FIRST-KEY = '2' AND SECOND-KEY = '2'
DISPLAY 'DUPLICATE KEY - VSAM-FILE'.
The values of the FILE STATUS bytes correspond to Table 15.1
END DECLARATIVES.
MAINLINE SECTION.
Remainder of Procedure Division is divided into sections
INVALID KEY is not specified as errors are handled through DECLARATIVES
WRITE VSAM-RECORD.

FIGURE 15.6 ***Use of Declarative Procedures***

Several features of Figure 15.6 bear mention.

1. The word DECLARATIVES immediately follows the Procedure Division header and in turn is followed by the declarative procedures. END DECLARATIVES precedes the remainder of the Procedure Division.
2. Declarative procedures must be *sections,* and consequently the remainder of the Procedure Division should be divided into sections as well. (D020-CHECK-VSAM-ERROR is a paragraph name in the declarative section D010-INVALID-KEY. The paragraph name is included because ANS 74 COBOL does not permit unnamed paragraphs.)
3. Declarative procedures are executed by the input/output control system after completing the standard input/output error routine, or upon recognition of the INVALID KEY or AT END conditions when these phrases have not been specified in the associated input/output statement. When the USE procedures are finished, control implicitly returns to the routine that caused the USE procedures to be invoked.
4. Declarative procedures may not reference any procedures appearing outside the DECLARATIVES section.

COBOL CASE STUDY—NONSEQUENTIAL FILE MAINTENANCE

Much of Chapter 14 was dedicated to the balance line algorithm, a truly general technique for *sequential* file maintenance. This section extends that technique to a *nonsequential* update.

Before proceeding further let us distinguish between the two methods of file maintenance. In a sequential update there are *two* distinct master files, an old and a new master. *Every record in the old master is rewritten to the new master regardless of whether it changes.* In a nonsequential update, however, there is a *single* file that functions as both the old and new master, and *only those records that change are rewritten.* In addition, a sequential update is driven by the *relationship between the old master and transaction files,* whereas a nonsequential update is driven by the transaction file(s) only; that is, transactions are processed until the file(s) are empty.

The choice between the two techniques is governed by the *activity* of the file to be updated. An active file, one with a "high" percentage of records to be changed, is best updated sequentially. On the other hand, an inactive file, one with a "low" percentage of changed records, should be updated nonsequentially. Unfortunately, quantitative guidelines as to what constitutes a high or low percentage of activity are not easily available.

Specifications for the nonsequential update follow.

Programming Specifications

Program Name:

Nonsequential Update

Narrative:

This program is a modified version of the sequential update from Chapter 14 (Figure 14.16). All processing requirements are identical, except that the master file is accessed nonsequentially.

Input File(s):

INDEXED-FILE
TRANSACTION-FILE
PROMOTION-FILE

Input Record Layout:

See Programming Specifications in Chapter 14, page 374.

Test Data:

See Figure 14.17.

Output File(s):

INDEXED-FILE (the same file is used for input and output)
DELETED-RECORD-FILE

Output Record Layout:

See Programming Specifications in Chapter 14, page 375.

Processing Requirements:

1. All requirements from the expanded maintenance program of Chapter 14 pertain to this project. In addition, consider items 2 and 3.
2. Use a *single* master file (i.e., an indexed file), which functions as both the old and new master; that is, this file is *read from* and *written to*. This file is to be accessed *randomly* for each value of the active key.
3. The incoming transaction and promotion files are sorted on Social Security number. (This assumption is perfectly reasonable if the update is done in a batch environment.) It is, in fact, desirable to presort the transaction file, particularly when multiple transactions are applied to a single indexed record. In this way the indexed file is read (and written or rewritten) only once for each value of the active key.

This section develops a COBOL program to update an indexed file nonsequentially and follows the requirements of the expanded maintenance program of Chapter 14 (Figure 14.16). Test data and associated output match Figure 14.17 and are not repeated. A hierarchy chart and pseudocode are shown in Figures 15.7 and 15.8, respectively.

Compare the hierarchy chart in Figure 15.7 to the sequential version in Chapter 14 noting the following changes:

1. The READ-OLD-MASTER-FILE module has disappeared from the second level of the hierarchy chart; the key of the old master record is *not* used in determining the active key.
2. The BUILD-NEW-MASTER and READ-OLD-MASTER-FILE modules from levels 3 and 4 have been replaced by a single module, READ-INDEXED-FILE.

In spite of these differences, the two hierarchy charts have more similarities than differences. *The logic of most modules is unchanged,* and the only module that changes significantly is CHOOSE-ACTIVE-KEY. The active key is now the smaller of *two* values, the transaction and promotion keys (as opposed to three: transaction, promotion, and old master).

Figure 15.8 contains pseudocode corresponding to the overall hierarchy chart. Figures 15.9 and 15.10 amplify the logic for processing transactions and promotions, respectively.

RECORD-KEY-ALLOCATED-SWITCH serves the same function as in the sequential version: It checks for duplicate additions and/or no matches. A second switch, RECORD-ORIGINALLY-THERE-SWITCH, is also required to decide if an updated indexed record is to be written, rewritten, or deleted. Both switches are initially set to 'YES' for each value of the active key. A random read of the indexed file sets both switches to 'NO' if the value of the active key is not in the indexed file.

RECORD-KEY-ALLOCATED-SWITCH is manipulated by itself on subsequent additions or deletions. It is set to 'YES' when a record is added and to 'NO' when a record is deleted. RECORD-ORIGINALLY-THERE-SWITCH is set only by the random read of the indexed file.

Figure 15.11 contains the completed program. The SELECT statement for INDEXED-FILE (lines 15–19) has the required ORGANIZATION IS INDEXED and RECORD KEY clauses and specifies ACCESS IS RANDOM. INDEXED-FILE is opened as I-O in line 135 because it serves as both the old and new master files; i.e., it is read from *and* written to.

The logic of 0010-UPDATE-MASTER-FILE closely parallels that of the sequential update except that an initial read is not done for the old master. Con-

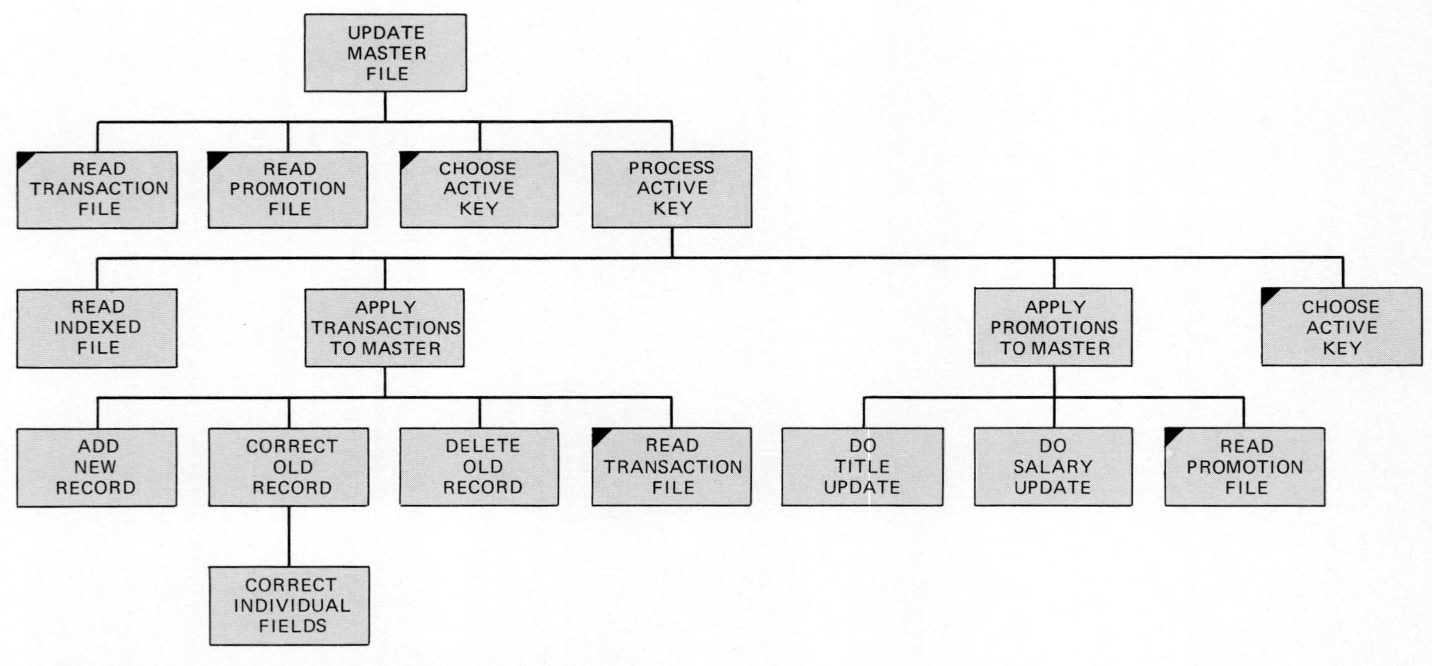

FIGURE 15.7 Hierarchy Chart for Nonsequential Update

```
OPEN FILES
READ TRANSACTION-FILE, AT END MOVE HIGH-VALUES TO TRANSACTION-KEY
READ PROMOTION-FILE, AT END MOVE HIGH-VALUES TO PROMOTION-KEY
CHOOSE FIRST ACTIVE-KEY
DO WHILE ACTIVE-KEY ≠ HIGH-VALUES
    MOVE ACTIVE-KEY TO INDEX-SOCIAL-SECURITY-NUMBER
    MOVE 'YES' TO RECORD-KEY-ALLOCATED-SWITCH
    MOVE 'YES' TO RECORD-ORIGINALLY-THERE-SWITCH
    READ INDEXED-FILE
       INVALID KEY MOVE 'NO' TO RECORD-KEY-ALLOCATED-SWITCH
                   MOVE 'NO' TO RECORD-ORIGINALLY-THERE-SWITCH
    DO WHILE TRANSACTION-KEY = ACTIVE-KEY     Expanded in Figure 15.9
    [APPLY TRANSACTION TO INDEXED-RECORD]
    READ TRANSACTION-FILE, AT END MOVE HIGH-VALUES TO TRANSACTION-KEY
    ENDDO
    DO WHILE PROMOTION-KEY = ACTIVE-KEY     Expanded in Figure 15.10
    [APPLY PROMOTION TO INDEXED-RECORD]

    READ PROMOTION-FILE, AT END MOVE HIGH-VALUES TO PROMOTION-KEY
    ENDDO
    IF RECORD-KEY-ALLOCATED-SWITCH = 'YES'
        IF RECORD-ORIGINALLY-THERE-SWITCH = 'YES'
            REWRITE RECORD
        ELSE (RECORD WAS ADDED TO INDEXED-FILE)
            WRITE RECORD
        ENDIF
    ELSE (RECORD IS NOT TO APPEAR IN INDEXED-FILE)
        IF RECORD-ORIGINALLY-THERE-SWITCH = 'YES'
            DELETE RECORD
        ELSE (A NO MATCH WAS PROCESSED)
            NEXT SENTENCE
        ENDIF
    ENDIF
    CHOOSE NEXT ACTIVE-KEY
ENDDO
CLOSE FILES
STOP RUN
```

FIGURE 15.8 Pseudocode for Nonsequential Update

sequently the logic of 0040-CHOOSE-ACTIVE-KEY has been modified to take the lesser of two values as the active key.

As in the sequential update, 0050-PROCESS-ACTIVE-KEY is executed repeatedly until the active key equals HIGH-VALUES. The first task in processing each value of the active key is to read the indexed file to determine if the current value is already allocated, i.e., whether the value of the active key exists in the indexed file. Note the use of switches in the INVALID KEY clause (lines 162–164), and how the switches are set to 'YES' immediately prior to the random read. Observe also that WS-ACTIVE-KEY is moved to INDEX-SOC-SEC-NUMBER (the field defined as the RECORD KEY in line 19) prior to the random read.

The contents of the intermediate and lower level modules (0070-APPLY-TRANS-TO-MASTER, 0075-APPLY-PROMO-TO-MASTER, 0090-ADD-NDX-

```
IF ADDITION
    IF RECORD-KEY ALLOCATED-SWITCH = 'YES'
        WRITE 'ERROR - DUPLICATE ADD'
    ELSE (ACTIVE-KEY IS NOT IN INDEXED-FILE)
        MOVE TRANSACTION-RECORD TO INDEXED-RECORD
        MOVE 'YES' TO RECORD-KEY-ALLOCATED-SWITCH
    ENDIF
ELSE IF CORRECTION
    IF RECORD-KEY-ALLOCATED-SWITCH = 'YES'
        PROCESS CORRECTION
    ELSE (ACTIVE-KEY IS NOT IN INDEXED-FILE)
        WRITE 'ERROR - NO MATCH'
    ENDIF
ELSE IF DELETION
    IF RECORD-KEY-ALLOCATED-SWITCH = 'YES'
        MOVE 'NO' TO RECORD-KEY-ALLOCATED-SWITCH
        PROCESS DELETION
    ELSE (ACTIVE-KEY IS NOT IN INDEXED-FILE)
        WRITE 'ERROR - NO MATCH'
    ENDIF
ENDIF
```

FIGURE 15.9 Pseudocode for APPLY-TRANSACTION-TO-INDEXED-RECORD

```
IF PROMOTION
    IF RECORD-KEY-ALLOCATED-SWITCH = 'YES'
        PROCESS PROMOTION
    ELSE (ACTIVE KEY IS NOT IN INDEXED-FILE)
        WRITE 'ERROR - NO MATCH'
    ENDIF
ELSE IF SALARY-RAISE
    IF RECORD-KEY-ALLOCATED-SWITCH = 'YES'
        PROCESS SALARY-RAISE
    ELSE (ACTIVE KEY IS NOT IN INDEXED-FILE)
        WRITE 'ERROR - NO MATCH'
    ENDIF
ENDIF
```

FIGURE 15.10 Pseudocode for APPLY-PROMOTION-TO-INDEXED-RECORD

```
       IDENTIFICATION DIVISION.
       PROGRAM-ID.   NONSEQUP.
       AUTHOR.        JACKIE CLARK.

       ENVIRONMENT DIVISION.
       CONFIGURATION SECTION.
       SOURCE-COMPUTER.     IBM-4341.
       OBJECT-COMPUTER.     IBM-4341.

       INPUT-OUTPUT SECTION.
       FILE-CONTROL.
           SELECT TRANSACTION-FILE
               ASSIGN TO UT-S-TRANS.

           SELECT INDEXED-FILE
               ASSIGN TO DA-VSAMMAST
```

FIGURE 15.11 Nonsequential Update

FIGURE 15.11 *(Continued)*

```
                ORGANIZATION IS INDEXED
                ACCESS IS RANDOM
                RECORD KEY IS INDEX-SOC-SEC-NUMBER.

            SELECT PROMOTION-FILE
                ASSIGN TO UT-S-PROMOTE.

            SELECT DELETED-RECORD-FILE
                ASSIGN TO UT-S-DELETE.

        DATA DIVISION.
        FILE SECTION.
        FD  TRANSACTION-FILE
            LABEL RECORDS ARE STANDARD
            BLOCK CONTAINS 0 RECORDS
            RECORD CONTAINS 80 CHARACTERS
            DATA RECORD IS TRANSACTION-RECORD.
        01  TRANSACTION-RECORD                      PIC X(80).

        FD  INDEXED-FILE
            LABEL RECORDS ARE STANDARD
            RECORD CONTAINS 80 CHARACTERS
            DATA RECORD IS INDEXED-RECORD.
        01  INDEXED-RECORD.
            05  INDEX-SOC-SEC-NUMBER                PIC X(9).
            05  REST-OF-INDEXED-RECORD              PIC X(71).

        FD  PROMOTION-FILE
            LABEL RECORDS ARE STANDARD
            BLOCK CONTAINS 0 RECORDS
            RECORD CONTAINS 80 CHARACTERS
            DATA RECORD IS PROMOTION-RECORD.
        01  PROMOTION-RECORD                        PIC X(80).

        FD  DELETED-RECORD-FILE
            LABEL RECORDS ARE STANDARD
            BLOCK CONTAINS 0 RECORDS
            RECORD CONTAINS 80 CHARACTERS
            DATA RECORD IS DELETED-RECORD.
        01  DELETED-RECORD                          PIC X(80).

        WORKING-STORAGE SECTION.
        01  FILLER                                  PIC X(14)
                VALUE 'WS BEGINS HERE'.

        01  WS-TRANS-RECORD.
            05  TR-SOC-SEC-NUMBER                   PIC X(9).
            05  TR-NAME.
                10  TR-LAST-NAME                    PIC X(15).
                10  TR-INITIALS                     PIC XX.
            05  TR-DATE-OF-BIRTH.
                10  TR-BIRTH-MONTH                  PIC 99.
                10  TR-BIRTH-YEAR                   PIC 99.
            05  TR-DATE-OF-HIRE.
                10  TR-HIRE-MONTH                   PIC 99.
                10  TR-HIRE-YEAR                    PIC 99.
            05  TR-LOCATION-CODE                    PIC X(3).
            05  TR-PERFORMANCE-CODE                 PIC X.
            05  TR-EDUCATION-CODE                   PIC X.
            05  TR-TITLE-DATA.
                10  TR-TITLE-CODE                   PIC 9(3).
                10  TR-TITLE-DATE                   PIC 9(4).
            05  TR-SALARY-DATA.
                10  TR-SALARY                       PIC 9(5).
                10  TR-SALARY-DATE                  PIC 9(4).
            05  TR-TRANSACTION-CODE                 PIC X.
                88  ADDITION        VALUE 'A'.
                88  CORRECTION      VALUE 'C'.
                88  DELETION        VALUE 'D'.
            05  FILLER                              PIC X(24).

        01  WS-NDX-MAST-RECORD.
            05  NDX-SOC-SEC-NUMBER                  PIC X(9).
            05  NDX-NAME.
                10  NDX-LAST-NAME                   PIC X(15).
                10  NDX-INITIALS                    PIC XX.
            05  NDX-DATE-OF-BIRTH.
                10  NDX-BIRTH-MONTH                 PIC 99.
                10  NDX-BIRTH-YEAR                  PIC 99.
            05  NDX-DATE-OF-HIRE.
```

Indicates nonsequential access.

Record key is defined within the index record.

FIGURE 15.11 *(Continued)*

```
00097                        10   NDX-HIRE-MONTH              PIC 99.
00098                        10   NDX-HIRE-YEAR               PIC 99.
00099                  05   NDX-LOCATION-CODE                 PIC X(3).
00100                  05   NDX-PERFORMANCE-CODE              PIC X.
00101                  05   NDX-EDUCATION-CODE                PIC X.
00102                  05   NDX-TITLE-DATA OCCURS 2 TIMES.
00103                        10   NDX-TITLE-CODE              PIC 9(3).
00104                        10   NDX-TITLE-DATE              PIC 9(4).
00105                  05   NDX-SALARY-DATA OCCURS 3 TIMES.
00106                        10   NDX-SALARY                  PIC 9(5).
00107                        10   NDX-SALARY-DATE             PIC 9(4).
00108
00109            01   WS-PROMOTION-RECORD.
00110                  05   PR-SOC-SEC-NUMBER                 PIC X(9).
00111                  05   PR-NAME.
00112                        10   PR-LAST-NAME                PIC X(15).
00113                        10   PR-INITIALS                 PIC XX.
00114                  05   PR-SALARY-DATA.
00115                        10   PR-SALARY                   PIC 9(5).
00116                        10   PR-SALARY-DATE              PIC 9(4).
00117                  05   PR-TITLE-DATA.
00118                        10   PR-TITLE-CODE               PIC 9(3).
00119                        10   PR-TITLE-DATE               PIC 9(4).
00120                  05   PR-PROMOTION-CODE                 PIC X.
00121                        88   SALARY-RAISE     VALUE 'R'.
00122                        88   PROMOTION        VALUE 'P'.
00123                  05   FILLER                            PIC X(37).
00124
00125
00126            01   WS-BALANCE-LINE-SWITCHES.
00127                  05   WS-ACTIVE-KEY                     PIC X(9).
00128                  05   WS-RECORD-KEY-ALLOCATED-SWITCH    PIC X(3).
00129                  05   WS-RECORD-ORIGINALLY-THERE-SW     PIC X(3).
00130
00131            PROCEDURE DIVISION.
00132            0010-UPDATE-MASTER-FILE.
00133                  OPEN INPUT TRANSACTION-FILE
00134                             PROMOTION-FILE              ── Indexed file serves as both old and new master.
00135                       I-O INDEXED-FILE
00136                       OUTPUT DELETED-RECORD-FILE.
00137                  PERFORM 0015-READ-PROMOTION-FILE.
00138                  PERFORM 0020-READ-TRANSACTION-FILE.
00139                  PERFORM 0040-CHOOSE-ACTIVE-KEY.
00140                  PERFORM 0050-PROCESS-ACTIVE-KEY
00141                       UNTIL WS-ACTIVE-KEY = HIGH-VALUES.
00142                  CLOSE TRANSACTION-FILE
00143                        PROMOTION-FILE
00144                        INDEXED-FILE
00145                        DELETED-RECORD-FILE.
00146                  STOP RUN.
00147
00148            0015-READ-PROMOTION-FILE.
00149                  READ PROMOTION-FILE INTO WS-PROMOTION-RECORD
00150                       AT END MOVE HIGH-VALUES TO PR-SOC-SEC-NUMBER.
00151
00152            0020-READ-TRANSACTION-FILE.
00153                  READ TRANSACTION-FILE INTO WS-TRANS-RECORD
00154                       AT END MOVE HIGH-VALUES TO TR-SOC-SEC-NUMBER.
00155
00156            0030-READ-INDEXED-FILE.
00157                  MOVE WS-ACTIVE-KEY TO INDEX-SOC-SEC-NUMBER.
00158                  MOVE 'YES' TO WS-RECORD-KEY-ALLOCATED-SWITCH.
00159                  MOVE 'YES' TO WS-RECORD-ORIGINALLY-THERE-SW.
00160
00161                  READ INDEXED-FILE INTO WS-NDX-MAST-RECORD        ── Nonsequential read.
00162                       INVALID KEY
00163                             MOVE 'NO' TO WS-RECORD-KEY-ALLOCATED-SWITCH
00164                             MOVE 'NO' TO WS-RECORD-ORIGINALLY-THERE-SW.
00165
00166            0040-CHOOSE-ACTIVE-KEY.
00167                  IF TR-SOC-SEC-NUMBER LESS THAN PR-SOC-SEC-NUMBER
00168                       MOVE TR-SOC-SEC-NUMBER TO WS-ACTIVE-KEY
00169                  ELSE
00170                       MOVE PR-SOC-SEC-NUMBER TO WS-ACTIVE-KEY.
00171                                                                   ── Active key is determined from
00172            0050-PROCESS-ACTIVE-KEY.                                  transaction and promotion files.
00173                  PERFORM 0030-READ-INDEXED-FILE.
00174
00175                  PERFORM 0070-APPLY-TRANS-TO-MASTER
00176                       UNTIL WS-ACTIVE-KEY NOT EQUAL TR-SOC-SEC-NUMBER.
```

```

    PERFORM 0075-APPLY-PROMO-TO-MASTER
        UNTIL WS-ACTIVE-KEY NOT EQUAL PR-SOC-SEC-NUMBER.

    IF WS-RECORD-KEY-ALLOCATED-SWITCH = 'YES'
        IF WS-RECORD-ORIGINALLY-THERE-SW = 'YES'
            REWRITE INDEXED-RECORD FROM WS-NDX-MAST-RECORD
        ELSE
            WRITE INDEXED-RECORD FROM WS-NDX-MAST-RECORD
    ELSE
        IF WS-RECORD-ORIGINALLY-THERE-SW = 'YES'
            DELETE INDEXED-FILE.

    PERFORM 0040-CHOOSE-ACTIVE-KEY.


0070-APPLY-TRANS-TO-MASTER.
    IF ADDITION
        PERFORM 0090-ADD-NDX-RECORD
    ELSE
        IF CORRECTION
            PERFORM 0100-CORRECT-NDX-RECORD
        ELSE
            IF DELETION
                PERFORM 0110-DELETE-NDX-RECORD.

    PERFORM 0020-READ-TRANSACTION-FILE.

0075-APPLY-PROMO-TO-MASTER.
    IF PROMOTION
        PERFORM 0120-DO-TITLE-UPDATE
    ELSE
        IF SALARY-RAISE
            PERFORM 0130-DO-SALARY-RAISE.

    PERFORM 0015-READ-PROMOTION-FILE.

0090-ADD-NDX-RECORD.
    IF WS-RECORD-KEY-ALLOCATED-SWITCH = 'YES'
        DISPLAY '    '
        DISPLAY '  ERROR DUPLICATE ADDITION: '
        DISPLAY '    TRANSACTION IN ERROR: ' WS-TRANS-RECORD
    ELSE
        MOVE 'YES' TO WS-RECORD-KEY-ALLOCATED-SWITCH
        MOVE SPACES TO WS-NDX-MAST-RECORD
        MOVE TR-SOC-SEC-NUMBER TO NDX-SOC-SEC-NUMBER
        MOVE TR-NAME TO NDX-NAME
        MOVE TR-DATE-OF-BIRTH TO NDX-DATE-OF-BIRTH
        MOVE TR-DATE-OF-HIRE TO NDX-DATE-OF-HIRE
        MOVE TR-LOCATION-CODE TO NDX-LOCATION-CODE
        MOVE TR-PERFORMANCE-CODE TO NDX-PERFORMANCE-CODE
        MOVE TR-EDUCATION-CODE TO NDX-EDUCATION-CODE
        MOVE TR-TITLE-DATA TO NDX-TITLE-DATA (1)
        MOVE TR-SALARY-DATA TO NDX-SALARY-DATA (1).

0100-CORRECT-NDX-RECORD.
    IF WS-RECORD-KEY-ALLOCATED-SWITCH = 'YES'
        PERFORM 0105-CORRECT-INDIVIDUAL-FIELDS
    ELSE
        DISPLAY '    '
        DISPLAY '  ERROR-NO MATCHING RECORD: '
        DISPLAY '    TRANSACTION IN ERROR: ' WS-TRANS-RECORD.

0105-CORRECT-INDIVIDUAL-FIELDS.
    IF TR-NAME NOT EQUAL SPACES
        MOVE TR-NAME TO NDX-NAME.
    IF TR-DATE-OF-BIRTH NOT EQUAL SPACES
        MOVE TR-DATE-OF-BIRTH TO NDX-DATE-OF-BIRTH.
    IF TR-DATE-OF-HIRE NOT EQUAL SPACES
        MOVE TR-DATE-OF-HIRE TO NDX-DATE-OF-HIRE.
    IF TR-LOCATION-CODE NOT EQUAL SPACES
        MOVE TR-LOCATION-CODE TO NDX-LOCATION-CODE.
    IF  TR-PERFORMANCE-CODE NOT EQUAL SPACES
        MOVE TR-PERFORMANCE-CODE TO NDX-PERFORMANCE-CODE.
    IF TR-EDUCATION-CODE NOT EQUAL SPACES
        MOVE TR-EDUCATION-CODE TO NDX-EDUCATION-CODE.
    IF TR-TITLE-CODE IS NUMERIC
        MOVE TR-TITLE-CODE TO NDX-TITLE-CODE (1).
    IF TR-TITLE-DATE IS NUMERIC
        MOVE TR-TITLE-DATE TO NDX-TITLE-DATE (1).
```

Existing records are rewritten.

Old records are removed through DELETE verb.

Identical modules as in sequential update.

```
00257           IF TR-SALARY IS NUMERIC
00258               MOVE TR-SALARY TO NDX-SALARY (1).
00259           IF TR-SALARY-DATE IS NUMERIC
00260               MOVE TR-SALARY-DATE TO NDX-SALARY-DATE (1).
00261
00262       0110-DELETE-NDX-RECORD.
00263           IF WS-RECORD-KEY-ALLOCATED-SWITCH = 'YES'
00264               MOVE 'NO' TO WS-RECORD-KEY-ALLOCATED-SWITCH
00265               WRITE DELETED-RECORD FROM WS-NDX-MAST-RECORD
00266           ELSE
00267               DISPLAY ' '
00268               DISPLAY '  ERROR-NO MATCHING RECORD: '
00269               DISPLAY '    TRANSACTION IN ERROR: ' WS-TRANS-RECORD.
00270
00271       0120-DO-TITLE-UPDATE.
00272           IF WS-RECORD-KEY-ALLOCATED-SWITCH = 'YES'
00273               MOVE NDX-TITLE-CODE (1) TO NDX-TITLE-CODE (2)
00274               MOVE NDX-TITLE-DATE (1) TO NDX-TITLE-DATE (2)
00275               MOVE PR-TITLE-CODE TO NDX-TITLE-CODE (1)
00276               MOVE PR-TITLE-DATE TO NDX-TITLE-DATE (1)
00277           ELSE
00278               DISPLAY ' '
00279               DISPLAY '  ERROR-NO MATCHING RECORD: '
00280               DISPLAY '    PROMOTION IN ERROR: ' WS-PROMOTION-RECORD.
00281
00282       0130-DO-SALARY-RAISE.
00283           IF WS-RECORD-KEY-ALLOCATED-SWITCH = 'YES'
00284               MOVE NDX-SALARY (2) TO NDX-SALARY (3)
00285               MOVE NDX-SALARY-DATE (2) TO NDX-SALARY-DATE (3)
00286               MOVE NDX-SALARY (1) TO NDX-SALARY (2)
00287               MOVE NDX-SALARY-DATE (1) TO NDX-SALARY-DATE (2)
00288               MOVE PR-SALARY TO NDX-SALARY (1)
00289               MOVE PR-SALARY-DATE TO NDX-SALARY-DATE (1)
00290           ELSE
00291               DISPLAY ' '
00292               DISPLAY '  ERROR-NO MATCHING RECORD: '
00293               DISPLAY '    PROMOTION IN ERROR: ' WS-PROMOTION-RECORD.
```

Same modules as in sequential update.

FIGURE 15.11 (Continued)

RECORD, 0100-CORRECT-NDX-RECORD, 0105-CORRECT-INDIVIDUAL-FIELDS, 0110-DELETE-NDX-RECORD, 0120-DO-TITLE-UPDATE, and 0130-DO-SALARY-RAISE) are the same as in the sequential update. However, the mechanics of writing, rewriting and deleting indexed records are more complicated than with a sequential file; hence the need for lines 181–188.

COBOL 8X:

Changes and Enhancements

A primary goal of COBOL 8X was to enhance the structured capabilities of the language. To that end, scope terminators and false condition branches have been added to a large number of statements. The power behind these new concepts has been mentioned several times in earlier chapters, and you have been previously referred to Appendix B for a complete discussion. Accordingly, we merely list the verbs covered in this chapter to which these extensions apply.

Scope Terminators:

END-WRITE, END-REWRITE, END-DELETE, END-START, END-READ

False Condition Branches:

NOT INVALID KEY (applies to several verbs), NOT AT END

A second major objective of the new compiler is to clarify many situations that were left undefined in COBOL 74. For example, reading past the end of a sequential file is an obvious error in program logic. The older language specification did not mandate a specific action but left the choice of what to do to the specific vendor implementation. By contrast, COBOL 8X defines a large number of new FILE STATUS conditions to provide for uniform treatment of various I/O errors. Nineteen additional conditions have been defined. You should consult the 8X specification for additional information.

Summary

This chapter discussed all necessary COBOL elements for processing indexed files and incorporated them in two complete programs. The first program contained statements necessary for sequential and nonsequential retrieval of both primary and secondary key. The second program extended the balance line algorithm of Chapter 14 and was accompanied by pseudocode and a hierarchy chart.

DECLARATIVES were covered in depth, with specific illustrations for interrogating the FILE STATUS bytes. (DECLARATIVES may be used with sequential files as well.) The COBOL 8X extensions pertain mostly to the definition of new FILE STATUS bytes.

True/False Exercises

1. ALTERNATE RECORD KEY should *always* be specified for indexed files to allow for future expansion.
2. The FILE STATUS clause is permitted only for indexed files.
3. A READ statement *must* contain either the AT END or INVALID KEY clause.
4. Declarative procedures may appear anywhere within the Procedure Division.
5. Inclusion of the INTO clause in a READ statement is not recommended, as it requires additional storage space.
6. RESERVE 0 AREAS is highly recommended to speed up processing.
7. Declarative procedures can be specified for both sequential and indexed files.
8. The value of RECORD KEY must be unique for every record in an indexed file.
9. The value of ALTERNATE RECORD KEY must be unique for every record in an indexed file.
10. The FILE STATUS clause is a mandatory entry in the SELECT statement for an indexed file.
11. An indexed file can be accessed sequentially and nonsequentially in the same program.
12. The first byte of an indexed record should contain either LOW- or HIGH-VALUES.
13. WRITE and REWRITE can be used interchangeably.
14. Records in an indexed file are deleted by moving HIGH-VALUES to the first byte.
15. The COBOL syntax for IBM VSAM files conforms to the ANS 74 standard.
16. Active files are best updated nonsequentially.

Problems

1. Describe the changes to Figure 15.3 if record keys 401, 723, 724, and 725 were added. What would happen if record keys 502 and 619 were deleted?

2. Assume that record key 289 is to be inserted in the first control area of the VSAM data set in Figure 15.3. Logically, it could be added as the *last* record in the first control interval or the *first* record in the second control interval. Is there a preference?
   In similar fashion, should record 620 be inserted as the *last* record in the third interval of the second area or as the *first* record in the first interval of the third area?
   Finally, will record 900 be inserted as the *last* record in the fourth control area, or will it require *creation of a fifth control area?* Can you describe in general terms how VSAM adds records at the end of control areas and/or control intervals?

3. A bank uses an indexed file for its outstanding loans. The record key is CUSTOMER-LOAN-NUMBER, which consists of a unique six-digit customer number and a three-digit sequence number. Each loan a customer receives is assigned a new sequence number. Customer 111111, for example, may have two outstanding loans with keys of 111111001 and 111111002. Develop code to retrieve all outstanding loans for a given customer. (*Hint:* Use the START verb.)

4. Given the COBOL definition

```
05 FILE-STATUS-BYTES      PIC 99.
```

   What is wrong with the following entries?

   (a)
```
IF FILE-STATUS-BYTES EQUAL '10'
    DISPLAY 'END OF FILE HAS BEEN REACHED'.
```
   (b)
```
IF FILE-STATUS-BYTES EQUAL 10
    DISPLAY 'ERROR – DUPLICATE KEY'.
```
   (c)
```
IF FILE-STATUS-BYTE EQUAL 1
    DISPLAY 'END OF FILE HAS BEEN REACHED'.
```
   (d)
```
IF FILE STATUS BYTES EQUAL 10
    DISPLAY 'END OF FILE HAS BEEN REACHED'.
```

5. Indicate whether each of the following entries are valid syntactically and logically. (Assume INDEXED-FILE and INDEXED-RECORD are valid as a file name and a record name, respectively.)

   (a)
```
OPEN INPUT INDEXED-FILE
    OUTPUT INDEXED-FILE.
```
   (b)
```
READ INDEXED-FILE.
```
   (c)
```
READ INDEXED-FILE.
    AT END MOVE 'YES' TO END-OF-FILE-SWITCH.
```
   (d)
```
READ INDEXED-FILE
    AT END MOVE 10 TO FILE-STATUS-BYTES.
```
   (e)
```
READ INDEXED-FILE
    AT END MOVE 21 TO FILE-STATUS-BYTES.
```
   (f)
```
READ INDEXED-FILE
    KEY IS SOCIAL-SECURITY-NUMBER
    INVALID KEY DISPLAY 'RECORD IS IN FILE'.
```
   (g)
```
WRITE INDEXED-RECORD.
```

(h) WRITE INDEXED-FILE
  INVALID KEY DISPLAY 'INVALID KEY'.
(i) REWRITE INDEXED-RECORD
  INVALID KEY DISPLAY 'INVALID KEY'.
(j) REWRITE INDEXED-FILE.
(k) DELETE INDEXED-RECORD.
(l) DELETE INDEXED-FILE RECORD.

Programming Specifications

Project 15–1

Program Name:
Indexed File Maintenance

Narrative:
This program illustrates nonsequential file maintenance and is an extension of the balance line algorithm of Chapter 14.

Input File(s):
INDEXED-FILE
TRANSACTION-FILE
PROMOTION-FILE

Input Record Layout:
See Project 14-1.

Test Data:
See Project 14-1.

Output File(s):
See Project 14-1.

Report Layout:
See Project 14-1.

Processing Requirements:
The processing specifications are the same as those in Project 14-1, with the following changes:

(a) Modify the nonsequential program of Figure 15.11 in lieu of the sequential version of Chapter 14.
(b) Expand the SELECT statement for the INDEXED-FILE to include the FILE STATUS clause. Delete the INVALID KEY clause in line 162, replacing it with an appropriate check for FILE STATUS bytes.
(c) Expand the SELECT statements for the TRANSACTION and PROMOTION files to include the FILE STATUS clause.
(d) Delete the AT END clauses in lines 150 and 154, substituting appropriate checks of the FILE STATUS bytes for these files.
(e) Recall that a nonsequential update reads and writes (rewrites) only those records which change. Hence it is not possible to fulfill processing requirement 2(i) from Project 14-1, which required a count of the records in the old master file.

COBOL 8X:

A Partial List of Changes and Highlights

The following represents the author's rather arbitrary selection of COBOL 8X features, thought to be of most interest to *beginning* programmers. Appropriate references are made to the text for detailed explanation. You may consult the ANSI document[1] for the complete, and rather lengthy, list.

ADD STATEMENT

The word TO is an optional word in the following format:

```
ADD {identifier} TO {identifier} GIVING identifier.
    {literal   }    {literal   }
```

This convenient change eliminates the all-too-prevalent compilation error that resulted in the natural combination of the TO and GIVING formats (see Chapter 4).

ALPHABETIC CLASS TEST INCLUDES LOWER CASE

In COBOL 8X the ALPHABETIC test is true for upper-case letters, lower-case letters, and the space character. The ALPHABETIC-UPPER test is true for upper-case letters and the space character. The ALPHABETIC-LOWER test is true for lower-case letters and the space character. There were no UPPER/LOWER tests in COBOL 74, and the ALPHABETIC test was true for upper-case letters and space characters (see Chapter 9).

[1]*Draft Proposed Revised X3.23 American National Standard Programming Language COBOL,* September 1983, Technical Committee X3J4, American National Standards Institute, New York, NY.

BLOCK CONTAINS CLAUSE

Omission of the BLOCK CONTAINS clause in COBOL 8X causes the system to take the blocking factor from the operating environment, i.e., the JCL. Omission of the clause in COBOL 74 caused a default to the implementor-designated number, regardless of what was specified in the JCL. (See Chapter 10.)

DAY-OF-WEEK

The DAY-OF-WEEK phrase has been added to the ACCEPT statement and returns an integer representing the day.

1 for MONDAY
2 for TUESDAY
3 for WEDNESDAY
4 for THURSDAY
5 for FRIDAY
6 for SATURDAY
7 for SUNDAY

(See Chapter 9.)

DE-EDITED MOVE

A numeric-edited data item may be moved to an unedited field; that is, de-editing takes place. This is useful in accepting numeric data from terminal input, as it permits user-friendly formats.

DISPLAY

The DISPLAY statement has two new features that facilitate formatting on a CRT. DISPLAY WITH NO ADVANCING causes the DISPLAY device to remain at the same line position after a DISPLAY is executed, and it allows displaying and accepting data on the same line. In addition, the ALL literal is permitted in a DISPLAY statement, e.g., DISPLAY ALL'–'. (See Chapter 9.)

ENVIRONMENT DIVISION

The Environment Division is optional. More realistically, within the Environment Division the Configuration Section, Source-Computer, and Object-Computer paragraphs are optional (see Chapter 3).

EVALUATE STATEMENT

The EVALUATE statement has been added to implement the case construct of structured programming (see Appendix B).

EXIT PROGRAM

EXIT PROGRAM need not be the only statement in a paragraph (see Chapter 10).

FALSE CONDITION BRANCH

A false condition branch has been added to all statements with conditional branches. These include

NOT ON SIZE ERROR:
    (ADD, SUBTRACT, MULTIPLY, DIVIDE, and COMPUTE)
NOT INVALID KEY:
    (DELETE, READ, REWRITE, START, WRITE)
NOT AT END:
    (READ, RETURN)

(See Chapter 9.)

FILE STATUS BYTES

Nineteen additional values have been defined for the FILE STATUS bytes (see Chapter 15).

FILLER

The word FILLER is optional and is no longer restricted to elementary data items; for example, one may code

```
01  HEADING-LINE.                FILLER need not be coded.
    05  [          ]             PIC X(10)   VALUE 'PAGE'.
    05  WS-PAGE-COUNT            PIC ZZZ9.
```

IF STATEMENT

END-IF has been added as a scope terminator (see Chapter 9).
THEN has been added as an optional reserved word.

INITIAL CLAUSE IN PROGRAM-ID PARAGRAPH

The INITIAL clause specifies a program that is initialized to its original state each time that the program is called (see Chapter 10).

INITIALIZE STATEMENT

The INITIALIZE statement provides a means of setting selected types of data fields to predetermined values. All numeric items are initialized to zeros, and all nonnumeric items to spaces.

LABEL RECORDS CLAUSE

The LABEL RECORDS clause in the FD is *optional* in COBOL 8X; if omitted, LABEL RECORDS ARE STANDARD is assumed.

NONNUMERIC LITERAL SIZE LIMIT

A nonnumeric literal has an upper limit of 160 characters in length. The upper limit is 120 characters in COBOL 74.

OCCURS CLAUSE WITH VALUE CLAUSE

The VALUE clause may be specified in a data-description entry that contains an OCCURS clause or in an entry that is subordinate to an entry containing an OCCURS clause. Neither situation was permitted in COBOL 74. The modification simplifies table initialization by eliminating the need for a REDEFINES clause (see Chapter 11).

PERFORM STATEMENT

The TEST AFTER phrase has been added to accommodate the DO UNTIL structure; that is, the condition is tested *after* the specified set of statements has been executed. The TEST BEFORE phrase tests the condition *prior* to execution of the designated statements and corresponds to the DO WHILE construct. Omission of both phrases defaults to TEST BEFORE, as is currently implemented in COBOL 74 (see Chapter 9).

The procedure name is optional in COBOL 8X, permitting an in-line PERFORM (see Appendix B).

QUALIFICATION

COBOL 8X has the capability of handling 50 levels of qualification. Five levels of qualification were defined in COBOL 74. (See Chapter 9.)

REFERENCE MODIFICATION

Reference modification can address a string of characters *within* another string by specifying the leftmost character and length for the data item. For example, the statement

```
05  DATA-NAME    PIC X(10)    VALUE 'ABCDEFGHIJ'.

MOVE DATA-NAME (6:2) TO FIELD-A.
```

will move "FG" to FIELD-A; that is, reference modification of DATA-NAME begins at the 6th character for a length of 2 (see Chapter 9).

RELATIONAL CONDITIONS

GREATER THAN OR EQUAL TO (>=) has been added as a relational condition. Previously, one had to specify NOT LESS THAN as the equivalent condition.

In similar fashion, LESS THAN OR EQUAL TO (< =) may be specified for NOT GREATER THAN (see Chapter 4).

REPLACE

This is a new statement with the intent of facilitating conversion from COBOL 74. It operates on COBOL source programs *before* they are compiled; an example is

```
REPLACE ==ALPHABETIC== BY ==ALPHABETIC-UPPER==
```

An installation might develop a standard conversion routine, which could then be copied into existing programs. The REPLACE statement should help to reduce the problems caused by the inadvertent use of a COBOL 8X reserved word as a COBOL 74 data name.

RESERVED WORDS

The following reserved words have been added:

ALPHABET
ALPHABETIC-LOWER
ALPHABETIC-UPPER
ALPHANUMERIC
ALPHANUMERIC-EDITED
ANY
CLASS
COMMON
CONTENT
CONTINUE
CONVERSION
CONVERTING
DAY-OF-WEEK
DEBUG-SUB-NUM
END-ADD
END-CALL
END-COMPUTE
END-DELETE
END-DIVIDE
END-EVALUATE
END-IF
END-MULTIPLY
END-PERFORM
END-READ
END-RECEIVE
END-RETURN
END-REWRITE
END-SEARCH
END-START
END-STRING
END-SUBTRACT
END-UNSTRING
END-WRITE
EVALUATE
EXTERNAL
FALSE
GLOBAL
INITIALIZE
NUMERIC-EDITED
ORDER
OTHER
PADDING
PURGE
REFERENCE
REPLACE
STANDARD-2
TEST
THEN
TRUE

The addition of any reserved word poses potential compatibility problems, when an existing data name corresponds to a new reserved word. The committee believed, however, that the benefits to be derived from each of the new reserved words outweighed the potential inconvenience. In addition, the REPLACE verb was introduced as an aid in conversion.

SCOPE TERMINATORS

Scope terminators mark the end of certain procedural statements; in addition, they enable the nesting of conditional statements. Scope terminators include

END-COMPUTE	END-WRITE	END-RETURN	END-SEARCH
END-ADD	END-REWRITE	END-RECEIVE	END-EVALUATE
END-SUBTRACT	END-DELETE	END-STRING	END-IF
END-MULTIPLY	END-START	END-UNSTRING	END-PERFORM
END-DIVIDE	END-READ	END-CALL	

SORT STATEMENT

The input and output procedures may contain explicit transfers of control to points outside the input or output procedure. (This effectively eliminates the need for a *forward* GO TO statement to branch to the end of either procedure. See Chapter 12.)

SUBPROGRAMS

There are three significant changes with respect to subprograms. One new convenience is that parameters passed in the USING phrase of a CALL statement may be other than 01- or 77-level data names, provided they are elementary items. COBOL 74 required either a 01- or 77-level entry.

The IS INITIAL clause of the PROGRAM-ID paragraph reinitializes all data names prior to the start of execution; for example, one may code

```
PROGRAM-ID.
    SUBPRGM IS INITIAL.
```

Finally, data items passed to a subprogram may have their values protected from modification by addition of the BY CONTENT clause; for example, one may code

```
CALL SUBPRGM
    USING BY CONTENT FIELD-A FIELD-B.
```

In this example the called program may not change the value of either FIELD-A or FIELD-B. However, the called program may change the value of the corresponding data item in the USING phrase of its own PROCEDURE DIVISION header. The BY REFERENCE phrase of the CALL statement causes the parameter in the CALL statement's USING phrase to be treated as it is currently specified in COBOL 74. That is, its value may be changed (see Chapter 10).

SUBSCRIPTS

Up to seven levels of subscripts are permitted in COBOL 8X (three was the former limit). This extension is unlikely to be used, as most programmers have all they can do to handle the old limit of three.

Relative subscripting is now permitted in COBOL 8X; hence one can reference DATA-NAME (SUBSCRIPT ± integer). Relative subscripting was *not* permitted in COBOL 74, although relative indexing was permitted (see Chapter 10).

COBOL 8X:

Appendix B

Structured Programming Enhancements

OVERVIEW

Every program appearing in the text has been run under the 74 compiler. Nevertheless, every program will also run under the 8X compiler, because they were designed to be upwardly compatible. However, in order to maintain compatibility, the sample programs have not utilized the COBOL 8X improvements. This has been done by design, to make you truly comfortable with either compiler.

This appendix highlights improvements in the 8X compiler, designed to improve the structured facilities of COBOL. We begin by discussing the evolution of the language. We continue with a thorough presentation of the structured programming enhancements and allude to other changes. We conclude with a final version of the Tuition Billing Program from Chapter 5 to illustrate the new features fully. □

EVOLUTION OF COBOL

At its inception in 1959, COBOL was designed as "open ended and capable of accepting change and amendment." The revision process is the province of the COBOL committee of CODASYL (COnference on DAta SYstems Languages), which meets periodically to publish a JOD (Journal of Development). This document is submitted to the X3J4 Technical Committee of the American National Standards Institute (ANSI), which publishes the actual standard. Until recently there have been two official standards, COBOL 68 and COBOL 74, the last version known officially as American National Standard COBOL X3.23-1974.

In 1977 the X3J4 committee began revising the 1974 standard based on the CODASYL JOD of 1976. Four intermediate publications, COBOL Information Bulletins 17, 18, 19, and 20, provided the public with its first glimpse of what to expect. CODASYL subsequently published a JOD in 1978 which revised the 1976 publication. Finally, in June 1981 the X3J4 committee completed its work and approved the content of a draft proposal to revise ANS COBOL X3.23-1974. The draft was made available in September 1981 for public comment, with the review period ending in February 1982. The proposed standard was again revised to reflect public reaction, and made available for review in the fall of 1984, with final approval expected shortly.

The long delay associated with approval of the new standard was the result of public concern over incompatibility with the existing compiler. Introduction of new reserved words, for example, poses compatibility problems if *existing* programs inadvertently use a (new) reserved word as a data name. Other incompatibilities result from the deletion, clarification, or reinterpretation of existing features. The hue and cry raised by the public, especially J. T. Brophy of the Traveller's Corporation, did much to minimize (but did not eliminate) conversion problems. Suffice it to say that the 1984 revision is a superior version to the 1981 proposal.

STRUCTURED PROGRAMMING ENHANCEMENTS

By far, the biggest improvement in COBOL 8X over its predecessor is its accommodation of structured programming concepts. The new standard is the first to be developed *after* the common acceptance of the structured methodology. An underlying objective of the standards committee was to make COBOL more conducive to current programming theory. Accordingly, COBOL 8X makes specific provision for:

- ☐ The DO WHILE and DO UNTIL constructs through modification of the PERFORM statement with a TEST BEFORE or TEST AFTER facility.
- ☐ Improved readability through introduction of *scope terminators,* such as END-IF, which make it possible to nest conditional statements.
- ☐ The case construct via introduction of the EVALUATE statement.
- ☐ False condition branch (e.g., NOT AT END), which provides structured symmetry to conditional clauses.

Each of these features is discussed in detail.

PERFORM

The UNTIL format of the PERFORM verb has been expanded to allow TEST AFTER and/or TEST BEFORE, with the latter as default:

```
PERFORM [procedure-name-1 [{THROUGH} procedure-name-2]]
                           {THRU   }

    [WITH TEST {BEFORE}] UNTIL condition-1
               {AFTER }

    [imperative-statement-1 END-PERFORM]
```

In other words, COBOL now accommodates both a DO WHILE and a DO UNTIL. The TEST BEFORE condition tests before performing the procedure and corresponds to a DO WHILE; *if the condition is satisfied initially, the designated procedure is never executed.* TEST AFTER, on the other hand, corresponds to the DO UNTIL construct; consequently, *if the condition is satisfied initially, the designated procedure will still be executed once.*

The new syntax shows the procedure name as an *optional* entry, enclosed in square brackets. This in turn provides an in-line capability; an example is

```
PERFORM
    statement-1
    statement-2
    .
    .
    .
    statement-n
END-PERFORM
```

An in-line PERFORM functions according to the general rules of a regular PERFORM statement, except that the statements executed are those contained *within* the PERFORM statement itself, i.e., between PERFORM and END-PERFORM. (Accordingly, omission of procedure-name-1 requires that both imperative-statement-1 and END-PERFORM be coded.) The in-line PERFORM does *not* provide any additional logic capability. Nevertheless, it is a welcome addition in that it can eliminate a degree of page turning and, further, gives COBOL a similar capability to that found in other block-oriented languages such as PASCAL and PL/I.

IF

The power and readability of the IF statement has been tremendously improved through inclusion of the END-IF *scope terminator.* An abbreviated format of the IF statement in COBOL 8X is

```
IF condition-1 THEN {statement-1} . . .
  {ELSE {statement-2} . . . [END-IF]}
  {END-IF                           }
```

An IF statement may be terminated by an ending period *or* an END-IF scope terminator. However, *it is strongly recommended that you use END-IF terminators exclusively* to eliminate the "column 73" problem that existed in COBOL 74. Consider Figure B.1, which contains apparently straightforward COBOL code and its surprising output.

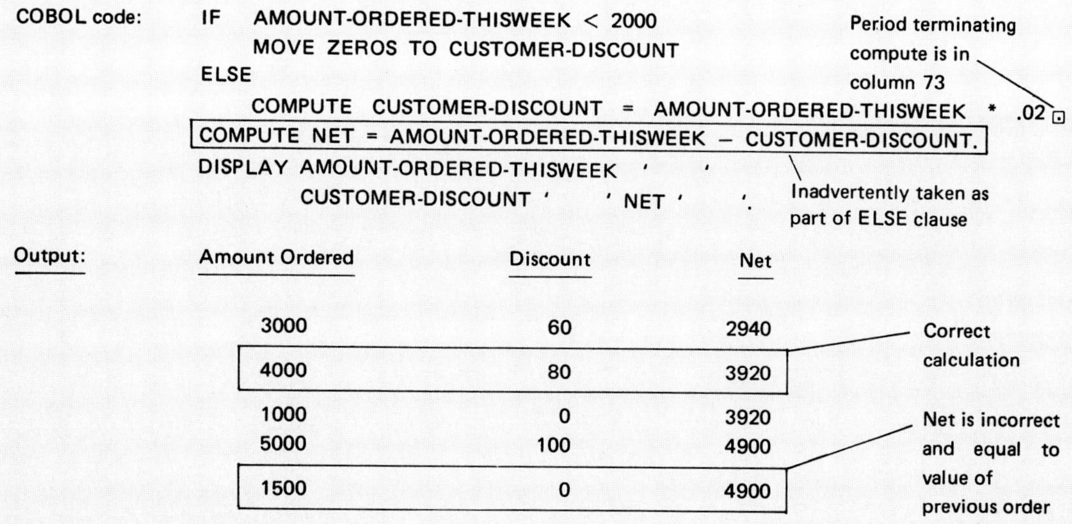

FIGURE B.1 The "Missing" Period

The logic in Figure B.1 is straightforward, yet the output is unexpected. An order of $2,000 or more receives a discount of 2% on the entire order. The amount due (NET) is equal to the amount ordered minus the discount. The code seems correct, yet the *calculated net amounts are wrong for any order less than 2,000*. The net amount printed for these orders equals the net for the previous order (i.e., the net for an order of 1,000 is *incorrectly* printed as 3,920, which was the correct net for the preceding order of 4,000). The net amount for an order of 1,500 was printed as 4,900, and so on. Why?

The only possible explanation is that the COMPUTE NET statement is not executed for net amounts less than 2,000. The only way that can happen is if the COMPUTE NET statement is taken as part of the ELSE clause, and that can happen only if the ELSE is not terminated by a period. The period is present, however, so we are back at ground zero—or are we? The period is present, but in *column 73,* which is ignored by the compiler. Hence the visual code does not match the compiler interpretation, and the resulting output is incorrect.

Note well that a period in column 73 is *not* a contrived problem. True, it may not have happened to you, but chances are it did happen to *someone* in your class. Inclusion of the END-IF delimiter will eliminate future errors of this type, and the IF statement should be recoded as follows:

```
IF AMOUNT-ORDERED-THISWEEK < 2000
    MOVE ZEROS TO CUSTOMER-DISCOUNT
ELSE
    COMPUTE CUSTOMER-DISCOUNT = AMOUNT-ORDERED-THISWEEK * .02
END-IF.
```

The END-IF scope terminator also provides additional logic capability by permitting the nesting of conditional statements. Consider Figure B.2 and its contrasting implementation in COBOL 74 and COBOL 8X.

The END-IF terminator effectively transforms a conditional statement to an imperative (i.e., complete) statement. Hence the required logic of Figure B.2*a* can be expressed as a single IF statement in COBOL 8X. By contrast, the COBOL 74 implementation requires an additional PERFORM statement. Scope terminators are available for a host of other verbs (e.g., READ AT END, COMPUTE SIZE ERROR) and are listed completely in Appendix A.

EVALUATE

Figure 7.4 depicted the *case* construct as a fourth permissible logic structure and a convenient way to express a multibranch situation. COBOL 74 was limited in its ability to implement this construct directly, as the programmer was forced to use either a multilevel nested IF or a GO TO DEPENDING statement. Although both methods work, neither is ideal and the resulting code was often obscure.

COBOL 8X remedies the situation through introduction of the EVALUATE statement, whose *abbreviated* format is shown:

```
         { identifier-1 }
EVALUATE {              }
         { expression-1 }

         { condition-1 }
    WHEN { TRUE        } imperative-statement-1 ...
         { FALSE       }

    [WHEN OTHER imperative-statement-2]

END-EVALUATE
```

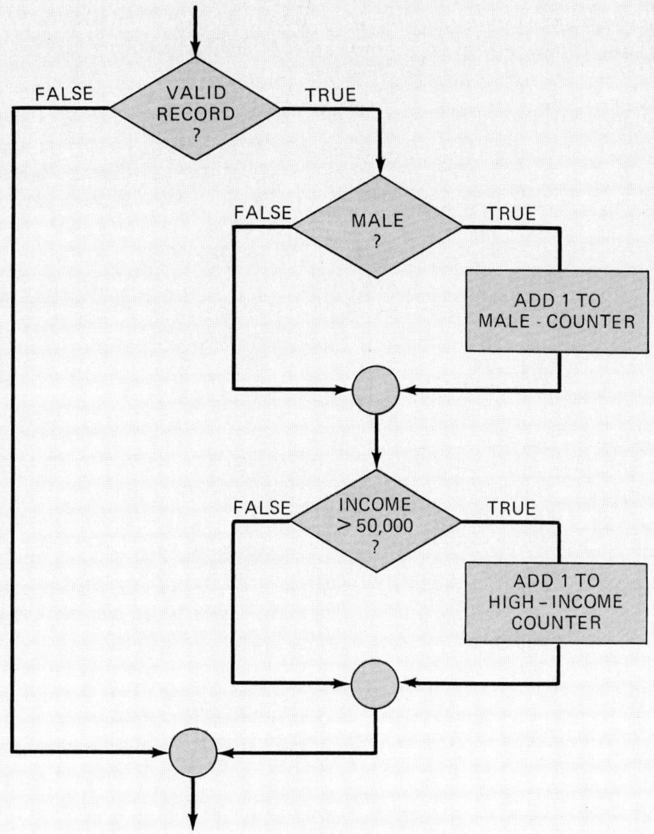

FIGURE B.2a ***Required Logic***

```
IF VALID-RECORD-SW = 'Y'
    IF SEX = 'M'
        ADD 1 TO MALE-COUNTER
    END-IF
    IF INCOME > 50000
        ADD 1 TO HIGH-INCOME-COUNTER
    END-IF
END-IF
```

FIGURE B.2b ***COBOL-8X Implementation***

```
    IF VALID-RECORD-SW = 'Y'
        PERFORM DO-ADDITIONAL-TESTS.
    .
    .
    .
DO-ADDITIONAL-TESTS.
    IF SEX = 'M'
        ADD 1 TO MALE-COUNTER.
    IF INCOME > 50000
        ADD 1 TO HIGH-INCOME-COUNTER.
```

FIGURE B.2c ***COBOL-74 Implementation***

Consider, for example, a program in which processing depends on the value of an incoming ''year in school'' code. When the code is equal to 1, a freshman routine is to be performed; when the code is equal to 2, a sophomore routine, and so on. The multibranch situation is easily implemented as follows:

```
EVALUATE YEAR-IN-SCHOOL
    WHEN 1 PERFORM FRESHMAN
    WHEN 2 PERFORM SOPHOMORE
    WHEN 3 PERFORM JUNIOR
    WHEN 4 PERFORM SENIOR
    WHEN OTHER PERFORM PROCESS-OTHER
END-EVALUATE.
```

In the example YEAR-IN-SCHOOL is evaluated. If it is equal to 1, FRESHMAN is performed; if it is equal to 2, SOPHOMORE is performed, and so on. Observe the use of the reserved word OTHER to accommodate an error-processing routine, and the terminating entry, END-EVALUATE.

False Condition Branch

A more complete syntax for the READ statement is as follows:

```
READ file-name
     [AT END imperative-statement-1]
     [NOT AT END imperative-statement-2]
[END-READ]
```

The addition of the NOT AT END clause provides a symmetry for the conditional branch that was not present in COBOL 74. Taken together with the new in-line PERFORM, these two statements neatly eliminate the need for a priming READ. Hence the ''mainline'' portion of a COBOL 8X program will now contain the following:

```
PERFORM UNTIL DATA-REMAINS-SWITCH = 'NO'
    READ INPUT-FILE
        AT END
            MOVE 'NO' TO DATA-REMAINS-SWITCH
        NOT AT END
            PERFORM PROCESS-RECORD
    END-READ
END-PERFORM.
```

THE TUITION BILLING PROGRAM

Figure B.3 is a final look at the Tuition Billing Program and is designed to highlight the COBOL 8X compiler. In actuality, it doesn't differ significantly from the listing in Chapter 5, save for the in-line PERFORM and NOT AT END statements in lines 108–115. The author believes this syntax to be superior to the COBOL 74 priming READ construct and advocates its use. Also of note are the END-IF delimiters and the omission of the Configuration Section in the Environment Division.

```
00001           IDENTIFICATION DIVISION.
00002           PROGRAM-ID.     TUITION.
00003           AUTHOR.         JACKIR CLARK.
00004
00005           ENVIRONMENT DIVISION.
00006           INPUT-OUTPUT SECTION.
00007           FILE-CONTROL.
00008               SELECT STUDENT-FILE
00009                   ASSIGN TO UT-S-SYSIN.
00010               SELECT PRINT-FILE
00011                   ASSIGN TO UT-S-SYSOUT.
00012
00013           DATA DIVISION.
00014           FILE SECTION.
00015           FD  STUDENT-FILE
00016               LABEL RECORDS ARE OMITTED
```

Configuration Section is not required.

FIGURE B.3 Tuition Billing Program in COBOL-8X

```
                 RECORD CONTAINS 80 CHARACTERS
                 DATA RECORD IS STUDENT-RECORD.
             01  STUDENT-RECORD.
                 05  STU-NAME                PIC X(20).
                 05  STU-SOC-SEC-NO          PIC 9(9).
                 05  STU-CREDITS             PIC 9(2).
                 05  STU-UNION-MEMBER        PIC X.
                 05  STU-SCHOLARSHIP         PIC 9(4).
                 05  FILLER                  PIC X(44).
             FD  PRINT-FILE
                 LABEL RECORDS ARE OMITTED
                 RECORD CONTAINS 133 CHARACTERS
                 DATA RECORD IS PRINT-LINE.
             01  PRINT-LINE                  PIC X(133).
             WORKING-STORAGE SECTION.
             01  DATA-REMAINS-SWITCH         PIC X(2)     VALUE SPACES.
             01  INDIVIDUAL-CALCULATIONS.
                 05  IND-TUITION             PIC 9(4)V99 VALUE ZEROS.
                 05  IND-ACTIVITY-FEE        PIC 9(2)     VALUE ZEROS.
                 05  IND-UNION-FEE           PIC 9(2)     VALUE ZEROS.
                 05  IND-BILL                PIC 9(6)V99 VALUE ZEROS.
             01  UNIVERSITY-TOTALS.
                 05  TOTAL-TUITION           PIC 9(6)V99 VALUE ZEROS.
                 05  TOTAL-SCHOLARSHIP       PIC 9(6)     VALUE ZEROS.
                 05  TOTAL-ACTIVITY-FEE      PIC 9(6)     VALUE ZEROS.
                 05  TOTAL-IND-BILL          PIC 9(6)V99 VALUE ZEROS.
                 05  TOTAL-UNION-FEE         PIC 9(6)     VALUE ZEROS.
             01  HEADING-LINE.
                 05  FILLER                  PIC X        VALUE SPACES.
                 05  FILLER                  PIC X(12)    VALUE 'STUDENT NAME'.
                 05  FILLER                  PIC X(10)    VALUE SPACES.
                 05  FILLER                  PIC X(11)    VALUE 'SOC SEC NUM'.
                 05  FILLER                  PIC X(2)     VALUE SPACES.
                 05  FILLER                  PIC X(7)     VALUE 'CREDITS'.
                 05  FILLER                  PIC X(2)     VALUE SPACES.
                 05  FILLER                  PIC X(7)     VALUE 'TUITION'.
                 05  FILLER                  PIC X(2)     VALUE SPACES.
                 05  FILLER                  PIC X(9)     VALUE 'UNION FEE'.
                 05  FILLER                  PIC X(2)     VALUE SPACES.
                 05  FILLER                  PIC X(7)     VALUE 'ACT FEE'.
                 05  FILLER                  PIC X(2)     VALUE SPACES.
                 05  FILLER                  PIC X(11)    VALUE 'SCHOLARSHIP'.
                 05  FILLER                  PIC X(2)     VALUE SPACES.
                 05  FILLER                  PIC X(10)    VALUE 'TOTAL BILL'.
                 05  FILLER                  PIC X(36)    VALUE SPACES.
             01  DETAIL-LINE.
                 05  FILLER                  PIC X        VALUE SPACES.
                 05  DET-STUDENT-NAME        PIC X(20).
                 05  FILLER                  PIC X(2)     VALUE SPACES.
                 05  DET-SOC-SEC-NO          PIC 999B99B9999.
                 05  FILLER                  PIC X(4)     VALUE SPACES.
                 05  DET-CREDITS             PIC 99.
                 05  FILLER                  PIC X(2)     VALUE SPACES.
                 05  DET-TUITION             PIC $$$$,$$9.99.
                 05  FILLER                  PIC X        VALUE SPACES.
                 05  DET-UNION-FEE           PIC $$$$,$$9.
                 05  FILLER                  PIC X(3)     VALUE SPACES.
                 05  DET-ACTIVITY-FEE        PIC $$$$,$$9.
                 05  FILLER                  PIC X(3)     VALUE SPACES.
                 05  DET-SCHOLARSHIP         PIC $$$$,$$9.
                 05  FILLER                  PIC X(3)     VALUE SPACES.
                 05  DET-IND-BILL            PIC $$$$,$$9.99.
                 05  FILLER                  PIC X(35)    VALUE SPACES.
             01  TOTAL-LINE.
                 05  FILLER                  PIC X(8)     VALUE SPACES.
                 05  FILLER                  PIC X(17) VALUE 'UNIVERSITY TOTALS'.
                 05  FILLER                  PIC X(17)    VALUE SPACES.
                 05  PR-TOT-TUITION          PIC $$$$,$$9.99.
                 05  FILLER                  PIC X        VALUE SPACES.
                 05  PR-TOT-UNION-FEE        PIC $$$$,$$9.
                 05  FILLER                  PIC X(3)     VALUE SPACES.
                 05  PR-TOT-ACTIVITY-FEE     PIC $$$$,$$9.
                 05  FILLER                  PIC X(3)     VALUE SPACES.
                 05  PR-TOT-SCHOLARSHIP      PIC $$$$,$$9.
```

```
00098              05  FILLER                PIC X(3)    VALUE SPACES.
00099              05  PR-TOT-IND-BILL       PIC $$$$,$$9.99.
00100              05  FILLER                PIC X(35)   VALUE SPACES.
00101
00102          PROCEDURE DIVISION.
00103          0010-PREPARE-TUITION-REPORT.
00104              OPEN INPUT   STUDENT-FILE
00105                   OUTPUT  PRINT-FILE.
00106              PERFORM 0015-WRITE-HEADING-LINE.
00107
00108              PERFORM UNTIL DATA-REMAINS-SWITCH = 'NO'
00109                  READ STUDENT-FILE
00110                      AT END
00111                          MOVE 'NO' TO DATA-REMAINS-SWITCH
00112                      NOT AT END
00113                          PERFORM 0020-PROCESS-A-RECORD
00114                  END-READ
00115              END-PERFORM.
00116
00117              PERFORM 0060-WRITE-UNIVERSITY-TOTALS.
00118              CLOSE STUDENT-FILE
00119                    PRINT-FILE.
00120              STOP RUN.
00121
00122          0015-WRITE-HEADING-LINE.
00123              MOVE HEADING-LINE TO PRINT-LINE.
00124              WRITE PRINT-LINE
00125                  AFTER ADVANCING PAGE.
00126
00127          0020-PROCESS-A-RECORD.
00128              PERFORM 0030-COMPUTE-INDIVIDUAL-BILL.
00129              PERFORM 0040-INCREMENT-ALL-TOTALS
00130              PERFORM 0050-WRITE-DETAIL-LINE.
00131
00132          0030-COMPUTE-INDIVIDUAL BILL.
00133              COMPUTE IND-TUITION = 127.50 * STU-CREDITS.
00134
00135              IF STU-UNION-MEMBER = 'Y'
00136                  MOVE 25 TO IND-UNION-FEE
00137              ELSE
00138                  MOVE ZERO TO IND-UNION-FEE
00139              END-IF.
00140
00141              MOVE 25 TO IND-ACTIVITY-FEE
00142
00143              IF STU-CREDITS > 6
00144                  MOVE 50 TO IND-ACTIVITY-FEE
00145              END-IF.
00146
00147              IF STU-CREDITS > 12
00148                  MOVE 75 TO IND-ACTIVITY-FEE
00149              END-IF.
00150
00151              COMPUTE IND-BILL = IND-TUITION + IND-UNION-FEE +
00152                  IND-ACTIVITY-FEE - STU-SCHOLARSHIP.
00153
00154          0040-INCREMENT-ALL-TOTALS.
00155              ADD IND-TUITION TO TOTAL-TUITION.
00156              ADD IND-UNION-FEE TO TOTAL-UNION-FEE.
00157              ADD IND-ACTIVITY-FEE TO TOTAL-ACTIVITY-FEE.
00158              ADD IND-BILL TO TOTAL-IND-BILL.
00159              ADD STU-SCHOLARSHIP TO TOTAL-SCHOLARSHIP.
00160
00161          0050-WRITE-DETAIL-LINE.
00162              MOVE SPACES TO PRINT-LINE.
00163              MOVE STU-NAME TO DET-STUDENT-NAME.
00164              MOVE STU-SOC-SEC-NO TO DET-SOC-SEC-NO.
00165              MOVE STU-CREDITS TO DET-CREDITS.
00166              MOVE IND-TUITION TO DET-TUITION.
00167              MOVE IND-UNION-FEE TO DET-UNION-FEE.
00168              MOVE IND-ACTIVITY-FEE TO DET-ACTIVITY-FEE.
00169              MOVE STU-SCHOLARSHIP TO DET-SCHOLARSHIP.
00170              MOVE IND-BILL TO DET-IND-BILL.
00171              MOVE DETAIL-LINE TO PRINT-LINE.
00172              WRITE PRINT-LINE
00173                  AFTER ADVANCING 1 LINE.
00174
00175          0060-WRITE-UNIVERSITY-TOTALS.
00176              MOVE SPACES TO PRINT-LINE.
00177              MOVE TOTAL-TUITION TO PR-TOT-TUITION.
00178              MOVE TOTAL-UNION-FEE TO PR-TOT-UNION-FEE.
```

PERFORM/END-PERFORM provides in-line PERFORM capability, eliminating the initial read.

READ statement has both scope terminator and false condition branch.

IF statements are terminated by END-IF delimiters.

```
            MOVE TOTAL-ACTIVITY-FEE TO PR-TOT-ACTIVITY-FEE.
            MOVE TOTAL-SCHOLARSHIP TO PR-TOT-SCHOLARSHIP.
            MOVE TOTAL-IND-BILL TO PR-TOT-IND-BILL.
            MOVE TOTAL-LINE TO PRINT-LINE.
            WRITE PRINT-LINE
                AFTER ADVANCING 2 LINES.
```

FIGURE B.3 (Continued)

Summary

Appendix B focused on structured programming enhancements in COBOL 8X. These included scope terminators, the EVALUATE statement, the TEST BEFORE and TEST AFTER clauses of the PERFORM verb, an in-line PERFORM capability, and false condition branches. These features were effectively combined in a final version of the Tuition Billing Program.

Remember that every listing in the text runs under the 74 compiler and will also run unchanged under the new compiler. However, these programs do not take advantage of the 8X enhancements that were discussed here.

True/False Exercises

Answer all questions with respect to the 8X compiler.

1. The COBOL 8X compiler will reject nonstructured code.
2. COBOL 8X is much better suited to implement structured programming theory than its predecessor.
3. COBOL 8X contains several structured programming enhancements.
4. Every IF statement must have a corresponding ELSE.
5. The EVALUATE statement facilitates implementation of the case construct.
6. An IF statement must be terminated by an END-IF scope terminator.
7. A PERFORM statement must specify either TEST BEFORE or TEST AFTER.
8. A PERFORM statement must specify a procedure name.
9. The reserved word THEN is required in an IF statement.
10. The READ statement may have both an AT END and a NOT AT END clause.
11. The READ statement *must* be terminated by an END-READ scope terminator.
12. A priming READ is far less significant in COBOL 8X than it was in COBOL 74.

Problems

1. COBOL 8X enhances COBOL's ability to implement structured programming theory, through the EVALUATE statement and extended formats for both the IF and PERFORM verbs. However, expanded capabilities required the introduction of several new reserved words.
   (a) List the new reserved words mandated by the COBOL enhancements discussed in this appendix.
   (b) Explain how the introduction of any new reserved word poses potential compatibility problems for existing programs. How would these problems be overcome?
   (c) Do you think the extended capabilities of COBOL 8X are worth the effort associated with overcoming the problems in part (b)? Why or why not?

2. The IF statement is only one of several COBOL verbs receiving a scope terminator to eliminate problems of the missing period. Can you think of any other COBOL verbs that would benefit from a similar capability?

3. How many times would PARAGRAPH-A be executed as a consequence of each of the following PERFORM statements?

(a)
```
PERFORM PARAGRAPH-A
    VARYING SUBSCRIPT FROM 1 BY 1
        UNTIL SUBSCRIPT > 5.
```
(b)
```
PERFORM PARAGRAPH-A
    VARYING SUBSCRIPT FROM 1 BY 1
        WITH TEST BEFORE
            UNTIL SUBSCRIPT > 5.
```
(c)
```
PERFORM PARAGRAPH-A
    VARYING SUBSCRIPT FROM 1 BY 1
        WITH TEST AFTER
            UNTIL SUBSCRIPT > 5.
```
(d)
```
PERFORM PARAGRAPH-A
    VARYING SUBSCRIPT FROM 1 BY 1
        UNTIL SUBSCRIPT = 5.
```
(e)
```
PERFORM PARAGRAPH-A
    VARYING SUBSCRIPT FROM 1 BY 1
        WITH TEST BEFORE
            UNTIL SUBSCRIPT = 5.
```
(f)
```
PERFORM PARAGRAPH-A
    VARYING SUBSCRIPT FROM 1 BY 1
        WITH TEST AFTER
            UNTIL SUBSCRIPT = 5.
```

4. Implement the logic in Figure B.4 in both COBOL 74 and COBOL 8X. Do you see any distinct advantages to the latter compiler?

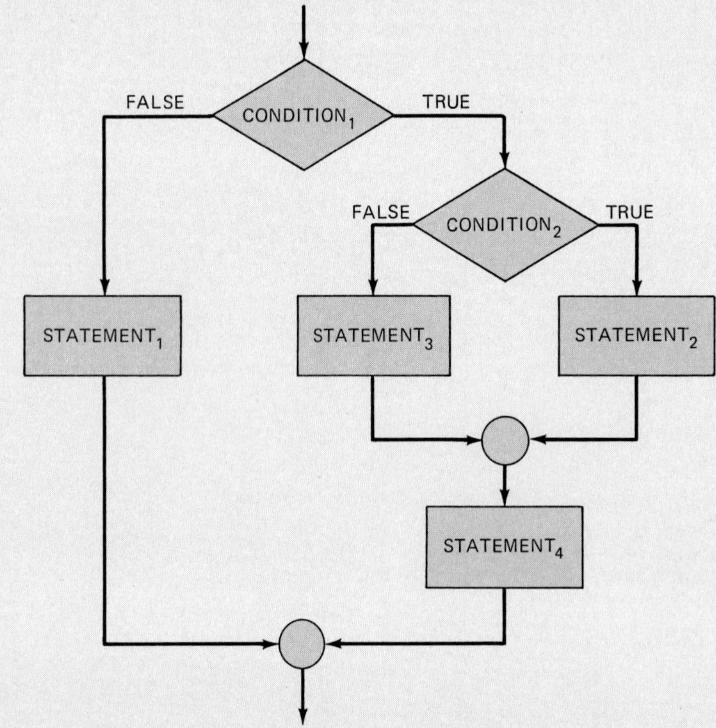

FIGURE B.4 **Flowchart for Problem 4**

VS COBOL II

Appendix C

Reserved Words[1]

ACCEPT
ACCESS
ADD
ADDRESS
ADVANCING
AFTER
ALL
ALPHABETIC
ALPHANUMERIC
ALPHANUMERIC-EDITED
ALSO
ALTER
ALTERNATE
AND
ANY
ARE
AREA
AREAS
ASCENDING
ASSIGN
AT
AUTHOR

BEFORE
BEGINNING
BLANK
BLOCK
BOTTOM
BY

CALL
CANCEL
CD
CF
CH
CHANGED
CHARACTER
CHARACTERS
CLOSE
COBOL
CODE
CODE-SET
COLLATING
COLUMN
COMM-REG
COMMA
COMMUNICATION
COMP
COMP-1
COMP-2
COMP-3
COMP-4
COMPUTATIONAL
COMPUTATIONAL-1
COMPUTATIONAL-2
COMPUTATIONAL-3
COMPUTATIONAL-4
COMPUTE
CONFIGURATION
CONTAINS
CONTENT
CONTINUE
CONTROL
CONTROLS
COPY
CORR
CORRESPONDING
COUNT
CURRENCY

DATA
DATE
DATE-COMPILED
DATE-WRITTEN
DAY
DE
DEBUG-CONTENTS
DEBUG-ITEM
DEBUG-LINE
DEBUG-NAME
DEBUG-SUB-1
DEBUG-SUB-2
DEBUG-SUB-3
DEBUGGING
DECIMAL-POINT
DECLARATIVES
DELETE
DELIMITED
DELIMITER
DEPENDING
DESCENDING
DESTINATION
DETAIL
DISABLE
DISPLAY
DISPLAY-1

[1]VS COBOL II is the first IBM compiler to support features of COBOL 8X. Reserved words new to this compiler are shown in color. Existing reserved words (in the OS/VS compiler) are shown in black type.

DIVIDE
DIVISION
DOWN
DUPLICATE
DYNAMIC

EGCS
EGI
ELSE
EMI
ENABLE
END
END-ADD
END-CALL
END-COMPUTE
END-DELETE
END-DIVIDE
END-EVALUATE
END-IF
END-MULTIPLY
END-OF-PAGE
END-PERFORM
END-READ
END-RETURN
END-REWRITE
END-SEARCH
END-START
END-STRING
END-SUBTRACT
END-UNSTRING
END-WRITE
ENDING
ENTER
ENTRY
ENVIRONMENT
EOP
EQUAL
ERROR
ESI
EVALUATE
EVERY
EXCEPTION
EXHIBIT
EXIT
EXTEND

FALSE
FD
FILE
FILE-CONTROL
FILLER
FINAL
FIRST
FOOTING
FOR
FROM

GENERATE
GIVING
GO
GOBACK
GREATER
GROUP

HEADING
HIGH-VALUE
HIGH-VALUES

I-O
I-O-CONTROL
ID
IDENTIFICATION
IF
IN
INDEX
INDEXED
INDICATE
INITIAL
INITIALIZE
INITIATE
INPUT
INPUT-OUTPUT
INSPECT
INSTALLATION
INTO
INVALID
IS

JUST
JUSTIFIED

KANJI
KEY

LABEL
LAST
LEADING
LEFT
LENGTH
LESS
LIMIT
LIMITS
LINAGE
LINAGE-COUNTER
LINE
LINE-COUNTER
LINES
LINKAGE
LOCK
LOW-VALUE
LOW-VALUES

MEMORY
MERGE
MESSAGE
MODE
MODULES
MORE-LABELS
MOVE
MULTIPLE
MULTIPLY

NAMED
NEGATIVE
NEXT
NO
NOT
NUMBER
NUMERIC
NUMERIC-EDITED

OBJECT-COMPUTER
OCCURS
OF
OFF
OMITTED
ON
OPEN
OPTIONAL
OR
ORGANIZATION
OTHER
OUTPUT
OVERFLOW

PAGE
PAGE-COUNTER
PASSWORD
PERFORM
PF
PH
PIC
PICTURE
PLUS
POINTER
POSITION
POSITIVE
PRINTING
PROCEDURE
PROCEDURES
PROCEED
PROCESSING
PROGRAM
PROGRAM-ID

QUEUE
QUOTE
QUOTES

RANDOM
RD
READ
READY
RECEIVE
RECORD
RECORDING
RECORDS
REDEFINES
REEL
REFERENCE
REFERENCES
RELATIVE
RELEASE

RELOAD
REMAINDER
REMOVAL
RENAMES
REPLACING
REPORT
REPORTING
REPORTS
RERUN
RESERVE
RESET
RETURN
RETURN-CODE
REVERSED
REWIND
REWRITE
RF
RH
RIGHT
ROUNDED
RUN

SAME
SD
SEARCH
SECTION
SECURITY
SEGMENT
SEGMENT-LIMIT
SELECT
SEND
SENTENCE
SEPARATE
SEQUENCE
SEQUENTIAL
SERVICE
SET
SIGN
SIZE
SKIP-1
SKIP-2
SKIP-3
SORT
SORT-CONTROL
SORT-MERGE
SORT-RETURN
SOURCE
SOURCE-COMPUTER
SPACE
SPACES
SPECIAL-NAMES
STANDARD
STANDARD-1
START
STATUS
STOP
STRING
SUB-QUEUE-1
SUB-QUEUE-2
SUB-QUEUE-3
SUBTRACT
SUM
SUPPRESS
SYMBOLIC
SYNCH
SYNCHRONIZED

TABLE
TALLYING
TAPE
TERMINAL
TERMINATE
TEST
TEXT
THAN
THEN
THROUGH
THRU
TIME
TIMES
TITLE
TO
TOP
TRACE
TRAILING
TRUE
TYPE

UNIT
UNSTRING
UNTIL
UP
UPON
USAGE
USE
USING

VALUE
VALUES
VARYING
WHEN
WHEN-COMPILED
WITH
WORDS
WORKING-STORAGE
WRITE

ZERO
ZEROES
ZEROS

COBOL 8X:

Reference Summary[1]

GENERAL FORMAT FOR IDENTIFICATION DIVISION

```
IDENTIFICATION DIVISION.

PROGRAM-ID. program-name [IS {|COMMON |} PROGRAM] .
                             {|INITIAL|}

[AUTHOR. [comment-entry] ... ]

[INSTALLATION. [comment-entry] ... ]

[DATE-WRITTEN. [comment-entry] ... ]

[DATE-COMPILED. [comment-entry] ... ]

[SECURITY. [comment-entry] ... ]
```

GENERAL FORMAT FOR ENVIRONMENT DIVISION

```
[ENVIRONMENT DIVISION.

[CONFIGURATION SECTION.

[SOURCE-COMPUTER. [computer-name [WITH DEBUGGING MODE].]]

[OBJECT-COMPUTER. [computer-name

    [PROGRAM COLLATING SEQUENCE IS alphabet-name-1]

    [SEGMENT-LIMIT IS segment-number].]]

[SPECIAL-NAMES. [[implementor-name-1

    {IS mnemonic-name-1 [ON STATUS IS condition-name-1 [OFF STATUS IS condition-name-2]]}
    {IS mnemonic-name-2 [OFF STATUS IS condition-name-2 [ON STATUS IS condition-name-1]]}
    {ON STATUS IS condition-name-1 [OFF STATUS IS condition-name-2]                     } ] ...
    {OFF STATUS IS condition-name-2 [ON STATUS IS condition-name-1]                     }
```

[1]This appendix reflects the *Draft Proposed X3.23 American National Standard Programming Language COBOL, September, 1983.*

```
[ALPHABET alphabet-name-1 IS

    ⎧ STANDARD-1                                              ⎫⎤
    ⎪ STANDARD-2                                              ⎪⎥
    ⎪ NATIVE                                                  ⎪⎥
    ⎨ implementor-name-2                                      ⎬⎥ ...
    ⎪ ⎧            ⎡⎧THROUGH⎫ literal-2      ⎤⎫               ⎪⎥
    ⎪ ⎨ literal-1  ⎢⎩THRU   ⎭                ⎥⎬ ...           ⎪⎥
    ⎩ ⎩            ⎣{ALSO literal-3} ...     ⎦⎭               ⎭⎦

[SYMBOLIC CHARACTERS {{{symbolic-character-1} ... {IS } {integer-1} ... } ...
                                                  {ARE}
    [IN alphabet-name-2]}] ...

[CLASS class-name IS {literal-4 [{THROUGH} literal-5]} ... ] ...
                                 {THRU   }
[CURRENCY SIGN IS literal-6]

[DECIMAL-POINT IS COMMA].]]]

[INPUT-OUTPUT SECTION.

 FILE-CONTROL.

    {file-control-entry} ...

[I-O-CONTROL.

    [[      [RECORD     ]                                          ]
    [[SAME  [SORT       ] AREA FOR file-name-1  {file-name-2} ...  ] ...
    [[      [SORT-MERGE ]                                          ]

    [MULTIPLE FILE TAPE CONTAINS

        {file-name-3  [POSITION IS integer-1] } ... ] ...  .]]]]
```

GENERAL FORMAT FOR FILE CONTROL ENTRY

SEQUENTIAL FILE:

```
SELECT  [OPTIONAL]  file-name-1

    ASSIGN TO {implementor-name-1} ...
              {literal-1         }

    [RESERVE integer-1 [AREA ]]
                       [AREAS]

    [[ORGANIZATION IS]  SEQUENTIAL]

    [PADDING CHARACTER IS {data-name-1}]
                          {literal-2  }

    [RECORD DELIMITER IS {STANDARD-1        }]
                         {implementor-name-2}

    [ACCESS MODE IS SEQUENTIAL]

    [FILE STATUS IS data-name-2].
```

RELATIVE FILE:

```
SELECT  [OPTIONAL]  file-name-1

    ASSIGN TO {implementor-name-1} ...
              {literal-1         }

    [RESERVE integer-1 [AREA ]]
                       [AREAS]

    [ORGANIZATION IS]  RELATIVE
```

```
[ACCESS MODE IS {SEQUENTIAL [RELATIVE KEY IS data-name-1]      }]
[               {{RANDOM }  RELATIVE KEY IS data-name-1        }]
[               {{DYNAMIC}                                     }]
[FILE STATUS IS data-name-2].
```

INDEXED FILE:

```
SELECT [OPTIONAL] file-name-1

   ASSIGN TO {implementor-name-1} ...
             {literal-1         }

   [RESERVE integer-1 [AREA ]]
   [                  [AREAS]]

   [ORGANIZATION IS] INDEXED

   [ACCESS MODE IS {SEQUENTIAL}]
   [               {RANDOM    }]
   [               {DYNAMIC   }]

   RECORD KEY IS data-name-1

   [ALTERNATE RECORD KEY IS data-name-2 [WITH DUPLICATES]] ...

   [FILE STATUS IS data-name-3].
```

SORT OR MERGE FILE:

```
SELECT file-name-1  ASSIGN TO {implementor-name-1} ... .
                              {literal-1         }
```

REPORT FILE:

```
SELECT [OPTIONAL] file-name-1

   ASSIGN TO {implementor-name-1} ...
             {literal-1         }

   [RESERVE integer-1 [AREA ]]
   [                  [AREAS]]

   [[ORGANIZATION IS] SEQUENTIAL]

   [PADDING CHARACTER IS {data-name-1}]
   [                     {literal-1  }]

   [RECORD DELIMITER IS {STANDARD-1        }]
   [                    {implementor-name-2}]

   [ACCESS MODE IS SEQUENTIAL]

   [FILE STATUS IS data-name-2].
```

GENERAL FORMAT FOR DATA DIVISION

```
[DATA DIVISION.

[FILE SECTION.

[file-description-entry

{record-description-entry} ... ] ...

[sort-merge-file-description-entry

{record-description-entry} ... ] ...

[report-file-description-entry] ... ]

[WORKING-STORAGE SECTION.
```

```
[77-level-description-entry ]
[record-description-entry   ] ...]

[LINKAGE SECTION.

[77-level-description-entry ]
[record-description-entry   ] ...]

[COMMUNICATION SECTION.

[communication-description-entry

[record-description-entry] ... ] ... ]

[REPORT SECTION.

[report-description-entry

{report-group-description-entry} ... ] ... ]]
```

GENERAL FORMAT FOR FILE DESCRIPTION ENTRY

SEQUENTIAL FILE:

```
FD  file-name-1

    [IS EXTERNAL]

    [IS GLOBAL]

    [BLOCK CONTAINS [integer-1 TO] integer-2 {RECORDS   }]
                                             {CHARACTERS}

    [       {CONTAINS integer-3 CHARACTERS                                         }]
    [RECORD {IS VARYING IN SIZE [[FROM integer-4] [TO integer-5] CHARACTERS]       }]
    [       {     [DEPENDING ON data-name-1]                                       }]
    [       {CONTAINS integer-6 TO integer-7 CHARACTERS                            }]

    [LABEL {RECORD IS   } {STANDARD}]
    [      {RECORDS ARE } {OMITTED }]

    [VALUE OF {implementor-name-1 IS {data-name-2}} ...]
    [                                {literal-1  }     ]

    [DATA {RECORD IS  } {data-name-3} ...]
    [     {RECORDS ARE}                  ]

    [LINAGE IS {data-name-4} LINES [WITH FOOTING AT {data-name-5}]
    [          {integer-8  }       [                {integer-9  }]

         [LINES AT TOP {data-name-6}] [LINES AT BOTTOM {data-name-7}]]
         [             {integer-10 }] [                {integer-11 }]]

    [CODE-SET IS alphabet-name-1].
```

RELATIVE FILE:

```
FD  file-name-1

    [IS EXTERNAL]

    [IS GLOBAL]

    [BLOCK CONTAINS [integer-1 TO] integer-2 {RECORDS   }]
                                             {CHARACTERS}

    [       {CONTAINS integer-3 CHARACTERS                                         }]
    [RECORD {IS VARYING IN SIZE [[FROM integer-4] [TO integer-5] CHARACTERS]       }]
    [       {     [DEPENDING ON data-name-1]                                       }]
    [       {CONTAINS integer-6 TO integer-7 CHARACTERS                            }]

    [LABEL {RECORD IS   } {STANDARD}]
    [      {RECORDS ARE } {OMITTED }]
```

```
[VALUE OF {implementor-name-1 IS {data-name-2}} ...]
                                 {literal-1  }

[DATA {RECORD IS  } {data-name-3} ...].
      {RECORDS ARE}
```

INDEXED FILE:

```
FD  file-name-1

    [IS EXTERNAL]

    [IS GLOBAL]

    [BLOCK CONTAINS [integer-1 TO] integer-2 {RECORDS   }]
                                             {CHARACTERS}

    [        {CONTAINS integer-3 CHARACTERS                                       }]
    [RECORD  {IS VARYING IN SIZE [[FROM integer-4] [TO integer-5] CHARACTERS]     }]
    [        {     [DEPENDING ON data-name-1]                                     }]
    [        {CONTAINS integer-6 TO integer-7 CHARACTERS                          }]

    [LABEL {RECORD IS  } {STANDARD}]
    [      {RECORDS ARE} {OMITTED }]

    [VALUE OF {implementor-name-1 IS {data-name-2}} ...]
                                     {literal-1  }

    [DATA {RECORD IS  } {data-name-3} ...].
          {RECORDS ARE}
```

SORT-MERGE FILE:

```
SD  file-name-1

    [        {CONTAINS integer-1 CHARACTERS                                       }]
    [RECORD  {IS VARYING IN SIZE [[FROM integer-2] [TO integer-3] CHARACTERS]     }]
    [        {     [DEPENDING ON data-name-1]                                     }]
    [        {CONTAINS integer-4 TO integer-5 CHARACTERS                          }]

    [DATA {RECORD IS  } {data-name-2} ...]
          {RECORDS ARE}
```

REPORT FILE:

```
FD  file-name-1

    [IS EXTERNAL]

    [IS GLOBAL]

    [BLOCK CONTAINS [integer-1 TO] integer-2 {RECORDS   }]
                                             {CHARACTERS}

    [        {CONTAINS integer-3 CHARACTERS                                       }]
    [RECORD  {IS VARYING IN SIZE [[FROM integer-4] [TO integer-5] CHARACTERS]     }]
    [        {     [DEPENDING ON data-name-1]                                     }]
    [        {CONTAINS integer-6 TO integer-7 CHARACTERS                          }]

    [LABEL {RECORD IS  } {STANDARD}]
    [      {RECORDS ARE} {OMITTED }]

    [VALUE OF {implementor-name-1 IS {data-name-2}} ...]
                                     {literal-1  }

    [CODE-SET IS alphabet-name-1]

    {REPORT IS  } {report-name-1} ...
    {REPORTS ARE}
```

GENERAL FORMAT FOR DATA DESCRIPTION ENTRY

FORMAT 1:

```
level-number [data-name-1]
             [FILLER     ]

     [REDEFINES data-name-2]

     [IS EXTERNAL]

     [IS GLOBAL]

     [{PICTURE} IS character-string]
     [{PIC    }                    ]

     [              {BINARY        }]
     [              {COMPUTATIONAL }]
     [[USAGE IS]    {COMP          }]
     [              {DISPLAY       }]
     [              {INDEX         }]
     [              {PACKED-DECIMAL}]

     [[SIGN IS] {LEADING } [SEPARATE CHARACTER]]
     [          {TRAILING}                     ]

     [OCCURS integer-2 TIMES                                                  ]
     [                                                                        ]
     [    [{ASCENDING } KEY IS {data-name-3} ...] ...                         ]
     [    [{DESCENDING}                         ]                             ]
     [                                                                        ]
     [    [INDEXED BY {index-name-1} ... ]                                    ]
     [OCCURS integer-1 TO integer-2 TIMES DEPENDING ON data-name-4            ]
     [                                                                        ]
     [    [{ASCENDING } KEY IS {data-name-3} ...] ...                         ]
     [    [{DESCENDING}                         ]                             ]
     [                                                                        ]
     [    [INDEXED BY {index-name-1} ... ]                                    ]

     [{SYNCHRONIZED} [LEFT ]]
     [{SYNC        } [RIGHT]]

     [{JUSTIFIED} RIGHT]
     [{JUST     }      ]

     [BLANK WHEN ZERO]

     [VALUE IS literal-1].
```

FORMAT 2:

```
66 data-name-1 RENAMES data-name-2 [{THROUGH} data-name-3] .
                                   [{THRU   }            ]
```

FORMAT 3:

```
88 condition-name-1 {VALUE IS  } {literal-1 [{THROUGH} literal-2]} ... .
                    {VALUES ARE} {          [{THRU   }          ]}
```

GENERAL FORMAT FOR COMMUNICATION DESCRIPTION ENTRY

FORMAT 1:

```
CD  cd-name-1

                          ┌[[SYMBOLIC QUEUE IS data-name-1]
                          │     [SYMBOLIC SUB-QUEUE-1 IS data-name-2]
                          │     [SYMBOLIC SUB-QUEUE-2 IS data-name-3]
                          │     [SYMBOLIC SUB-QUEUE-3 IS data-name-4]
                          │     [MESSAGE DATE IS data-name-5]
                          │     [MESSAGE TIME IS data-name-6]
                          │     [SYMBOLIC SOURCE IS data-name-7]
    FOR [INITIAL] INPUT   │     [TEXT LENGTH IS data-name-8]
                          │     [END KEY IS data-name-9]
                          │     [STATUS KEY IS data-name-10]
                          │     [MESSAGE COUNT IS data-name-11]]
                          │[data-name-1, data-name-2, data-name-3,
                          │     data-name-4, data-name-5, data-name-6,
                          │     data-name-7, data-name-8, data-name-9,
                          └     data-name-10, data-name-11]
```

FORMAT 2:

```
CD  cd-name-1 FOR OUTPUT
    [DESTINATION COUNT IS data-name-1]
    [TEXT LENGTH IS data-name-2]
    [STATUS KEY IS data-name-3]
    [DESTINATION TABLE OCCURS integer-1 TIMES
        [INDEXED BY {index-name-1} ... ]]
    [ERROR KEY IS data-name-4]
    [SYMBOLIC DESTINATION IS data-name-5].
```

FORMAT 3:

```
CD  cd-name-1

                          ┌[[MESSAGE DATE IS data-name-1]
                          │     [MESSAGE TIME IS data-name-2]
                          │     [SYMBOLIC TERMINAL IS data-name-3]
    FOR [INITIAL] I-O     │     [TEXT LENGTH IS data-name-4]
                          │     [END KEY IS data-name-5]
                          │     [STATUS KEY IS data-name-6]]
                          │[data-name-1, data-name-2, data-name-3,
                          └     data-name-4, data-name-5, data-name-6]
```

GENERAL FORMAT FOR REPORT DESCRIPTION ENTRY

```
RD  report-name-1

    [IS GLOBAL]

    [CODE literal-1]

    [{CONTROL IS  } {{data-name-1} ...             }]
    [{CONTROLS ARE} {FINAL [data-name-1] ...       }]

    [ PAGE [LIMIT IS  ] integer-1 [LINE ] [HEADING integer-2]
    [      [LIMITS ARE]           [LINES]
    [
    [      [FIRST DETAIL integer-3]  [LAST DETAIL integer-4]
    [
    [      [FOOTING integer-5]                               ].
```

GENERAL FORMAT FOR REPORT GROUP DESCRIPTION ENTRY

FORMAT 1:

```
01  [data-name-1]

    [LINE NUMBER IS {integer-1  [ON NEXT PAGE]}]
    [               {PLUS integer-2           }]

    [               {integer-3     }]
    [NEXT GROUP IS  {PLUS integer-4}]
    [               {NEXT PAGE     }]

                 ( {REPORT HEADING}                            )
                 ( {RH            }                            )
                 (                                             )
                 ( {PAGE HEADING}                              )
                 ( {PH          }                              )
                 (                                             )
                 ( {CONTROL HEADING} {data-name-2}             )
                 ( {CH             } {FINAL      }             )
                 (                                             )
     TYPE IS     ( {DETAIL}                                    )
                 ( {DE    }                                    )
                 (                                             )
                 ( {CONTROL FOOTING} {data-name-3}             )
                 ( {CF             } {FINAL      }             )
                 (                                             )
                 ( {PAGE FOOTING}                              )
                 ( {PF          }                              )
                 (                                             )
                 ( {REPORT FOOTING}                            )
                 ( {RF            }                            )

    [[USAGE IS]  DISPLAY].
```

FORMAT 2:

```
level-number  [data-name-1]

    [LINE NUMBER IS {integer-1  [ON NEXT PAGE]}]
    [               {PLUS integer-2           }]

    [[USAGE IS]  DISPLAY].
```

FORMAT 3:

```
level-number  [data-name-1]

    {PICTURE}  IS character-string
    {PIC    }

    [[USAGE IS] DISPLAY]

    [[SIGN IS]  {LEADING }  SEPARATE CHARACTER]
    [           {TRAILING}                    ]

    [ {JUSTIFIED}  RIGHT]
    [ {JUST     }       ]

    [BLANK WHEN ZERO]
```

```
[LINE NUMBER IS {integer-1  [ON NEXT PAGE]}]
[               {PLUS integer-2          }]

[COLUMN NUMBER IS integer-3]

{ SOURCE IS identifier-1                                          }
{ VALUE IS literal-1                                              }
{ {SUM  {identifier-2} ...  [UPON {data-name-2} ... ] } ...       }
{      [RESET ON  {data-name-3}]                                  }
{      [          {FINAL      }]                                  }

[GROUP INDICATE].
```

GENERAL FORMAT FOR PROCEDURE DIVISION

FORMAT 1:

```
[PROCEDURE DIVISION  [USING  {data-name-1} ... ].
[DECLARATIVES.
{section-name SECTION [segment-number].
    USE statement.
[paragraph-name.
    [sentence] ... ] ... } ...
 END DECLARATIVES.]
{section-name SECTION [segment-number].
[paragraph-name.
    [sentence] ... ] ... } ... ]
```

FORMAT 2:

```
[PROCEDURE DIVISION  [USING  {data-name-1} ... ].
{paragraph-name.
    [sentence] ... } ... ]
```

GENERAL FORMAT FOR COBOL VERBS

```
ACCEPT identifier-1  [FROM mnemonic-name-1]

                         {DATE       }
ACCEPT identifier-2 FROM {DAY        }
                         {DAY-OF-WEEK}
                         {TIME       }

ACCEPT cd-name-1 MESSAGE COUNT

ADD {identifier-1} ...   TO  {identifier-2 [ROUNDED]} ...
    {literal-1   }
   [ON SIZE ERROR imperative-statement-1]
   [NOT ON SIZE ERROR imperative-statement-2]
   [END-ADD]
```

```
ADD {identifier-1 | literal-1} ... TO {identifier-2 | literal-2}
    GIVING {identifier-3 [ROUNDED]} ...
    [ON SIZE ERROR imperative-statement-1]
    [NOT ON SIZE ERROR imperative-statement-2]
    [END-ADD]

ADD {CORRESPONDING | CORR} identifier-1 TO identifier-2 [ROUNDED]
    [ON SIZE ERROR imperative-statement-1]
    [NOT ON SIZE ERROR imperative-statement-2]
    [END-ADD]

ALTER {procedure-name-1 TO [PROCEED TO] procedure-name-2} ...

CALL {identifier-1 | literal-1} [USING {[BY REFERENCE] {identifier-2} ... | BY CONTENT {identifier-2} ...} ...]
    [ON OVERFLOW imperative-statement-1 [END-CALL]]

CALL {identifier-1 | literal-1} [USING {[BY REFERENCE] {identifier-2} ... | BY CONTENT {identifier-2} ...} ...]
    [ON EXCEPTION imperative-statement-1]
    [NOT ON EXCEPTION imperative-statement-2]
    [END-CALL]

CANCEL {identifier-1 | literal-1} ...

SW CLOSE {file-name-1 [{REEL | UNIT} [FOR REMOVAL] | WITH {NO REWIND | LOCK}]} ...

RI CLOSE {file-name-1 [WITH LOCK]} ...

COMPUTE {identifier-1 [ROUNDED]} ... = arithmetic-expression-1
    [ON SIZE ERROR imperative-statement-1]
    [NOT ON SIZE ERROR imperative-statement-2]
    [END-COMPUTE]

CONTINUE

DELETE file-name-1 RECORD
    [INVALID KEY imperative-statement-1]
    [NOT INVALID KEY imperative-statement-2]
    [END-DELETE]

DISABLE {INPUT [TERMINAL] | I-O TERMINAL | OUTPUT} cd-name-1

DISPLAY {identifier-1 | literal-1} ... [UPON mnemonic-name-1] [WITH NO ADVANCING]
```

```
DIVIDE {identifier-1} INTO {identifier-2 [ROUNDED]} ...
       {literal-1   }
   [ON SIZE ERROR imperative-statement-1]
   [NOT ON SIZE ERROR imperative-statement-2]
   [END-DIVIDE]
```

```
DIVIDE {identifier-1} INTO {identifier-2}
       {literal-1   }      {literal-2   }
   GIVING {identifier-3 [ROUNDED]} ...
   [ON SIZE ERROR imperative-statement-1]
   [NOT ON SIZE ERROR imperative-statement-2]
   [END-DIVIDE]
```

```
DIVIDE {identifier-1} BY {identifier-2}
       {literal-1   }    {literal-2   }
   GIVING {identifier-3 [ROUNDED]} ...
   [ON SIZE ERROR imperative-statement-1]
   [NOT ON SIZE ERROR imperative-statement-2]
   [END-DIVIDE]
```

```
DIVIDE {identifier-1} INTO {identifier-2} GIVING identifier-3 [ROUNDED]
       {literal-1   }      {literal-2   }
   REMAINDER identifier-4
   [ON SIZE ERROR imperative-statement-1]
   [NOT ON SIZE ERROR imperative-statement-2]
   [END-DIVIDE]
```

```
DIVIDE {identifier-1} BY {identifier-2} GIVING identifier-3 [ROUNDED]
       {literal-1   }    {literal-2   }
   REMAINDER identifier-4
   [ON SIZE ERROR imperative-statement-1]
   [NOT ON SIZE ERROR imperative-statement-2]
   [END-DIVIDE]
```

```
       {INPUT [TERMINAL]}
ENABLE {I-O TERMINAL    } cd-name-1
       {OUTPUT          }
```

```
         {identifier-1}  [     {identifier-2}]
         {literal-1   }  [     {literal-2   }]
EVALUATE {expression-1}  [ALSO {expression-2}] ...
         {TRUE        }  [     {TRUE        }]
         {FALSE       }  [     {FALSE       }]
 {{WHEN
   {ANY                                                                                   }
   {condition-1                                                                           }
   {TRUE                                                                                  }
   {FALSE                                                                                 }
   {      {{identifier-3             } [{THROUGH} {identifier-4             }]}           }
   {[NOT] {{literal-3                } [{THRU   } {literal-4                }]}           }
   {      {{arithmetic-expression-1  } [          {arithmetic-expression-2  }]}           }
  [ALSO
   {ANY                                                                                   }
   {condition-2                                                                           }
   {TRUE                                                                                  }
   {FALSE                                                                                 }
   {      {{identifier-5             } [{THROUGH} {identifier-6             }]}           }
   {[NOT] {{literal-5                } [{THRU   } {literal-6                }]}           } ] ...} ...
   {      {{arithmetic-expression-3  } [          {arithmetic-expression-4  }]}           }
  imperative-statement-1} ...
```

```
[WHEN OTHER imperative-statement-2]
[END-EVALUATE]

EXIT

EXIT PROGRAM

GENERATE {data-name-1  }
         {report-name-1}

GO TO [procedure-name-1]

GO TO {procedure-name-1} ... DEPENDING ON identifier-1

IF condition-1 THEN {{statement-1} ...} {ELSE {statement-2} ... [END-IF]}
                    {NEXT SENTENCE    } {ELSE NEXT SENTENCE               }
                                        {END-IF                           }

INITIALIZE {identifier-1} ...

  [REPLACING {{ALPHABETIC            }                               }    ]
  [          {{ALPHANUMERIC          }                               }    ]
  [          {{NUMERIC               } DATA BY {identifier-2}        } ...]
  [          {{ALPHANUMERIC-EDITED   }         {literal-1   }        }    ]
  [          {{NUMERIC-EDITED        }                               }    ]

INITIATE {report-name-1} ...

INSPECT identifier-1 TALLYING
{                  {CHARACTERS [{BEFORE} INITIAL {identifier-4}] ...                                        }     }
{identifier-2 FOR  {            {AFTER }         {literal-2   }                                             } ... } ...
{                  {{ALL    } {{identifier-3} [{BEFORE} INITIAL {identifier-4}] ...} ...                    }     }
{                  {{LEADING} {{literal-1   } [{AFTER }         {literal-2   }]     }                       }     }

INSPECT identifier-1 REPLACING
{CHARACTERS BY {identifier-5} [{BEFORE} INITIAL {identifier-4}] ...                                      }
{              {literal-3   } [{AFTER }         {literal-2   }]                                          } ...
{{ALL    } {{identifier-3} BY {identifier-5} [{BEFORE} INITIAL {identifier-4}] ...} ...                  }
{{LEADING} {{literal-1   }    {literal-3   } [{AFTER }         {literal-2   }]    }                      }
{{FIRST  }                                                                                               }

INSPECT identifier-1 TALLYING
{                  {CHARACTERS [{BEFORE} INITIAL {identifier-4}] ...                                        }     }
{identifier-2 FOR  {            {AFTER }         {literal-2   }                                             } ... } ...
{                  {{ALL    } {{identifier-3} [{BEFORE} INITIAL {identifier-4}] ...} ...                    }     }
{                  {{LEADING} {{literal-1   } [{AFTER }         {literal-2   }]     }                       }     }
REPLACING
{CHARACTERS BY {identifier-5} [{BEFORE} INITIAL {identifier-4}] ...                                      }
{              {literal-3   } [{AFTER }         {literal-2   }]                                          } ...
{{ALL    } {{identifier-3} BY {identifier-5} [{BEFORE} INITIAL {identifier-4}] ...} ...                  }
{{LEADING} {{literal-1   }    {literal-3   } [{AFTER }         {literal-2   }]    }                      }
{{FIRST  }                                                                                               }

INSPECT identifier-1 CONVERTING {identifier-6} TO {identifier-7}
                                {literal-4   }    {literal-5   }

   [{BEFORE} INITIAL {identifier-4}] ...
   [{AFTER }         {literal-2   }]

MERGE file-name-1 {ON {ASCENDING } KEY {data-name-1} ...} ...
                  {   {DESCENDING}                      }

   [COLLATING SEQUENCE IS alphabet-name-1]
```

```
USING file-name-2 {file-name-3} ...

{OUTPUT PROCEDURE IS procedure-name-1 [{THROUGH} procedure-name-2]}
{                                      {THRU   }                  }
{GIVING {file-name-4} ...                                         }

MOVE {identifier-1} TO {identifier-2} ...
     {literal-1   }

MOVE {CORRESPONDING} identifier-1 TO identifier-2
     {CORR         }

MULTIPLY {identifier-1} BY {identifier-2 [ROUNDED]} ...
         {literal-1   }
   [ON SIZE ERROR imperative-statement-1]
   [NOT ON SIZE ERROR imperative-statement-2]
   [END-MULTIPLY]

MULTIPLY {identifier-1} BY {identifier-2}
         {literal-1   }    {literal-2   }
   GIVING {identifier-3 [ROUNDED]} ...
   [ON SIZE ERROR imperative-statement-1]
   [NOT ON SIZE ERROR imperative-statement-2]
   [END-MULTIPLY]

S OPEN {INPUT {file-name-1  [WITH NO REWIND]} ...  } ...
       {OUTPUT {file-name-2  [WITH NO REWIND]} ... }
       {I-O {file-name-3} ...                      }
       {EXTEND {file-name-4} ...                   }

RI OPEN {INPUT {file-name-1} ...  } ...
        {OUTPUT {file-name-2} ... }
        {I-O {file-name-3} ...    }
        {EXTEND {file-name-4} ... }

W OPEN {OUTPUT {file-name-1 [WITH NO REWIND]} ... } ...
       {EXTEND {file-name-2} ...                  }

PERFORM [procedure-name-1 [{THROUGH} procedure-name-2]]
                           {THRU   }
   [imperative-statement-1 END-PERFORM]

PERFORM [procedure-name-1 [{THROUGH} procedure-name-2]]
                           {THRU   }
   {identifier-1} TIMES [imperative-statement-1 END-PERFORM]
   {integer-1   }

PERFORM [procedure-name-1 [{THROUGH} procedure-name-2]]
                           {THRU   }
   [WITH TEST {BEFORE}] UNTIL condition-1
              {AFTER }
   [imperative-statement-1 END-PERFORM]

PERFORM [procedure-name-1 [{THROUGH} procedure-name-2]]
                           {THRU   }
   [WITH TEST {BEFORE}]
              {AFTER }
```

```
    VARYING {identifier-2 }  FROM {identifier-3 }
            {index-name-1 }       {index-name-2 }
                                  {literal-1    }

         BY {identifier-4}  UNTIL condition-1
            {literal-2   }

     [ AFTER {identifier-5}  FROM {identifier-6 }
     [       {literal-3   }       {index-name-4 }
     [                            {literal-3    }

         BY {identifier-7}  UNTIL condition-2  ] ...
            {literal-4   }

    [imperative-statement-1 END-PERFORM]

  PURGE cd-name-1

SRI READ file-name-1 [NEXT] RECORD [INTO identifier-1]
        [AT END imperative-statement-1]
        [NOT AT END imperative-statement-2]
        [END-READ]

  R READ file-name-1 RECORD [INTO identifier-1]
        [INVALID KEY imperative-statement-3]
        [NOT INVALID KEY imperative-statement-4]
        [END-READ]

  I READ file-name-1 RECORD [INTO identifier-1]
        [KEY IS data-name-1]
        [INVALID KEY imperative-statement-3]
        [NOT INVALID KEY imperative-statement-4]
        [END-READ]

  RECEIVE cd-name-1 {MESSAGE} INTO identifier-1
                    {SEGMENT}
        [NO DATA imperative-statement-1]
        [WITH DATA imperative-statement-2]
        [END-RECEIVE]

  RELEASE record-name-1 [FROM identifier-1]

  RETURN file-name-1 RECORD [INTO identifier-1]
        AT END imperative-statement-1
        [NOT AT END imperative-statement-2]
        [END-RETURN]

  S REWRITE record-name-1 [FROM identifier-1]

 RI REWRITE record-name-1 [FROM identifier-1]
        [INVALID KEY imperative-statement-1]
        [NOT INVALID KEY imperative-statement-2]
        [END-REWRITE]
```

```
SEARCH identifier-1 [VARYING {identifier-2 }]
                             {index-name-1 }

    [AT END imperative-statement-1]

    {WHEN condition-1 {imperative-statement-2}} ...
                      {NEXT SENTENCE         }

    [END-SEARCH]

SEARCH ALL identifier-1  [AT END imperative-statement-1]

             {data-name-1 {IS EQUAL TO} {identifier-3             }}
    WHEN     {            {IS =       } {literal-]                }}
             {                          {arithmetic-expression-1  }}
             {condition-name-1                                     }

       [     {data-name-2 {IS EQUAL TO} {identifier-4             }}]
       [AND  {            {IS =       } {literal-2                }}] ...
       [     {                          {arithmetic-expression-2  }}]
       [     {condition-name-2                                     }]

       {imperative-statement-2}
       {NEXT SENTENCE         }

    [END-SEARCH]

SEND cd-name-1 FROM identifier-1

                                            {WITH identifier-2}
SEND cd-name-1  [FROM identifier-1]         {WITH ESI         }
                                            {WITH EMI         }
                                            {WITH EGI         }

    [{BEFORE}  ADVANCING  {{identifier-3} [LINE ]}]
    [{AFTER }             {{integer-1   } [LINES]}]
    [                     {{mnemonic-name-1}     }]
    [                     {{PAGE           }     }]

    [REPLACING LINE]

                                      {index-name-2}
SET {index-name-1} ...      TO        {identifier-2}
    {identifier-1}                    {integer-1   }

SET {index-name-3} ...   {UP BY  }  {identifier-3}
                         {DOWN BY}  {integer-2   }

SET {{mnemonic-name-1} ...  TO  {ON }} ...
                                {OFF}

SET {condition-name-1} ...   TO TRUE

SORT file-name-1 {ON {ASCENDING } KEY {data-name-1} ... } ...
                     {DESCENDING}

    [WITH DUPLICATES IN ORDER]

    [COLLATING SEQUENCE IS alphabet-name-1]

    {INPUT PROCEDURE IS procedure-name-1  [{THROUGH} procedure-name-2]}
    {                                     [{THRU   }                 ]}
    {USING  {file-name-2} ...                                         }

    {OUTPUT PROCEDURE IS procedure-name-3  [{THROUGH} procedure-name-4]}
    {                                      [{THRU   }                 ]}
    {GIVING  {file-name-3} ...                                         }

                        [     {IS EQUAL TO                    }             ]
                        [     {IS =                           }             ]
                        [     {IS GREATER THAN                }             ]
START file-name-1       [ KEY {IS >                           } data-name-1 ]
                        [     {IS NOT LESS THAN               }             ]
                        [     {IS NOT <                       }             ]
                        [     {IS GREATER THAN OR EQUAL TO    }             ]
                        [     {IS >=                          }             ]
```

```
    [INVALID KEY imperative-statement-1]

    [NOT INVALID KEY imperative-statement-2]

    [END-START]

STOP {RUN      }
     {literal-1}

STRING {{identifier-1}} ...  DELIMITED BY {identifier-2}} ...
       {{literal-1   }}                   {literal-2   }}
                                          {SIZE        }}

    INTO identifier-3

    [WITH POINTER identifier-4]

    [ON OVERFLOW imperative-statement-1]

    [NOT ON OVERFLOW imperative-statement-2]

    [END-STRING]

SUBTRACT {identifier-1} ...  FROM {identifier-3 [ROUNDED]} ...
         {literal-1   }

    [ON SIZE ERROR imperative-statement-1]

    [NOT ON SIZE ERROR imperative-statement-2]

    [END-SUBTRACT]

SUBTRACT {identifier-1} ...  FROM {identifier-2}
         {literal-1   }           {literal-2   }

    GIVING {identifier-3 [ROUNDED]} ...

    [ON SIZE ERROR imperative-statement-1]

    [NOT ON SIZE ERROR imperative-statement-2]

    [END-SUBTRACT]

SUBTRACT {CORRESPONDING} identifier-1 FROM identifier-2 [ROUNDED]
         {CORR         }

    [ON SIZE ERROR imperative-statement-1]

    [NOT ON SIZE ERROR imperative-statement-2]

    [END-SUBTRACT]

SUPPRESS PRINTING

TERMINATE {report-name-1} ...

UNSTRING identifier-1

    [DELIMITED BY [ALL] {identifier-2} [OR [ALL] {identifier-3}] ...]
                        {literal-1   }           {literal-2   }

    INTO {identifier-4 [DELIMITER IN identifier-5] [COUNT IN identifier-6]} ..

    [WITH POINTER identifier-7]

    [TALLYING IN identifier-8]

    [ON OVERFLOW imperative-statement-1]

    [NOT ON OVERFLOW imperative-statement-2]

    [END-UNSTRING]
```

```
                                                         {{file-name-1} ...}
                                                         {INPUT            }
USE [GLOBAL] AFTER STANDARD {EXCEPTION} PROCEDURE ON     {OUTPUT           }
                            {ERROR    }                  {I-O              }
                                                         {EXTEND           }
```

```
USE [GLOBAL] BEFORE REPORTING identifier-1
```

```
                          {cd-name-1                         }
                          {[ALL REFERENCES OF] identifier-1  }
USE FOR DEBUGGING ON      {file-name-1                       } ...
                          {procedure-name-1                  }
                          {ALL PROCEDURES                    }
```

```
S WRITE record-name-1  [FROM identifier-1]

    [                       {{identifier-2} [LINE ]}]
    [{BEFORE} ADVANCING     {{integer-1   } [LINES]}]
    [{AFTER }               {                      }]
    [                       {{mnemonic-name-1}     }]
    [                       {{PAGE           }     }]

    [AT {END-OF-PAGE} imperative-statement-1]
    [   {EOP        }                       ]

    [NOT AT {END-OF-PAGE} imperative-statement-2]
    [       {EOP        }                       ]

    [END-WRITE]
```

```
RI WRITE record-name-1  [FROM identifier-1]

    [INVALID KEY imperative-statement-1]

    [NOT INVALID KEY imperative-statement-2]

    [END-WRITE]
```

GENERAL FORMAT FOR COPY AND REPLACE STATEMENTS

```
COPY text-name-1  [{OF} library-name-1]
                  [{IN}               ]

    [           {{==pseudo-text-1==}    {==pseudo-text-2==}}    ]
    [REPLACING  {{identifier-1     } BY {identifier-2     }} ...]
    [           {{literal-1        }    {literal-2        }}    ]
    [           {{word-1           }    {word-2           }}    ]

REPLACE  {==pseudo-text-1==  BY  ==pseudo-text-2==} ...

REPLACE OFF
```

GENERAL FORMAT FOR CONDITIONS

RELATION CONDITION:

```
                         {IS [NOT] GREATER THAN        }
                         {IS [NOT] >                   }
                         {IS [NOT] LESS THAN           }
{identifier-1          } {IS [NOT] <                   } {identifier-2          }
{literal-1             } {IS [NOT] EQUAL TO            } {literal-2             }
{arithmetic-expression-1}{IS [NOT] =                   } {arithmetic-expression-2}
{index-name-1          } {IS GREATER THAN OR EQUAL TO  } {index-name-2          }
                         {IS >=                        }
                         {IS LESS THAN OR EQUAL TO     }
                         {IS <=                        }
```

CLASS CONDITION:

```
                            ⎧ NUMERIC          ⎫
                            ⎪ ALPHABETIC       ⎪
identifier-1 IS [NOT]       ⎨ ALPHABETIC-LOWER ⎬
                            ⎪ ALPHABETIC-UPPER ⎪
                            ⎩ class-name       ⎭
```

CONDITION-NAME CONDITION:

```
condition-name-1
```

SWITCH-STATUS CONDITION:

```
condition-name-1
```

SIGN CONDITION:

```
                                    ⎧ POSITIVE ⎫
arithmetic-expression-1 IS [NOT]    ⎨ NEGATIVE ⎬
                                    ⎩ ZERO     ⎭
```

NEGATED CONDITION:

```
NOT condition-1
```

COMBINED CONDITION:

```
condition-1  { {AND} condition-2 } ...
               {OR }
```

ABBREVIATED COMBINED RELATION CONDITION:

```
relation-condition  { {AND} [NOT] [relational-operator] object } ...
                      {OR }
```

QUALIFICATION

FORMAT 1:

```
                      ⎧ { {IN} data-name-2 } ... [ {IN} {file-name} ] ⎫
{data-name-1     }    ⎪   {OF}                     {OF} {cd-name  }   ⎪
{condition-name  }    ⎨                                               ⎬
                      ⎪ {IN} {file-name}                              ⎪
                      ⎩ {OF} {cd-name  }                              ⎭
```

FORMAT 2:

```
paragraph-name  {IN}  section-name
                {OF}
```

FORMAT 3:

```
text-name  {IN}  library-name
           {OF}
```

FORMAT 4:

```
LINAGE-COUNTER  {IN}  report-name
                {OF}
```

FORMAT 5:

```
{PAGE-COUNTER}  {IN}  report-name
{LINE-COUNTER}  {OF}
```

FORMAT 6:

```
              ⎧ ⎧IN⎫                ⎡⎧IN⎫              ⎤⎫
data-name-3   ⎨ ⎩OF⎭  data-name-4   ⎣⎩OF⎭  report-name ⎦⎬
              ⎪ ⎧IN⎫                                    ⎪
              ⎩ ⎩OF⎭  report-name                       ⎭
```

MISCELLANEOUS FORMATS

SUBSCRIPTING:

```
{condition-name-1}   ( {integer-1                        }  ... )
{data-name-1     }     {data-name-2 [{±} integer-2]      }
                       {index-name-1 [{±} integer-3]     }
```

REFERENCE MODIFICATION:

```
data-name-1 (leftmost-character-position: [length])
```

IDENTIFIER:

```
data-name-1 [{IN} data-name-2] ... [{IN} {cd-name    }]
            [{OF}            ]     [{OF} {file-name  }]
                                   [     {report-name}]

   [({subscript} ... ) ]  [(leftmost-character-position: [length])]
```

GENERAL FORMAT FOR NESTED SOURCE PROGRAMS

```
 IDENTIFICATION DIVISION.
 PROGRAM-ID.  program-name-1  [IS INITIAL PROGRAM].
[ENVIRONMENT DIVISION.  environment-division-content]
[DATA DIVISION.  data-division-content]
[PROCEDURE DIVISION.  procedure-division-content]
[[nested-source-program] ...
 END PROGRAM program-name-1.]
```

GENERAL FORMAT FOR NESTED-SOURCE-PROGRAM

```
 IDENTIFICATION DIVISION.
 PROGRAM-ID.  program-name-2  [IS {|COMMON |} PROGRAM] .
                              [   {|INITIAL|}        ]
[ENVIRONMENT DIVISION.  environment-division-content]
[DATA DIVISION.  data-division-content]
[PROCEDURE DIVISION.  procedure-division-content]
[nested-source-program] ...
 END PROGRAM program-name-2.
```

GENERAL FORMAT FOR A SEQUENCE OF SOURCE PROGRAMS

```
{IDENTIFICATION DIVISION.
 PROGRAM-ID. program-name-3 [IS INITIAL PROGRAM].
[ENVIRONMENT DIVISION. environment-division-content]
[DATA DIVISION. data-division-content]
[PROCEDURE DIVISION. procedure-division-content]
[nested-source-program] ...
 END PROGRAM program-name-3.} ...
 IDENTIFICATION DIVISION.
 PROGRAM-ID. program-name-4 [IS INITIAL PROGRAM].
[ENVIRONMENT DIVISION. environment-division-content]
[DATA DIVISION. data-division-content]
[PROCEDURE DIVISION. procedure-division-content]
[[nested-source-program] ...
 END PROGRAM program-name-4.]
```

Index